THE HERITAGE OF
WORLD CIVILIZATIONS

TEACHING AND LEARNING CLASSROOM EDITION

BRIEF THIRD EDITION

VOLUME ONE: TO 1700

Albert M. Craig
HARVARD UNIVERSITY

William A. Graham
HARVARD UNIVERSITY

Donald Kagan
YALE UNIVERSITY

Steven Ozment
HARVARD UNIVERSITY

Frank M. Turner
YALE UNIVERSITY

PEARSON

Prentice
Hall

Upper Saddle River, New Jersey 07458

Library of Congress Cataloging-in-Publication Data

The heritage of world civilizations / Albert M. Craig ... [et al].- Brief 3rd ed., volume one
  p. cm.
  Includes bibliographical references and index.
  ISBN 0-13-219694-8
    1. Civilizations–History–Textbooks.   I. Craig, Albert M.
  CB69.H45 2005

VP, Editorial Director: Charlyce Jones Owen
Executive Editor: Charles Cavaliere
Associate Editor: Emsal Hasan
Editorial Assistant: Maria Guarascio
Senior Media Editor: Deborah O'Connell
Editor-in-Chief, Development: Rochelle Diogenes
**AVP, Director of Production
  and Manufacturing:** Barbara Kittle
Senior Managing Editor: Joanne Riker
Production Liaison: Randy Pettit
Prepress and Manufacturing Manager: Nick Sklitsis
Prepress and Manufacturing Buyer: Ben Smith
Director of Marketing: Brandy Dawson
Marketing Manager: Emily Cleary
Creative Design Director: Leslie Osher
Interior and Cover Designer: Laura Gardner

Cartographer: CartoGraphics
Electronic Artists: Maria Piper, Mirella Signoretto,
  Bruce Killmer, Carey Davies
Director, Image Resource Center: Melinda Reo
Interior Image Specialist: Beth Brenzel
Cover Image Specialist: Karen Sanatar
Image Permission Coordinator: Michelina Viscusi
Photo Researcher: Elaine Soares
Color Scanning Services: Joe Conti, Greg Harrison, Cory
  Skidds, Rob Uibelhoer, Ron Walko
Editorial Production and Composition: GEX Publishing
  Services
Printer/Binder: The Courier Companies
Cover Printer: The Lehigh Press, Inc.

This detail of a gilded, wooden statue showing the reclining Buddha was made in Burma (modern-day Myanmar) in approximately 1700 C.E. The Theravada school of Buddhism took root in Burma early in the first millennium C.E., spread by missionaries and traders from India. The Buddha's cranial bump and elongated ears are common features in Buddhist imagery and suggest his supernatural being.

Credits and acknowledgments borrowed from other sources and reproduced, with permission, in this textbook appear on appropriate page within text or on page C-1

Pearson Education Ltd., London
Pearson Education Australia Pty., Limited, Sydney
Pearson Education Singapore, Pte., Ltd.

Pearson Education North Asia Ltd., Hong Kong
Pearson Education Canada, Ltd., Toronto
Pearson Educación de Mexico, S.A. de C.V.
Pearson Education — Japan, Tokyo

PEARSON
Prentice
Hall

Prentice Hall® is a registered trademark of
Pearson Education, Inc.

10 9 8 7 6 5 4 3 2 1

ISBN 0-13-219694-8

PART 2

EMPIRES AND CULTURES OF THE ANCIENT WORLD   54

Greek and Hellenistic Civilization   56

Iran, India, and Inner Asia to 200 C.E.   84

Visualizing The Past

Africa, Early History to 1000 C.E. 104

Republican and Imperial Rome 122

*China's First Empire
221 B.C.E.– 589 C.E.*   152

Visualizing The Past

PART 3
CONSOLIDATION AND INTERACTION OF WORLD CIVILIZATIONS 172

Religions of the World
Buddhism 224

Religions of the World

The Formation of Islamic Civilization 622–945   244

The Byzantine Empire and Western Europe to 1000   264

Islam in the Heartlands and Beyond, ca. 1000–1600   288

Visualizing The Past

The Divine in the Middle Ages 308

Ancient Civilizations of the Americas 310

Visualizing The Past

Mapping the World before 1500 334

Europe to the Early 1500s: Revival, Decline, and Renaissance 336

PART 4
THE WORLD IN TRANSITION 370

Europe 1500–1650: Expansion, Reformation and Religious Wars 372

Religions of the World

Christianity 412

Africa, ca. 1000–1800 414

18

Conquest and Exploitation: The Development of the Transatlantic Economy 434

19

East Asia in the Late Traditional Era 456

20
State Building and Society in Early Modern Europe   484

21

PART 5

ENLIGHTENMENT AND REVOLUTION IN THE WEST 534

22

23

Revolutions in the Transatlantic World 556

24

*Political Consolidation in Nineteenth-
Century Europe and North America,
1815–1880* 582

Visualizing The Past

**Imagining Women in the Eighteenth
and Nineteenth Centuries   614**

PART 6
INTO THE MODERN WORLD   616

*Northern Transatlantic Economy
and Society, 1815–1914*   618

26

Latin America from Independence to the 1940s   652

27

India, the Islamic Heartlands, and Africa: The Challenge of Modernity (1800–1945)   672

Religions of the World

PART 7

GLOBAL CONFLICT AND CHANGE 726

30

Depression, European Dictators, and the American New Deal 750

31

World War II 772

32

The West Since World War II   794

33

East Asia, The Recent Decades   818

34

Postcolonialism and Beyond: Latin America, Africa, Asia, and the Middle East 836

Visualizing The Past

Imperialism and Race in Modern Art 862

History's Voices

SPECIAL FEATURES

xxiii

Maps

SPECIAL FEATURES

SPECIAL FEATURES

Visualizing the Past

Religions of the World

PREFACE

The response of the United States to the events of September 11, 2001, including the war in Iraq and Afghanistan, have brought upon the world a new awareness of human history in a global context. Prior to the attacks on New York and Washington and the subsequent U.S. intervention in the Middle East, readers in North America generally understood world history and globalism as academic concepts. They now understand them as realities shaping their daily lives and experience. The immediate pressures of the present and of the foreseeable future draw us to seek a more certain and extensive understanding of the past.

The idea of globalization is now a pressing reality on the lives of nations, affecting the domestic security of their citizens, the deployment of armed forces, their standard of living, and the environment. Whether, as Samuel Huntington, the distinguished Harvard political scientist, contends, we are witnessing a clash of civilizations, we have certainly entered a new era in which no active citizen or educated person can escape the necessity of understanding the past in global terms. Both the historical experience and the moral, political, and religious values of the different world civilizations now demand our attention and our understanding. It is our hope that in these new, challenging times *The Heritage of World Civilizations* will provide one path to such knowledge.

THE ROOTS OF GLOBALIZATION

Globalization—that is, the increasing interaction and interdependency of the various regions of the world—has resulted from two major historical developments: the closing of the European era of world history and the rise of technology.

From approximately 1500 C.E. to the middle of the twentieth century, Europeans gradually came to dominate the world through colonization (most particularly in North and South America), state-building, economic productivity, and military power. That era of European dominance ended during the third quarter of the twentieth century after Europe had brought unprecedented destruction on itself during World War II and as the nations of Asia, the Near East, and Africa achieved new positions on the world scene. Their new political independence, their control over strategic natural resources, and the expansion of their economies (especially those of

the nations of the Pacific rim of Asia), and in some cases their access to nuclear weapons have changed the shape of world affairs.

Further changing the world political and social situation has been a growing discrepancy in the economic development of different regions that is often portrayed as a problem between the northern and southern hemispheres. Beyond the emergence of this economic disparity has been the remarkable advance of radical political Islamism during the past forty years. In the midst of all these developments, as a result of the political collapse of the former Soviet Union, the United States has emerged as the single major world power.

The second historical development that continues to fuel the pace of globalization is the advance of technology, associated most importantly with transportation, military weapons, and electronic communication. The advances in transportation over the past two centuries including ships, railways, and airplanes have made more parts of the world and its resources accessible to more people in ever shorter spans of time. Over the past century and a half, military weapons of increasingly destructive power enabled Europeans and then later the United States to dominate other regions of the globe. Now, the spread of these weapons means that any nation with sophisticated military technology can threaten other nations, no matter how far away. Furthermore, technologies that originated in the West from the early twentieth century to the present have been turned against the West. More recently, the electronic revolution associated with computer technology and most particularly the internet has sparked unprecedented speed and complexity in global communications. It is astonishing to recall that personal computers have been generally available for less than twenty-five years and the rapid personal communication associated with them has existed for less than fifteen years.

Why not, then, focus only on new factors in the modern world, such as the impact of technology and the end of the European era? To do so would ignore the very deep roots that these developments have in the past. More important, the events of recent years demonstrate, as the authors of this book have long contended, that the major religious traditions continue to shape and drive the modern world as well as the world of the past. The religious traditions link today's civilizations to their most ancient roots. We believe this emphasis on the great religious traditions recognizes not only a factor that has shaped the past, but one that is profoundly and dynamically alive in our world today.

STRENGTHS OF THE TEXT

Balanced and Flexible Presentation   In this edition, as in past editions, we have sought to present world history fairly, accurately, and in a way that does justice to its great variety. History has many facets, no one of which can account for the others. Any attempt to tell the story of civilization from a single perspective, no matter how timely, is bound to neglect or suppress some important part of that story.

Historians have recently brought a vast array of new tools and concepts to bear on the study of history. Our coverage introduces students to various aspects of social and intellectual history as well as to the more traditional political, diplomatic, and military coverage. We firmly believe that only through an appreciation of all pathways to understanding of the past can the real heritage of world civilizations be claimed.

The Heritage of World Civilizations, TLC Edition, is designed to accommodate a variety of approaches to a course in world history, allowing teachers to stress what is most important to them. Some teachers will ask students to read all the chapters. Others will select among them to reinforce assigned readings and lectures.

Clarity and Accessibility   Good narrative history requires clear, vigorous prose. Our goal has been to make our presentation fully accessible to students without compromising on vocabulary or conceptual level. We hope this effort will benefit both teachers and students.

Current Scholarship   As in previous editions, changes in this edition reflect our determination to incorporate the most recent developments in historical scholarship and the expanding concerns of professional historians. To better highlight the dynamic processes of world history, significant new coverage of the Silk Road, Byzantium, the Crusades, Southeast Asia, women in Islam, nineteenth-century European science, the homefront during World War II, and recent events in the Middle East has been added.

Pedagogical Features   This edition retains many of the pedagogical features of previous editions, while providing increased assessment opportunities.

- NEW • **Chapter Highlights** begin each chapter and provide a preview of the key developments and themes that are to follow.

- **Part Timelines** show the major events in five regions—Europe, the Near East and India, East Asia, Africa, and the Americas—side by side. Appropriate photographs enrich each timeline.

- **Chapter-Opening Questions**, organized by the main subtopics of each chapter, encourage careful consideration of important themes and developments. Each question is repeated at the appropriate place in the margin of the text.

- **Chronologies** within each chapter help students organize a time sequence for key events.

- **History's Voices**, including selections from sacred books, poems, philosophy, political manifestos, letters, and travel accounts, introduce students to the raw material of history, providing an intimate contact with the people of the past and their concerns. Questions accompanying the source documents direct students toward important, thought-provoking issues and help them relate the documents to the material in the text. They can be used to stimulate class discussion or as topics for essays and study groups.

- **Map Explorations** and **Critical-Thinking Questions** prompt students to engage with maps, often in an interactive fashion. Each Map Exploration is found on the Companion Website for the text.

- NEW • **Religions of the World** essays examine the historical impact of each of the world's great religious traditions: Judaism, Christianity, Islam, Buddhism, and Hinduism.

- **Visualizing the Past** essays, found at the end of selected chapters, analyze important aspects of world history through photographs, fine art, sculpture, and woodcuts. Focus questions and a running narrative guide students though a careful examination of the historical issues raised by each topic in question. Four new Visualizing the Past essays have been added to this edition: "Humans and Nature in the Ancient World," "The Silk Road," "Mapping the World before 1500," and "Imagining Women in the 18th and 19th Centuries."

- **Chapter Review** Questions help students focus on and interpret the broad themes of a chapter. These questions can be used for class discussion and essay topics.

- **Overview Tables** in each chapter summarize complex issues.

- **Quick Reviews**, found at key places in the margins of each chapter, encourage students to review important concepts.

- **Key Terms**, boldfaced in the text, are listed (with page reference) at the end of each chapter, and defined in the book's glossary.

- **Documents CD-ROM**, containing over 200 documents in world history, is bound with all new copies of the text. Relevant documents are listed at appropriate places in the margin of the text and at the end of each chapter.

- **NEW** • **Study in Time**, a laminated six-panel timeline of world history, provides a succinct overview of key developments in social, political, and cultural history in global history from earliest times to the present.

- **NEW** • **Online Essays**, located on the companion website for *The Heritage of World Civilizations*, provide additional learning opportunities. One set of essays examines technology and civilization from a cross-cultural perspective, while a second set introduces each chapter's content from a wider global viewpoint.

Content and Organization The many changes in content and organization in this edition of *The Heritage of World Civilizations* reflect our ongoing effort to present a truly global survey of world civilizations that at the same time gives a rich picture of the history of individual regions:

- **Strengthened Global Approach.** This new TLC edition more explicitly highlights the connections and parallels in global history among regions of the world.

Greater emphasis is now placed on cultural exchange, trade, encounter, and the diffusion of ideas.

- **Expanded and Improved Map Program.** The entire map program has been completely clarified and expanded. Several new maps graphically illustrate key global developments, such as trade in the classical world, the spread of Buddhism, the Islamicization of Southeast Asia, the Columbian exchange, world slavery, European global conflicts in the eighteenth century, global migration, and the Holocaust. Every single map in the text has been redesigned for greater visual appeal and accuracy. A listing of all the maps in the text can be found on pp. xxiv–xxvi.

- **Improved, Streamlined Organization.** To better accommodate typical teaching sequences, the number of chapters has been reduced to 34, with coverage of European society and state-building in the seventeenth and eighteenth centuries now treated in a single chapter. In addition, coverage of Han China (chapter 7) now immediately succeeds coverage of the Rome (chapter 6) making it easier to draw connections and parallels between these two empires. The final chapter has been exensively reorganized to better examine important recent events in the Middle East.

- **New Design and Photo Program.** The entire text has been set in a lively and engaging new design. Each of the 34 chapters includes photos never before included in previous editions of the text, the total number of illustrations in the text has been increased.

A Note on Dates and Transliteration We have used B.C.E. (before the common era) and C.E. (common era) instead of B.C. (before Christ) and A.D. (anno domini, the year of our Lord) to designate dates.

Until recently, most scholarship on China used the Wade-Giles system of romanization for Chinese names and terms. China, today, however, uses another system known as pinyin. Virtually all Western newspapers have adopted it. In order that students may move easily from the present text to the existing body of advanced scholarship on Chinese history, we now use the pinyin system throughout the text.

Also, we have followed the currently accepted English transliterations of Arabic words. For example, today Koran is being replaced by the more accurate Qur'an; similarly Muhammad is preferable to Mohammed and Muslim to Moslem. We have not tried to distinguish the letters 'ayn and hamza; both are rendered by a simple apostrophe (') as in shi'ite.

With regard to Sanskritic transliteration, we have not distinguished linguals and dentals, and both palatal and lingual s are rendered sh, as in Shiva and Upanishad.

ANCILLARY INSTRUCTIONAL MATERIALS

The Heritage of World Civilizations, TLC Edition, comes with an extensive package of ancillary materials.

For the Instructor

- **Instructor's Resource Binder** This innovative, all-in-one resource organizes the instructor's manual, the Test-Item File, and the transparency pack by each chapter of *The Heritage of World Civilizations* to facilitate class preparation. The Instructor's Resource Binder also includes an **Instructor's Resource CD-ROM**, which contains all of the maps, graphs, and many of the illustrations from the text in easily downloadable electronic files.

- The *Instructor Resource CD-ROM*, compatible with both Windows and Macintosh environments, provides instructors with such essential teaching tools as hundreds of digitized images and maps for classroom presentations, PowerPoint lectures, and other Instructional material. The assets on the IRCD-ROM can be easily exported into online courses, such as WebCT and Blackboard.

- *Test Manager* is a computerized test management program for Windows and Macintosh environments. The program allows instructors to select items from the test-item file to create tests. It also allows online testing.

- The *Transparency Package* provides instructors with full color transparency acetates of all the maps, charts, and graphs in the text for use in the classroom.

For the Student

- *History Notes* (Volumes I and II) provides practice tests, essay questions, and map exercise to help reinforce key concepts.

- *Documents in World History* (Volumes I and II) is a collection of 200 primary source documents in global history. Questions accompanying the documents can be used for discussion or as writing assignments.

- Produced in collaboration with Dorling Kindersley, the world's most respected cartography publisher, *The Prentice Hall Atlas of World History* includes approximately 100 maps fundamental to the study of world history—from early hominids to the twenty-first century.

- *Reading Critically About History* is a brief guide to reading effectively that provides students with helpful strategies for reading a history textbook.

- *Understanding and Answering Essay Questions* suggest helpful analytical tools for understanding different types of essay questions, and provides precise guidelines for preparing well-crafted essay answers.

- Prentice Hall is pleased to provide adopters of *The Heritage of World Civilizations* with an opportunity to receive significant discounts when copies of the text are bundled with Penguin Classics titles in world history. Contact your local Prentice Hall representative for details.

Media Resources

Key Prentice Hall's Online Resource, **OneKey** lets instructors and students in to the best teaching and learning resources—all in one place. This all-inclusive online resource is designed to help you minimize class preparation and maximize teaching time. Conveniently organized by chapter, OneKey for *The Heritage of World Civilizations*, TLC Edition, reinforces what students have learned in class and from the text. Among the student resources available for each chapter are: a complete, media-rich e-book version of *The Heritage of World Civilizations* TLC Edition; quizzes organized by the main subtopics of each chapter; over 200 primary-source documents; and interactive map quizzes.

For instructors, OneKey includes images and maps from *The Heritage of World Civilizations* TLC Edition, instructional material, hundreds of primary-source documents, and PowerPoint presentations.

Research Navigator.com *Prentice Hall One Search with Research Navigator: History 2005* This brief guide focuses on developing critical-thinking skills necessary for evaluating and using online sources. It provides a brief introduction to navigating the Internet with specific references to History web sites. It also provides an access code and instruction on using Research Navigator, a powerful research tool that provides entry to three exclusive databases of reliable source material: ContentSelect Academic Journal Database, the *New York Times* Search by Subject Archive, and Link Library.

The *Companion Website with Grade Tracker*™ (*www.prenhall.com/craig*) works in tandem with the text and features objectives, study questions, web links to related Internet resources, document exercises, interactive maps, online essays on technology and global history, and map labelling exercises.

World History Document CD-ROM Bound into every new copy of this textbook is a free World History Documents CD-ROM. This is a powerful resource for research and additional reading that contains more than 200 primary source documents central to World History. Each document provides essay questions that are linked directly to a website where short-essay answers can be submitted oline or printed out. A complete list of documents on the CD-ROM is found at the end of the text.

Pearson Prentice Hall is pleased to serve as a sponsor of the **The World History Association Teaching Prize** and **The World History Association and Phi Alpha Theta Student Paper Prize** (undergraduate and graduate divisions). Both of these prizes are awarded annually. For more information, contact *thewha@hawaii.edu*

Acknowledgments

We are grateful to the many scholars and teachers whose thoughtful and often detailed comments helped shape this as well as previous editions of *The Heritage of World Civilizations*. The advice and guidance provided by Magnus T. Bernhardsson of Williams College in the revision of the coverage of Islam is especially appreciated. We also thank Tianyuan Tan of Harvard University, who helped with conversion of Chinese words to the pinyin system and Gayle K. Brunelle, California State University (Fullerton), who provided invaluable input on strengthening the book's global approach.

Special thanks to A. Dan Frankforter of Pennsylvania State University who helped edit this new TLC edition.

Wayne Ackerson, *Salisbury State University*

Jack Martin Balcer, *Ohio State University*

Charmarie J. Blaisdell, *Northeastern University*

Deborah Buffton, *University of Wisconsin at La Crosse*

Loretta Burns, *Mankato State University*

Gayle K. Brunelle, *California State University, Fullerton*

Chun-shu Chang, *University of Michigan, Ann Arbor*

Mark Chavalas, *University of Wisconsin at La Crosse*

Anthony Cheeseboro, *Southern Illinois University at Edwardsville*

William J. Courteney, *University of Wisconsin*

Samuel Willard Crompton, *Holyoke Community College*

James B. Crowley, *Yale University*

Bruce Cummings, *The University of Chicago*

Stephen F. Dale, *Ohio State University, Columbus*

Clarence B. Davis, *Marian College*

Raymond Van Dam, *University of Michigan, Ann Arbor*

Bill Donovan, *Loyola University of Maryland*

Jaime Dunlap, *Olivet College*

Wayne Farris, *University of Tennessee*

Anita Fisher, *Clark College*

Suzanne Gay, *Oberlin College*

Katrina A. Glass, *United States Military Academy*

Robert Gerlich, *Loyola University*

Samuel Robert Goldberger, *Capital Community-Technical College*

Andrew Gow, *University of Alberta*

Katheryn L. Green, *University of Wisconsin, Madison*

David Griffiths, *University of North Carolina, Chapel Hill*

Louis Haas, *Duquesne University*

Joseph T. Hapak, *Moraine Valley Community College*

Kenneth E. Hendrickson, *Sam Houston State University*

Hue-Tam Ho Tai, *Harvard University*

David Kieft, *University of Minnesota*

Frederick Krome, *Northern Kentucky University*

Lisa M. Lane, *Mira Costa College*

Richard Law, *Washington State University*

David Lelyveld, *Columbia University*

Jan Lewis, *Rutgers University, Newark*

James C. Livingston, *College of William and Mary*

Moira Maguire, *University of Arkansas, Little Rock*

Richard L. Moore Jr., *St. Augustine's College*

Beth Nachison, *Southern Connecticut State University*

Robin S. Oggins, *Binghamton University*

Louis A. Perez Jr., *University of South Florida*

Jonathan Perry, *University of Central Florida*

Cora Ann Presley, *Tulane University*

Norman Raiford, *Greenville Technical College*

Norman Ravitch, *University of California, Riverside*

Thomas M. Ricks, *University of Pennsylvania*

Philip F. Riley, *James Madison University*

Thomas Robisheaux, *Duke University*

William S. Rodner, *Tidewater Community College*

David Ruffley, *United States Air Force Academy*

Dankwart A. Rustow, *The City University of New York*

James J. Sack, *University of Illinois at Chicago*

William Schell, *Murray State University*

Marvin Slind, *Washington State University*

Daniel Scavone, *University of Southern Indiana*

Roger Schlesinger, *Washington State University*

Charles C. Stewart, *University of Illinois*

Nancy L. Stockdale, *University of Central Florida*

Carson Tavenner, *United States Air Force Academy*

Truong-buu Lam, *University of Hawaii*

Harry L. Watson, *Loyola College of Maryland*

William B. Whisenhunt, *College of DuPage*

Paul Varley, *Columbia University*

Finally, we would like to thank the dedicated people who helped produce this revision: our acquisitions editor, Charles Cavaliere; Laura Gardner who created the handsome new design for this edition; Randy Pettit, our production Liaison; and Ben Smith our manufacturing buyer.

A.M.C.
W.A.G.
D.K.
S.O.
F.M.T.

ANNOUNCING A NEW SERIES IN WORLD HISTORY

✳ CONNECTIONS: KEY THEMES IN WORLD HISTORY
Series Editor: Alfred J. Andrea

The increasing pace and specialization of historical inquiry has caused an ever-widening gap between professional research and general surveys of world history. The titles in the Connections series are designed to bridge that gap by placing the latest research on selected topics of global significance, such as disease, trade, slavery, imperialism, decolonization, holy war, and revolution, into an easily accessible context for students. Brief and tightly focused, each Connections title examines cross-cultural themes by employing a combination of narrative, documents, and analysis to show students connections in world history.

PUBLISHED

- TRADING TASTES: *Commodity and Cultural Exchange to 1750*
  Erik Gilbert, *Arkansas State University*
  Jonathan Reynolds, *Northern Kentucky University*

- THE FIRST HORSEMAN: *Disease in Human History*
  John Aberth, *Castleton State College*

FORTHCOMING TITLES

- THE GLOBE ENCOMPASSED: *The Age of European Discovery*
  Glen Ames, *University of Toledo*

- JIHAD AND CRUSADE: *Islamic and Christian Holy Wars Through the Ages*
  Alfred J. Andrea, *University of Vermont*

- GENDER AND POWER: *Women and Nationalism, 1880–1960*
  Nupur Chaudhuri, *Texas Southern University*

- CHANGING THE COURSE OF HISTORY: *Revolutions Past and Present*
  Jack Goldstone, *George Mason University*

- CAPTIVES AS COMMODITIES: *The Trans-Atlantic Slave Trade*
  Lisa Lindsay, *University of North Carolina, Chapel Hill*

- AN IMPERIAL WORLD: *Empires and Colonies, 1750–1945*
  Douglas Northrop, *University of Michigan*

- CONFRONTING THE WEST: *Modernization in the Developing World, 1877–1936*
  Cyrus Veeser, *Bentley College*

Contact your local Prentice Hall representative for additional information regarding the Connections series.

ALBERT M. CRAIG is the Harvard-Yenching Research Professor of History at Harvard University, where he has taught since 1959. A graduate of Northwestern University, he took his Ph.D. at Harvard University. He has studied at Strasbourg University and at Kyoto, Keio, and Tokyo universities in Japan. He is the author of *Choshu in the Meiji Restoration* (1961), *The Heritage of Chinese Civilization* (2001), and, with others, of *East Asia, Tradition and Transformation* (1989). He is the editor of *Japan, A Comparative View* (1973) and co-editor of *Personality in Japanese History* (1970). At present he is engaged in research on the thought of Fukuzawa Yukichi. For eleven years (1976–1987) he was the director of the Harvard-Yenching Institute. He has also been a visiting professor at Kyoto and Tokyo Universities. He has received Guggenheim, Fulbright, and Japan Foundation Fellowships. In 1988 he was awarded the Order of the Rising Sun by the Japanese government.

WILLIAM A. GRAHAM is Albertson Professor of Middle Eastern Studies and Professor of the History of Religion at Harvard University, and Master of Currier House at Harvard University. From 1990–1996 he directed Harvard's Center for Middle Eastern Studies. He has taught for twenty-six years at Harvard, where he received the A.M. and Ph.D. degrees. He also studied in Göttingen, Tübingen, and Lebanon. He is the author of *Divine World and Prophetic World in Early Islam* (1977), awarded the American Council of Learned Societies History of Religions book prize in 1978, and of *Beyond the Written Word: Oral Aspects of Scripture in the History of Religion* (1987). He has published a variety of articles in both Islamic studies and the general history of religion and is one of the editors of the *Encyclopedia of the Qur'an*. He serves currently on the editorial board of several journals and has held John Simon Guggenheim and Alexander von Humboldt research fellowships. *Three Faiths, One God*, co-authored with Jacob Neusner and Bruce Chilton, published in January 2003.

DONALD KAGAN is Sterling Professor of History and Classics at Yale University, where he has taught since 1969. He received the A.B. degree in history from Brooklyn College, the M.A. in classics from Brown University, and the Ph.D. in history from Ohio State University. During 1958–1959 he studied at the American School of Classical Studies as a Fulbright Scholar. He has received three awards for undergraduate teaching at Cornell and Yale. He is the author of a history of Greek political thought, *The Great Dialogue* (1965); a four-volume history of the Peloponnesian war, *The Origins of the Peloponnesian War* (1969); *The Archidamian War* (1974); *The Peace of Nicias and the Sicilian Expedition* (1981); *The Fall of the Athenian Empire* (1987); and a biography of Pericles, *Pericles of Athens and the Birth of Democracy* (1991); *On the Origins of War* (1995), and *The Peloponnesian War* (2003). He is coauthor, with Frederick W. Kagan of *While America Sleeps* (2000). With Brian Tierney and L. Pearce Williams, he is the editor of *Great Issues in Western Civilization*, a collection of readings. He was awarded the National Humanities Medal for 2002.

STEVEN OZMENT is McLean Professor of Ancient and Modern History at Harvard University. He has taught Western Civilization at Yale, Stanford, and Harvard. He is the author of eleven books. *The Age of Reform, 1250–1550* (1980) won the Schaff Prize and was nominated for the 1981 National Book Award. Five of his books have been selections of the History Book Club: *Magdalena and Balthasar: An Intimate Portrait of Life in Sixteenth Century Europe* (1986), *Three Behaim Boys: Growing Up in Early Modern Germany* (1990), *Protestants: The Birth of A Revolution* (1992), *The Burgermeister's Daughter: Scandal in a Sixteenth Century German Town* (1996), and *Flesh and Spirit: Private Life in Early Modern Germany* (1999). His most recent publications are *Ancestors: The Loving Family of Old Europe* (2001), *A Mighty Fortress: A New History of the German People* (2004), and "Why We Study Western Civ," *The Public Interest* 158 (2005).

FRANK M. TURNER is John Hay Whitney Professor of History at Yale University, where he served as University Provost from 1988 to 1992. He received his B.A. degree at the College of William and Mary and his Ph.D. from Yale. He has received the Yale College Award for Distinguished Undergraduate Teaching. He has directed a National Endowment for the Humanities Summer Institute. His scholarly research has received the support of fellowships from the National Endowment for the Humanities and the Guggenheim Foundation and the Woodrow Wilson Center. He is the author of *Between Science and Religion: The Reaction to Scientific Naturalism in Late Victorian England* (1974), *The Greek Heritage in Victorian Britain* (1981), which received the British Council Prize of the Conference on British Studies and the Yale Press Governors Award, *Contesting Cultural Authority: Essays in Victorian Intellectual Life* (1993), and *John Henry Newman: The Challenge to Evangelical Religion* (2002). He has also contributed numerous articles to journals and has served on the editorial advisory boards of *The Journal of Modern History, Isis,* and *Victorian Studies.* He edited *The Idea of a University,* by John Henry Newman (1996). Since 1996 he has served as a Trustee of Connecticut College. In 2003, Professor Turner was appointed Director of the Beinecke Rare Book and Manuscript Library at Yale University.

*When writing history, historians use maps, tables, graphs, and visuals to help
their readers understand the past. What follows is an explanation of how to
use the historian's tools that are contained in this book.*

TEXT

Whether it is a biography of Gandhi, an article on the Ottoman Empire, or a survey of world history such as this one, the text is the historian's basic tool for discussing the past. Historians write about the past using narration and analysis. Narration is the story line of history. It describes what happened in the past, who did it, and where and when it occurred. Narration is also used to describe how people in the past lived, how they passed their daily lives and even, when the historical evidence makes it possible for us to know, what they thought, felt, feared, or desired. Using analysis, historians explain why they think events in the past happened the way they did and offer an explanation for the story of history. In this book, narration and analysis are interwoven in each chapter.

STUDY AIDS

A number of features in this book are designed to aid in the study of history. Each chapter begins with **Chapter Highlights**, mini-summaries that preview key themes and developments, and **Questions**, organized by the main subtopics of each chapter, which encourage careful consideration of important themes and developments. Each question is repeated at the appropriate place in the margin of the text.

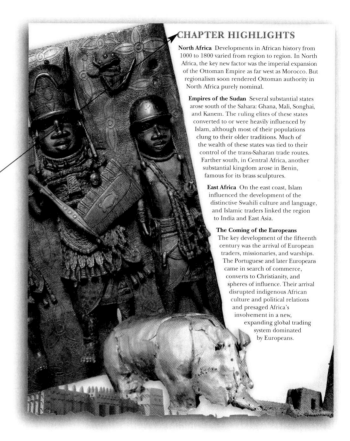

CHAPTER HIGHLIGHTS

North Africa Developments in African history from 1000 to 1800 varied from region to region. In North Africa, the key new factor was the imperial expansion of the Ottoman Empire as far west as Morocco. But regionalism soon rendered Ottoman authority in North Africa purely nominal.

Empires of the Sudan Several substantial states arose south of the Sahara: Ghana, Mali, Songhai, and Kanem. The ruling elites of these states converted to or were heavily influenced by Islam, although most of their populations clung to their older traditions. Much of the wealth of these states was tied to their control of the trans-Saharan trade routes. Farther south, in Central Africa, another substantial kingdom arose in Benin, famous for its brass sculptures.

East Africa On the east coast, Islam influenced the development of the distinctive Swahili culture and language, and Islamic traders linked the region to India and East Asia.

The Coming of the Europeans The key development of the fifteenth century was the arrival of European traders, missionaries, and warships. The Portuguese and later Europeans came in search of commerce, converts to Christianity, and spheres of influence. Their arrival disrupted indigenous African culture and political relations and presaged Africa's involvement in a new, expanding global trading system dominated by Europeans.

WHICH ECONOMIC factors led to the spread of slavery in the New World?

SLAVERY IN THE AMERICAS

*B*lack slavery was the final mode of forced or subservient labor in the New World. It extended throughout the Americas.

ESTABLISHMENT OF SLAVERY

As the numbers of Native Americans in South America declined, the Spanish and Portuguese turned to African slaves. By the late 1500s, in the West Indies and the cities of South America, black slaves surpassed the white population.

On much of the South American continent dominated by Spain, slavery declined during the late 17th century, but it continued to thrive in Brazil and in the Caribbean. In British North America, it began with the importation of slaves to Jamestown in 1619, and quickly became a fundamental institution.

The spread of slavery in Brazil and the West Indies was promoted by the market for sugar. Only slave labor could provide enough workers for the sugar

MAPS

Maps are important historical tools. They show how geography has affected history and concisely summarize complex relationships and events. Knowing how to read and interpret a map is important to understanding history. Map 11–1 from Chapter 11 shows Muslim conquests from 622–750 C.E. It has three features to help you read it: a **caption**, a **legend**, and a **scale**. The caption explains the rapid rise of Islam from its beginnings in Arabia to its domination of much of the Mediterranean and Persia.

The legend is situated on the bottom left corner of the map. The legend provides information for what each colored area of the map represents. The purple region is the Byzantine Empire. The dark orange represents Muhammad's conquests from 622–632. The areas in light orange were conquered in 632–661. The territories in brown were conquered between 661–750.

The scale, located on the top of the map, informs us that three-quarters of an inch equals 1000 miles (or about 1600 kilometers). With this information, estimates of distance between points on the map are easily made.

The map also shows the topography of the region—its mountains, rivers, and seas. This helps us understand the interplay between geography and history. For example, note how the spead of Islam stops at the Caucasus Mountains. Do you think the topography of this region played a role in limiting the Muslim advance?

Finally, a **critical-thinking question** asks for careful consideration of the spatial connections between geography and history.

MAP EXPLORATION

Interactive map: To explore this map further, go to **http://www.prenhall.com/craig/map11.1**

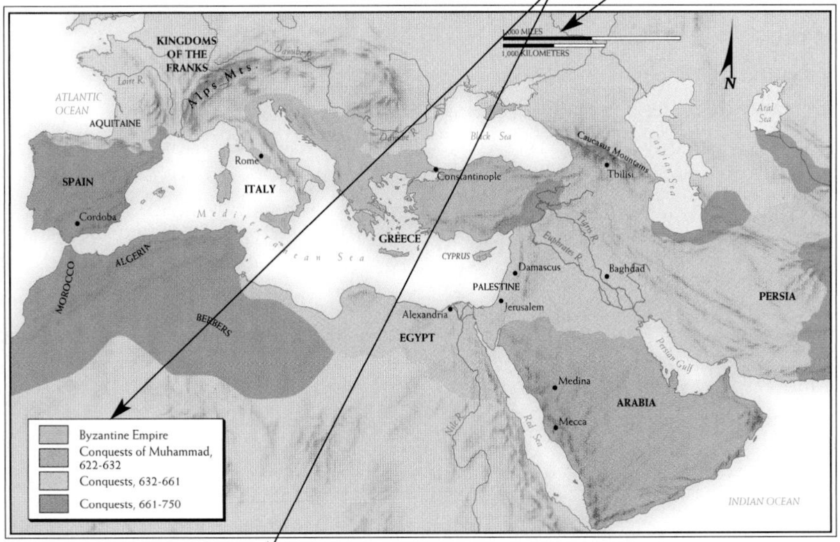

MAP 11–1
Muslim Conquests and Domination of the Mediterranean to about 750 C.E. The rapid spread of Islam (both religion and political-military power) is shown here. Within 125 years of Muhammad's rise, Muslims came to dominate Spain and all areas south and east of the Mediterranean.

WHY DID so many subject peoples welcome Islamic rule?

MAP EXPLORATIONS

Many of the maps in each chapter are provided in a useful interactive version on the text's Companion Website. These maps are easily identified by a bar along the top (see example above) that reads "**Map Exploration.**" An interactive version of Map 11.1 can be found at **www.prenhall.com/craig/map11.1**. The interactive version of this particular map provides an opportunity to move a timeline from left to right to see the progress of Muslim conquests.

ANALYZING VISUALS

Visual images embedded thoughout the text can provide as much insight into world history as the written word. Within photographs and pieces of fine art lies emotional and historical meaning. Captions also provide valuable information, such as in the example below. When studying the image, consider questions such as: "Who are these people?"; "What are their relationships to each other?"; "What are they doing?"; and "What can we learn from the way the people are dressed?" Such analysis allows for a fuller understanding of the way people lived in the past.

VISUALIZING THE PAST

These essays, found at the end of selected chapters, analyze important aspects of world history through photographs, fine art, sculpture, maps, and woodcuts. Focus questions and a running narrative guide the reader though a careful examination of the historical implications of each topic in question.

Plantation. In the American South, the islands of the Caribbean, and in Brazil, slaves labored on sugar plantations under the authority of overseers.

The Granger Collection.

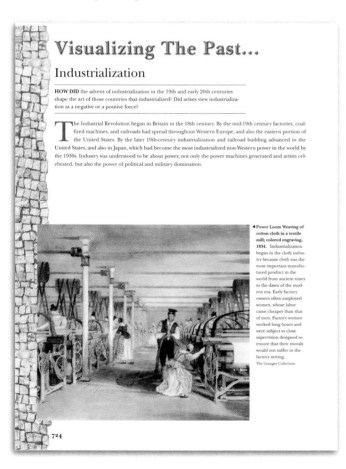

Visualizing The Past...

Industrialization

HOW DID the advent of industrialization in the 19th and early 20th centuries shape the art of those countries that industrialized? Did artists view industrialization as a negative or a positive force?

The Industrial Revolution began in Britain in the 18th century. By the mid-19th century factories, coal-fired machines, and railroads had spread throughout Western Europe, and also the eastern portion of the United States. By the later 19th-century industrialization and railroad building advanced in the United States, and also in Japan, which had become the most industrialized non-Western power in the world by the 1930s. Industry was understood to be about power, not only the power machines generated and artists celebrated, but also the power of political and military domination.

◄ **Power Loom Weaving of cotton cloth in a textile mill; colored engraving, 1834.** Industrialization began in the cloth industry because cloth was the most important manufactured product in the world from ancient times to the dawn of the modern era. Early factory owners often employed women, whose labor came cheaper than that of men. Factory women worked long hours and were subject to close supervision designed to ensure that their morals would not suffer in the factory setting.
The Granger Collection.

724

RELIGIONS OF THE WORLD

Each of these special, two-page essays examines one of the world's great religions and the impact it has had on history.

Religions of the World

JUDAISM

Monotheism, the belief in a unique God who is the creator of the universe and its all-powerful ruler, first became a central and lasting element in religion among the Hebrews, later called Israelites and also Jews. Their religion, more than the many forms of polytheistic worship that characterized the ancient world, demanded moral rectitude and placed ethical responsibilities both on individuals and on the community as a whole. Their God had a divine plan for human history, which was linked to the behavior of his chosen people. This vision of the exclusive worship of the true God, obedience to the laws governing the community that derive from him, and a strong ethical responsibility was connected to humanity's historical experience in this world. Ultimately it gave rise to three great religions: Judaism, Christianity, and Islam.

At the beginning of this tradition stands Abraham, whom all three religions recognize as their founder. According to the Torah (the first five books of the Hebrew Bible or the Christian Old Testament), Abraham entered into a covenant with God in which he promised to worship only this God, who in turn promised to make Abraham's descendants his own chosen people—chosen to worship him, to obey his laws, and to undertake a special set of moral responsibilities. God renewed the covenant with Moses at Mount Sinai when he freed the Israelites from Egyptian bondage. He promised them the land of Canaan (later called Palestine and part of which is now the state of Israel) and gave them the law (the Torah), including the Ten Commandments, by which they were to guide their lives. As long as they lived by his law, God would give them his guidance and protection.

In time the Israelites formed themselves into a kingdom which remained unified from about 1000 to 922 B.C.E. In the period after its division, prophets emerged. Thought to be inspired by God, the prophets chastised the Israelites for their lapses into idolatry and immorality. Even as the kingdom was disintegrating and the Israelites falling under the control of alien empires, the prophets preached social reform and a return to God's laws. They saw Israel's misfortune as punishment for failing to keep the covenant and predicted disaster if the Israelites did not change their ways. When disasters came—the Jewish kingdoms captured, the people enslaved and exiled—the prophets interpreted Israel's status as a chosen people to mean that their sufferings would make them "a light unto the nations," leading other nations to the true worship of one God

The prophets also preached that God was righteous and demanded righteousness from his people. But he was also a God of justice. Although he might need to punish his people for their sins, he would one day reward them with divine favor. Traditional Jewish belief expects that the Messiah, or Anointed One, will someday come and establish God's kingdom on earth. He will introduce an age of universal brotherhood in which all nations will acknowledge the one true God.

The Jews are "people of the Book," and foremost among their sacred texts is the Hebrew Bible, consisting of the Five Books of Moses (the Torah), the books of the prophets, and other writings. The Torah is the source of Jewish law. Over the centuries new experiences required new interpretation of the law, which was accomplished by the oral law, no less sacred than the written law. Compilations of interpretation and commentary by rabbis (wise and learned teachers) were brought together to form the Talmud.

▲ **Jonah Eaten by the Whale, from a Hebrew Bible, 1299.** Like the Christian illuminated manuscripts they closely resembled, Jewish medieval manuscripts were filled with images of scenes from the Torah and Jewish history. Hebrew writing also developed into an elaborately beautiful calligraphy. Many of these Jewish medieval illuminated manuscripts were, like their Christian counterparts, commissioned by wealthy and influential leaders of Jewish communities in Europe.
Instituto da Biblioteca Nacional, Lisbon, Portugal/Bridgeman Art Library.

50

OVERVIEWS

The **Overview** tables in this text are a special feature designed to highlight and summarize important topics within a chapter. The Overview table shown here, for example, summarizes the Columbian exchange.

OVERVIEW · THE COLUMBIAN EXCHANGE

The same ships that carried Europeans and Africans to the Americas also transported animals, plants, and diseases that had never before appeared in the New World. There was a similar transport back to Europe and Africa. Historians call this cross-continental flow "the Columbian exchange." The overall result was an ecological transformation that continues to shape the world.

To the Americas

Animals:	cattle, chickens, goats, horses, pigs, and sheep
Plants:	almonds, apples, apricots, bananas, barley, cabbage, cherries, dandelions, grapes, lemons, mangos, melons, oats, okra, olives, onions, oranges, peaches, pears, plums, radishes, rice, sugar cane, wheat, and other green vegetables
Diseases:	bubonic plague, chicken pox, diphtheria, influenza, malaria, measles, smallpox, typhoid, and typhus

From the Americas

Animals:	turkeys
Plants:	avocados, beans, blueberries, chilis, cocoa, guavas, maize, manioc (tapioca), peanuts, pecans, pineapples, potatoes, pumpkins, squash, sweet peppers, sweet potatoes, tobacco, and tomatoes
Diseases:	syphilis

QUICK REVIEWS

Quick reviews, placed at key locations in the margins of each chapter, provide pinpoint summaries of important concepts.

> **QUICK REVIEW**
>
> **Women Under the Qing and Ming**
> - Confucian family ideals changed little during the Ming and Qing eras
> - Footbinding spread among the upper classes and some commoners
> - As population grew, more women worked at home

Church and Empire

910	Monastery of Cluny founded
918	Henry I becomes King of Germany
951	Otto I invades Italy
955	Otto I defeats the Hungarians at Lechfeld
962	Otto I crowned emperor by Pope John XII
1077	Gregory VII pardons Henry IV at Canossa
1122	Concordat of Worms settles the investiture controversy
1152–1190	Reign of Frederick Barbarossa
1198–1215	Reign of Innocent III
1214	Collapse of the claims of Otto IV
1220	Frederick II crowned emperor
1232	Frederick II devolves authority to the German princes
1257	The German monarchy becomes elective

CHRONOLOGIES

Each chapter includes **Chronologies** that list, in chronological order, key events discussed in the chapter. The chronology shown here from Chapter 12, lists the dates of key events in the history of the Holy Roman Empire. Chronologies provide a review of important events and their relationship to one another.

WORLD HISTORY DOCUMENT CD-ROM

Bound into every new copy of this textbook is a free world. History Document CD-ROM. This is a powerful resource for research and additional reading that contains more than 200 primary source documents central to world History. Each document provides essay questions that are linked directly to a website where short-essay answers can be submitted online or printed out. Particularly relevant or interesting documents are called out at appropriate places in the margin of each chapter (see example). A complete list of documents on the CD-ROM is found at the end of the text.

11.1
Mansa Musa: The "King Who Sits on a Mountain of Gold"

PRIMARY SOURCE DOCUMENTS

Historians find most of their information in written records, original documents that have survived from the past. These include government publications, letters, diaries, newspapers—whatever people wrote or printed, including many private documents never intended for publication. Each chapter in the book contains a feature called **History's Voices**—a selection from a primary source document. The example shown here is a description by a Chinese traveler of India. Each **History's Voices** begins with a brief introduction followed by questions on what the document reveals.

HISTORY'S VOICES

A CHINESE TRAVELER'S REPORT ON THE GUPTA REALM

Fa-Hsien, a Chinese Buddhist monk, was the first of several Chinese known for traveling to India to study and bring back Buddhist scriptures from the intellectual centers of Buddhist thought there. He wrote an account of his travels, first through Central Asia, then all over India, and finally through Ceylon and Indonesia again to China (399–414 C.E.).

WHAT THINGS about India seem most to surprise Fa-Hsien? Is his image of Indian rule a positive one? What do his remarks say about the prestige of the Buddhist tradition and its monks in the Indian state? What does he tell us about Indian society?

On the sides of the river, both right and left, are twenty san ghârâmas [monasteries], with perhaps 3,000 priests. The law of the Buddha is progressing and flourishing. Beyond the deserts are the countries of Western India. The kings of these countries are all firm believers in the law of Buddha. They remove their caps of state when they make offerings to the priests. The members of the royal household and the chief ministers personally direct the food-giving; when the distribution of food is over, they spread a carpet on the ground opposite the chief seat (the president's seat) and sit down before it. They dare not sit on couches in the presence of the priests. The rules relating to the almsgiving of kings have been handed down from the time of Buddha till now. Southward from this is the so-called middle-country (Mâdhyadeśa). The climate of this country is warm and equable, without frost or snow. The people are very well off, without poll tax or official restrictions. Only those who till the royal lands return a portion of profit of the land. If they desire to go, they go; if they like to stop, they stop. The kings govern without corporal punishment; criminals are fined, according to circumstances, lightly or heavily. Even in cases of repeated rebellion they only cut off the right hand. The king's personal attendants, who guard him on the right and left, have fixed salaries. Throughout the country the people kill no living thing nor drink wine, nor do they eat garlic or onions, with the exception of Chandâlas [outcasts] only. The Chandâlas are named "evil men" and dwell apart from others; if they enter a town or market, they sound a piece of wood in order to separate themselves; then men, knowing who they are, avoid coming in contact with them. In this country they do not keep swine nor fowls, and do not deal in cattle; they have no shambles or wine-shops in their market places. In selling they use cowrie shells. The Chandâlas only hunt and sell flesh. Down from the time of Buddha's Nirvâna, the kings of these countries, the chief men and householders, have raised vihâras [monasteries] for the priests, and provided for their support by bestowing on them fields, houses, and gardens, with men and oxen. Engraved title-deeds were prepared and handed down from one reign to another; no one has ventured to withdraw them, so that till now there has been no interruption. All the resident priests having chambers (in these vihâras) have their beds, mats, food, drink, and clothes provided without stint; in all places this is the case. The priests ever engage themselves in doing meritorious works for the purpose of religious advancement (karma—building up their religious character), or in reciting the scriptures, or in meditation.

Source: "Buddhist Country Records," in Si-Yu-Ki, *Buddhist Records of the Western World*, trans. by Samuel Beal (London, 1884; reprint, Delhi: Oriental Books Reprint Corporation, 1969), pp. xxxvii–xxxviii. Reprinted by permission of Motilal Banarsidass Publishers Pvt. Ltd., Delhi, India.

Indigenous Reactions The vitality of so many of the cultures and traditions that bore the brunt of the Western onslaught has been striking. Arab, Iranian, Indian, African, and other encounters with Western material and intellectual domination produced different responses and initiatives. These have borne full fruit in political, economic, and intellectual independence only since 1945; however, most began much earlier, some even well before 1800.

One result of the imperial-colonial experience almost everywhere has been the sharpening of cultural self-consciousness and self-confidence among those peoples most negatively affected by Western dominance. The imperial-colonial experiences of the Third World nations may well prove to have been not only ones of misery and reversal, but also of transition to positive development and resurgence, despite the looming economic, educational, and demographic problems that plague many of them.

REVIEW QUESTIONS

1. What kind of policies did the British follow in India? What were the kinds of political activism against British rule were there in India after 1800?

2. How was the Islamic world internally divided after 1800? How did those divisions influence the coming of European powers?

3. How did nationalism affect European control in south Asia, Africa, and the Middle East?

4. What was the role of African nationalism in resisting foreign control?

KEY TERMS

bazaari (p. 681)
cantonments (p. 677)
Great Trek (p. 684)

mfecane (p. 684)
mujtahid (p. 680)
pan-Islamism (p. 682)

raj (p. 675)
scramble for Africa (p. 689)
Wahhabis (p. 679)

 For additional study resources for this chapter, go to:
www.prenhall.com/craig/chapter27

IMAGE KEY
for pages 672–673

a. A fez.
b. Kemal Ataturk.
c. ivory for sale, congo.
d. An Imperial procession, or *durbar*.
e. Mahatma Ghandi.
f. Bungandan Kabaka Mutesa I and members of his court.
g. A page from a 19th-century Moroccan Koran.
h. Imam Shamil of Dagestan.
i. Sepoy cavalry attacking British infantry at the Battle of Cawpore in 1857.

SUMMARIES, REVIEW QUESTIONS, AND ADDITIONAL STUDY RESOURCES

At the end of each chapter **summaries** and **review questions** reconsider the main topics. An Image Key provides information about the illustrations that appear at the beginning of the chapter. The URL for the Companion Website ™ is also found at the end of each chapter; this is an excellent resource for additional study aids. In addition, a laminated "Study in Time" chart is found at the front of the text and provides a succinct timeline of world history.

GLOSSARY/KEY TERMS

Significant historical terms are called out in heavy type throughout the text, defined in the margin, and listed at the end of each chapter with appropriate page numbers. These are listed alphabetically and defined in a glossary at the end of the book.

OneKey is all you need

EXPLORE THE POWER OF ONEKEY

OneKey is Prentice Halls' premium exclusive online resource for instructors and students. **OneKey** gives you access to the best online teaching and learning tools—all available 24/7. Harnessing the power of WebCT ✗WebCT, Blackboard **Bb**, and Course Compass 🧭 CourseCompass, OneKey puts all of your resources in one place for maximum convenience, simplicity and success.

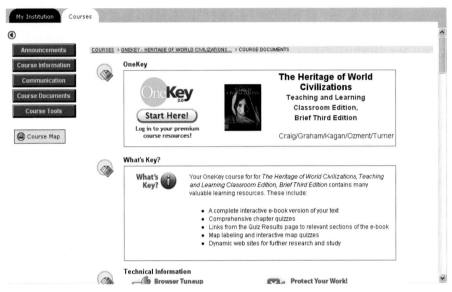

PRESENTATION RESOURCES FOR INSTRUCTORS

VISUALS

- Images
- Maps, Tables, Figures
- Map Outlines

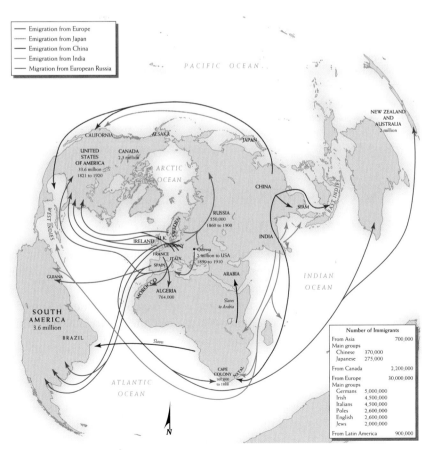

PowerPoint™ Presentations

- Lecture Aids—Visuals
- Lecture Aids—Text
- Lecture Aids—Lecture Outline

Changing Religious Life

❋ Religion in fifteenth-century life
- ◆ Clergy made up 6% to 8% of urban population
- ◆ Considerable political and religious power
- ◆ Monasteries were prominent and influential

❋ Religion in sixteenth-century life
- ◆ Numbers of clergy fell by 2/3
- ◆ Monasteries and nunneries nearly absent
- ◆ Worship conducted in the vernacular
- ◆ Clergy could marry, paid taxes

Animations and Activities

- Interactive Maps

Text

- Instructor's Manual

ASSESSMENT RESOURCES FOR STUDENTS

HOMEWORK

- Review Questions
- e-book

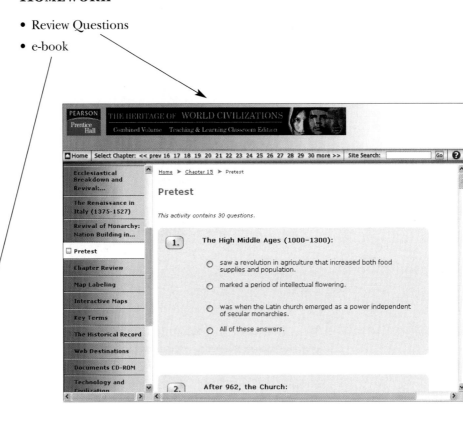

ADDITIONAL STUDENT RESOURCES

LINKS

- Companion Website
- e-themes in World History

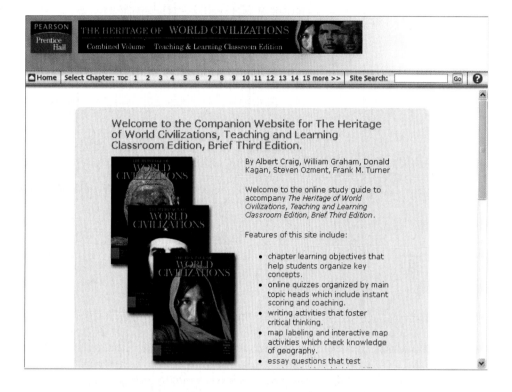

ADDITIONAL RESOURCES

 • Research Navigator

Take a tour at www.prenhall.com/onekey

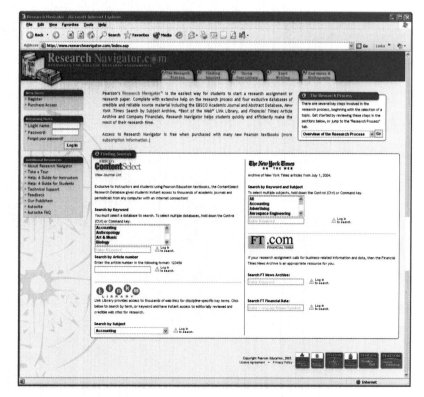

THE HERITAGE OF

WORLD CIVILIZATIONS

EUROPE

◄ Paleolithic sculpture

The Akkadian victory ►
stele of Naram-Sin
ca. 2230 B.C.E.

NEAR EAST / INDIA

ca. 8000 Neolithic Revolution, Mesopotamia

ca. 3500	Development of Sumerian cities
ca. 3000	Development of writing in Mesopotamia
ca. 2800–2370	Early Dynastic period of Sumerian city-states
ca. 2370	Sargon establishes Akkadian dynasty and Empire
ca. 2250–1750	Indus (Harappan) civilization; writing first appears in India
ca. 2125–2027	Third Dynasty of Ur
ca. 2000–1800	Establishment of Amorites in Mesopotamia
ca. 1800–1500	Aryan peoples invade northwestern India
ca. 1792–1750	Reign of Hammurabi
ca. 1550	Establishment of Kassite dynasty at Babylon

▲ Burial urn from China, Neolithic period

EAST ASIA

2205–1766	Traditional dates of Xia dynasty
1766	Bronze Age city-states, aristocratic charioteers, pictographic writing
1766–1050	Traditional dates of Shang dynasty; writing first appears in China

4000 B.C.E. Neolithic Revolution

Ceremonial food vessel, ►
Shang dynasty

AFRICA

3100–2700	Early Dynastic period (I–II), Egypt
ca. 3000	Writing first appears in Egypt
2700–2200	Old Kingdom (III–VI)
2200–2025	First Intermediate period (VII–XI)
2025–1630	Middle Kingdom (XII–XIII)
1630–1550	Second Intermediate period (XIV–XVII)
1550–1075	New Kingdom (XVIII–XX)

Neolithic statues from ►
Ain Ghazal, Jordan
ca. 8500–7000 B.C.E.

Seated Egyptian scribe ►
from the Fifth Dynasty

THE AMERICAS

ca. 4000 Neolithic Revolution in Mexico

ca. 2750 Monumental architecture at Aspero

624–545 Thales of Miletus
ca. 611–546 Anaximander
ca. 546 Anaximenes

469–399 Socrates
429–347 Plato
384–322 Aristotle
435–404 Great Peloponnesian War
ca. 460–400 Thucydides
ca. 400 Hippocrates of Cos
384–322 Demosthenes

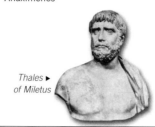

Thales ►
of Miletus

▲ Poseidon, Athena, Apollo, and Artemis, 5th century B.C.E.

---

ca. 1500–1000 Rig-Vedic period, India
ca. 1400–1200 Hittite Empire
ca. 1100 Rise of Assyrian Power

ca. 1000–961 Reign of King David
ca. 961–922 Reign of King Solomon
ca. 1000–500 Late Vedic period, India
ca. 1000–800/600 Composition of Brahmanas
ca. 800–500 Composition of major Upanishads
ca. 700–500 Probable reintroduction of writing
732–722 Assyrian conquest of Syria-Palestine
722 Assyrian conquest of Israel (Northern Kingdom)
612 Destruction of Assyrian capital at Nineveh
612–539 Neo-Babylonian (Chaldean) Empire
586 Destruction of Jerusalem; fall of Judah (southern kingdom); Babylonian captivity
539 Restoration of Temple; return of exiles
540–ca. 468 Mahavira, the Jina/Vardamana
ca. 566–ca. 486 Siddhartha Gautama, the Buddha

ca. 400 B.C.E.–200 C.E. Composition of great epics, the *Mahabharata* and *Ramayana*

Indus stone ►
stamp seal

◄ Ishtar Gate in Babylon

1050–256 Traditional dates of Zhou dynasty

500 Age of philosophers
370–290 Mencius
Fourth century Laozi
221 China is unified under the Qin

Confucius ►

Laozi ►

771 Iron Age territorial states
551–479 Confucius

671 Assyrian conquest of Egypt

◄ *Babylonian map of the world, 612–539 B.C.E.*

1500–400 The Olmec

800 B.C.E.–200 C.E. Chavin (Early) Horizon

200 B.C.E.–750 C.E. The Classic period in central Mexico
150 B.C.E.–900 C.E. The Classic period of Mayan civilization in the Yucatán and Guatemala

◄ *Olmec head*

Temple of the Sun ►

1 The Birth of Civilization

CHAPTER HIGHLIGHTS

The Emergence of Civilization Beginning in 10,000 B.C.E., human beings shifted from a hunter-gatherer way of life to one marked by settled agriculture and the domestication of animals. Between 4000 and 3000 B.C.E., civilization began to appear in the Tigris and Euphrates Valleys in Mesopotamia, then along the Nile River in Egypt, and somewhat later in the Indus Valley in India and the Yellow River Basin in China.

Mesopotamia The Sumerians founded the oldest Mesopotamian cities around 3000 B.C.E. Beginning around 2370 B.C.E., the Sumerian city states were conquered by the Akkadian, Babylonian, and Assyrian empires. The Sumerians passed much of their civilization down to their successors: a system of writing called *cuneiform*, the worship of gods based on natural forces, semi-divine kings, and a highly developed bureaucracy.

Egypt Watered by the Nile and protected by deserts and the sea, Egyptian civilization was more secure and peaceful than that of Mesopotamia. Religion dominated Egyptian life. The pharaohs were considered gods on whom the lives and prosperity of their people depended.

Indus Civilization By 2300 B.C.E. at least 70 Indus cities had developed a sophisticated urban culture. Indus civilization disappeared for unknown reasons between 1800 and 1700 B.C.E. In its place, Indo-European (or Aryan) invaders established the "Vedic" culture, named after the ritual writings known as the Vedas.

China The Shang dynasty and Zhou dynasty are the earliest known civilizations in China. By the fourth century B.C.E., as population and commerce expanded, many petty states clustered into a few large territorial units.

The Americas The first civilizations in the Americas arose in places that produced an agricultural surplus. In Mesoamerica, this was based on the cultivation of maize. In the Andes, it was based on a combination of agriculture and the rich marine resources of the Pacific. The Olmecs (1500–400 B.C.E.) established the first civilization in Mesoamerica, while the first monumental architecture appeared in the Andes around 2750 B.C.E.

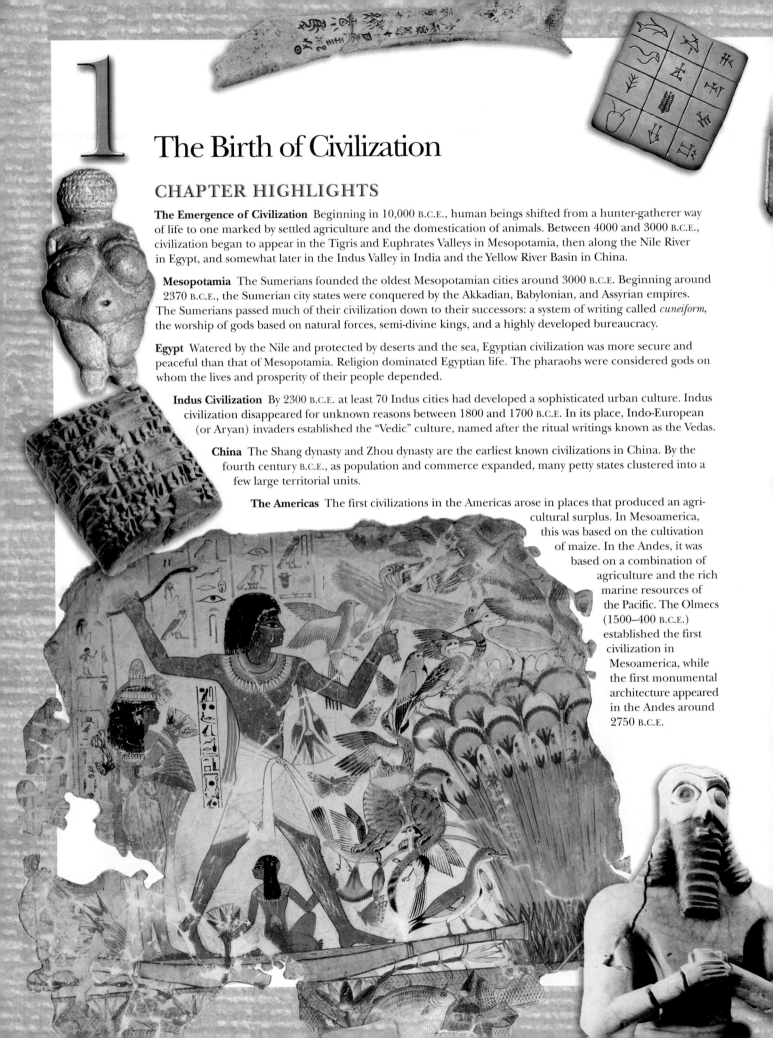

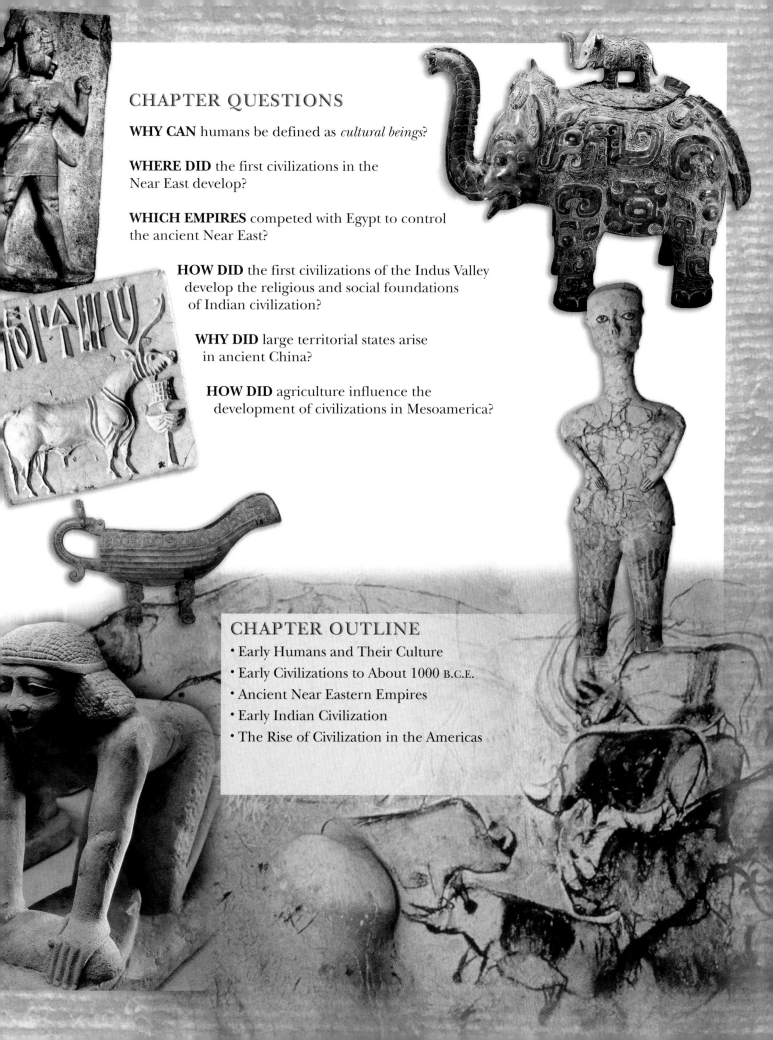

CHAPTER QUESTIONS

WHY CAN humans be defined as *cultural beings*?

WHERE DID the first civilizations in the
Near East develop?

WHICH EMPIRES competed with Egypt to control
the ancient Near East?

HOW DID the first civilizations of the Indus Valley
develop the religious and social foundations
of Indian civilization?

WHY DID large territorial states arise
in ancient China?

HOW DID agriculture influence the
development of civilizations in Mesoamerica?

CHAPTER OUTLINE
- Early Humans and Their Culture
- Early Civilizations to About 1000 B.C.E.
- Ancient Near Eastern Empires
- Early Indian Civilization
- The Rise of Civilization in the Americas

The earliest humans lived by hunting, fishing, and collecting wild plants. They learned to cultivate plants, herd animals, and make pottery only about 10,000 years ago. These discoveries transformed them from food gatherers to producers and allowed them to grow in number and to lead settled lives. About 5,000 years ago, a far more complex way of life began to appear in some parts of the world. In these places, humans learned how to increase harvests through irrigation and other methods and to sustain much larger populations than ever before. As villages grew into cities, centers of industry and commerce appeared. Writing was invented. Specialized occupations emerged, complex religions took form, and social classes developed. These events marked the birth of civilization.

EARLY HUMAN BEINGS AND THEIR CULTURE

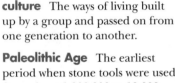

WHY CAN humans be defined as *cultural beings?*

Humans, unlike other animals, are cultural beings. **Culture** may be defined as the way of life built up by a group and passed on from generation to generation. Language, which appears to be a uniquely human trait, greatly facilitated the development and transmission of cultures.

THE PALEOLITHIC AGE

Anthropologists identify early human cultures by their tools. The earliest cultural period—the **Paleolithic Age** (from Greek, meaning "old stone")—dates from the first use of stone tools some 1 or 2 million years ago to about 10,000 B.C.E. During this long span of time, people survived by hunting, fishing, and gathering—but not by producing—food. They learned to make and control fire, to manufacture increasingly sophisticated tools, and to refine language.

Paleolithic technology could support only a thinly scattered population. If hunters became too numerous, game would not suffice. Paleolithic society was probably characterized by a division of labor by sex. Men most likely hunted, fished, and fought. Women, who were less mobile because of childbearing and nursing, probably gathered nuts, berries, and wild grains; wove baskets; and

culture The ways of living built up by a group and passed on from one generation to another.

Paleolithic Age The earliest period when stone tools were used, from about 1,000,000 to 10,000 B.C.E. From the Greek meaning "old stone."

Paleolithic Cave Drawings. Approximately 30,000 years ago in a Chauvet cave, near Avignon, France, Paleolithic artists decorated the walls with exquisite drawings of animals.

Jean Clottes/Corbis Sygma Photo News.

made clothing. By gathering food, women probably discovered how to plant and care for seeds, and they acquired the knowledge that eventually led to agriculture and the **Neolithic Revolution**.

THE NEOLITHIC AGE

However it happened, some 10,000 years ago people living in parts of what we now call the Middle East began to shift from the Paleolithic hunter-gatherer way of life to the settled agricultural lifestyle of the Neolithic Age ("new stone"). Neolithic people domesticated animal and plant species native to certain regions and then spread them to new lands. They invented pottery and learned to weave cloth from flax and wool. They nurtured crops from planting to harvest and built permanent buildings, usually in clusters near their richest fields. Everyone lived at much the same level. There was a little long-distance trade, but most villages were self-sufficient.

In the regions where agriculture and animal husbandry appeared, the number of human beings grew steadily. The Neolithic Revolution was a major step in human control of nature, and it was a vital precondition for the emergence of **civilization**. The earliest Neolithic societies appeared in the Middle East about 8000 B.C.E., in China about 4000 B.C.E., and in India about 5500 B.C.E. Settled agricultural societites began to become prevalent in Mesoamerica (modern Mexico and Central America) and in the Andean region of South America about 2500 B.C.E.

THE BRONZE AGE AND THE BIRTH OF CIVILIZATION

Between 4000 and 3000 B.C.E., civilization first appeared along the Tigris and Euphrates Rivers in the region called **Mesopotamia**. It developed a little later in the valley of the Nile River in Egypt, and somewhat later still in India's Indus Valley and China's Yellow River basin (see Map 1–1). Civilization was marked by the appearance of urban centers, monumental architecture, hierarchical societies, and the invention of writing. This period is called the **Bronze Age** because it coincided with the discovery of the technique for smelting tin and copper and combining them to make bronze, the first metal strong enough to be used for tools.

EARLY CIVILIZATIONS TO ABOUT 1000 B.C.E.

*A*bout 4000 B.C.E., people began to congregate in large numbers in the river-watered lowlands of Mesopotamia and Egypt. By about 3000 B.C.E., when the invention of writing signaled the transition from prehistory to history, urban life and centrally governed states appeared along the Tigris and Euphrates Rivers in Mesopotamia and the Nile in Egypt.

The concentration of people in cities created a new way of life. Many urban dwellers did not grow their own food, so urban life was possible only where farmers produced substantial surpluses and a method existed to collect and redistribute this resource. Organization was also encouraged by the need for intelligent management of water in the arid regions where civilization first appeared. Irrigation was essential in Mesopotamia, but it was difficult. Rivers flooded during the harvest season and water was in short supply at other times. Farmers had to build dikes and reservoirs to manage these challenges. Egypt's rivers flooded at a convenient time of year, making irrigation much simpler. Egypt's rivers were also confined to the floor of a valley, whereas Mesopotamia's rivers flowed through an open plain. Its rivers often changed their courses and forced people to relocate.

Venus of Willendorf. This famous statuette found near Willendorf, Austria, in 1908 may be 25,000 years old. It is only four and one-half inches tall.
Erich Lessing/Art Resource.

Neolithic Revolution The shift beginning 10,000 years ago from hunter-gatherer societies to settled communities.

civilization A form of human culture marked by urbanism, metallurgy, and writing.

Mesopotamia Modern Iraq. The land between the Tigris and Euphrates Rivers.

Bronze Age The name given to the earliest civilized era, ca. 4000 to 1000 B.C.E. The term reflects the importance of the metal bronze for the people of this age in making weapons and tools.

WHERE DID the first civilizations in the Near East develop?

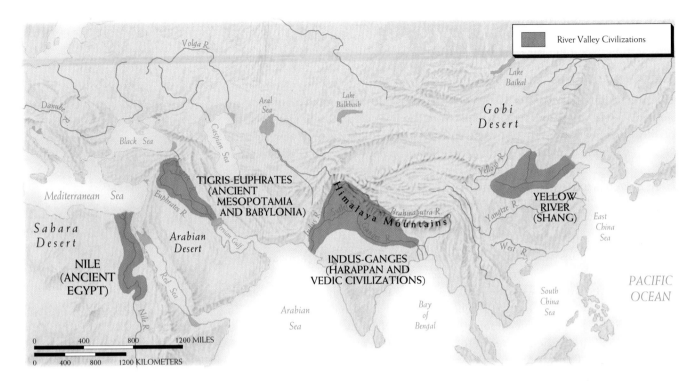

MAP 1–1

The Four Great River Valley Civilizations to ca. 1000 B.C.E. By ca. 2000 B.C.E., urban life was established along the Tigris and Euphrates Rivers in Mesopotamia, the Nile River in Egypt, the Indus and Ganges Rivers in India, and the Yellow River in China.

WHY DID the first civilizations in the Near East and Asia develop in river valleys?

MESOPOTAMIAN CIVILIZATION

The oldest Mesopotamian cities appear to be those founded by the Sumerians around 3000 B.C.E. in the southern half of Babylonia. From about 2800 to 2370 B.C.E., the Early Dynastic period, several Sumerian city-states arose in southern Mesopotamia. They formed leagues, fought among themselves incessantly, and, as stronger towns conquered weaker ones, kingdoms appeared.

The region immediately upstream from the principal Sumerian city-states was primarily occupied by people who spoke a language that belongs to the same family as modern Arabic and Hebrew (i.e., a Semitic language). These people established a kingdom with a capital at Akkad, near the site where the famous city of Babylon was later founded. The Akkadian king, Sargon, conquered the Sumerian cities and created an empire. The dynasty of Semitic kings he founded, about 2370 B.C.E., ruled Sumer and Akkad for two centuries. When it succumbed to internal weakness and external attack, smaller independent states appeared. About 2125 B.C.E. the city of Ur, under its Third Dynasty, restored unity to the region, and Sumerian civilization flowered for the final time. When it fell about 2027 B.C.E., the Sumerians disappeared as an identifiable group—though their language survived as a scholarly tongue preserved by subsequent Middle Eastern civilizations.

About 1900 B.C.E., a people called the Amorites gained control of the region and established a government with its seat at Babylon. The Amorite, or Old Babylonian, dynasty dominated Mesopotamia for about 300 years. Its high point was the reign of Hammurabi (r. ca. 1792–1750 B.C.E.), who is best known for

HISTORY'S VOICES

THE CODE OF HAMMURABI

The Code of Hammurabi (r. 1792–1750 B.C.E.) was only one of many collections of laws produced by Mesopotamian societies. Mesopotamian law codes, such as that of Hammurabi, seem unjust, in that they prescribed different rights, responsibilities, and punishments, depending on the gender, class, and slave or free status of the persons involved. But Hammurabi's code represents an enormous advance in legal thought because it organized and standardized laws and punishments, which made the legal process less dependent on the whims of rulers and judges. Hammurabi's code also provides invaluable information for historians about the social structures and culture of Babylonian society.

WHAT DO the passages suggest about Mesopotamians' views on the role of marriage in society and on the role of women in marriage? If you formed your judgment about the roles women played in Babylonian society from passages 129, 137, and 138 alone, you might assume that women primarily reared children and were confined to the home. What do the other passages reveal about other roles that women played in this culture? What does this difference suggest about the importance of evidence and the accidents of its survival in understanding the lives of women in history?

109. If rebels meet in the house of a wineseller and she does not seize them and take them to the palace, that wineseller shall be slain.

110. If a priestess who has not remained in the temple shall open a wine-shop, or enter a wine-shop for a drink, that woman shall be burned.

117. If a man has contracted a debt, and has given his wife, his son, his daughter for silver or for labor, three years shall they serve in the house of their purchaser or bondsmaster; in the fourth year they shall regain their original condition.

129. If the wife of a man is found lying with another male, they shall be bound and thrown into the water. If the husband lets his wife live, then the king shall let his servant live ...

137. If a man had decided to divorce ... a wife who has presented him with children, then he shall give back to that woman her dowry, and he shall give her the use of field, garden, and property, and she shall bring up her children. After she has brought up her children, she shall take a son's portion of all that is given to her children, and she marry the husband of her heart.

138. If a man divorces his spouse who has not borne him children, he shall give to her all the silver of the bride-price, and restore to her the dowry which she brought from the house of her father, and so he shall divorce her.

Source: *The Human Record*, vol. I, Afred J. Andrea, James H. Overfield, eds., pp. 14–15. Their source is Chilperic Edwards, *The Hammurabi Code* (1904), pp. 23–80.

the law code that bears his name. Hammurabi's laws document a society strictly divided into classes: nobles, commoners, and slaves. Punishments were harsh, but less so for privileged people than for the lower classes. Hammurabi claimed the king-mediated law and justice came from the gods to the people (see "The Code of Hammurabi"). Invaders from the north and east brought down the Babylonian kingdom about 1600 B.C.E.

Writing and Mathematics   The Sumerians invented a writing system we call **cuneiform** (from *cuneus*, Latin for "wedge") because of the wedge-shaped marks

cuneiform A writing system invented by the Sumerians that used a wedge-shaped stylus, or pointed tool, to write on wet clay tablets that were then baked or dried (*cuneus* means "wedge" in Latin). The writing was also cut into stone.

Key Events and People in Mesopotamian History

ca. 3500 B.C.E.	Sumerians arrive
ca. 2800–2370 B.C.E.	Sumerian city-states
ca. 2370 B.C.E.	Sargon establishes Semitic dynasty at Akkad
ca. 2125–2027 B.C.E.	Third Dynasty of Ur
ca. 1900 B.C.E.	Amorites at Babylon
ca. 1792–1750 B.C.E.	Reign of Hammurabi
ca. 1600 B.C.E.	Invasion by Hittites and Kassites

QUICK REVIEW

Mesopotamian Religion
- Sumerians worshipped gods with human forms
- Babylonians sought evidence of divine action in movements of heavenly bodies
- Religion played an important part in Mesopotamian art and literature

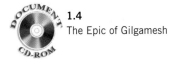

1.4
The Epic of Gilgamesh

they made with reed styluses on clay tablets. The Sumerian writing system used several thousand characters, some of which stood for words and some for sounds. It was difficult to learn, and literacy was confined to a circle of highly educated scribes.

The Sumerians also began the development of mathematics. At first, people did not conceive of numbers apart from counting specific things. Therefore, they developed different numerals for counting different things. Once the abstract concept of number was grasped, however, mathematics developed rapidly. The Sumerian system was sexagesimal (based on the number 60), not decimal. The convention of the 60-minute hour and circle of 360 degrees still survives. Mathematics enabled the Sumerians to develop, by means of observation of the heavenly bodies, the first calendars.

Religion   The Sumerians and their successors worshipped gods in human form, who were usually identified with the forces of nature. Priests flourished, for they alone commanded the knowledge needed to influence the gods. Armies of scribes compiled the many kinds of information that learned priests needed for their work. The Babylonians' belief that the movements of the heavenly bodies revealed the will of the gods led to the development of astrology.

Religious myths dominated the literature and art of Mesopotamia. The Mesopotamians believed that the human race was created to labor for the gods, who were imagined to need and enjoy the same kinds of things that human beings did. Mesopotamian temples were literally homes for gods. Their staffs provided banquets, changes of clothing, and entertainment for their deities. Human beings, on the other hand, did not anticipate much for themselves. There was no reward for virtuous living. All the dead were thought to descend to a gloomy netherworld where they suffered from hunger and thirst unless their needs were supplied by their living descendants.

The Babylonians believed in omens and developed elaborate means for divining the future. They also wrote epics to explain the creation of the world, and some of their stories (e.g., a great flood that almost destroyed human life, and an island paradise from which a god was expelled for eating forbidden plants) have entered the Wester n religious tradition through the Bible.

Society   The many sections of the Code of Hammurabi that are devoted to debts, rates of interest, security, and default indicate how important commerce was to the ancient Babylonians. Other sections of the code deal with builders, surgeons, and various kinds of professionals; with land tenure; and with the family. Marriages were arranged by parents. A husband whose wife was childless or ill could take a second wife. Extramarital relations between a married man and concubines, slaves, and prostitutes were accepted.

The law appears to have protected wives as individuals with rights. Divorce was relatively easy, and women who were divorced by their husbands without good cause received their dowries back. A woman who sought a divorce could also recover her dowry if her husband could not convict her of wrongdoing. However, a woman's place was definitely thought to be in the home.

Slavery: Chattel Slaves and Debt Slaves Slavery in Mesopotamia usually arose from debt. Parents could sell their children into slavery or pledge themselves and their family members as surety for loans. Some slaves worked for the king and the state, others for the temple and the priests, and still others for private citizens. Slaves were property, were subject to their master's will, and had little legal protection. But slaves could engage in business and hold property. Those who acquired sufficient wealth could buy their freedom. Slaves could marry free men or women, and the children of these unions were free.

EGYPTIAN CIVILIZATION

The center of Egyptian civilization was the Nile River. From its source in central Africa, the Nile runs in long navigable stretches broken by several cataracts north some 4,000 miles to the Mediterranean Sea. Ancient Egypt included the 750 miles of the valley from the First Cataract to the sea. The narrow valley of the Nile constituted Upper (southern) Egypt, and Lower (northern) Egypt occupied the river's broad delta, which fans out along 150 miles of the Mediterranean coast. The Nile alone made life possible in Egypt's almost rainless desert. Each year the river flooded and covered the land. When it receded, it left behind a fertile mud that renewed the land and produced two crops a year. The construction of irrigation ditches to utilize the river's water and careful planning and organization of agricultural work produced prosperity for Egypt that was unmatched in the ancient world.

The Nile served as a highway connecting the long, narrow country and encouraged its unification. By 3100 B.C.E., Upper and Lower Egypt were unified as a single kingdom. Nature helped protect and isolate the ancient Egyptians from outsiders. The cataracts, the sea, and the desert made it difficult for foreigners to reach Egypt for either friendly or hostile purposes. Egypt knew far more peace and security than Mesopotamia. This, along with the sunny, predictable climate, gave the Egyptians a more optimistic attitude toward life than that manifested by their Mesopotamian neighbors.

Events in the more than 3,000-year span of ancient Egyptian history are traditionally dated by reference to the reigns of 31 royal dynasties, which modern historians cluster into eight periods.

The Old Kingdom (2700–2200 B.C.E.) By the Third Dynasty, Egypt's kings had achieved absolute supremacy over their subjects. Ruling from Memphis in Upper Egypt, just above the entrance to the delta, they had the resources of a huge, prosperous nation at their disposal. Kings (the title **pharaoh**, meaning "great house" or "palace," was not used until later in Egyptian history) governed through their families, appointing and removing officials at their pleasure. Peasants were carefully regulated and heavily taxed.

Babylonian World Map. This clay tablet from the Neo-Babylonian period (612–539 B.C.E.) shows a map of the world as seen by the Babylonians. The "Salt Sea" is shown as a circle. An arc inside it is labeled "Mountains." Below it is a rectangular box marked "Babylon," and to the right of the box is a small circle marked "Assyria."
Courtesy of the Trustees of the British Museum. ©The British Museum.

pharaoh The god-kings of ancient Egypt. The term originally meant "great house" or palace.

QUICK REVIEW

Egyptian Kingship
- Egyptian kings were considered gods
- Kings were the direct source of law and justice
- Egyptian government was an aspect of religion

Periods in Ancient Egyptian History (dynasties in Roman numerals)

ca. 3100–2700 B.C.E.	Early Dynastic period (I–II)
ca. 2700–2200 B.C.E.	Old Kingdom (III–VI)
ca. 2200–2052 B.C.E.	First Intermediate period (VII–X)
ca. 2052–1786 B.C.E.	Middle Kingdom (XI–XII)
ca. 1786–1575 B.C.E.	Second Intermediate period (XIII–XVII)
ca. 1700 B.C.E.	Hyksos invasion
ca. 1575–1087 B.C.E.	New Kingdom (or Empire) (XVIII–XX)
ca. 1087–30 B.C.E.	Post Empire (XXI–XXXI)

An Egyptian king was considered a god on whom the lives, safety, and prosperity of his people depended. The land was his personal possession, and the people his servants. Because his will defined justice for his people, Egypt published no law codes. Religion dominated Egyptian life and government. The gods appeared in many guises, as animals, humans, and natural forces. Elaborate conventions governed the burial of the dead and the equipment of graves with items the departed were believed to need for a pleasant life after death. Bodies were mummified to preserve them. Tombs were beautifully decorated with paintings, and offerings of food were regularly brought to the dead.

Nothing better illustrates the extent of royal power than the three great pyramids built as tombs by the kings of the Fourth Dynasty. They are remarkable not only for the great technical skill needed to erect them, but also for the concentration of power and resources they represent.

The First Intermediate Period and Middle Kingdom (2200–1786 B.C.E.) About 2200 B.C.E. the Old Kingdom collapsed. After a period of confusion (the First Intermediate period, ca. 2200–2052 B.C.E.), the governors of Thebes in Upper Egypt established the Middle Kingdom. The Middle Kingdom's Twelfth Dynasty (2052–1786 B.C.E.) restored order, peace, and prosperity to Egypt. Its pharaohs were less absolute, distant god-kings than their predecessors and more directly concerned for the well-being of their subjects. They encouraged trade and extended Egyptian power and influence into Palestine and Ethiopia.

The Second Intermediate Period and New Kingdom (1786–1087 B.C.E.) The resurgent power of the local nobility and the erosion of central authority mark the end of the Middle Kingdom and the beginning of the Second Intermediate period. A people called the Hyksos—Semitic peoples from the eastern Mediterranean—controlled the Nile Delta for about a century (beginning ca. 1700 B.C.E.). Then a dynasty from Thebes drove them out and reunited Egypt, marking the beginning of the New Kingdom or Empire.

The rulers of the New Kingdom (ca. 1575–1087 B.C.E.) built a powerful army that pushed out Egypt's frontiers up the Nile to the south and east across Palestine and Syria to the upper Euphrates. Egyptian expansion was finally checked by the powerful Hittite Empire of Asia Minor. Egypt survived, but its period of greatest glory came to an end. Throughout the Post–Empire period (1087–30 B.C.E.) it repeatedly fell to foreign invaders.

Language and Literature The idea of writing may have come to Egypt from Mesopotamia, but the Egyptians independently invented a script that the Greeks later called **hieroglyphs** ("sacred carvings"). Although this writing script utilized hundreds of picture signs and was very difficult and complex, it remained relatively unchanged for more than 3,000 years. The Egyptian literature it recorded consisted of sacred hymns, myths, and magical formulas, as well as tales of secular business, letters, travel stories, and "wisdom literature" (bits of advice to help one get on well in the world).

hieroglyphics The writing script of ancient Egypt. It combined picture writing with pictographs and sound signs. Hieroglyph means "sacred carvings" in Greek.

Religion: Gods and Temples   Egyptian religion encompassed concepts that appear inconsistent to the modern mind. There were, for instance, three separate explanations for the origin of the universe. The Egyptian gods also cannot be organized into an orderly pantheon, for their functions and natures combine and overlap. Worship of the sun took a variety of forms in this hot, arid land, and for a brief period the pharaoh Akhenaten elevated a new sun god over all Egypt's traditional deities. The gods, often represented as having animal heads on human bodies, were thought to inhabit their lavish temples. Ordinary people did not worship there, but the gods' images were occasionally carried out and paraded before the masses.

Worship and the Afterlife   Most Egyptians worshipped at small local shrines. Their homes also had niches for images of household deities. They worshipped their ancestors, and they believed strongly in magic, dreams, and oracles. They wore amulets to ward off evil. Magic, they assumed, was essential for escaping the dangers that confronted souls in the afterlife. Originally, only the pharaoh was thought to have a hope of immortality, but gradually this privilege extended to all who could make the necessary preparations. Preservation of the body was considered essential for survival in the afterlife.

Old Kingdom Statue.   A hallmark of the early river civilizations was the development of techniques to increase harvests. This statue from the Old Kingdom in Egypt (ca. 2700–2200 B.C.E.) shows a woman grinding wheat for bread.

Kenneth Garrettings/National Geographic Society.

Women in Egyptian Society   A woman's primary role was management of a household, but she was not confined to her home. Although women could not hold office or receive the kind of education that fit men for public functions and crafts, they could control their own property, sue for divorce, and enjoy equal legal protection. Royal women occasionally had great power. Hatshepsut, daughter of Thutmosis I, ruled as pharaoh for nearly 20 years.

Slaves   Slaves were not numerous in Egypt until the Middle Kingdom, when Egypt launched military campaigns that built its empire. Black Africans from Nubia and Asians from the East were taken captive, branded, and brought to Egypt as slaves. Slaves performed numerous tasks. Some were common laborers, while others served as policemen and soldiers. They could be freed, but that appears rarely to have been done.

ANCIENT MIDDLE EASTERN EMPIRES

While the Eighteenth Dynasty ruled Egypt, new groups of peoples established themselves in the Middle East. Among them were the Kassites in Babylonia and the Hittites in Asia Minor. These groups forged an empire that lasted 200 years (see Map 1–2).

WHICH EMPIRES competed with Egypt to control the ancient Near East?

THE HITTITES

By about 1500 B.C.E., the Hittites had established a strong, centralized kingdom with its seat near Ankara, the capital of modern Turkey. Between 1400 and 1200 B.C.E., they contested Egypt's control of Palestine and Syria, but about 1200 B.C.E., their kingdom fell to waves of migrants from Europe. The Hittites appear to have been responsible for a great technological advance—the smelting of iron. They also played an important role in transmitting the ancient cultures of Mesopotamia and Egypt to the Greeks, who lived on their western frontier.

THE KASSITES

A people of unknown origin, the Kassites succeeded the Amorites as the rulers of Babylon. Their dynasty survived for 500 years. They were organized into large tribal families and are particularly memorable for their contributions to Babylonian literature. Their power was maintained with the aid of the prestige weaponry of their age—an aristocratic corps of charioteers.

THE MITANNIANS

The Mitannians were part of a large group called the Hurrians, some of whom traced their roots in Mesopotamia and Syria back to the days of Akkad and Ur. The Mitannians were important mediators of Mesopotamian culture to Syria and Anatolia, and they developed the art of chariot warfare and horse training to a high degree. The Hittites eventually overthrew and absorbed them.

THE ASSYRIANS

The Assyrians inhabited the upper reaches of the Tigris River. Their language was related to Babylonian. Their capital, Assur, was an early trade center, but it emerged as a political power in the 14th century B.C.E. as the Mitannians declined. This First Assyrian Empire collapsed at the end of the second millennium and the Arameans, Semitic nomads, invaded Assyria. The Aramean language became one of the common tongues of the ancient Middle East.

Key Events in the History of Ancient Middle Eastern Empires

ca. 1400–1200 B.C.E.	Hittite Empire
ca. 1100 B.C.E.	Rise of Assyrian power
ca. 732–722 B.C.E.	Assyrian conquest of Palestine-Syria
ca. 671 B.C.E.	Assyrian conquest of Egypt
ca. 612 B.C.E.	Destruction of Assyrian capital at Nineveh
ca. 612–539 B.C.E.	Neo-Babylonian (Chaldean) Empire

THE SECOND ASSYRIAN EMPIRE

About 1000 B.C.E., the Assyrians began steadily to expand their territory, and by 665 B.C.E., they controlled all of Mesopotamia, and much of Asia Minor, Syria, Palestine, and Egypt. The Assyrians succeeded thanks to a large, well-disciplined army and a society that valued military virtues. Fierce and cruel, the Assyrians boasted of their brutality, which was a useful strategy for terrorizing opponents into submission.

Unlike earlier empires, the Assyrians systematically exploited the area they held, using various methods of control. They collected tribute from some regions, stationed garrisons in others, and sometimes pacified districts by deporting and scattering their native peoples.

The Assyrian Empire grew too large to be managed efficiently, but the precise reasons for its fall are unclear. A civil war may have divided the Assyrians and made them vulnerable to attack by the Medes, a powerful people from

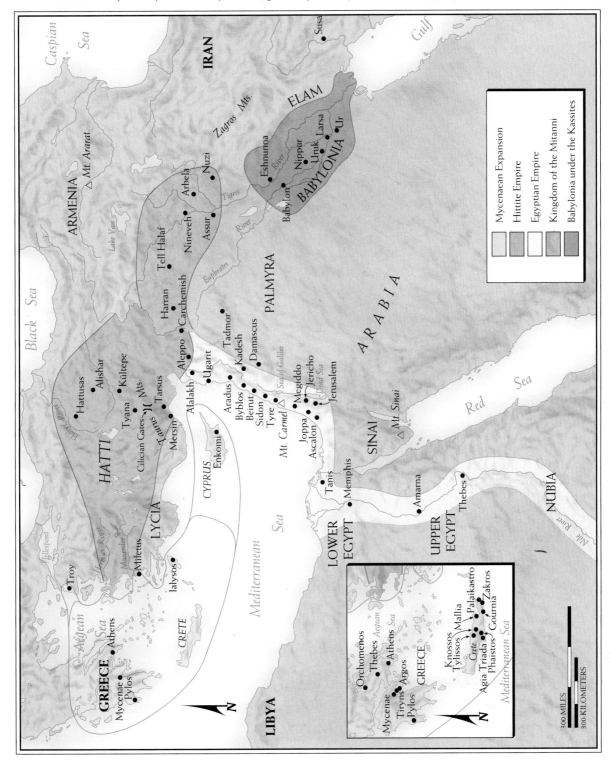

MAP 1–2

The Near East and Greece ca. 1400 B.C.E.   About 1400 B.C.E., the Near East was divided among four empires. Egypt extended south to Nubia and north through Palestine and Phoenicia. Kassites ruled in Mesopotamia, Hittites in Asia Minor, and the Mitannians in Assyrian lands. In the Aegean, the Mycenaean kingdoms were at their height.

WHY WERE there so many empires during this period in the ancient Middle East?

Assyrian Palace Relief. This eighth-century B.C.E. relief of a hero gripping a lion formed part of the decoration of an Assyrian palace. The immense size of the figure and his powerful limbs and muscles may well have suggested the might of the Assyrian king.

Giraudon/Art Resource, N.Y.

western and central Iran. The Medes were assisted by the Babylonians, who had been restive subjects of Assyria's empire, and in 612 B.C.E. the great Assyrian cities were destroyed.

THE NEO-BABYLONIANS

The Medes did not follow up their conquests. This opened the way for the Babylonian king, Nebuchadnezzar, to take over much of the former Assyrian territory. Babylon, his capital, prospered as a center of world trade, although his dynasty did not long survive. Confusion and mismanagement by his successors cleared the way for Babylon to fall to Persian conquerors from Iran in 539 B.C.E. (see Chapter 4).

EARLY INDIAN CIVILIZATION

The Indian subcontinent's earliest literate, urban civilization arose in the valley of the Indus River sometime after 2600 B.C.E. By about 2300 B.C.E., the people of this region were trading with Mesopotamia. Known as the **Harappan** or Indus culture, early Indian civilization lasted only a few centuries. The second identifiable contribution to the region's civilization came from the Vedic Aryans, named for an **Indo-European** (or "**Aryan**") immigrant people who composed influential holy texts, the **Vedas**. Their arrival dates to about 1500 B.C.E., and their power endured for nearly a millennium. They created no cities and no writing system, but commingled religious and social traditions with older cultures to shape the civilization that has flourished in India for the past two and a half millennia.

THE INDUS CIVILIZATION

No one knew of the Indus culture until archaeologists discovered its remains at the site of Harappa in the 1920s. Since then, some 70 cities, the largest being Harappa and Mohenjo-Daro, have been identified. The Indus civilization had a diversified social and economic organization. These early Indian people created cities, bronze tools, and writing, and engineered covered drainage systems. Indus life is the least understood of the early civilizations, but enough evidence remains to reconstruct something of its culture.

General Character   The Indus culture was remarkably homogeneous. City layouts, building construction, a refined system of weights and measures, seal inscriptions, fine-patterned pottery and figurines, and even the kind of burnt brick used for buildings and floodwalls are unusually uniform throughout all Indus towns. This suggests an integrated economic system and good internal communications.

Indus culture was also remarkably constant over time. Because the main cities and towns lay in river lowlands subject to periodic flooding, they were rebuilt often. Each new level of construction closely followed its precursor's pattern. Similarly, the Indus script shows no evidence of change over time. This stability, regularity, and traditionalism have led scholars to speculate that this far-flung society was centrally governed, perhaps by a conservative priestly organization rather than a less stable royal dynasty.

Cities   Harappa and Mohenjo-Daro may each have had populations exceeding 35,000 people. They were meticulously laid out. To the west of each stood a large, walled citadel on a raised rectangular platform. The citadel contained the main public buildings. The town proper was laid out on a north-south, east-west grid of main avenues. The town "blocks" formed by the main avenues were crisscrossed by small, less rigidly planned lanes lined by private houses. The typical house was built around a central courtyard, and its walls facing the street were blank and windowless.

Perhaps the most striking features of these cities were their complex drainage systems. Private houses had wells, bathrooms, and latrines. The sewers that served these facilities were engineering feats unrivaled in the ancient world until the time of the Romans nearly 2,000 years later.

Economic Life   The Indus state or states were supported by a thriving agricultural economy. The Indus people wove cloth from cotton, made metal tools, and used the potter's wheel. Evidence shows that they traded with Mesopotamia. Metals and semiprecious stones were imported from present-day Iran, Afghanistan, and Central Asia, from the southern Indian peninsula, and perhaps from Arabia. Artistic styles suggest that trade contacts inspired the borrowing of ideas from other cultures.

Material Culture   Among the most striking accomplishments of the Indus culture are fine sculptures and artifacts, including copper and bronze tools and vessels, painted pottery, stonework, figurines and toys, jewelry, and dyed fabrics. Except for some decorative brickwork, no monumental friezes, mosaics, or sculpture have been found.

Religion   Elaborate bathing facilities suggest that the Indus religion may have utilized washing as an important purification ritual. The many images of male animals, such as the humped bull, that have been found imply that animals may have been worshipped as symbols of power and fertility. A recurring human male figure with leafy headdress and horns, often seated in a posture associated later in India with yogic meditation, suggests the Vedic Aryan "Lord of All Creatures" of the Indian god Shiva. Figurines of females, often pregnant or holding a child, resemble female images in several prehistoric cultures. They may represent an element of pre-Aryan religion that reemerged later to figure in Hindu culture.

The Passing of Indus Civilization   Between 1800 to 1700 B.C.E., Indus civilization faded away. Warlike Aryan invaders, abnormal flooding, and a long period of dessication may have contributed to its decline. Today, the Indus culture remains in the shadows of prehistory and its influence has yet to be accurately gauged.

HOW DID the first civilizations of the Indus Valley develop the religious and social foundations of Indian civilization?

QUICK REVIEW

Harappa and Mohenjo-Daro
- Both cities had populations of more than 35,000 people
- The cities were laid out in grids
- Both had complex systems of drains and sewers

Harappan Term used to describe the first civilization of the Indus Valley.

Indo-European A widely distributed language group that includes most of the languages spoken in Europe, Persian, Sanskrit, and their derivatives.

Aryans Indo-European people who invaded India and Iran in the second and first millenia B.C.E.

Vedas Sacred texts of the ancient Aryan invaders of India. The Rig Veda is the oldest material in the Vedas.

Indus stone stamp seal. Note the familiar humped bull of India.
© Scala/Art Resource, N.Y.

3.1
Rig Veda

Mahabharata and Ramayana
Two classical Indian epics.

THE VEDIC ARYAN CIVILIZATION

The Aryan culture, which effectively "refounded" Indian civilization around 1500 B.C.E., is known primarily through the "winged words" of the Vedas, the Aryan sacred texts. For this reason, the culture is called Vedic. The Vedas are ritual, priestly, speculative works, not histories. The texts offer little about events but provide insight into the religion, society, values, and thought of early Aryan India.

Veda means "knowledge." The Vedas are the four major compilations of Vedic ritual texts. The Rig Veda, the oldest material, dates from ca. 1000 B.C.E. to perhaps 1700–1200 B.C.E. when the Aryans spread across the northern plains to the upper reaches of the Ganges. It recounts the history of the early Aryans through a collection of 1,028 religious hymns.

Aryan, a different kind of term, was apparently the name of a people who originated in the steppeland between Eastern Europe and Central Asia and emigrated to Europe, Greece, Anatolia, the Iranian plateau, and India during the second and first millennia B.C.E. Those who came to India are more precisely designated *Indo Aryans* or *Vedic Aryans*.

In the 19th century, Aryan was the term applied to the widespread language group known more commonly today as Indo-European. Greek, Latin, the Romance and Germanic languages, the Slavic tongues, and the Indo-Iranian languages, including Persian and Sanskrit and their derivatives, all belong to the Indo-European family. The Nazis perversely misused Aryan to refer to a white "master race." Today, Aryan usually refers to the Indo-European speakers who invaded India and the Iranian plateau in the second millennium B.C.E. It is also the name linguists use for the Indo-Iranian languages.

"Aryanizing" of North India   The Vedic Aryans were seminomadic warriors who reached India through the mountain passes of the Hindu Kush. They probably entered India gradually in small tribal groups. The Vedic Aryans were horsemen and cattle herders rather than farmers and city builders. They left their mark not on material culture but in the languages, social organization, techniques of warfare, and religions of the regions they overran.

The Vedic Aryans first penetrated the Punjab and the Indus Valley (1800–1500 B.C.E.). Their horses, chariots, and copper-bronze weapons likely gave them military superiority. Echos of early conflicts can be heard in some Rigvedic hymns. The extent of their conquests during the Rigvedic age (ca. 1700–1000 B.C.E.) is not clear, but their main locus remained the Punjab and the plains west of the Yamuna River. From about 1000 to 500 B.C.E., the Later Vedic age, the Vedic Aryans spread across the plains between the Yamuna and the Ganges, northeast to the Himalayan foothills, and southeast along the Ganges, occupying what was to become the cradle of subsequent Indian civilization.

The Later Vedic period is also called the Brahmanic age because it was dominated by the priestly religion of the Brahman class, which is documented in commentaries called the *Brahmanas* (ca. 1000–800 or 600 B.C.E.). It was the setting for India's two classical epics, the **Mahabhrarata** and the **Ramayana**, both of which reflect complex cultural and social mixing of Aryan and earlier subcontinent peoples.

By about 200 C.E., this mixing had spread a distinctive new "Indian" civilization over most of the subcontinent. Its basis was clearly Aryan, but its language, social organization, and religion incorporated many non-Aryan elements.

OVERVIEW   THE FIRST CIVILIZATIONS

Civilization is a form of human culture usually marked by the development of cities, the ability to make and use metal tools and instruments, and the invention of a system of writing. The first civilizations appeared in the Middle East between 4004 and 3000 B.C.E., and by the second millennium B.C.E., there were civilized societies in Eurasia, China, and the Americas.

Mesopotamia	Sumerians arrive in the Tigris-Euphrates River Valley, ca. 3500 B.C.E., and establish the first city-states ca. 2800 B.C.E.
Egypt	Egyptian civilization develops along the Nile River, ca. 3100 B.C.E. Egypt becomes a unified state ca. 2700 B.C.E.
Indus Valley	Flourishing urban civilization develops in northern India along the Indus River, ca. 2250 B.C.E.
China	City-states appear in the Yellow River basin ca. 1766 B.C.E.
Americas	Agricultural surplus gives rise to the first cities in Mesoamerica, ca. 1500 B.C.E., and to the first Andean civilization in South America, ca. 2750 B.C.E.

Vedic Aryan Society Aryan society was apparently patrilineal; that is, succession and inheritance passed down in the male line. Gods were predominantly male. Marriage appears to have been monogamous, but widows could remarry. Related families belonged to larger kin groups, and the largest social grouping was the tribe, ruled by a chieftain or **raja** ("king" in Sanskrit). By the Brahmanic age, the power of the priestly class increased, along with that of the king, who, with the sanction of the priestly establishment, became a hereditary ruler claiming divine qualities.

Aryan society seems at first to have had only two basic divisions: noble and common. In time, the Dasas—the darker, conquered peoples—formed a third group of the socially excluded. Eventually, a rigid scheme of four social classes (excluding the non-Aryan Dasas) evolved: the priestly (Brahman), the warrior/noble (Kshatriya), the peasant/tradesman (Vaishya), and the servant (Shudra). By the late Rigvedic period, these four divisions, or *varnas*, had become so basic to society as to be sanctioned explicitly in religious theory. Only the members of the three upper classes participated fully in social, political, and religious life. This scheme underlies the rigid caste system that later became fundamental to Indian society.

Material Culture The early, seminomadic Aryans had little impressive material culture. They lived simply in wood and thatch or, later, mud-walled dwellings. They measured wealth in cattle and were accomplished at carpentry and bronze work. They cultivated some crops, especially grains.

The Brahmanic age is poor in material remains. Mud-brick towns appeared, but urban culture was undeveloped. Established kingdoms with fixed capitals existed. Trade grew. Later texts mention artisans, such as goldsmiths, basketmakers, weavers, potters, and entertainers.

Writing had been reintroduced to India some time earlier, perhaps around 700 B.C.E., and its use became common about 500 B.C.E. The prestige of oral transmission for the Vedas remained so high among the Brahman class, however, that writing continued to be scorned for truly sacred texts.

raja An Indian king.

Ancient India

ca. 2250–1750 B.C.E.	Indus (Harappan) civilization
(2500–1500?)	Written script still undeciphered
ca. 1800–1500 B.C.E.	Aryan peoples invade northwestern India
ca. 1500–1000 B.C.E.	Rigvedic period: composition of Rigvedic hymns; Punjab as center of Indo-Aryan civilization
ca. 1000–500 B.C.E.	Later Vedic period; Doab as center of Indo-Aryan civilization
ca. 1000–800/600 B.C.E.	Composition of *Brahmanas* and other Vedic texts
ca. 800–500 B.C.E.	Composition of major Upanishads
ca. 700–500 B.C.E.	Probable reintroduction of writing
ca. 400 B.C.E.–200 C.E.	Composition of great epics, the *Mahabharata* and *Ramayana*

Upanishads Vedic texts most concerned with speculation about the universe.

WHY DID large territorial states arise in ancient China?

Religion   The earliest Indo-Aryans probably worshipped numerous gods. The Rigvedic hymns address anthropomorphic deities linked to natural phenomena such as the sky, the clouds, and the sun. Chief among them was Indra, god of war and the storm.

Ritual sacrifice was the central focus of Vedic religion. Its goal apparently was to invoke the presence of the gods to whom the offering was made rather than to expiate sins or express thanksgiving. An intoxicant (soma juice) was drunk as a prominent feature of the sacrificial ritual. A recurring theme of the Vedic hymns that accompanied such religious ceremonies is the desire for the good things of this life: prosperity, health, and victory. Burnt offerings were particularly important and feature in both public and private worship.

By Brahmanic times, a considerable body of mystical speculation had developed around sacrificial ritual. The god, the offering, the sacrifice, and the sacrificer were all identified with one another. The word *Brahman*, which originally meant a ritual utterance or word of power, came to refer to the generalized divine power present in the sacrifice. In the **Upanishads**, some of the latest Vedic texts and the ones most concerned with speculation about the universe, *Brahman* was expanded to refer to the Absolute, the transcendent principle of reality. As the guardian of ritual and the master of the sacred word, the priest was known throughout the Vedic Aryan period by a related word, *Brahmana* (*Brahman* in English). Echoes of these associations lent force in later Hindu tradition to the special status of the Brahman caste groups as the highest social class (see Chapter 4).

EARLY CHINESE CIVILIZATION

NEOLITHIC ORIGINS IN THE YELLOW RIVER VALLEY

Agriculture began in China about 4000 B.C.E. in the basin of the southern bend of the Yellow River. The chief crop of China's agricultural revolution was millet. The early Chinese cleared land and burned its cover to plant millet and cabbage and, later, rice and soybeans. When the soil became exhausted, fields and sometimes villages were abandoned. The Chinese used stones to make a variety of tools (axes, hoes, spades, and sickle-shaped knives) and pottery to store grain. They domesticated pigs, sheep, cattle, dogs, and chickens.

The first Chinese cultivators lived in wattle-and-daub pit dwellings with wooden support posts and sunken, plastered floors. Their villages occupied isolated clearings along slopes of river valleys. They buried their dead in cemeteries with jars of food. Tribal leaders wore rings and beads of jade.

EARLY BRONZE AGE: THE SHANG

The traditional history of China postulates the existence of three ancient dynasties: Xia (2205–1766 B.C.E.), Shang (1766–1050 B.C.E.), and Zhou (1050–256 B.C.E.). Until early in the 20th century, modern historians believed the first two to be legendary. Then, in the 1920s, archaeological excavations near present-day An Yang uncovered the ruins of a walled city that had been a late Shang capital. More Shang cities have since been discovered. The archives of the department of divination of the Shang court, containing thousands of "oracle bones" incised with archaic Chinese writing, have been found in the ruins. The names of kings recovered from artifacts almost perfectly correspond to the names that feature in the traditional historical record. The discovery that the Shang existed increases the probability that there was also a real Hsia dynasty.

The city-state was the characteristic political institution of Bronze Age China. Cities were walled compounds containing public buildings, altars, and the residences of the aristocracy. They were surrounded by a sea of Neolithic tribal villages. By late Shang times, several such cities were scattered across the north China plain.

The military aristocracy rode to war in chariots, supported by levies of foot soldiers. The Shang fought against barbarian tribes and, occasionally, against Chinese city-states that rebelled against Shang rule. Captured prisoners were enslaved.

The three most notable features of Shang culture were writing, bronzes, and the appearance of social classes. Scribes at the Shang court kept records on strips of bamboo, few of which have survived. Large numbers of inscriptions on bronze artifacts and oracle bones, however, have survived. Some bones contain the question put to the oracle, the oracle's answer, and the outcome. Oracles were asked such questions as: Which ancestor is causing the king's earache? Will the king's child be a son? Was a particular sacrifice acceptable to ancestral deities?

Our knowledge of Shang religion derives from inscriptions on oracle bones. The Shang believed in a supreme "Deity Above," who had authority over the human world. There were lesser natural deities—the sun, moon, earth, rain, wind, and the six clouds—who served at the court of the Deity Above. Even the Shang king, however, did not presume to sacrifice to the Deity Above but only to his ancestors, who interceded with the Deity Above on the king's behalf. Kings, while alive at least, were not considered divine but were regarded as the high priests of the state.

In Shang times, as later, religion in China was closely associated with cosmology. The Shang people observed the movements of the planets and stars and noted eclipses. Celestial happenings were seen as omens from the gods, and chief cosmologists maintained records of them at court. The Shang calendar had a month of 30 days and a year of 360 days. An extra month was inserted periodically to keep the solar and lunar years in sync. The king used the calendar to tell his people when to sow and reap.

Bronze, which appeared in China about 2000 B.C.E., was used for weapons, armor, chariot fittings, and ceremonial vessels.

A class hierarchy defined life in the Chinese city-state. The king and the officials of his court lived within the walled city. Their lifestyle was, for ancient times, opulent. A far larger population of agricultural workers lived hard, meager lives in cramped pit

Bronze Vessel from the Shang Dynasty. The little elephant on top forms the handle of the lid. Wine was poured through the spout formed by the big elephant's trunk.

The Freer Gallery of Art, Smithsonian Institution, Washington, D.C.

dwellings outside the city. Nowhere was the gulf between the royal lineage and the baseborn more apparent than in the Shang institution of human sacrifice. When a king died, hundreds of slaves or prisoners of war, sometimes together with people who had served the king during his lifetime, might be buried with him. Similar sacrifices were made when a palace or an altar was dedicated.

LATE BRONZE AGE: THE WESTERN ZHOU

To the west of the area of Shang rule lived the Zhou people. They were less civilized and more warlike than the Shang. By 1050 B.C.E., the last Shang kings had been debilitated by campaigns against nomads in the north and rebellious tribes in the east. Taking advantage of this opportunity, the Zhou swept in, conquering the Shang.

The Zhou continued the Shang pattern of life and rule. The agrarian-based city-state remained the basic unit of society, and by the 8th century B.C.E. there were about 200 urban centers. The Zhou also assimilated Shang culture and continued the development of China's ideographic writing.

The Zhou kept their primary capital in the west but set up a secondary capital at Loyang along the southern bend of the Yellow River. They appointed kinsmen or aristocratic allies as rulers of other city-states. Blood or lineage ties were fundamental to the organization of Zhou government. The Zhou king was the head of the senior branch of the family and performed sacrifices for the entire family. The rank of a lord of princely state depended on how closely he was related to the senior line of Zhou kings.

The Zhou, having conquered the Shang, needed a rationale for why they, and not the Shang, had become China's rightful rulers. Their argument was that heaven had withdrawn its mandate from the Shang, awarding it instead to the Zhou. The concept of the **Mandate of Heaven** was subsequently invoked by every dynasty in China down to the 20th century.

IRON AGE: THE EASTERN ZHOU

In 771 B.C.E., the Wei valley capital of the Western Zhou was overrun by barbarians. The heir to the throne escaped to the secondary capital at Loyang and inaugurated the Eastern Zhou period.

The first phase of the Eastern Zhou lasted until 481 B.C.E., but the Zhou kings were never able to reestablish their old authority. By the early seventh century B.C.E., kinship and religious ties to the Zhou house had worn thin, and its leaders no longer had the military strength to reimpose its rule. During the seventh and sixth centuries B.C.E., numerous small principalities maintained political equilibrium on the north-central plain. Larger, autonomous territorial states occupied the borders of the plain and gradually expanded by conquering the states on their peripheries.

The second phase of the Eastern Zhou is called the Warring States period. (It is named for a chronicle that treats the years from 401 to 256 B.C.E.) By the fifth century B.C.E., all defensive alliances had collapsed, and the stronger states had swallowed their weaker neighbors. As the border states grew in size and power, conflicts increased until the fourth century B.C.E., when only eight or nine great territorial states existed. It remained to be seen which one would defeat the others and unify China.

Mandate of Heaven The Chinese belief that heaven entrusts or withdraws a ruler's or a dynasty's right to govern.

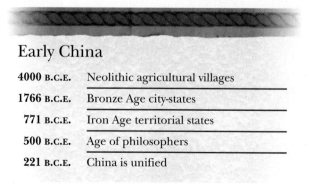

Early China

4000 B.C.E.	Neolithic agricultural villages
1766 B.C.E.	Bronze Age city-states
771 B.C.E.	Iron Age territorial states
500 B.C.E.	Age of philosophers
221 B.C.E.	China is unified

Three basic changes in Chinese society contributed to the rise of large territorial states. One development was the expansion of population and agricultural lands. The walled cities of the Shang and Western Zhou had resembled oases in the wilds. They were bounded by plains, marshes, and forests. But in the Eastern Zhou, the wilds started to disappear as the population grew. States began to abut, and friction arose over boundaries. These changes accelerated after the start of the Iron Age in the late sixth century B.C.E. With iron tools, farmers expanded agricultural resources by clearing new lands and plowing deeper. Irrigation and drainage canals appeared. By the third century B.C.E., China had about 20 million people and was the most populous country in the world, a distinction it has never lost.

The second change that promoted the growth of large states was the rise of commerce. Roads built for war were used by merchants. Products of one region were traded for those of another. Copper coins joined bolts of silk and precious metals as media of exchange. Zhou tombs show that the material and artistic culture of China leaped ahead during this period despite endemic warfare.

2.3
Ch'u Yuan and Sung Yu:
Individual Voices in a
Chaotic Era

A third factor that encouraged the development of large city-states was the rise of a new kind of army. War chariots of the old aristocracy, which were effective only on level terrain, gave way to cavalry armed with crossbows. Most of the fighting was done by conscript foot soldiers, and professional commanders replaced the old nobility. Territorial states could field armies numbering in the hundreds of thousands. Military tactics were bloody and ruthless, and prisoners were often massacred.

Government also changed. Lords of the new territorial states began to call themselves kings, taking a title that previously only Zhou royalty had enjoyed. The hereditary nobility began to decline, supplanted by ministers appointed for their knowledge of statecraft. To survive, new states mobilized their agricultural and commercial wealth for support of their military, necessitating administration by a literate bureaucracy. Its members constituted a category of people called the *shih*, a term that came to mean "scholar-bureaucrat." The shih included petty nobility, warriors, landlords, merchants, and commoners. From this class, as we will see in Chapter 2, came the philosophers who transformed the culture of China.

THE RISE OF CIVILIZATION IN THE AMERICAS

HOW DID agriculture influence the development of civilization in Mesoamerica?

During the last Ice Age, the Bering region between Siberia and Alaska was dry land. Perhaps as early as 30,000 years ago, humans crossed this land bridge. These Asian immigrants moved south and east until they reached the tip of South America and the eastern regions of North America.

The earliest immigrants to the Americas, like all other Paleolithic peoples, lived by hunting, fishing, and gathering. However, many parts of North and South America were poor in animal resources when compared to Africa and Eurasia. Neither horses nor cattle were to be found on the American continents. Where fish or small game were insufficiently plentiful, people relied on protein from vegetable sources. In the exploitation of plants that provided protein, America far outpaced Europe. One of the most important early achievements was the development of useful species of maize. Wherever maize (corn) could be extensively grown, the food supply was essentially secured. Maize appears to have been cultivated in Mexico by 4000 B.C.E., as were other important foods such as potatoes, manioc, squash, beans, peppers, and tomatoes.

Early Civilizations of Mesoamerica

1500–400 B.C.E.	The Olmec
200 C.E.–750 C.E.	The Classic period in Central Mexico. Dominance of Teotihuacán in the Valley of Mexico and Monte Alban in the Valley of Oaxaca
150 C.E.–900 C.E.	The Classic period of Maya civilization in the Yucatán and Guatemala

Mesoamerica Region of North America that extends from the central part of modern Mexico to Central America.

Olmec Head. This colossal Olmec head, now in the Museo Nacional de Antropologia in Mexico City, was excavated at San Lorenzo. Carved of basalt, it may be a portrait of an Olmec ruler. Olmec civilization thrived between 1500 and 800 B.C.E.

Josephus Daniels/Photo Researchers, Inc.

Eventually, **Mesoamerica** and the Andean region of South America saw the emergence of strong, long-lasting states. In regions that lacked maize-based agriculture and settled village life—notably the North American Southwest—food supplies might have been too insecure to support the development of states.

Mesoamerica, which extends from the central part of modern Mexico into Central America, ranges from tropical rainforest to semiarid mountains (see Map 1–3). Archaeologists divide its preconquest history into three broad periods: Preclassic or Formative (2000 B.C.E.–150 C.E.), Classic (150–900 C.E.), and Post-Classic (900–1521). The earliest Mesoamerican civilization, that of the Olmecs, arose during the Preclassic on the Gulf Coast about 1500 B.C.E. The Olmec centers at San Lorenzo (ca. 1200–ca. 900 B.C.E.) and La Venta (ca. 900–ca. 400 B.C.E.) exhibit many of the characteristics of later Mesoamerican cities: symmetrical arrangement of large platforms, plazas, and monumental structures situated along a central axis. Writing developed in Mesoamerica during the late Formative period.

The Andes rise abruptly from the coastal plain and then descend gradually into the Amazon basin to the east. Agriculture is possible on the coast only in the valleys of the many rivers that flow from the Andes into the Pacific. The earliest monumental architecture in the Andean region was built on the coast at the site of Aspero by people who depended on a combination of agriculture and the Pacific's rich marine resources. It dates to about 2750 B.C.E. and is contemporary with the Great Pyramids of Egypt's Old Kingdom.

From 800 B.C.E. to 200 B.C.E., a civilization associated with the site of Chavín de Huantar in the highlands of Peru exerted great influence in the Andes. Artifacts in the distinctive Chavín style of this period can be found over a large area, which archaeologists call the Early Horizon. In many places this was a time of technical innovation with pottery, textiles, and metallurgy. The spread of the Chavín style may be due to political integration or the influence of a strong religious center. The period following the decline of Chavín, which archaeologists call the Early Intermediate period, saw the development of distinctive cultures in several regions. Most notable are the Moche culture on the northern coast of Peru and the Nazca culture on the southern coast. A second period of transregional integration, called the Middle Horizon, occurred around 600 C.E. and was probably caused by the rise of empires centered on the highland sites of Huari and Tiahuanaco. The Late Intermediate period was dominated on the northern coast of Peru by the Chimu successors of the Moche state. This era ended with the founding of the vast, tightly controlled empire of the Incas in the 14th and 15th centuries C.E.

MAP 1–3

Early Civilization in Mesoamerica and the Andean Region.   Both Mesoamerica and the Andean region of South America saw the development of a series of civilizations beginning between 1500 and 1000 B.C.E.

WHY DID the first civilizations in the Americas develop in Mesoamerica and the Andes?

Summary

The Emergence of Civilization Beginning in 10,000 B.C.E., human beings shifted during the Neolithic Revolution from a hunter-gather way of life to one marked by settled agriculture and the domestication of animals. Between 4000 and 3000 B.C.E., civilization began to appear along the Tigris and Euphrates Rivers in Mesopotamia, then along the Nile River in Egypt, and somewhat later in the Indus Valley in India and the Yellow River basin in China. Each of these early civilizations developed urban centers, monumental architecture, a hierarchical society, and a system of writing. The period is known as the Bronze Age because it coincided with the discovery of the technique for making bronze tools and weapons.

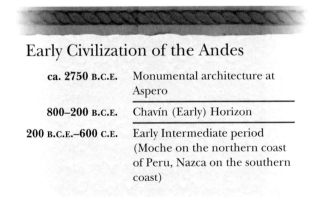

Early Civilization of the Andes

ca. 2750 B.C.E.	Monumental architecture at Aspero
800–200 B.C.E.	Chavín (Early) Horizon
200 B.C.E.–600 C.E.	Early Intermediate period (Moche on the northern coast of Peru, Nazca on the southern coast)

IMAGE KEY
for pages 4–5

a. Bone from China
b. Sumerian stone with cuneiform writing
c. Theban tomb of Nebamum
d. Tablet with cuneiform writing
e. Neolithic stone figure
f. Venus of Willendorf
g. Votive statue of Sumerian priest
h. Hittite warrior
i. Indian stone stamp seal
j. Zhou dynasty ritual water vessel
k. Egyptian Old Kingdom statue
l. Paleolithic cave painting

Mesopotamia The Sumerians founded the oldest Mesopotamian cities around 3000 B.C.E. Beginning around 2370 B.C.E., the Sumerian city-states were conquered and absorbed in turn by the Akkadian, Babylonian, and Assyrian empires. The Sumerians passed down much of their civilization to their successors: a system of writing on clay tablets called cuneiform, the worship of gods based on natural forces, semi-divine kings, and a highly developed bureaucracy.

Egypt Watered by the Nile River and protected by deserts and the sea, Egyptian civilization was more secure and peaceful than that of Mesopotamia. Egypt became a unified kingdom around 2700 B.C.E. Religion dominated Egyptian life. The kings, or pharaohs, were considered gods on whom the lives and prosperity of their people depended. Egyptian history is divided into three main periods: Old Kingdom (2700–2200 B.C.E.), Middle Kingdom (2052–1786 B.C.E.), and New Kingdom (1575–1087 B.C.E.). Under the New Kingdom, Egypt contended for mastery of the Middle East with the Hittite Empire.

Indus Civilization By 2300 B.C.E. at least 70 Indus cities, the largest being Harappa and Mohenjo-Daro, had developed a sophisticated urban culture. Indus civilization disappeared for unknown reasons between 1800 and 1700 B.C.E. In its place, Indo-European (or Aryan) invaders established the Vedic culture, named after sacred texts called the Vedas. In turn, Vedic culture evolved into a "new" Indian civilization that spread over the whole subcontinent.

China The Shang dynasty (1766–1050 B.C.E.) founded the earliest known Bronze Age civilization in China. The Shang and their successors, the Zhou (1050–256 B.C.E.), ruled as warrior aristocrats from city-states that fought outsiders and each other. By the 4th century B.C.E., as population and commerce expanded, rulers needed bigger armies to defend their states and trained bureaucrats to administer them. The result was the consolidation of many petty states into a few large territorial units.

The Americas The first civilizations in the Americas arose in places that produced an agricultural surplus. In Mesoamerica (central Mexico and Central America), the civilization was based on the cultivation of maize; in the Andes valleys, it was based on a combination of agriculture and the rich marine resources of the Pacific. The Olmecs (1500–400 B.C.E.) established the first civilization in Mesoamerica, and the first monumental architecture appeared in the Andes region around 2750 B.C.E.

REVIEW QUESTIONS

1. How was life in the Paleolithic era different from that in the Neolithic period? Is it or is it not appropriate to speak of a Neolithic "revolution"?

2. What defines civilization? What are the similarities and differences among the world's earliest civilizations?

3. Why were the Assyrians so successful in establishing their Middle Eastern Empire? Did this empire advance the developoment of civilization in the Middle East? Did it have a weakness?

4. How does the early history of Indian civilization differ from that of the riverine civilizations of China, Mesopotamia, and Egypt?

5. What were the stages of early Chinese history?

6. What factors gave rise to civilization in the Americas?

KEY TERMS

Aryans (p. 17)

Bronze Age (p. 7)

civilization (p. 7)

culture (p. 6)

cuneiform (p. 9)

Harappan (p. 17)

hieroglyphics (p. 12)

Indo-European (p. 17)

Mahabharata **and**

Ramayana (p. 18)

Mandate of Heaven (p. 22)

Mesoamerica (p. 24)

Mesopotamia (p. 7)

Neolithic Revolution (p. 7)

Paleolithic Age (p. 6)

pharaoh (p. 11)

raja (p. 19)

Upanishads (p. 20)

Vedas (p. 17)

 For additional study resources for this chapter, go to:
www.prenhall.com/craig/chapter1

2 The Four Great Revolutions in Thought and Religion

CHAPTER HIGHLIGHTS

The Four Great Philosophical and Religious Revolutions
Between 800 and 300 B.C.E., four philosophical and religious revolutions arose that were to shape the subsequent history of the world.

Chinese Philosophy Traditional Chinese philosophical thought, which took shape with the teachings of Confucius in the sixth century B.C.E., remained dominant in China until the early twentieth century. It was concerned with social and political issues and sought to teach human beings how to live harmoniously and ethically under Heaven. Other Chinese philosophies were Daoism, a mystical way of thought that offered a refuge from social responsibilities, and Legalism, which taught that a good society requires a strong state that enforces the law and punishes wrongdoers.

Indian Religion Hinduism took shape by 400 B.C.E. Indian religion saw existence as an endless alteration between life and death. The escape from this dilemma lay in the concept of *karma*, the idea that good actions (*dharma*) could lead to rebirth as a higher being. Another Indian religious tradition, the Jains, sought to liberate the soul from the bonds of the material world. Buddhism traces its origins to the teachings of an Indian, Siddhartha Gautama (b. ca. 566 B.C.E.). Buddhism holds that escape from *samsara* lies in following a moral path of right actions and in having compassion for all beings.

Hebrew Monotheism Monotheism is the faith in a single, all-powerful God. The Hebrews were the first people to emphasize the moral demands that the one God, Yahweh, placed on individual and community. The Hebrews, or Jews, were the first people in history to be defined by shared religious faith and practice. Through the Christian and Muslim traditions, Judaic monotheism would change the face of much of the world.

Greek Philosophy The Greeks were the first to initiate the unreservedly rational investigation of the universe. They thus became the forerunners of Western philosophy and science. Greek thinkers sought to explain natural phenomena without recourse to divine intervention. In the later fifth century and the fourth century B.C.E., philosophers such as Socrates, Plato, and Aristotle, applied the same rational, inquisitive approach to the study of moral and political issues.

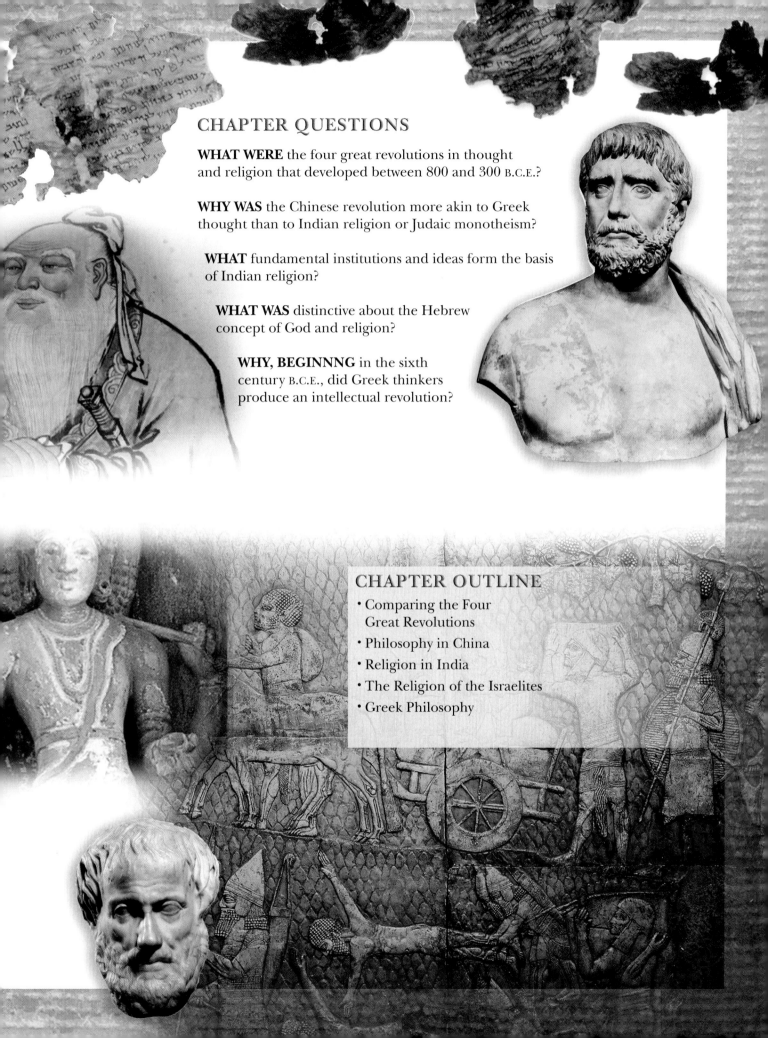

CHAPTER QUESTIONS

WHAT WERE the four great revolutions in thought and religion that developed between 800 and 300 B.C.E.?

WHY WAS the Chinese revolution more akin to Greek thought than to Indian religion or Judaic monotheism?

WHAT fundamental institutions and ideas form the basis of Indian religion?

WHAT WAS distinctive about the Hebrew concept of God and religion?

WHY, BEGINNNG in the sixth century B.C.E., did Greek thinkers produce an intellectual revolution?

CHAPTER OUTLINE

- Comparing the Four Great Revolutions
- Philosophy in China
- Religion in India
- The Religion of the Israelites
- Greek Philosophy

All human cultures develop religious or philosophical systems. Some people have speculated that human beings may be biologically "hard-wired" for religious faith. Whatever the explanation, it is clear that religion and philosophy respond to profound human psychological needs. They address our curiosity about our ultimate origins, our final destiny, and the meaning of our lives.

COMPARING THE FOUR GREAT REVOLUTIONS

WHAT WERE the four great revolutions in thought and religion that developed between 800 and 300 B.C.E.?

The religious revolution that took place in China provides the clearest example of how philosophical breakthroughs emerged from the legacies of the earliest civilizations. Natural barriers isolated China and prevented outside forces from influencing its development. In India, by contrast, it was not until the culture of the Indo-Aryan immigrants replaced the original Indus civilization that the foundation was laid for the great tradition of Indian thought and religion. The situation in the Mediterranean world was even more complex. No direct ties have been traced from the early Mesopotamian and Egyptian civilizations to Greek philosophy and Judaic monotheism, but they drew on the complex amalgam of cultures that the early Middle Eastern civilizations inspired. The full impact of Greek and Hebrew thought was not felt in the West until centuries later when Christianity and Islam emerged as a second stage in their evolution.

PHILOSOPHY IN CHINA

WHY WAS the Chinese revolution more akin to Greek thought than to Indian religion or Judaic monotheism?

Of the four great intellectual revolutions of the first millennium B.C.E., China's was closer to Greece's than to India's or to Judaic monotheism. Greece produced many different philosophers, and Chinese tradition claimed "one hundred schools." But whereas Greek thought was speculative and interested in natural phenomena, Chinese thought was practical and sociopolitical. Chinese thought also had far greater staying power than Greek thought, which only a few centuries after the glory of Athens was submerged by Christianity. It became the handmaiden of theology and did not reemerge as an independent force until the Italian Renaissance. In contrast, Chinese philosophy, although challenged by Buddhism, remained dominant until the early 20th century. How were these early philosophies able to maintain such a grip on China when the cultures of every other part of the world fell under the sway of religions?

Part of the answer is that most Chinese philosophy had a religious dimension. But it was a different kind of religion, with assumptions unlike those derived from Judaic roots. In the Christian or Islamic worldview, there is a God who, however concerned with humankind, is not of this world. This worldview leads to dualism, the distinction between a supernatural other world and this world.

In the Chinese worldview, the two spheres are not separate: The cosmos is single, continuous, and nondualistic. It includes Heaven, Earth, and humanity. Heaven is above. Earth is below. Humanity, ideally guided by a wise and virtuous ruler, stands in between and harmonizes the cosmological forces of Heaven and Earth by virtuous living and ritual sacrifice.

CONFUCIANISM

Confucius was born in 551 B.C.E. in a minor state in northeastern China. Since he received an education in writing, music, and rituals, he probably belonged to the lower nobility or the knightly class. His father died when Confucius was young, so

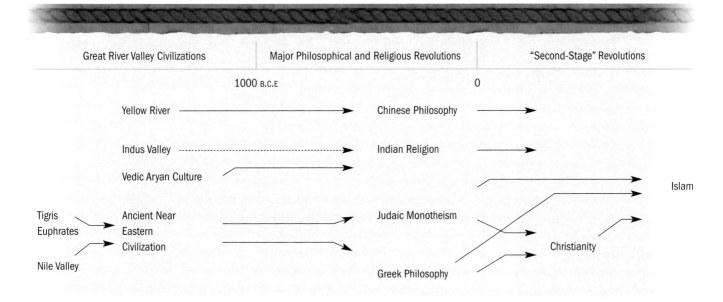

Great River Valley Civilizations	Major Philosophical and Religious Revolutions	"Second-Stage" Revolutions

1000 B.C.E   0

Yellow River ⟶ Chinese Philosophy ⟶

Indus Valley ⤏ Indian Religion ⟶

Vedic Aryan Culture ⟶

Tigris / Euphrates ⟶ Ancient Near Eastern Civilization ⟶ Judaic Monotheism ⟶ Islam

Nile Valley ⟶

Christianity

Greek Philosophy ⟶

he may have known privation. He made his living by teaching, and he traveled with his disciples from state to state, seeking a ruler who would put his ideas into practice. Although he may once have obtained a minor post, his ideas were usually rejected as impractical. He died in 479 B.C.E., honored as a teacher and scholar but having failed to find a ruler who would implement his ideas. *Confucius* is the Latinized form of *K'ung Fu-tzu,* or *Master K'ung,* as he is known in China.

The only records of Confucius's teachings are the *Analects,* collections of his sayings made by his disciples. The picture that emerges from them is of a man of moderation, propriety, optimism, good sense, and wisdom. In an age of cruelty and superstition, he was humane, rational, and upright, demanding much of others and more of himself. Characteristically, when asked about death, he turned the questioner's attention back to this life: "You do not understand even life. How can you understand death?"[1]

Confucius described himself as a transmitter and a conservator of tradition, not an innovator. He idealized the early Shang and Zhou kings as paragons of virtue and imagined early Zhou society as a golden age. He sought the secrets of its success in its writings, some of which became Confucian classics. Throughout most of Chinese history they have had an authority not unlike Scripture in the West.

Confucius proposed to resolve the turmoil of his own age by a return to the good old ways of the early Zhou. When asked about government, he said, "Let the ruler be a ruler, the subject a subject, the father a father, the son a son." His vision was of an unbroken social harmony (extending from the individual family member to the monarch) based on five categories of relationship: ruler-subject, father-son, husband-wife, older brother-younger brother, and friend-friend. China, however, was undergoing a dynamic transition, and it was not enough simply to stress basic human relationships.

The genius of Confucius was to transform the old aristocratic code into a new ethical system that any educated Chinese could practice. His reinterpretation of the early Zhou tradition can be seen in his concept of the ***chun-tzu,*** literally "the son of the ruler" (or of an aristocrat). Confucius redefined it as a person with the inner virtues of humanity, integrity, righteousness, altruism, and loyalty,

[1]Confucius, *The Analects,* trans. by D. C. Lau (Penguin Books, 1979).

QUICK REVIEW

Confucius

• Born in 551 B.C.E. in northeastern China

• Probably belonged to the lower nobility or knightly class

• Made his living as a teacher and a scholar

2.4
Confucius: *Analects*

chun-tzu The Confucian term for a person who behaves ethically, in harmony with the cosmic order.

Confucius. The philosopher is depicted here wearing the robes of a scholar of a later age.

Collection of the National Palace Museum, Taiwan, Republic of China.

Daoism A Chinese philosophy that teaches that wisdom lies in becoming one with the *Dao*, the "way," which is the creative principle of the universe.

matched by an outward demeanor of propriety. This redefinition was not unlike the change that has taken place in the meaning of *gentleman*, from "one who is gentle-born" to "one who is gentle-behaved." But whereas *gentleman* remained a fairly superficial category in the West, in China *chun-tzu* went deeper. Confucius saw ethics as grounded in nature. The true gentleman was in touch with his basic nature, and through it, with the cosmic order.

Confucius taught that good government depended on the appointment to office of good men, who would serve as models for the multitude: "The virtue of the gentleman is like wind; the virtue of the small man is like grass. Let the wind blow over the grass and it is sure to bend." Above the gentleman was the sage king, who possessed an almost mystical virtue and power.

Confucianism was not adopted as the official philosophy of China until the second century B.C.E., during the Han dynasty (202 B.C.E.–9 C.E.; see Chapter 7). But two other important Confucian philosophers had appeared in the meantime. Mencius (370–290 B.C.E.) is famous for his argument that humans tend toward the good just as water runs downward. The role of education, therefore, is to uncover and cultivate that innate goodness. Moreover, just as humans tend toward the good, so does Heaven possess a moral will. The will of Heaven is that a government should see to the education and well-being of its people. The rebellion of people against a government is the primary evidence that Heaven has withdrawn its mandate. At times in Chinese history, only lip service was paid toward concern for the people, but the idea that government should care for the people became a permanent part of the Confucian tradition.

The other influential Confucian philosopher was Xunzi (300–237 B.C.E.), who felt that Heaven was amoral and indifferent to whether China was ruled by a tyrant or a sage. He believed human nature was bad or at least that human desires and emotions, if unchecked and unrefined, caused conflict. He emphasized etiquette and education as restraints on unruly human nature, and good institutions, including punishments and rewards, as a means for shaping behavior. These ideas influenced the thinkers of the Legalist school.

DAOISM

Daoism (pronounced "Dah-oh-ism") offered a refuge from the burden of social responsibilities. The classics of the school are the *Lao-tzu*, dating from the fourth century B.C.E., and the *Chuang-tzu*, dating from about a century later.

The central concept of the religion is the *Dao*, or way. It is the mysterious, unnameable creator, the sustainer, and the process or flux of the universe. The Dao functions on a cosmic scale. As the *Lao-tzu* puts it, "Heaven and Earth are ruthless, and treat the myriad creatures as straw dogs; the sage (in accord with the Dao) is ruthless, and treats the people as straw dogs."[2] But the sage is also described as one who "excels in saving people." By realizing the Dao, he transcends disruptive action and allows nature to flourish.

The sage follows the rhythms of nature, the *Lao-tzu* says, by regaining or returning to an original simplicity. To attain this state, one must "learn to be without learning." Knowledge is bad because it creates distinctions and leads to a succession of ideas and images that interfere with participation in the Dao. One must also learn to be without desires beyond the immediate and simple needs of nature.

Along with the basic Daoist prescription of becoming one with the Dao are two other assumptions or principles. One is that any action pushed to an extreme

[2] *Tau Te Ching*, trans. by D. C. Lau (Penguin Books, 1963).

will initiate a countervailing reaction in the direction of the opposite extreme. The other is that too much government, even good government, can become oppressive by its very weight. As the *Lao-tzu* put it, "Govern a large state as you would cook small fish"; that is, without too much stirring.

LEGALISM

A third great current in classical Chinese thought was **Legalism**. Legalists were also concerned about ending the wars that plagued China. True peace, they felt, required a strong state. The Legalists did not seek a model in the distant past nor model their state on a heavenly order of values. They began with the assumption that human nature is selfish and in need of restraint by a strong state. Severe laws, rewards for service that strengthens the state, and punishment for acts that weaken it are the means to a good society.

Legalism was the philosophy of the state of Qin, which destroyed the Zhou in 256 B.C.E. and unified China in 221 B.C.E. Because Qin laws were cruel and severe, and because Legalism put human laws above an ethic modeled on Heaven, later generations of Chinese execrated its doctrines. Yet its legacy of administrative and criminal laws survived. Even Confucian statesmen could not do without them.

China

551–479 B.C.E.	Confucius
370–290 B.C.E.	Mencius
300–237 B.C.E.	Xunzi
Fourth century B.C.E.	Lao-Tzu
221 B.C.E.	Qin unifies China

RELIGION IN INDIA

*B*y 400 B.C.E., new social and religious forms took shape in the Indian subcontinent. A tradition was created whose fundamental institutions and ideas came to prevail virtually throughout the subcontinent. Despite staggering internal diversity and divisions and long periods of foreign rule, this Indian culture has survived for more than 2,000 years.

WHAT FUNDAMENTAL institutions and ideas form the basis of Indian religion?

"HINDU" AND "INDIAN"

The word **Hindu** lumps together an immense diversity of social, racial, linguistic, and religious groups. It is not a term for any single or uniform religious community. "Indian," on the other hand, commonly refers today to all native inhabitants of the subcontinent, including Muslims, Sikhs, and Christians. We, however, shall use *Indian* to refer to the distinctively Indian tradition of thought and culture that achieved its classical formulation in the Hindu society of the first millennium C.E. (before the arrival of Muslim culture ca. 1000 C.E.). The Jains of India and the Buddhists of wider Asia were also its heirs.

HISTORICAL BACKGROUND

We saw in Chapter 1 how, in the later Vedic or Brahmanic period, a priest-centered cult dominated the upper classes of Aryanized northern Indian society. By the sixth century B.C.E., this cult had apparently grown so extreme that most people had little or no access to it. Elaborate animal sacrifices on behalf of Aryan rulers imposed economic burdens on peasants whose religious concerns they did not address.

The latest Vedic texts themselves reflect a reaction against excessive emphasis on the power of sacrifice and ritual formulas, accumulation of worldly wealth and power, and hope for an afterlife in paradise. Treatises called the **Brahmanas** (ca. 1000–800 B.C.E.) dealt with the ritual applications of the old Vedic texts, the

Legalism Chinese philosophical school that argued that a strong state was necessary to have a good society.

Hindu Term applied to the diverse social, racial, linguistic, and religious groups of India.

Brahmanas Texts dealing with the ritual application of the Vedas.

Sacred Texts

- Latest Vedic texts were a reaction against excessive emphasis on ritual and sacrifice
- *Brahmanas* dealt with ritual application of Vedic text
- Upanishads were an extended reflection on meaning of ritual and nature of *Brahman*

explanation of Vedic rites and mythology, and the theory of the sacrifice. Initially they had focused on methods for controlling the sacred power (*Brahman*) of the sacrificial ritual, but they gradually came to emphasize the acquisition of this power through knowledge instead of ritual acts.

This tendency became central to the Upanishads (ca. 800–500 B.C.E.), and extended meditations on the meaning of ritual and the nature of *Brahman*. The Upanishadic sages and the early Jains and Buddhists shared certain revolutionary ideas and concerns. Their thinking and piety influenced not only all later Indian thought but, through the spread of the Buddhist tradition, much of the intellectual and religious life of East and Southeast Asia as well. Thus, the middle centuries of the first millennium B.C.E. in India began a religious and philosophical revolution that, like China's, marks a turning point in the history of civilization.

THE UPANISHADIC WORLDVIEW

The Upanishads emphasized two new ideas: that knowledge is more important than ritual, and that immortality is not an afterlife but escape from existence itself. An early Upanishadic prayer said, "From the unreal lead me to the Real. From death lead me to immortality." The first sentence suggests the Upanishadic focus on speculation about the nature of things, the quest for ultimate truth. Here ritual takes a backseat to meditation, and knowledge, not sacred words or acts, becomes the source of power. The second sentence reflects a novel belief that true immortality is liberation from existence in any earthly, heavenly, or other sense. These two Upanishadic beliefs changed the shape of Indian thought forever and provide the key to understanding its basic worldview.

The Nature of Reality The Upanishadic quest for knowledge focused on discovering the nature of the individual self (*atman*) and the self's relation to ultimate reality (*Brahman*). The gods are seen as part of the total scheme of things, subject to the laws of existence, and not on the same plane with the transcendent Absolute. Prayer and sacrifice to particular gods for their help continues; but the higher goal is realization of *Brahman* through intellect alone, not ritual.

The culmination of Upanishadic speculation is the suggestion that the way to the Absolute is through the self. Through contemplation, ***Atman-Brahman*** is recognized not as a deity, but as the very principle of reality itself—the unborn, uncreated, unchanging infinite. Because the ultimate cannot be conceptualized or described in finite terms, all that can be said of this reality is that it is "neither this nor that." Beneath the impermanence of ordinary reality lies the changeless *Brahman*, to which every being's immortal self belongs. The difficulty is in recognizing this self (and with it the Absolute) while one is enmeshed in mortal existence.

A second, and related, focus of Upanishadic thought is inquiry into the nature of "normal" existence. The realm of life is seen to be ultimately impermanent and ever changing. Things that appear to be "substantial"—the physical world, our bodies and personalities, worldly success—are revealed in the Upanishads as ultimately ephemeral. Even happiness is transient. Existence, therefore, can never be satisfying in any fundamental sense. Only *Brahman* is enduring, eternal, unchanging, for it is the unmoved ground of being. Here we see the roots of the Buddhist belief that impermanence and suffering are the fundamental facts of existence as we know it.

Atman-Brahman The unchanging, infinite principle of reality in Indian religion.

Life After Death   The Upanishadic sages conceived of existence as a ceaseless cycle, a never-ending alternation between life and death. The concept of *samsara*, the endless cycle of existence, became the basic assumption of all Indian thought and the key to its understanding of reality. It regards the prospect of endless "redeath" as the dismal lot of all beings in this world

Karma   The concept of *karma* helped make sense of the cycle of *samsara*. It holds that every action has inevitable effects. Good deeds bring good results, perhaps even rebirth in a heaven or as a god, and evil deeds bring evil consequences, whether in this life or by rebirth in the next. Because of the fundamental impermanence of everything in existence, both good and evil are temporary. The flux of existence knows only movement, change, endless cause and effect far transcending a mere human life span.

Solutions   The Indian tradition developed two kinds of solutions to the problem of *samsara*. The first recommends a strategy of maximizing good actions and minimizing bad actions to achieve the best possible rebirth in one's next round of existence. The second, and more radical, solution seeks "liberation" (*moksha*) from existence: escaping all karmic effects by escaping action itself.

The first strategy has been characterized as the "ordinary norm," as opposed to the "extraordinary norm" (a path possible only for a select elite). Essentially, the ordinary norm aims at living in accordance with a code of social and moral responsibility. The most significant such codes in Indian history are those of the Hindus, Buddhists, and Jains. The seekers of the "extraordinary norm" usually follow an ascetic discipline aimed at helping them to withdrawal from the karmic cycle altogether and win release (*moksha*) from cause and effect, good and evil, birth and rebirth. These two responses to the problem posed by *samsara* underlie the fundamental forms of Indian thought and piety that took shape in the mid- to late-first millennium B.C.E.

Social Responsibility: *Dharma* as Ideal   The "ordinary norm" of life in the various traditions of Indian religiousness can be summarized as life lived according to *dharma*. *Dharma* has many meanings, but its most common is "the right (order of things)," "moral law," "right conduct," or "duty." It includes the cosmic order (comparable to the Chinese Dao) as well as individual moral responsibility and the right conduct of political, commercial, social, and religious affairs. For most people, life according to *dharma* is the life of moral action that will lead to a better birth in the next round of existence.

Life according to *dharma* accepts action in the world of *samsara* as necessary and legitimate. It demands acceptance of the responsibilities associated with one's sex, class and caste group, stage in life, and other circumstances. It allows for legitimate self-interest—the right to do whatever acquires merit for one's eternal *atman* and to avoid whatever brings evil consequences. Rebirth in heaven, in paradise, is the highest goal attainable through the life of *dharma*, but every achievement in the *dharma* realm (the world of *samsara*), even the attainment of Heaven, is ultimately impermanent and is subject to change.

Ascetic Discipline: *Moksha* as Ideal   Persons who have the mental and physical capacity to abandon the world of ordinary life and pursue freedom from *samsara* pursue a way of life in direct contrast to the "ordinary norm." First, any action, good or bad, is counterproductive, for action produces only more action,

samsara The endless cycle of existence, of birth, and rebirth.

karma Indian belief that every action has an inevitable effect. Good deeds bring good results; evil deeds have evil consequences.

dharma Moral law or duty.

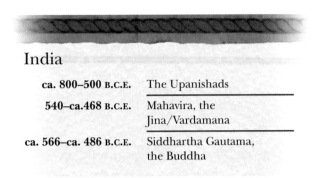

India

ca. 800–500 B.C.E.	The Upanishads
540–ca.468 B.C.E.	Mahavira, the Jina/Vardamana
ca. 566–ca. 486 B.C.E.	Siddhartha Gautama, the Buddha

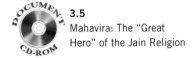

3.5

Mahavira: The "Great Hero" of the Jain Religion

more *karma*, more rebirth. Second, nonaction is achieved only by withdrawing from "normal" existence. The person seeking release from *samsara* has to move beyond the usual responsibilities of family and society. Most often, this involves becoming a "renouncer" (*sannyasi*)—whether a Hindu hermit, yogi, or wanderer, or a Jain or Buddhist monk. Third, true renunciation of the world demands selflessness, the elimination of ego. One must give up the desires and attachments that normally enable the self to function in the world. Fourth, the highest goal is not rebirth in Heaven, but liberation (*moksha*) from all rebirth. *Moksha* is permanent. Its realization means no more becoming, no more suffering in the realm of *samsara*. Eternity, transcendence, and freedom from suffering are its attributes.

Seekers of the Extraordinary Norm   The ideas that inspired some people to live by what was called the extraordinary norm were first developed in the Upanishads. They appealed to individuals who wanted to abandon both ritualistic religious practices and the class distinctions and material concerns of their societies. Many of these were of warrior-noble (*Kshatriya*), not Brahmanic, birth. They lived as hermits and pursued spiritual power through yogic meditation and radical self-denial. They hoped to transcend bodily existence and experience the absolute.

In the sixth century B.C.E., teachers of new ideas appeared in the region of modern Bihar. They rejected traditional practices and the authority of the Vedas in favor of ascetic discipline. Two of these teachers founded lasting traditions of piety and faith: those of the Jains and Buddhists.

MAHAVIRA AND THE JAIN TRADITION

The **Jains** are an Indian community that traces its tradition to Vardhamana, known as Mahavira ("the great hero"), who is traditionally believed to have lived from about 540 to 468 B.C.E. Mahavira is hailed by the Jains as the final Jina ("victor" over *samsara*). The Jains (or *Jainas*, "adherents of the *Jina*") do not regard Mahavira as a god, but as a human teacher who found and taught the way to extricate the self, or soul, from the bonds of the material world and its karmic accretions. Mahavira's path to release focused on the elimination of evil thoughts and acts, especially those harmful to others. His radical ascetic practice aimed at destroying karmic defilements and, ultimately, all actions leading to karmic bondage.

In the Jain view, there are only innumerable, ceaseless cycles of generation and degeneration. The universe is alive with an infinite number of souls, all immortal, omniscient, and pure, but trapped in *samsara*. Any thought, word, or deed attracts karmic matter that encumbers the soul. The greatest quantity of such matter comes from evil acts, especially those done out of cruelty to another being. Jains are vegetarians and regard *ahimsa* ("noninjury") to any being as paramount. Compassion is the great virtue for them, as for Buddhists. Today, as in earlier centuries, there is a thriving lay community of perhaps three million Jains, mostly resident in western India.

THE BUDDHA'S "MIDDLE PATH"

The Buddhist tradition remains one of the great universalist forms of faith in the world today. Despite the fact that Buddhism originated in India, few of its people are now Buddhists. It did, however, leave its mark on Hindu and Jain religion and culture.

Jains Indian religious community that teaches compassion for all beings.

Like the two other great universalist traditions, Christianity and Islam, Buddhism traces its origins to a single figure who has loomed larger than life in the community of the faithful for centuries. He is Siddhartha Gautama, known as the Buddha, or "enlightened/awakened one." Like his contemporary, Mahavira, Gautama was born (ca. 566 B.C.E.) in apparently comfortable circumstances.

At the age of 29, Gautama was struck by the reality of human existence: aging, sickness, and death. He abandoned his home and family to seek a solution to the dilemma of the endless cycle of mortal existence. After this "Great Renunciation," he studied with renowned teachers. Then he adopted extreme ascetic disciplines and, still unsatisfied, turned finally to intense yogic meditation under a pipal tree near Varanasi (Banaras) known as Gaya. On one historic night, he moved through different levels of trance, during which he reviewed his past lives, grasped the nature of the cycle of existence that entraps all beings, and discovered how to stop the karmic outflows that fuel suffering. Thus he became the Buddha, the one fully enlightened by omniscient consciousness of reality as it truly is.

Gautama devoted the last of his earthly lives before his final release to teaching others his "middle path" between asceticism and indulgence. This path has been the core of Buddhist faith and practice ever since. It begins with acceptance of the "four noble truths": (1) all life is *dukkha*, or suffering; (2) the source of suffering is desiring; (3) the cessation of desiring is the way to end suffering; and (4) the path to this end is eightfold: right view, thought, speech, action, livelihood, effort, mindfulness, and concentration. The key idea of the Buddha's teaching, or *dharma*, is that everything in the world of existence is causally linked. The essential fact of existence is *dukkha*, suffering, for no pleasure—no matter how great—is permanent (the Buddhist endorsement of the fundamental Indian theme of *samsara*).

Dukkha comes from desire, from craving, from attachment to self, and Buddhism recommends the moral "eightfold path" and the cardinal virtue of compassion for all beings as the way to eliminate the selfish desiring that is the root of *samsara* and its unavoidable suffering. The Buddha himself attained this goal. When he died (ca. 486 B.C.E.) after a life of teaching others how to master desiring, he passed from the round of existence forever. In Buddhist terminology, he attained nirvana, the extinguishing of karmic bondage (see History's Voices: The "Turning of the Wheel of *Dharma*": Basic Teachings of the Buddha). The Buddhist movement, like the Jain, included not only those who were willing to renounce marriage and normal occupations to become part of the Buddha's communities of monks or nuns, but also laypersons who strove to live by the Buddha's high moral standards and support those who sought final release by becoming mendicants. Buddhist tradition embraced seekers of both the extraordinary and the ordinary norms, and this dual community has remained characteristic of all forms of Buddhism.

Fasting Buddha. Before Gautama arrived at the "Middle Path," he practiced severe austerities for six years. This fourth- to second-century B.C.E. statue of a fasting Buddha from Gandhara (in present-day Pakistan) reflects Greek influence on early Buddhist sculpture.

Borromeo, EPA/Art Resource, N.Y.

QUICK REVIEW

Siddhartha Gautama

- Great Renunciation: at 29 left home to seek answers to eternal questions
- Unsatisfied with study with renowned teachers
- Achieved status as the Buddha through yogic meditation

HISTORY'S VOICES

THE "TURNING OF THE WHEEL OF THE DHARMA": BASIC TEACHINGS OF THE BUDDHA

Following are selections from the sermon said to have been the first preached by the Buddha. It was directed at five former companions with whom he had practiced extreme austerities. When he abandoned asceticism to meditate under the Bodh tree, they had left him, but this sermon is said to have persuaded them to become his first followers. Because it set in motion the Buddha's teaching, or Dharma, it is described as "setting in motion the wheel of Dharma." The text is from the Dhammacakkappavattanasutta.

WHAT EXTREMES does the Middle Path try to avoid? What emotion drives the chain of suffering? How does the "knowledge" that brings salvation compare to the knowledge sought in the Hindu tradition?

Thus have I heard. The Blessed One was once living in the Deer Park at Isipatana (the Resort of Seers) near Baranasi (Benares). There he addressed the group of five bhikkhus.

"Bhikkhus, these two extremes ought not to be practiced by one who has gone forth from the household life. What are the two? There is devotion to the indulgence of sense-pleasures, which is low, common, the way of ordinary people, unworthy and unprofitable; and there is devotion to self-mortification, which is painful, unworthy and unprofitable.

"Avoiding both these extremes, the Tathagata has realized the Middle Path: it gives vision, it gives knowledge, and it leads to calm, to insight, to enlightenment, to Nibbana. And what is that Middle Path? It is simply the Noble Eightfold Path, namely, right view, right thought, right speech, right action, right livelihood, right effort, right mindfulness, right concentration. This is the Middle Path realized by the Tathagata, which gives vision, which gives knowledge,

and which leads to calm, to insight, to enlightenment, to Nibbana. . . .

"The Noble Truth of suffering (*Dukkha*) is this: Birth is suffering; aging is suffering; sickness is suffering; death is suffering; sorrow and lamentation, pain, grief and despair are suffering; association with the unpleasant is suffering; dissociation from the pleasant is suffering; not to get what one wants is suffering—in brief, the five aggregates of attachment are suffering.

"The Noble Truth of the origin of suffering is this: It is this thirst (craving) which produces re-existence and re-becoming, bound up with passionate greed. It finds fresh delight now here and now there, namely, thirst for nonexistence (self-annihilation).

"The Noble Truth of the Cessation of suffering is this: It is the complete cessation of that very thirst, giving it up, renouncing it, emancipating oneself from it, detaching oneself from it.

"The Noble Truth of the Path leading to the Cessation of suffering is this: It is simply the Noble Eightfold Path. . . .

"But when my vision of true knowledge was fully clear regarding the Four Noble Truths, then I claimed to have realized the perfect Enlightenment that is supreme in the world with its gods, in this world with its recluses and brahmanas, with its princes and men. And a vision of true knowledge arose in me thus: My heart's deliverance is unassailable. This is the last birth. Now there is no more re-becoming (rebirth)."

This the Blessed One said. The group of five bhikkhus was glad, and they rejoiced at his words.

—*Samyutta-nikaya, LVI, II*

Source: *What the Buddha Taught* by Walpola Rahula. Copyright © 1974 by W. Rahula, pp. 92–94. Used by permission of Grove Atlantic Inc.

THE RELIGION OF THE ISRAELITES

he ancient Near East was a **polytheistic** world. Everywhere people worshiped local or regional gods and goddesses who were represented largely as capricious, amoral beings, no more affected by the actions of humans than were the natural forces that some of them represented. Out of this polytheistic world came the great tradition of ethical monotheistic faith represented historically in the Jewish, Christian, and Islamic communities. This tradition traces its origin to the small nation of the Israelites, or Hebrews.

Monotheism, faith in a single, all-powerful God as the sole creator, sustainer, and ruler of the universe, may be older than the Hebrews, but its first clear historical manifestation was with them. It was among the Hebrew tribes that emphasis on the moral demands and responsibilities that the one God placed on individual and community was first definitively linked to human history itself, and that history to a divine plan.

WHAT WAS distinctive about the Hebrew concept of God and religion?

FROM HEBREW NOMADS TO THE ISRAELITE NATION

The history of the Hebrews, later known as Israelites, is pieced together from various sources. The Hebrews are mentioned only rarely in the records of their ancient Middle Eastern neighbors, so we must rely on their own accounts as compiled in the Hebrew Bible (the "Old Testament" in Christian terminology). Scholars once tended to dismiss the Bible as a reliable source of history, but the trend today is to use it cautiously and critically.

Tradition maintains that Abraham, the ancestor of the Hebrews, came from Ur in southern Mesopotamia and wandered west with his clan to the land later known as Palestine. Precise dating of the arrival of the Hebrews in Palestine is impossible, but it was likely between 1900 and 1600 B.C.E.

It was Moses, however, early in the 13th century B.C.E., who led the Hebrews clearly onto the stage of history. Some of Abraham's people had settled in the Palestinian region, but others wandered into Egypt. As the biblical narrative tells it, there they had become a settled but subjected, even enslaved, people. Under Moses, part of the Egyptian Israelites fled Egypt to find a new homeland in Canaan, the province of Palestine that is described in the Bible as the homeland God promised them. This is the key event in the sacred history of the Hebrews or Israelites: the forging of the covenant, or mutual pact, between God *(Yahweh)* and His people. In secular terms, the Exodus marked the emergence of the Israelites as a nation, a people with a sense of community and a common faith.

By about 1200 B.C.E., the Israelites had displaced the Canaanite inhabitants of ancient Palestine. About two centuries later, the now-settled people reached the peak of their power under their kings David (r. ca. 1000–961 B.C.E.) and Solomon (r. ca. 961–922 B.C.E.). But their nation split into two parts in the ninth century B.C.E.: Israel in the north and Judah, with its capital at Jerusalem, in the south (see Map 2–1).

The rise of great empires in the Middle East spelled disaster for the Israelites. The northern kingdom fell to the Assyrians in 722 B.C.E., and its people were scattered.

polytheism The worship of many gods.

monotheism The worship of one universal God.

The Israelites

ca. 1000–961 B.C.E.	Reign of King David
ca. 961–922 B.C.E.	Reign of King Solomon
722 B.C.E.	Assyrian conquest of Israel (northern kingdom)
586 B.C.E.	Destruction of Jerusalem; fall of Judah (southern kingdom); Babylonian captivity
539 B.C.E.	Restoration of temple; return of exiles

MAP EXPLORATION

Interactive map: To explore this map further, go to
http://www.prenhall.com/craig/map2.1

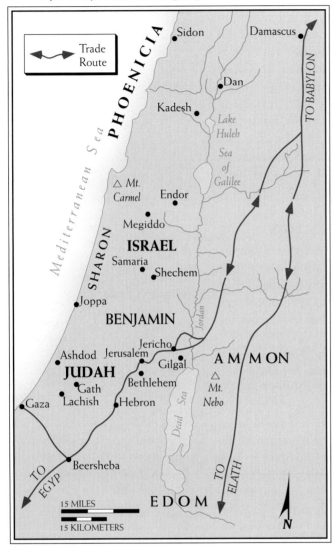

MAP 2–1
Ancient Palestine.   The Hebrews established a unified kingdom under Kings David and Solomon in the 10th century B.C.E. After Solomon, the kingdom was divided into Israel in the north and Judah, with its capital, Jerusalem, in the south. North of Israel were the great commercial cities of Phoenicia.

WHICH NEAR Eastern empire was responsible for the destruction of the Hebrew kingdoms?

   **1.9**
Hebrew Scriptures

Only the residents of Judah remained, the Jews. In 586 B.C.E., Judah was conquered by the Neo-Babylonian king Nebuchadnezzar II (d. 562 B.C.E.). He destroyed the great temple built by Solomon and sent the Jewish nation into exile in Babylon. There, in the "Babylonian captivity" of the Exile, without a temple, the Jews clung to their traditions and faith. After the Persians defeated the Babylonians in 539 B.C.E., the Jews were allowed to return to Jerusalem, and by about 516 B.C.E., a second temple had been erected.

The new Judaic state continued for centuries to be dominated by other nations, but its people maintained their religious and political identity. However, Judah was again destroyed and its people dispersed after the Romans sacked Jerusalem in 70 C.E. and again in 132 C.E. By then, however, the Jews had developed a religious worldview that could thrive without the support of a Judaic state.

THE MONOTHEISTIC REVOLUTION

This small nation developed a tradition of faith that amounted to a revolution in ways of thinking about the human condition, the meaning of life and history, and the nature of the Divine. The revolutionary character of the faith lay in its uniquely moralistic understanding of human life and history and the uncompromising monotheism on which it was based.

At the root of this monotheistic tradition stands Abraham, whom Jews, Christians, and Muslims honor as the symbolic founder of their faith. Abraham probably conceived of his Lord as one deity among many other divinities whom he might have worshiped. But the biblical account recognizes him as the "Father of the Faithful," for Abraham promised exclusive loyalty to God. Abraham was the first Hebrew patriarch to make a covenant with God. He pledged to serve only God, and God promised in exchange that Abraham's descendants would become His special people.

When Moses renewed the covenant at Mount Sinai, he and his followers may not yet have conceived of a purely monotheistic faith. The covenant united the Israelites as a people with a special relationship to God, and at Sinai they received both God's holy law (the Torah) and God's promise of protection so as long as they kept the law. This pivotal moment launched the monotheistic revolution that came to fruition several hundred years later. Exclusive loyalty to one God became belief in only one God.

The monotheistic revolution might be said to have begun with Abraham or Moses. Historically, we can trace it to the period when the Israelite kingdom divided (922 B.C.E.). At this time, *prophets*—inspired messengers of God—appeared to call their people back from false gods to faith in the one true God and to obedience to God's commandments. The prophets' concerns with purifying Jewish faith and with morality, focused on two ideas that are central to Judaic monotheism.

The first is the significance of history in the divine plan. The prophets saw in Israel's troubles God's punishment for the people's failure to fulfill their covenant duties. But they also saw Israel as the "suffering servant" of God, as the instrument God would use to purify other nations and bring them to knowledge of God. The prophets transcended the nationalistic focus of earlier Israelite religion and proclaimed a universalist monotheism: Yahweh was God of all.

The second idea fundamental to monotheism centered on the nature of Yahweh. God was a righteous God who expected righteousness from human beings. He was a moral God who demanded goodness, not blood offerings or empty prayers.

The crux of the breakthrough to ethical monotheism lay in linking the Lord of the Universe to history and morality. The Almighty Creator was seen as concerned with the actions and fates of His human creatures (as exemplified by Israel). History thus took on transcendent meaning. God had created humankind for a good purpose; people were called to be just and good like their Creator, for they were involved in the fulfillment of His divine purpose. The prophets promised that this fulfillment would come for the Israelites in their restoration as a people purifed of sins.

Although the Exile came to an end, however, the prophesied days of peace and blessedness under God's rule still did not come. This sparked the idea that history would culminate in a future Messianic age. The faith and morality that the Jews had long seen as keys to human destiny became in later Jewish teaching a prediction of a day of judgment that would cap the golden age of the **Messiah**. These ideas played a key role in the later formation of Christian and Muslim expectations for a Messianic deliverer, a resurrection of the body, and a life after death.

The other key element in the monotheistic revolution of the Jews was the role accorded to the law embodied in the five books of Torah (Genesis, Exodus, Leviticus, Numbers, and Deuteronomy). The law enabled Jews who lived in exile to survive the loss of their Temple and its priestly cult. Observation of the Torah,

Messiah The redeemer whose coming, Jews believed, would establish the kingdom of God on earth. Christians considered Jesus to be the Messiah (Christ means Messiah in Greek).

Scroll from the Dead Sea. This photograph shows part of one of the ancient scrolls found in 1947 in a remote cave at Khirbat near the Dead Sea in Jordan. The passage from the Hebrew Bible contains part of the Ten Commandments in the Book of Deuteronomy. The scrolls were written sometime between 200 B.C.E. and 68 C.E. They contain documents that suggest they belonged to a monastic sect of Jews called Essenes whose beliefs bear some similarity to those of John the Baptist and Jesus. ASAP/David Harris.

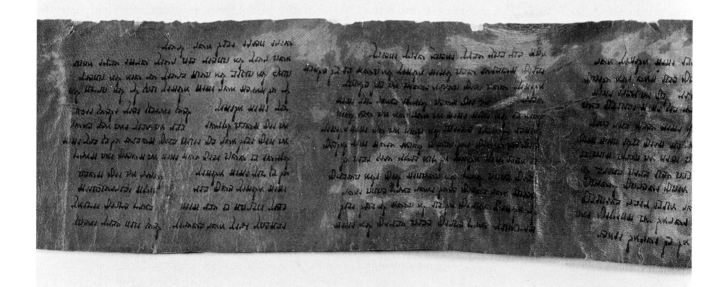

OVERVIEW   FOUR GREAT SYSTEMS OF THOUGHT AND RELIGION

Between 800 B.C.E. and 300 B.C.E., four philosophical or religious revolutions occurred that shaped the subsequent history of the world. These revolutions, which were attempts to answer universal questions about the human condition, established cultural patterns that have endured to the present day.

Chinese Philosophy	Three principal schools: Confucianism, Daoism, Legalism. Each school was concerned with social and political issues, with how individuals interact with each other and the state, and with the question of how to lead an ethical life that was in harmony with nature and the cosmos.
Indian Religion	Hinduism, Jains, Buddhism. Indian religion saw existence as an endless cycle of birth and rebirth (*samsara*). *Karma*, the concept that every action has good or evil effects, was the key to resolving the dilemma of *samsara*. Good actions could result in a person's being reborn in a higher state, even as a god. Complete withdrawal from the world could lead to escape from *samsara* into nonexistence.
Hebrew Monotheism	The Hebrews, or Israelites, were the first people in history to base their identity as a nation faithful to a single, all-powerful God who made ethical demands and placed responsibilities on them as individuals and as a community. History, itself, was the unfolding of a divine plan for human beings. Through the Christian and Muslim traditions, Hebrew monotheism would profoundly influence much of the world.
Greek Philosophy	Beginning in the sixth century B.C.E., Greek thinkers were the first to try to explain the natural world without reference to supernatural powers. Later Greek thinkers used rational analysis to investigate ethical, political, and social problems: how human beings should govern themselves, live in society, and act toward each other. The Greek tradition of rational inquiry lies at the root of all subsequent Western science and philosophy.

the earthly focus of their faith, enabled them to preserve their special identity as God's people.

In the second century B.C.E., the role of Torah was ensured by its compilation, together with the books of the prophets and other writings, as the Holy Scriptures or Bible (from Greek *bibloi*, "books"). A holy, authoritative, divinely revealed scripture put the seal on the monotheistic revolution that had made the sovereignty and righteousness of God the foci of faith.

GREEK PHILOSOPHY

WHY, BEGINNING in the sixth century B.C.E., did Greek thinkers produce an intellectual revolution?

*M*any, if not most, Greeks in the ancient world must have lived with assumptions about life and the universe similar to those held by people in other ancient cultures. But some Greeks innovated ideas that set a part of humankind on a new path. As early as the sixth century B.C.E., Greeks began to raise questions about the natural world and proposed explanation for its processes that made no reference to supernatural powers. A historian has explained the originality of Thales of Miletus (624–545 B.C.E.), the first Greek philosopher, in this way:

> In one of the Babylonian legends it says: "All the lands were sea. Marduk bound a rush mat upon the face of the waters, he made dirt and piled it beside the rush mat." What Thales did was to leave Marduk out. He, too,

said that everything was once water. But he thought that earth and every-thing else had been formed out of water by a natural process, like the silt-ing up of the Delta of the Nile. It is an admirable beginning, the whole point of which is that it gathers together into a coherent picture a num-ber of observed facts without letting Marduk in.[3]

By looking for an explanation for the world's origin in nature, Thales may have initiated the rational investigation of the universe and both Western philosophy and Western science. The same rational approach was applied to questions about the gods. In the same century as Thales, Xenophanes of Colophon expressed the opinion that humans think of gods as resembling themselves. Thus, Africans believed in flat-nosed, black-faced gods, and Thracians in gods with blue eyes and red hair.[4] In the fifth century B.C.E., Protagoras of Abdera (ca. 490–ca. 420 B.C.E.) verged on agnosticism, saying: "About the gods I can have no knowledge either that they are or that they are not or what is their nature."[5]

This rationalistic, skeptical attitude also affected thinking about practical matters. Hippocrates of Cos (ca. 400 B.C.E.) attempted to understand and cure disease without recourse to supernatural forces, and by the fifth century B.C.E., the historian Thucydides (ca. 460–ca. 400 B.C.E.) was analyzing and explaining events completely in terms of human nature and chance, leaving no place for the gods. The relative unimportance of divine or supernatural forces also characterized Greek views of law and justice. Greeks believed that laws were made by humans and derived their authority from the fact that they represented the consent of the citizens they governed.

Ideas of this kind contrasted dramatically with earlier approaches to under-standing the world and inaugurated discussions of issues that remain major con-cerns for modern thinkers: What is the nature of the universe? How can it be controlled? Are there divine powers? If there are, what is humanity's relationship to them? Are law and justice human, divine, or both? How should human soci-eties balance freedom and obedience to authority?

Thales of Miletus, the First Greek Philosopher. His explanation for the origin of the world was based on reason and the observation of nature without any need for the supernatural.

Corbis-Bettmann.

REASON AND THE SCIENTIFIC SPIRIT

The rational spirit characteristic of Greek culture blossomed in the sixth cen-tury B.C.E. into the methods for seeking an understanding of the physical world and humanity's place in it that we call *philosophy*. The first steps along this path were taken in Ionia on the coast of Asia Minor, which was in touch with the learning of the East.

Thales (mentioned above) believed that the Earth floated on water and that water was the primary substance from which all things originated. Thales noted that water exists in all the states found in nature: liquid, solid, and gas. He believed that it "created" land by alluvial deposit, and he knew that it was neces-sary for all life. It seemed to him, therefore, that water could account for the phenomena of nature without the need to postulate any supernatural activity.

[3]Benjamin Farrington, *Greek Science* (London: Penguin Books, 1953) p. 37.
[4]H. Frankfort et al., *Before Philosophy* (1949), pp. 14–16.
[5]Hermann Diels, *Fragmente der Vorsokratiker*, 5th ed., ed. by Walther Kranz (Berlin: Weidmann, 1934–1938), Frg. 4.

Later Greek philosophers accepted his assumption that the world was knowable, rational, and simple.

Another native of Miletus, Anaximander (ca. 611–546 B.C.E.), suggested that the primal element was the "unlimited," something combining all attributes. The world emerged from this basic element as the result of an interaction of opposite forces—wet and dry, hot and cold. Anaximander pictured the universe as eternally fluctuating, with all things emerging from the "unlimited," then decaying and returning to it. He also theorized that human beings originated in water and had evolved to their present state through several stages, including that of fish.

Heraclitus of Ephesus, who lived near the end of the sixth century B.C.E., carried the dialogue further. His fundamental hypothesis was: "All is motion." This raised important questions, for if all is constantly in motion, nothing ever really exists. Heraclitus argued, however, that the world had order, for it was governed by a guiding principle, the *logos* ("word," "language," "speech," and "reason"). Phenomena changed, but the *logos* did not. Heraclitus's point was that the physical world obeyed rational laws that could be comprehended by rational minds. The study of nature, therefore, necessitated speculation about language, the essence of human thought and knowledge itself.

Parmenides of Elea and his pupil Zeno disagreed with Heraclitus. They argued that change was an illusion. Reality had to be unchanging, for if something new (i.e., a change) appeared, it would have to originate from nothing—and it was rationally impossible for nothing to create something. Empedocles of Acragas (flourished ca. 450 B.C.E.) postulated the existence of four basic elements (fire, water, earth, and air) as a compromise between Heraclitus and Parmenides. He argued that reality was permanent but not unchanging. The elements did not change, but they were constantly recombined by two primary forces, Love and Strife, or, as we might say, attraction and repulsion.

Leucippus of Miletus (flourished fifth century B.C.E.) and Democritus of Abdera (ca. 460–370 B.C.E.) proposed something similar. They believed that the world consisted of tiny, solid particles (atoms, "indivisibles") that could not be divided or modified. Atoms moved about in the void, and their size and combinations produced the things that our senses perceive. Anaxagoras of Clazomenae (ca. 500–428 B.C.E.) had previously postulated the existence of tiny fundamental particles called *seeds* that were arranged in rational ways by a force called *nous* ("mind"). He assumed that mind was distinct from matter, but the **atomists** regarded "mind" as material. They believed that everything was guided by purely physical laws. These debates began the continuing dialogue between materialism and idealism.

A separate category of philosophers did not speculate about the physical universe but applied reasoned analysis to human beliefs and institutions. They were professional teachers in the mid-fifth century B.C.E. called **Sophists**. They traveled about and were paid to teach practical techniques of persuasion, such as rhetoric. The Sophists explored the tension, perhaps contradiction, between nature and custom or law. The more traditional among them argued that law was in accord with nature. This view strengthened traditional beliefs about the *polis*, the Greek city-state (see Chapter 3). Others argued that laws were based in nature, and were merely agreements among people aimed at preventing them from harming one another. The most extreme Sophists even insisted that law was contrary to nature, and that laws were a strategy the strong used to dominate the weak.

Atomists School of ancient Greek philosophy founded in the fifth century B.C.E. by Leucippus of Miletus and Democritus of Abdera. It held that the world consists of innumerable, tiny, solid, indivisible, and unchangeable particles called atoms.

Sophists Professional teachers who emerged in Greece in the mid-fifth century B.C.E. who were paid to teach techniques of rhetoric, dialectic, and argumentation.

polis The basic Greek political unit. Usually, but incompletely, translated as "city-state," the Greeks thought of the polis as a community of citizens theoretically descended from a common ancestor.

POLITICAL AND MORAL PHILOSOPHY

Like thinkers in other parts of the world in the mid-first millennium B.C.E., some Greeks were vitally concerned with the formulation of moral principles for the governance of the state and the regulation of individual lives, as well as with abstract problems of the nature of existence and transcendence. Nowhere is the Greek concern with ethical, political, and religious issues clearer than in the philosophical tradition that began with Socrates in the latter half of the fifth century B.C.E. That tradition continued with Socrates' pupil Plato and with Plato's pupil Aristotle. Aristotle also made major contributions to the scientific understanding of the physical world and to later Western and Islamic metaphysics.

The starting point for all three was the social and political reality of the Greek city-state, the polis. The greatest crisis for the polis was the Great Peloponnesian War (435–404 B.C.E.; see Chapter 3). The life and teachings of Socrates (469–399 B.C.E.) should be viewed in this political context. Our knowledge of him comes chiefly from his disciples Plato and Xenophon (ca. 435–354 B.C.E.) and from later tradition.

Socrates was committed to the search for truth and for the understanding of human affairs that he believed reason could uncover. His strategy was to question and cross-examine his fellow Greeks. The result of these encounters was always the same. He demonstrated that those whom he questioned might have some technical information and skill, but they seldom demonstrated any knowledge of the fundamental principles of human behavior. Athenians understandably were disturbed by Socrates' unrelenting intellectual challenges, and they concluded that he was undermining the beliefs and values of the polis. Socrates' unconcealed contempt for democracy, a political system that he said allowed ignorant amateurs to make important political decisions, also angered them. His insistence on pursuing his individual philosophical agenda even against the wishes of his fellow citizens further prejudiced them against him.

But Socrates, unlike the Sophists, did not accept pay for his teaching. It was not wealth or pleasure or power that motivated him, but he insisted that he sought "the greatest improvement of the soul." Also, despite his criticism of democracy, he did not question the legitimacy of the polis' claim on its citizens. He proved that in 399 B.C.E., after he was condemned to death by an Athenian jury. Given a chance to escape, he refused because of his respect for the laws that had condemned him.

Socrates' career set the stage for later approaches to dealing with the problems raised by the polis as a system of government and a way of life. Although he refused to play an active role in politics, he did not reject the idea of the polis. He fought as a soldier in its defense, obeyed its laws, and tried to find rational justifications for its fundamental values.

The Cynics Socrates' concern with personal morality and the soul, disdain for worldly pleasure and wealth, and withdrawal from political life became, in exaggerated form, the basis for the teachings of the Cynics. Antisthenes (ca. 455–360 B.C.E.), one of Socrates' followers, was said to be their founder, but their most famous representative was Diogenes of Sinope (ca. 400–325 B.C.E.). To show his contempt for convention, he performed shameful acts in public, dressed in rags, and lived in a tub. He taught that happiness lay in satisfying natural needs in the simplest, most direct way. The Cynics also ridiculed all religious observances. Plato described Diogenes as Socrates gone mad.

Major Greek Philosophers

469–399 B.C.E.	Socrates
429–347 B.C.E.	Plato
384–322 B.C.E.	Aristotle

Plato Plato (429–347 B.C.E.) was the most important of Socrates' associates. He was the first systematic philosopher and, therefore, the first thinker to situate political ideas in a broader philosophical context. He was also a writer of genius, who composed 26 philosophical discussions in the form of dramatic dialogues. In 386 B.C.E., Plato founded the Academy, a center of philosophical investigation and a school for training statesmen and citizens. It survived into the sixth century C.E.

Like Socrates, Plato firmly believed in the polis and its values of order, harmony, and justice. One of its goals was to produce good people. He accepted Socrates' argument that virtue was a form of knowledge, and he believed that knowledge was *episteme*, science, a body of true and unchanging wisdom obtained by only a few philosophers whose training, character, and intellect allowed them to comprehend truth. They were the only people qualified to rule. Although they would prefer lives devoted to contemplation, they would accept the responsibility entailed by their gifts and serve society as philosopher-kings. The training of these people required specialization and subordination of individual to community interests. Plato claimed that true justice lay in each person doing only that one thing to which his nature was best suited.

The polis in Plato's day suffered from terrible internal stress, class struggle, and factional divisions. Plato, however, believed that harmony could be restored by moral and political reforms that would eliminate the causes of strife. Among these causes were private property and the family—things that individuals were tempted to put before their devotion to the common good represented by the polis.

Plato asked the traditional questions: What is a good man, and how is he made? Given that doing the good necessitated knowing the good, a theory of knowledge and an investigation into the nature of knowledge was where Plato believed the discussion had to begin. The search for an understanding of what made ideas true led Plato into metaphysics. Once the nature of the good was established, however, the question remained: How could the state bring its citizens to knowledge of the good? This issue forced Plato to develop a theory of education. Purely logical and metaphysical questions were pursued as part of the quest for solutions to political challenges. Plato's need to polster the beleaguered polis thus contributed to the birth of systematic philosophy.

Aristotle Aristotle (384–322 B.C.E.) was a pupil of Plato whose different experience and cast of mind led him in new directions. In 336, he founded his own school at Athens, the Lyceum. The Lyceum's mission differed from that of the Academy. Its members concentrated on gathering, ordering, and analyzing the data that was the basis for all human knowledge. Aristotle and his students prepared collections of information that advanced scientific studies of logic, physics, astronomy, biology, ethics, rhetoric, literary criticism, and politics.

In each field, Aristotle's method was the same. He began with observation of empirical evidence, which in some cases was physical and in others was common opinion. He then rationally examined this body of information to uncover inconsistencies or other difficulties. To deal with these, he developed metaphysical models. His approach to metaphysics, like Plato's, was teleological; that is, he believed in goals apart from and greater than the wills of individual human beings. Plato characterized those goals as ideas or forms—transcendental concepts beyond human experience. But for Aristotle, they could be inferred by observing the behavior of things in our world.

The most striking characteristics of Aristotle's thought are moderation and common sense. His epistemology (i.e., theory of knowledge) acknowledges the importance of both reason and experience. His metaphysics honors both mind and body. His ethical system envisions a good life that is contemplative and humane—acknowledging as legitimate concerns moderate wealth, comfort, and pleasure.

In politics Aristotle, like Plato, opposed the Sophists' assertion that the polis was contrary to human nature and the result of mere convention. The teleology that he saw in all nature also gave him an explanation for politics. Matter, he claimed, existed to achieve an end, and it developed until it fully realized its end, its form or potential. The primitive instincts of the individual could be seen as the matter out of which the human's potential as a political being could be realized. As the culmination of a series of institutions (marriage, household, village, and finally, polis) that brought human beings together, it served the natural end of enabling them to continue their species. For Aristotle, the purpose of the polis was neither economic nor military, but moral: "The end of the state is the good life," the life lived "for the sake of noble actions," a life of virtue and morality. [6]

Characteristically, Aristotle was less interested in the best state—a utopia ruled by idealized philosopher kings—than in the best state practically possible, one that enabled ordinary people to enjoy both justice and stability. He characterized the constitution for such a state as a *politeia*, not the best system, but the next best—the one most possible for most states. Its quality was moderation. It empowered neither the extremes of the rich or the poor, but the middle class. For the health of the state, he claimed that the middle class should be the largest class. It possessed essential virtues. Because its wealth was moderate, the middle class was not tempted to the arrogance of the rich, and it did not excite the malice of the poor. It fostered stability, a condition that was also promoted by what Aristotle called a mixed constitution (a combination of democracy and oligarchy). Aristotle was both a visionary and a policial realist.

The desire to understand nature in a purely rational, scientific way remained strong through the fifth century B.C.E. It culminated in the work of the atomic theorists, Democritus and Leucippus, and in the medical school founded by Hippocrates of Cos. In the mid-fifth century B.C.E., however, men like the Sophists and Socrates turned their attention to humankind and to ethical, political, and religious questions. This latter tradition of inquiry led, by way of Plato, Aristotle (in his metaphysical thought), and the Stoics, to Christianity, and it had a substantial impact on Judaic and Islamic thought. The former tradition of thought, following a line from the natural philosophers, the Sophists, Aristotle (in his scientific work), and the Epicureans, had to wait until the Renaissance in western Europe to exert influence. Since the 18th century, however, it has been the more influential force in Western civilization. The other tradition has, however, never been forgotten, and since the Enlightenment of the 18th century, the Western world has been engaged in a dialogue between the two intellectual communities the Greeks founded. As Western influence has spread throughout the world, that dialogue has assumed new importance, for other societies have not separated the religious and philosophical from the scientific and physical realms as radically as has the modern West.

4.8b
Aristotle, Virtue and Redemption: The Doctrine of the Mean

[6]Aristotle, *Politics*, 1280b, 1281a.

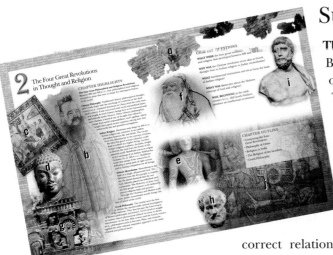

IMAGE KEY

for pages 28–29

a. The dead sea scrolls in Washington D.C.
b. Confucius
c. School of Plato
d. Mathura sculpture head of Buddha
e. Shiva sculpture carved into a granite wall niche
f. Painting of Confucius
g. An early carving showing the *chakra* or wheel of *Dharma*
h. Aristotle
i. Thales of Miletus, the first Greek philosopher
j. Assyrian wall carving depicting the Jews with their cattle and baggage going into exile.

SUMMARY

The Four Great Philosophical and Religious Revolutions Between 800 and 300 B.C.E., four philosophical and religious revolutions arose that shaped the subsequent history of the world. These were Chinese philosophy, Indian religion, Hebrew monotheism, and Greek philosophy.

Chinese Philosophy Traditional Chinese philosophical thought, which took shape with the teachings of Confucius in the sixth century B.C.E., remained dominant in China until the early 20th century. It was concerned with social and political issues and sought to teach human beings how to live harmoniously and ethically under Heaven by prescribing the correct relationships between ruler-subject, father-son, husband-wife, older brother-younger brother, and friend-friend. Confucianism became the official philosophy of China in the second century B.C.E. Other Chinese philosophies were Daoism, a mystical way of thought that offered a refuge from social responsibilities, and Legalism, which taught that a good society requires a strong state that enforces the law and punishes wrongdoers.

Indian Religion Hinduism, the dominant Indian religious tradition, took shape by 400 B.C.E. Indian religion saw existence as an endless alteration between life and death (*samsara*). The escape from this dilemma lay in the concept of *karma*, the idea that good actions (*dharma*) could lead to rebirth as a higher being, even a god, or to escape the cycle entirely and cease to exist entirely (*moksha*).

Another Indian religious tradition, the Jains, sought to liberate the soul from the bonds of the material world by eliminating evil acts. Although there are few Indian Buddhists today, Buddhism traces its origins to the teachings of an Indian, Siddhartha Gautama (b. ca. 566 B.C.E.). Buddhism holds that escape from *samsara* lies in following a moral path of right understanding and actions and in having compassion for all beings.

Hebrew Monotheism Monotheism is the faith in a single, all-powerful God as the sole creator, sustainer, and ruler of the universe. The Hebrews were the first people to emphasize the moral demands that the one God, Yahweh, placed on the individual and community and to see history as the unfolding of a divine plan. The Hebrews, or Jews, were the first people to be defined by shared religious faith and practice. Through the Christian and Muslim traditions, Judaic monotheism was to change the face of much of the world.

Greek Philosophy The Greeks were the first to initiate the unreservedly rational investigation of the universe. They became the forerunners of Western philosophy and science. In the sixth and fifth centuries B.C.E., Greek thinkers, such as Thales of Miletus and Heraclitus, sought to explain natural phenomena without recourse to divine intervention. In the later fifth century and the fourth century B.C.E., philosophers, such as Socrates, Plato, and Aristotle, applied the same rational, inquisitive approach to the study of moral and political issues in the life of the Greek city-state, or polis.

REVIEW QUESTIONS

1. What are the differences and similarities among Confucianism, Daoism, and Legalism?

2. What fundamental assumptions about the world, the individual, and reality do the Jain, Hindu, and Buddhist traditions share?

3. How did the concept of monotheism develop? Why was is it regarded as a radical innovation in the context of ancient Middle-Eastern civilization?

4. How did the approach to understanding the world taken by the Greeks differ from that of other ancient peoples? What did Socrates contribute to philosophy? How do Aristotle's political and ethical ideas compare with those of Confucius?

KEY TERMS

Atman-Brahman (p. 34)   **Hindu** (p. 33)   **monotheism** (p. 39)

atomists (p. 44)   **Jains** (p. 36)   **polis** (p. 44)

Brahmanas (p. 33)   **karma** (p. 35)   **polytheism** (p. 39)

Chun-tzu (p. 31)   **Legalism** (p. 33)   **samsara** (p. 35)

dharma (p. 35)   **Messiah** (p. 41)   **Sophists** (p. 44)

Daoism (p. 32)

 For additional study resources for this chapter, go to:
www.prenhall.com/craig/chapter2

JUDAISM

Monotheism, the belief in a unique God who is the creator of the universe and its all-powerful ruler, first became a central and lasting element in religion among the Hebrews, later called Israelites and also Jews. Their religion, more than the many forms of polytheistic worship that characterized the ancient world, demanded moral rectitude and placed ethical responsibilities both on individuals and on the community as a whole. Their God had a divine plan for human history, which was linked to the behavior of his chosen people. This vision of the exclusive worship of the true God, obedience to the laws governing the community that derive from him, and a strong ethical responsibility was connected to humanity's historical experience in this world. Ultimately it gave rise to three great religions: Judaism, Christianity, and Islam.

At the beginning of this tradition stands Abraham, whom all three religions recognize as their founder. According to the Torah (the first five books of the Hebrew Bible or the Christian Old Testament), Abraham entered into a covenant with God in which he promised to worship only this God, who in turn promised to make Abraham's descendants his own chosen people—chosen to worship him, to obey his laws, and to undertake a special set of moral responsibilities. God renewed the covenant with Moses at Mount Sinai when he freed the Israelites from Egyptian bondage. He promised them the land of Canaan (later called Palestine and part of which is now the state of Israel) and gave them the law (the Torah), including the Ten Commandments, by which they were to guide their lives. As long as they lived by his law, God would give them his guidance and protection.

In time the Israelites formed themselves into a kingdom which remained unified from about 1000 to 922 B.C.E. In the period after its division, prophets emerged. Thought to be inspired by God, the prophets chastised the Israelites for their lapses into idolatry and immorality. Even as the kingdom was disintegrating and the Israelites falling under the control of alien empires, the prophets preached social reform and a return to God's laws. They saw Israel's misfortune as punishment for failing to keep the covenant and predicted disaster if the Israelites did not change their ways. When disasters came—the Jewish kingdoms captured, the people enslaved and exiled—the prophets interpreted Israel's status as a chosen people to mean that their sufferings would make them "a light unto the nations," leading other nations to the true worship of one God

The prophets also preached that God was righteous and demanded righteousness from his people. But he was also a God of justice. Although he might need to punish his people for their sins, he would one day reward them with divine favor. Traditional Jewish belief expects that the Messiah, or Anointed One, will someday come and establish God's kingdom on earth. He will introduce an age of universal brotherhood in which all nations will acknowledge the one true God.

The Jews are "people of the Book," and foremost among their sacred texts is the Hebrew Bible, consisting of the Five Books of Moses (the Torah), the books of the prophets, and other writings. The Torah is the source of Jewish law. Over the centuries new experiences required new interpretation of the law, which was accomplished by the oral law, no less sacred than the written law. Compilations of interpretation and commentary by rabbis (wise and learned teachers) were brought together to form the Talmud.

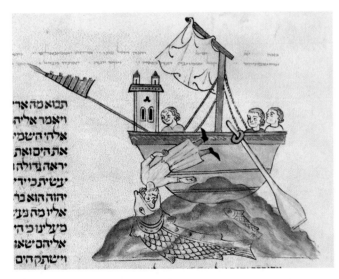

Jonah Eaten by the Whale, from a Hebrew Bible, 1299. Like the Christian illuminated manuscripts they closely resembled, Jewish medieval manuscripts were filled with images of scenes from the Torah and Jewish history. Hebrew writing also developed into an elaborately beautiful calligraphy. Many of these Jewish medieval illuminated manuscripts were, like their Christian counterparts, commissioned by wealthy and influential leaders of Jewish communities in Europe.

Instituto da Biblioteca Nacional, Lisbon, Portugal/Bridgeman Art Library.

The destruction of their temple in Jerusalem by the Romans in 70 C.E. hastened the scattering of the Jews throughout the empire. Thereafter almost all Jews lived in the Diaspora (dispersion), without a homeland, a political community, or a national or religious center. In the fifth and sixth centuries the decline of the Sassanid Empire in Iran and the collapse of the Western Roman Empire undermined the institutions in which the Jews had found a stable way of life. In the seventh and eighth centuries, the missionary zeal of the Christian church also brought hard times for the Jews in Western Europe and in the Byzantine East. In the West, their condition improved in the ninth century under Charlemagne and his successors.

Under Islam, Jews, like Christians, were tolerated as people of the Book. Jewish settlements flourished throughout the Islamic world. After the Islamic conquest of Spain in 711, the Jews there enjoyed an almost 300-year-long golden age. During this period of extraordinary intellectual and cultural accomplishment, Jews practiced their religion openly and flourished economically.

The beginning of the Crusades in the 11th century brought renewed persecution of the Jews in both the Christian and Islamic worlds. In the wake of the Christian reconquest of Spain, Jews were persecuted, killed, forced to convert, and finally expelled in 1492.

By the Middle Ages, Jews had divided into two distinct branches: those who lived in Christian Europe, called *Ashkenazim*, and those in the Muslim world, particularly Spain, called *Sephardim*. The Sephardim, with greater opportunities, developed a more secular lifestyle. Their language, Ladino, combined Hebrew and Spanish elements. The Ashkenazim, scattered in tiny communities, were forced to turn inward. Centered in German lands, they developed Yiddish, a combination of Hebrew and German. In time, Yiddish became the language of most Jews in northern Europe, although the Torah was always read and studied in Hebrew.

Two of the dominant influences on modern Judaism have been Zionism—the effort to found a Jewish nation—and the death of some 6 million Jews in the Holocaust of World War II. Bolstered by the determination of Jews never again to find themselves victimized by the forces of anti-Semitism, the Zionist movement culminated in the founding of the state of Israel in 1948.

Adherents of Judaism are divided into several groups—Reform, Reconstruction, Conservative, and Orthodox—each holding significantly different views about the place of tradition and traditional law in the modern world. All, however, would give assent to the saying of Hillel, the great Talmudic teacher of the first century B.C.E.: "What is distasteful to you do not to your fellow man. This is the Law, all the rest is commentary. Now go and study."

- In what ways did Judaism differ from the polytheistic religions?
- What elements of the religion helped it persist through the ages?

Visualizing The Past

Humans and Nature in Antiquity

WHY DID the natural world figure so prominently in the culture and religions of ancient peoples? What does this tell us about the relationship between humans and the natural world in antiquity?

Animism—the idea that everything in the natural world, from inanimate objects to humans, is in some way alive and sentient, part of single connected cosmos—describes the belief systems of many ancient peoples. Animals, in particular, were integral to ancient religions. They were admired for their strength, wisdom and other virtues, and were either worshipped as gods or played central roles in the religious ceremonies of ancient peoples across the world.

Shaman. A reproduction of a ▶ 20,000-year-old cave painting, from the Grotto of Les Trois Freres in the French Pyrenees, of a barefooted **shaman**, or sorcerer, dressed in a deerskin costume. Shamans often dressed fantastically, clothing themselves in deer or bear skins, antlers or claws. The shaman depicted here may be performing a dance as part of a healing ritual. Shamans still form an important part of many non-sedentary societies across the world today.

Sheila Terry/Photo Researchers, Inc.

◀ **Images of Animals.** These 4,250-year old seals from the ancient Harappan civilization of the Indus valley in present-day Pakistan show various animals, including a rhinoceros, an elephant, and a bull. Images of bulls are widespread in the ancient world and the depiction of one here suggests that the sacred status of cows and bulls in Hinduism has its roots in the first civilization of the Indus valley.

Seals from Mohenjo Doro (Indus Valley culture). National Museum of Pakistan, Karachi, Pakistan. Copyright Scala/Art Resource, N.Y.

◄ **Pharoahs and Gods.** The pharoah Ramses I kneels between the jackal-headed god of the underworld Anubis and the falcon-headed god Horus, from a painted limestone relief in the Ramses's tomb, circa 1292–1290 B.C.E., from the Valley of the Kings in Egypt. Anubis and Horus were one of many Egyptian gods who were imagined as part human, part animal.

The Art Archive/Dagli Orti

Lamassus. This human-headed, winged ► lion is from the palace of the Assryian ruler Ashurnasirpal II (r.883–859 B.C.E.) at Nimrud, present-day Iraq. It demonstrates the admiration of the warlike Assyrians for powerful animals, which are combined into a fanciful creature, a *lamassus*—divine guardian protectors of palaces and throne rooms.

Human-headed winged bull and winged lion (lamassu). Alabaster (ypsum); Gateway support from the Palace of Ashurnasirpal II (ruled 883–859 B.C.E.). Limestone. H: 10'3½". L: 9'1". W: 2"½". The Metropolitan Museum of Art, Gift of John D. Rockefeller, Jr., 1932. (32.143.2) Photography © 1981 The Metropolitian Museum of Art.

PART TWO   EMPIRES AND CULTURES OF THE ANCIENT WORLD

EUROPE

| ca. 2500–1100 | Minoan civilization on Crete |
| ca. 1600–1100 | Mycenaean civilization on Greek mainland |

ca. 1100–800	Greek "dark ages"
800	Etruscan civilization begins in Italy
ca. 750–550	Rise of the polis
594	Solon's legislation at Athens
509	Foundation of the Roman Republic
508	Democracy established in Athens

Sixth-century B.C.E. Attic jar ▶

NEAR EAST / INDIA

ca. 3500–3000	Emergence of Sumerian city-states
ca. 3000	Emergence of civilization along the Nile River
ca. 2300	Emergence of Harappan civilization in Indus valley
2276–2221	Sargon of Akkad creates the first Mesopotamian Empire
ca. 2000	*Epic of Gilgamesh*
1750	Hammurabi's code

ca. 1500	Aryan peoples migrate into northwestern India
960–933	Rule of Hebrew king Solomon
ca. 628–551	Traditional dates of Zarathushtra
ca. 537–486	Siddhartha Gautama
559–529	Cyrus the Great creates the Persian Empire

◀ *Ruins of pyramids in Ancient Kingdom of Kush-Sudan*

EAST ASIA

ca. 4000	Neolithic cultures in China
ca. 8000–300	Jōmon culture in Japan
ca. 1766–1050	Shang dynasty in China with city-states and writing

1027–771	Western Chou dynasty, China
771–256	Eastern Chou dynasty in China
ca. 771	Iron Age territorial states in China
551–479	Confucius in China

◀ *Homo habilis skull*

AFRICA

ca. 3000	Practice of agriculture spreads from Nile River Valley to the Sudan
ca. 2000	Ivory and gold trade between Kush (Nubia) and Egypt
ca. 1500	Practice of agriculture spreads from the Sudan to Abyssinia and the savanna region

750	Kushite king Kashta conquers Upper Egypt; founds 25th Egyptian dynasty
ca. 720	Kushite king Piankhy completes conquest of Egypt and reigns as king of Kush and Egypt
ca. 600	Meroitic period of Kushan civilization begins

THE AMERICAS

| ca. 4000 | Maize already domesticated in Mexico |

| ca. 1500–800 | Olmec civilization in Mesoamerica |
| ca. 800–200 | Chavín (Early) Horizon in Andean South America |

◀ *Olmec monument, La Venta*

480–479	Persian invasion of Greece
478	Foundation of Delian League/Athenian Empire
431–404	Peloponnesian Wars
338	Battle of Chaeronia; Macedonian conquest of Greece
336–323	Career of Alexander the Great

◄ *The Charioteer of Delphi, ca. 470 B.C.E.*

264	Rome rules all of Italy
146	Rome destroys Carthage; rules all of western Mediterranean
44–31	Civil wars destroy Roman Republic
31	Rome rules Mediterranean
31 B.C.E.–14 C.E.	Principate of Augustus

96–180	The good emperors rule Rome
180–284	Breakdown of the *Pax Romana*
306–337	Constantine reigns
313	Edict of Milan
325	Council of Nicaea
391	Theodosius makes Christianity the official imperial religion
ca. 400–500	The Germanic invasions
426	*The City of God*, by Augustine
476	The last Western emperor is deposed

▲ *Arch of Constantine*

ca. 540–468	Vardhamana Mahavira, founder of Jain tradition
334	Alexander begins conquest of the Near East; invades India in 327
321–181	Mauryan Empire in India

◄ *The Great Stupa at Sanchi*

ca. 300	Foundation of Seleucid dynasty in Anatolia, Syria, and Mesopotamia; Ptolemaic dynasty in Egypt
269–232	Mauryan emperor Ashoka patronizes Buddhism
247 B.C.E.–224 C.E.	Parthian dynasty controls Persia
180 B.C.E.–320 C.E.	India politically divided

▲ *The Lion Capital of Sarnath*

30	Crucifixion of Jesus
70	Romans destroy the Temple at Jerusalem
216–277	Mani
ca. 224	Fall of Parthians, rise of Sasanids, in Persia
ca. 320–500	Gupta Dynasty in India
ca. 400	Chandra Gupta (r. 375–415) conquers western India; increases trade with Near East and China
ca. 450	The Huns invade India

ca. 500–200	Rise of Mohist, Taoist, and Legalist schools of thought in China
401–256	Period of the Warring States in China
ca. 300	Old Stone Age Jōmon culture in Japan replaced by Yayoi culture

256–206	Ch'in dynasty in China
221	Ch'in emperor unites all of China
206 B.C.E.–8 C.E.	Former Han dynasty in China
179–104	Han philosopher Tung Chung-shu
145–90	Han historian Ssu-ma Chien
141–187	Emperor Wu Ti of China reigns

Standing attendant, ▶ *Han dynasty*

Han dynasty ▶ *sculpture*

25–220	The Later Han dynasty, China
ca. 220–590	Spread of Buddhism in China
220–589	Six Dynasties period in China
ca. 300–500	Barbarian invasions of China
ca. 300–680	Archaic Yamato state in Japan

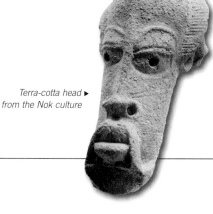

Terra-cotta head ▶ *from the Nok culture*

25	Romans sack Kushite capital of Napata
100 B.C.E.–1 C.E.	Probable first Indonesian migrations to east African coast

ca. 200	Camel first used for trans-Saharan transport
ca. 200–900	Expansion of Bantu people
ca. 250	Aksum (Ethiopia) controls the Red Sea trade
ca. 300–400	Rise of kingdom of Ghana
ca. 350	Kush ceases to exist

ca. 200–600	Early Intermediate period in Andean South America; Moche and Nazca cultures
ca. 150–900	Classic period; dominance of Teotihuacán in central Mexico, Tikal in southern Yucatán

ca. 500–200	Founding of Monte Alban

3

Greek and Hellenistic Civilization

CHAPTER HIGHLIGHTS

Early Greece   Greek civilization is divided into several periods. In the Minoan and Mycenaean ages, the Greek states were ruled by powerful kings. By 750 B.C.E., during the archaic period, Greek society took its characteristic form: the *polis* (plural *poleis*), a self-governing city-state. The most important *poleis* were Athens and Sparta. At first governed by land-owning aristocrats, then by tyrants, many *poleis* evolved more democratic forms of government by 500 B.C.E. In an effort to avoid the pressures of overpopulation and land hunger, the Greeks established colonies around the shores of the Mediterranean and Black Seas.

Classical Greece   After defeating two Persian attempts to conquer them in the early fifth century B.C.E., the Greeks entered their golden age. The greatest achievements in art, literature, and philosophy of Classical Greece took place in Athens, where the government was the most democratic seen until modern times. Among the accomplishments of Greek artists, writers, and thinkers were naturalistic sculpture, tragedy and comedy, secular history, and systematic logic, all of which still influence Western art and thought.

Hellenistic Greece   The *polis* went into political and cultural decline after Sparta defeated Athens in the Great Peloponnesian War (435–404 B.C.E.). Alexander the Great's (r. 336–323 B.C.E.) conquest of the Persian Empire spread Greek culture over a wide area and ushered in the Hellenistic era. Hellenistic Greek culture, which was fostered by the kingdoms that succeeded Alexander's empire, was more accessible to outsiders than that of classical Greece. Hellenistic scholars made Greek literature and science available to many different peoples who adopted it as their own. The Romans were particularly impressed. They spread Hellenistic culture across the Mediterranean world and transmitted it to later generations in the West.

CHAPTER QUESTIONS

HOW WERE the Greek states organized during the Mycenaean period?

WHY WAS the *polis* the most characteristic Greek instittion?

WHAT FEATURES distinguished archaic Greek society?

WHY WERE the Greeks able to defeat the Persians?

WHAT WERE the causes and results of the Peloponnesian War?

WHAT WERE the main cultural achievements of Classical Greece?

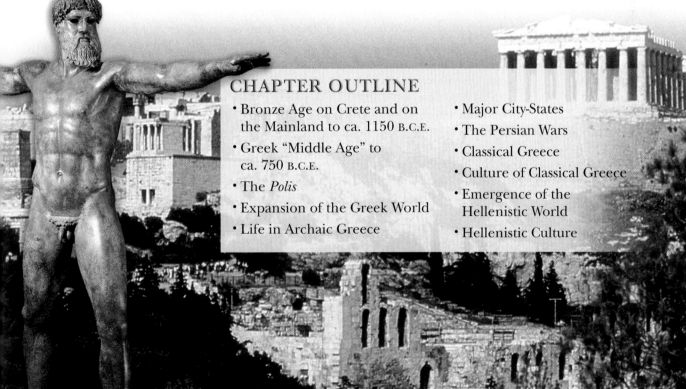

CHAPTER OUTLINE

- Bronze Age on Crete and on the Mainland to ca. 1150 B.C.E.
- Greek "Middle Age" to ca. 750 B.C.E.
- The *Polis*
- Expansion of the Greek World
- Life in Archaic Greece

- Major City-States
- The Persian Wars
- Classical Greece
- Culture of Classical Greece
- Emergence of the Hellenistic World
- Hellenistic Culture

About 2000 B.C.E., Greek-speaking peoples settled the lands surrounding the Aegean Sea, where they came in contact with the more advanced and earlier civilizations of the Middle East. Adapting from these predecessors, the Greeks forged their own way of life, forming a set of ideas, values, and institutions that would spread far beyond their homeland. The foundation of this way of life was the independent city-state, or polis (plural poleis).

HOW WERE the Greek states organized during the Mycenaean period?

BRONZE AGE ON CRETE AND ON THE MAINLAND TO CA. 1150 B.C.E.

he large island of Crete provided a cultural bridge between the older civilizations of the Middle East and the new ones of the Greeks.

THE MINOANS

In the third and second millennia B.C.E., a Bronze Age civilization arose on Crete that powerfully influenced the islands of the Aegean and the mainland of Greece. This civilization is called **Minoan**, after Minos, the legendary king of Crete. Scholars have divided Minoan history into three periods—Early, Middle, and Late Minoan.

The civilization of the Middle and Late Minoan periods in eastern and central Crete centered on a few great palaces. The distinctive and striking art and architecture of these palaces reflect the influence of Syria, Asia Minor, and Egypt, but they have a uniquely Cretan style and quality. Minoan cities lacked strong defensive walls, suggesting that they were not built with defense in mind.

Excavations at Minoan sites have revealed clay writing tablets like those found in Mesopotamia. Tablets found at the royal palace at Cnossus, accidentally preserved when a great fire that destroyed the palace hardened them, have three distinct kinds of writing on them. The Minoans were not Greeks, but one of these writing systems was an early form of Greek. The contents of the tablets reveal an organization centered on the palace and ruled by a king who was supported by an extensive bureaucracy. This sort of organization is typical of early civilizations in the Middle East but is nothing like that of the Greeks after the Bronze Age. The development of Greek civilization on the mainland was encouraged by contacts between Crete and the mainland's Helladic culture during the Bronze Age.

THE MYCENAEANS

In the third millennium B.C.E., most of the Greek mainland, including many of the sites of later Greek cities, was settled by people who used metal, built some impressive houses, and traded with Crete and the islands of the Aegean. The names they gave to places make it clear that they were not Greeks and that they spoke a language that was not Indo-European (the language family to which Greek belongs). Not long after 2000 B.C.E., many of the Early Helladic sites were destroyed, abandoned, or yielded to an invading people. These signs of invasion probably signal the arrival of the Greeks.

The shaft graves cut into the rock at the royal palace-fortress of Mycenae show

Minoan Bronze Age civilization that arose in Crete in the third and second millennia B.C.E.

Minoan Fresco. Acrobats leaping over a charging bull, from the east wing of the Minoan-period palace at Cnossus on the island of Crete. It is not known whether such acrobatic displays were for entertainment or for part of some religious ritual.

Scala/Art Resource, N.Y.

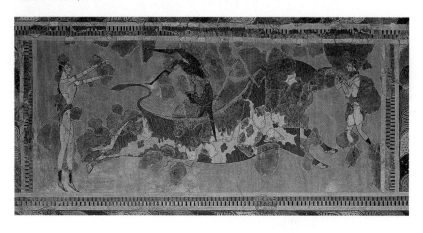

that by the Late Helladic, the conquerors had prospered. At Mycenae the richest finds come from the period after 1600 B.C.E. The city's wealth and power reached their peak at this time, and the culture of the whole mainland during this period goes by the name **Mycenaean**. Greek invaders also established themselves in Crete, and at the height of Mycenaean power (1400–1200 B.C.E.), Crete was part of the Mycenaean world.

Excavations at Mycenaean sites reveal a culture influenced by, but different from, Minoan culture. Mycenaean cities were built on hills commanding the neighboring territory. The Mycenaean people were warriors led by strong kings who, with their retainers, lived in palaces protected by defensive walls while most of the population lived outside the walls. Like the palaces of Crete, Mycenaean palaces were adorned with murals, but instead of the peaceful pursuits and games depicted on the Cretan murals, the Mycenaean murals depicted scenes of war and boar hunting.

About 1500 B.C.E., *tholos* tombs—large, beehivelike chambers cut into hillsides—replaced the shaft graves. The tholos tombs, built of enormous cut and fitted stones, were approached through unroofed passages carved into the sides of the hills that enclosed them. Only a strong king could undertake such a project. His wealth probably came from plundering raids, piracy, and trade. Some of this trade went to Italy and Sicily, but most was with the Aegean islands, Asia Minor, Syria, Egypt, and Crete. The Mycenaeans exchanged pottery, olive oil, and animal hides for jewels and other luxuries.

Further evidence that the Mycenaean world was made up of a number of independent, powerful, and well-organized monarchies comes from the many clay tablets with Mycenaean writing found throughout the mainland. These reveal a society similar to that of Cnossus on Crete. A king, whose title was *wanax*, held a royal domain, appointed officials, commanded servants, and kept a close record of what he owned and what was owed to him.

The Fall of Mycenaean Power   At the height of their power (1400–1200 B.C.E.), the Mycenaeans enlarged their cities, expanded their trade, and even established commercial colonies in the east. Sometime about 1250 B.C.E. they probably sacked Troy, found on the coast of northwestern Asia Minor, an event memorialized in the epic poems of Homer, the *Iliad* and the *Odyssey*. Around the year 1200 B.C.E., however, the Mycenaean world showed signs of trouble. By 1100 B.C.E., it was gone. Reasons for the collapse of Mycenaean civilization are unclear. Greek legends attribute the fall to a new wave of Greek invaders, the Dorians, from the north—a rude people who spoke a Greek dialect unlike that of the Mycenaeans.

GREEK "MIDDLE AGE" TO CA. 750 B.C.E.

*T*he immediate effects of the Mycenaean collapse were disastrous. Palaces were destroyed, kings and bureaucrats were swept away, and wealth and organization evaporated. Greece entered a dark "Middle Age" about which little is known.

The turmoil surrounding the Mycenaean collapse launched a migration of Greek-speaking people eastward from the mainland to the Aegean islands and the coast of Asia Minor (Ionia). This turned the Aegean into a Greek lake. Trade, however, diminished, and each community was left largely to its own devices. However, because the Middle East was also in disarray, no great power arose to

Mycenaean Bronze Age civilization of mainland Greece that was centered at Mycenae.

The *Iliad* and the *Odyssey* Epic poems by Homer about the "Dark Age" heroes of Greece who fought at Troy. The poems were written down in the eighth century B.C.E. after centuries of being sung by bards.

WHAT KIND of society does Homer depict in the *Iliad* and the *Odyssey*?

The "Trojan Horse." The legend of the Trojan horse is depicted on this seventh-century B.C.E. Greek vase. According to legend, the Greeks finally defeated Troy by pretending to abandon their siege of the city, leaving a giant wooden horse behind. Soldiers hidden in the horse opened the gates of the city to their compatriots after the Trojans had brought it within their walls. Note the wheels on the horse and the Greek soldiers who are hiding inside it.

Deutsches Archäologisches Institut, Athens.

impose its ways on the helpless people who lived around the Aegean, and the Greeks were free to create a unique style of life.

AGE OF HOMER

Homer provides the best picture of society in these poorly documented "dark ages." His epic poems, the *Iliad* and the *Odyssey*, emerged from a tradition of oral poetry whose roots reached back to the Mycenaean Age. Through the centuries bards had sung tales of the heroes who had fought at Troy, and in this way preserved some very old material. In the eighth century B.C.E., the oral poetry was reworked as the poems attributed to Homer. Although the poems tell of the deeds of Mycenaean heroes, the world they describe resembles that of the 10th and ninth centuries B.C.E. more than Mycenaean.

Government Kings in the Homeric poems have much less power than Mycenaean rulers had. Homeric kings were expected to make important decisions in consultation with a council of their followers. The right to speak in this council was limited to noblemen, but common people could not be ignored. If a king planned a major change of policy, he would call the common soldiers to an assembly. They could not take part in debate, but they could express their feelings by acclamation. Homer shows that even in these early times Greeks practiced a form of constitutional government.

Society Homeric society was aristocratic. Noble status was hereditary and usually associated with wealth. Below the nobles were two other classes: *thetes* and slaves. Thetes were landless laborers. They endured the worst conditions in Homeric society. In a world where membership in a settled group provided the only security, free laborers were desperately vulnerable. Slaves were attached to family households, so they were at least protected and fed. Slaves were few in number and were mostly women who served as maids and concubines. Agriculture mostly utilized free labor throughout Greek history.

4.1
Homer: *The Iliad*

Homeric Values Homer's poems became the schoolbooks of the Greeks, who memorized his texts and emulated the behavior and cherished the values displayed in them. The values of the Homeric poems—physical prowess, courage, and fierce protection of family, friends, property—reflected an aristocratic code that influenced all future Greek thought. Defense of personal honor and reputation was of supreme importance. The great hero of the *Iliad*, Achilles, withdraws from the field of battle at Troy and allows his fellow Greeks to be almost defeated, when Agamemnon wounds his honor. He returns to the army not out of a sense of duty but to avenge the death of his friend Patroclus.

The highest virtue in Homeric society was *arete*—manliness, the excellence proper to a hero. Arete was best demonstrated by competing in a contest, an *agon*. Homeric battles are primarily individual matches between champions, and the major entertainment for Homer's heroes are athletic contests. The central ethical idea in Homer's epics is found in the instructions that fathers of heroes give to their sons: "Always be the best and distinguished above others"; "Do not bring shame on the family of your fathers." The chief aristocratic values of Homer's world—to vie for individual supremacy in *arete* and to defend and increase the honor of the family—would remain as prominent Greek values long after Homeric society was only a memory.

THE POLIS

The characteristic Greek institution was the *polis*. The common translation of that word as "city-state" says both too much and too little. Because all Greek poleis began as agricultural villages or towns and many stayed small, the word "city" does not accurately describe them. All of them were states in the sense of being independent political units, but they were much more than that. The polis was thought of as a community of relatives; all its citizens were theoretically descended from a common ancestor. They were organized into subgroups on the basis of presumed blood relationships: fighting brotherhoods (*phratries*), clans, and tribes. They worshipped the same ancestral gods with the same traditional rituals.

Aristotle (see Chapter 2) claimed that the human being is by nature "an animal who lives in a polis." Humans alone have the power of speech—a social attribute—and from it derive the ability to distinguish good from bad and right from wrong, "and the sharing of these things is what makes a household and a polis." Without law and justice, humans are the worst and most dangerous of the animals. With them, they can be the best, but justice can be maintained only with the aid of the institutions of a polis.

DEVELOPMENT OF THE POLIS

Originally the word *polis* referred to a citadel, an elevated, defensible rock to which the farmers of the neighboring area could retreat when attacked. The **Acropolis** in Athens and the hill called Acrocorinth in Corinth are examples. For some time such high places and the adjacent farms made up the polis. Towns grew up around these fortresses gradually and without planning. For centuries they had no walls. The availability of farmland and of a natural fortress determined where poleis sprang up. They were usually situated well inland or at least far enough away from the sea to avoid raids by pirates. Only later and gradually did an **agora**—a marketplace and civic center—appear within the polis. The agora provided the setting for development of the Greeks' unique fascination with conversation and public debate.

Some poleis probably appeared early in the eighth century B.C.E., and all the colonies established by the Greeks after 750 B.C.E. took the form of poleis. Once the new institution had been fully established, true monarchy disappeared. The original form of the polis was an aristocratic republic dominated by a council of nobles who also monopolized all political offices.

THE HOPLITE PHALANX

A new military strategy promoted development of the polis. In earlier times the brunt of fighting had been carried on by small troops of cavalry and individual "champions." Toward the end of the eighth century B.C.E., however, the **hoplite phalanx** came into being and remained the basis of Greek warfare thereafter.

WHY WAS the *polis* the most characteristic Greek institution?

Acropolis Religious and civic center of Athens. It is the site of the Parthenon.

agora Greek marketplace and civic center. It was the heart of the social life of the polis.

hoplite phalanx Basic unit of Greek warfare in which infantrymen fought in close order, shield to shield, usually eight ranks deep.

class conflicts slow to develop

WHY DID the Greeks establish colonies?

Magna Graecia Meaning "Great Greece" in Latin. The name given by the Romans to southern Italy and Sicily because there were so many Greek colonies in the region.

Panhellenic Meaning "all-Greek." The sense of cultural identity that all Greeks felt in common with each other.

A hoplite was a heavily armed infantryman who fought with a spear and a large shield. Hoplites were arrayed in close order in a formation called a phalanx that was at least eight ranks deep. The success of a hoplite army depended on the discipline, strength, and courage of its individual soldiers. At its best, the phalanx could withstand cavalry charges and defeat less disciplined infantries. Until the Roman legion appeared, it was the dominant military force in the Mediterranean.

The usual hoplite battle in Greece involved the armies of two poleis quarreling over a piece of land. One army invaded the territory of the other when its crops were almost ready for harvest. The defending army had to protect the fields. If the defenders were beaten, the fields were captured or destroyed. The farmer-soldier-citizen, who defended the polis, usually hoped to settle a dispute quickly by a single decisive battle and then get back to work. It was to the advantage of an agriculturally based society to keep wars short and limit their cost.

Service in the phalanx created a bond between the aristocrats and the family farmers who fought side by side. This may explain why class conflicts were slow to develop, but it also meant that aristocratic monopolies of political power within a poleis would eventually be challenged.

EXPANSION OF THE GREEK WORLD

From the mid-eighth century B.C.E. until well into the sixth, a burst of colonizing activity planted poleis from Spain to the Black Sea. A century earlier a few Greeks had established trading posts in Syria, and about 750 B.C.E., they borrowed a writing system from one of the local Semitic scripts. By adding vowels to it, they created the first true alphabet. The Greek alphabet, which was easier to learn than any earlier writing system, enabled literacy to spread widely in Greek communities.

GREEK COLONIES

Syria and its neighboring territory were too strong to penetrate, so the Greeks sought out less populated regions for their colonies. Before long, there were so many Greek colonies in southern Italy and Sicily that the Romans began to call those lands *Magna Graecia* ("Great Greece"). The Greeks also established colonies in Spain, southern France, around the Black Sea, and on the north African coast. Most colonies were independent, but they maintained a special relationship with their mother cities (see Map 3–1).

Colonization relieved the pressure of a growing population on the Greek mainland, and confrontations between Greek colonists and diverse peoples made the Greeks acutely aware of their own cultural identity. They cultivated a **Panhellenic** ("all-Greek") spirit through the establishment of common religious festivals, the most important of which were at Olympia, Delphi, Corinth, and Nemea.

Colonization also encouraged trade and industry. The influx of new wealth and the increased demand for goods stimulated a more intensive use of land. Crops were rasied for export, chiefly olives and wine grapes. Craftsmen also manufactured pottery, tools, weapons, fine metalwork, and perfumed oil (the soap of the ancient Mediterranean) for a world market. The opportunities created by the growing economy made some men, who were not nobles, wealthy. They constituted a troublesome element in the aristocratically dominated poleis, for they resented being barred from political power, religious privileges, and social acceptance by the nobility. This led to crises in the many states that culminated, between 700 and 500 B.C.E., in the establishment of tyrannies.

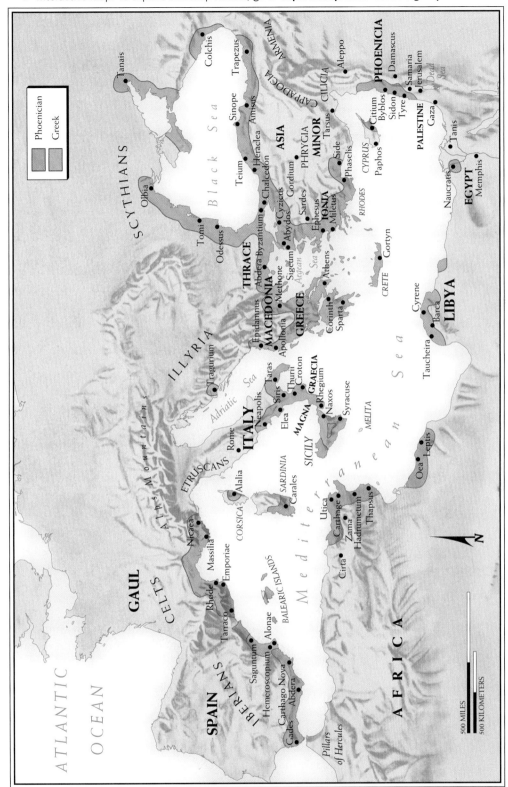

MAP 3–1

Phoenician and Greek Colonization. Most of the coastline of the Mediterranean and Black Seas was populated by Greek or Phoenician colonies. The Phoenicians were a commercial people who planted their colonies in North Africa, Spain, Sicily, and Sardinia, chiefly in the ninth century B.C.E. The height of Greek colonization came later, between ca. 750 and 550 B.C.E.

WHAT IMPACT did colonization have on Phoenician and Greek societies?

Rise of Greece

ca. 2900–1150 B.C.E.	Minoan period
ca. 1900 B.C.E.	Probable date of the arrival of the Greeks on the mainland
ca. 1600–1150 B.C.E.	Mycenaean period
ca. 1250 B.C.E.	Sack of Troy (?)
ca. 1200–1150 B.C.E.	Destruction of Mycenaean centers in Greece
ca. 1100–750 B.C.E.	Dark Ages
ca. 750–500 B.C.E.	Major period of Greek colonization
ca. 725 B.C.E.	Probable date of Homer
ca. 700 B.C.E.	Probable date of Hesiod
ca. 700–500 B.C.E.	Major period of Greek tyranny

THE TYRANTS (CA. 700–500 B.C.E.)

A tyrant was a monarch who had gained power in an unorthodox but not necessarily wicked way and who exercised a strong one-man rule that might be both beneficent and popular.

The Rise of Tyranny   The founding tyrant was usually a member of the ruling aristocracy who either had a personal grievance against members of his own class or who led an ambitious faction. He sought the support of disgruntled elements within the polis: the politically powerless, newly wealthy, and poor farmers. He often expelled his aristocratic opponents, terminated the privileges of the aristocrats, and divided their land among his supporters. Tyrants presided over a period of population growth in the Greek world, and to maintain popular support they fostered trade and colonization. They sponsored programs of public works, founded new festivals, and provided patronage for the arts.

The End of the Tyrants   Tyranny, however, could turn oppressive, and there was something about the concept of tyranny that was inimical to the idea of the polis. The notion of the polis as a community for which each of its members was responsible, the connection of justice with that community, and the natural aristocratic hatred of monarchy all made tyranny seem alien and offensive to the Greeks. By the end of the sixth century B.C.E., tyranny had disappeared from the Greek world, and the last tyrants were remembered with bitterness. The tyrants had, however, helped secure the prosperity of Greece and had cultivated technology, the arts, and literature. Most importantly, they had broken the grip of the aristocracy on Greek society.

LIFE IN ARCHAIC GREECE

WHAT FEATURES distinguished archaic Greek society?

SOCIETY

As the "dark ages" came to an end, the features that would distinguish Greek society took shape. Most people farmed the land, but the role of the artisan and the merchant grew increasingly important.

Farmers   The poet Hesiod (ca. 700 B.C.E.) described himself as a small farmer, and his *Works and Days* gives us an idea of the life of a Greek farmer. His crops included grain (chiefly barley but some wheat), grapes for wine, olives for oil (used for cooking, lighting, and washing), green vegetables, and fruit. Sheep and goats provided milk and cheese, but ordinary farmers usually ate meat only when animals were sacrificed at religious festivals. Life was continual toil under the burning sun and in the freezing cold, and pleasures were few.

symposion   Carefully organized drinking party that was the center of Greek aristocratic social life. It featured games, songs, poetry, and even philosophical disputation.

Aristocrats   Most aristocrats employed hired laborers, sharecroppers, and some slaves, to work their lands. This gave them leisure for other activities. Aristocratic social life revolved around the drinking party, or *symposion*, a carefully organized activity for men only. Symposium guests might play games, enjoy professional entertainment, or amuse themselves with songs, poetry, or even philosophical disputes. Often, their activities took the form of contests, with a prize for the winner. Aristocratic values emphasized competition, the need to excel, and the desire to be recognized for one's achievements.

This aspect of aristocratic life explains the popularity of the athletic contests that became widespread early in the sixth century B.C.E. The games included running events, boxing, wrestling, and the chariot race. Only the rich could afford racehorses, so the chariot race was a special preserve of aristocracy. Wrestling, however, was also favored by the nobility, and the *palaestra* where they practiced became an important social center for nobles and men of leisure. The contrast between the hard, drab life of the peasant and the leisured and lively one of the aristocrat could hardly be greater.

RELIGION

Like most ancient peoples, the Greeks were polytheists, and religion played an important part in their lives.

The Greek pantheon consisted of the 12 gods who lived on Mount Olympus. They were

- Zeus, the father of the gods

- Hera, his wife

- Zeus's siblings:
  Poseidon, his brother, god of the seas and earthquakes
  Hestia, his sister, goddess of the hearth
  Demeter, his sister, goddess of agriculture and marriage

- Zeus's children:
  Aphrodite, goddess of love and beauty
  Apollo, god of the sun, music, poetry, and prophecy
  Ares, god of war
  Artemis, goddess of the moon and the hunt
  Athena, goddess of wisdom and the arts
  Hephaestus, god of fire and metallurgy
  Hermes, messenger of the gods, connected with commerce and cunning

The gods were assumed to behave like humans, from whom they differed primarily in strength and immortality. Also, like humans, the Olympians were believed to be subordinate to the Fates. Zeus, however, was not an arbitrary ruler but a defender of justice. Each polis honored one of the Olympians as its guardian deity, but all the gods were Panhellenic. In the eighth and seventh centuries B.C.E., common shrines were established at Olympia for the worship of Zeus, at Delphi for Apollo, and at Corinth for Poseidon. Each shrine held athletic contests in honor of its deity, to which all Greeks were invited and for which a sacred truce was declared.

The worship of the Olympian deities did not inspire intense emotion. Worshippers offered a god prayer, libations, and gifts in hope of currying protection and favors. Greek religion offered little moral teaching. Most Greeks seem to have thought that civic virtue consisted of worshipping the state deities in the traditional way, performing required public services, and fighting in defense of

Attic Jar. From late in the sixth century B.C.E., this jar shows how olives, one of Athens's most important crops, were harvested.

Courtesy of the Trustees of the British Museum.

the state. Private ethics required only that one do good to one's friends and harm to one's enemies.

In the sixth century B.C.E., the cult and oracle of Apollo at Delphi began to exercise great influence. The priests of Apollo preached moderation. They urged self-control and warned that arrogance (*hubris*) caused moral blindness and invited divine vengeance. Famous mottos summed up their advice: "Know thyself," and "Nothing in excess."

To assuage human fears, hopes, and passions, the Greeks turned to deities who were worshipped with more emotional rites. Of these, the most popular was Dionysus, a god of nature and fertility, of the grape and drunkenness, and of ecstacy and sexual abandon.

POETRY

The great changes that swept through the Greek world were reflected in a new genre of poetry, the lyric. Sappho of Lesbos, Anacreon of Teos, and Simonides of Cous treated personal themes, often describing the pleasure and agony of love. Alcaeus of Mytilene, an aristocrat driven from his city by a tyrant, wrote bitter invective. But the most interesting poet from a political point of view was Theognis of Megara, the spokesman for the old, defeated aristocracy of birth. He divided Greeks into two classes—the noble and the base. The former were good and the latter bad. Only nobles could aspire to virtue, for he said that only they possessed critical moral and intellectual qualities. These things could not be taught. They were innate and were lost if a noble wed a commoner. These prejudices remained strong in aristocratic circles throughout the next century and greatly influenced later thinkers, Plato among them.

MAJOR CITY-STATES

Generalization about the poleis is difficult, for although the states had much in common, some of them developed in unique ways. Sparta and Athens became the two most powerful Greek states.

SPARTA

About 725 B.C.E., population pressure and land hunger led the Spartans to conquer their western neighbor, Messenia. The Spartans now had as much land as they would ever need, and because they reduced the Messenians to serfs, or **Helots**, they no longer had to work this land themselves. About 650 B.C.E., the Helots rebelled, and the Spartans faced a turning point. To keep down the Helots, who outnumbered them perhaps 10 to 1, they turned their city into a permanent military academy and camp.

Society The new system exerted control over each Spartan from birth, when officials of the state decided which infants, male and female, were sufficiently strong to be raised. At age 7, the Spartan boy was taken from his mother and turned over to young instructors who trained him in athletics and the military arts. The Spartan youth was enrolled in the army at age 20 and lived in barracks until he was 30. He could marry, but could visit his wife only by stealth. At age 30 he became a full citizen, an "equal," and was allowed to live in his own house with his wife, although he took his meals at a public mess in the company of 15 comrades. His food, a simple diet without much meat or wine, was provided by his own plot of land, which was worked for him by Helots. Only when he reached 60 could the Spartan retire from military service to his home and family.

HOW DID Spartan society and government differ from that of Athens?

QUICK REVIEW

Spartan Society
- Spartan system controlled Spartan life from birth
- At age 7 Spartan boys began military training
- Spartan girls were also indoctrinated with idea of service to state

4.5
The City-State of Sparta

Helots Hereditary Spartan serfs.

Spartan girls were permitted greater freedom than other Greek females and were, like their brothers, indoctrinated with the idea of service to Sparta. The entire system was designed to subordinate the natural feelings of devotion to family to a more powerful commitment to the polis. Privacy, luxury, and even comfort were sacrificed to produce the best soldiers in the world. Nothing that might turn the mind away from duty was permitted.

Government   Sparta was governed by two kings, a council of elders, and an assembly. The power of the kings was limited. The council of elders—28 men over age 60 who were elected for life—was consulted before any proposal was put before the assembly. The assembly, which consisted of all males over age 30, could only ratify, not debate, the decisions of magistrates, elders, and kings. Sparta also had a board of ephors, five men elected annually by the assembly. The ephors controlled foreign policy, oversaw the generalship of the kings, presided at the assembly, and guarded against rebellion by the Helots.

Suppression of the Helots required all the Spartans' effort and energy. They did not try to expand their borders, but they did force their neighbors to follow their lead in foreign affairs and supply them with troops on demand. This formed an alliance known as the Peloponnesian League, which made Sparta the most powerful polis in Greece.

ATHENS

In the seventh century B.C.E., Athens and the region of Attica constituted a typical aristocratic polis. The state was governed by the **Areopagus**, a council of nobles. Annually the council elected nine magistrates, called *archons*, who became members of the council after their year in office. A broad-based citizens' assembly, the Areopagus had little power. It represented the four tribes into which Attica's inhabitants were divided.

Pressure for Change   In the seventh century B.C.E., quarrels within the nobility and the beginnings of an agrarian crisis disturbed the peaceful life of Athens. A shift to more intensive agricultural techniques forced the less successful farmers to borrow from wealthy neighbors. Many defaulted and were enslaved for their debts. Some were sold abroad. The poor began to demand the abolition of debt and a redistribution of the land.

Reforms of Solon   In 594 B.C.E., as tradition has it, the Athenians elected Solon (ca. 639–559 B.C.E.) to revise Athens' governing institutions. Solon immediately canceled debts, forbade debt slavery, and brought back Athenians enslaved abroad. He forbade the export of wheat, a food staple, but encouraged production of olive oil and wine for sale abroad. This nudged the Athenians toward a commercially based economy that utilized their land most efficiently for cash crops, such as olives and grapes.

Solon changed the way Athens was governed. He expanded citizenship to include immigrant artisans and merchants, and divided the citizenry into four classes on the basis of wealth. Only men of the wealthiest two classes could be archons and sit on the Areopagus. Men of the third class could be hoplites and serve on a council of 400 chosen by the assembly of all male citizens.

The Charioteer of Delphi, ca. 470. **B.C.E.** This freestanding statue, the *Charioteer of Delphi*, is one of the few full-scale bronze sculptures that survive from the fifth century B.C.E. Polyzalus, the tyrant of the Greek city of Gela in Sicily, dedicated it after winning a victory in the chariot race in the Pythian games, either in 478 or 474. The games were held at the sacred shrine of the god Apollo at Delphi, and the statue was placed within the god's sanctuary, not far from Apollo's temple. Greek (Classical). Bronze, H: 180 cm. Archaeological Museum, Delphi, Greece. Photograph © Nimatallah/Art Resource, N.Y.

Areopagus Governing council of Athens, originally open only to the nobility. Named after the hill on which it met.

Key Events in the Early History of Sparta and Athens

ca. 725–710 B.C.E.	First Messenian War
ca. 650–625 B.C.E.	Second Messenian War; Solon institutes reforms at Athens
ca. 560–550 B.C.E.	Sparta defeats Tegea; beginning of Peloponnesian League
ca. 546–527 B.C.E.	Pisistratus reigns as tyrant at Athens (main period)
ca. 510 B.C.E.	Hippias, son of Pisistratus, deposed as tyrant of Athens
ca. 508–501 B.C.E.	Clisthenes institutes reforms at Athens

Pisistratus the Tyrant Despite Solon's reforms, Pisistratus (605?–527 B.C.E.), a nobleman and military hero, seized power in 546 B.C.E. and made himself the city's first tyrant. Pisistratus sought to increase the power of the central government at the expense of the nobles. He made no formal change in the institutions of government, but saw to it that his supporters filled key offices. The unintended effect was to give more Athenians more experience with participatory government and a growing taste for it. The tyranny ended with Pisistratus's son, Hippias (r. 527–510 B.C.E.). When his rule became harsh and unpopular, his aristocratic opponents, with Sparta's help, rallied and drove him into exile (510 B.C.E.).

Clisthenes, the Founder of Democracy Some factions in the Athenian aristocracy tried to restore the aristocracy to the position of dominance it held before Solon. Their plans were upset by Clisthenes, an aristocrat who proposed a program that won him the backing of the masses. A central aim of Clisthenes' reforms was to diminish the political influence of the tribal territories into which Attica was divided, for these territories were the power bases of the noble families. Clisthenes replaced Attica's traditional four tribes with 10 new tribes composed of units drawn from all parts of Attica, rather than each tribe representing a single locale. The new organization increased devotion to the polis by weakening regional loyalties.

Clisthenes vested final authority in all things in the assembly of all adult male Athenian citizens. Debate in the assembly was free and open; any Athenian could submit legislation, offer amendments, or argue the merits of any question.

THE PERSIAN WARS

WHY WERE the Greeks able to defeat the Persians?

*T*he Greeks' period of isolation and freedom from interference by the outside world ended in the sixth century B.C.E. The first to be threatened were the Greek cities on the coast of Asia Minor, which came under the control of the rapidly expanding Persian Empire (see Chapter 4).

IONIAN REBELLION

At first, the cities of Ionia (the central part of the west coast of Asia Minor and nearby islands) prospered under Persian rule and did not resist Persian domination. The private troubles of an ambitious tyrant of Miletus named Aristagoras, however, ended this calm. Aristagoras had urged a Persian expedition against the island of Naxos. When it failed, he tried to avoid punishment from Persia by raising a rebellion in Ionia (499 B.C.E.). When he turned to the mainland Greeks for help, Athens agreed to send a fleet. In 498 B.C.E., the Athenians and their allies burned Sardis, the seat of the Persian governor. The revolt spread. But after the Athenians withdrew, the Persians reimposed their will. In 494 B.C.E. they wiped out Miletus and put down the Ionian rebellion.

THE WAR IN GREECE

In 490 B.C.E. the Persian king, Darius (r. 521–486 B.C.E.), sent an expedition to punish Athens. Miltiades (d. 489 B.C.E.), an Athenian who had fled from Persian service, led the city's army to a confrontation with the invaders at Marathon, a plain north of Athens, and won a decisive victory.

The Great Invasion For the Persians, however, Marathon was only a temporary defeat. In 481 B.C.E., Darius's successor, Xerxes (r. 486–465 B.C.E.), gathered an army of at least 150,000 men and a navy of more than 600 ships for the conquest of Greece. By then, Themistocles (ca. 525–462 B.C.E.) had become Athens' leading politician. His policies were aimed at making Athens a major naval power, and by 480 B.C.E., when Xerxes invaded, Athens had more than 200 ships. It was the Athenian navy that defeated the Persians.

Darius had launched a naval attack on the Greek mainland, but Xerxes invaded by land. His huge army had to keep in touch with its fleet for supplies. Themistocles reasoned that if the Greeks could defeat the Persian navy, the Persian army would have to retreat. His strategy was to try to delay the advance of the Persian army until he could fight the kind of naval battle he might hope to win.

The Spartans led a Greek army that made a famous, but futile, attempt to block the Persian invasion at a place called Thermopylae. The fate of Greece was subsequently decided by the Athenians in a sea battle in the narrow straits to the east of the island of Salamis. When they destroyed more than half of Xerxes' fleet, he retreated to Asia with a good part of his army.

The Persian general Mardonius was left behind to continue the fight. The Spartan regent, Pausanias (d. ca. 470 B.C.E.), amassed the largest army of Greek allies yet assembled, and at Plataea, in the summer of 479 B.C.E., it killed Mardonius and routed the remaining Persian forces. Meanwhile, the Ionian Greeks urged King Leotychidas, the Spartan commander of the fleet, to fight the Persian fleet. At Mycale, near Samos, he destroyed the Persian camp and fleet, and the Persians withdrew from the Aegean and Ionia.

CLASSICAL GREECE

*T*he repulse of the Persians marks the beginning of the Classical period in Greece, 150 years of intense cultural achievement that has rarely if ever been matched (see Map 3–2). Although it was an era of progress for civilization, the Classical period was not a time of peace and stability for the Greeks. It was plagued by destructive conflicts among the poleis that left them weakened and vulnerable.

THE DELIAN LEAGUE

Greek unity gave way within two years of the Persian retreat. Two spheres of influence emerged—one dominated by Sparta, the other by Athens. The developments that led to the split were motivated by a need to protect the Ionian Greeks and make sure that the Persians did not return to the Aegean. Athens, Greece's largest naval power, was best equipped to direct this campaign.

In the winter of 478–477 B.C.E., the Aegean islanders, the Greeks from the coast of Asia Minor, and some from other Greek cities met with the Athenians on the sacred island of Delos to swear a permanent alliance under Athenian leadership. Known as the **Delian League**, the alliance kept the Persians at bay and cleared the Aegean of pirates. To create a workable system, some Greek states were forced into the league, and some who wished to resign were prevented from doing so. The Delian League and Athens were led at this time by a statesman and soldier named Cimon (d. 449 B.C.E.). His policy was to aggressively attack Persia while maintaining friendly relations with Sparta. He worked

Greek Hoplite Attacking a Persian Soldier. The contrast between the Greek's metal body armor, large shield, and long spear and the Persian's cloth and leather garments indicates one reason why the Greeks won.

Greek. Vase, Red-figured. Attic. ca. 480–470 B.C. Neck amphora, Nolan type. SIDE 1: "Greek warrior attacking a Persian." Said to be from Rhodes. Terracotta. H. 13-11/16 in. The Metropolitan Museum of Art, Rogers Fund, 1906 (Acc. # 06.1021.117) Photograph © The Metropolitan Museum of Art.

WHAT WERE the causes and results of the Peloponnesian War?

Delian League Alliance of Greek states under the leadership of Athens that was formed in 478–477 B.C.E. to resist the Persians.

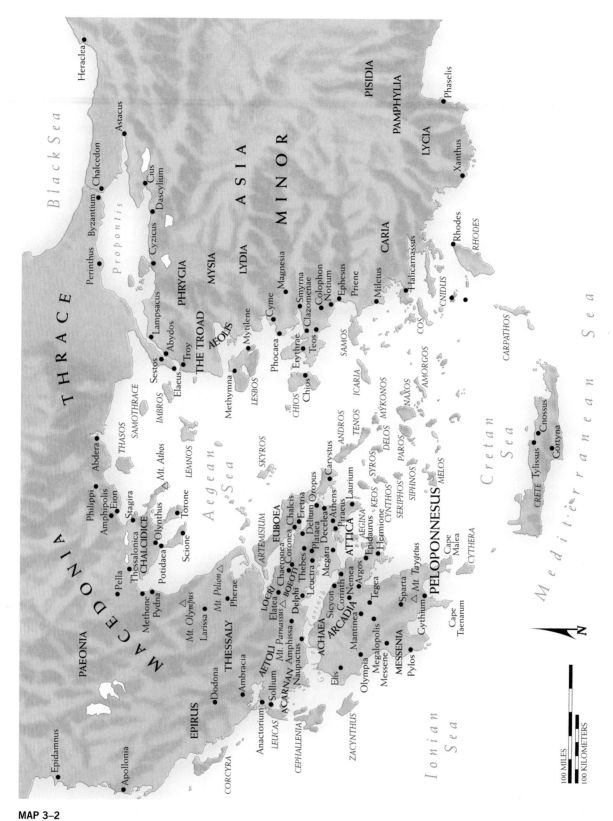

MAP 3–2

Classical Greece. Greece in the Classical period (ca. 480–338 B.C.E.) centered on the Aegean Sea. Although there were important Greek settlements in Italy, Sicily, and all around the Black Sea, the area shown in this general reference map embraced the vast majority of Greek states.

WHY WERE most Greek cities located close to the sea?

within the constraints of the popular democratic constitution that Clisthenes had given Athens.

THE FIRST PELOPONNESIAN WAR

The Fall of Cimon In 465 B.C.E., the island of Thasos rebelled against the league. Cimon's suppression of this rebellion began the transformation of the league into an Athenian empire. Despite his success abroad, at home Cimon faced challenges from a faction led by Pericles (ca. 495–429 B.C.E.). Although Pericles was a member of a distinguished Athenian family, he wanted to increase the power of ordinary Athenians and break with the Spartans, traditional allies of some Athenian aristocrats.

In 461 B.C.E. Cimon's opponent engineered his exile, and Athens allied with Argos, Sparta's enemy in the Peloponnese. Almost overnight, Cimon's domestic and foreign policies were overturned.

Outbreak of War The policies of Athens' new regime helped incite a conflict with Sparta known as the First **Peloponnesian War**. The Athenians made great gains during the war's early years. They seemed invulnerable, winning control of some neighboring states and dominating the sea.

In 454 B.C.E., however, the tide turned. An Athenian fleet, which was dispatched to help the Egyptians rebel against Persia, was destroyed, and revolts broke out within the Delian League. Athens moderated its behavior and agreed to a peace of 30 years with Sparta. Greece was divided into two blocs: Sparta and its allies on the mainland and Athens and what had become the Athenian Empire in the Aegean.

THE ATHENIAN EMPIRE

The Athenians moved the Delian League's treasury from Delos to Athens and began to keep one-sixtieth of the league's annual revenues for themselves. Athens gave up the pretext of being the leader of a free alliance.

Greek Wars Against Persia

ca. 560–546 B.C.E.	Greek cities of Asia Minor conquered by Croesus of Lydia
546 B.C.E.	Cyrus of Persia conquers Lydia and gains control of Greek cities
499–494 B.C.E.	Greek cities rebel (Ionian rebellion)
490 B.C.E.	Battle of Marathon
480–479 B.C.E.	Xerxes' invasion of Greece
480 B.C.E.	Battles of Thermopylae and Salamis
479 B.C.E.	Battles of Plataea and Mycale

Peloponnesian Wars
Protracted struggle between Athens and Sparta to dominate Greece between 465 and Athens' final defeat in 404 B.C.E.

WHAT WERE the main cultural achievements of classical Greece?

The Acropolis. It was both the religious and civic center of Athens. In its final form the Acropolis is the work of Pericles and his successors in the late fifth century B.C.E. This photograph shows the Parthenon and, to its left, the Erechtheum.

Meredith Pillon, Greek National Tourism Organization.

Key Events in Athenian History Between the Persian War and the Great Peloponnesian War

478–477 B.C.E.	Delian League founded
ca. 474–462 B.C.E.	Cimon leading politician
465–463 B.C.E.	Rebellion of Thasos
462 B.C.E.	Pericles rises to leadership
461 B.C.E.	Cimon ostracized
ca. 460 B.C.E.	First Peloponnesian War begins
454 B.C.E.	Athens defeated in Egypt; crisis in the Delian League
445 B.C.E.	Thirty Years' Peace ends First Peloponnesian War

The league had become an empire that was the key to Athens' prosperity and security.

ATHENIAN DEMOCRACY

While the Athenians tightened their control over their subjects, they expanded democracy for themselves at home. Under the leadership of Pericles they evolved the freest government the world had yet seen. Property qualifications for offices were removed, opening all offices to all adult male citizens. Pericles introduced pay for jury service, which allowed the poor to take time off from work to serve. Judges traveled circuits to provide swift impartial justice for the poor who were living in the countryside. As the privileges of Athenian citizenship grew, however, access to citizenship was sharply restricted. Only those who had two citizen parents could claim what had become a valuable commodity.

Athens was governed as a direct democracy. Every political decision had to be approved by the popular assembly—the people themselves, not their representatives. Every judicial decision was subject to appeal to a popular court chosen from the Athenian male population. Many officials were selected by lot, which made class irrelevant. Elected officials generally continued to be members of noble families and were almost always rich men, but the people were free to choose whomever they wanted. All public officials could be removed from office and were held to a compulsory accounting at the end of their terms. There was no standing army; no police force, open or secret; and no way to coerce the people.

Pericles was elected to the generalship (a military office with important political influence) 15 years in a row and 30 times in all. After the First Peloponnesian War, he instituted a conservative policy designed to preserve the empire in the Aegean and peace with Sparta.

WOMEN OF ATHENS

Subjection   Greek society was dominated by men, and democracry did nothing to challenge male supremacy in Athens. Women were excluded from most aspects of public life. They could not vote, take part in political assemblies, or hold office. Their only public function—an important one—was participation in certain rituals and festivals of the state religion.

In private life, women were always under the control of a male guardian—a father, husband, or relative. Women married young, usually between the ages of 12 and 18, whereas men typically did not marry until the age of 30. Marriages were arranged; the woman normally had no choice of husband, and her dowry was controlled by a male relative. To obtain a divorce, a woman needed the approval of a male relative.

The main function of an Athenian woman of a citizen family was to produce male heirs for her husband's household (*oikos*). Because the pure and legitimate lineage of offspring was important for ensuring transmission of rights to citizenship, women were segregated from men outside the family and confined to women's quarters in their homes. Respectable women stayed home, raised children, and oversaw their households. Their husbands spent most of their time outside the home and were free to seek whatever sexual gratification they wanted.

It may be that the role played by Athenian women was more complex than their legal status suggests, for myths, pictorial art, and the tragedies and comedies performed at Athenian religious festivals often feature women as central characters and powerful figures in both the public and the private spheres (see "Lysistrata Ends the War").

THE GREAT PELOPONNESIAN WAR

The Thirty Years' Peace of 445 B.C.E. endured little more than 10 years. About 435 B.C.E., Athens and Sparta plunged back into conflict. This new war shook the foundations of Greek civilization.

The Spartan strategy was traditional: to invade the enemy's country and threaten the crops, forcing the enemy to defend them in a hoplite battle. The Athenian strategy was to retreat to their impregnable city, allow the devastation of their land, and raid the Peloponnesian coast to put pressure on Sparta by harrassing its allies. The Athenian plan required restraint, and it was abandoned after Pericles died in 429 B.C.E. After 10 years of fruitless fighting, the war ended in stalemate.

In 415 B.C.E., Alcibiades (ca. 450–404 B.C.E.), a young and ambitious kinsman of Pericles, persuaded the Athenians to invade Sicily. When the entire expedition was destroyed, Athens' power and prestige were greatly diminished. Subjects of Athens' empire rebelled, and Sparta reopened the war—with Persian aid.

The Athenians fought on and won several important victories at sea, but their resources steadily diminished. When their fleet was destroyed at Aegospotami in 405 B.C.E., they could not rebuild it. The Spartans, under Lysander (d. 395 B.C.E.) blockaded Athens and cut off its food supply. In 404 B.C.E. Athens surrendered unconditionally.

STRUGGLE FOR GREEK LEADERSHIP

The Hegemony of Sparta   The collapse of the Athenian empire opened the way for Spartan dominance of the Aegean. Lysander installed boards of 10 local oligarchs loyal to him and supported by Spartan garrisons in most of the cities along the European coast and the islands of the Aegean. These tributaries brought Sparta almost as much revenue as the Athenians had collected.

Some of Sparta's allies, especially Thebes and Corinth, were alienated by Sparta's increasingly arrogant policies. The oligarchic government that Lysander installed in Athens in 404 B.C.E. came to be called the "Thirty Tyrants" by Athenians who resented its heavy-handed policies. When supporters of democracy fled to Thebes and Corinth and recruited an army to challenge the oligarchs' hold on Athens, Sparta's conservative king, Pausanias, arranged a peaceful settlement and the restoration of democracy. Thereafter, Athenian foreign policy remained under Spartan control, but otherwise Athens was free.

Theban Hegemony   Sparta's actions grew increasingly arrogant and lawless. In 382 B.C.E., Sparta seized Thebes during peacetime without warning or pretext. In 379 B.C.E., a Spartan army made a similar attempt on Athens. This move persuaded the Athenians to join with Thebes, which had rebelled from Sparta. In 371 B.C.E. the Thebans defeated the Spartans at Leuctra. They helped

The Great Peloponnesian War

432 B.C.E.	Sparta declares war on Athens
431 B.C.E.	Peloponnesian invasion of Athens
421 B.C.E.	Peace of Nicias
415–413 B.C.E.	Athenian invasion of Sicily
405 B.C.E.	Battle of Aegospotami
404 B.C.E.	Athens surrenders

HISTORY'S VOICES

LYSISTRATA ENDS THE WAR

ristophanes, the greatest of the Athenian comic poets, presented the play Lysistrata in 411 B.C.E., two decades into the Great Pelopennesian War. The plot's central idea is that the women of Athens, led by Lysistrata, tire of the privations imposed by the war and decide to take matters into their own hands to bring the war to an end. Their plan is to get the women on both sides to deny their marital favors to their husbands until the men agree to make peace. Their sexual strike quickly succeeds. Before the following passage, Lysistrata has set the terms the Spartans must accept. Next she turns to the Athenians. The play is a masterful example of Athenian Old Comedy, which was almost always full of contemporary and historical political satirical references and sexual and erotic puns and jokes. The references to "Peace" in the stage directions are to an actor playing the goddess Peace.

WHAT WAS the real role of women in Athenian political life, and what does the play tell us about it?

LYSISTRATA
(*Turning to the Athenians*)
—Men of Athens, do you think I'll let you off?
Have you forgotten the Tyrant's days, when you wore the smock of slavery, when the Spartans turned to the spear, cut down the pride of Thessaly, despatched the friends of tyranny, and dispossessed your oppressors?
Recall:
On that great day, your only allies were Spartans; your liberty came at their hands, which stripped away your servile garb and clothed you again in Freedom!

SPARTAN
(*Indicating Lysistrata*)
Hain't never seed no higher type of woman.

KINESIAS
(*Indicating Peace*)
Never saw one I wanted so much to top.

LYSISTRATA
(*Oblivious to the byplay, addressing both groups*)

With such a history of mutual benefits conferred and received, why are you fighting? Stop this wickedness! Come to terms with each other! What prevents you?

SPARTAN
We'd a heap sight druther make Peace, if we was indemnified with a plumb strategic location.
(*Pointing at Peace's rear*)
We'll take thet butte.

LYSISTRATA
Butte?

SPARTAN
The Promontory of Pylos—Sparta's Back Door.
We've missed it fer a turrible spell.
(*Reaching*)
Hev to keep our hand in.

KINESIAS
(*Pushing him away*)
The price is too high—you'll never take that!

LYSISTRATA
Oh, let them have it.

KINESIAS
What room will we have left for maneuvers?

LYSISTRATA
Demand another spot in exchange.

KINESIAS
(*Surveying Peace like a map as he addresses the Spartan*)
Then you hand over to us—uh, let me see—let's try Thessaly—
(*Indicating the relevant portions of Peace*)
First of all, Easy Mountain ...
then the Maniac Gulf behind it ...
and down to Megara for the legs ...

SPARTAN
You cain't take all of thet! Yore plumb out of yore mind!

LYSISTRATA

(*To Kinesias*)

Don't argue. Let the legs go.

(*Kinesias nods. A pause, general smiles of agreement*)

KINESIAS

(*Doffing his cloak*)

I feel an urgent desire to plow a few furrows.

SPARTAN

(*Doffing his cloak*)

Hit's time to work a few loads of fertilizer in.

LYSISTRATA

Conclude the treaty and the simple life is yours.
If such is your decision, convene your councils,
and then deliberate the matter with your allies.

KINESIAS

Deliberate? Allies?
We're over-extended already!

Wouldn't every ally approve of our position—
Union Now?

SPARTAN

I know I kin speak for ourn.

KINESIAS

And I for ours.

They're just a bunch of gigolos.

LYSISTRATA

I heartily approve. Now first attend to your purification, then we, the women, will welcome you to the Citadel and treat you to all the delights of a home-cooked banquet. Then you'll exchange your oaths and pledge your faith, and every man of you will take his wife and depart for home.

Source: Aristophanes, *Lysistrata* trans. by Douglass Parker in *Four Comedies by Aristophanes*, ed. by W. Arrowsmith (Ann Arbor: University of Michigan Press, 1969), pp. 79–81. Reprinted by permission of the University of Michigan Press.

the Arcadian cities of the central Peloponnesus to form a federal league and freed the Helots, who founded a city of their own. Sparta's population had shrunk, and hemmed in by hostile neighbors and deprived of much of its farmland and of the slaves who had worked it, Sparta ceased to be a first-rank power. Its aggressive policies had led to ruin.

The Second Athenian Empire   In 378 B.C.E. Athens organized a second confederation aimed at resisting Spartan aggression in the Aegean. Its constitution was designed to prevent the abuses that had turned the Delian League into an Athenian Empire, but the Athenians tried to revert to their old habits. This time, however, they did not have the power to dominate their allies, and when the threats posed by Sparta, Thebes, and Persia receded, their allies rebelled. After two centuries of almost continual warfare, the Greeks returned to the chaotic disorganization that had characterized the era before the founding of the Peloponnesian League.

CULTURE OF CLASSICAL GREECE

The term *classical* often suggests calm and serenity, but the word that best describes Greek life, thought, art, and literature during the Classical period is *tension*. Among the achievements of this era (discussed in Chapter 2) were the philosophical works of Socrates (469–399 B.C.E.), Plato (427?–347 B.C.E.), and Aristotle (384–322 B.C.E.). The same curiosity about the nature and place in the universe of human beings that motivated the philosophers also animated the arts of the period.

Spartan and Theban Hegemonies

404–403 B.C.E.	Thirty Tyrants rule at Athens
401 B.C.E.	Expedition of Cyrus, rebellious prince of Persia; Battle of Cunaxa
400–387 B.C.E.	Spartan War against Persia
398–360 B.C.E.	Reign of Agesilaus at Sparta
395–387 B.C.E.	Corinthian War
382 B.C.E.	Sparta seizes Thebes
378 B.C.E.	Second Athenian Confederation founded
371 B.C.E.	Thebans defeat Sparta at Leuctra; end of Spartan hegemony
362 B.C.E.	Battle of Mantinea; end of Theban hegemony

The Striding God from Artemisium.
This bronze statue, dating from ca.
460 B.C.E., was found in the sea near
Artemisium, the northern tip of the
large Greek Island of Euboea, and is
now on display in the National
Archaeological Museum in Athens.
Exactly whom this god represents is
not known. Some have thought him to
be Poseidon holding a trident; others
believe that he is Zeus hurling a thun-
derbolt. In either case he is a splendid
representative of the early classical
period of Greek sculpture.

National Archaeological Museum, Athens.

FIFTH CENTURY B.C.E.

Two sources of tension contributed to the artistic outpouring of fifth-century-B.C.E. Greece. One arose from the conflict between the Greeks' pride in their accomplishments and their concern that overreaching would bring retribution. The second was the conflict between the hopes and achievements of individuals and the claims and limits put on them by their fellow citizens in the polis. These tensions were felt throughout Greece. They had the most spectacular consequences, however, in Athens in its Golden Age, between the Persian and Peloponnesian Wars.

Attic Tragedy   Nothing reflects these concerns better than Attic (Athenian) tragedy, which emerged in the fifth century B.C.E. The tragedies were selected in a contest and presented as part of public religious observations in honor of the god Dionysus. Poets who wished to compete submitted their works to the archon. The three best competitors were each awarded three actors and a chorus. The actors were paid by the state and the chorus was provided by a wealthy citizen. Most of the tragedies were performed in the theater of Dionysus, which accommodated up to 30,000.

Attic tragedy raised vital issues. Until late in the century the tragedies, drawing mostly on mythological subjects, dealt solemnly with religion, politics, ethics, or morality. The plays of the dramatists Aeschylus (525–456 B.C.E.) and Sophocles (ca. 496–406 B.C.E.) follow this pattern. The plays of Euripides (ca. 480–406 B.C.E.) are more concerned with individual psychology.

Old Comedy   Comedy was introduced into the Dionysian festival early in the fifth century B.C.E. The great master of the genre called Old Comedy, Aristophanes (ca. 450–385 B.C.E.), wrote political comedies filled with scathing invective and political satire.

Architecture and Sculpture   Beginning in 448 B.C.E., Pericles undertook a great building program on the Acropolis with funds from the empire. The new buildings visually projected Athenian greatness, emphasizing the city's intellectual and artistic achievements and providing tangible proof that Athens was the intellectual center of Greece.

History   The first prose history ever written was a description of the Persian War by Herodotus (484?–425? B.C.E.), "the father of history." His account attempts to explain human actions and draw instruction from them. Herodotus sometimes treated legends and oracles as sources for history—although not uncritically—and often explained human events in terms of divine intervention. Yet his *History* also stresses the importance of human intelligence in guiding events. Herodotus recognized the significance of institutions. He claimed that the Greek polis inspired voluntary obedience to the law in its citizen soldiers whereas fear of punishment motivated the Persians.

Thucydides, the historian of the Peloponnesian War, was born about 460 B.C.E. and died about 400. He took great pains to achieve factual accuracy and tried to use his evidence to discover meaningful patterns of human behavior. He believed that human nature was essentially unchanging, so that a wise person, equipped with an understanding of history, might foresee events and guide them.

FOURTH CENTURY B.C.E.

The power of the poleis waned after the Great Peloponnesian War. Some Greeks tried to shore up its weakening institutions; others despaired and looked for radical alternatives; and still others turned their back on public life altogether. All these attitudes are reflected in the literature, philosophy, and art of the period.

Drama   The tendency to forsake the public for the private sphere is clear in a new genre that emerged in the fourth century B.C.E.: Middle Comedy. Old Comedy had dealt amusingly with serious subjects, but the themes of Middle Comedy were ordinary daily life, intrigue, and domestic satire. This tendency was magnified in New Comedy, which focused entirely on domestic scenes, the foibles of ordinary people, and the travails of lovers. The art of tragedy declined, but the great works of the previous century were revived, and Euripides, who had explored the psyches of individual characters, found his most appreciative audiences.

EMERGENCE OF THE HELLENISTIC WORLD

The term *Hellenistic* was coined in the 19th century to describe a period of three centuries during which Greek culture spread from its homeland to Egypt and Asia. The result was a new civilization that combined Greek and Asian elements. The Hellenistic world was larger than the world of classical Greece, and its major political units were much larger than the poleis. Hellenistic civilization had its roots in the rise to power of a dynasty in Macedonia whose armies conquered Greece and the Persian Empire.

HOW DID the diffusion of Greek culture affect the cultures of Egypt and Asia?

MACEDONIAN CONQUEST

The kingdom of Macedon, north of Thessaly, had long served as a buffer between the Greek states and barbarian tribes farther to the north. The

OVERVIEW   GREEK CIVILIZATION

Historians divide ancient Greek civilization into periods marked by different forms of social and political organizations and by significant cultural achievements.

Minoan	Based on the island of Crete, ca. 2900–1150 B.C.E., sea-based power, probably ruled by kings. Palace architecture, vivid frescoes.
Mycenaean	Mainland Greece, ca. 1600–1150 B.C.E., city-states ruled by powerful kings assisted by an elaborate bureaucracy. Monumental architecture, gold, and bronzework.
Archaic	Colonization from Greece to Asia Minor, southern Italy, and the coasts of the Black Sea, 700–500 B.C.E.. Characteristic form of government was the polis, a city-state dominated by land-holding aristocrats or ruled tyrants. Lyric poetry, natural philosophy.
Classical	Golden age of Athenian civilization, fifth century B.C.E.. Athens and other poleis became much more democratic. Drama, sculpture in marble and bronze, architecture (the Acropolis), philosophy, history.
Hellenistic	Conquests of Alexander the Great (356–323 B.C.E.) spread Greek culture to Egypt and as far east as the Indus Valley. Decline of the polis. Domination of the Greek world by large monarchical states. Stoic and Epicurean philosophy, realistic sculpture, advances in mathematics and science.

Macedonians were of the same stock as the Greeks and spoke a Greek dialect. Macedon's kings sought to bring Greek culture to their court. By Greek standards, however, Macedon was semi-barbaric. It had no poleis. The king gained his throne through acclamation by the army, and a council of nobles checked his power. Constant internal conflict prevented Macedon from playing much of a part in Greek affairs up to the fourth century B.C.E., but once unified under a strong king, that changed.

Philip of Macedon   That king was Philip II (r. 359–336 B.C.E.). Like many of his predecessors, he admired Greek culture. His natural talents for war and diplomacy and his boundless ambition made him the ablest king in Macedonian history. After he won control of a lucrative gold and silver mining region, he used his resources to turn his army into the finest fighting force in the world.

4.6

The First Philippic: A Great Orator Warns of Macedonian Imperialism

Invasion of Greece   In 340 B.C.E., Philip besieged Perinthus and Byzantium, the lifeline of Athenian commerce. The Athenian fleet saved both cities, so Philip marched into Greece, and in 338 B.C.E., he defeated Athens and Thebes at Chaeronea in Boeotia. Chaeronea marked the end of the era of freedom and autonomy for the Greek polis. Poleis retained their institutions and control over their internal affairs for some time, but new political realities began to chart Greece's future.

ALEXANDER THE GREAT AND HIS SUCCESSORS

In 337 B.C.E., Philip announced his intention to invade Persia, but in the spring of 336 B.C.E., as he prepared to begin the campaign, he was assassinated. Philip's son, Alexander III (356–323 B.C.E.), later called Alexander the Great, succeeded his father at the age of 20, and inherited his plans for the conquest of Persia.

The Conquest of Persia   In 334 B.C.E., Alexander crossed into Asia. His army consisted of about 30,000 infantry and 5,000 cavalry; he had no navy and little money. Consequently, he needed a quick and decisive battle, and the Persianss obliged him. Alexander met them at the Granicus River (see Map 3–3), where he won a smashing victory. Alexander then captured the coastal cities, denying them access to the Persian fleet.

In 333 B.C.E., Alexander marched inland to Syria, meeting the main Persian army under King Darius III (r. 336–330 B.C.E.) at Issus, and sent Darius fleeing to the east. Marching on to Egypt, he was greeted as liberator and proclaimed pharaoh and son of the god Re.

In the spring of 331 B.C.E., Alexander left Egypt and marched east into Mesopotamia. At Gaugamela, near the ancient Assyrian city of Nineveh, he met Darius again. Alexander's tactical genius and personal leadership carried the day. The Persians fled, and Alexander moved on to occupy Babylon and burn Persepolis, the Persian capital.

Darius was murdered by his relative Bessus as he fled east to escape Alexander. Alexander pursued and captured Bessus and then continued east to the frontier of India. His strategy for consolidating the territories he conquered was to encourage an amalgamation of their people. To this end, he married a Bactrian princess, Roxane, and enrolled 30,000 young Bactrians in his army.

In 327 B.C.E., Alexander conquered the lands around the Indus River (modern Pakistan). He hoped to continue east to the river called Ocean that the Greeks believed encircled the world, but his weary men rebelled and refused to go any further. By the spring of 324 B.C.E., the army was back at the Persian Gulf.

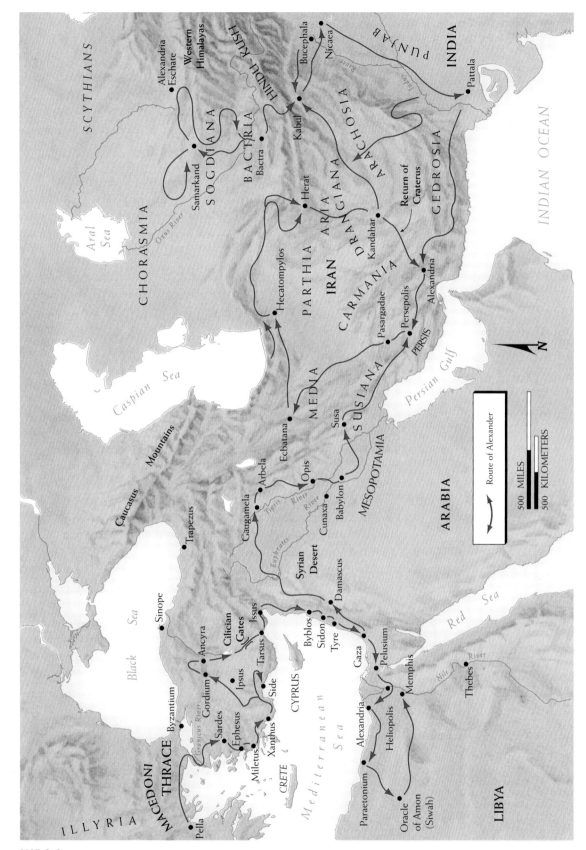

MAP 3–3

Alexander's Campaigns. The route taken by Alexander the Great in his conquest of the Persian Empire, 334–323 B.C.E. Starting from the Macedonian capital at Pella, he reached the Indus Valley before being turned back by his own restive troops. He died of fever in Mesopotamia.

GIVEN THE extent of Alexander's conquests, why do you think his empire was divided after his death?

Rise of Macedon

359–336 B.C.E.	Reign of Philip II
338 B.C.E.	Battle of Chaeronea; Philip conquers Greece; founding of League of Corinth
336–323 B.C.E.	Reign of Alexander III, the Great
334 B.C.E.	Alexander invades Asia
333 B.C.E.	Battle of Issus
331 B.C.E.	Battle of Gaugamela
330 B.C.E.	Fall of Persepolis
327 B.C.E.	Alexander reaches Indus Valley
323 B.C.E.	Death of Alexander

Alexander's Death and His Successors   Alexander was filled with plans for the future, but in June 323 B.C.E., he took ill and died in Babylon at the age of 33. He quickly entered myth and legend, and a debate began about his goals, his personality, and his achievements that has continued to the present day.

Alexander had no child at the time of his death, and he made no arrangements for a successor. He left his enormous empire without an obvious heir. After prolonged warfare, three of his generals founded dynasties that continued the spread of Hellenistic culture:

- Ptolemy I, 367?–283 B.C.E.; founder of the 31st Dynasty in Egypt, the Ptolemies, of whom Cleopatra, who died in 30 B.C.E., was the last
- Seleucus I, 358?–280 B.C.E.; founder of the Seleucid dynasty in Mesopotamia
- Antigonus I, 382–301 B.C.E.; founder of the Antigonid dynasty in Asia Minor and Macedon

For the first 75 years or so after the death of Alexander, the world ruled by his successors enjoyed prosperity. The vast sums of money he and they had put into circulation increased economic activity. The opening of vast new territories to Greek trade, the increased demand for Greek products, and the greater availability of things Greeks wanted all helped stimulate commerce. The new prosperity, however, was not evenly distributed. The urban Greeks, the Macedonians, and the Hellenized natives who made up the upper and middle classes lived in comfort and even luxury, but native peasants did not.

Eventually, war and inflation produced economic crises. The kings bore down heavily, but the middle classes skillfully avoided their exactions, and peasants and city laborers reacted by slowing work and striking. In Greece, economic pressures caused clashes between rich and poor and civil wars.

These internal difficulties made the Hellenistic kingdoms vulnerable to attack, and by the middle of the second century B.C.E. Rome had absorbed all of them except for Egypt. The two centuries of Hellenistic rule had, however, promoted economic and cultural cohesion throughout the eastern Mediterranean coast, Greece, Egypt, Mesopotamia, and the old Persian Empire.

HELLENISTIC CULTURE

HOW DID Hellenistic culture differ from that of classical Greece?

*A*lexander's empire and its successor kingdoms ended the role the autonomous polis had played in Greek affairs, and this marked a turning point in Greek literature, philosophy, religion, and art. The Greek cities lost the kind of political freedom that was basic to the outlook of the Classical period. They became municipalities within military empires. Deprived of political influence, their citizens turned inward and focused on their private hopes and fears. The confident, sometimes arrogant, humanism of the fifth century B.C.E. gave way to a kind of resignation to fate, a recognition of helplessness before forces too great for humans to manage.

PHILOSOPHY

These developments explain the direction philosophy took during the Hellenistic era. Plato's Academy and Aristotle's Lyceum continued to operate, but changed their foci. The Academy drifted toward skepticism, and the Lyceum abandoned scientific work for literary and historical studies Two especially influential new schools appeared: the Epicureans and the Stoics.

Epicureans   Epicurus of Athens (342–271 B.C.E.) claimed that the highest good was happiness, a state achieved by living according to the dictates of reason. Reason, the **Epicureans** believed, indicates that reality is only a construct of atoms continually falling through the void. When combintations of atoms strike our sense organs, they create the things we perceive in the world. When we die, the atoms that compose our bodies disperse so that we have no further existence or perception. There is, therefore, nothing to fear after death. Epicurus also believed that gods took no interest in human affairs.

The purpose of Epicurean physics was to liberate people from the fear of death and the supernatural. Epicurean ethics identified happiness with pleasure, but a pleasure that was chiefly negative: the absence of pain. The goal was *ataraxia*, the condition of being undisturbed, without trouble, pain, or responsibility. To achieve it, one should ideally have sufficient means to withdraw from worldly affairs; Epicurus even advised against marriage and children. He preached a life of restrained selfishness, which might appeal to intellectuals of means but was not widely attractive.

Stoics   The Stoic school, established by Zeno of Citium (335–263 B.C.E.), took its name from the *Stoa Poikile*, or Painted Portico, in the Athenian Agora, where Zeno and his disciples met. The **Stoics** also sought the happiness of the individual, but Stoic philosophy was almost indistinguishable from religion. The Stoics believed that god and nature are the same and that humans must live in harmony within themselves and with nature. The guiding principle in nature is divine reason (*logos*), or fire. Every human has a spark of this divinity, and after death it returns to the eternal divine spirit. From time to time the world is destroyed by fire, from the ashes of which a new world arises.

Happiness, according to the Stoics, lies in living virtuously—that is, living in accordance with natural law. Wisdom is needed to distinguish good from evil and both from things that are "indifferent" (neutral). Good and evil are dispositions of the mind or soul. Prudence, justice, courage, and temperance are good; folly, injustice, and cowardice are evil. Life, health, pleasure, beauty, strength, and wealth are "indifferent" in that they have no innate moral worth. Morally indifferent things, such as these, become sources of misery when they inspire passion, an irrational mental response. The wise seek *apatheia*, or freedom from passion.

The Stoics viewed the world as a single large polis and all people as children of god. Many Stoics were politically active, but they were indifferent to many concerns that often produced political arguments. With their striving for inner harmony and a life lived in accordance with the divine will, their fatalistic attitude, and their pursuit of a form of apathy, the Stoics fit the post-Alexandrian world well. The spread of Stoicism eased the creation of a new political system that relied on the docile submission of the governed.

LITERATURE

The literary center of the Hellenistic world in the third and second centuries B.C.E. was Alexandria, Egypt, where the Ptolemies founded the museum—a great research institute that provided patronage for scientists and scholars and a library that included a comprehensive collection of the literature of the ancient world. Alexandrian scholars collected, copied, edited, and wrote commentaries on a vast

Epicureans   School of philosophy founded by Epicurus of Athens (342–271 B.C.E.). It sought to liberate people from fear of death and the supernatural by teaching that the gods took no interest in human affairs and that true happiness consisted in pleasure, which was defined as the absence of pain.

Stoics   Philosophical school founded by Zeno of Citium (335–263 B.C.E.) that taught that humans could only be happy with natural law.

logos   Divine reason, or fire, which according to the Stoics, was the guiding principle in nature.

One of the masterpieces of Hellenistic sculpture, the *Laocoön*. This is a Roman copy. According to legend, Laocoön was a priest who warned the Trojans not to take the Greeks' wooden horse within their city. This sculpture depicts his punishment. Great serpents sent by the goddess Athena, who was on the side of the Greeks, devoured Laocoön and his sons before the horrified people of Troy.

Direzione Generale Musei Vaticani.

heliocentric theory The theory, now universally accepted, that the Earth and the other planets revolve around the sun. First proposed by Aristarchos of Samos (310–230 B.C.E.).

amount of material. To them we owe the preservation of most of what has survived of ancient literature.

ARCHITECTURE AND SCULPTURE

The Hellenistic monarchies lavishly funded the work of architects and sculptors as well as scholars, and they competed for the services of prominent artists. In general, Hellenistic art continued a drift that began in the fourth century B.C.E. toward the sentimental, emotional, and realistic.

MATHEMATICS AND SCIENCE

Among the most spectacular intellectual accomplishments of the Hellenistic age were those in mathematics and science. Indeed, Alexandrian scholars were responsible for most of the scientific knowledge available to the West until the Scientific Revolution of the 16th and 17th centuries C.E.

Euclid's Elements (written early in the third century B.C.E.) is still the foundation for courses in plane and solid geometry. Archimedes of Syracuse (ca. 287–212 B.C.E.), who also made advances in geometry, established the theory of the lever in mechanics and invented hydrostatics.

As early as the fourth century, Heraclides of Pontus (ca. 390–310 B.C.E.) argued that Mercury and Venus circulate around the sun and not the Earth. He made other suggestions leading in the direction of a **heliocentric theory** of the universe, but it was Aristarchus of Samos (ca. 310–230 B.C.E.) who clearly asserted that the sun, along with the other fixed stars, did not move and that the Earth rotated on its axis while revolving around the sun. The heliocentric theory, however, was not generally accepted. More popular was the geocentric model of the universe proposed by Hipparchus of Nicea (b. ca. 190 B.C.E.). It was complicated, but it did a good job of accounting for the movements of the sun, the moon, and the planets. Ptolemy of Alexandria (second century C.E.) adopted Hipparchus's system with a few improvements, and it remained dominant until the work of Copernicus, in the 16th century C.E.

Hellenistic scientists mapped the Earth as well as the sky. Eratosthenes of Cyrene (ca. 275–195 B.C.E.) accurately calculated the circumference of the Earth and wrote a treatise on geography based on mathematical and physical reasoning and the reports of travelers.

SUMMARY

Early Greece Greek civilization is divided into several periods. In the Minoan and Mycenaean ages, the Greek states were ruled by powerful kings supported by elaborate bureaucracies. Invaders from the north destroyed Mycenaean civilization around 1150 B.C.E. By 750 B.C.E., during the Archaic period, Greek society took its characteristic form: the polis (plural poleis), a self-governing city-state. The most important poleis were Athens and Sparta. At first governed by land-owning aristocrats, then by tyrants, many poleis evolved more democratic forms of government by 500 B.C.E. In an effort to avoid the pressures of overpopulation and land hunger, the Greeks established colonies around the shores of the Mediterranean and Black Seas.

Classical Greece After defeating two Persian attempts to conquer them in the early fifth century B.C.E., the Greeks entered their golden age. The greatest achievements in art, literature, and philosophy of Classical Greece took place in Athens, where the government was the most democratic seen until modern times. Among the accomplishments of Greek artists, writers, and thinkers were naturalistic sculpture, tragedy and comedy, secular history, and systematic logic, all of which still influence Western art and thought.

Hellenistic Greece The polis went into political and cultural decline after Sparta defeated Athens in the Great Peloponnesian War (435–404 B.C.E.). Macedon under Philip II (r. 359–336 B.C.E.) and Alexander the Great (r. 336–323 B.C.E.) came to dominate first Greece and then all the Middle East from Asia Minor to northern India. Alexander's conquest of the Persian Empire spread Greek culture over a wide area and ushered in the Hellenistic Era. Hellenistic Greek culture, which was fostered by the kingdoms that succeeded Alexander's empire, was more accessible to outsiders than that of Classical Greece. Hellenistic scholars made Greek literature and science available to many different peoples who adopted it as their own. The Romans were particularly impressed. They spread Hellenistic culture across the Mediterranean world and transmitted it to later generations in the West.

IMAGE KEY
for pages 56—57

a. A gold jewelry pendant with the shape of bees
b. Fifth century B.C.E. Greek vase
c. Column capital from Temple of Artemis at Ephesus
d. Lyre
e. The "Alexander Sarcophagus" from the Phoenician royal necropolis at Sidon
f. Ancient Greek Athenian Coin
g. Scene on an Attic jar showing how olives were harvested
h. Attic vase, 475 B.C.E.
i. Artemisian statue, 460 B.C.E.
j. The Acropolis

REVIEW QUESTIONS

1. How did the Greek world of the Minoan and Mycenaean period compare with the classical era?

2. What was a polis? How did it influence classical Greek civilization?

3. Why did Sparta develop its unique form of government? How did Athens become a democracy between 600 and 500 B.C.E.?

4. Why did the Greeks and Persians go to war in 490 and 480 B.C.E.? Why were the Greeks able to defeat the Persians? What were the consequences of their victory?

5. Why did Sparta win the Peloponnesian War?

6. How did Alexander's conquests change Greek civilization?

KEY TERMS

Acropolis (p. 61)
agora (p. 61)
Areopagus (p. 67)
Delian League (p. 69)
Epicureans (p. 81)
heliocentric theory (p. 82)

Helots (p. 66)
hoplite phalanx (p. 61)
The *Iliad* and the *Odyssey* (p. 59)
logos (p. 81)
Magna Graecia (p. 62)
Minoan (p. 58)

Mycenaean (p. 59)
Panhellenic (p. 62)
Peloponnesian War (p. 71)
Stoics (p. 81)
symposion (p. 64)

 For additional study resources for this chapter, go to:
www.prenhall.com/craig/chapter3

4

Iran, India, and Inner Asia to 200 C.E.

CHAPTER HIGHLIGHTS

Indo-Iranian Empires Between 600 B.C.E. and 200 C.E., imperial governments arose in the Indo-Iranian world whose power and influence surpassed that of any before them. The Achaemenid Empire based in Iran, the Mauryan Empire in India, and the Hellenistic empire of the Seleucids provided the security and wealth that permitted trade and culture to flourish from the Mediterranean to India. The Achaemenid Empire established two centuries of tolerant, stable, prosperous rule from Egypt to the borders of India. The Mauryans created the first Indian empire, while Seleucid rule fostered the spread of Greek culture in Western Asia.

Cross-cultural Contacts In Asia these empires enabled widely influential, lasting religious traditions—Zoroastrianism, Buddhism, Hinduism—to come of age and spread. The empires also fostered an increase of cross-cultural contact, especially in Central Asia where Greek, Iranian, Indian, and steppe-people languages, ideas, arts, customs, and religious practices intermingled. These contacts and influences were manifested in new peoples, structures of government, technological innovations, specialized skills and arts, and ethical and religious ideas.

CHAPTER QUESTIONS

WHAT WERE the main teachings of Zoroaster
and how did Zoroastrianism influence other traditions?

WHAT WERE the chief achievements
of the Achaemenid Empire?

HOW WAS the Mauryan Empire created?

HOW DID Hellenistic Greek culture influence
Iranian and northern Indian civilization?

CHAPTER OUTLINE

IRAN
- Ancient History
- The First Iranian Empire
  (550–330 B.C.E.)

INDIA
- The First Indian Empire
  (321–185 B.C.E.)

- Consolidation of
  Indian Civilization
  (ca. 200 B.C.E.–300 C.E.)

GREEK AND ASIAN DYNASTIES
- Seleucids
- Indo-Greeks
- Steppe Peoples

From the Mediterranean to China, the period from about 600 B.C.E. to 200 C.E. saw the rise of centralized empires on an unprecedented scale. Well before the Qin unification (221–207 B.C.E.) or the Han dynasty (202 B.C.E.–9 C.E.) in China, and long before imperium *replaced republic in Rome, imperial states flourished in Iran. The Achaemenids (ca. 539–330 B.C.E.), an Aryan dynasty from the mountains of southwestern Iran, created an empire based in Babylonia and Iran that was the greatest yet seen anywhere. Two centuries later the Mauryans, a northeast Indian dynasty centered in the Ganges basin, founded the first great Indian Empire (ca. 321–ca. 185 B.C.E.). Both of these empires, like their later Chinese and Roman counterparts, built sophisticated bureaucracies, professional armies, and strong communication systems. They also contributed to new cultural, political, and religious developments in their domains.*

Another characteristic of this period was increased and sustained contact among the major centers of culture from the Mediterranean to China. Alexander the Great's conquest (334–323 B.C.E.) of the Persian Empire and the regions eastward to north India increased the growing contact among diverse cultures, races, and religious traditions.

A third characteristic of this period was the rise, spread, and consolidation of major religious traditions that would affect later history from Africa to China.

IRAN

"Iran" designates the vast expanse of southwest Asia bounded by the Caspian Sea and Jaxartes (Syr Darya) River to the north and northeast, the Indus Valley to the southeast, the Arabian Sea and Gulf to the south, the Tigris-Euphrates to the west, and the Caucasus to the northwest. The heart of this region is the vast Iranian plateau, bounded on all sides by mountains.

The great Asian trade routes put Iran at the heart of east–west interchange. Their location, as well as the locations of the cities and towns that flourished because of them, was determined largely by mountain passes, river fords, and plateau crossings.

ANCIENT HISTORY

WHAT WERE the main teachings of Zoroaster and how did Zoroastrianism influence other traditions?

THE ELAMITES

The Elamites were a non-Semitic people who built a flourishing civilization in the southwestern lowlands on the eastern frontier of Mesopotamia. They were repeatedly at war with the Sumerians, Babylonians, and Assyrians from around 2700 B.C.E. until their destruction by the Assyrian emperor Asshurbanipal in 639. The Elamite language long outlived the Elamite state and was one of the three official languages of the Persian Empire.

THE IRANIANS

The forefathers of the Iranian dynasts were Aryans. The oldest texts in ancient Persian dialects show that Aryan people settled on the Iranian plateau sometime around 1100 B.C.E. Like their Vedic or Indo-Aryan relations in North India, these people were evidently pastoralists—horse-breeders—from the Eurasian or Central Asian steppes. The most prominent of these ancient Iranians were the Medes and the Persians. By the eighth century B.C.E., they had spread around the deserts of the plateau to settle and control its western and southwestern reaches, which were named for them: Media and Persis (later Fars).

The Medes developed a tribal confederacy in western Iran. By 612 B.C.E., they and the Neo-Babylonians had defeated the mighty Assyrians. But by 550 B.C.E., their supremacy on the Iranian plateau had ended. The Achaemenid clan, led by Cyrus the Great, incorporated the region into the sprawling Persian Empire. Many of the institutions of his empire (such as the satrapy system of provincial administration) were based on Median practices, some of which had been drawn from Babylonian and Assyrian models. The Achaemenids' unparalleled success in building and ruling a far-flung empire owed much to the use of existing institutions.

ANCIENT IRANIAN RELIGION

We know more about religious traditions of ancient Iran than about other aspects of its culture because our only pre-Achaemenid texts are religious. These texts suggest that old Iranian culture and religion were similar to those of the Vedic Aryans. The emphasis was on moral order, or the "Right." The supreme heavenly deity was Ahura Mazda, the "Wise Lord."

ZOROASTER AND THE ZOROASTRIAN TRADITION

The first person who stands out in Iranian history was not Cyrus, the founder of the Achaemenid Empire, but the great prophet-reformer of Iranian religion, Zarathushtra, commonly known in the West as Zoroaster. It is clear from his hymns that, like the Hebrew prophets, the Buddha, and Confucius, Zoroaster urged moral reform on an age of materialism, political opportunism, and ethical indifference.

Zoroaster was evidently trained as a priest in the old Iranian tradition, but his hymns reflect a new religious vision. Zoroaster's personal religious experience inspired him to reinterpret the sacrificial fire of the old faith as a symbol of Ahura Mazda. He called on people to abandon worship of and sacrifice to all lesser deities, whom he dismissed as demons, not gods. He urged his people to reform their morality and warned of a "final reckoning," when the good would be rewarded with "future glory" but the wicked with "long-lasting darkness, ill food, and wailing."

By the mid-fourth century B.C.E., the Zoroastrian reform had spread into western as well as eastern Iran. The quasi-monotheistic worship of Ahura Mazda, the Wise Lord, was rapidly accommodated to the veneration of older Iranian gods. The old Iranian priestly clan of the *Magi*, as reforms, may have integrated Zoroastrian ideas and texts into their polytheistic tradition. The name "magi" was later used for the priests of the faith now called "Zoroastrian."

Zoroastrianism probably influenced not only Jewish, Christian, and Muslim ideas of angels, devils, the messiah, the last judgment, and the afterlife, but some important Buddhist concepts as well. Zoroastrianism was wiped out as a major force in Iran by the spread of Islam in the seventh and eighth centuries C.E. However, its tradition continues in the faith and practice of the Parsis, most of whom live in western India.

THE FIRST IRANIAN EMPIRE (550–330 B.C.E.)

THE ACHAEMENIDS

Achaemenid regional power in southwestern Iran (Persis) went back at least to Cyrus I (d. 600 B.C.E.), but the rise of Iran as a major civilization and empire is usually dated from the reign of his famous grandson, Cyrus the Great (559–530 B.C.E.).

A Fifth-Century B.C.E. Achaemenid Amphora. This amphora from southwestern Iran has double tube-handles.

Gisela Croon/Bildarchiv Preussischer Kulturbesitz.

Zoroastrianism A quasi-monotheistic Iranian religion founded by Zoroaster (ca. 628–551 B.C.E.) who preached a message of moral reform and exhorted his followers to worship only Ahura Mazda, the Wise Lord.

WHAT WERE the chief achievements of the Achaemenid Empire?

Iran to the Third Century C.E.

ca. 2000–1000 B.C.E.	Indo-Iranian (Aryan) tribes move south into the Punjab of India and the Iranian plateau
ca. 628–551 B.C.E. (or before 1000 B.C.E.?)	Traditional life of Zoroaster, probably in eastern/northeastern Iran (perhaps originally in Herat?)
559–530 B.C.E.	Reign of Cyrus the Great Persian Achaemenid ruler
539–330 B.C.E.	Achaemenid Empire
331–330 B.C.E.	Alexander (d. 323 B.C.E.) conquers Achaemenid Empire
312–ca. 125 B.C.E.	Seleucid rule in part of Achaemenid realm
ca. 248 B.C.E.–224 C.E.	Parthian Empire of the Arsacids in Iran, Babylonia

The empire founded by Cyrus the Great was anticipated in many ways by the large but loosely controlled empire of his predecessors, the Medes. Cyrus defeated the last Median king about 550 B.C.E. He then subdued northern Assyria, Cilicia, and the kingdom of Lydia, near the Aegean coast of Asia Minor. The Lydian capital, Sardis, became a provincial capital of the growing Persian state. Next, Cyrus defeated the last Babylonian king.

The conquest of Babylon, in 539 B.C.E., symbolically marks the beginning of the Achaemenid Empire, for it joined the Mesopotamian and Iranian spheres for the first time under one rule (see Map 4–1). Cyrus subsequently extended Achaemenid rule in the east where he died fighting steppe tribes. His readiness to utilize local elites and institutions rather than impose new political superstructures was perhaps his most notable legacy.

He and his successors ruled what was really a tribal confederation. They adopted so many Median administrative practices and employed so many Medes in their government that the Achaemenid rulers are referred to in the Bible and other sources as the "Medes and Persians." What the Medes had set in motion, Cyrus and his heirs consolidated and expanded to create an Iranian Empire that was the most extensive the world had ever seen. Among its beneficiaries were the Jews, whose Babylonian exile Cyrus brought to an end (see Chapter 2).

Cyrus's successor, Cambyses (r. 529–522 B.C.E.), added Egypt to the empire, but his brief reign was followed by a succession struggle. The winner, Darius I (521–486 B.C.E.), enjoyed a prosperous reign in which the Achaemenid Empire reached its greatest extent—from Egypt northeast to southern Russia and Sogdiana (Transoxiana) and east to the Indus Valley.

The next five rulers (486–359 B.C.E.) fared less well, and after 478 B.C.E., the Persians found the Greeks pulling ahead of them militarily. They utilized diplomacy to keep the Greeks divided and at bay, but Greek cultural influence steadily grew in Asia Minor. Egyptian rebellions, succession struggles, renewed conflict with Scythian steppe tribes, and poor leadership plagued the empire. The capable and energetic Artaxerxes III (r. 359–338 B.C.E.) might have solved these problems had he not been poisoned in a palace coup just as Philip of Macedon was unifying the Greeks. When Philip's son Alexander succeeded him, the days of Achaemenid rule were numbered.

THE ACHAEMENID STATE

Perhaps the greatest achievement of the Achaemenids was the relative stability of their empire. To justify their sovereignty—and the title of ***Shahanshah***, "king of kings"—they claimed that Ahura Mazda had entrusted them with universal sovereignty. The emperor acted as priest and sacrificer in the court rituals; his role as cosmic ruler was symbolized by a special royal fire that burned throughout his reign. The Achaemenids were, however, tolerant of other cultural and religious traditions in ways earlier empires had not been.

The Achaemenids built a powerful army, but much of their success derived from their administrative abilities and willingness to learn and to borrow from

Shahanshah "King of kings," the title of the Persian ruler.

MAP EXPLORATION

Interactive map: To explore this map further, go to **http://www.prenhall.com/craig/map4.1**

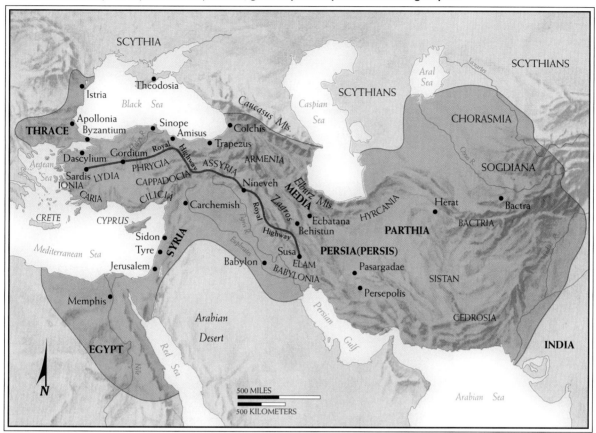

MAP 4–1

The Achaemenid Persian Empire.   The empire created by Cyrus reached its fullest extent under Darius when Persia attacked Greece in 490 B.C.E. It extended from India to the Aegean, and even into Europe, encompassing the lands formerly ruled by Egyptians, Hittites, Babylonians, and Assyrians.

WHY WERE the Persians able to govern such a large empire for so long?

predecessors such as the Medes or Babylonians. Most of their leaders worked to maintain what has been termed a *pax Achaemenica.*[1] They preserved continuity as their state evolved from a tribal confederation into a sophisticated monarchy supported by a noble class, professional armies (led by Persian elite troops), provinces ruled by governors called ***satraps***, and fixed-yield levies of revenue.

Communication and propaganda systems illustrated the excellence of Achaemenid administration. Couriers linked imperial outposts with the heartlands over a well-kept highway system. Herodotus called the greatest of these highways, which ran from Sardis to Susa, "the King's Road." A network of reporters and royal inspectors kept the court abreast of activities beyond the capital. An efficient chancery served administrative needs. The adoption of the Aramaic language by the bureaucracy helped link east and west, and Achaemenid inscriptions emphasized the provision of universal justice through the rule of law.

The Achaemenid court rotated among a series of palaces and never had a single, fixed capital. Whole states were incorporated intact into the empire as

satraps Governors of provinces in the Persian Empire.

[1]Richard N. Frye, *The Heritage of Persia* (New York: New American Library, 1966), p. 110.

Persepolis The ruins of the famous royal complex at Persepolis, begun ca. 518 B.C.E. The foundation of the treasury is in the foreground; part of the restored women's quarters is visible on the left; and the tall pillars of the main audience hall stand in the rear.

Giraudon/Art Resource, N.Y.

satrapies. This caused little disruption to local customs and encouraged conquered people to accept Achaemenid rule. Some satraps rebelled from time to time, but the centralized power of the "king of kings" succeeded remarkably at governing diverse provinces.

THE ACHAEMENID ECONOMY

The success of the Achaemenid government boosted economic activity from Greece to India. Coinage gradually displaced in-kind payments and stimulated banking operations. The Achaemenids levied taxes on estates, livestock, mines, trade, and production. Wages were regulated and monetary values for goods were published (e.g., the worth of a sheep might be set at three shekels). Agriculture remained the basic industry for most free men. Serfs and slaves provided much of the labor. Where water was scarce, the government created irrigation systems using both subterranean and surface canals.

The quality of life under the *pax Achaemenica* helps to explain why the empire was fairly stable for more than two centuries. Its stability and cosmopolitan culture facilitated the Hellenization of western Asia that flourish in the wake of Alexander's conquests.

OVERVIEW   IRANIAN AND INDIAN EMPIRES

From 600 B.C.E. to 200 C.E. a series of centralized empires arose on the Iranian plateau and in India. These states built sophisticated bureaucracies, professional armies, and effective communication systems. They also contributed to new cultural, religious, and social developments.

Achaemenid Empire, 539–330 B.C.E.	Founded by Cyrus the Great (r. 559–530 B.C.E.), the empire was based in Iran and ran from Egypt to northern India. It provided a tolerant, stable, and prosperous cosmopolitan environment that paved the way for the eventual Hellenization of western Asia under Alexander the Great and his successors.
Mauryan Empire, 321–185 B.C.E.	The first Indian empire, it stretched from northern India to the Deccan. Its greatest ruler was Ashoka (r. ca. 272–232 B.C.E.), who converted to Buddhism. The Mauryans helped spread Buddhism, developed strong administrative and communications systems that helped give India a sense of unity, established contact with the West, and fostered the growth of cities and the flourishing of art and literature.
Seleucid Empire, 312–125 B.C.E.	A successor state to Alexander's empire. The Seleucids controlled much of the Middle East from the Mediterranean to northern India. By fusing Greek and Persian cultural and political elements, the Seleucids helped to spread Hellenistic culture throughout western Asia.

INDIA

Large-scale imperial expansion came much later to the South Asian, or Indian, subcontinent than to Iran. A cultural and religious heritage going back to the Aryan invaders of North India left its mark on the subsequent history of this vast and diverse subcontinent. However, on only four occasions has a substantial part of the whole come under a single rule: in the Mauryan, Gupta, Mughal, and British imperial epochs.

THE FIRST INDIAN EMPIRE (321–185 B.C.E.)

*A*lexander the Great conquered the northwest Indian provinces of Gandhara and the Indus Valley in 327 B.C.E., but this had little or no impact on the Indian subcontinent. Only under the Mauryan emperors was much of North India incorporated into the first true Indian empire.

HOW WAS the Mauryan Empire created?

POLITICAL BACKGROUND

The basis for an empire in North India was the rise of regional states between the seventh and the fourth centuries B.C.E., the strongest of which were the monarchies of the Ganges plains. Farther north, tribal republics were more common. King Bimbisara (d. 493 B.C.E.) of Magadha built the first centralized state strong enough to attempt imperial expansion, but his successors fell behind in competition with the Mauryans.

The Lion Capital of Sarnath. This famous Ashokan column capital was taken by India as its state seal after independence in 1947. It reflects both Persian and Greek influences. Originally the capital stood atop a mighty pillar some 50 feet high; the lions supported a huge stone chakra, the Buddhist "Wheel of the *Dharma*," the symbol of universal law.

Bridgeman-Giraudon/Art Resource, N.Y.

THE MAURYANS

The first true Indian empire was established by Chandragupta Maurya (r. ca. 321–297 B.C.E.), an adventurer who made Pataliputra (modern Patna) his capital (see Map 4–2). He pushed westward into the vacuum that was created when Alexander the Great's army returned to Babylon (326 B.C.E.) and brought the Indus region and much of west-central India under his control. A treaty with Seleucus (ca. 358–280 B.C.E.), Alexander's successor in Bactria, added Gandhara and Arachosia to his empire.

Chandragupta's son and successor, Bindusara (r. ca. 297–272 B.C.E.), continued his father's imperial expansion. He moved swiftly to conquer the Deccan, the great plateau that covers central India and divides the far south (Tamilnad) from North India.

Ashoka The third and greatest Mauryan, Ashoka (r. ca. 272–232 B.C.E.), commissioned numerous rock inscriptions that record information about his reign and character. He conquered Kalinga, the last independent kingdom in North India and the Deccan, and extended Mauryan control over the whole subcontinent except the far south.

The bloodship provoked by the Kalinga war revolted Ashoka and prompted his religious conversion. He devoted himself to the Buddhist "middle path" in both personal and public affairs. He abandoned hunting and meat eating and championed nonviolence. He eschewed aggression in favor of "conquest by righteousness" (*dharma*), winning others to humanitarian values by example. He looked on all his subjects as his "children." His edicts show that he pursued the layman's version of the Buddhist *dharma*, a striving to win heaven by the merit of good actions. He stressed tolerance for all traditions, but sent envoys abroad to spread Buddhist teaching. He appointed "dharma officials" to investigate public welfare problems and foster just government at the local level (see "The Edicts of Ashoka").

Ashoka eased burdens imposed on his people by earlier rulers and instituted beneficial public works. However, by the end of his reign, the empire's size hindered its administration, and under his successors, Mauryan rule fell apart. Ashoka's memory survived, however, to create the model for the ideal king in later Hindu and Buddhist thought. As a symbol of enlightened rule, he has few equals in the history of East or West.

The Mauryan State Mauryan bureaucracy was marked by centralization, standardization, and efficiency in communications, civil and military organization, tax collection, and information gathering (by a secret service). The fundamental unit of government was the village, with its headman and council. Groups of villages formed districts within the larger provincial unit. The provinces were controlled by governors sent from the capital or by native rulers, like the Achaemenids' satraps (probably the model for the Mauryan imperial system).

The king directly administered the empire with the aid of an advisory council. Revenues came primarily from taxing the produce of the land, which

was regarded as the king's property. Urban trade and production were also heavily taxed. Slavery existed, but most slaves did domestic labor.

The Mauryan Legacy   An imperial ideal, a strengthened Buddhist movement, and strong central administration were not the Mauryans' only gifts to Indian culture. They left behind new cosmopolitan traditions of external relations and internal communication that encouraged cultural development and discouraged provincialism. Their many contacts with the West reflect their international perspective, as do the Ashokan edicts, which were executed in various languages and scripts. Writing and reading must have been common by this time, or the edicts would have had no purpose. The Mauryans' excellent road system would later provide routes for Buddhism's spread to Central Asia and China, as well as corridors for successive invaders of the subcontinent.

3.6
Ashoka: How a Life Was Turned Around

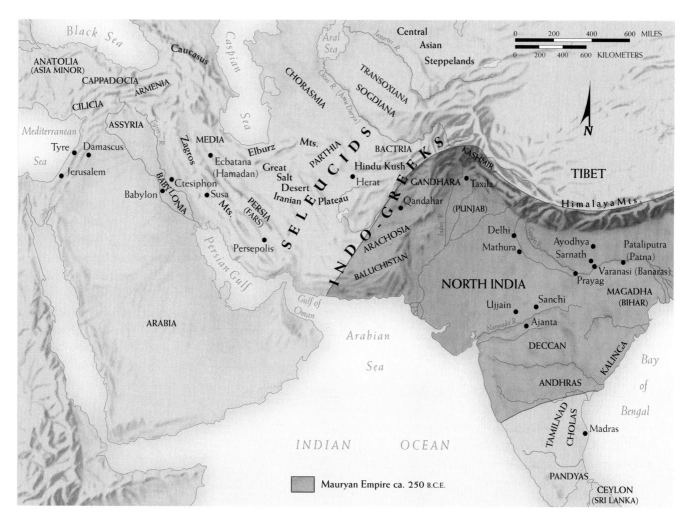

MAP 4–2
Southwest Asia and India ca. 250 B.C.E.   This map shows not only the major cities and regions of greater Iran and the Indian subcontinent, but also the neighboring eastern Mediterranean world. Although the Mediterranean was closely tied to Iran from Achaemenid times onward, its contacts with India in the wake of the conquests of Alexander the Great were many and varied.

WHICH STATES helped spread Greek culture from the Mediterranean to northern India?

HISTORY'S VOICES

THE EDICTS OF ASHOKA

I n the first of the two following excerpts from Ashokan edicts, the monarch explains his change of heart and conversion to nonviolence after the Kalinga war and states his determination to follow dharma. "The Beloved of the Gods" was the common royal epithet Ashoka used for himself. The second excerpt is from the end of Ashoka's reign and speaks of his efforts to better his and other people's lives by rule according to the dictates of dharma.

WHAT DOES Ashoka suggest is the role of the monarch? What is his concept of "conquest?" What does he think of those of other faiths and what does he want for them? What reforms does Ashoka propose, and why? Can you reconcile his expressed abhorrence of killing with his words to the forest tribes? How do these edicts compare to other approaches to law, leadership, and government? See, for example, "The Code of Hammurabi" (Chapter 1).

FROM THE THIRTEENTH ROCK EDICT

When the king, Beloved of the Gods and of Gracious Mien, had been consecrated eight years Kalinga was conquered, 150,000 people were deported, 100,000 were killed, and many times that number died. But after the conquest of Kalinga, the Beloved of the Gods began to follow Righteousness [*dharma*], to love Righteousness, and to give instruction in Righteousness. Now the Beloved of the Gods regrets the conquest of Kalinga, for when an independent country is conquered people are killed, they die, or are deported, and that the Beloved of the Gods finds very painful and grievous . . . The Beloved of the Gods will forgive as far as he can, and he even conciliates the forest tribes of his dominions; but he warns them that there is power even in the remorse of the Beloved of the Gods, and he tells them to reform, lest they be killed.

For all beings the Beloved of the Gods desires security, self-control, calm of mind, and gentleness. The Beloved of the Gods considers that the greatest victory is the victory of Righteousness; and this he has won here [in India] and even five hundred leagues beyond his frontiers in the realm of the Greek king Antiochus, and beyond Antiochus among the four kings Ptolemy, Antigonus, Magas, and Alexander. Even where the envoys of the Beloved of the Gods have not been sent, men hear of the way in which he follows and teaches Righteousness, and they too follow it and will follow it. Thus he achieves a universal conquest, and conquest always gives a feeling of pleasure; yet it is but a slight pleasure, for the Beloved of the Gods only looks on that which concerns the next life as of great importance . . . .

FROM THE SEVENTH PILLAR EDICT

In the past kings sought to make the people progress in Righteousness, but they did not progress ... And I asked myself how I might uplift them through progress in Righteousness . . . Thus I decided to have them instructed in Righteousness, and to issue ordinances of Righteousness, so that by hearing them the people might conform, advance in the progress of Righteousness, and themselves make great progress . . . For that purpose many officials are employed among the people to instruct them in Righteousness and to explain it to them. . . .

Moreover I have had banyan trees planted on the roads to give shade to man and beast; I have planted mango groves, and I have had ponds dug and shelters erected along the roads at every eight kos. Everywhere I have had wells dug for the benefit of man and beast. But this benefit is but small, for in many ways the kings of olden time have worked for the welfare of the world; but what I have done has been done that men may conform to Righteousness . . . .

I have enforced the law against killing certain animals and many others, but the greatest progress of Righteousness among men comes from exhortation in favor of noninjury to life and abstention from killing living beings.

I have done this that it may endure as long as the moon and sun, and that my sons and my great-grandsons may support it; for by supporting it they will gain both this world and the next.

From *Sources of Indian Tradition* by William Theodore de Bary. Copyright © 1988 by Columbia University Press. Reprinted with permission of the publisher.

This era also saw the flourishing of cities across the empire. They were centers for arts, crafts, industry, literature, and education. The stone buildings and sculpture of the Ashokan period reflect sophisticated aesthetics and technique, as well as strong Persian and Greek influence.

CONSOLIDATION OF INDIAN CIVILIZATION (CA. 200 B.C.E.–300 C.E.)

*I*n the post-Mauryan period, North India was dominated by the influx of various foreign peoples. In the rest of the subcontinent, indigenous Indian dynasties held sway. Autonomous regional and local governments continued unbroken until the rise of the empire built by the Guptas (320 C.E.–ca. 550; see Chapter 10). However, the centuries between the Mauryans and Guptas saw religious and cultural consolidation of transregional patterns and styles that helped to shape Indian and, through the diffusion of Buddhism, Asian civilization ever after.

HOW WAS the period between 200 B.C.E. and 300 C.E. formative in the development of Indian civilization?

THE ECONOMIC BASE

Although agriculture remained the basis of the economy, commerce flourished amid the post-Mauryan political fragmentation. The fine Mauryan road system facilitated trade throughout India (see Map 4–3). Chinese and Roman demand for Indian luxury goods made India a magnet for world trade, and wealth flowed in. Guild organizations provided technical education in crafts, and kings as well as merchants invested in guilds. Coin minting increased after Mauryan times, and banking flourished.[2]

HIGH CULTURE

During this era, the major achievements in the arts were inspired by Buddhism. Northwestern India saw the rise of the Gandharan school of Buddhist art. It joined Hellenistic naturalism with the more recent Indian tradition of Buddha images, and it created relief and freestanding sculptural figures with flowing, draped garments through which the muscular lines of the human body are discerned. In central India as early as the first century B.C.E., artists were producing stone-relief sculpture with the naturalistic, yet flowing, plastic human and animal forms that would become earmarks of the "classical" style of Indian art.

Language and literature during this period employed the sophisticated Sanskrit grammar of Panini (ca. 300 B.C.E.?). Two masterpieces of Sanskrit culture, the epics of the *Mahabharata* and the *Ramayana*, probably took general shape by 200 C.E. The first is a composite work concerned largely with the nature of dharma (see Chapter 2). Included in its earlier, narrative portions is the Bhagavad Gita, or "Song of the Blessed Lord," the most influential of all Indian religious texts.

India from the Sixth Century B.C.E. to the End of Mauryan Rule

ca. 600–400 B.C.E.	Late Upanishadic age: local/regional kingdoms and tribal republics along the Ganges and in Himalayan foothills, the Punjab, and northwestern India
ca. 540–ca. 468 B.C.E.	Vardhamana Mahavira, Jain founder
ca. 537–ca. 486 B.C.E.	Siddhartha Gautama, the Buddha
ca. 550–324 B.C.E.	Regional empire of Maghadan kings
330–325 B.C.E.	Alexander campaigns in Indus Valley, Soghdiana, Bactria, and Punjab
324–ca. 185 B.C.E.	Mauryan Empire controls most of northern India and the Deccan
ca. 272–232 B.C.E.	Reign of the Mauryan emperor Ashoka

[2]Romila Thapar, *A History of India*, vol. I (Harmondsworth, U.K.: Penguin Books, 1966), pp. 105–118.

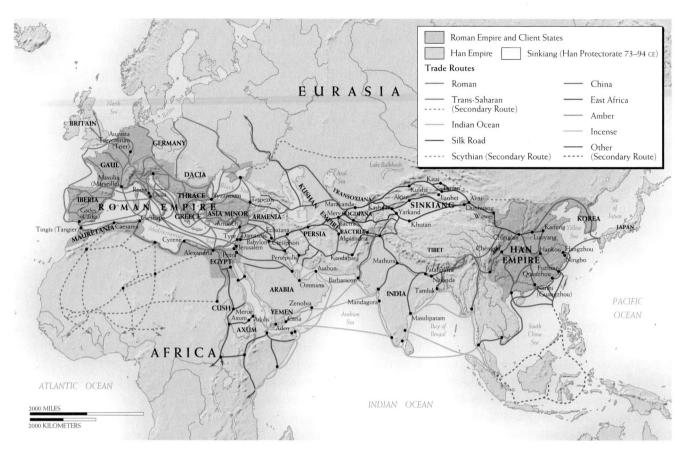

MAP 4–3

Eurasian Trade Routes ca. 100 C.E. An extensive network of overland and sea routes connected Eurasia from the Mediterranean to China.

HOW CENTRAL were Iran, India, and Inner Asia in the Eurasian trade networks of the ancient world?

RELIGION AND SOCIETY

The post-Mauryan period saw Buddhist monasticism and lay devotionalism thrive across the subcontinent. However, the Brahmans continued to dominate Vedic learning and ritual. Toward the end of this age, Buddhism in its Mahayana form began to spread from India to Central Asia and eventually to China and Japan.

Hindu Tradition What is now called Hinduism emerged at this time. The major developments shaping Hindu tradition were: (1) the consolidation of the caste system, Brahman ascendancy, and the "high" culture of Sanskrit learning; (2) the increasing dominance of theistic devotionalism (especially the cults of Vishnu and Shiva); and (3) the intellectual reconciliation of these developments with older ascetic and speculative traditions deriving from the Upanishadic age.

Buddhist Tradition Indian Buddhist monastic communities prospered under mercantile and royal patronage. Buddhist lay devotion figured prominently in Indian religious life, especially in the Ganges basin. The Buddha and

Buddhist saints were naturally identified with popular Indian deities, and popular Buddhist practice was indistinguishable from countless other devotional cults that began to dominate the Indian scene. One reason why Buddhist tradition remained only one among many Indian religious options was Buddhism's absorption into the religious variety that then and now typifies the Hindu religious scene.

GREEK AND ASIAN DYNASTIES

SELEUCIDS

Alexander's successors in the Achaemenid lands were the Greek general Seleucus and his heirs. They ruled most of the former Achaemenid realm from about 312 to 246 B.C.E. and lesser portions until about 125 B.C.E. Alexander's policies of Greco-Persian fusion helped make the Seleucid rule of many eastern areas viable. The new "cities" that Alexander founded provided bases for Seleucid control. As a foreign minority, the Seleucids relied on mercenary troops to hold their domain, but it was the leaders of these troops and of the Seleucid satrapies who gradually whittled away at Seleucid rule. Neither Seleucus (r. 311–281 B.C.E.; see Chapter 3) nor the strongest of his successors, Antiochus the Great (r. 223–187 B.C.E.), ever secured lasting dominion on the scale of the Achaemenids.

Alexander's strategy of joining Hellenes with Iranians in political power, marriage, and culture bore fruit more lasting than the empire. During the second century B.C.E., Hellenistic culture and law spread new ideals among the Seleucid elites, and the Seleucids welcomed into the ruling classes those non-Hellenes who were willing to be Hellenized.

Zoroastrian religious tradition declined with the loss of its imperial-cult status. The many syncretic cults of the Mediterranean Hellenistic world made inroads even in the East in Seleucid and Parthian times. Mystery and savior cults were becoming more popular. The new Hellenistic urban centers may have provided an environment in which the individual was less rooted in established traditions of culture and religious life. This would have enhanced the attractiveness of the focus on individual salvation common to many lesser Hellenistic cults and to emerging traditions such as the Christian, Mahayana Buddhist, Manichaean, and Hindu devotionalist that came to dominate Eurasia.

INDO-GREEKS

The farthest reach of Hellenization in the East came not under the Seleucids but with the **Indo-Greeks** of Bactria. About 246 B.C.E., Bactria's Greek satrap broke away from the Seleucids. His successor, Euthydemus (r. ca. 235–ca. 200 B.C.E.),

Indo-Greek, Iranian, Indian, and Steppe Dynasties After Alexander

312–ca. 125 B.C.E.	Seleucid rule in part of the old Achaemenid realm
ca. 247 B.C.E.–224 C.E.	Parthian Empire of the Arsacids in Iran, Babylonia
246–ca. 50 B.C.E.	Indo-Greek ("Graeco-Bactrian," "Euthydemid") rulers of region from modern Afghanistan to Oxus
ca. 171–138 B.C.E.	Reign of Arsacid king Mithradates I
ca. 130 B.C.E.–ca. 100 C.E.	Movements west and south of Yüeh Chih (including Kushans) and Sythians (Sakas) into Sogdiana, then Bactria, then northwestern India
ca. C.E. 50–ca. 250	Height of Kushan power in Oxus to Ganges region
ca. 100–150 C.E.	Accession of King Kanishka to Kushan throne in Taxila (ruled about 28 years)

 3.7
"King Milinda": The Greek Worlds Incursion into India

HOW DID Hellenistic Greek culture influence Iranian and northern Indian civilizations?

Indo-Greeks Bactrian rulers who broke away from the Seleucid Empire to found a state that combined elements of Greek and Indian civilizations.

steppe peoples Nomadic tribespeople who dwelled on the Eurasian plains from eastern Europe to the borders of China and Iran. They frequently traded with or invaded more settled cultures.

WHAT IMPACT did nomadic steppe peoples have on Eurasian history in antiquity?

The Great Stupa at Sanchi is an outstanding example of early Buddhist relic mounds. The mound, seated on an Ashokan foundation, was added to over the centuries. Magnificent carvings adorn its stone railings and gateways, one of which is shown in the left foreground. Sanchi is located in north-central India.

Dale Williams.

extended his sway north and southwest. His son Demetrius exploited the growing Mauryan weakness to conquer Arachosia. Demetrius and his successor, Menander, made Taxila their capital. Most of the Indo-Greeks were Indian in language, culture, and religion, as their coins and inscriptions show.

Before their demise at the hands of invading steppe peoples (ca. 130–100 B.C.E.), these Indo-Greeks left their mark on civilization in all the areas around their Bactrian center. Bactria was a major source of the later Greco-Buddhist art of Gandhara, one of history's remarkable examples of cross-cultural influence. The Indo-Greeks also probably helped spread Buddhism from India to Central Asia.

STEPPE PEOPLES

The history of North India and the Iranian plateau was dominated from about 250 B.C.E. to 300 C.E. by incursions of Iranian tribal peoples originally from the Central Asian steppes. Although commonly ignored, the nomadic **steppe peoples** have been a major force in Eurasian history.

PARTHIANS

The Parni, said to be related to the Scythians, were probably the major group of Iranian steppe peoples who first settled the area south of the Aral

Sea and Oxus. In late Achaemenid times, they moved south into Parthia. Thenceforward we can call them Parthians. The independent control of Parthia by the dynastic family of the Arsacids dates from about 247 B.C.E. For decades they were only a regional power, but under Mithradates I (ca. 171–138 B.C.E.) they became a new Eurasian imperial force and the true successors to the Achaemenids.

The Parthian Empire stretched across the Iranian plateau from Mesopotamia to Arachosia. Its center was Ctesiphon, on the Tigris. From the time of their victory over the Romans at Carrhae in 53 B.C.E. (see Chapter 6) until their fall in 233 C.E., the Parthians were the major Eurasian power alongside Rome. Eventually, wars with Rome and the pressure of the Kushan Empire in the east weakened them sufficiently for a new Persian dynasty to replace them.

Culturally, the Parthians were oriented toward the Hellenistic world of their Seleucid predecessors until the mid-first century C.E., when they experienced a kind of Iranian revival. Similarly, the magi preserved the worship of Ahura Mazda despite the success of other eastern and western cults and the tendency to assimilate Greek and Iranian gods. The Parthians, however, tolerated religious plurality.

SAKAS AND KUSHANS

The successors of the Indo-Greeks were steppe peoples who played a major political and cultural role in Asia for several centuries. They reflect the cosmopolitan nature of Central Asia, eastern Iran, and northwestern India at this time.

Beginning about 130 B.C.E., Scythian (Saka) tribes from beyond the Jaxartes (Syr Darya) overran northeastern Iran, conquering Sogdiana's Hellenic cities and then Bactria. One group of Sakas extended their domain into North India. Another went southwest into Herat and Sistan. In northwestern India the Sakas were, in turn, defeated by invading Iranians known as the Pahlavas.[3]

The Sakas had been displaced earlier in Sogdiana by another steppe people, known from Chinese sources as the Yüeh Chih. These peoples, led by the Kushan tribe, drove the Sakas out of Bactria in the mid-first century B.C.E. About a hundred years later, they swept over the mountains into northwestern India. Here they ended Pahlava rule and founded a long-lived Indian Kushan dynasty.

The Kushan kingdom of India was—along with Rome, China, and the weakened Parthian Empire of Iran—one of four major centers of civilization in Eurasia around 100 C.E. Its greatest ruler, Kanishka, reigned either around 100 or possibly 150 C.E. He was the greatest patron of Buddhism since Ashoka.

Parthian Warrior. The Parthians were superb fighters and were particularly noted for the "Parthian shot," firing arrows backward while mounted on a galloping horse. It is not difficult to imagine the fear that must have gripped sedentary peoples at the sight of such swift and mobile cavalrymen.

Werner Forman Archive.

QUICK REVIEW

The Parthians
- Settled area south of the Aral Sea and Oxus
- Control of Parthia by Arsacids dates from 247 B.C.E.
- Empire stretched across the Iranian plateau from Mesopotamia to Arachosia

---

[3]Tradition gives one of their rulers, Gondophares, the role of host to Saint Thomas, who is said to have brought Christianity to India. But because Gondophares probably ruled in the early to mid-first century C.E., it may be a confused report. Even if traditions of Thomas's mission to India are correct, some connect him instead with southern India.

At its height in the first to third centuries C.E., Kushan power in Central Asia facilitated the missionary activity that carried Buddhism across the steppes into China. A lasting Kushan contribution was the school of Greco-Buddhist art fostered in Gandhara by Kanishka and his successors and supported by a later Kushan dynasty for another 500 years.

SUMMARY

Indo-Iranian Empires Between 600 B.C.E. and 200 C.E. imperial governments arose in the Indo-Iranian world whose power and influence surpassed that of any before them. The Achaemenid Empire based in Iran, the Mauryan Empire in India, and the Hellenistic Empire of the Seleucids provided the security and wealth that permitted trade and culture to flourish from the Mediterranean to India. The Achaemenid Empire established two centuries of tolerant, stable, prosperous rule from Egypt to the borders of India. The Mauryans created the first Indian empire, while Seleucid rule fostered the spread of Greek culture in Western Asia.

Cross-cultural Contacts In Asia these empires enabled widely influential, lasting religious traditions—Zoroastrianism, Buddhism, Hinduism—to come of age and spread. These empires also fostered an increase of cross-cultural contact, especially in Central Asia where Greek, Iranian, Indian, and steppe-people languages, ideas, arts, customs, and religious practices intermingled. These contacts and influences were manifested in new peoples, structures of government, technological innovations, specialized skills and arts, and ethical and religious ideas.

IMAGE KEY
for pages 84–85

a. Barley seeds (Mai Ya)
b. Achaemenid Goldwork Winged Lion
c. Archaemenid Gold Chariot 5th-4th Century B.C.E., Persia Antiques
d. Wheat stalks
e. Gandharan gold pendant depicting Hariti
f. Coin of a Parthian monarch
g. Head of Achaemenid Prince
h. Gold winged lion set in a circle
i. The Lion Capital of Sarnath
j. Persepolis treasury relief of Darius I receiving tributes
k. A fifth-century B.C.E. Achaemenid amphora

REVIEW QUESTIONS

1. What key factors contributed to the long survival of the Achaemenid Empire?
2. How did Ashoka develop Mauryan power and prestige?
3. How do Buddhism and Hinduism compare?
4. What roles did the Kushans, Sakas, and other inner-Asian groups play in world history?

KEY TERMS

Indo-Greeks (p. 97)   **Shahanshah** (p. 88)   **Zoroastrianism** (p. 87)
satraps (p. 89)   **steppe peoples** (p. 98)

For additional study resources for this chapter, go to:
www.prenhall.com/craig/chapter4

Visualizing The Past

Goddesses and the Female Form in Ancient Art

ANCIENT ARTISTS created images of women as often as men in their art, but there were key differences in how they depicted the female versus the male form. What were these differences, why did they come about, and what did they signify?

Artists celebrated male gods and human men alike for their roles in society as priests, warriors, or commoners. By contrast, from ancient times to the present, sexuality has been central to artistic conceptualizations of women and the female role in the divine and human realms. In most societies, earthly women and goddesses alike were usually drawn or sculpted nude, at least from the waist down, and, given the link between female sexuality and fertility, with breasts and hips prominent or even exaggerated. Goddesses in the ancient world tended to have a dual nature, of death and regeneration, and to be linked to symbols of earth, love, death, and war, and often also to mastery of snakes, a prominent symbol in many cultures of male fertility. Biology thus tended to be the primary factor in how artists conceived of women's role in ancient societies and how they depicted the female form in art.

Innana-Ishtar, ca. 2025–1763 B.C.E., ▶ Babylonian goddess of love and death.
Inanna-Ishtar has a lovely feminine form but taloned feet, denoting her dual nature. She stands upon her symbol, the lion; holds a rod and a ring, symbols of kingship; and is surrounded by two owls, symbols of her mastery over death.
Rèunion des Musées Nationaux/Art Resource, N.Y.

"Snake Goddess," Minoan, c. 1650 B.C.E.

Strong cultural and economic ties linked Mediterranean and Near Eastern cultures, as can be seen in the similarities between this small statuette of a Minoan goddess and the preceding image of Innana-Ishtar. As was typical in Minoan and Greek art, this goddess is nude only to the waist. Like Innana-Ishtar, however, her arms are raised and she holds symbols of power, in this case snakes rather than a rod (although both are symbols of male sexual power).

Photograph ©Erich Lessing/Art Resource.

Fertility Goddess, India, Third Century B.C.E.

Even before Alexander the Great reached India in 327 B.C.E., trade brought Greek objects and artistic influences to India, where Indian artists assimilated them into Indian aesthetics and religion. This life-sized statue of a fertility goddess resembles Hellenistic statues such as the Venus de Milo (c. 150 B.C.E.) in that she is a free-standing figure and nude to the waist. Her prominent breasts, like those of the Minoan "Snake Goddess," symbolize female fertility. Hindu ▼ culture and religion have traditionally celebrated female beauty and sexual power more than most other world religions.

Dirk Bakker.

◄ Coatlicue, Aztec mother goddess.

Although hailing from the New World, and depicted in a radically different artistic tradition, Coatlicue, the "goddess of the serpent skirt," shares with goddesses of the Old World an emphasis on mastery of male sexual power (her serpent skirt), fertility and motherhood (she was the mother of the powerful Aztec god Huitzilopochtli), and death (she craved human sacrifices).

Mexican National Tourist Council.

5 Africa
Early History to 1000 C.E.

CHAPTER HIGHLIGHTS

Geography and History The human species, *homo sapiens* (*sapiens*) probably originated in Africa. Africa's geography and climate, however, limited Africans' contact with peoples outside the continent. Nonetheless, Africa cannot be considered a dark continent without a history. Within Africa itself, archaeology reveals that there were extensive migrations of peoples across the continent from the earliest days of African history with widespread crosscultural influences.

Contact with Other Cultures In three parts of Africa, there was considerable contact with non-African civilizations. In the Nile River Valley, Egypt had extensive interaction with the Nubian peoples to its south. Nubian kingdoms— Kush, Napata, Meroe, and Axum (Ethiopia)— adopted many features of Egyptian civilization and sometimes dominated Egypt itself. Axum adopted Christianity in the fourth century C.E.

On the coast of East Africa, trade across the Red Sea and the Indian Ocean with Arabia and east Asia fostered a distinct and sophisticated culture. Extensive trade across the Sahara between North Africa and the western and central Sudan enabled products and ideas from the Mediterranean to reach the African interior in exchange for African products, such as gold, ivory, and salt.

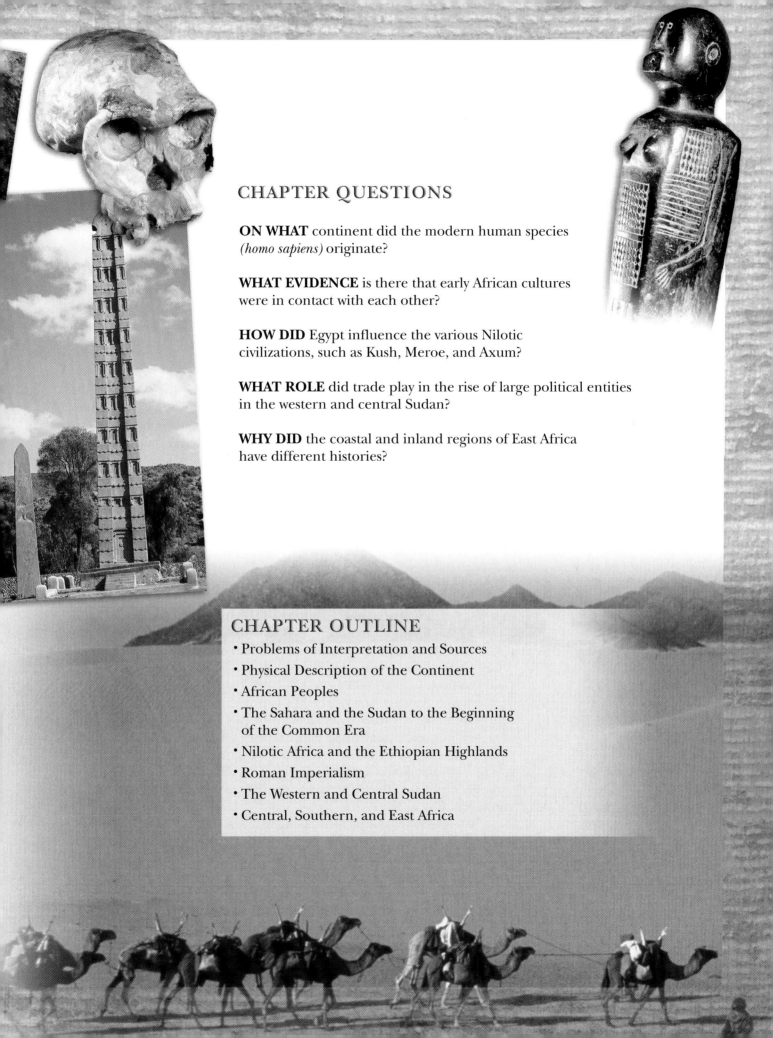

CHAPTER QUESTIONS

ON WHAT continent did the modern human species *(homo sapiens)* originate?

WHAT EVIDENCE is there that early African cultures were in contact with each other?

HOW DID Egypt influence the various Nilotic civilizations, such as Kush, Meroe, and Axum?

WHAT ROLE did trade play in the rise of large political entities in the western and central Sudan?

WHY DID the coastal and inland regions of East Africa have different histories?

CHAPTER OUTLINE

• Problems of Interpretation and Sources
• Physical Description of the Continent
• African Peoples
• The Sahara and the Sudan to the Beginning of the Common Era
• Nilotic Africa and the Ethiopian Highlands
• Roman Imperialism
• The Western and Central Sudan
• Central, Southern, and East Africa

Africa, the world's second largest continent, forms the southern frontier of the Mediterranean world and connects to Asia through the Arabian peninsula and the Indian Ocean. Evidence suggests that the first humans emerged from eastern Africa, and the continent's subsequent history is one of ongoing interaction, both internally and with the rest of the world.

Problems of Interpretation and Sources

The Question of Civilization

The narrow definition of "civilization" emphasizes social complexity (e.g., cities) and technological developments (e.g., writing, metallurgy), but people may lack these and have a level of intellectual, cultural, and artistic sophistication that merits identifying them as civilized. Until recently, outside the Nile valley and the Ethiopian highlands, most African societies may not have been civilizations in the narrow sense, but they were hardly uncivilized in the broader sense of the term.

The Source Problem

Stateless societies, such as those that characterized much of sub-Saharan Africa, leave few historical records. Surviving oral traditions and scattered reports by outside observers provide some insight into recent centuries, but there is much that is unknown. Archaeologists have recovered evidence of large, advanced societies whose existence had been forgotten. But the tropical climate of sub-Saharan Africa has destroyed many artifacts, and few traces remain of the continent's smaller communities. Beginning about 950 C.E., descriptions of Africa by outsiders become available, but these are often distorted by preconceptions and biases.

Physical Description of the Continent

Africa makes up over one-fifth of the Earth's landmass. It is geologically massive, with unusually high relief over virtually its entire expanse. The result is a dearth of natural harbors and islands and generally steep escarpments surmounting narrow coasts. This has made access to, as well as egress from, its interior difficult. All of Africa's major rivers (the Niger, Kongo [Zaïre], Nile, Zambezi, and Orange) lie largely in plateau basins and are navigable in their inland reaches. They are not, however, navigable across the cataracts they traverse before they reach the coastlands. (Only the Nile has a relatively long navigable stretch below its cataracts in upper Egypt.) The vast size and sharp physical variations—from high mountains to swamp lands, tropical forests, and deserts—have also made rapid long-distance communication and movement difficult.

The special character of various regions is due in considerable part to Africa's position astride the equator. As a whole, its climate is hot. North and south of the equator, dense rain forests dominate a west-east band of tropical woodland territory. North and south of this band, the lush rain forests give way to the **savannah**—open woodlands and grassy plains. This, in turn, passes into steppe and semidesert (the **Sahel**) and finally into true desert. Africa contains two of the world's greatest and driest deserts. The **Sahara** is the world's largest desert and historically has hindered contact between the Mediterranean world and sub-Saharan Africa. The **Kalahari** in southwestern Africa partially cuts off

ON WHAT continent did the modern human species (*homo sapiens*) originate?

savannah An area of open woodlands and grassy plains.

Sahel An area of steppe and semi-desert that borders the Sahara.

Sahara The world's largest desert. It extends across Africa from the Atlantic to the eastern Sudan. Historically, the Sahara has hindered contact between the Mediterranean and sub-Saharan Africa.

Kalahari A large desert in southwestern Africa that partially isolates southern Africa from the rest of the continent.

the southern plateau and coastal regions from central Africa.

Other natural factors are of importance to Africa's history. Its soils contain meager amounts of humus, or vegetable mold. Because they are easily leached of mineral and nutrient content, they are not highly productive for extended periods. Water shortage is another perennial problem for agriculture in most of Africa and a potent factor in its history. Crop pests and insects have also hampered both farming and pastoralism in Africa; the tsetse fly has blocked the spread of domesticated cattle and horses to the forested portions of the continent. However, in most regions Africa's abundant animal life has always been a major resource sustaining hunting and fishing.

Africa has great mineral wealth, and this has long stimulated trade. The market for salt, for example, was motivating merchants to cross the Sahara, linking the western Sudan with North Africa, as early as the first millennium C.E. Iron, copper, and gold were also traded in significant quantities.

The African continent contains seven distinct regions:

1. *North Africa*—the Mediterranean coastal regions from modern Morocco through modern Libya and the northern Sahara, including the Sahel that marks the transition from mountains to true desert.

2. **Nilotic Africa** (i.e., the lands of the Nile), roughly the area of modern Egypt and Sudan.

3. *The Sudan*, the broad belt of Sahel and savannah below the Sahara, stretching from the Atlantic east across the entire continent.

4. *West Africa*, including the woodland coastal regions and the desert, Sahel, and savannah of the western Sudan as far east as the Lake Chad basin.

5. *East Africa*, from the Ethiopian highlands south over modern Kenya and Tanzania.

6. *Central Africa*, the region north of the Kalahari, from the Chad basin across the Zaïre basin and southeast to Lake Tanganyika and south to the Zambezi River.

7. *Southern Africa*, from the Kalahari desert and Zambezi south to the Cape of Good Hope.

AFRICAN PEOPLES

AFRICA AND EARLY HUMAN CULTURE

Archaeological research indicates that our ancestors evolved in the Great Rift region of highland East Africa at least 1.5 to 1.8 million years ago. It was probably also here that, sometime before 100,000 B.C.E., modern humans—the species *homo sapiens* (*sapiens*)—appeared and moved out to populate the rest of Africa and the world.

Excavation in Progress at Blombos Cave, South Africa. The recent discovery of bone tools, decorated ochre blocks, and polished spear points that have been dated to about 70,000 years ago indicate that earliest evidence of tools and artwork come from Africa.

National Science Foundation.

Nilotic Africa The lands along the Nile River.

WHAT EVIDENCE is there that early African cultures were in contact with each other?

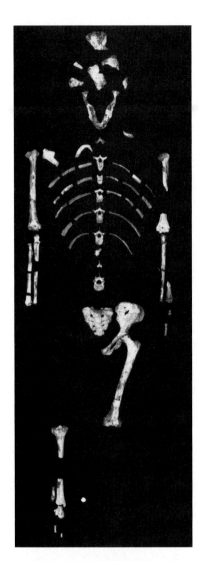

"Lucy." One of the most famous fossils found in the north end of the Great Rift Valley, an area rich in fossils of species ancestral to humans, Lucy represents one of the earliest species to walk upright.

Cleveland Museum of Natural History.

HOW DID the Sahara impact the early history of Africa?

The once popular view of sub-Saharan Africa as a vast region isolated from civilization until its "discovery" by Europeans distorts reality. Although its interior and southern reaches were isolated from direct contact with Eurasia until relatively recent times, African goods circulated for centuries through Indian Ocean and Mediterranean trade. Archaeological research documents the existence and substantial internal movements of peoples—and hence languages, cultures, and technologies—both north-south and east-west within the continent in ancient times.

DIFFUSION OF LANGUAGES AND PEOPLES

Despite continental barriers, Africans have not been separated from one another. As many as 3,000 languages or dialects are spoken in Africa. The precolonial tongues belong to four major families: Afro-Asiatic, Nilo-Saharan, Niger-Kongo, and "Khoisan." The first originated near the Red Sea and includes Arabic, Hebrew, Aramaic, Syriac, ancient Egyptian, and other tongues spoken in north and northeastern Africa. The second is found from the upper reaches of the Nile across the Sahara to Moroccan highlands. The third lie in a belt west and south of this region, and the fourth is found today in southern Africa. The Afro-Asiatic tongues probably began to spread from the Jordan and Nile valleys across North Africa about 8000 B.C.E. The Nilo-Saharan languages may have originated in the Nubian region and spread west about 5000 B.C.E. The Niger-Kongo family appeared in the forested districts of west and central Africa. Its largest subgroup, the Bantu speakers, spread southward through equatorial and rain forests to the savannahs. Khoisan at one time covered most of the southern half of the continent, but yielded much of its territory to the Bantu language.

RACIAL DISTINCTIONS

In recent times lighter-skinned Caucasoid Africans have predominated in the Sahara, North Africa, and Egypt and darker-skinned Negroid peoples have been the majority in the rest of the continent. The Greeks called Negroid people *Ethiopians*, "burnt skins," and the Arabs referred to sub-Saharan Africa as *Bilad al-Sudan*, "Land of the Blacks." Attempts have been made to link race with cultural and historical developments, but race itself is a problematic concept, and African populations are so mixed that most Africans are best seen as members of one race or none—regardless of color or physical attributes.

THE SAHARA AND THE SUDAN TO THE BEGINNING OF THE COMMON ERA

EARLY SAHARAN CULTURES

One of the most striking and imposing physical features of the African continent is the Sahara. Since the second millennium B.C.E., this vast arid wilderness has separated the North African and Egyptian worlds from the wide expanse of the Sudan and, farther south, West and central Africa. Still, this desert barrier never fully blocked north-south contact and exchange. The Nile valley and the Great Rift plateau provided one corridor for movement of ideas and peoples south to north and vice versa. Similarly, the Red Sea, the Atlantic and Indian Ocean coasts, and a few routes through the Sahara itself allowed people, goods, and ideas to breach the great Saharan barrier as far back as our evidence takes us.

What is hard to imagine, however, is that until about 2500 B.C.E. the Sahara was arable land with lakes and rivers, trees, grasses, and a reasonable climate.

Then climatic changes caused the Sahara to undergo a relatively rapid desiccation. By 1000 B.C.E., the drying-up process had made the Sahara an immense east-west expanse of largely uninhabitable desert, separating the greater part of the African continent from the Mediterranean coastal rim and the Middle Eastern centers of early civilization.

NEOLITHIC SUDANIC CULTURES

Most interesting to speculate about are the repercussions of the Saharan desiccation for later settled communities, especially those in the Sahel and savannah of the Sudan. From the first millennium B.C.E., preliterate, but complex agricultural communities with Neolithic and early Iron Age cultures dotted the central and western reaches of the great belt of the sub-Saharan Sudan. We may surmise that these peoples had once been spread farther north in the then-arable Saharan lands that they would then have shared with ancestors of the Berber-speaking peoples of contemporary west-Saharan and North Africa.

OVERVIEW   THE GEOGRAPHY OF AFRICA

Geography has played a large role in the history and culture of Africa, limiting its contacts with non-African peoples and influencing patterns of trade and settlement. Africa is divided into a number of geographical zones and cultural regions.

North Africa	The region along the Mediterranean coast, extending from Morocco in the west to Egypt in the east. This area has long had extensive contacts with Europe and the Near East and has been dominated by Islam since the seventh century C.E.
Sahara	The world's largest desert. It extends across Africa from the Atlantic to the eastern Sudan. Historically, the Sahara has hindered contact between the Mediterranean and sub-Saharan Africa.
Sahel	An area of steppe and semidesert that borders the Sahara.
Savannah	Areas of open woodlands and grassy plains that border the Sahel.
Rain forests	Large areas of dense vegetation along the equator and much of the West African coast.
Kalahari	A large desert in southwestern Africa that partially isolates southern Africa from the rest of the continent.
Nilotic Africa	The lands along the Nile River Valley. It extends from the Mediterranean coast of Egypt south to include the modern Republic of Sudan and Ethiopia. Historically, it has been one of the African regions most open to outside cultural, religious, and economic influences.
Sudan	The broad belt of savannah and Sahel below the Sahara that extends east across the continent from the Atlantic.
West Africa	The woodland coastal regions, savannah, Sahel, and desert that extends as far east as the Lake Chad basin. Many of the slaves caught up in the Atlantic slave trade from the 16th to the 19th centuries came from this region.
East Africa	Extends from Ethiopia south over modern Kenya and Tanzania. Historically, East Africa has had extensive trade and cultural contacts with Arabia and east Asia.
Central Africa	Extends from the Chad basin across the Congo to Lake Tanganyika and the Zambezi River.
Southern Africa	Extends from the Kalahari desert and the Zambesi River south to the Cape of Good Hope.

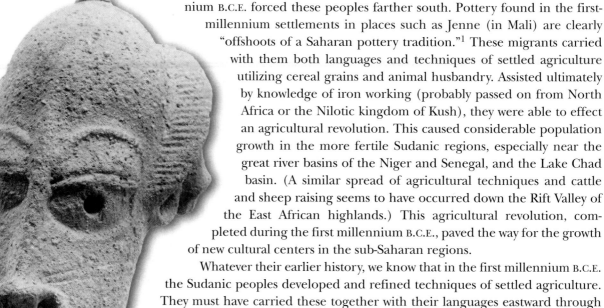

A Terra-cotta Head. This is from the Iron Age Nok culture, which occupied what is today northeastern Nigeria from about 900 B.C.E. to about 200 C.E.

© Werner Forman Archive/Art Resource, N.Y./ Jos Museum, Nigeria.

One theory proposes that the progressive desiccation of the second millennium B.C.E. forced these peoples farther south. Pottery found in the first-millennium settlements in places such as Jenne (in Mali) are clearly "offshoots of a Saharan pottery tradition."[1] These migrants carried with them both languages and techniques of settled agriculture utilizing cereal grains and animal husbandry. Assisted ultimately by knowledge of iron working (probably passed on from North Africa or the Nilotic kingdom of Kush), they were able to effect an agricultural revolution. This caused considerable population growth in the more fertile Sudanic regions, especially near the great river basins of the Niger and Senegal, and the Lake Chad basin. (A similar spread of agricultural techniques and cattle and sheep raising seems to have occurred down the Rift Valley of the East African highlands.) This agricultural revolution, completed during the first millennium B.C.E., paved the way for the growth of new cultural centers in the sub-Saharan regions.

Whatever their earlier history, we know that in the first millennium B.C.E. the Sudanic peoples developed and refined techniques of settled agriculture. They must have carried these together with their languages eastward through the savannahs and southward, largely along the rivers, into the tropical rain forests of central and West Africa. This changed the face of sub-Saharan Africa, which previously had been dominated by small groups of hunter-gatherers. Knowledge of iron smelting enabled these settled peoples to develop larger and more complex societies than their predecessors.

THE EARLY IRON AGE AND THE NOK CULTURE

Common features of the oldest iron-smelting furnaces found in widely scattered sites across Africa suggest that Africa's iron-working technology was invented within the continent, probably in Egypt and Nubia, or possibly in the central Saharan highlands of the Tibesti, Ahaggar, and Aïr. Thence it likely spread southward into western, central, and eastern regions. Some of the most significant Iron Age sites have been found in northeastern Nigeria. Near the village of Jos, archaeological digs have yielded evidence of an Iron Age people, the Nok culture, dating between 900 B.C.E. and 200 C.E. The Nok people cleared substantial woodlands from the plateau and practiced both agriculture and cattleherding.

The Nok culture is significant for two reasons. First, the Nok people, who mastered the relatively difficult art of smelting as early as 500 B.C.E., had the earliest Iron Age culture in West Africa, and their probable acquisition of this art by way of the Aïr Mountains to the north is evidence of early contacts among African cultures. Second, Nok culture offers extraordinary sculptural art, most vividly evident in magnificent burial or ritual masks. The apparent continuities of Nok sculptural traditions with those of other, later West African cultures to the south suggest that this culture had an important impact on later West and central African life. These continuities indicate that ancient communities of considerable sophistication laid a foundation for subsequent, better-known Sudanic civilizations. (See Map 5–1.)

[1]S. J. and R. J. McIntosh, *Prehistoric Investigations at Jenne, Mali* (Oxford, U.K.: B.A.R., 1980), p. 436.

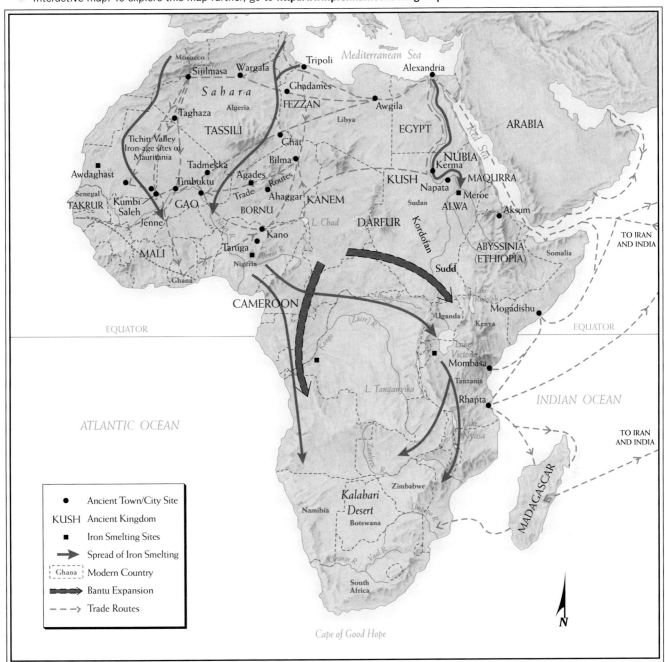

MAP 5–1
Ancient African Kingdoms and Empires.

WHAT EFFECT did the migrations of people and the spread of technology have on early African history?

Meroitic Pottery. The people of Meroe produced many examples of fine pottery. This fired clay jar is decorated with giraffes and serpents.

University of Pennsylvania Museum of Archaelogy and Anthropology.

NILOTIC AFRICA AND THE ETHIOPIAN HIGHLANDS

THE KINGDOM OF KUSH

The land of Kush lies in the upper Nile basin, just above the first cataract. It was here that an Egyptianized segment of Nilo-Saharan-speaking Nubians built the earliest (except for Pharaonic Egypt) known literate and politically unified civilization in Africa. The Old Kingdom pharaohs subjugated and colonized Nubia, but in the early second millennium B.C.E., an independent kingdom arose in Kush just above the third cataract of the Nile. As early as 2000 B.C.E., its capital, Kerma, had become a major trading outpost for Middle Kingdom Egypt.

The early Kushite kingdom reached its zenith in the years between the Middle and New Kingdoms of Egypt about 1700–1500 B.C.E. It appears to have been wealthy and prosperous by any standard. Egypt's revival under the pharaohs of the New Kingdom restored Egyptian colonial rule in Nubia and hence stronger Egyptian influences. Then, sometime after 1000 B.C.E., as the New Kingdom floundered, a new Kushite state reasserted itself. By about 900 B.C.E. it had conquered lower as well as upper Nubia.

THE NAPATAN EMPIRE

This new Kushite empire, with its center first at Napata and then at Meroe, survived from the 10th century B.C.E. until the fourth century C.E., when the Ethiopian Aksumites replaced Kush as the dominant power in northeastern Africa. It was the true successor to Pharaonic Egypt. The kings who ruled at Napata saw themselves as Egyptian. They practiced the Pharaonic custom of marrying their sisters. They embalmed their royalty and buried them in pyramids in traditional Egyptian style. They used Egyptian protocol and titles. In the eighth century B.C.E., they conquered Egypt and ruled it for about a century as its Twenty-Fifth Dynasty. The Kushite pharaohs were driven out of Egypt proper by Assyria around the middle of the seventh century B.C.E. (see "Kushite Conquest of Memphis").

THE MEROITIC EMPIRE

Forced back above the lower cataracts of the Nile by the Assyrians and kept there by the Persians, the Napatan kingdom became increasingly isolated and evolved in distinctive ways. After Napata was sacked by an Egyptian army in 591 B.C.E., Meroe became the kingdom's political and cultural capital. In the sixth century B.C.E., it was the center of a flourishing iron industry, which may have spread knowledge of iron smelting west and south to the sub-Saharan world. Certainly the Kushites traded widely to the west across the Sudan as well as with the Hellenistic world and beyond. The Meroitic state maintained a wide network of internal African and external, intercontinental commercial relations. The empire survived until it was defeated and divided in the fourth century C.E. by Nuba peoples from west of the upper Nile. It was replaced as the dominant regional power by a rival trading state, Aksum on the Abyssinian plateau.

Culture and Economy The heyday of Meroitic culture was from the mid-third century B.C.E. to the first century C.E. The kingdom mediated various African goods to the Mediterranean and Near East: animal skins, ebony

HISTORY'S VOICES

KUSHITE CONQUEST OF MEMPHIS

T*he following text comes from a granite pillar, a victory stela that the Kushite king Piankhi had erected near Napata to commemorate his conquest of Egypt in the decade before 750 B.C.E. It describes the siege and capture of Memphis.*

WHAT ELEMENTS in the description might be slight exaggerations or hyperbole rather than sober chronicling?

When day broke, at early morning, his majesty reached Memphis. When he had landed on the north of it, he found that the water had approached to the walls, the ships mooring at [the walls of] Memphis. Then his majesty saw that it was strong, and that the wall was raised by a new rampart, and battlements manned with mighty men. There was found no way of attacking it. Every man told his opinion among the army of his majesty, according to every rule of war. Every man said: "Let us besiege it—; lo, its troops are numerous." Others said: "Let a causeway be made against it; let us elevate the ground to its walls. Let us bind together a tower; let us erect masts and make the spars into a bridge to it. We will divide it on this [plan] on every side of it, on the high ground and on the north of it, in order to elevate the ground at its walls, that we may find a way for our feet."

Then his majesty was enraged against it like a panther; he said: "I swear, as Re loves me, as my father, Amon (who fashioned me), favors me, this shall befall it, according to the command of Amon . . . I will take it like a flood of water. I have commanded . . ." Then he sent forth his fleet and his army to assault the harbor of Memphis; they brought to him every ferryboat, every (cargo) boat, every (transport), and the ships, as many as there were, which had moored in the harbor of Memphis, with the bow-rope fastened among its houses. [There was not] a citizen who wept, among all the soldiers of his majesty.

His majesty himself came to line up the ships, as many as there were. His majesty commanded his army: "Forward against it! Mount the walls! Penetrate the houses over the river. If one of you gets through upon the wall, let him not halt before it (so that) the (hostile) troops may not repulse you . . ."

Then Memphis was taken as (by) a flood of water, a multitude of people were slain therein, and brought as living captives to the place where his majesty was.

Source: J. H. Breasted, *Ancient Records of Egypt* (Chicago: University of Chicago Press, 1906), Vol. 4, pars. 861 ff. Reprinted in Basil Davidson, *The African Past* (New York: Grosset and Dunlap, 1967), pp. 51–52.

and ivory, gold, oils and perfumes, and slaves. The Kushites traded with the Hellenistic-Roman world, southern Arabia, and India. They shipped high-quality iron to Aksum and the Red Sea, and the Kushite lands between the Nile and the Red Sea were a major source of gold for Egypt and the Mediterranean world. Cattle breeding, other animal husbandry, and agriculture were their economic mainstays. Cotton cultivation in Kush preceded that of Egypt and may have been an early export.

Many monuments were built, including royal pyramids and the storied palace and walls of the capital. Meroitic culture is especially renowned for two kinds of pottery: The first was wheel-turned by males and attuned apparently to market demands; the second was hand-thrown by women largely for domestic use. This latter pottery seems to have come from an older tradition of African pottery craft found well outside the region of Kush—an indication of ancient traditions shared among regions of Africa and of the antiquity of internal trade within Africa.

Early African Civilizations

ca. 7500–2500 B.C.E.	"Wet Holocene" period
ca. 2500 B.C.E.	Rapid desiccation of Saharan region begins
ca. 2000–1000 B.C.E.	Increasing Egyptian influence in Nubia
ca. 1000–900 B.C.E.	Kushite kingdom with capital at Napata becomes independent of Egypt
751–663 B.C.E.	Kushite kings Piankhi and Taharqa rule all Egypt
ca. 600–500 B.C.E.	Meroe becomes new Kushite capital
ca. 500 B.C.E.–330 C.E.	Meroitic kingdom of Kush (height of Meroitic Kushite power ca. 250 B.C.E.–50 C.E.)
ca. 500 B.C.E.–500 C.E.?	Nok culture flourishes on Jos plateau in western Sudan (modern central Nigeria)
First century C.E.	Rise of Aksum as trading power on Ethiopian (Abyssinian) plateau
ca. 330 C.E.	Aksumite conquest of Kush

Nilotic Africa and the Ethiopian Highlands

ca. 500 B.C.E.	Yemenites (southern Arabians) enter and settle the Ethiopian plateau
30 B.C.E.	Egypt becomes part of Roman Empire of Octavian
ca. 1–100 C.E.	Earliest mention (in Latin and Greek writers) of the kingdom of Aksum on Ethiopian plateau
ca. 330 B.C.E.	Fall of Kushite empire to Ezana of Aksum
ca. 200–400 C.E.	Heyday of Aksumite Ethiopia
ca. 500–600 C.E.	Christianizing of the major Nubian states of Maqurra and Alwa
652 C.E.	Maqurra and Alwa make peace with Arab Muslim armies from Egypt

Rule and Administration The political system of the Meroitic Empire, like the Pharaonic, was evidently stable over many centuries. Although the king was considered a living god—an idea found in both ancient Egypt and many other African societies—he seems to have ruled by customary law. According to Greek accounts, his actions were limited by firm taboos. Royal succession was not from father to son, but it stayed within the royal family, often passing through the maternal rather than the paternal line. (Evidence suggests that matrilineal succession was a widespread norm in ancient Africa.) Succession to the throne was by election. The priests presented several candidates for king, from whom the god would choose the heir. (We are not told how.) The role of the queen mother in the election appears to have been crucial—another parallel to African practices elsewhere. Indeed, the queen mother seems to have adopted her son's wife upon his succession. In the second century B.C.E., a woman became monarch and initiated a long line of queens.

We know very little about Meroitic administration. The empire seems to have been under the autocratic control of its sovereign, perhaps on the Egyptian model. He or she presided over a central administration run by numerous high officials. The provinces were delegated to princes.

Society and Religion Limited sources mean that we can only speculate about social groups outside the ruling class of monarch, royal relatives, priests, courtiers, and nobles. Slaves are mentioned, most commonly female domestics, but there were also male laborers taken as prisoners of war. Cattle breeders, farmers, traders, artisans, and minor government functionaries probably formed an intermediate class or classes between slaves and rulers.

Kushite religious practices followed Egyptian traditions for centuries. To judge from the great temples dedicated to him, Amon was the highest god for the earlier kings. By the third century B.C.E., however, gods unknown to Egypt rose in importance alongside Amon and the Egyptian gods. Most notable was Apedemak, a warrior god with a lion's head. The many lion temples associated with him reflect his importance. Such gods were likely local deities who grew increasingly popular.

THE AKSUMITE EMPIRE

A highland people who had developed their own commercially powerful trading state to the south of Kush delivered the final blow to the weakened Kushite Empire, apparently about 330 C.E. This was the newly Christianized state of Aksum, which centered in the northern Ethiopian, or Abyssinian, highlands where the Blue Nile rises. With the ascendancy of Aksum, our sources lapse into relative silence concerning the Nubian regions of the Nile. Not until the rise of Christian Nubian states in the mid-sixth century is there again much information about the heirs to the land of Kush.

The peoples of Aksum were the product of a linguistic, cultural, and genetic mixing of African Kushitic speakers with Semitic speakers from Yemenite southern Arabia. This mixing occurred after southern Arabians settled on the Ethiopian plateau around 500 B.C.E., giving Aksum, and later Ethiopia, Semitic speech and script closely related to South Arabian. Greek and Roman sources attest to the existence of an Aksumite kingdom from at least the first century C.E. By this time, the kingdom, through its chief port of Adulis, had already become the major ivory and elephant market of northeastern Africa.

In the first two centuries C.E., its location on the Red Sea made Aksum a strategic site on the increasingly important Indian Ocean trade routes that linked India and the East Indies, Iran, Arabia, and the East African coast with the Roman Mediterranean. Aksum also controlled trade between the African interior and the extra-African world, from Rome to Southeast Asia—notably exports of ivory, but also of elephants, obsidian, slaves, gold dust, and other inland products.

By the third century C.E., Aksum was one of the most impressive states of its age in the African or western Asian world, as the remains of its major cities—Aksum, Adulis, and Matara—attest. From the late second century onward, the Aksumites often held tributary territories across the Red Sea in southern Arabia. They also gained control of northern Ethiopia and conquered Meroitic Kush. Thus, by the third and fourth centuries they controlled some of the most fertile cultivated regions of the ancient world: their own plateau, the rich Yemenite highlands of southern Arabia, and much of the eastern Sudan across the upper Nile as far as the Sahara.

The resulting empire was ruled by a king of kings in Aksum through tribute-paying vassal kings in the other subject states. Aksum's minting of gold, silver, and copper coins (the first by a tropical African state) indicate its political and economic power. Goods from the Roman-Byzantine world and India and Sri Lanka, as well as of neighboring Meroe, flowed into Aksum, and its vast herds and good agricultural land helped to ensure its prosperity.

The pre-Christian paganism of Aksum resembled the pre-Islamic paganism of southern Arabia, with various gods and goddesses associated with natural phenomena such as the sun, moon, and stars. There is also evidence that Jewish, Meroitic, and even Buddhist minorities lived in the major cities of Aksum—an indication of its cosmopolitanism.

An inscription from the reign of the powerful fourth-century king, Ezana, records his conversion to Christianity, the start of the Christianizing of the kingdom

A Giant Stela at Aksum. Dating probably from the first century C.E., this giant carved monolith is the only one remaining of seven giant stelae—the tallest of which reached a height of 33 meters—that once stood in Aksum amid numerous smaller monoliths. Although the exact purpose of the stelae is not known, the generally accepted explanation is that they were commemorative funerary monuments. Erecting them required engineering of great sophistication.

Werner Former Archive/Art Resource, N.Y.

as a whole. This was the work of Frumentius, a Syrian bishop of Aksum who served as secretary and treasurer to the king. Subsequently, under Alexandrian influence, the Ethiopian church embraced the Monophysite belief that Christ had only one, divine nature. Constantinople persecuted Monophysites within its empire, but religious disagreement did not hamper its trade with Aksum. In the fifth century C.E., the native Semitic language, Ge'ez, began to replace Greek in the liturgy, a major step toward the development of a distinctive Ethiopic or Abyssinian Christian Church.

ISOLATION OF CHRISTIAN ETHIOPIA

Aksumite trade continued to thrive through the sixth century, despite the decay of Rome. Strong enough at times to extend to the Yemen, Aksumite power was eclipsed in the end by the rise of Arab Islamic power. Aksum ceased to be a center of foreign trade and became increasingly isolated. Its center of gravity shifted south from the coast to the more rugged parts of the plateau. There, surrounded largely by Muslim peoples, a Monophysite Christian, Ge'ez-speaking culture emerged (modern Ethiopia) and survived in relative isolation until modern times.

Ethiopia's northern neighbors, the Christian states of Maqurra and Alwa, also survived for centuries in the former Meroitic lands of the Nilotic Sudan. However, incursions from Muslim Egypt in the 14th and 15th centuries and Arab migration from about 1300 led ultimately to the Islamization of the whole Nubian region. Ethiopia was left as the sole predominantly Christian state in Africa.

THE WESTERN AND CENTRAL SUDAN

AGRICULTURE, TRADE, AND THE RISE OF URBAN CENTERS

By the first or second century C.E., most of the inhabitants of the western Sudan had become settled farmers using iron tools, and their way of life was spreading into forest regions farther south. The savannah areas seem to have experienced a substantial population explosion, especially around major water sources: along the Senegal River, around the great northern bend in the Niger River, and in the Lake Chad basin. The largest political organizations remained villages or chiefdoms consisting of several villages. As time went on, their growth led to the development of larger towns and political units.

Trade promoted, or accompanied, the eventual rise of larger political entities in the western and central Sudan. Regional and interregional trade networks here date to ancient times. Extensive east-west trade connected the western Sahel to Egypt and the Nilotic Sudan. From the western Sahel, traders also found Saharan routes leading to the north (see Map 5–2).

By the latter half of the first millennium B.C.E., substantial urban settlements—such as Gao, Kumbi (or Kumbi Saleh), and Jenne—had emerged in the western Sahel. Excavations at Jenne, in the upper Niger (the so-called Inland Delta), date settlement there from 250 B.C.E. and indicate that its population reached more than 10,000 by the late first millennium C.E.[2]

> **WHAT ROLE** did trade play in the rise of large political entities in the western and central Sudan?

The Western and Central Sudan: Probable Dates for Founding of Regional Kingdoms

ca. 400 C.E.	Takrur (Senegal River valley) or earlier
400–600 C.E.	Ghana (in Sahel between great northern bends of the Senegal and Niger Rivers)
ca. 700–800 C.E.	Gao (on the Niger River or before southeast of great bend)
ca. 700–900 C.E.	Kanem (northeast of Lake Chad)

[2]S. J. and R. J. McIntosh, pp. 41–59, 434–461; and R. Oliver, *The African Experience* (1991) pp. 90–101.

MAP 5–2
Africa: Early Trade Routes and Early States of the Western and Central Sudan.   This map shows some of the major routes of north–south trans-Saharan caravan trade and their links with Egypt and with Sudanic and forest regions of West Africa.

HOW DID Africa's geography help determine its trade routes?

These early urbanized areas were supported by a mix of farming, fishing, and hunting. All of them developed in oasis or river regions rich enough to sustain dense populations and trade. Over time, the relatively autonomous settlements formed loose confederations or widely dispersed imperial networks.

The introduction of the domesticated camel from the east around the beginning of the Christian era greatly increased the viability of trans-Saharan trade. By the early Christian centuries, the West African settled communities had developed trading centers of considerable importance on their northern

QUICK REVIEW

Trade
• Trade contributed to rise of larger political entities
• Regional and interregional trade networks date to ancient times
• Trade routes connected western and central Sudan with Egypt

A Camel Caravan Crossing the Sahara.
Use of the camel as a beast of burden
from the first century C.E. onward
greatly increased trans-Saharan trade.

© Michael S. Lewis/Corbis.

WHY DID the coastal and inland
regions of East Africa have
different histories?

peripheries in the Sahel near the edge of the true
desert. Salt and gold were the prime commodities
exchanged.

Towns such as Awdaghast, Walata, Timbuktu,
Gao, Tadmekka, and Agades were the most famous
southern terminals for trade over the centuries.
These centers allowed the largely Berber middlemen who plied the desert routes to cross the ever-
dangerous Sahara via oasis stations en route to the
North African coasts and Egypt. Because a typical
crossing could take two to three months, this was
not an easy route for transporting goods.

FORMATION OF SUDANIC KINGDOMS IN THE FIRST MILLENNIUM

The first millennium C.E. saw the growth of settled
agricultural populations and the expansion of
trans-Saharan and other internal trade. These
developments coincided with the rise of sizable
states in the western and central Sudan. The most important of these were
located in Takrur on the Senegal River, from the fifth century or earlier; Ghana,
between the northern bends of the Senegal and the Niger, from the fifth or
sixth century; Gao, on the Niger southeast of the great bend, from before the
eighth century; and Kanem, northeast of Lake Chad, from the eighth or ninth
century. Each represents the first of a series of large political entities in its
region. All continued to figure prominently in subsequent West African history
(see Chapter 18).

The states developed by the Fulbe people of Takrur and the Soninke people of Ghana thrived by obtaining gold for the Saharan trade with Morocco from
the savannah region west of the upper Senegal. Of all the sub-Saharan kingdoms
of the late first millennium, Ghana was the most famous outside of the region,
thanks to the major role it played in the gold trade. Its people built a large
regional empire with its capital at Kumbi (or Kumbi Saleh). Its throne passed
through matrilineal descent, and its king was regarded as semidivine. The king's
subjects approached him through a hierarchy of government ministers. In contrast to the Soninke of Ghana, the Songhai rulers of Gao had no gold trade until
the 14th century, and Gao, unlike its western neighbors, was oriented through its
forest trade routes toward the lower, not the upper, Niger basin and in its
Saharan ties toward eastern Algeria, not Morocco.

These states were supported by settled, farming populations. By contrast,
the power of Kanem, on the northwestern side of Lake Chad, originated in the
borderlands of the central Sudan and southern Sahara from a nomadic federation of black tribal peoples that persisted long enough for the separate tribes to
merge as a single people, the Kanuri. Their kingdom controlled the southern
terminus of perhaps the best trans-Saharan route—that running north via good
watering stations to the oasis region of Fezzan in modern central Libya and
thence to the Mediterranean (see Chapter 17).

CENTRAL, SOUTHERN, AND EAST AFRICA

The African subcontinent is the part of central, southern, and East Africa that lies
south of a line from roughly the Niger delta and Cameroon across to southern

Somalia on the east coast. Paucity of sources makes it difficult to reconstruct in any detail the history of this region before 1,000 C.E. Some relatively certain facts and reasonable hypotheses have, however, emerged from linguistic, archaeological, and other research.

BANTU MIGRATIONS AND DIFFUSION

In the southern subcontinent, most people speak one of more than four hundred languages that belong to a single language group known as *Bantu*. These languages are as closely related as are the Germanic or Romance tongues of Europe. Although the place of origin and routes of diffusion of Bantu tongues have long been debated, there is increasing consensus that the location of the proto-Bantu language was the region south of the Benue River, in eastern Nigeria and modern Cameroon. During the later centuries B.C.E. and the first millennium C.E., migrations of Bantu-speaking peoples must have carried their languages in two basic directions: (1) south into the lower Zaïre (Kongo) basin and ultimately to the southern edge of the equatorial forest in present-day northern Katanga; and (2) east around the equatorial forests into the lakes of highland East Africa. How the Bantu peoples managed to impose their languages on the earlier cultures of these regions remains unexplained. In any case, Bantu cultures became fully interwoven with those of the peoples among whom they settled. For example, Bantu-Arab mixing on the eastern coasts produced the Swahili culture (see Chapter 18). We find Bantu-speaking peoples as slash-and-burn farmers in the Zaïre River savannah, as cattle herders in the East African high plains, as perennial floodplain cultivators on the Zambezi River, and as terracing and irrigating farmers among the highland Kikuyu and Chagga peoples.

EAST AFRICA

The history of East Africa along the coast before Islam differed from that of the inland highlands. Long-distance travel was easy and common along the seashore but less so inland. The coast had had maritime contact with India, Arabia, and the Mediterranean via the Indian Ocean and Red Sea trade routes from at least as early as the second century B.C.E. By contrast, we know little about the long-distance contacts of inland regions with the coastal areas until after 1000 C.E. Nonetheless, both regional inland and coastal trade must also be ancient. Both coastal and overseas trade remained important and interdependent over the centuries, because the Indian Ocean trade depended on the monsoon winds and could, therefore, use only the northernmost coastal trading harbors of East Africa for round-trip voyages in the same year. The monsoon winds blow from the northeast from December to March and thus can carry sailing ships south from Iran, Arabia, and India only during those months; the winds blow from the southwest from April to August, so ships can sail from Africa northeast during those months. Local coastal shipping had to haul cargoes from south of Zanzibar and then transfer them to other ships for the annual round-trip voyages to Arabia and beyond.

Long-distance trade came into its own in Islamic times—about the ninth century—as an Arab monopoly. However, long before the coming of

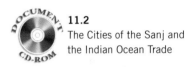

11.2
The Cities of the Sanj and the Indian Ocean Trade

Prehistoric San rock painting from southern Africa.

Christopher and Sally Gable© Dorling Kindersley.

Islam, trade was apparently largely in Arab hands. Many Arabs had settled in the East African coastal towns and in Iran and India to handle this international commerce. We have documentation of Greco-Roman contact with these East African centers of Red Sea and Indian Ocean trade from as early as the first century C.E.

Overseas trade was, however, evidently even more international than the earliest sources indicate. Today, Malagasy, the imported Malayo-Polynesian language of Madagascar, points to the antiquity of substantial contact with the East Indies via the coastal trading routes of Asia's ancient southern rim. Evidence of an Indonesian migration even before the beginning of our era is seen in the spread of bananas, coconut palms, and other food crops indigenous to Southeast Asia across the entire African continent as staple foods. Further, as a result of the early regular commercial ties to distant lands of Asia, extra-African ethnic and cultural mixing has long been the rule for the East African coast; even today, its linguistic and cultural traditions are rich and varied (see Chapter 18).

Other African imports included Persian Gulf pottery, Chinese porcelain, and cotton cloth. The major African export, around which the east coast trade revolved, was ivory. The slave trade was also important. Slaves were exported to the Arab and Persian world, as well as to India or China.

The history of inland East Africa south of Ethiopia is much more difficult to trace than that of the coast, again because of the absence of written sources and the immense difficulty of access until relatively recent times. We can, however, infer from linguistic clues and other evidence some key developments in the eastern highlands. These regions had seen an early diffusion of peoples from the north, and changing conditions of subsistence over the centuries continued to propel movements of small groups into new areas. Of the early migrants from the north, first came peoples speaking Kushitic languages of the Afro-Asiatic family, likely cattle herders and grain cultivators. Perhaps as early as 2000 B.C.E., they pushed from their homeland on the Ethiopian plateau south down the Rift Valley as far as the southern end of Lake Tanganyika.

Later, by about 1000 C.E., Nilotic-Saharan speakers moved from the southwestern side of the Ethiopian plateau west over the upper Nile valley. Then they pushed east and south, following older Kushite paths, to spread across the Rift Valley area (by the 15th century) and subsequently much of the East African highlands of modern-day Uganda, Kenya, and Tanzania. Here they all but completely supplanted their Kushite predecessors. Two of these Nilotic peoples were the Lwo and Maasai. The Lwo populated over a 900-mile-long swath of modern Uganda and parts of southern Sudan and western Kenya. They mixed readily with other peoples, absorbing new cultural elements and adapting to new situations wherever they went. The Maasai, on the other hand, were and still are cattle pastoralists fiercely proud of their separate language, way of life, and cultural traditions. These features have distinguished them sharply from the farming or hunting peoples whose settlements abutted their pasturages at the top of the southern Rift Valley in modern Kenya and Tanzania. Here, the Maasai have concentrated and remained.

These migrations from the north and those of the Bantu peoples, who also entered the eastern highlands over

Movement and Contact of Peoples in Central, Southern, and East Africa

ca. 1300–1000 B.C.E.	Kushitic-speaking peoples migrate from Ethiopian plateau south along Rift Valley
ca. 400 B.C.E.–1000 C.E.	Probable era of major Bantu migrations into central, East, and southeastern Africa
200–100 B.C.E.	East African coast becomes involved in Indian Ocean and Red Sea trade
ca. 100 B.C.E.	Probable time of first Indonesian immigration to East African coast
ca. 100–1500 C.E.	Nilotic-speaking peoples spread over upper Nile valley; Nilotic peoples spread over Rift Valley region

many centuries from the west, have made the highlands a melting pot for an immense diversity of languages and cultures. Here the radical diversity of peoples and cultures of the entire African continent is mirrored by a single region.

SUMMARY

Geography and History The human species, *homo sapiens* (*sapiens*) probably originated in Africa. Africa's geography and climate limited Africans' contact with peoples outside the continent and their development and preservation of historical records. Nonetheless, Africa does have a significant history. Archaeology produces evidence for extensive migrations of peoples across the continent from the earliest times diffusing cross-cultural influences throughout huge regions.

Contact with Other Cultures In three parts of Africa, there was considerable contact with non-African civilizations. In the Nile River valley, Egypt had extensive interaction with the Nubian peoples to its south. Nubian kingdoms—Kush, Napata, Meroe, and Axum (Ethiopia)—adopted many features of Egyptian civilization and sometimes dominated Egypt itself. Axum adopted Christianity in the fourth century C.E.

On the coast of East Africa, trade across the Red Sea and the Indian Ocean with Arabia and east Asia fostered a distinct and sophisticated culture. Extensive trade across the Sahara between North Africa and the western and central Sudan enabled products and ideas from the Mediterranean to reach the African interior in exchange for African products, such as gold, ivory, and salt.

IMAGE KEY
for pages 104–105

a. Great battle of Archers
b. Cave painting-prehistory; women gathering grain
c. Camel
d. Nigeria, Nok head
e. Homo habilis skull (reconstructed)
f. Cattle in a Saharan rock painting from Tassili n'Ajjer
g. Ruins of pyramids in ancient kingdom of Kush-Sudan
h. A carving from the ancient site of Great Zimbabwe
i. A giant stela at Aksum; perhaps a funerary monument
j. A Saharan camel train

REVIEW QUESTIONS

1. Were early African societies truly civilized? What unique conditions hamper current understanding of their histories?

2. How did the diffusion of peoples and languages affect early African history?

3. How did the political systems of the Meroitic Empire and Egypt compare?

4. How did Aksum become a Christian state?

5. What were the most important goods for African internal trade? Which products were traded abroad?

6. How did geography influence early African history?

KEY TERMS

Kalahari (p. 106)   **Sahara** (p. 106)   **savannah** (p. 106)
Nilotic Africa (p. 107)   **Sahel** (p. 106)

For additional study resources for this chapter, go to:
www.prenhall.com/craig/chapter5

6 Republican and Imperial Rome

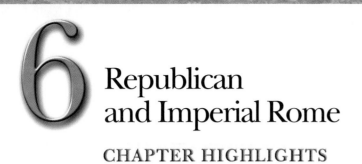

CHAPTER HIGHLIGHTS

Republican Rome Rome began as a small settlement ruled by kings; it became a republic in 509 B.C.E. The Roman constitution divided power between elected magistrates, an appointed Senate, and popular assemblies. During the third century B.C.E., the aristocratic patricians were forced to share power with the common people, the plebians.

Roman Expansion By the early fourth century, Rome had expanded to control all of Italy. Between 264 and 146 B.C.E., Rome fought three wars with Carthage for control of the western Mediterranean. These Punic Wars ended with the destruction of Carthage.

In the third century B.C.E., Rome turned to the east and defeated the Hellenistic monarchies that had succeeded Alexander's empire. This led to the rapid Hellenization of Roman culture. By the first century B.C.E., Rome controlled most of the Mediterranean world.

The Empire The Roman Republic was destroyed by social unrest and rivalry among ambitious generals and politicians, the most successful of whom was Julius Caesar. After Caesar's assassination in 44 B.C.E., his nephew Octavian emerged as the most powerful man in Rome. Under the title of Augustus, he set up a system that, while preserving the façade of republican institutions was in fact a monarchy.

Peace and stability prevailed throughout the Empire for two centuries. Christianity, which arose in the Roman province of Judaea in the first century C.E., spread throughout the empire despite occasional persecutions by the Roman state, which itself became Christian in the late fourth century.

Decline and Fall In the third century C.E., the Roman peace collapsed under the pressure of invasions by barbarians in the west and the Persians in the east. The emperors Diocletian and Constantine managed to arrest the decline, but in the fifth century C.E. Roman authority in the West collapsed. In the East, however, a Christian Roman Empire based in the city of Constantinople survived and evolved into the Byzantine Empire.

CHAPTER QUESTIONS

HOW DID the Etruscans influence early Rome?

WHY DID Rome and Carthage fight the Punic Wars?

HOW DID the Roman Republic come to an end?

WHAT ROLE did cities play in the Roman Empire?

HOW DID a Catholic Church emerge from early Christianity?

HOW DID the Roman Empire change under Diocletian and Constantine?

CHAPTER OUTLINE

- Prehistoric Italy
- The Etruscans
- Royal Rome
- The Republic
- Civilization in the Early Roman Republic: Greek Influence
- Roman Imperialism
- The Fall of the Republic
- The Augustan Principate

- Civilization of the Ciceronian and Augustan Ages
- Peace and Prosperity: Imperial Rome (14–180 c.e.)
- The Rise of Christianity
- The Crisis of the Third Century
- The Late Empire
- Arts and Letters in the Late Empire
- The Problem of the Decline and Fall of the Empire in the West

The ancient Romans were responsible for one of the most remarkable achievements in history. From their city in central Italy, they conquered most of the Near East and much of Europe. They brought peace, prosperity, and unity to this vast region for the only time in history.

Rome's legacy was not just military prowess and superb political organization. The Romans transformed the intellectual and cultural achievements of the Greeks, creating the Graeco-Roman tradition in literature, philosophy, and art. This tradition remains the heart of Western civilization.

PREHISTORIC ITALY

bout 1000 B.C.E. bands of warlike people speaking related Italic dialects (belonging to the Indo-European family of languages) began to infiltrate Italy. They spread through the peninsula's Apennine mountains and then contested control of the western agricultural plains with earlier settlers. The Romans were the descendants of some of these hardy folk.

THE ETRUSCANS

HOW DID the Etruscans influence early Rome?

truscan civilization, which was to have a powerful influence on the Romans, arose about 800 B.C.E. The **Etruscans** constituted a military ruling class, dominating the native people they had dispossessed. From their base in northern Italy (modern Tuscany), they took to the sea and established trade contacts with the Greeks and the Cartholginians of North Africa. Their influence spread south to the plains of Latium and Campania in the seventh and sixth centuries, but their power declined rapidly after 500 B.C.E.

ROYAL ROME

ome, which was located on the northeastern rim of the plain of Latium, came under the control of Etruscan kings in the sixth century B.C.E. Geographical location made Rome a center for communication and trade. With Etruscan leadership, the Roman army conquered most of Latium.

GOVERNMENT

Roman kings had the awesome power of *imperium*, the right to issue commands and enforce them by fines, arrests, and physical punishment, including execution. Although the crown tended to remain in families, kingship was elective. The Roman Senate approved the candidate, and the Roman people, voting in assembly, formally granted him the *imperium*. This procedure—the granting of great power to executive officers contingent on the approval of the Senate and ultimately the people—remained a characteristic of Roman government.

The Senate, the second branch of the early Roman government, ostensibly had neither executive nor legislative power, but its authority was great. Senators, like kings, served for life. The Senate enrolled the most powerful men in the state. They provided continuity for government and experienced counsel.

The third branch of government, the curiate assembly, was made up of all citizens. The body of citizens was divided into 30 groups. Voting was by group; a majority within each group determined its single vote, and decisions were made by majority vote of the groups. Group voting remained the custom for future forms of Roman political assembly.

Etruscans A people of central Italy who exerted the most powerful external influence on the early Romans.

imperium In ancient Rome, the right to issue commands and to enforce them by fines, arrests, and even corporal and capital punishment.

FAMILY

The center of Roman life was the family. At its head stood the father, whose power and authority resembled those of the king within the state. He held broad powers analogous to *imperium* over his children; he could sell them into slavery and might even kill them. Over his wife he had less power; he could not sell or kill her. In practice his power to dispose of his children was limited by other family members, by public opinion, and, most of all, by tradition. A wife could be divorced only for serious offenses. The Roman woman had a respected position and significant responsibility as the primary manager of her husband's household.

CLIENTAGE

Clientage was one of Rome's most important institutions. The client was said to be in the *fides*, or trust, of his patron, giving the relationship a moral dimension. The patron provided his client with physical and legal protection and economic support. In return, the client would fight for his patron, work his land, and support him politically. These mutual obligations were enforced by public opinion and tradition. Because the client-patron relationship was hereditary and was sanctioned by religion and custom, it was a major factor in the organization of Roman society and political life.

PATRICIANS AND PLEBEIANS

Roman society was divided into two classes based on birth. The wealthy **patrician** upper class held a monopoly of power and influence. Its members alone could conduct state religious ceremonies, sit in the Senate, or hold office. They formed a closed caste by forbidding marriage outside their own group.

The **plebeian** lower class may have originally consisted of poor, dependent small farmers, laborers, and artisans, the clients of the nobility. As Rome grew, some of these nonpatrician plebeian families acquired wealth, and some patrician families fell into poverty from incompetence or bad luck. The line between the classes and the monopoly of privileges nevertheless remained firm.

patricians   Hereditary upper class of early republican Rome.

plebeians   Hereditary lower class of early republican Rome.

THE REPUBLIC

oman legend claimed that outrageous behavior by the last kings provoked the city's noble families to revolt in 509 B.C.E. They abolished monarchy and reorganized Rome as a republic.

WHY DID Rome and Carthage fight the Punic Wars?

CONSTITUTION

The Roman constitution was an unwritten accumulation of laws and customs that evolved over many generations.

Consuls   The Romans granted consuls, their chief magistrates, the power of the *imperium* that kings had exercised. Like the kings, the consuls led the army, had religious duties, and served as judges. But the power of the consul was kept in check in two ways. Two men held consulships simultaneously, and each could overrule the other. Both were limited to a term of only one year. Their *imperium* was also limited. Although the consuls had full powers of life and death in the field with the army, within the city of Rome, citizens could appeal to the popular assembly any cases involving capital punishment. After their year in office, a consul also knew that he would spend the rest of his life as a member of the Senate, so only a reckless consul would ignore its advice. In serious crises, the consuls

A Roman warship. Rome became a naval power late in its history, in the course of the First Punic War. Roman sailors initially lacked the skill and experience in sea warfare of their Carthaginian opponents, who could maneuver their oared ships to ram the enemy. To compensate for this disadvantage, the Romans sought to make a sea battle more like an encounter on land by devising ways to grapple enemy ships and board them with armed troops. In time they also mastered the skillful use of the ram. This picture shows a Roman ship, propelled by oars, with both ram and soldiers, ready for either kind of fight.

Direzione Generale Musei Vaticani.

censor Official of the Roman republic charged with conducting the census and compiling the lists of citizens and members of the Senate.

tribunes Roman officials who had to be plebeians and were elected by the plebeian assembly to protect plebeians from the arbitrary power of the magistrates.

could, with the advice of the Senate, appoint a single *dictator*, who would hold *imperium* not subject to appeal both inside and outside the city for six months.

Financial officials called *quaestors* assisted consuls, and in 325 B.C.E., the Romans created the office of *proconsul*, which permitted a consul in the field to retain command for more than a year during a long campaign. Another new office, that of *praetor*, was primarily judicial. After the middle of the fifth century B.C.E., the job of identifying citizens and classifying them according to age and property was delegated to a **censor**. The Senate elected two censors every five years. They conducted a census and drew up the citizen rolls, and by the fourth century B.C.E. could exclude senators from the Senate on moral as well as financial grounds. The office was regarded as the ultimate prize of a political career.

Senate and Assembly The end of the monarchy increased the power of the Senate. It was the only ongoing deliberative body in the Roman state and soon took control of finances and foreign policy.

The *centuriate assemble*, the early republic's most important popular assembly, was, in a sense, the Roman army acting in a political capacity. Its basic unit was the century, 100 fighting men who fought with the same kind of equipment. Because each man equipped himself, this divided the assembly into classes according to wealth—that is, according to the weapons a man could afford.

Struggle of the Orders Patricians monopolized power in the early republic. Plebeians, however, made up much of the Roman army, and this gave them great political leverage. Their fight for political, legal, and social equality, the "struggle of the orders," lasted 200 years. They won the right to a plebeian tribal assembly led by elected officials called *tribunes*. A tribune could veto any action of a magistrate or any bill proposed in a Roman assembly or by the Senate. In 367 B.C.E., one of the consulships was opened to men of plebeian rank. In 287 B.C.E., the plebeians secured the passage of a law making the decisions of the plebeian assembly binding on all Romans without the approval of the Senate.

The victory of the plebeians in the "struggle of the orders" primarily benefited wealthy plebeian families by allowing them to share the political privileges of the patrician aristocracy. The *nobiles*—a small group of wealthy families, both patrician and plebeian—dominated the Senate and controlled the highest offices of the state.

CONQUEST OF ITALY

Initial Expansion and Gallic Invasion By the beginning of the fourth century B.C.E., the Romans had become the chief power in central Italy. In 340 B.C.E., the city's Latin neighbors, the Latin League, sought to curtail Rome's expansion, but in 338 B.C.E., the Romans defeated the league and dissolved it.

Roman Policy Toward the Conquered   The Romans did not destroy any of the Latin cities. To some near Rome they granted full citizenship. To others farther away they granted municipal status, which included the right to local self-government and the right to trade and intermarry with Romans. Still other states became allies of Rome. The Romans established permanent colonies of veteran soldiers in conquered lands. The colonists remained Roman citizens and deterred rebellion. A network of durable roads—some still in use—connected the colonies to Rome.

Rome divided its enemies and extended its influence through military force and diplomatic skill. Rebels were punished harshly, but Rome was generous to those who submitted. Loyal allies could gain full Roman citizenship. This policy gave allies a stake in Rome's future and, as a result, most remained loyal.

ROME AND CARTHAGE

In the ninth century B.C.E., the Phoenician city of Tyre had planted a colony on the North African coast, calling it Carthage. In the sixth century B.C.E., Carthage became independent and expanded west and east. Carthage claimed an absolute monopoly on trade in the western Mediterranean.

First Punic War (264–241 B.C.E.)   Sicily was strategically important to both Carthage and Rome. It was there, in 264 B.C.E., that the two expanding powers first came to blows. Because the Romans called the Carthaginians *Poeni* or *Puni* (meaning "Phoenician"), the conflicts between them are called the **Punic Wars**.

Because Rome's strength was its army and Carthage's power was its navy, neither side could make much progress against the other in the First Punic War until the Romans built a fleet. Once they were able to blockade the Carthaginian ports in Sicily, the tide turned. Carthage capitulated in 241 B.C.E., giving up Sicily and agreeing to pay a war indemnity. Neither side was to attack the allies of the other.

Second Punic War (218–202 B.C.E.)   After 241 B.C.E., Carthage recovered strength by building a rich empire in Spain. In 221 B.C.E., Hannibal (247–182 B.C.E.) took command of Carthaginian forces in Spain. A few years earlier, Rome had received an offer of alliance from the Spanish town of Saguntum. The Romans accepted, and the Saguntines, confident of Rome's protection, began to stir up Spanish tribes allied with Hannibal. The Romans warned Hannibal to let Saguntum alone, but he ignored Rome's warning and captured it. Rome declared war in 218 B.C.E., but Hannibal struck first, marching overland from Spain to launch a swift and daring invasion of Italy. His army defeated the Romans in three battles, but his hopes for final victory were pinned on persuading Rome's allies to switch sides.

In 216 B.C.E., at Cannae, Hannibal destroyed a Roman army of 80,000 men. It was the worst defeat in Roman history, and many of Rome's allies went over to Hannibal. In 215 B.C.E., Philip V (r. 221–179 B.C.E.), king of Macedon, allied with Hannibal and launched a war to recover his influence on the Adriatic. For more than a decade Hannibal was free to roam Italy and do as he pleased, but victory was denied him so long as crucial

Punic Wars   Three wars between Rome and Carthage for dominance of the western Mediterranean that were fought from 264 B.C.E. to 146 B.C.E.

The Punic Wars

264–241 B.C.E.	First Punic War
238 B.C.E.	Rome seizes Sardinia and Corsica
221 B.C.E.	Hannibal takes command of Punic army in Spain
218–202 B.C.E.	Second Punic War
216 B.C.E.	Battle of Cannae
202 B.C.E.	Battle of Zama
149–146 B.C.E.	Third Punic War
146 B.C.E.	Destruction of Carthage

5.1
A Hero Under Fire: Livy Relates the Trials and Tribulations of Scipio Africanus

allies remained loyal to Rome. He had neither the numbers nor the supplies to besiege the city itself.

The turning point in the conflict came when the Romans appointed Publius Cornelius Scipio (237–183 B.C.E.), later called Scipio Africanus, to the command in Spain. He was almost as talented as Hannibal. Within a few years Scipio had conquered all Spain and deprived Hannibal of help from that region. In 204 B.C.E., Scipio invaded Africa and forced Hannibal to return to protect Carthage. In 202 B.C.E., Scipio defeated Hannibal at Zama. Carthage was stripped of its empire, and Rome emerged dominant at seas and over the Mediterranean coast from Italy westward.

The New Imperial System The old practice of extending citizenship in exchange for loyalty to Rome to defeated opponents stopped at the borders of Italy. The Romans made Sicily, Sardinia, and Corsica provinces. The governors of these provinces exercised an *imperium* free of the limits put on the power of officials in Rome. The natives of provinces became tribute-paying subjects of a Roman empire. Rome collected their taxes by "farming them out"; that is, by auctioning the right to collect taxes to the man who made the highest bid. The treasury got a guaranteed sum, and the tax collector made a profit by exploiting the provincials. Provincial government spread so much corruption that it strained the constitution and traditions of Rome and threatened to destabilize the republic.

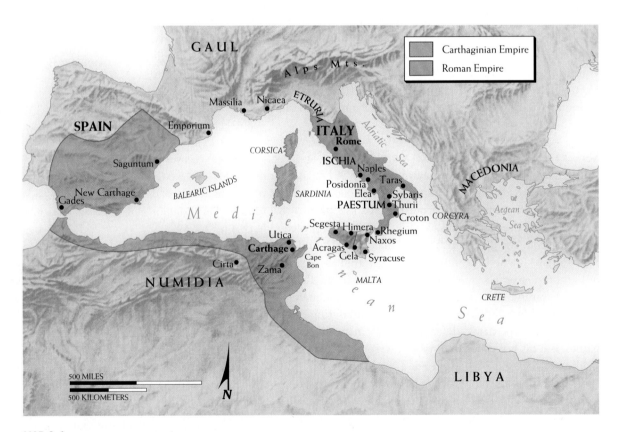

MAP 6–1
The Western Mediterranean Area During the Rise of Rome. This map covers the theater of conflict between the growing Roman dominions and those of Carthage in the third century B.C.E. The Carthaginian Empire stretched westward from Carthage along the North African coast and into southern Spain.

WHY WAS conflict between Rome and Carthage inevitable?

HISTORY'S VOICES

SALLUST ON FACTIONS AND THE DECLINE OF THE REPUBLIC

Sallust *(86–35 B.C.E.) was a supporter of Julius Caesar and of the political faction called* populares, *translated here as "the democratic party," opponents of the* optimates, *translated here as "the nobility." In this selection from his monograph on the Jugurthine War, Sallust tries to explain Rome's troubles in the period after the destruction of Carthage in 146 B.C.E.*

WHY DID Sallust think the destruction of Carthage marked the beginning of the decline of the Roman republic? Does his account of events seem fair and dispassionate? How would a member of "the nobility" have evaluated the same events? Is the existence of factions or "parties" inevitably harmful to a republic?

The division of the Roman state into warring factions, with all its attendant vices, had originated some years before, as a result of peace and of that material prosperity which men regard as the greatest blessing. Down to the destruction of Carthage, the people and Senate shared the government peaceably and with due restraint, and the citizens did not compete for glory or power; fear of its enemies preserved the good morals of the state. But when the people were relieved of this fear, the favourite vices of prosperity—licence and pride—appeared as a natural consequence. Thus, the peace and quiet which they had longed for in time of adversity proved, when they obtained it, to be even more grievous and bitter than the adversity. For the nobles started to use their position, and the people their liberty, to gratify their selfish passions, every man snatching and seizing what he could for himself. So the whole community was split into parties, and the Republic, which hitherto had been the common interest of all, was torn asunder. The nobility had the advantage of being a close-knit body, whereas the democratic party was weakened by its loose organization, its supporters being dispersed among a huge multitude. One small group of oligarchs had everything in its control alike in peace and war—the treasury, the provinces, public offices, all distinctions and triumphs. The people were burdened with military services and poverty, while the spoils of war were snatched by the generals and shared with a handful of friends. Meantime, the soldiers' parents or young children, if they happened to have a powerful neighbour, might well be driven from their homes. Thus, the possession of power gave unlimited scope to ruthless greed, which violated and plundered everything, respecting nothing and holding nothing sacred, till finally it brought about its own downfall. For the day came when noblemen rose to power who preferred true glory to unjust dominion: then the state was shaken to its foundations by civil strife, as by an earthquake.

Excerpt from Sallust, *The Jugurthine War: The Conspiracy of Catiline*, trans. by S. A. Hanford (London: Penguin Classics, 1963). Copyright © S. A. Hanford, 1963.

THE REPUBLIC'S CONQUEST OF THE HELLENISTIC WORLD

The East By the mid-third century B.C.E., the eastern Mediterranean had reached a stable balance of power. That equilibrium was threatened by two aggressive monarchs, Philip V of Macedon and the Seleucid emperor Antiochus III (223–187 B.C.E.). In 200 B.C.E., the Romans ordered Philip not to attack any Greek city and to pay reparations to the kingdom of Pergamum in Asia Minor. Philip refused. Two years later, the Romans demanded that Philip withdraw from Greece entirely. In 197 B.C.E., with Greek support, they defeated Philip in Thessaly. The Greek cities taken from Philip were made autonomous and declared free.

QUICK REVIEW

Rome Conquers Greece
- Romans forbid interference in Greek cities by Macedonia
- Rome saw Greek cities as a kind of protectorate
- Rome responded with force to sign of anti-Roman feeling in Greek cities

Soon after, Antiochus landed an army on the Greek mainland. The Romans drove him from Greece, and in 189 B.C.E. they crushed his army at Magnesia in Asia Minor. The Romans left Greek cities free, but they regarded Greece and Asia Minor as protectorates in which they could intervene as they chose.

In 179 B.C.E., Perseus (r. 179–168 B.C.E.) succeeded Philip V as king of Macedon. He tried to gain popularity in Greece by favoring the democratic and revolutionary forces in the cities. The Romans defeated him in 168 B.C.E. and divided Macedon into four separate republics. The new policy reflected a stern, businesslike policy promoted by the conservative censor Cato (234–149 B.C.E.). Leaders of anti-Roman factions in the Greek cities were punished severely, and in 146 B.C.E., the city of Corinth was destroyed. The Roman treasury benefited so much from these wars that Rome abolished direct property taxes on its citizens. Romans were learning that foreign campaigns could bring profit to the state, rewards to soldiers, and wealth, fame, and power to their generals.

The West Although Carthage posed no threat, some Romans could not shake their hatred and fear of the enemy that had come so close to defeating them. In 146 B.C.E., Scipio Aemilianus took the city, and the Romans incorporated Carthage as the province of Africa (see "Sallust on Factions and the Decline of the Republic").

HOW DID Greek culture influence Roman civilization?

CIVILIZATION IN THE EARLY ROMAN REPUBLIC: GREEK INFLUENCE

*A*mong the most important effects of Rome's expansion overseas were changes in the Roman style of life and thought. Such Roman aristocrats as the Scipios surrounded themselves with Greek intellectuals. Even conservatives, such as Cato, learned Greek and absorbed Greek culture.

RELIGION

Almost from the beginning, the Romans identified their gods with Greek equivalents and incorporated Greek mythology into their own. However, in the third century B.C.E. important new cults were introduced from the east: the worship of Cybele, the Great Mother goddess from Asia Minor, and of Dionysus, or Bacchus. Interest in Babylonian astrology also grew.

humanitas Roman name for a liberal arts education.

A Master Among His Students.
This carved relief from the second century C.E. shows a schoolmaster and his pupils. The student at the right is arriving late.

Rheinisches Landesmuseum, Triern, Germany/ Alinari/Art Resource, N.Y.

EDUCATION

Education was entirely the responsibility of the Roman family. It is not clear whether girls received any education in early Rome, although they did later on. Boys' education aimed at making them moral, pious, patriotic, law-abiding, and respectful of tradition. Contact with the Greeks of southern Italy produced momentous changes in Roman curricula. Greek teachers introduced the study of language, literature, and philosophy, as well as the idea of a liberal education, or what the Romans called *humanitas*.

Schools were established in which the teacher

taught his students the Greek language and its literature, particularly the works of Homer. Thereafter, educated Romans were expected to be bilingual. Roman boys of the upper classes studied rhetoric, which was of great use in legal disputes and political life.

By the last century of the Roman republic, the new Hellenized education had become dominant. Latin literature formed part of the course of study, but much of it was modeled after Greek examples.

Girls of the upper classes were educated similarly to boys. They were probably taught by tutors at home, although they were usually married by the age when men were pursuing higher education. Still, some women became prose writers or poets.

A rich, socially ambitious Roman might support a Greek philosopher in his own home, so that his son could acquire through conversation the learning and polished thought necessary for the fully cultured gentleman. Some, like the great orator Cicero (106–43 B.C.E.), traveled to Greece to study with great teachers of rhetoric and philosophy. This style of education made the Romans part of the culture of the Hellenistic world, a world they ruled and, therefore, needed to understand.

ROMAN IMPERIALISM

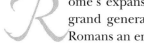 ome's expansion in Italy and overseas was accomplished without a grand general plan. But whether intended or not, it brought the Romans an empire, and with it, power, wealth, and responsibilities.

AFTERMATH OF CONQUEST

War and expansion changed the economic, social, and political life of Italy. The Second Punic War did terrible damage to the Italian farmland. Many veterans found it impossible or unprofitable to go back to their farms. Most became tenant farmers or hired hands. Often the land they abandoned was acquired by the wealthy who converted these farms, later called *latifundia*, into large plantations.

Land was inexpensive, and slaves conquered in war provided cheap labor. By fair means and foul, large landholders obtained sizable quantities of public land and forced small farmers off it. These changes separated the people of Rome and Italy more sharply into rich and poor, landed and landless, privileged and deprived. The result was conflict that threatened the republic.

THE GRACCHI

By the middle of the second century B.C.E., the problems caused by Rome's rapid expansion troubled perceptive Roman nobles. Tiberius Gracchus (168–133 B.C.E.) tried to solve these problems. He became tribune in 133 B.C.E. on a program of land reform. The program aroused great hostility. When Tiberius put it before the tribal assembly, another tribune vetoed it. Tiberius responded by persuading the assembly to remove from office the tribune who had blocked his popular legislation. Tiberius then proposed and passed a second bill, harsher than the first and even more appealing to the people. Because no tribune dared to oppose him, he got his way. But the cost was the destruction of the Roman constitution.

Tiberius understood the danger to himself and to prospects for implementing his reforms once his term as tribune came to an end, so he announced his candidacy for a second successive term. This violated the term limits posed by

WHY WAS there social unrest in Rome after the Second Punic war?

latifundia Large plantations for growing cash crops owned by wealthy Romans.

Roman Overseas Engagements

215–205 B.C.E.	First Macedonian War
200–197 B.C.E.	Second Macedonian War
196 B.C.E.	Proclamation of Greek Freedom
189 B.C.E.	Battle of Magnesia; Antiochus defeated in Asia Minor
172–168 B.C.E.	Third Macedonian War
168 B.C.E.	Battle of Pydna
154–133 B.C.E.	Roman wars in Spain
134 B.C.E.	Numantia taken

populares Roman politicians who sought to pursue a political career based on the support of the people rather than just the aristocracy.

equestrians Literally "cavalrymen" or "knights." In the earliest years of the Roman republic, those who could afford to serve as mounted warriors.

the Roman constitution. Having no legal recourse left, a mob of senators and their clients resorted to violence. They killed Tiberius and some 300 of his followers and threw their bodies into the Tiber River.

The tribunate of Tiberius Gracchus and the violent acts that ended it created a new situation. Tiberius had shown the Romans how to build a political career that was based not on aristocratic influence but on pressure from the people. In the last century of the republic, such politicians were called *populares*, whereas those who supported the traditional role of the Senate were called *optimates* ("the best men").

The tribunate of Gaius Gracchus (ca. 159–121 B.C.E.), brother of Tiberius, was much more dangerous to the Senate than that of Tiberius because all the tribunes were Gaius's supporters. There could be no veto, and tribunes could now be reelected (and, therefore, monopolize power). Gaius courted popularity by establishing colonies for landless veterans and passing a law stabilizing the price of grain in Rome. He also divided the wealthy, by winning the backing of the equestrian order in his struggles with the Senate. The **equestrians** were rich men who supplied goods and services to the Roman state and collected its taxes in the provinces. They had a special interest in Roman expansion and in the exploitation of the provinces. When Pergamum became the Roman province of Asia in 129 B.C.E., Gaius gave them the right to collect taxes there.

Gaius easily won reelection as tribune for 122 B.C.E., but then he made a misstep. He proposed giving citizenship to Italian allies, but the common people did not want to share the advantages of their Roman citizenship. The Senate seized on this to drive a wedge between Gaius and his supporters. After Gaius failed reelection in 121 B.C.E., a hostile consul provoked an incident that led to violence. Gaius was killed, and 3,000 of his followers were put to death without trial.

MARIUS AND SULLA

Before long the senatorial oligarchy faced a stronger opponent who got his start in a war with Jugurtha (d. 104 B.C.E.), king of Numidia. When the war dragged on, the people elected Gaius Marius (157–86 B.C.E.) to the consulship for 107 B.C.E. Marius was a *novus homo*, a political outsider, the first man from his family to win a consulship. He did so by promising the voters that popular military reforms would lead to speedy victory. He eliminated the traditional property qualification for military service and opened the ranks to volunteers, mostly dispossessed farmers and rural proletarians. They enlisted for long terms of service, looked on the army as a career, and expected land as a bonus when they retired. They became semiprofessional clients of their general and backed the politician who seemed most likely to be able to get them what they wanted. They looked to their commander rather than to the state for their rewards. Marius had to obtain grants from the Senate to maintain his power and reputation. But with a large, loyal army behind him, he could frighten the Senate into doing his bidding. Marius's innovation created both the opportunity and the necessity for military leaders to challenge the authority of civilian government.

Marius quickly routed Jugurtha, but a guerrilla war dragged on. Finally, Marius's subordinate, Lucius Cornelius Sulla (138–78 B.C.E.), captured Jugurtha and ended the war. Marius, however, took the credit, leaving Sulla to plot his revenge.

WAR AGAINST THE ITALIAN ALLIES (90–88 B.C.E.)

For a decade, Rome ignored the grievances of its Italian allies. In frustration, they took up arms. By 88 B.C.E., the revolt was put down, largely by giving the Italians what they wanted. They became Roman citizens, but their municipalities retained local self-government. The forging of Romans and Italians into a single people helped Italy to flourish.

SULLA'S DICTATORSHIP

Sulla was elected consul for 88 B.C.E. He backed the Senate in a war against Marius and his supporters, and following its victorious conclusion, he had himself appointed dictator. He used his power to restore the traditional Roman constitution and the power of the Senate. He could not, however, undo the effect of his example. Sulla had taken possession of Rome with its own army and led Romans in slaughtering Romans. Others were soon to do the same.

FALL OF THE REPUBLIC

POMPEY, CRASSUS, AND CAESAR

Marcus Licinius Crassus (115–53 B.C.E.) and Cnaeus Pompey (106–48 B.C.E.) won election to the consulship for the year 70 B.C.E. and repealed most of Sulla's laws. In 67 B.C.E., a special law gave Pompey *imperium* for three years over the entire Mediterranean and 50 miles in from the coast to rid the area of pirates. When he returned to Rome in 62 B.C.E., he had more power, prestige, and popular support than any Roman in history.

Crassus had the most reason to fear Pompey's return. Although rich and influential, he did not have the confidence of the Senate, a firm political base of his own, or the kind of military support needed to rival Pompey. During the 60s B.C.E., therefore, he allied himself with a promising young soldier politician, Gaius Julius Caesar (100–44 B.C.E.).

FIRST TRIUMVIRATE

To general surprise, Pompey disbanded his army and returned to Italy as a private citizen. He needed a grant of land for his veterans from the Senate and was dismayed when the fearful Senate decided to try to turn his men against him by refusing his request. This drove Pompey into an alliance with Crassus and Caesar called the First Triumvirate.

DICTATORSHIP OF JULIUS CAESAR

Caesar was elected consul for 59 B.C.E. and enacted the Triumvirate's program. Caesar got an opportunity to raise a great army for the conquest of Gaul; Crassus got a similar military command in the Middle East; and Pompey got land for his veterans and confirmation of his treaties from the Senate. By the time Caesar had conquered Gaul and was ready to return to Rome, the Triumvirate had dissolved. Crassus's invasion of Parthia had ended with his death at Carrhae in 53 B.C.E., and Pompey had allied with the Senate against Caesar.

HOW DID the Roman republic come to an end?

Fall of the Roman Republic

133 B.C.E.	Tribunate of Tiberius Gracchus
123–122 B.C.E.	Tribunate of Gaius Gracchus
111–105 B.C.E.	Jugurthine War
104–100 B.C.E.	Consecutive consulships of Marius
90–88 B.C.E.	War against the Italian allies
70 B.C.E.	Consulship of Crassus and Pompey
60 B.C.E.	Formation of First Triumvirate
58–50 B.C.E.	Caesar in Gaul
53 B.C.E.	Crassus killed in Battle of Carrhae
49 B.C.E.	Caesar crosses Rubicon; civil war begins
46–44 B.C.E.	Caesar's dictatorship
43 B.C.E.	Formation of Second Triumvirate
42 B.C.E.	Battle of Philippi
31 B.C.E.	Octavian defeats Antony at Actium

Early in January of 49 B.C.E., when Caesar's term as governor came to its end, the Senate ordered him to lay down his command. Instead, Caesar's legions crossed the Rubicon River, the boundary of his province. This began a civil war that ended in 45 B.C.E. with Caesar's victory over Pompey and the Senate.

Caesar made few changes in the government of Rome, but his monopoly of military power made a sham of the republic. His Senatorial enemies conspired against him, and on March 15, 44 B.C.E., they stabbed him to death at a meeting of the Senate. The assassins expected his death automatically to restore the republic, but 13 more years of civil war ensued and fatally undercut what was left of the republic.

SECOND TRIUMVIRATE AND THE EMERGENCE OF OCTAVIAN

Caesar's heir was his grandnephew, Octavian (63 B.C.E.–14 C.E.). Marcus Antonius (Mark Antony) (ca. 83–30 B.C.E.) and Lepidus (d. 13 B.C.E.), two of Caesar's officers, joined him in forming the Second Triumvirate, an alliance dedicated to punishing Caesar's assassins. The triumvirs defeated their enemy in 42 B.C.E., but soon quarreled among themselves. Octavian gained control of the western part of the empire. Antonius, together with Cleopatra (r. 51–30 B.C.E.), queen of Egypt, ruled the east. In 31 B.C.E., Octavian crushed the fleet and army of Antony and Cleopatra at Actium and ended the civil war. Octavian emerged in control of the Mediterranean world but faced a daunting challenge. He had to restore peace, prosperity, and confidence, without making the mistake that had cost Caesar his life. He had to excercise the power of a king without appearing to threaten the republican traditions to which his fellow Romans were passionately attached.

THE AUGUSTAN PRINCIPATE

Octavian's constitutional solution was to drape a monarchy in republican trappings by apparently sharing authority with the Senate. All real power, however, lay with the ruler, whether he was called by the unofficial title of "first citizen" (*princeps*) like Octavian, or "emperor" (*imperator*) like those who followed. The outline of his plan emerged in 27 B.C.E.: He was to rule the provinces of Spain, Gaul, and Syria with proconsular power for military command and retain a consulship in Rome. The Senate would govern the other provinces. Twenty of Rome's 26 legions just happened to be stationed in Octavian's provinces, giving him effective control of the empire. The Senate, however, was grateful to him for establishing peace after Rome's long civil war, and it voted him many honors, including the semireligious title "**Augustus**," which connoted veneration, majesty, and holiness. Historians refer to Octavian in his role as Rome's first emperor as Augustus and characterize his regime as the Principate, a government that tried to conceal the naked power on which it rested.

ADMINISTRATION

Augustus made important changes in the government of Rome, Italy, and the provinces to reduce inefficiency and corruption, to eliminate the threat to peace and order by ambitious individuals, and to reduce the distinction between Romans and Italians, senators and equestrians. Augustus controlled the elections and saw to it that promising young men, whatever their origin, served the state.

WHAT WERE the bases of Augustus's power?

imperator   Under the Roman republic, the title given to a victorious general. Under Augustus and his successors, it became the title of the ruler of Rome, meaning "emperor."

Augustus   Title given to Octavian in 27 B.C.E. and borne thereafter by all Roman emperors.

QUICK REVIEW

The Army Under Augustus
- Augustus professionalized army
- 20-year enlistment with good pay and pension
- 300,000 men formed frontier army

Equestrians and Italians who had no connection with the Roman aristocracy were admitted to the Senate, which Augustus treated with respect and honor.

The Augustan period was prosperous. Its economy was stimulated by wealth from newly conquered Egypt, by a general peace that stimulated commerce and industry, by a vast program of public works, and by a revival of small farming on the lands granted to Augustus's veterans.

THE ARMY AND DEFENSE

Under Augustus, Rome's soldiers became true professionals. Enlistment was for 20 years, but the pay was good, and there were bonuses and a pension on retirement. The citizen legions, together with auxiliary units staffed by provincials, stationed about 300,000 men on the empire's frontiers—barely enough to hold the line. The army in the provinces brought Roman culture to the natives. The soldiers spread their language and customs, often marrying local women and settling down there. They attracted merchants, who became the nuclei of new towns that became centers of Roman civilization. As time passed, the provincials on the frontiers became Roman citizens and helped strengthen Rome's defenses against the barbarians.

RELIGION AND MORALITY

A century of political strife and civil war had undermined Roman society. Augustus believed that restoration of traditional family and religious values would give the Romans the strength they needed to hold their empire. He curbed adultery and divorce, encouraged marriage and the procreation of legitimate children, and restored the dignity of formal Roman religion by building temples and reviving cults. Like Julius Caesar, he was deified after his death, and a state cult was dedicated to his worship.

Emperor Augustus (r. 27 B.C.E.–14 C.E.). This statue, now in the Vatican, stood in the villa of Augustus's wife Livia. The figures on the elaborate breastplate are all of symbolic significance. At the top, for example, Dawn in her chariot brings in a new day under the protective mantle of the sky god; in the center, Tiberius, Augustus's successor, accepts the return of captured Roman army standards from a barbarian prince; and at the bottom, Mother Earth offers a horn of plenty.

Charitable Foundation, Gemeinnutzige Stiftung Leonard von Matt.

CIVILIZATION OF THE CICERONIAN AND AUGUSTAN AGES

oman civilization reached its peak in the late republican era and during the Principate of Augustus.

WHAT WERE the main achievements of Augustan civilization?

THE LATE REPUBLIC

Cicero (106–43 B.C.E.) Cicero is most famous for his orations delivered in the law courts and the Senate. Many of his letters also survive, giving us a fuller insight into his mind than we have of any other figure in antiquity. He also wrote treatises on rhetoric, ethics, and politics, and believed in a world governed by divine and natural law. He looked to law, custom, and tradition to produce both stability and liberty.

Law The period from the Gracchi to the fall of the republic was important for the development of Roman law. The edicts of the magistrates who dealt with foreigners developed the idea of a comprehensive *jus gentium*, or "law of peoples," as opposed to a law based strictly on Roman custom. In the first century B.C.E., under the influence of the Greeks, the *jus gentium* was equated with the *jus naturale*, or "natural law," taught by the Stoics.

Poetry Two of Rome's greatest poets, Lucretius and Catullus, were citizens of the late republic. The Hellenistic literary theorists believed that poetry should educate as well as entertain, a task Lucretius (ca. 99–ca. 55 B.C.E.) undertook in his epic poem *De Rerum Natura* (*On the Nature of Things*). It explained and advocated the scientific and philosophical theories of Epicurus and Democritus, which Lucretius believed would liberate people from superstition and the fear of death.

Catullus's (ca. 84–ca. 54 B.C.E.) poems were personal. He wrote of the joys and pains of love, and amused himself composing witty poetic exchanges. He illustrates the mindset of the proud, independent, pleasure-seeking, late republican nobility.

THE AGE OF AUGUSTUS

The literary works of the Augustan Age, the Golden Age of Roman literature, reflected the new conditions of society. As the old aristocratic order declined, poets lost their traditional patrons, the nobility. Henceforth, support for artists flowed from the *princeps*.

Virgil Virgil (70–19 B.C.E.) was the most important of the Augustan poets. His greatest work is the *Aeneid*, a long epic that linked the history of Rome with the Homeric tradition of the Greeks. Its hero, the Trojan Aeneas, personifies the ideal Roman qualities of duty, responsibility, serious purpose, and patriotism. Virgil celebrated the peace and prosperity Augustus established for the empire and supported Augustus's program for the revival of traditional Roman virtues.

Horace Horace's (65–8 B.C.E.) great skills as a lyric poet are best revealed in his *Odes*. Many of them glorify the new Augustan order, the imperial family, and the empire.

Ovid Ovid (43 B.C.E.–18 C.E.) wrote entertaining love elegies that reveal the sophistication and the loose sexual conduct of the Roman aristocracy. His most popular work is *Metamorphoses*, a graceful, lively poem of epic length that retells Greek myths as charming stories.

History The most important and influential prose writer of the time was Livy (59 B.C.E.–17 C.E.). His *History of Rome* traced the period from Rome's legendary origins until 9 B.C.E. Only one-fourth of his work survives. His great achievement was the creation of a continuous, impressive narrative encompassing the full sweep of Roman history. Its purpose was to promote traditional morality and patriotism. He glorified Rome's greatness and, like Augustus, grounded it in Rome's hardy virtues.

Architecture and Sculpture Augustus embarked on a building program that beautified Rome, glorified his reign, contributed to the general prosperity, and enhanced his popularity. The greatest sculptural monument of the age is the Altar of Peace (*Ara Pacis*), dedicated in 9 B.C.E. Its walls show a procession in which

Augustus and his family appear to move forward, followed by the magistrates, the Senate, and the people of Rome. There is no better symbol of the new order.

Imperial Procession from the Frieze of the Ara Pacis. The altar was dedicated in 9 B.C.E. It was part of a propaganda campaign—involving poetry, architecture, myth, and history—that Augustus undertook to promote himself as the savior of Rome and the restorer of peace.

Saturnia, Tellus, Goddess of Earth, Air and Water. Panel from the Ara Pacis. 13–9 B.C.E. Museum of the Ara Pacis, Rome. Nimatallah/Art Resource, N.Y.

PEACE AND PROSPERITY: IMPERIAL ROME (14–180 C.E.)

Augustus tried to cloak the monarchical nature of his government, but his successors soon abandoned all pretense. They were called *imperator*—from which comes our word *emperor*—as well as *Caesar*. The latter title signified connection with the imperial house, and the former indicated the military power on which their authority was based. Augustus designated his heirs by giving them a share in the imperial power and responsibility (see Map 6–2).

WHAT ROLE did cities play

in the Roman Empire?

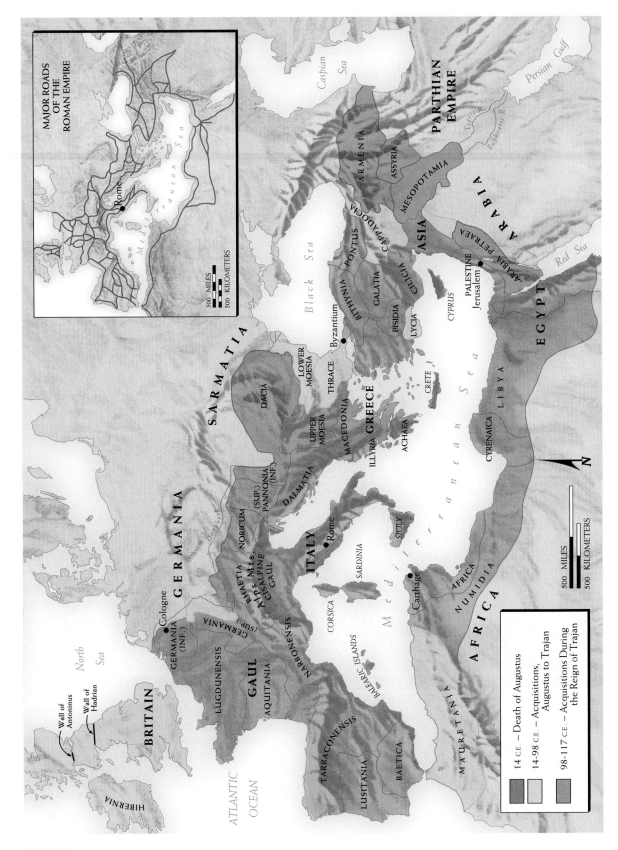

MAP 6–2

Provinces of the Roman Empire to 117 C.E.   The growth of the empire to its greatest extent is shown in three states—at the death of Augustus in 14 B.C.E., at the death of Nerva in 98 C.E., and at the death of Trajan in 117 C.E. The division into provinces is also indicated. The inset outlines the main roads that tied together the far-flung empire.

WHY WAS the Mediterranean central to the Roman Empire?

Tiberius (emperor 14–37 C.E.), Gaius (Caligula, 37–41 C.E.), Claudius (41–54 C.E.), and Nero (54–68 C.E.) descended from Augustus's family. After their line died out in 68 C.E., various Roman armies marched on Italy and elevated four men in rapid succession to the throne.

Vespasian (69–79 C.E.) emerged victorious from the chaos, and his sons, Titus (79–81 C.E.) and Domitian (81–96 C.E.), carried forward his line, the Flavian dynasty. Vespasian was the first emperor who did not come from the old Roman nobility.

Following Domitian's assassination, the Senate appointed Nerva (96–98 C.E.) emperor. He was the first of the five "good emperors": Trajan (98–117 C.E.), Hadrian (117–138 C.E.), Antoninus Pius (138–161 C.E.), and Marcus Aurelius (161–180 C.E.). Until Marcus Aurelius, none of these men had sons, so they were each free to choose an able successor. The result was almost a century of excellent administration. This ended when Marcus Aurelius's incompetent son, Commodus (180–192 C.E.), succeed him. The "good emperors" had all enlisted the cooperation of the upper class by courteous and modest deportment.

ADMINISTRATION OF THE EMPIRE

The empire was a collection of cities and towns. Roman policy during the Principate was to raise urban centers to the status of Roman municipalities. The upper classes of the provinces were enlisted in the governments of their regions. This spread Roman culture and won the loyalty of influential people.

As the imperial bureaucracy grew and became more efficient, however, the scope of its functions grew. The importance and autonomy of the municipalities shrank as the central administration took a greater role in local affairs. Efficient centralized control was obtained at the cost of the vitality of the cities.

Augustus and his successors had not tried to expand the empire, but Trajan launched a sustained offensive into neighboring territory. Between 101 and 106 C.E., he established the new province of Dacia north of the Danube. His intent was probably to defend the empire by driving wedges into enemy territory. The same strategy led him to invade the Parthian Empire in the east (113–117 C.E.).

Hadrian retreated to a defensive posture, and gradually the military initiative passed to the barbarians. Marcus Aurelius spent most of his reign repulsing their attacks on the frontiers. This put enormous pressure on the empire's resources.

CULTURE OF THE EARLY EMPIRE

Literature   In Latin literature, the years between the death of Augustus and Marcus Aurelius are known as the Silver Age. Writers of the Silver Age were gloomy, negative, and pessimistic. They were prone to criticism and satire. Historians of the era wrote about remote periods to avoid the risk of offending an emperor's sensibilities. Scholarship was encouraged, but we hear little of poetry. Romances written in Greek became popular as an escape from contemporary realities.

Rulers of the Early Empire

27 B.C.E.–14 C.E.	Augustus
The Julio-Claudian Dynasty	
14–37 C.E.	Tiberius
37–41 C.E.	Gaius (Caligula)
41–54 C.E.	Claudius
54–68 C.E.	Nero
69 C.E.	Year of the four emperors
The Flavian Dynasty	
69–79 C.E.	Vespasian
79–81 C.E.	Titus
81–96 C.E.	Domitian
The "Good Emperors"	
96–98 C.E.	Nerva
98–117 C.E.	Trajan
117–138 C.E.	Hadrian
138–161 C.E.	Antoninus Pius
161–180 C.E.	Marcus Aurelius

Pompeiian Woman. The Roman provincial city of Pompeii, near the Bay of Naples, was buried by an eruption of Mount Vesuvius in 79 c.e. As a result, the town, together with its private houses and their contents, was remarkably well preserved until recovery in the 18th century. Among the discoveries were a number of works of art, including pictorial mosaics and paintings. This depiction of a young woman, on a round panel from a house in Pompeii, is part of a larger painting that includes her husband holding a volume of Plato's writings. The woman is holding a stylus and a booklet of wax tables and is evidently in the process of writing. Her gold earrings and hair net show that she is a fashionable person of some means. Late first century c.e. Diameter: 14 5/8 inches.

Sappho, idealized portrait of a girl poising as a poetess. Fresco from Pompeii, Insula occidentale. Museo Archeologico Nazionale, Naples, Italy, © Erich Lessing/Art Resource, N.Y.

Architecture   The prosperity and relative stability of the first two centuries of imperial Rome brought Roman architecture to full flower. Roman contributions to the building arts were largely advances in engineering that made huge structures feasible. To the basic post-and-lintel construction used by the Greeks, the Romans added the semicircular arch, borrowed from the Etruscans. When used internally in the form of vaults and domes, the arch permitted great buildings like the Roman baths. Romans also made good use of concrete, a building material first used by the Hellenistic Greeks. The arena in Rome called the Colosseum, which was built by the Flavian emperors, is an excellent example of Roman architecture. The only major Roman temple to survive intact is the Pantheon, a building roofed by a great dome. Roman engineers also spread impressive bridges, roads, and aqueducts throughout the empire.

Society   The first two centuries of the Roman Empire deserve their reputation as a Golden Age, but by the second century c.e., troubles had arisen—troubles that foreshadowed difficult times ahead. In the first century c.e., the upper classes had vied for election to municipal office, but by the second century, emperors were having to force the ruling classes to accept public office. The reluctance to serve was caused largely by the imperial practice of holding magistrates and councilmen personally and collectively responsible for the revenues that were due from their communities.

These difficulties reflected more basic problems. The prosperity created in Augustus's day by the end of the civil war and the influx of wealth from the east could not be sustained. Population also seems to have declined. The cost of government, however, kept rising, for emperors had to maintain an expensive standing army, keep the people in Rome quiet with "bread and circuses," pay for an increasingly large bureaucracy, and defend frontiers against dangerous and determined enemies. The ever-increasing need for money compelled the emperors to oppress their subjects and debase the coinage. The result was a series of crises that destroyed the empire.

LIFE IN IMPERIAL ROME: THE APARTMENT HOUSE

The civilization of the Roman Empire was the product of the vitality of its cities. The typical city had about 20,000 inhabitants; Rome probably had in excess of half a million.

Most of its residents were squeezed into tall apartment buildings, which the Romans called *insulae* ("islands"). The buildings, which were five or more stories tall, were uncomfortable and dangerous. Built cheaply, they were prone to collapse, and they were easily set on fire by the many torches, candles, oil lamps, and braziers their inhabitants used. They had no running water or other conveniences. Little wonder that Romans spent most of their time out of doors.

RISE OF CHRISTIANITY

*T*he story of how Christianity ultimately conquered the Roman Empire is one of the most remarkable in history. Christianity was opposed by the established religious institutions of its native Judaea and had to compete not only against the official cults of Rome and the sophisticated philosophies of the educated classes, but also against **"mystery" religions** such as the cults of Mithra, Isis, and Osiris. Christians were also at times officially persecuted by the state. But despite all this, Christianity became the official religion of the empire.

JESUS OF NAZARETH

An attempt to understand the triumph of Christianity must begin with Jesus of Nazareth. The Gospel authors believed that Jesus was the son of God who came to redeem humanity and bring immortality to those who followed his way; to the Gospel writers, Jesus' resurrection was striking proof of his teachings.

Jesus was born in Judaea in the time of Augustus and was a most effective teacher in the tradition of the Jewish prophets. This tradition promised the coming of a Messiah (in Greek, *christos—Jesus Christ* means "Jesus the Messiah"), a redeemer who would make Israel triumph over its enemies and establish the kingdom of God on Earth. Jesus seems to have insisted that the Messiah would not establish an earthly kingdom but, at the Day of Judgment, God would reward the righteous and condemn the wicked. Until that day, which his followers believed would come soon, Jesus taught the faithful to abandon sin and worldly concerns; to follow the moral code described in the Sermon on the Mount, which preached love, charity, and humility; and to believe in him and his divine mission.

Jesus won a following, especially among the poor. This provoked the hostility of Jerusalem's religious leaders, and they convinced the Roman governor that Jesus and his followers might be dangerous revolutionaries. He was put to death in Jerusalem by the cruel and degrading method of crucifixion, probably in 30 C.E. His followers believed that he was resurrected on the third day after his death, and that belief became a critical element in their religion.

HOW DID a Catholic Church emerge from early Christianity?

"mystery" religions Cults of Isis, Mithra, and Osiris, which promised salvation to those initiated into the secret or "mystery" of their rites.

Although faith in Jesus as the Christ spread to some Jewish communities in Syria and Asia Minor, without Saint Paul it might have remained a small, heretical cult within Judaism.

PAUL OF TARSUS

Paul (?5–67 C.E.), whose Hebrew name was Saul, was born in Tarsus in Asia Minor. He had an excellent Hellenistic education and held Roman citizenship. He was also a **Pharisee**, a strict adherent of the Jewish law. He persecuted the early Christians until his own sudden conversion while travelling to Damascus about 35 C.E. The great problem facing the early Christians, like Paul, was their relationship to Judaism. If the new faith was a version of Judaism, then it must adhere to the Jewish law and seek converts only among Jews. James, called the brother of Jesus, held that view, whereas Hellenist Jews tended to see Christianity as a new and universal religion.

Paul supported the position of the Hellenists and soon won many converts among the gentiles. He believed that the followers of Jesus were called to be evangelists ("messengers"), to spread the gospel ("good news") of God's gracious gift of salvation during the short time that remained before Jesus returned for the Day of Judgment. Faith in Jesus as the Christ was necessary for salvation, but salvation was a gift of God's grace, not something earned by good works.

ORGANIZATION

The new religion had its greatest success in the cities and among the poor and uneducated. The rites of the early Christians appear to have been simple and few. Baptism by water removed original sin and permitted participation in the community and its activities. The central ritual was a common meal called the *agape* ("love feast"), followed by the ceremony of the *Eucharist* ("thanksgiving"), a celebration of the Lord's Supper in which unleavened bread was eaten and unfermented wine drunk. There were also prayers, hymns, and readings from works that eventually became the Christian scriptures.

At first the churches had little formal organization, but by the second century C.E., most cities had leaders called bishops (*episkopoi* or "overseers"), who administered their Christian congregations. The doctrine of Apostolic Succession asserted that the message and authority Jesus had entrusted to his original disciples were passed on from bishop to bishop by the rite of ordination.

The bishops maintained discipline within their churches and dealt with the civil authorities. In time they began coming together in councils to settle difficult questions, define orthodox belief, and expel those who would not accept it. Christianity could probably not have survived without such strong internal organization and government.

PERSECUTION OF CHRISTIANS

The new faith soon incurred the distrust of the pagan world and of the imperial government. The Christians' refusal to demonstrate their patriotism by worshipping the emperor was considered treason. By the end of the first century, membership in the Christian community had become a crime.

EMERGENCE OF CATHOLICISM

Most Christians held to traditional, simple, conservative beliefs. This body of majority opinion and the church that enshrined it came to be called **Catholic**, which means "universal." Its doctrines were deemed **orthodox**; those holding contrary opinions were called **heretics**.

Pharisees Group that was most strict in its adherence to Jewish law.

agape Meaning "love feast." A common meal that was part of the central ritual of early Christian worship.

Eucharist Meaning "thanksgiving." Celebration of the Lord's Supper. Considered the central ritual of worship by most Christians. Also called Holy Communion.

Catholic Meaning "universal." The body of belief held by most Christians enshrined within the church.

orthodox Meaning "holding the right opinions." Applied to the doctrines of the Catholic Church.

heretics Persons whose religious beliefs differ from the official doctrines of their faith.

Christ's Arrest. This Early Christian art shows Christ arrested by soldiers on the night before his crucifixion. Note that Christ is portrayed clean-shaven and dressed in the toga of a Roman aristocrat.

Hirmer Fotoarchiv, Munich.

By the end of the second century, an orthodox scriptural canon had emerged that included the Old Testament, the Gospels, and the Epistles of Paul. The orthodox declared the church the guardian of authentic Christian belief and granted bishops power to define it. They drew up creeds, brief statements of faith to which true Christians should adhere. By the end of the second century, an orthodox Christian—that is, a member of the Catholic Church—had to accept its creed, its canon of holy writings, and the authority of the bishops.

ROME AS A CENTER OF THE EARLY CHURCH

The church in the city of Rome acquired special prominence. Rome benefited from the tradition that both Jesus' apostles Peter and Paul were martyred there. Peter was thought to be the first bishop of Rome, and the Gospel of Matthew (16:18) reported Jesus saying to Peter, "Thou art Peter [in Greek, *Petros*] and upon this rock [in Greek, *petra*] I will build my church." Subsequent bishops of Rome claimed supremacy over the Catholic Church as heirs to the role Jesus granted to Peter.

THE CRISIS OF THE THIRD CENTURY

Pressure on Rome's frontiers reached massive proportions in the third century C.E. In the east, a new Iranian dynasty, the Sasanids, reinvigorated Persia (see Chapter 10) and raided Roman territory. On the western and northern frontiers the threat came from German tribes.

WHAT PROBLEMS did Rome experience during the third century?

BARBARIAN INVASIONS

Developments within the empire made it difficult for the Romans to meet the challenges to their empire. Septimius Severus (emperor 193–211 C.E.) and his successors changed the character of the Roman army. Septimius subordinated civil society to the support of a militarized monarchy and drew recruits for his army from peasants from the less civilized provinces. The result was a barbarization of Rome's military forces and a deline in their patriotism.

ECONOMIC DIFFICULTIES

Inflation had forced Commodus (r. 180–192 C.E.) to raise the soldiers' pay, but the Severan emperors had to double it to keep up with prices. This increased the imperial budget by as much as 25 percent. The emperors invented new taxes, debased the coinage, and even sold the palace furniture to raise money. Even then it was hard to recruit troops.

As external threats distracted the emperors, they were less able to preserve domestic peace. Piracy, brigandage, and the neglect of roads and harbors hampered trade. So, too, did inflation. As the money supply deteriorated, the government began to demand payment in food, supplies, and labor. The upper classes in the cities were ordered to serve as administrators without pay and to meet deficits in revenue out of their own pockets. Rebellions erupted in some provinces, and peasants and even town administrators fled to escape their burdens. The result was further diminishment of the Roman economy.

THE SOCIAL ORDER

The new conditions caused important changes in the social order. The state began to take on a military appearance. People's clothing became a kind of uniform that indicated their status. Titles were assigned to ranks in civilian society as to ranks in the army. The most important distinction was the one formally established by Septimius Severus between the *honestiores* (senators, equestrians, municipal aristocracy, and soldiers) and the lower classes, or *humiliores*. Septimius granted the *honestiores* legal privileges: lighter punishments, exemption from torture, and right of appeal to the emperor. It became more difficult to move from the lower order to the higher. Freedom and private initiative were suppressed as the state's needs forced it steadily to increase its control over its citizens.

CIVIL DISORDER

By the mid-third century, the empire seemed on the point of collapse, but a series of able military emperors gave it new life. Rome and other cities were given defensive walls to guard them from barbarian attack. The best troops were withdrawn from the frontiers to the emperor's command post. Rome relied on a newly organized heavy cavalry and a mobile army composed largely of German mercenaries whose loyalty was to the emperor, not the empire. Their officers became a new, if foreign, hereditary aristocracy. They increasingly filled the high administrative posts within the empire and some became emperors. In effect, the Roman people succumbed to an army of mercenaries they hired to protect them.

THE LATE EMPIRE

THE FOURTH CENTURY AND IMPERIAL REORGANIZATION

The reigns of Diocletian (r. 284–305 C.E.) and Constantine (r. 306–337 C.E.) marked an era of reconstruction and reorganization.

Diocletian Diocletian rose to the throne through the army. He concluded that the job of defending and governing the entire empire was too great for one man. He, therefore, devised a new administrative system, a **tetrarchy**, a

HOW DID the Roman Empire change under Diocletian and Constantine?

tetrarchy Diocletian's (r. 306–337 C.E.) system for ruling the Roman Empire by four men with power divided territorially.

division of territorial responsibility for the empire among four men: two emperors and two assistants who were designated as their successors.

Constantine   In 305, Diocletian retired and compelled his co-emperor to do the same. But his plan for a smooth succession failed. By 310, five men were competing for the throne. In 324, Constantine emerged as sole emperor.

The emperor had now become almost unapproachable. Those admitted to his presence had to prostrate themselves before him and kiss the hem of his robe. He was addressed as *dominus* ("lord"), and he claimed a divine right to rule. Remoteness and ceremony helped to secure the emperor against assassination by making him an awe-inspiring figure.

Constantine moved the capital of the empire to a new city called Constantinople on the site of ancient Byzantium on the Bosphorus. Its strategic location was excellent. The city was surrounded on three sides by water and was easily defended, and it enabled the emperor to stay in close touch with the endangered eastern and Danubian frontiers.

Administration and Finance   The autocratic emperors governed through a civilian bureaucracy, which was kept separate from the army to divide power and reduce the temptation an official might have to challenge the emperor. The system was kept under surveillance by a network of spies and secret police, but they failed to eliminate corruption and inefficiency.

The cost of maintaining a 400,000-man army, a vast civilian bureaucracy, and an expensive imperial court, strained an already weak economy. Peasants unable to pay their taxes and officials unable to collect them fled their posts. Wealthy individuals moved from cities to their rural estates, and many peasants sought protection from the government's tax collectors by becoming tenant farmers on these estates. They were tied to the land, as were their descendants, as a caste system hardened.

Division of the Empire   The peace and unity established by Constantine did not last. The Germans in the west attacked along the Rhine, but even greater trouble was brewing along the Danube where the Visigoths had been driven from their home in the Ukraine by the Huns. The Emperor Valentinian (r. 364–375) saw that he could not defend the empire alone and appointed his brother Valens (r. 364–378) as co-ruler in the east. The empire was again divided in two, and the cultures of Latin west and Greek east grew increasingly distinct. In 376, the Goths began to plunder the Balkan provinces. In 378, Valens met them in battle at Adrianople in Thrace, and he was cut down with most of the eastern army. Theodosius (r. 379–395), an able and experienced general, unified the empire, but at his death in 395 it was divided between his sons and never reunited again.

The west became increasingly rural as barbarian invasions grew. The villa, a fortified country estate, became the basic unit of society. *Coloni* (tenant farmers) served local magnates in return for economic assistance and protection. Cities were depopulated and shrank to tiny walled fortresses ruled by military commanders and bishops. The upper classes left the cities and moved to the country to escape the imperial authorities. The inability of the central authority to maintain and police roads curtailed trade and communications, and living conditions became increasingly primitive. By the fifth century, the west was devolving into rural enclaves ruled by independent aristocrats and worked by a dependent

5.7
Sidonius Appolinaris: Rome's Decay and the Glimpse of the New Order

labor force. The only unifying institution was the Christian church. The pattern of life that was to prevail in the west during the early Middle Ages had been generally established.

While the west was being overrun by barbarians, the Roman Empire, in altered form, persisted in the east. Constantinople flourished as the "New Rome." Although its people continued to call themselves "Romans," their lifestyles were so different from those of ancient Rome that historians refer to them as subjects of medieval *Byzantine* empire. Constantinople's defensible location, the services of some skillful emperors, and the resources of its base in Asia Minor, enabled the eastern empire to deflect and repulse barbarian attacks. A strong Byzantine navy allowed commerce to flourish and cities to prosper. Emperors generally kept the upper hand in dealing with restive aristocratic elements. Byzantine civilization was a unique combination of classical culture, Christian religion, Roman law, and eastern artistic influences. When historians speak of the decline and fall of the Roman Empire in the fourth and fifth centuries, they reference only the west. A form of classical culture persisted in Byzantium for another thousand years.

TRIUMPH OF CHRISTIANITY

Religious Currents in the Empire   In the troubled fourth and fifth centuries people sought the help of powerful, personal deities. It was by no means unusual for people to worship new deities alongside traditional ones and to intertwine features of several gods to create new ones, a phenomenon called **syncretism**. Christianity bore some resemblance to other new faiths of the period, but none of them developed its universal appeal.

syncretism   In religion, the equating or combining of deities.

The Triumph of Christianity

ca. 4 B.C.E.	Jesus of Nazareth born
ca. 30 C.E.	Crucifixion of Jesus
64 C.E.	Fire at Rome: persecution by Nero
ca. 70–100 C.E.	Gospels written
ca. 250–260 C.E.	Major persecutions by Decius and Valerian
303 C.E.	Persecution by Diocletian
311 C.E.	Galerius issues Edict of Toleration
312 C.E.	Battle of Milvian Bridge; conversion of Constantine to Christianity
325 C.E.	Council of Nicaea
ca. 330 C.E.	Georgia and Armenia become first Christian kingdoms
395 C.E.	Christianity becomes official religion of Roman Empire

Imperial Persecution   In 303, Diocletian had launched the most serious persecution inflicted on the Christians in the Roman Empire. It failed to stem the Christian tide. Ancient states could not carry out a program of terror with the thoroughness of modern totalitarian governments, and the witness of Christian martyrs may have strengthened the faith. In short order, Christians witnessed a miraculous reversal of fortune.

The conversion of Diocletian's ultimate successor, Constantine, and his ascent as sole ruler of the empire transformed Christianity's prospects. Constantine provided lavish patronage for the church and encouraged widespread conversion. In 394, the emperor Theodosius forbade the celebration of pagan cults, and by the time he died, Christianity had become the official religion of the Roman Empire.

Temptations of power and privilege constituted new threats to the moral standards and spiritual fervor of some Christians. State support for the faith threatened to subordinate the church to the state, as the pagan cults of empire had been. In the east, that was generally the church's fate, but in the west, the weakness of emperors permitted church leaders to exercise independence. In 390, when Ambrose (ca. 339–397), bishop of Milan, excommunicated

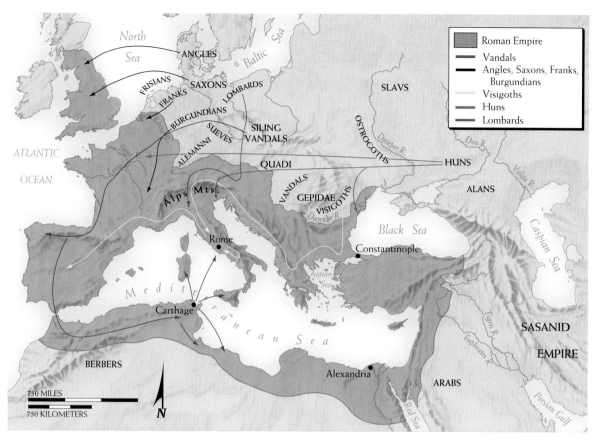

MAP 6–3

The Empire's Neighbors. In the fourth century the Roman Empire was nearly surrounded by more threatening neighbors. The map shows where these so-called barbarians lived and the invasion routes many of them took in fourth and fifth centuries.

HOW DID barbarian invasions transform the Roman world?

Emperor Theodosius, the emperor submitted to his authority and did penance. This set an important precedent for future assertions of the church's autonomy and authority.

Arianism and the Council of Nicea   The Christian emperors hoped to unify their increasingly decentralized realms by imposing Christianity as the only religion, but Christianity divided society in new ways. Safety from persecution allowed Christians the freedom to fight among themselves, and disputes over doctrine spread through the general population and caused serious disturbances as Christians sought to distinguish orthodox from heretical teachings. The most important controversy concerned **Arianism**, a debate begun by a priest named Arius of Alexandria (ca. 280–336). Arius's view that Jesus was not co-equal and co-eternal with God the Father was dismissed by his orthodox opponents, who argued that it undercut Jesus' power as savior. In 325, Constantine summoned a great church, **council of Nicaea**, to settle the issue. The **Nicene Creed** the council issued endorsed the doctrine of the Trinity: the belief that God is three persons (Father, Son, and Holy Spirit) who share one substance. Arianism, however, survived and spread and continued to create political difficulties for generations.

Arianism Belief formulated by Arius of Alexandria (ca. 280–336 C.E.) that Jesus was a created being, neither fully man nor fully God, but something in between.

Council of Nicea Council of Christian bishops at Nicaea in 325 C.E. that formulated the Nicene Creed, a statement of Christian belief that rejected Arianism in favor of the doctrine that Christ is both fully human and fully divine.

Nicene Creed A declaration of faith that the Council of Nicaea hoped would be endorsed by all Christians.

OVERVIEW   THE FALL OF THE ROMAN EMPIRE IN THE WEST

For centuries scholars have proposed theories to explain why the ancient world collapsed, but the great English historian Edward Gibbon (1737–1794), the author of *The Decline and Fall of the Roman Empire*, said that we should really ask not why Rome fell but how so vast an empire managed to survive for so long. The following are some of the explanations scholars have proposed for the fall of Rome. They range from the plausible to the ridiculous.

Cause	Explanation
Climate change	A gradual drying and cooling climate destroyed the productivity of ancient agriculture on which the empire depended.
Soil exhaustion	Depleted soil around the Mediterranean no longer produced enough food to feed the population, which weakened and declined.
Lead poisoning	Use of lead pipes for drinking and cooking water led to widespread lead poisoning and sterility, especially among the upper classes who had most access to running water.
Racial pollution	Eastern immigrants to Rome—Syrians, Greeks, and Jews—sapped the vitality of the Romans and destroyed their ability to rule and defend themselves.
Slavery	The prevalence of slavery made the Romans lazy and undercut free labor.
Intellectual stagnation	Failure to make advances in science and technology—to achieve a scientific revolution—led the empire to an intellectual and economic dead end.
Social disorder	The destruction of the middle class through civil war, invasion, and over taxation wiped out the most productive and culturally aware part of the Roman population. Third-century emperors encouraged the rural poor to plunder the middle and upper classes.
Excessive government	Government exactions and regulations destroyed the operation of a market economy, which was the basis for prosperity.
Christianity	Adoption of Christianity as the official religion of the empire in the fourth century weakened the Roman state, diverted scarce resources to building and staffing churches and monasteries, and led large segments of the population to embrace pacifism.
Immorality	Gluttony, sloth, and sexual depravity replaced the old Roman virtues that had enabled Rome to conquer its empire.

HOW IS late antiquity a transition period from the Classical to the Medieval?

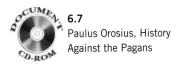

6.7
Paulus Orosius, History Against the Pagans

ARTS AND LETTERS IN THE LATE EMPIRE

The art and literature of the late empire reflect both the confluence of pagan and Christian ideas and traditions and the conflict between them. Much of the literature is polemical, and much of the art is propaganda.

PRESERVATION OF CLASSICAL CULTURE

One of the major accomplishments of this period was the preservation of many of the great works of classical literature at a time when declining literacy and education threatened their loss. Books that were fundamental to the classical tradition were reproduced in many copies. Scholars saved some materials by condensing long works (e.g., Livy's *History of Rome*) into shorter versions, and they wrote learned commentaries and grammars that enabled later generations to comprehend their legacy from the ancient world.

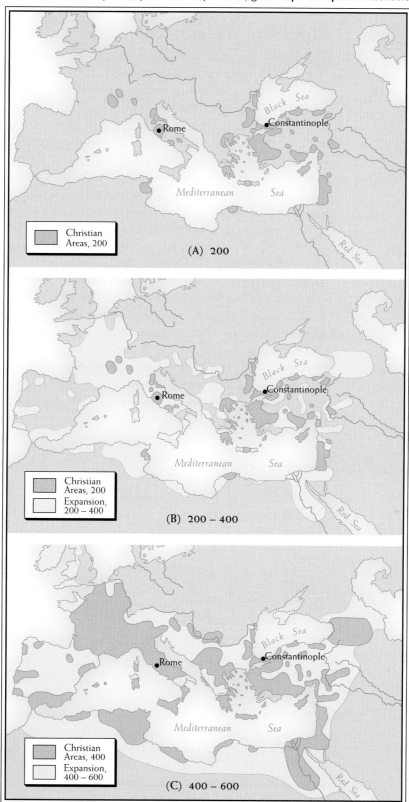

(A) 200

Christian
Areas, 200

(B) 200 – 400

Christian
Areas, 200
Expansion,
200 – 400

(C) 400 – 600

Christian
Areas, 400
Expansion,
400 – 600

MAP 6–4

The Spread of Christianity.   Christianity grew swiftly in the third, fourth, fifth, and sixth centuries—especially after the conversion of the emperors in the fourth century. By 600, on the eve of the birth of the new religion of Islam, Christianity was dominant throughout the Mediterranean world and most of Western Europe.

WHICH AREAS remained largely non-Christian at the end of the seventh century?

CHRISTIAN WRITERS

Christianity inspired scholars who did important original work. Jerome (348–420), a Christian who had superb classical education, used his linguistic skills to create the Vulgate, a revised version of the Bible in Latin. It became the official version of the Bible used by the medieval Catholic Church.

The most important Christian scholar in the east may have been Eusebius of Caesarea (ca. 260–ca. 340). His *Ecclesiastical History* attempted to develop a Christian theory of history as a working out of God's will. All of history, he claimed, had divine significance and direction. Constantine's victory and the subsequent unity of empire and church was its culmination.

The closeness and complexity of the relationship between classical pagan culture and the Christianity of the late empire are nowhere better displayed than in the career and writings of Augustine (354–430), bishop of Hippo in North Africa. His skill in pagan rhetoric and philosophy made him peerless among his contemporaries as a defender of Christianity and a theologian. His greatest works are his *Confessions*, an autobiography that describes his conversion, and *The City of God*. The latter was a response to Rome's sack by the Goths in 410. Augustine separated the fate of Christianity from that of the Roman Empire. He contrasted the secular world—the city of Man—with the spiritual—the City of God. The former was selfish, the latter unselfish; the former evil, the latter good. All states, even a Christian Rome, were part of the City of Man and therefore corrupt, mortal, and destined to pass away. Only the City of God was eternal and unaffected by earthly calamities.

SUMMARY

Republican Rome Rome began as a small settlement in Latium in central Italy ruled by Etruscan kings; Rome became a republic in 509 B.C.E. The Roman constitution divided power between elected magistrates, the chief of whom were two consuls: an appointed Senate, whose members served for life; and popular assemblies. During the third century B.C.E., the aristocratic patricians were forced to share power with the common people, the plebians. The institution of clientage by which clients pledged their loyalty to powerful patrons in return for legal and political protection was an important part of Roman political life.

Roman Expansion By the early fourth century, Rome had expanded to control all of Italy through a policy of conquest, alliances, colonies of Roman veterans, and generosity to foes who submitted. Between 264 and 146 B.C.E., Rome fought three wars with Carthage for control of the western Mediterranean. These Punic Wars ended with the destruction of Carthage, but led to resolve social and political disorder in Italy. Many small farmers lost their land, and efforts by the Gracchi brothers to resolve the problems ended in their murders.

In the third century B.C.E., Rome turned to the east and defeated the Hellenistic monarchies that had succeeded Alexander's empire. Macedon and Greece fell under Roman rule. This led to the adoption of Greek culture by the Roman aristocracy and the rapid Hellenization of Roman culture. By the first century B.C.E., Rome controlled most of the Mediterranean world.

The Empire The Roman republic was destroyed by social unrest and rivalry among ambitious generals and politicians, the most successful of whom was Julius Caesar. After a civil war that followed Caesar's assassination in 44 B.C.E., his nephew Octavian emerged as the most powerful man in Rome. Under the title of Augustus, he set up a system that, while preserving the façade of republican institutions, was in fact a monarchy.

The Roman Empire stretched from Scotland to Iraq. Rome fostered the growth of cities, developed the rule of law, built a vast network of roads and other public works, and established two centuries of peace and stability. Christianity, which arose in the Roman province of Judaea in the first century C.E., spread throughout the empire despite occasional persecutions by the Roman state, which itself became Christian in the late fourth century.

Decline and Fall In the third century C.E., the Roman peace collapsed under the pressure of invasions by barbarians in the west and the Persians in the east. Rival generals murdered emperors and usurped the throne. The economy declined. The state exacted more and more taxes and resources from its citizens. The emperors Diocletian and Constantine managed to arrest the decline, but in the fifth century C.E. Roman authority in the west collapsed. In the East, however, a Christian Roman Empire based in the city of Constantinople survived and evolved into the Byzantine Empire that did much to preserve the Greek and Roman heritage for 1,000 years.

REVIEW QUESTIONS

1. How did the institutions of family and clientage help to organize the early Roman republic?

2. What events and motives led Rome to bring Italy, Greece, and Asia Minor under its control?

3. How did Rome's victories over Carthage change Rome?

4. Why was the Roman republic plagued by civil war throughout the last century B.C.E.?

5. Why was the Roman population willing to accept Augustus's empire?

6. Why were Christians persecuted by Roman authorities? What explains Christianity's success?

IMAGE KEY
for pages 122–123

a. A Roman warship
b. Clay Plaque showing emblem of 20th Roman Legion - charging Boar
c. Pompeian, Boscoreale. "Lady playing the cithara"
d. Ancient bronze Roman flutes
e. Detailed scale model of the Roman Coliseum
f. Sarcophagus of an Etruscan couple, sixth century B.C.E.
g. A relief from Titus's Arch of Victory in the Roman Forum
h. Statue of Emperor Augustus of Prima Porta, Rome
i. Reconstruction of a large house and apartments at Ostia
j. Early Christian art showing the arrest of Christ
k. Arch of Constantine, Rome, Italy

KEY TERMS

agape (p. 142)
Arianism (p. 147)
Augustus (p. 134)
Catholic (p. 142)
censor (p. 126)
Council of Nicaea (p. 147)
equestrians (p. 132)
Etruscans (p. 124)
Eucharist (p. 142)

heretics (p. 142)
humanitas (p. 130)
imperator (p. 134)
imperium (p. 124)
latifundia (p. 131)
"mystery" religions (p. 141)
Nicene Creed (p. 147)
orthodox (p. 142)

patricians (p. 125)
Pharisee (p. 142)
plebeians (p. 125)
populares (p. 132)
Punic Wars (p. 127)
syncretism (p. 146)
tetrarchy (p. 144)
tribunes (p. 126)

 For additional study resources for this chapter, go to:
www.prenhall.com/craig/chapter6

7

China's First Empire
221 B.C.E. – 589 C.E.

CHAPTER HIGHLIGHTS

Unification of China China first became a unified state under the Qin dynasty (256–206 B.C.E.). The first Qin emperor built the Great Wall to contain the northern nomadic peoples. The Ch'in ruled through a strong bureaucracy, but their centralized administration collapsed after the death of the first emperor.

Han Dynasty Under the Han (256 B.C.E.–220 C.E.), China's centralized administration was revived. The bureaucracy grew, population expanded, and culture flourished. The Confucian classics became the standard for education. Buddhism arrived in China in the first century C.E. Under the Han it spread across China and adapted itself to Chinese culture. The Han eventually collapsed through a welter of court intrigue, rebellion, and military seizure of power.

CHAPTER QUESTIONS

HOW DID the Qin unify China?

WHAT WAS the dynastic cycle?

HOW DID the Han empire collapse?

TO WHAT extent did China become Buddhist under the Han dynasty?

CHAPTER OUTLINE

- Qin Unification of China
- Former Han Dynasty (206 B.C.E.–8 C.E.)
- Later Han (25–220 C.E.) and Its Aftermath
- Han Thought and Religion

154 **CHAPTER 7** CHINA'S FIRST EMPIRE 221 B.C.E.–220 C.E.

One hallmark of Chinese history is its striking continuity of culture, language, and geography. The Shang and Zhou dynasties were centered in north China along the Yellow River or its tributary, the Wei. The capitals of China's first empire were in exactly the same areas, and north China has remained China's political center up to the present. If Western civilization had experienced similar continuity, it would have progressed from Thebes in the valley of the Nile to Athens on the Nile; Rome on the Nile; and then, in time, to Paris, London, and Berlin on the Nile; and each of these centers of civilization would have spoken Egyptian and written in Egyptian hieroglyphics.

The many continuities in its history did not mean, however, that China was unchanging. One key turning point came in the third century B.C.E., when the old, quasi-feudal, multistate Zhou system gave way to a centralized bureaucratic government. The new centralized state built an empire stretching from the steppe in the north to Vietnam in the south.

The history of the first empire is composed of three segments: the Qin dynasty, the Former Han dynasty, and the Later Han dynasty. The English word China *is derived from the name of the first dynasty. The Qin overthrew the previous Zhou dynasty in 256 B.C.E. and went on to unify China in 221 B.C.E. In reshaping China, the Qin developed such momentum that it overextended, and its realm collapsed only a generation after the unification. The succeeding Han dynasties each lasted about 200 years, the Early Han from 206 B.C.E. to 8 C.E., the Later Han (founded by a descendant of the Former Han rulers) from 25 to 220 C.E. Historians usually treat each of the Han dynasties as separate periods, although they were almost back to back and shared many institutions and cultural traits. So deep was the impression left by these two dynasties on the Chinese that even today they call themselves—in contrast to Mongols, Manchus, Tibetans, and other minorities—the "Han people," and their ideographs, "Han writing."*

QIN UNIFICATION OF CHINA

HOW DID the Qin unify China?

Of the territorial states of the Late Zhou era, none was more innovative and ruthless than Qin. Its location on the Wei River in northwest China—the same area from which the Zhou had launched their expansion a millennium earlier—gave it strategic advantages: It controlled the passes leading to the Yellow River plain, so it was easy to defend and was a secure base from which to attack other states. In the late fourth century B.C.E., the Qin conquered a part of Szechwan. This, with its home territory, gave the Qin control over two of the most fertile regions of ancient China. It welcomed Legalist administrators, who developed policies for enriching the country and strengthening its military. Despite the Qin's harsh laws, the order and stability of its society attracted farmers from other areas. Its armies had been forged by centuries of warfare against the nomadic raiders by whose lands it was half encircled. To counter their raid, Qin soldiers learned the skills of the nomads and developed cavalry in the fourth century. Other states saw the Qin as tough, crude, and brutal, but recognized its formidable strengths.

In 246 B.C.E., the man who would unify China succeeded to the Qin throne at the age of 13. Vigorous, ambitious, intelligent, and decisive, the First Qin Emperor is famous as a Legalist autocrat; but he was well liked by his ministers, whose advice he usually followed (see Chapter 2 for a description of Legalism). In 232 B.C.E., at the age of 27, he began the campaigns that destroyed the six remaining territorial states. In 221 B.C.E., he signified his victory and declared his superiority to the kings he conquered by adopting a glorious title. We translate it as "emperor," but it is a combination of ideographs hitherto used only for gods or mythic heroes. Then, aided by officials of great talent, this First Emperor implemented reforms throughout China that had been tried and found effective in his own realm. His accomplishments in the 11 years before his death, in 210 B.C.E., were stupendous.

Having conquered the civilized world of north China and the Yangtze River basin, the First Emperor sent his armies farther afield. They reached the northern edge of the Red River basin in what is now Vietnam. They occupied China's southeastern coast and the area about the present-day city of Canton (see Map 7–1). In the north and the northwest, the emperor's armies fought against the Hsiung Nu, Altaic-speaking Hunnish nomads. During the late Zhou, northern border states had built long walls to protect settled lands from incursions by nomadic horsemen. The Qin emperor joined into a single Great Wall that extended 1,400 miles from the Pacific Ocean into Central Asia. Construction of the Great Wall cost the lives of vast numbers of conscripted laborers—by some accounts, 100,000; by others, as many as 1 million.

The most significant Qin reform, carried out by the Legalist minister Li Si, extended the Qin system of bureaucratic government to the entire empire. Li Si divided China into 40 prefectures, which were further subdivided into counties. The county heads were responsible to prefects, who, in turn, were responsible to the central government. Officials were chosen by ability. Bureaucratic administration was impersonal, based on laws to which all were subject. No one, for example, escaped Qin taxation. This kind of bureaucratic centralism broke sharply with the old Zhou pattern of creating dependent principalities for members of a ruler's family. Furthermore, to ensure the smooth functioning of local government offices, former aristocrats of the territorial states were removed from their lands and resettled in the Qin capital, near present-day Xian. They were housed in mansions on one side of the river, from which they could gaze across at the enormous palace of the First Emperor.

Other policies contributed to the unity of the First Emperor's vast domain. Roads were built radiating out from the capital city. The emperor decreed a system of uniform weights and measures. He regulated the Chinese writing system, establishing standard ideographs to replace the great variety that had hitherto prevailed. He established uniform axle lengths for carts. Even thinkers were expected to conform to the government's standards. Following the precepts of Legalism, the emperor and his advisers launched a campaign for which they have been execrated throughout Chinese history. They collected and burned the books of the Confucian and other schools and were said to have buried alive several hundred scholars who rejected the Legalist philosophy. Only books considered useful—on agriculture, medicine, or Legalist teachings—were spared.

The Qin changed too much too quickly. To pay for the roads, canals, and the Great Wall, burdensome taxes were levied. Commoners hated conscription and labor service, and nobles resented their subordination to government authority. Merchants felt exploited, and scholars (except for Legalists) oppressed.

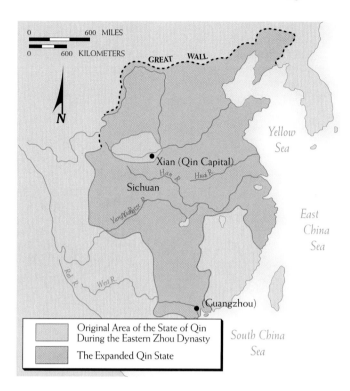

MAP 7–1

Unification of China by the Qin State.   Between 232 and 221 B.C.E., the Qin state expanded and unified China.

WHY DID Qin expansion fail to move westward?

QUICK REVIEW

Ch'in Reforms

- Extension of Ch'in bureaucracy to entire empire
- Building of roads
- Creation of a unified writing system
- Creation of unified system of weights and measures

2.7
Sima Qian: The Historian's Historian writes about the builder of the Great Wall

A Chinese historian later wrote: "The condemned were an innumerable multitude; those who had been tortured and mutilated formed a long procession on the roads. From the princes and ministers down to the humblest people everyone was terrified and in fear of their lives."[1] After the First Emperor died, in 210 B.C.E., intrigues broke out at court, and rebellions arose in the land. At the end, the Qin was destroyed by the domino effect of its own legal codes. When the generals sent to quell a rebellion were defeated, they joined the rebellion rather than returning to the capital to suffer the severe punishment decreed for failure. The dynasty collapsed in 206 B.C.E.

In 1974, a farmer near Xian discovered the army of 8,000 life-size terracotta horses and soldiers that guarded the tomb of the First Emperor. The historical record tells us that in the tomb itself, under a mountain of earth, are a replica of his capital; a relief model of the Chinese world with quicksilver rivers; other warriors with chariots of bronze; and the remains of horses, noblemen, and criminals sacrificed to accompany in death the emperor whose dynasty was to have lasted for 10,000 generations.

FORMER HAN DYNASTY (206 B.C.E.–8 C.E.)

THE DYNASTIC CYCLE

WHAT WAS the dynastic cycle?

Confucian historians of China have seen a pattern in every dynasty of long duration. They call it the **dynastic cycle**. The stages of the cycle are explained as the "Mandate of Heaven." The cycle begins with internal wars that eventually lead to the military unification of China. Unification is proof that heaven has given the unifier the mandate to rule. Strong and vigorous, the first ruler consolidated his political power and restores peace and order to China. Economic growth follows, almost automatically. The peak of the cycle is marked by public works, more energetic reforms, and aggressive military expansion. During this phase, China

dynastic cycle Term used to describe the rise, decline, and fall of China's imperial dynasties.

[1]C. P. Fitzgerald, *China, A Short Cultural History* (New York: Praeger, 1935), p. 147.

OVERVIEW   THE DYNASTIC CYCLE

Confucian historians of China saw a pattern in the rise and fall of China's imperial dynasties that they called the "dynastic cycle." They saw it as a process under which a ruling family won and eventually lost "the Mandate of Heaven," the divine sanction to rule China. The dynastic cycle had the following stages:

Internal wars	China is wracked by disorder and divisions.
Unification	Eventually a strong ruler quells the disorder and reunifies China. His success is proof that he enjoys the Mandate of Heaven.
Strong government	His successors are wise and upright rulers under whom the economy flourishes, China expands, and public works and reforms are promoted. China appears invincible.
Decline	Government costs exceed revenues. The imperial court becomes overly luxurious and riven by intrigues. Emperors neglect their duties. Central controls weaken.
Collapse	Finally, public works decay, floods and plague occur, rebellions break out, and the dynasty collapses. Confucians consider the last emperors in the cycle morally culpable. They have lost the Mandate of Heaven.

appears invincible. But then the cycle turns downward. The costs of expansion, coupled with increasing opulence at court, place a heavy burden on tax revenues just as they are beginning to decline. The vigor of the monarchs wanes. Intrigues develop at court. Central controls loosen, and provincial governors and military commanders gain autonomy. Finally, public works fall into disrepair, floods and pestilence occur, rebellions break out, and the dynasty collapses. For Confucian historians, the last emperors in a cycle are not only politically weak but morally culpable.

EARLY YEARS OF THE FORMER HAN DYNASTY

The first 60 years of the Han may be thought of as the early phase of its dynastic cycle. After the collapse of the Qin, one rebel general gained control of the Wei basin and went on to unify China. He became the first emperor of the Han dynasty and is known by his posthumous title of Gaozu (r. 206–195 B.C.E.). He rose from plebeian origins to become emperor, which only happened one other time in Chinese history. Gaozu built his capital at Chang'an, not far from the former capitals of the Western Zhou and the Qin. It took Gaozu and his immediate successors many years to consolidate their power, for they wanted to avoid the appearance of reinstituting the hated Qin despotism. They made punishments less severe and reduced taxes. Good government prevailed, the economy rebounded, granaries were filled, and the government accumulated vast cash reserves. Later historians often singled out the early Han rulers as model sage-emperors.

HAN WUDI

The second phase of the dynastic cycle began with the rule of Wudi (the "martial emperor"), who came to the throne in 141 B.C.E. at the age of 16 and ruled for 54 years (141–87 B.C.E.). Wudi was daring, vigorous, and intelligent, but also superstitious, suspicious, and vengeful. He wielded tremendous personal authority.

Building on the prosperity achieved by his predecessors, Wudi initiated new economic policies. A canal was built from the Yellow River to the capital in

A soldier. From the army of life-size terracotta soldiers, this was found in the tomb of the first emperor of the Qin dynasty (256–206 B.C.E.).

Adam Crowley/Getty Images, Inc./PhotoDisc, Inc.

northwest China, linking the two major economic regions of north China. "Ever-level granaries" were established throughout the country so that the surplus from bumper crops could be bought and then resold in time of scarcity. To increase revenues, taxes were levied on merchants, the currency was debased, and some offices were sold. Wudi also moved against merchants who had built fortunes in untaxed commodities by reestablishing government monopolies—a practice of the Qin—on copper coins, salt, iron, and liquor. For fear of Wudi, no one spoke out against the monopolies, but a few years after his death, a famous debate took place at court.

Known as the "Salt and Iron Debate," from the title of the chronicle that records it, the discussion was frequently cited thereafter in China, Japan, and Korea. Quasi-Legalist officials argued that the state should enjoy the profits from the sale of salt and iron. They were opposed by Confucians, who argued that these resources should be left in private hands, for the moral purity of officials would be sullied if they had to deal with merchants. The Confucian scholars who compiled the chronicle made themselves the winners in the debate; but state monopolies became a regular part of Chinese government finance.

Wudi also aggressively expanded Chinese territory—a policy that would characterize every strong dynasty. His armies swept south into what is today northern Vietnam and northeast across Manchuria to establish a military outpost in northern Korea that survived until 313 C.E.

THE XIONGNU

The principal threat to the Han was from the Xiongnu Empire to the north. Their mounted archers could raid China and flee before an army could be mobilized to send against them. Wudi responded by developing policies that became standard thereafter. When possible, he "used the barbarian to control the barbarian," making allies of border nomads against more distant nomads. These allies were allowed to trade with Chinese merchants; they were awarded titles and honors; and their kings were sent Chinese princesses as brides. When this method did not work, Wudi used force. Between 129 and 119 B.C.E. he sent several armies of more than 100,000 troops into the steppe, destroying Xiongnu power south of the Gobi Desert in southern Mongolia. To establish a strategic line of defense aimed at the heart of the Xiongnu Empire farther to the west, Wudi then sent 700,000 Chinese colonists to the arid Kansu panhandle and extended the Great Wall to the Jade Gate outpost at the eastern end of the Tarim basin. From this outpost, Chinese influence was extended over the rim oases of Central Asia, establishing the **Silk Road** that linked Ch'ang-an with Rome (see Map 7–2).

GOVERNMENT DURING THE FORMER HAN

To demonstrate their difference from the Qin emperor, the early Han emperors set up some Zhou-like principalities: small, semiautonomous states with independent lords. This, however, was a token gesture. The principalities were closely superintended and then curtailed after several generations. Basically, despite its repudiation of the Qin and all its works, the Han continued the Qin form of centralized bureaucratic administration. Officials were organized by grades and were paid salaries in grain, plus cash or silk. They were recruited by sponsorship or recommendation. Provincial officials had the duty of recommending promising candidates, and a school that trained them at Chang'an was said to have 30,000 students by the Later Han. The bureaucracy grew until, by the first century B.C.E., there were

Silk Road Trade route from China to the West that stretched across Central Asia.

MAP EXPLORATION
Interactive map: To explore this map further, go to **http://www.prenhall.com/craig/map7.2**

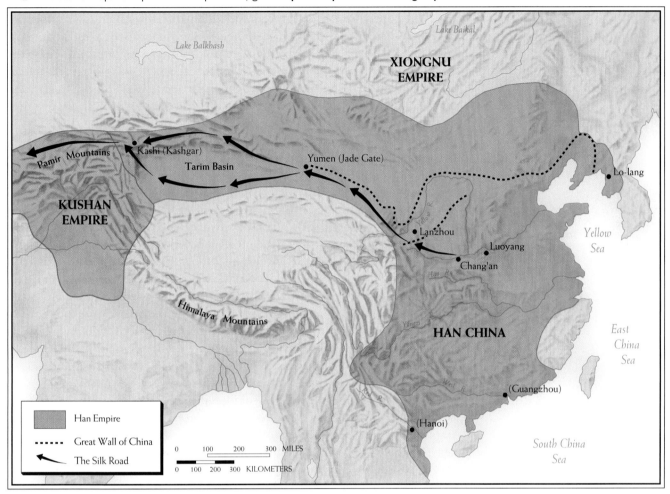

MAP 7–2

The Han Empire 206 B.C.E.–220 C.E.   At the peak of Han expansion, Han armies advanced far out into the steppe north of the Great Wall and west into Central Asia. The Silk Road to Rome passed through the Tarim basin to the Kushan Empire, and on to western Asia and the Middle East.

WHY DID the Han seek to expand their empire to the west and south?

more than 130,000 officials. This, however, may not have been too many for a population that, by then, numbered 60 million.

During the Han dynasty, this Legalist governmental system was slowly and partially Confucianized. The first Han emperor despised Confucians as bookish pedants—he once urinated in the hat of a scholar! But Confucian ideas proved useful. The Mandate of Heaven provided an ethical justification for dynastic rule. The vast bookkeeping the empire entailed engendered respect for old records and the written word. The Confucian classics gradually were accepted as the standard texts for educating government officials. Confucius taught that ethical cultivation could transformation the self, and he envisioned a benevolent government by virtuous, talented men who needed no external constraint

This painted banner is from the tomb of an aristocratic lady, Hunan Province, China, Han dynasty, ca. 160 B.C.E.

to keep them honest. No one attempted to replace laws with a code of etiquette, but increasingly laws were interpreted and applied by men with a Confucian education.

The court during the Han dynasty exhibited features that would appear in later dynasties as well. Everything centered on the emperor, the all-powerful "son of heaven." The will of a strong adult emperor was paramount. If he was weak, however, or ascended the throne when still a child, others competed to rule in his name. Four types of contenders for this surrogate role appeared and reappeared throughout Chinese history: court officials, the empress dowager, court eunuchs, and military commanders.

Court officials were selected for their ability. They staffed the apparatus of government and directly advised the emperor on matters of policy. Apart from the emperor himself, they were usually the most powerful men in China. Their position, however, was often precarious. Few officials escaped being removed from office or banished at least once or twice during their careers. Of the seven prime ministers who served Wudi, five were executed by his order.

Of the emperor's many wives, the empress dowager was the one whose child was designated heir to the throne. Her influence sometimes continued even after her son became an adult, but she was most powerful as a regent for an emperor during his minority. On Gaozu's death in 195 B.C.E., for example, the Empress Lu became the regent for her child, the new emperor. Aided by her relatives, she seized control of the court and murdered a rival. When her son was about to come of age, she killed him and made a younger son the heir so that she could continue to rule as regent. When she died in 180 B.C.E., loyal adherents of the imperial family who had opposed her rule massacred her relatives.

Court eunuchs came mostly from families of low social status. They were brought to court as boys, castrated, and assigned to work as servants in the emperor's harem. They were thus in contact with the future emperor from the day he was born. They became his childhood confidants, and they often continued to advise him after he had gained the throne. Emperors found eunuchs, who had no family ties, useful as counterweights to officials. But the scholars who wrote China's history characterized the eunuchs as greedy half men, given to evil intrigues.

Military leaders, whether generals or rebels, were the usual founders of dynasties. In the later phase of most dynasties, regional military commanders often became semi-independent rulers. A few even usurped the throne. Yet they were less powerful at the Chinese court than they were, for example, in imperial Rome, partly because military men were regarded as inferior in prestige to the better-educated civil officials. The court also took great pains to prevent its generals from establishing bases of personal power. An appointment to command a Han army was given only for a specific campaign, and commanders were appointed in pairs so that each would check the other.

Another characteristic of government during the Han and subsequent dynasties was that its functions were limited. It collected taxes, maintained military forces, administered laws, supported the imperial household, and carried out public works that were beyond the powers of local jurisdictions. But government in a district that remained orderly and paid its taxes was left largely in the hands of local notables and large landowners. This pattern was not, to be sure, unique to China. Most premodern governments, even those that were bureaucratic, were not able to reach down and interfere in the everyday lives of their subjects.

THE SILK ROAD

Romans loved Chinese silks, and the Chinese coveted Roman glass and gold. No single caravan conveyed these goods from one empire to the other, but they were passed through many hands, like batons in a relay race. During the Han and later dynasties, a route began to evolve that ran from the Chinese capital to Kashgar and then north through Tashkent and Samarkand or south through Teheran and Bagdad to Mediterranean ports such as Tyre, Antioch, and Byzantium. Only a small portion of the original shipments made it to the end of the line, a journey of thousands of miles that took more than half a year. Only the most valuable goods were worth the effort of moving them so far.

The Chinese and Romans had no direct contact. Each was unsure of the other's location and knew little about the civilization of the land with which it traded. Ideas and technologies, however, moved along the silk road and were more important than exotic luxury goods. China borrowed the chariot, compound bow, wheat, the domesticated horse, the stirrup, and maybe even the technology for bronze casting from western Asia. Papermaking, iron casting, water-powered mills, shoulder collars for draft animals, compasses, and gunpowder spread from China to the West. Plants and animals were exchanged. Religions migrated, and horrific plagues swept from one region to the other.

DECLINE AND USURPATION

During the last decade of Wudi's rule in the early first century B.C.E., military expenses began to run ahead of revenues. His successor cut back on military costs, eased economic controls, and reduced taxes. But over the next several generations, large landowners used their growing influence in provincial politics to avoid paying taxes. State revenues declined. The tax burden on smaller landowners and free peasants grew heavier. In 22 B.C.E., rebellions broke out in several parts of the empire. At the court, too, decline set in through a series of weak emperors, intrigues, nepotism, and factional struggles. Officials worried that Heaven had withdrawn its mandate and that the dynastic cycle approached its end.

Galloping Horse. China traded with steppe merchants to obtain the horses needed to equip its armies against steppe warriors. Especially desired by the Chinese were the fabled "blood sweating" horses of far-off Ferghana (present-day Tajikistan).

The New York Public Library for the Performing Arts/Art Resource.

Many courtiers urged Wang Mang, the regent for the infant emperor and the nephew of an empress, to take the throne and found a new dynasty. Wang Mang refused several times—to demonstrate his lack of eagerness—and then, in 8 C.E., accepted. He drew up a program of sweeping reforms based on ancient texts. He was a Confucian, but he relied on new institutional arrangements rather than moral reform to improve society. He revived ancient titles, expanded state monopolies, abolished private slavery (affecting about 1 percent of the population), made loans to poor peasants, and confiscated large private estates.

These reforms alienated many. Merchants disliked the monopolies. Large landowners resisted the expropriation of their lands. Even nature seemed to turn against Wang Mang. The Yellow River overflowed its banks, changed its course, and destroyed the northern Chinese irrigation system. Several years of poor harvests resulted in famines. The Xiongnu overran China's northern borders. In 18 C.E., a peasant secret society rose in rebellion, and in 23 C.E., rebels attacked Chang'an. Wang Mang was killed and eaten by rebel troops. He had tried to found a new

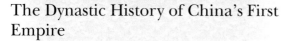

The Dynastic History of China's First Empire

256–206 B.C.E.	Qin dynasty
206 B.C.E.–8 C.E.	Former Han dynasty
25–220 C.E.	Later Han dynasty

HOW DID the Han empire collapse?

dynasty from within a decrepit court, but without a base of military support, the attempt was futile. Internal wars continued in China for two more years until a large landowner, the leader of a rebel army, emerged triumphant (25 C.E.). He was from a branch line of the imperial family, and his new dynasty was seen as a restoration of the Han.

LATER HAN (25–220 C.E.) AND ITS AFTERMATH

FIRST CENTURY

The founder of the Later Han moved his capital east to Loyang. Under the first emperor and his two successors there was a return to strong central government and a laissez-faire economy. Agriculture and population recovered. By the end of the first century C.E., China was as prosperous as it had been during the good years of the Former Han. And as in the case of the Former Han, military expansion followed pacification and recuperation. This time the transition came much earlier. South China and Vietnam were retaken during the reign of the first emperor. Dissension among the Xiongnu enabled the Chinese to secure an alliance with some of the southern tribes in 50 C.E., and in 89 C.E. Chinese armies crossed the Gobi Desert and defeated the northern Xiongnu. This defeat sparked the migrations that some historians believe sent the Xiongnu across the southern Russian steppes and then, in the fifth century C.E., to Europe, where they were known as the Huns. In 97 C.E., a Chinese general led an army to the shores of the Caspian Sea. The Chinese expansion in inner Asia, coupled with more lenient government policies toward merchants, facilitated the camel caravans that carried Chinese silk across the Tarim basin to Iran, Palestine, and Rome.

DECLINE DURING THE SECOND CENTURY

Until 88 C.E. the emperors of the Later Han were vigorous, but their successors were ineffective and short-lived. Empresses plotted to advance the fortunes of their families. Emperors turned for help to palace eunuchs, whose power at times surpassed that of officials. In 159 C.E., a group of eunuchs in the service of an emperor slaughtered the family of a scheming empress dowager and took over the court. When officials and students protested against the eunuch dictatorship, more than 100 were killed and 1,000 were tortured or imprisoned. In another incident in 190 C.E., a general deposed one emperor, installed another, killed the empress dowager, and massacred most of the eunuchs at the court.

In the countryside, large landowners who had been powerful from the start of the dynasty grew more so. They harbored private armies. Farmers on their estates were reduced to serfs, and they used their influence to avoid taxes. Great numbers of free farmers escaped their taxes by fleeing south, leaving the remaining freeholders obligated for ever-increasing taxes and labor services. Many peasants turned to neo-Daoist religious movements that provided the justification and organization they needed to turn their discontent into action. In 184 C.E., rebellions organized by members of the religious movements broke out against the government. Han generals suppressed the rebellions but then took personal control of the provinces they had pacified. In 220 C.E., they deposed the last Han emperor.

AFTERMATH OF EMPIRE

For more than three and a half centuries after the fall of the Han, China was fragmented. For several generations it was divided into three kingdoms, whose heroic warriors and scheming statesmen were made famous by wandering storytellers. These characters are included in the *Tale of the Three Kingdoms*, a Chinese romantic epic.

Chinese history during the post-Han centuries had two characteristics. The first was the dominant role played by the great aristocratic landowning families. With vast estates, huge numbers of serfs, fortified manor houses, and private armies, no king could control them. Because they took over many of the functions of local government, some historians see post-Han China as reverting to the quasi-feudalism of the Zhou. The second feature of this period was divergence in the ways that northern and southern China were developing.

In the south, a succession of ever weaker dynasties centered on Nanjing. Although the period of Chinese history from 220 C.E. to 589 C.E. is called the Six Dynasties era, these six southern states were in fact short-lived kingdoms, plagued by intrigues, usurpations, and coups d'état. They were frequently at war with northern states and in constant fear of their own generals. The main developments in the south were: (1) continuing economic growth and the emergence of Nanking as a thriving center of commerce, (2) the ongoing absorption of tribal peoples into Chinese society and culture, (3) large-scale immigrations of Chinese fleeing the north, and (4) the penetration of Buddhism to the heart of Chinese culture.

In the north, state formation depended on interaction between nomads and the Chinese. During the Han dynasty, Chinese invasions of the steppe had led to the establishment of semi-Sinicized Xiongnu as the northernmost tier of the Chinese defense system—just as Germanic tribes protected the late Roman Empire. But as the Chinese state weakened, the highly mobile nomads broke loose, joined with other tribes, and began to invade China. The short-lived states that they formed are usually referred to as the "Sixteen Kingdoms." One was founded by invaders of Tibetan stock. Most spoke Altaic languages: the Xianbii (proto-Mongols), the Tuoba (proto-Turks), and the Ruan Ruan (who would later appear in eastern Europe as the Avars). But differences were less important than these tribes' similarities:

1. All began as steppe nomads with a way of life different from that of agricultural China.

2. After forming states, all became at least partially Sinicized. Chinese from great families, which had preserved Han traditions, served as their tutors and administrators.

3. All were involved in wars—among themselves, against southern dynasties, or against conservative steppe tribes that resisted Sinicization.

4. Buddhism was as powerful in the north as in the south. As a universal religion, it acted as a bridge between "barbarians" and Chinese—just as Christianity was a unifying force in post-Roman Europe. The barbarian rulers of the north were especially attracted to its magical side and usually made Buddhism their state religion. Of the northern states, the most durable was the Northern Wei (386–534 C.E.), famed for its Buddhist sculpture.

TO WHAT extent did China become Buddhist under the Han dynasty?

HAN THOUGHT AND RELIGION

*P*oems describe the splendor of Chang'an and Luoyang: broad boulevards, tiled gateways, open courtyards, watchtowers, and imposing walls. Most splendid of all were the palaces of emperors, with their audience halls, vast chambers, harem quarters, and parks containing artificial lakes and rare animals and birds. Today, however, little remains of the grandeur of the Han. Whereas Roman ruins abound in Italy and circle the Mediterranean, in China nothing remains above ground. Only from pottery, bronzes, musical instruments, gold and silver jewelry, lacquerware, and clay figurines that were buried in tombs can we get a feeling for the rich material culture of the Han period. And only from paintings on the walls of tombs do we know of its art. But a wealth of written records survives to document the intellectual achievements of Han culture, particularly in the fields of philosophy and history.

HAN CONFUCIANISM

A major accomplishment of the early Han was the recovery of texts lost during the Qin persecution of scholars. Some were retrieved from the walls of houses where they had been hidden; others were reproduced from memory by scholars. (The degree of authenticity of the texts was debated then as now.) In 51 B.C.E. and again in 79 C.E., councils were held to determine the true meaning of the Confucian classics. In 175 C.E., an approved, official version of the texts was inscribed on stone tablets. Han scholars also began writing commentaries on the classics, a major scholarly activity throughout Chinese history. Scholars learned the classics by heart and used classical allusions in their writing.

The first dictionary was compiled about 100 C.E. Containing about 9,000 characters, it helped promote a uniform system of writing. In Han times, as today, Chinese from the north could not converse with Chinese from the southeastern coast. But a common written language bridged differences of pronunciation and fostered Chinese unity.

Han philosophers augmented Zhou Confucianism with ideas characterized as cosmological naturalism. Zhou Confucianists had assumed that the moral force of a virtuous emperor would both order society and harmonize nature. Han Confucianists explained why. Dong Zhongshu (ca. 179–104 B.C.E.), for example, held that all nature was a single, interrelated system. Just as summer always follows spring, so does one color, one virtue, one planet, one element, one number, and one officer of the court always take precedence over another. All

Han Dynasty Tomb Painting. Court figures painted on ceramic tile in a Han dynasty tomb (Gray earthenware; hollow tiles painted in ink and colors on a whitewashed wound 73.8 × 204.7 cm).

"Lintel & Pediment of a Tomb." China, Western Han dynasty, first century B.C. Gray earthenware; hollow tiles painted in ink & colors on a whitewashed ground. 73.8 × 204.7 cm. Denman Waldo Ross Collection, & Gift of C.T. Loo. Courtesy Museum of Fine Arts, Boston.

reflect the systematic workings of yang and yin and the five elements. And just as one dresses appropriately for each season, so was it important for the emperor to choose policies appropriate to the sequences inherent in nature. If he was moral, if he acted in accord with heaven's natural system, then all would go well. But if he acted inappropriately, then heaven would send a portent as a warning—a blue dog, a rat holding its tail in its mouth, an eclipse, or a comet. If the portent was not heeded, wonders and then misfortunes would follow. It was the Confucian scholars themselves, of course, who claimed to understand these omens, a skill that made them essential advisers to emperors.

It is easy to criticize Han philosophy as a pseudo-scientific or mechanistic view of nature. But it represented a new effort by the Chinese to comprehend the interrelationships of the natural world. This effort led to inventions like the seismograph and to advances in astronomy, music, and medicine. It was also during the Han that the Chinese invented paper, the wheelbarrow, the stern-post rudder, and the compass (known as the "south-pointing chariot").

HISTORY

The Chinese were the greatest historians of the premodern world. They wrote more history than anyone else, and what they wrote was usually more accurate than other accounts. Apart from the *Spring and Autumn Annals* and the scholarship of Confucius himself, history writing in China began during the Han dynasty. Various explanations are proposed for why the Chinese were so history-minded. It may be because Chinese tradition is this-worldly or because veneration of the Confucian classics created respect for the written word. It could be because history was seen as a lesson book (the Chinese called it a mirror) for statesmen, and thus knowledge of it was a necessity for the literate men who ran the Chinese state.

The practice of using actual documents and firsthand accounts of events began with Sima Qian (d. 85 B.C.E.), who attempted to write a history of the known world from the most ancient times down to the age of the emperor Wudi. His *Historical Records* consisted of 130 substantial chapters. It was divided into "Basic Annals"; "Chronological Tables"; "Treatises" (on rites, music, astronomy, the calendar, and so on); "Hereditary Houses"; and "Biographies" (70 chapters including descriptions of foreign people). A second great work, *The Book of the Han*, was written by Ban Gu (d. 92 C.E.). It applied the analytical schema of Sima Qian to a single dynasty, the Former Han, and established the pattern by which each dynasty wrote the history of its predecessor.

NEO-DAOISM

As the Han dynasty waned, the effort to realize the Confucian ethic in the sociopolitical order became increasingly difficult. Some scholars abandoned Confucianism altogether in favor of **Neo-Daoism**, or "mysterious learning," as it was called. A few wrote commentaries on the classical Daoist texts that had been handed down from the Zhou. The *Zhuangzi* was especially popular. Other scholars, defining the natural as the pleasurable, withdrew from society to engage in witty "pure conversations." They discussed poetry and philosophy, played the lute, and drank wine. The most famous were the Seven Sages of the Bamboo Grove of the third century C.E. One sage was always accompanied by a servant carrying a jug of wine and a spade—the one for his pleasure, the other to dig his grave should he die. Another wore no clothes at home. When criticized, he replied that the cosmos was his home, and his house his clothes. "Why are you in my pants?" he asked a discomfited visitor. Still another took a boat to visit a friend on a snowy night, but on

Chinese Historians
- Greatest historians of premodern world
- History seen as a lesson book for statesmen
- Practice of using actual documents and firsthand accounts began with Sima Qian (d. 85 B.C.E.)

Neo-Daoism A revival of Daoist "mysterious learning" that flourished as a reaction against Confucianism during the Han dynasty.

arriving at his friend's door, turned around and went home. When pressed for an explanation, he said that it had been his pleasure to go, and that when the impulse died, it was his pleasure to return. This story reveals a scorn for convention coupled with an admiration for an inner spontaneity, however eccentric (see "The Peach Blossom Spring").

Another concern of Neo-Daoism was the achievement of immortality. Some people sought it in dietary restrictions and Yogalike meditation, some in sexual abstinence or orgies. Others, trying to discover elixirs to prolong life, dabbled in alchemy, and although no magical formula was ever found, the schools of alchemy to which the search gave rise are credited with the discovery of medicines, dyes, glazes, and gunpowder. Popular religious cults arose among the common people that, because they included the Daoist classics among their sacred texts, are considered Neo-Daoist. Like most folk religions, they were an amalgam of beliefs, practices, and superstitions. They had a pantheon of gods and immortals and taught that the good or evil done in this life would be rewarded or punished in the innumerable heavens or hells of an afterlife. These cults had priests, shamans who practiced faith healing, seers, and sorceresses. For a time, they also had hierarchical religious organizations, but these were smashed at the end of the second century C.E. Local Daoist temples and monasteries, however, survived until modern times. With many Buddhist accretions, they furnished the religious beliefs of the bulk of the Chinese population. Today, these sects continue in Taiwan and in Chinese communities in Southeast Asia. They were suppressed in China during the Maoist era but revived during the 1990s.

BUDDHISM

Central Asian missionaries, following the trade routes east, brought Buddhism to China in the first century C.E. It was at first viewed as a new Daoist sect, which is not surprising because early translators used Daoist terms to render Buddhist concepts. *Nirvana*, for example, was translated as "not doing" (*wuwei*). In the second century C.E., confusion about the two religions led to the very Chinese view that Laozi had gone to India, where the Buddha had become his disciple, and that Buddhism was the Indian form of Daoism.

Then, as the Han sociopolitical order collapsed in the third century C.E., Buddhism spread rapidly. We are reminded of the spread of Christianity at the end of the Roman Empire. Although an alien religion in China, Buddhism had some advantages over Daoism:

1. It was a doctrine of personal salvation, offering several routes to that goal.
2. It upheld high standards of personal ethics.
3. It had systematic philosophies, and during its early centuries in China, it continued to receive inspiration from India.
4. It drew on the Indian tradition of meditative practices and psychologies, which were the most sophisticated in the world.

By the fifth century C.E. Buddhism had spread over all of China (see Map 7–3 on page 166). Occasionally it was persecuted by Daoist emperors—in the north between 446 and 452 C.E., and again between 574 and 578 C.E. But most courts supported Buddhism. The "Bodhisattva Emperor" Wu of the southern Liang dynasty three times dedicated himself to a monastery and had to be ransomed back by his disgusted courtiers. Temples and monasteries abounded in both the north and the south. There were communities of women as well as of men. Chinese produced Buddhist painting and sculpture of surpassing beauty, and

nirvana In Buddhism the attainment of release from the wheel of *karma*.

HISTORY'S VOICES

THE PEACH BLOSSOM SPRING

*T*he poet Dao Qian wrote in 380 C.E. of a lost village without taxes and untouched by the barbarian invasions and wars of the post-Han era. The simplicity and naturalness of his utopian vision were in accord, perhaps, with certain strains of Neo-Daoist thought. It struck a chord in the hearts of Chinese, and then Koreans and Japanese, inspiring a spate of paintings, poetry, and essays.

UTOPIAS ARE often based on religion, but this one is not. What does this suggest regarding the Chinese view of human nature?

During the T'ai-yuan period of the Ch'in [Qin] dynasty a fisherman of Wuling once rowed upstream, unmindful of the distance he had gone, when he suddenly came to a grove of peach trees in bloom. For several hundred paces on both banks of the stream there was no other kind of tree. The wild flowers growing under them were fresh and lovely, and fallen petals covered the ground—it made a great impression on the fisherman. He went on for a way with the idea of finding out how far the grove extended. It came to an end at the foot of a mountain whence issued the spring that supplied the stream. There was a small opening in the mountain and it seemed as though light was coming through it. The fisherman left his boat and entered the cave, which at first was extremely narrow, barely admitting his body; after a few dozen steps it suddenly opened out onto a broad and level plain where well-built houses were surrounded by rich fields and pretty ponds. Mulberry, bamboo and other trees and plants grew there, and criss-cross paths skirted the fields. The sounds of cocks crowing and dogs barking could be heard from one courtyard to the next. Men and women were coming and going about their work in the fields. The clothes they wore were like those of ordinary people. Old men and boys were carefree and happy.

When they caught sight of the fisherman, they asked in surprise how he had got there. The fisherman told the whole story, and was invited to go to their house, where he was served wine while they killed a chicken for a feast. When the other villagers heard about the fisherman's arrival they all came to pay him a visit. They told him that their ancestors had fled the disorders of Ch'in [Qin] times and, having taken refuge here with wives and children and neighbors, had never ventured out again; consequently they had lost all contact with the outside world. They asked what the present ruling dynasty was, for they had never heard of the Han, let alone the Wei and the Ch'in [Qin]. They sighed unhappily as the fisherman enumerated the dynasties one by one and recounted the vicissitudes of each. The visitors all asked him to come to their houses in turn, and at every house he had wine and food. He stayed several days. As he was about to go away, the people said, "There's no need to mention our existence to outsiders." After the fisherman had gone out and recovered his boat, he carefully marked the route. On reaching the city, he reported what he had found to the magistrate, who at once sent a man to follow him back to the place. They proceeded according to the marks he had made, but went astray and were unable to find the cave again.

Source: *The Poetry of Ta'o Ch'ien* by J. R. Hightower. Copyright © 1970 Clarendon Press. pp. 254–255. Reprinted by permission of Oxford University Press.

thousands of monk-scholars labored to translate sutras and philosophical treaties. Chinese monks went on pilgrimages to India. The record left by Fa Xian, who traveled to India overland and back by sea between 399 and 413 C.E., became a prime source of Indian history. The Tang monk Xuanzang went to India from 629 until 645. Several centuries later, a novelized version of his pilgrimage (combining faith, magic, and adventure) appeared under the title *Journey to the West.*

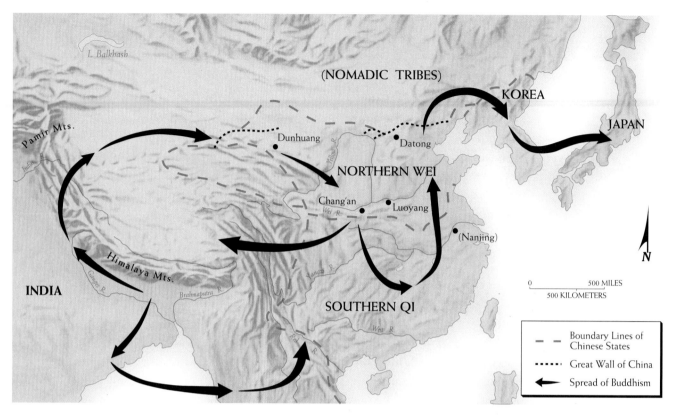

MAP 7–3

The Spread of Buddhism and Chinese States in 500 C.E.   Buddhism originated in a Himalayan state in northwest India and spread in one wave south to India and on to Southeast Asia as far as Java. But Buddhism also spread into northwest India, Afghanistan, Central Asia, and then to China, Korea, and Japan.

WHAT IS the relationship between the spread of Buddhism and trade?

Buddha.   A giant statue of the Buddha dwarfs visitors to the Yungang Grotto in Datong, China. Note the little Buddhas in the walls of the grotto.

China Tourism Press/Chan, Yat Nin/Getty Images, Inc.

A comparison of Indian and Chinese Buddhism highlights some distinctive features of its spread. Buddhism in India had begun as a reform movement. The Buddha had advised people to forget speculative philosophies and elaborate metaphysics and concentrate on simple truths: Life is suffering; the cause of suffering is desire; death does not stop the endless cycle of birth and rebirth; only the attainment of *nirvana* releases one from the "wheel of *karma*." In this most otherworldly of world religions, the cosmic drama of salvation was compressed into single figure—the Buddha meditating under the Bodhi tree. Over the centuries, however, Indian Buddhism developed contending philosophies and conflicting sects. It became virtually indistinguishable from Hinduism and was reabsorbed after 1000 C.E.

In China, there were a number of sects with different doctrinal positions. But the Chinese genius was more syncretic. It adopted the sutras and meditative practices of early Buddhism. It took in the Mahayana philosophies that depicted a succession of Buddhas, cosmic and historical, past and future, all embodying a single ultimate reality. It also honored the sutras and practices of Buddhist devotional sects. Finally, in the Tiantai sect, the Chinese joined together these various elements, explaining them as different levels of a single truth. Thus, the monastic routine of a Tiantai monk would include reading sutras, meditating, and practicing devotional exercises.

Socially, too, Buddhism adapted to China. Ancestor worship demanded heirs to perform the sacrifices. Without progeny, ancestors might become "hungry ghosts." Hence, the first son would be expected to marry and have children, whereas the second son, if he were so inclined, might become a monk. The practice also arose of holding Buddhist masses for dead ancestors. Still another difference between China and India was the more extensive regulation of Buddhism by the state in China. Just as Buddhism was not to threaten the integrity of the family, so Buddhism was not to reduce the taxes paid on land. As a result, limits were placed on the number of monasteries, nunneries, and monastic lands, and men and women had to get permission from the state before they could abandon the world to enter a religious establishment. This regulation, to be sure, was not always enforced.

SUMMARY

Unification of China China first became a unified state under the Qin dynasty (256–206 B.C.E.). In the north, the first Qin emperor built the Great Wall to contain the northern nomadic peoples. The Qin ruled through a strong bureaucracy, but their centralized administration collapsed after the death of the first emperor.

Han Dynasty Under the Han (256 B.C.E.–220 C.E.), China's centralized administration was revived. The Han made such a profound impression on Chinese history that the Chinese still speak of themselves as the "Han people." The Confucian classics became the standard for education and Buddhism arrived in China in the first century C.E.. The Han eventually collapsed through a welter of court intrigue, rebellion, and military seizure of power.

REVIEW QUESTIONS

1. What were the main features of Qin administration? Why did the Qin collapse?

2. What was the "Mandate of Heaven?" What was the "dynastic cycle?"

3. Who were the players who sought power at the Han court? Did the means they used reflect differences in their positions?

4. Did Buddhism "triumph" in China in the same sense in which Christianity triumphed in the Roman world? What problems did both China and the Roman Empire face and how did they try to resolve them?

KEY TERMS

dynastic cycle (p. 156)   **nirvana** (p. 166)

Neo-Daoism (p. 165)   **Silk Road** (p. 158)

IMAGE KEY
for pages 152–153

a. Bronze horse bit from Han Dynasty
b. Great Wall near Peking, China
c. "Prince Charming"—stem with flowers
d. Ancient Chinese armored terra cotta soldier
e. China, Xian, The army of terracotta warriors, close-up
f. Han sculpture of Chinese galloping horse
g. Bronze mirror, Han Dynasty
h. The lintel of an ancient tomb from the Western Han dynasty
i. Scabbard from the Dian Kingdom
j. A Chinese seismograph
k. A pottery model of a Later Han dynasty watch tower
l. A tomb figure; Former Han dynasty

 For additional study resources for this chapter, go to:
www.prenhall.com/craig/chapter7

Visualizing The Past

Visualizing the Past: The Silk Road in Late Antiquity

WHAT IS the relationship between trade and cultural exchange?
Why is the Silk Road a uniquely Eurasian phenomenon?

In late antiquity Eurasia was connected by a series of political, economic, and cultural networks that extended from China to Rome. The Silk Road (see page 161) was the most important link in this nexus of trade and cultural exchange. Along this great route ideas, religions, and artistic styles were transmitted across Eurasia.

◄ **The Story of the Silk Princess.** This sixth-century C.E. wooden panel comes from a Buddhist sanctuary in Khotan, a Central Asian kingdom that flourished along the Silk Road in late antiquity. This scene illustrates the introduction of silk moths to Khotan from China, which first domesticated the insect around 5000 B.C.E and strenuously tried to prevent the spread of silk cultivation. A Chinese princess (second from left) defied the emperor's embargo by hiding mulberry seeds and eggs of the silk moth in her crown and smuggled them past a border-post. An attendant draws the viewer's attention to this by pointing to her head-dress. The basket of cocoons between them signifies the mission's success. On the far right, a figure holding a comb stands in front of a loom with a reel of thread behind. The four-armed deity is the patron of weaving.

Standing Buddha. In the early centuries of the first millennium C.E. the Kushan empire straddled the trade routes that intersected the steppes of Central Asia to become an influential power facilitating the spread of culture and ideas. One of the legacies of Kushan is the Gandharan school of art which fused Greek (Hellenistic) and Indian influences into its own unique style (see chapter 4), as exemplified by this standing Buddha.
National Museum of New Delhi.

Shapur II. Located on the western end of the Silk Road, the Sasanian ▶ Empire (224–651 C.E.), the last Persian dynasty before the advent of Islam, extended its cultural reach far beyond its borders. Sasanian ideals of kingship would later influence Arab notions of imperial splendor as well as the pretensions of regional powers, such as Armenia and Georgia. This silver plate depicts the great fourth-century Sasanian emperor Shapur II (r. 531–579) slaying a deer. The ideal of the king as a mighty hunter is a common motif in late antiquity.
4th century C.E. British Library/London/Great Britain. Hunting Scene. Plate. Sasanian (224–649 C.E.). Shapur II (310–379). Silver. HIP/Art Resource, N.Y.

◀ **Nestorian Christianity in China.** The spread of Christianity along the Silk Road perfectly illustrates the close connection between missionary activity and trading routes in late antiquity. The Nestorians (named after Nestorius, a fifth-century Greek theologian) were an early Christian sect that flourished initially in what is present-day Iraq and Iran. They stressed the human as opposed to the divine aspect of Jesus Christ. Although the Nestorians had little impact on Christian communities in the Mediterranean and Europe, their faith extended east along the Silk Road. The **stele** depicted here, built in 781 C.E., commemorates the introduction of Nestorian Christianity in China.
Musée des Arts Asiatiques–Guimet, Paris, France. Réunion des Musée Nationaux/Art Resource, N.Y.

PART THREE   CONSOLIDATION AND INTERACTION OF WORLD CIVILIZATIONS

EUROPE

511	Death of Clovis, Frankish ruler of Gaul
529	Benedict of Nursia founds Benedictine Order
590–604	Pontificate of Gregory I, "the Great"
768–814	Charles the Great (Charlemagne)

◄ Crown of the Holy Roman Emperor
Kunsthistorisches Museum, Vienna.

▲ Charlemagne

ca. 800–1000	Invasions of England and the Carolingian Empire (Vikings, Magyars, and Muslims)
843	Treaty of Verdun divides Carolingian Empire
910	Cluny Monastery founded
1019–1054	Yaroslav the Wise reigns; peak of Kievan Russia
1054	Schism between Latin and Greek churches
1066	Norman Conquest of England
1073–1085	Investiture controversy
1096–1270	The Crusades

▲ Battle of Hastings

NEAR EAST / INDIA

527–565	Justinian's reign
531–579	Reign of Chosroes Anosharvian in Iran
ca. 570–632	Muhammad
622	The Hijra
616–657	Reign of Harsha; neo-Gupta revival in India
651	Death of last Sasanid ruler
661–750	Umayyad dynasty
680	Death of Al-Husayn at Karbala; second civil war begins
ca. 710	First Muslim invasion of India
750–1258	Abbasid dynasty
786–809	Caliph Harun Al-Rashid reigns

800–1200	Period of feudal" overlordship in India
900–1100	Golden age of Muslim learning
909–1171	Fatimids in North Africa and Egypt
945–1055	Buyid rule in Baghdad
994–1186	Ghaznavid rule in northwestern India, Afghanistan, and Iran
1055–1194	Seljuk rule in Baghdad
1071	Seljuk Turks capture Jerusalem
1081–1118	Byzantine emperor Alexius Comnenus reigns
ca. 1000–1300	Turko-Afghan raids into India

◄ Song dynasty wine pot

Manichaean priests ►

EAST ASIA

589–618	Sui dynasty reunifies China
607	Japan begins embassies to China
618–907	Tang dynasty in China
701–762	Li Bo, Tang poet
710–784	Nara court, Japan's first permanent capital
712	*Records of Ancient Matters,* in Japan
713–756	Emperor Hsuan Tsung reigns in China
755	An Lushan rebellion in China
794–1185	Heian (Kyoto) court in Japan

856–1086	Fujiwara dominate Heian court
960–1279	Song dynasty in China
ca. 1000	*Pillow Book* by Sei Shōnagon and *Tale of Genji* by Murasaki Shikibu
1037–1101	Su Dungpo, Song poet

AFRICA

ca. 500	States of Takrur and Ghana founded
ca. 500–700	Political and commercial ascendancy of Aksum (Ethiopia)
ca. 600–1500	Extensive slave trade from sub-Saharan Africa to Mediterranean
ca. 700–800	Ghanians begin to supply gold to Mediterranean
ca. 700–900	States of Gao and Kanem
ca. 800	Appearance of the Kanuri people around Lake Chad

ca. 800–900	Decline of Aksum
ca. 900–1100	Kingdom of Ghana; capital city, Kumbi Saleh
ca. 1000–1100	Islam penetrates sub-Saharan Africa
1000–1500	"Great Zimbabwe" center of Bantu Kingdom in southeastern Africa

◄ Stela at Aksum

THE AMERICAS

ca. 150–900	Classic period. Dominance of Teotihuacán in central Mexico, Tikal in southern Yucatán

ca. 600–1000	Middle (Huari/Tiwanaku) Horizon in Andean South America

Ruins of Tikal ►

1154–1158	Frederick Barbarosa invades Italy
1182–1226	St. Francis of Assisi
1198–1216	Pontificate of Innocent III
ca. 1100–1300	Growth of trade and towns
1215	Magna Carta granted
ca. 1225–1274	St. Thomas Aquinas
1265–1321	Dante Alighieri

1337	Hundred Years' War begins
ca. 1340–1400	Geoffrey Chaucer
1347–1349	The Black Death
1375–1527	The Italian Renaissance
1485	Battle of Bosworth Field; accession of Henry Tudor to the throne of England
1492	Columbus's first voyage to the New World

*Book of Hours ▶
(15th century)*

1174–1193	Saladin reigns
1192	Muslim conquerors end Buddhism in India
1206–1526	Delhi Sultanate in India; Indian culture divided into Hindu and Muslim
ca. 1220	Mongol invasions of Iran, Iraq, Georgia, Armenia, Syria, India
1258	Hulagu Khan, Mongol leader, conquers Baghdad
1260–1335	Il-Khans rule Iran

1250–1517	Mamluk rule in Egypt
1366–1405	Timur (Tameriane) reigns
1405–1494	Timurids rule in Transoxiana and Iran
1453	Byzantine Empire falls to the Ottoman Turks, with capture of Constantinople

◀ Bronze Shiva

1130–1200	Zhu Xi, Song philosopher
1167–1227	Genghis Khan, founder of Mongol Empire
1185–1333	Kamakura shogunate in Japan
1274–1281	Mongol invasions of Japan
1279–1368	Mongol (Yuan) dynasty in China

◀ Genghis Khan

1336–1467	Ashikaga shogunate in Kyoto
1368–1644	Ming dynasty in China
1405–1433	Voyages of Cheng Ho to India and Africa
1467–1568	Warring States era in Japan
1472–1529	Wang Yang-ming, Ming philosopher

▲ Sesshū painting of a market day in Japan

ca. 1100–1897	Kingdom of Benin in tropical rain forest region
1194–1221	Kanem Empire achieves greatest expansion
1203	Kingdom of Ghana falls to Sosso people
1230–1255	King Sundiata, first ruler of Mali Empire; Walata and Timbuktu become centers of trade and culture
ca. 1230–1450	Kingdom of Mali Empire

▲ Fatimid ceramic bowl

1307–1332	Mansa Musa, greatest king of Mali
1490s	Europeans establish trading posts on western African coast
mid-1400s	Decline of Mali Empire; creation of Songhai Empire
1468	Sonni Ali captures Timbuktu
1476–1507	Reign of King Mai Ali of Bornu in central Sudan
1493–1528	Songhai ruler Askia Muhammed reigns; consolidates Songhai Empire

ca. 800–1400	Chimu Empire on north coast of Peru

1325	Founding of Aztec capital of Tenochtitlán
1428–1519	Period of Aztec expansion
1492	European encounter with America
1519	Cortes conquers Aztec Empire
ca. 1350–1533	Inca Empire in Peru
1533	Pizarro executes Inca ruler Atahualpa

*Pre-Columbian ▶
Aztec sun stone*

8 Imperial China
589 B.C.E. – 1368 C.E.

CHAPTER HIGHLIGHTS

Sui and Tang Dynasties The Sui and Tang dynasties (589–907) reunited China's empire. Under the Tang, China expanded into Central Asia, taking control of much of the lucrative Silk Road along which trade moved to the West. Chang'an, the Tang capital, became the largest city in the world. Tang culture was rich and cosmopolitan, much influenced by its contacts with other cultures. The Tang dynasty was also the golden age of Buddhism in China.

Song Dynasty Under the Song dynasty (960–1279), China experienced an agricultural revolution in which large aristocratic estates worked by serfs gave way to small land holdings owned by free farmers. Advances in technology led to the invention of printing and the development of a coal and iron-smelting industry. The growth of a money economy encouraged the expansion of trade. Song culture was particularly rich in philosophy, poetry, and painting.

The Mongols After their unification by Genghis Khan (1167–1227), the Mongols created the greatest empire in history. The highly mobile Mongol cavalry overwhelmed Chinese armies. By 1279 the Mongols ruled all of China. But Mongol rule in China was short lived and enjoyed only shallow Chinese support. Mongol rule in China ended in 1368.

CHAPTER QUESTIONS

WHY WERE the Sui and Tang dynasties able to recreate China's empire?

WHAT WAS the agricultural revolution that occurred under the Song dynasty?

WHY WERE the Mongols able to conquer such a vast empire?

CHAPTER OUTLINE

- Re-establishment of Empire: Sui (589–618) and Tang (618–907) Dynasties
- Transition to Late Imperial China: The Song Dynasty (960–1279)
- China in the Mongol World Empire: The Yuan Dynasty (1279–1368) and Its Aftermath

If Chinese dynasties from the late sixth to the mid-14th centuries were given numbers like those of ancient Egypt, the Sui and Tang dynasties would be called the Second Empire; the Song, the Third; and the Yuan, the Fourth. Numbers, however, would not convey the distinct personalities of these dynasties. The Tang (618–907) is everyone's favorite dynasty: open, cosmopolitan, expansionist, exuberant, and creative. It was the example of Tang China that decisively influenced the formation of states and high cultures in Japan, Korea, and Vietnam. Poetry during the Tang attained a peak that has not been equaled since. The Song (960–1279) rivaled the Tang in the arts; it was China's great age of painting and the most significant period for philosophy since the Zhou, when Chinese philosophy began. Although not militarily strong, the Song dynasty also witnessed an important commercial revolution. The Yuan (1279–1368) was a short-lived dynasty of Mongol rulers during which China became the most important unit in the largest empire the world has yet seen.

REESTABLISHMENT OF EMPIRE: SUI (589–618) AND TANG (618–907) DYNASTIES

WHY WERE the Sui and Tang dynasties able to recreate China's emperor?

In the period corresponding to the European early Middle Ages, the most notable feature of Chinese history was the reunification of China, the recreation of a centralized bureaucratic empire consciously modeled on the earlier Han dynasty (206 B.C.E.–220 C.E.). Reunification, as usual, began in the north. The first steps were taken by the Northern Wei (386–534), the most enduring of the northern Sino-Turkic states. It moved its court south to Luoyang, made Chinese the language of the court, and adopted Chinese dress and surnames. It also used the leverage of its nomadic cavalry to impose a new land tax, mobilizing resources for state use. The Northern Wei was followed by several short-lived kingdoms. Because the emperors, officials, and military commanders of these kingdoms came from the same aristocratic stratum, none had an advantage over the others, and the throne was often in contention among them.

THE SUI DYNASTY

QUICK REVIEW

Sui Wen-ti (d. 605)
- Founder of the Sui dynasty (589–618)
- Talented ruler who unified China
- Grand Canal constructed and Great Wall rebuilt during his reign

A general of mixed Chinese-Turkic ancestry, Sui Wen-ti (d. 605), who came to power in 581 and began the Sui dynasty (589–618), was no exception to this rule. He was, however, talented and succeeded in unifying the north, restoring the tax base, and reestablishing a centralized bureaucratic government. He went on to conquer and unify southern China. Huge palaces arose in his Wei valley capital. The Great Wall was rebuilt. The Grand Canal was constructed, linking the Yellow and Yangtze Rivers. This canal enabled the northern conquerors to tap the wealth of central and southern China. Peace was maintained with the Turkic tribes along China's northern borders. Eastern Turkic khans (chiefs) were honored with Chinese princesses as brides.

The early years of the Second Sui emperor were also constructive, but then meddling in the politcs of the steppe peoples stirred up wars. The hardships and casualties created by campaigns against Korea and along China's northern border spawned discontent. Natural disasters occurred. The court became bankrupt and demoralized. Rebellions broke out, and a free-for-all again broke out among the armies of aristocratic military commanders. The winner, and the founder of the Tang dynasty, was a relative of the Sui empress and a Sinobarbarian aristocrat of the same social background as those who had ruled before him.

Chinese historians often compare the short-lived Sui dynasty with that of the Qin (256–206 B.C.E.). Each unified China after centuries of fragmentation.

Each achieved a great deal and then fell to be replaced by a long-lasting dynasty. The Tang built on the foundations that had been laid by the Sui, just as the Han had built on those of the Qin.

THE TANG DYNASTY

The first Tang emperor took over the Sui capital, renamed it Chang'an, and made it his own. Within a decade the Tang had extended its authority over all of China. It collected adequate tax revenues to govern effectively, and it inaugurated military campaigns that brought more territory than ever before under Chinese control (see Map 8–1). Confucian scholars served the court. Buddhist temples and monasteries flourished, and good order prevailed throughout the land, particularly from 624 to 755.

Government   The first Tang emperor had been a provincial governor before he became a rebel general. Many of those whom he appointed to posts in the new Tang administration were former Sui officials who had served with him. In building the new administration, he and his successors had to reconcile two conflicting sets of interests. On the one hand, the emperor wanted a bureaucratic

9.1
The T'ang Dynasty (618–907): The Art of Government

MAP EXPLORATION

Interactive map: To explore this map further, go to **http://www.prenhall.com/craig/map8.1**

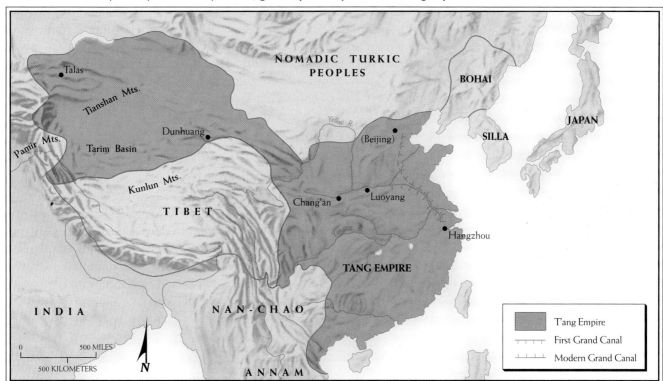

MAP 8–1
The Tang Empire at its Peak During the Eighth Century.   The Tang expansion into Central Asia reopened trade routes to the Middle East and Europe. Students from Bohai, Silla (Korea), and Japan studied in the Tang capital of Chang'an, and then returned, carrying with them Tang books and technology.

WHY DID the Chinese Empire continually seek to expand into Central Asia?

government in which authority was centralized in his own person. On the other hand, he had to make concessions to the aristocrats whose dominance of Chinese society during the late Han continued during the early Tang.

The degree to which political authority was centralized was apparent in the formal organization of the bureaucracy. At the highest level were three organs: Military Affairs, the **Censorate**, and the Council of State. Military Affairs supervised the Tang armies, of which the emperor was commander-in-chief. The Censorate had watchdog functions; it reported instances of misgovernment directly to the emperor and could also remonstrate with the emperor when it considered his behavior improper. The Council of State, which was made up of the heads of the Secretariat, was the most important body. It met daily with the emperor. The Secretariat drafted policies. The Chancellery reviewed them, and State Affairs carried them out. Beneath State Affairs were the Six Ministries, which remained the core of the central government down to the 20th century. Beneath them were several levels of local administration.

The tax system made concessions to the aristocratic families. All land was declared to be the property of the emperor. He distributed it to able-bodied cultivators, who owed him taxes in labor and grain for its use. Because all able-bodied adult males received an equal allotment of land (women got less), the land-tax system was called the "equal field system." Aristocrats, however, were given exemptions and grants of "rank" and "office" lands that, in effect, allowed them to preserve their estates.

Aristocrats were also favored in the recruiting of officials. Most officials either were recommended for posts or received posts because their fathers had been officials. They were drawn almost exclusively from the aristocracy. A tiny percentage were recruited by the Confucian system of examinations. Those who passed the examinations had the highest prestige and were more likely to have brilliant careers. But as only well-to-do families could afford the years of study needed to pass the rigorous examinations, even the examination bureaucrats were usually noble. Entrance to government schools at Chang'an and the secondary capital at Luoyang was restricted to the sons of nobles and officials.

The Empress Wu Women of the inner court continued to play a role in government. Wu Zhao (626–ca. 706), a young concubine of the strong second emperor, so entranced his weak heir that when he succeeded to the throne, he recalled her from the nunnery to which all the former wives of deceased emperors were routinely consigned and installed her at the court. She poisoned or otherwise removed her rivals and became his empress. She also murdered or exiled the statesmen who opposed her. When the emperor suffered a stroke in 660, she completely dominated the court. After his death in 683 she ruled for seven years as regent and then, deposing her son, became emperor herself, the only woman in Chinese history to hold the title. Empress Wu moved the court to Luoyang in her native area and proclaimed a new dynasty. A fervent Buddhist with an interest in magic, she saw herself as the incarnation of the messianic Buddha Maitreya and built temples throughout the land. She patronized the White Horse Monastery, appointing one of her favorites as its abbot. Her sexual appetites were said to have been prodigious. She ruled China until 705, when at the age of 80 she was deposed.

After Empress Wu, no woman would ever become emperor again; yet her machinations did not seriously weaken the court. So highly centralized was power during these early years of the dynasty that the ill effects of her intrigues could be absorbed without provinces breaking away or military commanders becoming

Censorate Branch of the imperial Chinese government that acted as a watchdog, reporting instances of misgovernment directly to the emperor and remonstrating when it considered the emperor's behavior improper.

autonomous. In fact, her struggle for power may have strengthened the central government, for she sought help in controling the old northwestern Chinese aristocrats, not from her family, but from men who passed through the examination system, the Scholars of the North Gate. This broadened her government's base by bringing in aristocrats from other regions of China. The dynamism of a young dynasty may also explain why her rule coincided with the maximal geographical expansion of Tang military power.

The Chang'an of Emperor Xuan Zong   Only a few years after Empress Wu was deposed—years filled with tawdry intrigues—Xuan Zong (r. 713–756) came to the throne. In reaction to Empress Wu, he shifted favor from examination bureaucrats and established government commissions headed by distinguished aristocrats to reform government finances. The Grand Canal was repaired and extended. A new census added to the tax rolls, and wealth and prosperity inspired a cultural flowering. Years later, the great poet Li Bo (701–762) recalled the exhilaration of his youth and the glory of the capital of Xuan Zong:

Long ago, among the flowers and willows,

We sat drinking together at Chang'an.

The Five Barons and Seven Grandees were of our company,

But when some wild stroke was afoot

It was we who led it, yet boisterous though we were

In the arts and graces of life we could hold our own

With any dandy in the town—

In the days when there was youth in your cheeks

And I was still not old.

We galloped to the brothels, cracking our gilded whips,

We sent in our writings to the palace of the Unicorn,

Girls sang to us and danced hour by hour on tortoise-shell mats.

We thought, you and I, that it would be always like this.

How should we know the grasses would stir and dust rise on the wind?

Suddenly foreign horsemen were at the Hsien-ku Pass

Just when the blossom at the palace of Ch'in was opening on the sunny boughs.[1]

Chang'an was an imperial city, an administrative center that lived on taxes. It was designed to exhibit the power of the emperor and the majesty of his court. At

Tang Government Organization

```
                          Emperor
                             |
Military Affairs      Council of State      Censorate
                             |
   Secretariat         State Affairs        Chancellery
                             |
                       Six Ministries
                         Personnel
                         Revenues
                           Rites
                         Military
                          Justice
                       Public Works
                             |
                      10–20 Circuits
                             |
                      358 Prefectures
                             |
                      1,573 Districts
```

[1]Arthur Waley, *The Poetry and Career of Li Po* © 1950, George Allen & Unwin Ltd, an imprint of HarperCollins Publishers, Ltd.

QUICK REVIEW

Chang'an
- Chang'an was an administrative center that lived on taxes
- Designed to show power and majesty of emperor and his court
- City was laid out on a grid

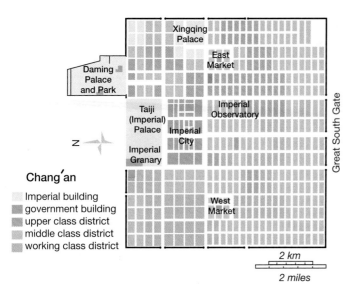

MAP 8–2

Chang'an. The great city of Chang'an had been a Chinese capital since the Han period. By the eighth century there were around a million people within the city walls with the same number close by outside, making it the largest city in the world at the time. The rigorous grid structure accommodates a variety of districts, each with its own function.

HOW DOES the layout of Chang'an exhibit the power of the emperor?

the far north of the city, the palace faced south. The placement was traditional: Confucius, speaking of Shun, said he had only "to hold himself in a respectful posture and to face due south." In front of the palace was a complex of government offices from which an imposing 500-foot-wide avenue led to the main southern gate. The city was laid out on a north-south, east-west grid, which one Tang poet compared to a chessboard. Each block of the city was administered as a ward with interior streets and gates that were locked at night. Enclosed by great walls, the city covered 30 square miles. It was the largest city in the world, having a population of more than one million (half within the walls; the other half in suburbs). The population of China in the year 750 was about 50 million—about 4 percent of the country's present-day population. Chang'an was also a trade center from which caravans set out across Central Asia. Merchants from India, Iran, Syria, and Arabia hawked the wares of the Middle East and all of Asia in its two government-controlled markets.

The Tang Empire A Chinese dynasty is like an accordion, first expanding into the territories of its barbarian neighbors and then contracting back toward its original, densely populated core. The principal threats to the Tang state were from Tibetans in the west, Turks in the northwest and north, and Khitan Mongols in Manchuria.

OVERVIEW CHINESE POLICY TOWARD BARBARIANS

Nomadic peoples from the west and north, whom the Chinese considered to be barbarians, posed a recurrent threat to the Chinese Empire for much of its history. The imperial Chinese government adopted a variety of strategies for dealing with this threat.

Armies	When nothing else worked, the Chinese went on the offensive and sent armies against the nomads. But armies were expensive, and victories over nomads were transitory. Within a few years the tribes would regroup and menace China anew.
Nomads against nomads	The Chinese were adept at inducing their nomadic neighbors to fight among themselves. This distracted the nomads and diverted their energy and attention away from China.
Defense	The Chinese fortified their northern borders, most conspicuously with the Great Wall. At times China also put its frontier provinces under military rule.
Diplomacy	China sought to neutralize its neighbors by loosely attaching them to its empire. Nomadic tribes, Central Asian states, and Korea became "tributaries" of the emperor. Their rulers sent embassies bearing gifts ("tribute") to the imperial court, which fed and housed them, and sent them home with even costlier gifts and reports of China's power, wealth, splendor, and cultural achievements. The Chinese hoped that these "barbarians" would be too overawed to pose a threat.

To protect their border, the Tang employed a four-tier policy. When nothing else would work, the Tang dispatched an army. But armies were expensive, and using them against nomads was like sweeping back the waves with a broom. A victory might dissolve a tribal confederation, but a decade or two later the federation would reorganize under a new leader. For example, in 630 Tang armies defeated the eastern Turks; in 648, they took the Tarim basin and kept trade routes to western Asia open for almost a century. In 657, they defeated the western Turks and extended Chinese influence across the Pamir Mountains to petty states near Samarkand. By 698, however, the Turks were again invading northeastern China, and from 711 to 736 they controlled the steppe from the Oxus River to China's northern frontier.

China's experience with Tibet was much the same. From 670 Tibet expanded and threatened China. In 679, it was defeated, but in 714 it rose again. More wars were fought from 727 to 729. A settlement was reached in 730, but wars then broke out again. In 752, Tibet allied with the state of Nan Chao in Yunnan. In 763, Tibetan forces captured and looted Chang'an. They were driven out, but even at the height of Tang power, no final victory was possible.

The second defensive strategy the Chinese employed was to use nomads against nomads. The critical development for the Tang was the rise to power of the Uighur Turks. From 744 to 840, the Uighurs controlled Central Asia and were staunch allies of the Tang. Without their support, the Tang dynasty would never have lasted as long as it did.

The third option was to station military along China's borders, including the Great Wall. At mid-dynasty, whole frontier provinces in the north and the northwest were assigned to military commanders, who in time came to control civil as well as military affairs. The bulk of the Tang military was stationed in frontier commands. At times the autonomy and rebel potential of these forces were as much a threat to the Tang court as to the nomadic enemy.

Diplomacy is always cheaper than war, and the fourth line of defense was to bring potential enemies into the empire as tributaries. The Tang defined "tributary" broadly. It included principalities that were truly dependent on China, Central Asian states conquered by China, enemy states (such as Tibet or the Thai state of Nan Chao in Yunnan) when they were not actually at war with China, the Korean state of Silla (which had unified the peninsula with Tang aid but then blocked Tang armies that tried to impose Chinese hegemony), and wholly independent states, such as Japan. All sent embassies and gifts to the Tang court, which hosted them and sent them home with costly presents.

For some countries these embassies had a special significance. As the only "developed nation" in eastern Asia, China was a model for countries still in the throes of state formation. Foreign embassies to the Chinese court were exposed to Tang culture and technology: its philosophy and literature; its administrative and land systems; its Buddhism; and its arts, architecture, and medicine. In 640, there were 8,000 Koreans, mostly students, in Chang'an. Never again would China exert such an influence, for never again would its neighbors be at such a formative and receptive stage of development.

Rebellion and Decline In the mid–eighth century, signs of decline began to appear. China's frontiers started to contract. Tribes in Manchuria became unruly. Tibetans threatened China's western border. In 751, an overextended Tang army led by a Korean general was defeated

Imperial China

589–618	Sui dynasty
618–907	Tang dynasty
960–1279	Song dynasty
1279–1368	Yuan (Mongol) dynasty

by Arabs near Samarkand in western Asia, shutting down China's caravan trade with the West for more than five centuries. Furthermore, in 755 a Sogdian general, An Lu-shan, who commanded three Chinese provinces on the northeastern frontier, led his 160,000 troops in a rebellion that swept across northern China, capturing Luoyang and then Chang'an. The emperor fled to Sichuan.

The event contained an element of romance. Ten years earlier the emperor Xuan Zong had taken a young woman, Yang Guifei, from the harem of his son. (He gave his son another beauty in exchange.) So infatuated was he that he neglected not only the other "3,000 beauties of his inner chambers" but the business of government as well. For a while this did not matter because he had an able chief minister. But when the minister died and Xuan Zong appointed his concubine's second cousin to the post, he set a train of events in motion that led to a rebellion. En route to Sichuan, his soldiers, blaming Yang Guifei for their plight, strangled her. The event was later immortalized in a poem that described her "snow-white skin," "flowery face," and "moth eyebrows," as well as the 72-year-old emperor's "eternal sorrow." After a decade of wars and much devastation, a new emperor restored the dynasty with the help of the Uighur Turks, who rewarded themselves by looting Chang'an. The recovery and the century of relative peace and prosperity that followed testify to the resilience of Tang institutions. China was smaller, but military governors secured its diminished frontiers. Provincial governors were more autonomous, but they still sent taxes to the capital. Occasional rebellions were suppressed by imperial armies, sometimes led by eunuchs. Most of the emperors were weak, but three were strong and able to implement reforms. Edwin O. Reischauer, who translated the diary of a Japanese monk who studied in China during the early ninth century, commented that the "picture of government in operation" that the diarist painted "is amazing for the ninth century, even in China:"

> The remarkable degree of centralized control still existing, the meticulous attention to written instructions from higher authorities, and the tremendous amount of paper work involved in even the smallest matters of administration are all the more striking just because this was a period of dynastic decline.[2]

Of the reforms of this era, none was more important than the reorganization of the land system. The official census, on which land allotments and taxes were based, showed a drop in population from 53 million before the An Lushan rebellion to 17 million afterward. Unable to find enough people to fill the registers, the government's revenue from land fell below what it received from salt and iron. It, therefore, replaced the equal field system with a fixed quota of taxes levied on each province and paid twice a year. The new system began in 780 and continued into the 16th century.

During the second half of the ninth century the government weakened further. Most provinces were autonomous and ruled by military commanders who resisted efforts to enforce centralized control. Wars were fought with the state of Nan Chao in the southwest. Bandits appeared. Droughts sparked peasant uprisings. By the 880s, warlords had divided China into independent kingdoms, and in 907 the Tang dynasty fell. Within half a century, however, a new dynasty arose. The fall of the Tang did not lead to centuries of division as had the collapse of the Han. Something had changed within China.

Tang Figurine. During the Tang dynasty (618–907), well-to-do families placed glazed pottery figurines in the tombs of their dead. Perhaps they were intended to accompany and amuse the dead in the afterlife. Note the fancy chignon hairstyle of this female flutist, one figure in a musical ensemble. Today these figurines are sought by collectors around the world.

Werner Forman/Art Resource, N.Y.

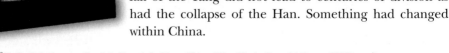

[2]E. O. Reischauer, *Ennin's Travels in Tang China* (New York: Ronald Press, 1955), p. 7.

Relief of Tang Emperor's Horse. A bearded "barbarian" groom tends the charger of the second Tang emperor (r. 626–649). This stone relief was found on the emperor's tomb. Note the stirrup, a Chinese invention of the fourth century C.E.

A Relief of Emperor T'ai T'song's Horse, "Autumn Dew." University of Pennsylvania Museum, Philadelphia (NEG.# S8-62840).

Tang Culture   The creativity of the Tang period arose from the juxtaposition and interaction of cosmopolitan, medieval Buddhist, and secular elements—a development rooted in the wealth and the social order of the recreated empire. Tang culture was cosmopolitan not just because of its broad contacts with other cultures and peoples but also because of its openness to them. Buddhist pilgrims journeyed to India, and Indian art and thought returned to China. The influence of voluptuous Indian painting and sculpture can be seen, for instance, in the Tang representation of the *bodhisattva*. Commercial contacts were also widespread, and foreign goods were sold in Chang'an marketplaces. Communities of central and western Asians were established in the capital, and Arab and Iranian quarters grew in the seaports of southeastern China. Merchants imported religions as well as goods: Nestorian Christianity, Zoroastrianism, Manichaeism, Judaism, and Islam. Most of these were suppressed by persecution during the ninth century, but Islam and small pockets of Judaism survived until the 20th century. Central Asian music and musical instruments became so popular as almost to displace the native traditions. Tang ladies adopted foreign hairstyles. Foreign dramas and acrobatic performances by western Asians could be seen in the streets of the capital. Even among the pottery figurines customarily placed in tombs were representations of western Asian traders and Central Asian grooms, along with those of horses, camels, and court ladies that today may be seen in museums around the world. In Tang poetry, too, what was foreign was not shunned but judged on its own merits or presented as exotically attractive.

The Tang dynasty was slightly less an age of faith than the preceding Six Dynasties, but it was, nonetheless, the golden age of Buddhism in China. Patronized by emperors and aristocrats, the Buddhist establishment acquired vast landholdings and great wealth. Temples and monasteries were constructed

Caravaneer on a Camel. The animal's shaggy mane indicates that it is a Bactrian camel from Central Asia.

Réunion des Musées/Art Resource, N.Y.

Amitabha Buddha Buddhist Lord of the Western Paradise, or Pure Land.

Zen A form of Buddhism, which taught that Buddha was only a man and exhorted each person to attain enlightenment by his or her own efforts.

throughout China. To gain even an inkling of the beauty and sophistication of the temple architecture, the wooden sculpture, or the paintings on the temple walls, one must see Hryji or the ancient temples of Nara in Japan, for little of note has survived in China. The single exception is the Caves of the Thousand Buddhas at Dunhuang in China's far northwest, which were sealed during the 11th century for protection from Tibetan raiders and not rediscovered until the 20th century. They contained stone sculptures, Buddhist frescoes, and thousands of manuscripts in Chinese and Central Asian languages.

Only during the Tang did China have a religious institution that was at all comparable to medieval Europe's church, but even then it was subservient to the far stronger Tang state. Buddhist wealth and learning entailed secular obligations. Tang temples served as schools, inns, and even bathhouses. The temples lent money. Priests performed funerals and dispensed medicines. Occasionally the state recaptured revenues gifted to temples. The fortunes of Chinese Buddhism began to decline when, between 841 and 845, an ardent Daoist emperor confiscated millions of acres of tax-exempt lands, put 260,000 monks and nuns back on the tax registers, and destroyed 4,600 monasteries and 40,000 shrines.

During the early Tang, the principal Buddhist sect was the Tiantai, but after the mid-ninth-century suppression of Buddhist temples, other sects came to the fore:

1. One devotional sect focused on Maitreya, a Buddha of the future, who would create a paradise on earth. Maitreya was a cosmic messiah, not a human figure. The messianic teachings of the sect often furnished the ideology for popular uprisings and rebellions like the White Lotus, which claimed that it was renewing the world in anticipation of Maitreya's coming.

2. Another devotional sect worshiped the **Amitabha Buddha**, the Lord of the Western Paradise or Pure Land. This sect taught that in the early centuries after the death of the historical Buddha, his teachings had been accurately transmitted and people could obtain enlightenment by their own efforts, but that at present the Buddha's teachings had become so distorted that only by reliance on Amitabha could humans obtain salvation. All who called on Amitabha with a pure heart and perfect faith would be saved. Developing a congregational form of worship, this sect became the largest in China and deeply influenced Chinese popular religion.

3. A third sect, and the most influential among the Chinese elites, was known in China, where it began, as Chan and is better known in the West by its Japanese name, **Zen**. Zen had no cosmic Buddhas. It taught that the historical Buddha was only a man and exhorted each person to attain

enlightenment by his or her own efforts. Although its monks were often the most learned in China, Zen was anti-intellectual in its emphasis on direct intuition into one's own Buddha-nature. Enlightenment was to be obtained by a regimen of physical labor and meditation. To jolt the monk into enlightenment—after preparation by long hours of meditation— some Zen sects used little problems not answerable by normal ratiocination: "What was your face before you were conceived?" "If all things return to the One, what does the One return to?" "From the top of a hundred-foot pole, how do you step forward?" The psychological state induced by attempting to deal with these problems is compared to that of "a rat pursued into a blocked pipe" or "a mosquito biting an iron ball." The discipline of meditation, combined with a Zen view of nature, profoundly influenced the arts in China and subsequently in Korea and Japan as well.

Another characteristic of Tang culture was the reappearance of secular scholarship and letters. The reestablishment of a centralized bureaucratic government stimulated the tradition of learning that had been partially interrupted by the fall of the Han dynasty in the third century C.E. Most men of letters were officials, and most high-ranking officials were also painters or poets. An anthology of Tang poetry compiled during the Ming period (1368–1644) contained 48,900 poems by almost 2,300 authors. This secular stream of Tang culture was not ideologically anti-Buddhist. Officials were often privately sympathetic to Buddhism. But as men of affairs active in government, their values became increasingly this-worldly.

Court historians of the Tang revived the Han practice of writing official histories of preceeding dynasties. For the first time scholars wrote comprehensive institutional histories and regional and local gazetteers. They compiled dictionaries and wrote commentaries on the Confucian classics. Other scholars wrote ghost stories or tales of adventure, using the literary language. Buddhist sermons were often written in the vernacular, and more paintings were Buddhist than secular. Chinese landscape painting originated during the Tang. Nowhere, however, was the growth of a secular culture more evident than in poetry, the greatest achievement of Tang letters.

Li Bo (701–762) was exceptional among Tang poets in never having sat for the civil service examinations. Whether he can be called wholly secular is questionable. Li Bo might better be called Daoist. But he clearly was not Buddhist. Born in Sichuan, his poetic reputation won him an official post at Chang'an, which he held for a short time. Large and muscular, he was a swordsman and a carouser. Of the 20,000 poems he is said to have composed, 1,800 have survived, and a fair number have titles like "Bring on the Wine" or "Drinking Alone in the Moonlight." According to legend, he drowned while drunkenly attempting to embrace the reflection of the moon in a lake. His poetry is clear, powerful, passionate, and always sensitive to beauty (see "A Poem by Li Bo").

Du Fu (712–770), an equally famous Tang poet, was from a literary family. He failed the metropolitan examination at the age of 23 and spent years in wandering and poverty. At 39, he received an official appointment after presenting his poetry to the court. Four years later he was given a military post. He fell into rebel

Great Wild Goose Pagoda at Ci'en Temple, Xi'an, China, Tang Dynasty, 645. During the Tang dynasty, Buddhism reached its greatest development, although under the patronage of the later Tang emperors a conservative reaction reasserted Confucian influence at the expense of Buddhism.

HISTORY'S VOICES

A POEM BY LI BO

* **IT HAS** been said that concreteness of imagery is the genius of Chinese poetry. How does this poem support that contention?

THE RIVER MERCHANT'S WIFE: A LETTER

While my hair was still cut straight across my
 forehead
I played about the front gate, pulling flowers.
You came by on bamboo stilts, playing horse,
You walked about my seat, playing with blue plums.
And we went on living in the village of Chokan:
Two small people, without dislike or suspicion.
At fourteen I married My Lord you.
I never laughed, being bashful.
Lowering my head, I looked at the wall.
Called to, a thousand times, I never looked back.
At fifteen I stopped scowling,
I desired my dust to be mingled with yours
Forever and forever and forever.
Why should I climb the look out?

At sixteen you departed,
You went into far Ku-to-yen, by the river of swirling
 eddies,
And you have been gone five months.
The monkeys make sorrowful noise overhead.
You dragged your feet when you went out.
By the gate now, the moss is grown, the different
 mosses,
Too deep to clear them away!
The leaves fall early this autumn, in wind.
The paired butterflies are already yellow with August
Over the grass in the West garden;
They hurt me. I grow older.
If you are coming down through the narrows of the
 river Kiang,
Please let me know beforehand,
And I will come out to meet you,
As far as Cho-fu-Sa.

Source: "The River Merchant's Wife: A Letter" by Ezra Pound, from *Personae.* Copyright © 1926 by Ezra Pound. Reprinted by permission of New Directions Publishing Corp.

hands during the An Lushan rebellion but escaped. He was reappointed to a civil post, but was ultimately dismissed and condemned to further hardships. His poetry is less lyrical and more allusive than Li Bo's. It also reflects more compassion for human suffering. For example, he writes about the mother whose sons have been conscripted and sent to war; the brothers scattered by war; his own family, to whom he returned after having been given up for dead. Like Li Bo, he felt that humans are short-lived and that only nature endures. Visiting the ruins of the palace of the second Tang emperor, he saw "grey rats scuttling over ancient tiles" and "in its shadowed chambers ghost fires green." In describing the ruins, he writes, "Its lovely ladies are the brown soil" and only "tomb horses of stone remain." His response to this sad scene was somewhat Stoic and un-Buddhist:

> Sing wildly, let the tears cover your open hands.
>
> Then go ever onward and on the road of your travels,
>
> Meet none who prolong their fated years.[3]

---

[3]S. Owen, *The Great Age of Chinese Poetry: The High Tang.* © 1980, New Haven, CT: Yale University Press, pp. 223–224. Reprinted by permission.

TRANSITION TO LATE IMPERIAL CHINA: THE SONG DYNASTY (960–1279)

*M*ost traditional Chinese history was written to illustrate what Chinese scholars assumed to be an inevitable dynastic cycle—a pattern of rise and fall, of expansion and contraction, that was the fate of every dynasty. Certainly the Song fit this model. It reunified China in 960 and established its capital at Kaifeng on the Yellow River (see Map 8–3). It provided effective government for 170 years, a period called the Northern Song. In 1127, the Song lost control over the north, but for another 150 years it continued to rule the south from a new capital at Hangzhou in east-central China. The Southern Song fell before the Mongol onslaught in 1279.

But there is more to Chinese history than a repetitive dynastic cycle. Important longer-term changes cut across dynasties. One such set of changes began during the late Tang and continued into the Song period. Its affects on economy, society, state, and culture help to explain why China after the Tang did not relapse into centuries of disunity as it had after the Han—and why China never again experienced more than brief intervals of disunity. Fundamental transformations contributed more to these changes than emperors, empresses, eunuchs, and generals.

AGRICULTURAL REVOLUTION OF THE SONG: FROM SERFS TO FREE FARMERS

Landed aristocrats had dominated local society in China during the Sui and Tang periods. The tillers of their estates were little more than serfs. Labor service was the heaviest tax, and whether performed on the lands aristocrats held by office or rank, or on other government lands, it created a system of social subordination.

The aristocracy declined under the Tang and after the Tang's fall. Estates shrank as they were divided among all a man's male children after his death. Artistocracts, whose local property diminished, were attracted to the capital where they became a metropolitan elite. After the fall of the Tang, the aristocratic estates were often seized by warlords. The fading power of the aristocracy and changes in the land and tax systems worked in favor of those who tilled the soil. The end of the equal field system freed farmers to buy and sell land, and ownership of land as private property gave cultivators greater independence. They could now move about as they pleased. Taxes paid in grain gave way during the Song to taxes in money. The commutation of the labor tax to a money tax gave farmers more control over their time. Conscription, the cruelest and heaviest labor tax of all, disappeared as the conscript armies of the early and middle Tang were replaced by professional soldiers.

Changes in technology also benefited the cultivator. New strains of an early-ripening rice permitted double cropping. In the Yangzi region, extensive water-control projects were carried out, and more fertilizers were used. New commercial crops were developed. Tea, which had been introduced during the Six Dynasties as a medicine and had been drunk by monks during the Tang, became widely cultivated. Cotton also became a common crop. Because taxes paid in money tended to become fixed, much of the profit generated by increased productivity accrued to the cultivator. Of course, not all benefited equally. Landlords and landless tenants as well as independent small farmers still existed.

MAP 8–3

The Northern Song and Liao Empires (Top) and the Southern Song and Jin Empires (Bottom). During the Northern Song, the Mongol Liao dynasty ruled only the extreme northern edge of China. During the Southern Song, in contrast, the Manchurian Jin dynasty ruled half of China.

WHY DID the authority of the Song dynasty not extend beyond southern China after 1279?

The disappearance of the aristocrats also increased the authority of district magistrates, who no longer had to contend with their interference in local affairs. The Song magistrate became the sole representative of imperial authority in each locality, but there were too many villages in his district for him to be involved regularly in their internal governance. As long as taxes were paid and order maintained, affairs were left in the hands of the village elites. The Song farmer, therefore, enjoyed rising income, greater freedom, and substantial self-government.

One other development that began during the Song—and became vastly more important later—was the appearance of a scholar-gentry class. The typical gentry family lived in the district seats or market towns and had at least one member who had passed the provincial civil service examination. Socially and culturally, these gentry were closer to magistrates than villagers, but they usually owned land in the villages and thus shared some interests with the local landholders. Although much less powerful than the former aristocrats, the gentry took a hand in local affairs and at times functioned as a buffer between the village and the magistrate's office.

COMMERCIAL REVOLUTION OF THE SONG

Changes in the countryside contributed to, and were stimulated by, several factors: demographic shifts, innovative technologies, growth of cities, spread of money, and rising trade. The effects of these developments varied by region, but overall the Song economy reached new heights of prosperity.

Emergence of the Yangzi Basin Until late in the Tang, the north had been China's most populous and productive region. But from the late ninth-century the center of gravity of China's population, agricultural production, and culture shifted to the lower and eastern Yangzi region. Between 800 and 1100, the population of the region tripled as China's total population increased to about 100 million. The Yangzi's rice paddies yielded more per acre than the wheat or millet fields of the north, making rice the tax base of the empire. The area's wealth led to the establishment of so many schools that the government set quotas for the examination system to prevent the Yangzi region from dominating China. The Northern Song capital itself was kept in the north for strategic reasons, but it was situated at Kaifeng, further east than Luoyang, at the point where the Grand Canal, which carried tax rice from the south, joined the Yellow River.

New Technology During the Northern Song a coal and iron-smelting industry developed in north China, providing the Chinese with better tools and weapons. Using coke and bellows to heat furnaces to temperatures required for carbonized steel, Song technology was the most advanced in the world.

Printing began in China with the use of carved seals. The earliest woodblock texts, mostly on Buddhist subjects, appeared in the seventh century. By the 10th century, a complete edition of the classics had been published, and by the mid-Song books printed with movable type were fairly common. Other advances during the Song were the abacus, the use of gunpowder in grenades and projectiles, and improvements in textiles and porcelains.

Irrigation Methods on a Farm in the Yangzi Valley. A farmer and his wife use their legs and feet to work the square-pallet chain pump, a boy drives a water buffalo to turn a water-pumping device, and another boy fishes.

© Photograph by Wan-go Weng/Collection of H. C. Weng.

Rise of a Money Economy Exchange during the Tang had been based on silk. Coins had been issued, but their circulation was limited. During the Northern Song large amounts of copper cash were coined, but the demand rose more rapidly than the supply. Coins were made with holes in the center so that they could be strung together (a string of 1,000 was the usual unit for large transactions). In the Southern Song, silver began to be minted to complement copper cash (10 times as much silver in the late 12th century as in the early 11th century). Letters of credit were used by merchants, and various kinds of paper money were issued. The penetration of money into the village economy was such that by 1065 tax receipts paid in money had risen to 38 million strings of cash—compared with a mere two million in mid-Tang.

Trade The growth of trade spurred the demand for money. During the Tang most cities had been administrative centers supported by taxes from the countryside. The salaries and government expenditures made possible by these taxes created a demand for services and commercial products that turned these cities into islands of commerce in a noncommercial hinterland. In most of China's seven or eight economic regions, this pattern continued during the Song, but in the capital and the economically advanced regions along the Yangzi, cities became the hubs of regional commercial networks, with district seats or market towns serving as secondary centers for the local markets beneath them.

As this transition occurred, cities with more than 100,000 households almost quadrupled in number. The Northern Song capital at Kaifeng had 260,000 households—probably more than one million inhabitants—and the Southern Song capital at Hangzhou had 391,000 households. Compare these capitals to those of backward Europe: London during the Northern Song had a population of about 18,000; Rome during the Southern Song had 35,000; and Paris even a century later had fewer than 60,000.

Furthermore, these Song capitals, unlike Chang'an with its walled wards that closed at night, were open within and spread beyond their outer walls. As in present-day Chinese cities, their main avenues were lined with shops. Merchant guilds replaced government officials as the managers of marketplaces. Growing

Chinese Ladies Preparing Silk. The manufacture of silk was an important part of the Song economy and was exported abroad.

Emporer Hui Tsung, Chinese, 1082–1135. Ladies Preparing Newly Made Silk, Part 11. Chinese scroll painting, Song Dynasty. Courtesy, Museum of Fine Arts, Boston. Reproduced with permission. © 2006 Museum of Fine Arts, Boston. All Rights Reserved.

wealth also led to a taste for luxury and an increasingly secular lifestyle. Restaurants, theaters, wine shops, and brothels abounded. Entertainment quarters with fortunetellers, jugglers, chess masters, acrobats, and puppeteers sprang up. Such amusements had previously been available in Chang'an, but now their numbers increased, and they catered to traders and rich merchants as well as to officials.

Trade between regions during the Song was limited mainly to luxury goods like silk, lacquerware, medicinal herbs, and porcelains. Only where transport was cheap—along rivers, canals, or the coast—was interregional trade in bulk commodities economical, and even there it usually thrived only temporarily to make up for specific shortages.

Foreign trade also reached new heights during the Song. In the north, Chinese traders bought horses from Tibetan, Turkic, and Mongol border states, and sold silks and tea. Along the coast, Chinese merchants took over the port trade that during the Tang had been in the hands of Korean, Arab, and Persian merchants. The new hegemony of Chinese merchants was based on improved ships using both sail and oars and equipped with watertight compartments and better rudders. Chinese captains, navigating with the aid of the compass, came to dominate the sea routes from Japan in the north to Sumatra in the south. The products traded overseas reflected China's advanced economy. China imported raw materials and exported finished goods. Porcelains were sent to Southeast Asia and then were carried by Arab ships to medieval trading centers on the Persian Gulf and down the coast of East Africa as far south as Zanzibar.

GOVERNMENT: FROM ARISTOCRACY TO AUTOCRACY

The millennium of late imperial China after the Tang is often spoken of as the age of autocracy or as China's era of absolute monarchy. Earlier emperors were often personally powerful, but beginning with the Song, changes occurred that made it easier for emperors to be autocrats.

Song emperors had the advantage of direct personal control over more offices than their Tang predecessors. Also, the Board of Academicians, an advisory office, presented the emperor with policy options separate from those presented by the Secretariat-Chancellery. The emperor could thus use the one against the other and prevent bureaucrats in the Secretariat-Chancellery from dominating his government.

The central government of the Song was better funded than previous administrations. Revenues in 1100 were three times the peak revenues of the Tang. Income was derived from increasing population and agricultural wealth, government monopolies (on salt, wine, and tea), and various duties, fees, and taxes levied on domestic and foreign trade. During the Northern Song these commercial revenues rivaled the land tax; during the Southern Song they surpassed it. Confucian officials continued to stress the primacy of land, but throughout late imperial China, commerce was a vital source of revenues.

Another change that strengthened the emperors was the disappearance of the aristocracy. During the Tang the emperor had come from the same Sino-Turkic nobility of northwestern China as most of his principal ministers, and he was essentially the organ of a state that ruled on behalf of this aristocracy. Aristocrats monopolized the high posts of government. They married among themselves and with the imperial family. They called the emperor the Son of Heaven, but they knew he was one of them. During the Song, however, government officials were commoners and mostly products of the examination system. They were separated from the emperor by an enormous social gulf and saw him as a person apart.

The Song examination system was larger than that of the Tang, but smaller than under later dynasties. Whereas only 10 percent of officials had been recruited by examination during the Tang, the Song figure rose to more than 50 percent and included the most important officials. The first examination was given at regional centers. The applicant took the examination in a walled cubicle under close supervision. To ensure impartiality, his answers were recopied by clerks and his name was replaced by a number before his examination was sent to the officials who graded it. Of those who sat for the examination, only a tiny percentage passed. The second hurdle was the metropolitan examination at the national capital, where the precautions were equally elaborate. Only one in five, or about 200 a year, passed. The average successful applicant was in his mid-30s. The final hurdle was the palace examination, which weeded out a few more and assigned rankings to the rest.

9.2
Song China: Imperial
Examination System

To pass the examinations, the candidate had to memorize the Confucian classics, interpret selected passages, write in the literary style, compose poems on themes given by the examiners, and propose solutions to contemporary problems in terms of Confucian philosophy. The quality of the officials produced by the Song system was impressive. A parallel might be drawn with 19th-century Britain, where students in the classics at Oxford and Cambridge went on to become generalist bureaucrats. The Chinese examination system that flourished during the Song continued, with some interruptions, into the 12th century. The continuity of Chinese government during this millennium depended on the common culture and values of the examination elite.

The examination meritocracy was sustained by land, education, and office. Landed wealth paid the costs of education. A poor peasant or city dweller could not afford the years of study needed to pass the examinations, and without passing the examinations, an official position was unobtainable. Family wealth, however, could not be preserved unless one held an office. The Chinese pattern of inheritance, as noted earlier, divided property at each change of generation. China's extended-family or clan system, however, meant that bright children were often educated by a wealthy relative who held an office. Some families passed the civil service examinations for several generations running. More often, the sons of well-to-do officials did not study as hard as those with scant means. The adage "shirt sleeves to shirt sleeves in three generations" describes a common fate during the Song and later dynasties.

How the merchants related to this system is unclear. They had wealth but were despised by scholar-officials as grubby profit seekers and were barred from taking the examinations. Some merchants avoided the system altogether, for an education in the Confucian classics did little to fit a merchant's son for a career in commerce. Others bought land for status and security, and their sons or grandsons became eligible to take the exams. Similarly, a small peasant might build up his holdings, become a landlord, and educate a son or grandson. The system was steeply hierarchical, but it was not closed and did not produce a new, self-perpetuating aristocracy.

SONG CULTURE

As society and government changed during the Tang-Song transition, so too did culture. Song culture retained some of the energy of the Tang while becoming more intensely and perhaps more narrowly Chinese. The rich Song culture was encouraged by a rising economy, an increase in the number of schools, higher literacy rates, and the spread of printing. Song culture was less aristocratic, less cosmopolitan, and more closely associated with the officials and the scholar-gentry, who were both its practitioners and its patrons. It also was less Buddhist than the Tang had been. Only the Buddhist Zen (Chan) sect remained vital, and many Confucians were outspokenly anti-Buddhist and anti-Daoist. The secular culture of officials that originated during the Tang broadened to become the mainstream during the Song.

Chinese believe that the Song dynasty marked the peak of their traditional culture. It was, for example, China's greatest age of pottery and porcelains. High-firing techniques were developed, and kilns were established in every area. There was a rich variety of beautiful glazes. Shapes were restrained and harmonious. Song pottery, like nothing produced in the world before it, made ceramics a major art form in East Asia. This was also an age of great historians. Sima Guang (1019–1086) wrote *A Comprehensive Mirror for Aid in Government*, which treated not a single dynasty but all Chinese history. His work was more sophisticated than previous histories in that it included a discussion of documentary sources and an explanation of why he chose to rely on one source rather than another. The greatest achievements of the Song, however, were in philosophy, poetry, and painting.

An Elegant Song Dynasty Wine Pot. This pot has green celadon glaze (24.8 cm high).

Ewer with carved flower sprays. Porcelain with molded and carved low-relief decoration in grayish-green glaze approx. 1000–12000. Northern Song Dynasty (960–1127) H. 9 5/8 in × W. 5 1/4 in × D. 7 3/4 in, H. 24.5 cm × W. 13.4 cm × D. 19.7 cm. China; Shaanxi province. © Gift of The Asian Art Museum Foundation.

Philosophy   The Song was second only to the Zhou as a creative age in philosophy. A series of original thinkers culminated in the towering figure of Zhu Xi (1130–1200). Zhu Xi studied Daoism and Buddhism in his youth, along with Confucianism. A brilliant student, he passed the metropolitan examination at the age of 18. During his 30s, he focused his attention on Confucianism, deepening and making more systematic its social and political ethics by drawing on Buddhist and native metaphysical elements. He pioneered a new Confucianism as a viable alternative to Buddhism for Chinese intellectuals. Zhu Xi became famous as a teacher at the White Deer Grotto Academy, and his writings were widely distributed. Before the end of the Song, his version of Confucianism had become the standard interpretation used in the civil service examinations, and it remained so until the 20th century.

Comparable figures in other traditions include Saint Thomas Aquinas (1224–1274) of medieval Europe and the Islamic theologian al-Ghazali (1058–1111), both of whom produced a new synthesis or worldview that lasted for centuries. Aquinas combined Aristotle and Latin theology just as Zhu Xi combined Confucian philosophy and metaphysical notions from other sources. Because Zhu Xi used terms such as the "great ultimate" and because he emphasized a Zen-like meditation called "quiet sitting," some contemporary critics claimed that his Neo-Confucian philosophy was a Buddhist wolf in the clothing of a Confucian sheep. This was unfair. Whereas Aquinas would make philosophy serve religion, Zhu Xi made religion or metaphysics serve philosophy. In his hands, the "great ultimate" or *li* ("principle") lost its otherworldly character and became a constituent of all things in the universe. Perhaps Zhu Xi's philosophy should be characterized as innerworldly.

Later critics often argued that Zhu Xi's teachings encouraged metaphysical speculation at the expense of practical ethics. Zhu Xi's followers replied that, on the contrary, his teachings gave practical ethics a systematic underpinning and positively contributed to individual moral responsibility. What was discovered within by Neo-Confucian quiet sitting was just those positive ethical truths enunciated by Confucius more than 1,000 years earlier. The new metaphysics did not change the Confucian social philosophy.

Zhu Xi urged that scholar-officials be chosen by schools rather than by examinations, and it is ironic that his teachings became a new orthodoxy that was maintained by the channelizing effect of the civil service examinations. However, Zhu Xi's teachings may have contributed to the stability of late imperial China, for like the examination system, the imperial institution, the scholar-gentry class, and the land system, his interpretation of Confucianism maintained continuity and impeded change. Some historians fault the Zhu Xi orthodoxy for stifling intellectual creativity during later dynasties, but this probably overstates its power. There were always contending schools.

Poetry   Song poets were in awe of those of the Tang, yet Song poets were also among China's best. A Japanese authority on Chinese literature wrote:

> Tang poetry could be likened to wine, and Song poetry to tea. Wine has great power to stimulate, but one cannot drink it constantly. Tea is less stimulating, bringing to the drinker a quieter pleasure, but one which can be enjoyed more continuously.[4]

The most famous poet of the Northern Song was Su Dungpo (1037–1101), a man skilled in all the cultural activities of his era. He was a painter and a calligrapher who was particularly knowledgeable about inks. He practiced Zen and wrote commentaries on the Confucian classics. Su superintended engineering projects, and he was a connoisseur of cooking and wine. His life was shaped by politics. He was a conservative, who believed in a limited role for government and in relying on morality to maintain social control. Opponents in the Song bureaucracy, the reformers, stressed law and an expanded role for government.

Passing the metropolitan examination, Su rose through a succession of posts to become the governor of a province—a position of immense power. One of his poems reflected on his duty to authorize death sentences, which could not be carried over into a new year:

New Year's Eve—you'd think I could go home early

But official business keeps me.

I hold the brush and face them with tears:

Pitiful convicts in chains,

Little men who tried to fill their bellies,

Fell into the law's net, don't understand disgrace.

And I? In love with a meager stipend

Song Dynasty Philosopher Zhu Xi (1130–1200). His Neo-Confucian ideas remained central up to the 20th century.

Collection of the National Palace Museum, Taiwan, R.O.C.

宋微國朱文公遺像

[4]Kojiro Yoshikawa, *An Introduction to Song Poetry*, trans. by Burton Watson (Cambridge: Harvard University Press, Harvard-Yenching Institute Monograph Series, 1967), p. 37.

> I hold on to my job and miss the chance to retire.
>
> Do not ask who is foolish or wise;
>
> All of us alike scheme for a meal.
>
> The ancients would have freed them a while at New Year's—Would
>
> I dare do likewise? I am silent with shame.[5]

Eight years later, when the reformers came to power, Su himself was arrested and spent 100 days in prison, awaiting execution on a charge of slandering the emperor. Instead, he was released and exiled. He wrote:

> "Out the gate, I do a dance, wind blows in my face; our galloping horses
> race along as magpies cheer."[6]

Arriving at his place of exile, he reflected:

> Between heaven and earth I live,
>
> One ant on a giant grindstone,
>
> Trying in my petty way to walk to the right
>
> While the turning of the mill wheel takes me endlessly left.
>
> Though I go the way of benevolence and duty,
>
> I can't escape from hunger and cold.[7]

Su turned his place of exile into a work of art. He farmed a plot of land at the "eastern slope" from which he took his literary name, Dungpo. Of his work there, he wrote:

> A good farmer hates to wear out the land;
>
> I'm lucky this plot was ten years fallow.
>
> It's too soon to count on mulberries;
>
> My best bet is a crop of wheat.
>
> I planted seed and within the month
>
> Dirt on the rows was showing green.
>
> An old farmer warned me,
>
> Don't let seedlings shoot up too fast!
>
> If you want plenty of dumpling flour
>
> Turn a cow or sheep in here to graze.
>
> Good advice—I bowed my thanks;
>
> I won't forget you when my belly's full.[8]

The conservatives regained control of the government in 1086, and Su resumed his official career. In 1094 power shifted once more, and Su was again exiled to the distant southern island of Hainan. Su was on his way back to the capital after another change of government when he died in 1101.

Painting   In the West, penmanship and painting are quite separate, one merely a skill and the other esteemed as an art. In China, calligraphy and painting were

[5]Yoshikawa, p. 119

[6]Yoshikawa, p. 117

[7]Yoshikawa, p. 105

[8]Yoshikawa, p. 119–120

equally appreciated and were seen as related. A scholar spent his life with brush in hand. The same qualities of line, balance, and strength needed for calligraphy carried over to painting. Chinese calligraphy is immensely pleasing even to the untutored Western eye, and it is not difficult to distinguish between the elegant strokes of Huineng, the last emperor of the Northern Song, and the powerful brushwork of the Zen monk Zhang Jizhi.

Song painters chose a wide variety of subjects—birds, flowers, fish, insects, horses, monkeys, water buffalo, scholars, emperors, Buddhas, and Daoist immortals. But its crowning achievement was landscape. Song landscapes are different from those of the West. Each stroke of the brush on silk or paper was final, for a mistake could not be covered up. Each element within a painting was represented in its most pleasing aspect; the painting as a whole was not constrained by single-point perspective. It had no single source of illumination, but an overall diffusion of light. Space was an integral part of its composition. A typical painting might have craggy rocks or twisted pine trees in the foreground, then mist or clouds or rain to create distance, and in the background the outlines of mountains or cliffs. If the painting contained human figures at all, they were tiny elements set in a world of nature that was very large. Chinese painting thus reflected the same worldview as Chinese philosophy and poetry. The painter sought to grasp the inner reality of a scene and not to be preoccupied by surface details.

In paintings by monks or masters of the Zen school, the presentation of an intuitive vision of an inner reality became even more pronounced. A Zen "broken ink" landscape might feature rocks, water, mountains, and clouds, each represented by a few explosive strokes of the brush. Paintings of Bodhidharma, the legendary founder of the Zen sect, are often dominated by a single powerful downstroke of the brush, defining the edge of his robe. Paintings of patriarchs tearing up sutras or sweeping dust from the mirror of the mind with a broom are almost calligraphic.

CHINA IN THE MONGOL WORLD EMPIRE: THE YUAN DYNASTY (1279–1368)

*T*he Mongols created the greatest empire in the history of the world. Their domain extended from the Caspian Sea to the Pacific Ocean; from Russia, Siberia, and Korea in the north to Persia and Burma in the south. Invasion fleets were even sent to Java and Japan, although without success. Mongol rule in China is one chapter of this larger story.

WHY WERE the Mongols able to conquer such a vast empire?

RISE OF THE MONGOL EMPIRE

The Mongols were a nomadic people who lived to the north of China on grasslands where they raised horses and herded sheep. They lived in felt tents (yurts) and sometimes called themselves "the people of the felt tents." Women performed much of the work and were freer and more easygoing than women in China. Families belonged to clans, and related clans to tribes. Tribes would gather during the annual migration from the summer plains to winter pasturage. Chiefs were elected, most often from noble lineages, and chosen for their courage, military prowess, judgment, and leadership. Like Manchu or Turkic, the Mongol tongue was Altaic. The Mongols worshipped nature deities and a supreme sky god. (Sky blue was their sacred color.) They communicated with their gods through religious specialists called *shamans*. Politically divided, they traded and warred among themselves and with settled peoples on the borders of their vast grassland domains.

The founder of the Mongol Empire, Temujin, was born in 1167, the son of a tribal chief. While Temujin was still a child, his father was poisoned. He fled and after wandering for some years, returned to the tribe, avenged his father, and in time became chief himself. By the time he was forty, Temujin's shrewd alliances and remarkable skill as a survivor had enabled him to unite the Mongol tribes and become their great khan or ruler. It is by the title *Genghis* (also spelled *Jenghiz* or *Chinggis*) *Khan* that he is known to history. Genghis possessed an extraordinary charisma, and his sons and grandsons were wise and talented leaders. Why the Mongol tribes, almost untouched by the higher civilizations of the world, should have produced such leaders at this point in history is difficult to explain.

A second conundrum is how the Mongols, who numbered only about 1.5 million, created the army that conquered vastly denser populations. Part of the answer is institutional. Genghis organized his armies into "myriads" of 10,000 troops, with decimal subdivisions of 1,000, 100, and 10. Elaborate signals were devised so that in battle, even large units could be manipulated like the fingers of a hand. Mongol tactics were superb: Units would retreat, turn, flank, and destroy their enemies. The historical record makes amply clear that Genghis's nomadic cavalry had a paralytic effect on its opponents. The most dreaded weapon of the peerless Mongol horseman was the compound bow. It was short enough to be shot from the saddle yet more powerful than the English longbow.

The Mongol cavalry was astonishingly mobile. Men carried their own supplies, and, trailing remounts, they covered vast distances quickly. By 1241, a Mongol army had reached Hungary, Poland, and the shore of the Adriatic. It was poised to continue its advance into western Europe when word of the death of the great khan caused it to hasten back to Mongolia to help choose his successor.

Conquered enemies taught the Mongols how to use siege weapons to take walled cities. Chinese engineers were employed in campaigns in Persia. The Mongols also used terror as a weapon. Inhabitants of cities that refused to surrender were put to the sword. Large areas in north China and Sichuan were devastated and depopulated. Descriptions of the Mongols by those whom they conquered dwell on their physical toughness and pitiless cruelty.

But Mongol strength was more than military. Genghis opened his armies to recruits from the Uighur Turks, the Manchus, and other nomadic peoples. As long as they complied with the military discipline demanded of his forces, they could share his triumphs. In 1206, Genghis promulgated laws designed to prevent the traditional wrangling and warring between tribes that might otherwise have undermined his empire. Genghis also obtained pledges of personal loyalty from thousands of his followers, and he used these "vassals"

Kublai Khan. Wearing an ermine coat, the Mongol emperor sits on a horse among Mongol warriors at the hunt.

National Palace Museum, Taiwan, R.O.C.

to command his armies and staff his government. This gave his forces an inner coherence that countered the divisive effect of tribal loyalties.

Mongol conquests were all the more impressive in that, unlike the earlier Arab expansion, the Mongols lacked the unifying force of religious zeal. To be sure, at an assembly of chiefs in 1206, an influential shaman revealed that it was the sky god's will that Genghis conquer the world. Yet other unabashedly frank words attributed to Genghis may reveal a truer image of what lay behind the Mongol drive to conquest: "Man's highest joy is in victory: to conquer one's enemies, to pursue them, to deprive them of their possessions, to make their beloved weep, to ride on their horses, and to embrace their wives and daughters."[9]

Genghis divided his far-flung empire among his four sons. Trade and communications were maintained between the parts, but over several generations, each of the four khanates became independent. The khanate of Chagatai was in Central Asia and remained purely nomadic. A second khanate of the Golden Horde ruled Russia from the lower Volga. The third was in Persia, and the fourth, led by those who succeeded Genghis as great khans, centered first in Mongolia and then in China (see Map 8–4).

MONGOL RULE IN CHINA

The standard theory used to organize Chinese history is the dynastic cycle, but a second theory explains Chinese history in terms of the interaction between the settled peoples of China and the nomads of the steppe. When strong states emerged in China, their wealth and population enabled them to expand militarily onto the steppe. But when China was weak, as was more often the case, the steppe peoples overran China. To review briefly:

1. During the Han dynasty (206 B.C.E.–220 C.E.), the most pressing problem in foreign relations was the Hsiung Nu Empire to the north.

2. During the centuries that followed the Han, various nomadic peoples invaded and ruled northern China.

3. The energy and institutions of these Sino-Turkic rulers of the northern dynasties shaped China's reunification during the Sui (589–618) and Tang (618–907) dynasties. The Uighur Turks also played a major role in Tang defense policy.

4. Northern border states became even more important during the Song. The Northern Song (960–1126) bought peace with payments of gold and silver to the Liao. The Southern Song (1126–1279), for all its cultural brilliance, was little more than a tributary state of the Chin dynasty, which had expanded into northern China.

From the start of the Mongol pursuit of world hegemony, the riches of China were a target. But Genghis proceeded cautiously, determined to leave no enemy at his back. He first disposed of the Tibetan state to the northwest of China and then the Manchu state of Chin that ruled north China. Mongol forces took Beijing in 1227, the year Genghis died. They went on to take Luoyang and the southern reaches of the Yellow River in 1234, and all of north China by 1241. During this time, the Mongols were interested mainly in loot. Only later did Chinese advisers persuade them that more wealth could be obtained by taxation.

---

[9]J. K. Fairbank, E. O. Reischauer, and A. M. Craig, *East Asia, Tradition and Transformation* (Boston: Houghton Mifflin, 1973), p. 164.

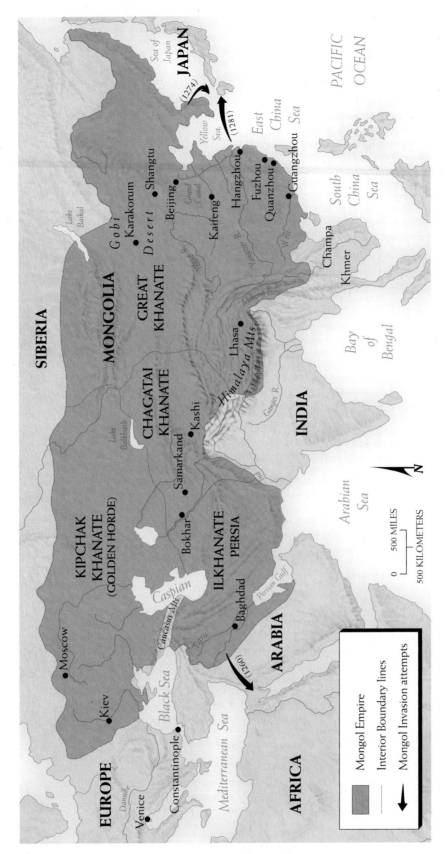

MAP 8–4

The Mongol Empire in the Late 13th Century. Note the four khanates: the Golden Horde in Russia, the Ilkhanate in Persia, Chagatai in Central Asia, and the Great Khanate extending from Mongolia to southern China.

HOW DID the size of the Mongol Empire facilitate trade and communication?

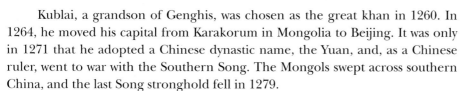

Kublai, a grandson of Genghis, was chosen as the great khan in 1260. In 1264, he moved his capital from Karakorum in Mongolia to Beijing. It was only in 1271 that he adopted a Chinese dynastic name, the Yuan, and, as a Chinese ruler, went to war with the Southern Song. The Mongols swept across southern China, and the last Song stronghold fell in 1279.

Kublai Khan's rule in Beijing reflected the mixture of cultural elements in Mongol China. From Beijing, Kublai could rule as a Chinese emperor, which would not have been possible in Karakorum. He adopted the Chinese custom of hereditary succession. He rebuilt Beijing as a walled city. It was known to the West as Cambulac, "the city (baliq) of the khan." Beijing was far to the north of any previous Chinese capital, away from centers of wealth and population, and the Grand Canal had to be extended to provision it. But from Beijing, Kublai could watch over Manchuria and Mongolia and maintain ties with the other khanates. Residence in the city proper was limited to Mongols. Chinese were segregated in an adjoining walled city. The palace of the khan was designed in a Central Asian style by an Arab architect. Kublai also maintained a summer palace at Shangdu (the "Xanadu" of Samuel Taylor Coleridge's poem) in Inner Mongolia, where he could hawk and ride and hunt in Mongol style.

Early Mongol rule in northern China was rapacious and exploitative, but it later came to employ Chinese forms of government and taxation, especially in the south and at the local level. As a foreign military occupation, its civil administration was highly centralized. Under the emperor was a Central Secretariat, and beneath it were 10 "Moving Secretariats," which became provinces under later dynasties. These highly centralized institutions and the arbitrary style of Mongol decision making accelerated the trend toward absolutism that had started during the previous dynasty.

About 400,000 Mongols lived in China during the Yuan period. For such a tiny minority to control the Chinese majority, it had to maintain itself as a separate and distinct people. One technique was to limit military service to Mongols and their nomadic allies and to station garrisons throughout China, while maintaining a strategic reserve on the steppe. Military officers were always regarded as more important than civil officials. A second technique for assuring Mongol superiority was to use ethnic classifications when appointing civil officials. Mongols held the top civil and military posts. The second rank category of high civilian offices was open to Persians, Turks, and other non-Chinese. The third rank admitted the northern Chinese, including Manchus and other border peoples, and the fourth employed the southern Chinese. Even when the examination system was sporadically revived after 1315, the Mongols and their allies were favored by easier examinations. Their quota was as large as that for the much more numerous Chinese, and they were appointed to higher offices.

The net result was an uneasy symbiosis. Chinese officials at the lower levels directly governed the Chinese populace, collecting taxes, settling disputes, and maintaining local order. Few of them learned to speak Mongolian, but without their cooperation, Mongol rule in China would have been impossible. The Mongols, concentrated in Beijing, large cities, and in garrisons, spoke Mongolian among themselves and usually did not bother to learn Chinese. A few exceptional Mongols learned to write poetry in Chinese and to paint in the Chinese style, but most were content to communicate through interpreters. When a Chinese district magistrate sent a query to the court, the response was written in Mongolian with a word-for-word Chinese translation.

(The Mongols borrowed the alphabet of the Uighurs to transcribe their tongue.) As the two languages are syntactically very different, the resulting Chinese was grotesque.

FOREIGN CONTACTS AND CHINESE CULTURE

11.5
William of Rubruck:
*Impressions of the
Medieval Mongols*

11.6
The Book of Ser
Marco Polo

Diplomacy and trade within the greater Mongol Empire brought China into contact with other higher civilizations for the first time since the Tang period. Persia and the Arab world were especially important. Merchants, missionaries, and diplomats voyaged from the Persian Gulf and across the Indian Ocean to seaports in southeastern China. The Arab communities in Canton and other ports were larger than they had been during the Song. Camel caravans carrying silks and ceramics left Beijing to pass through the Central Asian oases and on to Baghdad. Although the Mongols did not favor Chinese merchants and most trade was in other hands, Chinese trade expanded. Chinese communities were established in Tabriz, the center of trading in western Asia, and in Moscow and Novgorod. During this period knowledge of printing, gunpowder, and Chinese medicine spread to western Asia. Chinese ceramics influenced those of Persia, and Chinese painting influenced Persian miniatures.

In Europe, knowledge of China was transmitted by the Venetian trader Marco Polo, who said he had served Kublai as an official between 1275 and 1292. His book, *A Description of the World*, was translated into most European languages. Many readers doubted that a land of such wealth and culture could exist so far from Europe, but the book excited an interest in geography. When Christopher Columbus set sail in 1492, his goal was to reach Polo's Zipangu (Japan). A great Muslim explorer, Ibn Battuta (1304–c. 1370) of Morocco, also toured much of the Mongol world and left us a description of customs of the peoples he encountered. He characterized the Chinese as wealthy, but disinclined to flaunt their riches.

Other cultural contacts were fostered by the Mongol toleration or encouragement of religion. Nestorian Christianity spread from Persia to Central Asia and reentered China during the Mongol era. Churches were built in main cities. The mother of Kublai Khan was a Nestorian Christian. Several papal missions were sent from Rome to the Mongol court. An archbishopric was established in Beijing, where a church was built, sermons preached in Turkish and Mongolian, and choirboys sang hymns. Kublai gave Marco Polo's father and uncle a letter for the pope asking him to send 100 educated men to Kublai's court.

Tibetan Buddhism, with its magical doctrines and elaborate rites, was the religion most favored by the Mongols, but Chinese Buddhism also flourished. Priests and monks of all religions were given tax exemptions. Half a million Chinese became Buddhist monks during the Mongol century. The foreign religion that

The Journey of Marco Polo. Marco Polo and compagnions en route to China on the Silk Road.

Getty Images, Inc/Hulton Archive Photos.

made the greatest gains was Islam. It took permanent root in Central Asia and western China. Mosques were built in these areas, in Beijing, and in southeastern port cities. Confucianism was regarded as a religion by the Mongols. Its teachers were exempted from taxes, but as the scholar-gentry rarely obtained important offices, they saw the Mongol era as a time of hardship.

Despite these wide contacts with other peoples and religions, the high culture of China appears to have changed little if at all—partly because China had little to learn from other areas, and partly because the centers of Chinese culture were in the south, the last area to be conquered and the area least affected by Mongol rule. In reaction to the Mongol conquest, Chinese culture became conservative and turned in on itself. Scholars wrote poetry in the style of the Song. New schools of painting appeared, but they evolved within the Chinese tradition. The greatest Yuan paintings continued the style of the Song. The head of the court bureau of historiography was a Mongol, but the histories produced by his Chinese staff were in the traditional mold. As the dynasty waned, unemployed scholars wrote essays professing loyalty to the Song and satirizing the Mongols. Their works were not censored, for the Mongols either could not read them or did not care.

The major contribution to Chinese arts during the Yuan was by dramatists. They combined poetic arias with vaudeville theater to produce a new operatic drama. Performed by traveling troupes, the operas used few stage props and relied for effect on makeup, costumes, pantomime, and stylized gestures. Female roles were usually played by men. Except for the arias—the highlights of the performance—the dramas used vernacular Chinese to appeal to a popular audience. The unemployed scholars who wrote the scripts drew on the entire repertoire of the Song storyteller. Among the stock figures of the operas were a Robin Hood-like bandit, a famous detective-judge, a Tang monk who traveled to India, warriors and statesmen of the Three Kingdoms, and an assortment of romantic heroes, villains, and ghosts. Justice always triumphed, and the dramas usually ended happily. In several famous plays the hero got the girl, despite objections by her parents and seemingly insurmountable obstacles, by passing the civil service examinations in first place. As the examinations were not employed during most of the Yuan, this resolution of the hero's predicament harked back to the Song traditions of government. Yuan drama continued almost unchanged in later dynasties, and during the 19th century it merged with a form of southern Chinese theater to become today's Beijing Opera.

LAST YEARS OF THE YUAN

Despite the Mongol military domination of China and the highly centralized institutions of the Mongol court, the Yuan was the shortest of China's major dynasties. Little more than a century elapsed between Kublai's move to Beijing in 1264 and the dynasty's collapse in 1368. The rule of Kublai and his successor had been effective, but thereafter decline set in. By then, the Mongol Empire as a whole no longer lent strength to its parts. The khanates became separated by religion and culture as well as distance. Tribesmen in Mongolia rebelled now and then against the great khans in Beijing, who, in their eyes, had become too Chinese. The court at Beijing had never gained legitimacy. Some Chinese officials served it loyally to the end, but most Chinese viewed it as a government of carpetbaggers and Mongol rule as a military occupation. When succession disputes, bureaucratic factionalism, and pitched battles between

Mongol generals broke out, the Chinese showed little inclination to rally to the support of the dynasty.

Problems also arose in the countryside. Taxes were heavy, and some local officials were corrupt. The government issued excessive paper money and then refused to accept it in payment for taxes. The Yellow River changed its course, flooding the canals that carried grain to the capital. At great cost and suffering, a labor force of 150,000 workers and 20,000 soldiers rerouted the river to the south of the Shandung Peninsula. Further natural disasters during the 1350s led to popular uprisings. The White Lotus sect preached the coming of Maitreya. Regional military commanders, who combated the rebellions, broke free from central control, and became independent warlords. Important economic regions were devastated and partially depopulated. At the end, a rebel army threatened Beijing, and the last Mongol emperor and his court fled on horses to Shangdu. When it fell, they fled deeper into Mongolia.

SUMMARY

Sui and Tang Dynasties The Sui and Tang dynasties (589–907) reunited China's empire. Under the Tang, China expanded into Central Asia, taking control of much of the lucrative Silk Road along which trade moved to the West. Chang'an, the Tang capital, became the largest city in the world. Tang culture was rich and cosmopolitan, much influenced by its contacts with other cultures. The Tang dynasty was also the golden age of Buddhism in China, and a variety of Buddhist sects flourished.

Song Dynasty Under the Song dynasty (960–1279), China experienced an agricultural revolution in which large aristocratic estates worked by serfs gave way to small land holdings owned by free farmers. Advances in technology led to the invention of printing and the development of a coal and iron-smelting industry. The growth of a money economy encouraged the expansion of trade, both within China and with foreign countries. Song culture was particularly rich in philosophy, poetry, and painting.

The Mongols After their unification by Genghis Khan (1167–1227), the Mongols created the greatest empire in history. The highly mobile Mongol cavalry overwhelmed Chinese armies. By 1279, the Mongols controlled all of China. Mongol rulers, however, enjoyed only shallow Chinese support, and their reign came to an end in 1368.

IMAGE KEY

for pages 174–175

a. Song dynasty philosopher Chu Hsi (1130–1200)

b. A painting of irrigation methods on a farm south of the Yangtze

c. Animal-shaped vessel from China

d. Longquanware celadon jar with lotus petal lid

e. Song dynasty wine pot

f. Chinese, Song Dynasty incense burner (possibly Lao-Tzu on a Water buffalo)

g. A Mongol warrior's boots

h. Tang poet Li Po, as imagined by Song artist Liang Kai

i. Stone sculpture of bodhisattva

j. Pottery figures of court ladies playing polo, seventh century, Tang dynasty

k. Kublai Khan with Mongol warriors at the hunt

l. A "Barbarian" groom tends his steed

REVIEW QUESTIONS

1. Why was China able to reestablish its empire just 400 years after the fall of the Han, when Rome could not?

2. How did the Chinese economy and government change from the Tang to the Northern Song to the Southern Song?

3. What position did poets occupy in Chinese society?

4. How were the Mongols able to conquer most of the known world? What was the Chinese response to Mongol rule?

KEY TERMS

Amitabha Buddha (p. 184)   **Censorate** (p. 178)   **Zen** (p. 184)

 For additional study resources for this chapter, go to:
www.prenhall.com/craig/chapter8

9 Japan
Early History to 1467

CHAPTER HIGHLIGHTS

Yamato Japan Early Japanese history has two main turning points. The first occurred in the third century B.C.E. when an Old Stone Age Japan became an agricultural, metal-working society. The new technologies came to Japan from Korea. By the fifth century C.E., the Yamato court ruled most of Japan. It was heavily influenced by Korea until the seventh century when, in the second main turning point of their history, the Japanese began to adopt and adapt many features of Chinese culture, including Buddhism and Chinese writing, literature, and political institutions.

Nara and Heian Japan In this period, Japan was ruled by a civil aristocracy under the emperor. An enormous gulf existed between aristocrats and commoners. Japanese government was heavily influenced by the Chinese imperial system. Japanese culture, however, was increasingly self-confident and was aristocratic in its tastes and forms of expression. Noblewomen wrote many of the great works of Japanese literature during this age. Buddhism, heavily influenced by Shintoism, became increasingly assimilated in Japan.

The Early Feudal Age In the eighth century, mounted warriors called *samurai* began to dominate local government. By the late 1100s, power passed from the civil bureaucracy to military aristocrats. A series of *shōguns*, military officials, ruled in the emperor's name. The *shōguns'* power was based on their ability to command the loyalty of military vassals. Minamoto Yoritomo's seizure of power in 1185 marked the beginning of Japan's feudal age. He established *bakufu*, or "tent government." It would endure in Japan until the mid-nineteenth century. In 1274 and 1281, the Japanese, with the help of storms that destroyed the Mongol fleet, managed to defeat Mongol invaders sent by Kublai Khan.

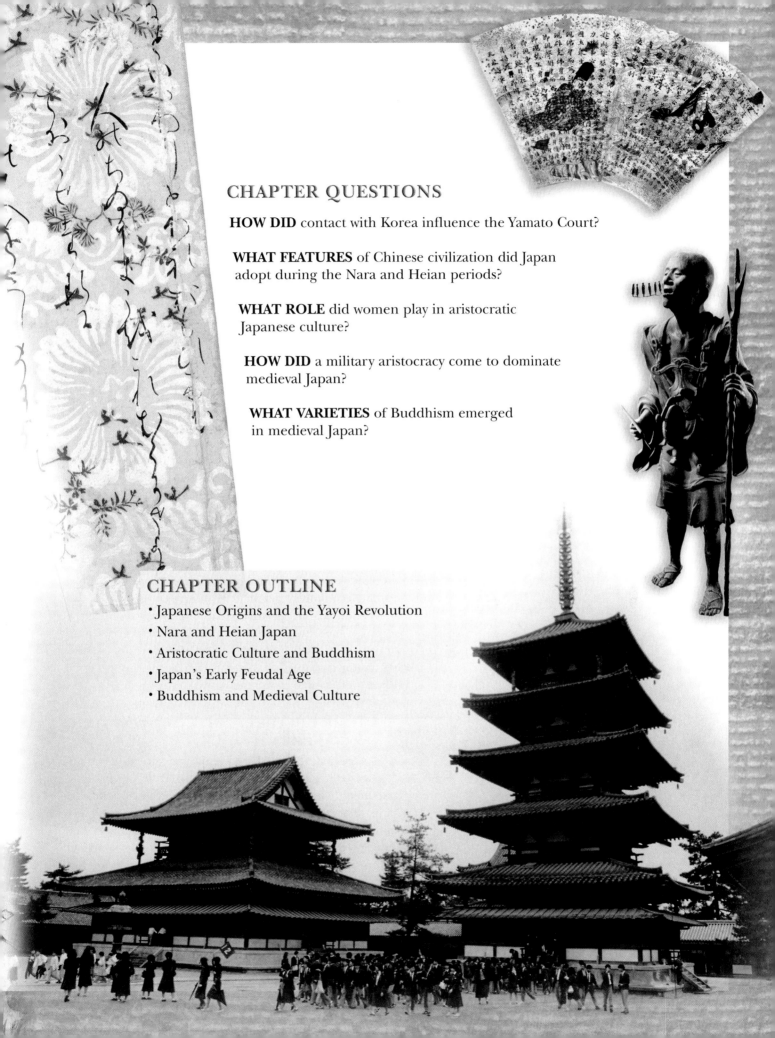

CHAPTER QUESTIONS

HOW DID contact with Korea influence the Yamato Court?

WHAT FEATURES of Chinese civilization did Japan adopt during the Nara and Heian periods?

WHAT ROLE did women play in aristocratic Japanese culture?

HOW DID a military aristocracy come to dominate medieval Japan?

WHAT VARIETIES of Buddhism emerged in medieval Japan?

CHAPTER OUTLINE

- Japanese Origins and the Yayoi Revolution
- Nara and Heian Japan
- Aristocratic Culture and Buddhism
- Japan's Early Feudal Age
- Buddhism and Medieval Culture

Japanese history has three main turning points, each marked by a major influx of an outside culture and each followed by a massive restructuring of Japanese institutions. The first was in the third century B.C.E., when an Old Stone Age Japan became an agricultural, metal-working society. The second turning point came during the seventh century, when whole complexes of Chinese culture entered Japan directly, and Japan made the leap to a higher historical civilization, associated with the writing system, technologies, and philosophies of China, and with Chinese forms of Buddhism. Japan remained within this cultural sphere until the third turning point, in the 19th century, when it encountered the West.

HOW DID contact with Korea influence the Yamato Court?

Jōmon Figurine. Along with the cord-patterned pots, the hunting and gathering Jōmon people produced mysterious figurines. Is this a female deity? Why are the eyes slitted like snow goggles? Earthenware with traces of pigment (Kamegaoka type); 24.8 cm high.

Asia Society, N.Y.: Mr. and Mrs. John D. Rockefeller 3rd Collection.

JAPANESE ORIGINS AND THE YAYOI REVOLUTION

The earliest evidence of human habitation in Japan dates from about 30,000 B.C.E. Pottery, the oldest in the world, appeared about 10,000 B.C.E., and from about 8000 B.C.E. the Jōmon or "cord-pattern" pottery style developed. Archaeologists are baffled by its appearance in an Old Stone Age society, for in all other early societies pottery does not predate New Stone Age cultures.

After 8,000 years of Jōmon culture, the second phase of Japanese prehistory began about 300 B.C.E. It is called the Yayoi culture, after a place in Tokyo where its distinctive hard, pale orange pottery was first unearthed. There is no greater break in the cultural history of Japan than that between the Jōmon and the Yayoi. For at the beginning of the third century B.C.E., the agricultural revolution, the bronze revolution, and the iron revolution simultaneously burst on Japan. The new technologies were brought to Japan from Korea and rapidly replaced Jōmon culture as far east in Japan as the modern city of Nagoya. After that, the Yayoi culture diffused more slowly overland into eastern Japan, where conditions were less favorable for agriculture and a mixed agricultural-hunting economy lingered.

By the first century C.E., the Yayoi population had so expanded that wars were fought for the best land. From these wars emerged a more peaceful order of regional states ruled by a class of aristocratic warriors. During the third century C.E., a temporary hegemony was established over a number of these states.

TOMB CULTURE, THE YAMATO STATE, AND KOREA

A period (300–600 C.E.) emerged directly from the Yayoi culture that was characterized by giant tomb mounds. (They still dot the landscape of the Nara-Osaka region.) The early tombs imitated Korean models: circular mounds of earth built atop megalithic burial chambers. Like the Yayoi graves that preceded them, the tombs contained mirrors, jewels, and other ceremonial objects. From the fifth century C.E., these objects were replaced by armor, swords, spears, and military trappings. The change reflected a new wave of continental influences from the Korean peninsula—a flow of people and culture into Japan that began with Yayoi was continuous into historical times.

Japan appeared in Chinese chronicles in the fifth century C.E., a period also covered in the earliest Japanese accounts of their own history, the *Records of Ancient Matters* (*Kojiki*), compiled in 712, and the *Records of Japan* (*Nihongi*), dating from 720. A picture emerges of regional aristocracies under the loose hegemony of the Yamato "great kings" whose courts were located on the Yamato plain, near present-day Osaka, ancient Japan's richest agricultural region. The Yamato rulers held lands and granaries throughout Japan. The tomb of the great king Nintoku, which is 486 meters long and 36 meters high, has twice the volume of material found in the Great Pyramid of Egypt. By the fifth century C.E., the great kings must have had great authority to be able to commandeer laborers for a project on such a scale.

The great kings awarded Korean-type titles to court and regional aristocrats, titles that implied a national hierarchy centering on the Yamato court. Regional rulers used a similar system to govern their populations.

The basic social unit of Yamato aristocratic society was the extended family (*uji*). Groups of specialist workers and peasants called *be* were attached to these families. Yamato society had a small class of slaves, but many peasants were neither slaves nor members of aristocratic clans or specialized workers' groups.

The court was the scene of incessant struggles for power between aristocratic families and an ongoing campaign to control outlying regions. Rebellions were frequent, and there were constant wars with "barbarian tribes" in southern Kyushu and eastern Honshu on the frontiers of "civilized" Japan. Under the Yamato court, a three-cornered military balance emerged on the Korean peninsula between the states of Paekche, Silla, and Koguryo (see Map 9–1). Japan was an ally of Paekche, and the Paekche connection enabled the Yamato court to expand its power within Japan. Imports of iron weapons and tools increased its military strength. The migration to Japan of Korean artisans expanded its wealth and influence, and many immigrants founded noble families. Paekche also served as a conduit for elements of Chinese culture to reach Japan. Chinese writing was adopted for the transcription of Japanese names during the fifth or sixth century. Confucianism entered in 513 and Buddhism in 538.

In 532, Paekche turned against Japan, but by this time Japan had established direct relations with China.

RELIGION IN EARLY JAPAN

The indigenous religion of Yamato Japan was an animistic worship of the forces of nature, later given the name of *Shintō*, or "the way of the gods," to distinguish it from Buddhism. Shintō, which probably appeared in Japan as part of Yayoi culture, saw the underlying forces of nature embodied in a waterfall, a twisted tree, a strangely shaped boulder, a mountain, or in a great leader who would be worshipped as a deity after his death. Mount Fuji was regarded as holy not because it was thought to be the abode of a god, but because the mountain itself was an upwelling of a vital force of nature. Even today in Japan, a gnarled tree trunk may be girdled with a straw rope to mark it as an object of veneration. The sensitivity to nature and natural beauty that pervades Japanese art and poetry owes much to Shintō.

Early Japanese History

8000–300 B.C.E.	Jōmon culture

Early Continental Influences

300 B.C.E.–300 C.E.	Yayoi culture
300–680 C.E.	Tomb culture and the Yamato state
680–850 C.E.	Chinese Tang pattern in Nara and Early Heian Japan

Shintō "The way of the gods." The animistic worship of the forces of nature that is the indigenous religion of Japan.

Terra-cotta Tomb Figurine. A clay statue of a Japanese warrior in armor from an ancient tomb.

Tokyo National Museum.

MAP 9–1

Yamato Japan and Korea (ca. 500 c.e.). Paekche was Japan's ally on the Korean peninsula. Silla, Japan's enemy, was the state that would eventually unify Korea. (Note: Nara was founded in 710; Heian in 794.)

HOW DID Japan's proximity to Korea and China influence its cultural development?

A second aspect of early Shintō was its connection with the state and the aristocracy. The more potent forces of nature such as the sea, the sun, the moon, the wind, and thunder and lightning became personified as deities. Each clan, or extended family, had its own myth centering on a nature deity (*kami*) that it claimed as its original ancestor. Aristocratic families developed genealogies to trace their descent from such a deity, and the head of a clan was the chief priest who led its worship. When Japan was unified by the Yamato court, the myths of several clans apparently were joined into a composite national myth. The deity of the Yamato great kings was the sun goddess, so she became the chief deity.

The *Records of Ancient Matters* and *Records of Japan* narrate myths of Japan's origin and the deeds and misdeeds of gods, but in mid-volume the stories of the gods give way to stories about early emperors and events in Japanese history. The Japanese emperors, today the oldest royal family in the world, were viewed

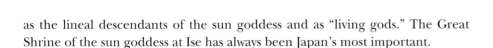

as the lineal descendants of the sun goddess and as "living gods." The Great
Shrine of the sun goddess at Ise has always been Japan's most important.

Nara and Heian Japan

The second major turning point in Japanese history was its adoption of the
higher civilization of China. This is a prime example of the worldwide
process (described in Chapter 2) by which the heartland civilizations
spread into outlying areas. In Japan, this happened between the seventh and
12th centuries and can best be understood as occurring in three stages. First, the
Japanese studied China. Then, during the eighth and ninth centuries, they
imported Chinese institutions, and finally they adapted these institutions to fit
conditions in Japan. By the 11th century, the creative reworking of Chinese elements had created a Japanese culture distinct from China's and that of the
Yamato court.

Court Government

Japan began to send official embassies—traders, students, and Buddhist
monks—to China in 607 C.E. Like Third World students who study abroad today,
Japanese who studied in China returned home with technology, art, Buddhism,
and a knowledge of Tang legal and governmental systems. Large-scale institutional changes inspired by the Tang model began in the
680s with the Emperor Temmu and his successor, the
Empress Jito (r. 686–697).

Temmu usurped the throne from his nephew and
then used Chinese systems to consolidate his power. A
Chinese-type law code greatly augmented his authority.
He styled himself "heavenly emperor" (*tennō*), which
thereafter replaced the title of "great king." He
rewarded his supporters with court ranks and positions
in government patterned after the Tang example. He
extended the authority of the court and increased its
revenues by a survey of agricultural lands and a census.
In short, although admiration for Chinese things must
have been enormous, much of the borrowing was dic-
tated by Japanese concerns.

Until the eighth century, the capital was usually
moved each time an emperor died. Then, in 710 a new
capital was laid out at Nara on a checkerboard grid pattern (similar to the Chinese capital at Chang'an). The
capital was intended to be permanent, but it was moved
again in 794 to Heian (later Kyoto) on the plain north
of Nara. The imperial capital remained there until its
relocation to Tokyo in 1869.

The superimposition of a Chinese-type capital on
a still backward Japan produced a stark contrast. In the
villages, peasants lived in pit dwellings and either
planted in crude paddy fields or used slash-and-burn
techniques of dry-land farming. In the capital, the
emperor and nobles, believed to be descendants of the
gods, dwelt in pillared palaces, drank wine, wore silk,

WHAT FEATURES of Chinese
civilization did Japan adopt during
the Nara and Heian periods?

tennō "Heavenly emperor."
The official title of the emperor
of Japan.

Prince Shōtoku (574–622). Shown
here with two of his sons, he was a
Buddhist and a reformer who began
sending regular embassies to China
in 607.

Corbis/Bettmann.

9.4
Prince Shotoku's
Seventeen Article
Constitution

9.5
Pilgrimage to
China (840) Ennin

and enjoyed the paintings, perfumes, and pottery of the Tang. Clustered about the capital were Buddhist temples with soaring pagodas and tile roofs.

Emperors at the Heian court were seen both as Confucian rulers with the majesty accorded by Chinese law and as Shintō rulers descended from the sun goddess. Their lineage was never usurped. Japanese history constitutes a single dynasty, although a few emperors were killed and replaced by other family members.

Beneath the emperor, the same modified Chinese pattern prevailed. A Council of State representing leading clans manipulated the authority of an emperor who usually reigned but did not rule. Beneath this council were eight ministries, including the Imperial Household Ministry. Size affected function: Where China had a population of 60 million, Japan had only four or five million. There were no significant external enemies, and local rule, in the Yamato tradition, was mostly in the hands of local clans. Consequently, much of the business of court government concerned the court itself. Of the 6,000 persons in the central ministries, more than 4,000 were concerned with the care of the imperial house.

Under the central court government were about 60 provinces, subdivided into districts and villages. Provincial governors were sent out from the capital. This change reduced the regional aristocrats to district magistrates and increased the power of the central aristocracy.

Japanese court government was, in other regards, unlike China's. There were no eunuchs. There was little tension between the emperor and the bureaucracy. (The main struggles were between clans.) The Tang shift from aristocracy

OVERVIEW   DEVELOPMENT OF JAPANESE WRITING

No two languages could be more different than Chinese and Japanese. Chinese is nonsyllabic, uninflected, and tonal. Japanese is polysyllabic, highly inflected, and atonal. To adopt Chinese writing for use in Japanese was thus no easy task. What the Japanese did at first—when they were not simply learning to write in Chinese—was to use certain Chinese ideographs as a phonetic script. For example, in the *Man'yōshū*, the eighth-century poetic anthology, *shira-nami* (white wave) was written with 之 for *shi*, 良 for *ra*, 奈 for *na*, and 美 for *mi*. Over several centuries, these phonetic ideographs evolved into a unique Japanese phonetic script:

Original Chinese Ideograph	Simplified Ideograph	Phonetic Script (kana)
之	之	し
良	良	ら
奈	奈	な
美	美	み

It is apparent in the above examples how the original ideograph was first simplified according to the rules of calligraphy and was then further simplified into a phonetic script known as *kana*. In modern Japanese, Chinese ideographs are used for nouns, verb stems, and adjectives, and the phonetic script is used for inflections and particles.

学生 は 図書館 へ 行きました Students/as for/library/to/went. (The students went to the library.)

In the above sentence, the Chinese ideographs are the forms with many strokes, and the phonetic script is shown in the simpler, cursive form.

toward meritocracy did not take place, and only aristocrats were appointed to important official posts. A feeble attempt to establish an examination meritocracy on the Chinese model failed completely. Japan simply did not need the elaborate structures of Chinese imperial government. In the early Heian period, three new departments outside the Chinese system handled most of the functions of government: an office of auditors handled taxation, a bureau of archivists exercised executive power through the drafting of decrees, and police commissioners enforced laws and maintained order in the capital. Power shifted during the Heian period, but always revolved around the emperor. Until the mid-ninth century, some emperors ruled directly. In 856, the northern branch of the Fujiwara clan began to establish a stranglehold on power which was not broken until the last half of the 11th century. In 1072, the Emperor Shirakawa regained control of the government and strengthened the imperial family, but by then the capital was increasingly isolated and threatening developments were taking place in the countryside.

Land and Taxes

The last Japanese embassy to China was in 839. By then, the Japanese were sufficiently self-confident to use Chinese ideas in innovative ways. The 350 years that followed until the end of the 12th century were a time of assimilation and evolutionary change. Nowhere was this more evident than in the system of taxation.

The land system of early Heian Japan was patterned after China's equal field system. All land belonged to the emperor. It was redistributed to all able-bodied persons every six years, and taxes were levied on them, not on the land. The system was complex, requiring land surveys, the redrawing of boundaries, and elaborate land and population registers. Even China, with its sophisticated bureaucracy, could not prevent the system from breaking down. The attempt to implement the system demonstrates the energy and ability of the early Japanese.

The evolution of taxation in late Heian Japan was a messy affair driven by haphazard local developments. Court officials were not able to maintain the elaborate records needed to administer the equal field system, so they simply assigned each governor a fixed sum to be collected from his province. The governor assigned quotas to district magistrates, who collected as much as they could and pocketed the surplus. This began the evolution of a new local ruling class.

Nobles and powerful temples in Kyoto used their influence at court to obtain exemptions from taxation for their lands. From the ninth century, many cultivators of small holdings began to commend their land to such nobles, judging that they would be better off as serfs on tax-free estates than as free farmers subject to taxation. The estates were managed by stewards, appointed from among local notables. They took a share of the harvests for themselves and thus had a vital interest in upholding local order.

Rise of the Samurai

During the Nara period, Japan followed China's example and experimented with conscripted armies. These, however, proved inefficient, and in 792, the court ended conscription and established a system of mounted warriors whose taxes were remitted in exchange for military service. They were stationed in the capital and in the provinces. The Japanese verb "to serve" is *samurau*, so those who served became known as **samurai**. Nonofficial private bands of local warriors

samurai Professional Japanese warriors.

Japanese Sword. From medieval times, Japanese artisans made the world's finest swords. They became a staple export to China. Worn only by samurai, they were also an emblem of class status, distinguishing them from commoners.

Philip Gatward © Dorling Kindersley.

sprang up to replace the official appointees, and they constituted Japan's military until the 15th and 16th centuries, when a new emphasis was placed on foot soldiers.

Being a samurai was expensive. Horses, armor, and weapons were costly, and their use required long training. The primary weapon was the bow and arrow, used from the saddle. Most samurai were from well-to-do local families. Their initial function was to preserve local order and, possibly, to help with tax collection. But at times they contributed to disorder. District magistrates sometimes led local forces against provincial governors to protest taxation.

Regional military coalitions or confederations formed and first made history in 935–940, when a descendant of an emperor, who headed such a group, became involved in a tax dispute. He captured several provinces and declared himself emperor. The Kyoto court recruited another military band as its champion, and quelled the rebellion. It, however, was only the first of a number of conflicts between regional military bands. By the mid-12th century, local and regional military bands existed in every part of Japan. In 1156, a power struggle at court enabled a band led by Taira Kiyomori to seize control of Kyoto and the emperor. But, like the earlier Fujiwara family, he did not change the system. He only imposed a new stratum atop the many power centers already established at court.

ARISTOCRATIC CULTURE AND BUDDHISM

*I*f the features of a culture could be weighed, the culture of Nara and early Heian Japan would appear to have been consisted largely of Shintō religious practices and village folkways—an extension of the culture of the late Yamato period. The aristocracy was small and encapsulated at court, just as Buddhist monks were contained within their monastic environment. The early Heian aristocracy comprised one-tenth of 1 percent of Japan's population, and most of its court culture had only recently been imported from China. There had not been time for commoners to ape their betters or for the powerful force of the indigenous culture to reshape that of the elite.

The resulting cultural gap helps explain why the aristocrats believed that commoners were hardly human. The writings of courtiers reflect little sympathy for the people. Heian high culture resembled a hothouse plant. It was protected by the political influence of the court and nourished by the flow of tax revenues and income from estates. Its indulged aristocrats developed a unique way of life guided by canons of elegance and taste that are striking even today.

CHINESE TRADITION IN JAPAN

Education at the Nara and Heian courts was largely a matter of reading Chinese books and acquiring the skills to compose poetry and prose in Chinese. These were daunting tasks, but the challenge was met. From the Nara period until the 19th century, most philosophical and legal writings, as well as most of the histories, essays, and religious texts in Japan, were written in Chinese.

Not only were Japanese writings in Chinese a vital part of the Japanese cultural tradition, but the original Chinese works themselves also became a part of the same tradition. Chinese history was read, and its stock figures provided the types of heroes and villains through whom the Japanese

Who Was in Charge at the Nara and Heian Courts?

710–856	Emperors or combinations of nobles
856–1086	Fujiwara nobles
1086–1160	Retired emperors
1160–1180	Military house of Taira

viewed their own history. Chinese history became the mirror in which Japan saw itself, despite the differences between the two societies. Buddhist stories and the books of Confucianism also became Japanese classics. A Western parallel might be the role that "foreign books," such as the Bible and works of Plato and Aristotle, played in medieval and Renaissance England.

BIRTH OF JAPANESE LITERATURE

Stimulated by Chinese models, the Japanese began to compose poetry in their native tongue. The first major anthology, the *Collection of Ten Thousand Leaves* (*Man'yōshū*), dates from about 760 and contains 4,516 poems. Sentiments in the poems reveal a deep sensitivity to nature and strong human relationships between husband and wife, parents and children. They also display a love for the land of Japan and links to a Shintō past.

An early obstacle to the development of a Japanese poetic tradition was the difficulty of transcribing Japanese sounds. In the *Ten Thousand Leaves*, Chinese characters were used as phonetic symbols. But because there was no standardization for transcription, it soon became unintelligible. In 951, a committee of poets deciphered the work and put it into *kana*, a new syllabic script or alphabet that had developed during the ninth century.

The invention of *kana* opened the gate to the most brilliant developments of the Heian period. Most of the new works and certainly the greatest were by women—particularly Sei Shōnagon and Murasaki Shikibu. Both were daughters of provincial officials serving at the Heian court. The *Pillow Book of Sei Shōnagon* contains sharp, satirical, amusing essays and literary jottings that illustrated the demanding aristocratic taste of the early 11th-century Heian court.

The *Tale of Genji*, written by Murasaki Shikibu (about 1010), is the world's first novel. *Genji* is a work of sensitivity, originality, and acute psychological delineation of character. It had no Chinese model. It tells of the life, loves, and sorrows of Prince Genji, son of an imperial concubine, and, after his death, of his son Kaoru. The novel spans three-quarters of a century and may be seen as having had a "definite and serious purpose." In one passage Genji twits a court lady whom he finds reading an extravagant romance. But then Genji says:

> I think far better of this art than I have led you to suppose. Even its practical value is immense. Without it what should we know of how people lived in the past, from the Age of the Gods down to the present day? For history books such as the *Chronicles of Japan* show us only one small corner of life; whereas these diaries and romances, which I see piled around you contain, I am sure, the most minute information about all sorts of people's private affairs.[1]

[1]R. Tsunoda, W. T. deBary, and D. Keene, eds., *Sources of the Japanese Traditon* (New York: Columbia University Press, 1958), p. 181.

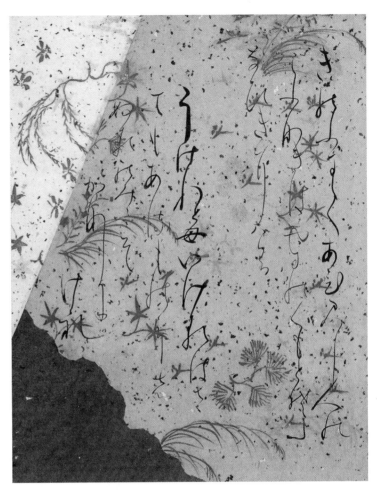

An Album Leaf. This album leaf from the Ishiyama-gire is part of a collection from the works of 36 poets compiled in the early 12th century. The poem is by Ki no Tsurayuki (868?–945?), who in the preface to another anthology wrote: "The poetry of Japan has its roots in the human heart and flourishes in the countless leaves of words . . . Hearing the warbler sing among the blossoms and the frog in his fresh waters—is there any living being not given to song? It is poetry which, without exertion, moves heaven and earth, stirs the feelings of gods and spirits invisible to the eye, softens the relations between men and women, calms the hearts of fierce warriors." The calligraphy is by Fujiwara no Sadanobu (1088–1154). The poem is written on layered rice paper with gold and silver and foliage designs. Even to the untutored eye, the effect is elegant.

Freer Gallery of Art, Smithsonian Institution, Washington, D.C.

NARA AND HEIAN BUDDHISM

The Six Sects of the Nara period each represented a separate philosophical doctrine within Mahayana Buddhism. Their monks, trained in monastic communities set apart from the larger society, studied, read sutras, copied texts, meditated, and joined in rituals. As in China, monasteries and temples were tied closely to the state. Tax revenues supported them, and monks prayed for the health of the emperor and for rain in time of drought.

Japan in the seventh and eighth centuries was much less culturally developed than China. The Japanese came to Buddhism not from the philosophical perspectives of Confucianism or Daoism but from the magic and mystery of Shintō. What appealed to the early Japanese in Buddhism was, consequently, its colorful and elaborate rituals; the gods, demons, and angels of the Mahayana pantheon; and, above all, the beauty of Buddhist art. The philosophy took longer to establish itself.

Japan's cultural identity was also different. In China, Buddhism was always viewed as Indian and alien—a factor leading to the Chinese persecution of Buddhists during the ninth century. In contrast, Japan's cultural identity or cultural self-consciousness took shape only during the Nara and early Heian periods. One element in that identity was the imperial cult derived from Shintō, but Shintō was no match for Buddhism as a religion. Buddhism was no more foreign to Japan than Confucianism and the rest of the Chinese culture that had helped reshape the Japanese identity, so there was no bias against it. Consequently,

The Hōryūji Temple. Built by Prince Shōtoku in 607, it contains the oldest wooden buildings in the world. They are the best surviving examples of Chinese Buddhist architecture. Note the groups of visiting students in the foreground.

Susumu Takahashi/Reuters/Corbis-Bettmann.

Buddhism entered deeply into Japanese culture and retained its vitality longer than in China. Not until the 17th or 18th centuries did Japanese elites became so Confucian as to be anti-Buddhist. In 794, when the court moved to Heian (Kyoto), the two great new Buddhist sects were Tendai and Shingon.

Tendai's champion was a monk named Saichō (767–822) who, in 785, founded a temple on Mount Hiei to the northwest of Kyoto. He went to China to study in 804 and returned the following year imbued with the teachings of the Tendai sect. He taught that salvation could be attained by all who led a life of contemplation and moral purity. He instituted strict monastic rules and a 12-year training curriculum for novices who sought admission to his monastery. The sect grew until thousands of temples had been built on Mount Hiei. Many later Japanese sects emerged from the Tendai fold.

The Shingon sect was begun by Kūkai (774–835), who became a monk at the age of 18. In 804, he went to China with Saichō. He returned two years later bearing the Shingon doctrines and founded a monastery on Mount Kōya. Kūkai was a bridge builder, a poet, an artist, and one of the three great calligraphers of his age. He is sometimes credited with inventing the *kana* syllabary and with introducing the Japanese to tea. Shingon doctrines center on an eternal and cosmic Buddha, of whom all other Buddhas are manifestations. *Shingon* means "true word" or "mantra," a verbal formula with mystical powers. It is sometimes called *esoteric Buddhism* in that it had secret teachings that were passed from master to disciple. In China, Shingon died out as a sect in the persecutions of the mid-ninth century, but in Japan its doctrines even influenced the Tendai center on Mount Hiei.

During the later Heian period, Buddhism began to be more widely assimilated. At the village level, the folk religion of Shintō took in many Buddhist elements. In the high culture of the capital, Shintō was almost absorbed by Buddhism. Shintō deities came to be seen as the local manifestations of universal Buddhas. The cosmic or "Great Sun Buddha" of the Shingon sect, for example, was easily identified with the sun goddess. Often, great Buddhist temples had smaller Shintō shrines on their grounds. Not until the mid-19th century was Shintō disentangled from Buddhism, and then the motive was political, not religious.

JAPAN'S EARLY FEUDAL AGE

HOW DID a military aristocracy come to dominate medieval Japan?

The year 1185, or 1160, if we include Taira rule in Kyoto, marked the shift from centuries of rule by a civil aristocracy to centuries of rule by military nobles. It saw the formation of the *bakufu* (tent government), a completely non-Chinese type of government. During this time the *shōgun* emerged as the de facto ruler of Japan, although in theory he was a military official of the emperor. The year marked the beginning of new cultural forms and initiated changes in family and social organization.

THE KAMAKURA ERA

Taira Kiyomori's seizure of Kyoto in 1160 fell short of establishing a national military hegemony, for other bands flourished elsewhere in Japan beyond his control. After Kiyomori's victory, the Taira embraced the elegant lifestyle of the Kyoto court. They expected their tutelage over the court to be as enduring as that of the Fujiwara. But in 1180, Minamoto Yoritomo (1147–1199) responded to a call to

bakufu "Tent government." Military regime that governed Japan under the shguns.

shōgun Military official who was the actual ruler of Japan in the emperor's name from the late 1100s until the mid-19th century.

Minamoto Yoritomo. Founder of the Kamakura Shogunate. He is depicted here in court robes as a statesman and official, though he was, above all, a warrior-general.

Seka Bunka Photo.

Japanese Scroll Painting. Mongol invaders battling with an intrepid samurai horseman. Note the bomb bursting in the air at the upper right of this late 13th-century Japanese scroll painting.

© Museum of Imperial Collections–Sannomaru Shozo Kan. Courtesy of the International Society for Educational Information, Inc.

arms by a disaffected prince, seized control of eastern Japan (the rich Kanto plain), and began the war that ended in 1185 with the downfall of the Taira.

Yoritomo's authority was national, for his armies had ranged over most of Japan. After his victory in 1185, warriors from every area became his vassals. Wary of Kyoto, Yoritomo set up his headquarters at Kamakura, 30 miles south of present-day Tokyo, at the edge of his base of power in eastern Japan. He called his government the bakufu in contrast to the civil government in Kyoto. The offices he established were few and practical: one to deal with his samurai retainers, one to administer and execute his policies, and one to hear legal suits. Each office was staffed by vassals. Yoritomo also appointed military governors in each province and military stewards on the former estates of the Taira and of others who had fought against him. These appointments carried the right to some income from the land, but the rest of the income went to Kyoto as taxes or as revenues for the noble owners of these estates.

When Yoritomo died in 1199, his widow and her Hōjō kinsmen moved to usurp the power of the Minamoto house. The widow, having taken holy orders after her husband's death, was known as the Nun Shōgun. One of her sons was pushed aside. The other became Shōgun but was murdered in 1219. After that, the Hōjō ruled as regents for a puppet Shōgun. The Kyoto court led an armed uprising against Kamakura in 1221, but it was suppressed. Any society based on personal bonds faces the problem of how to transfer loyalty from one generation to another. That the Kamakura vassals fought for the Hōjō in 1221 suggests that they were loyal to the bakufu, which guaranteed their income from land. Their personal loyalty to the Minamoto had ended with the death of Yoritomo.

The Mongols In 1266, Kublai Khan (see Chapter 8) sent envoys demanding that Japan submit to his rule. He had subjugated Korea in 1258. The Hōjō at Kamakura refused. The first Mongol invasion fleet arrived with 30,000 troops in 1274, but withdrew after initial victories. A second invasion force arrived in 1281. Carrying 140,000 troops, the scale of this amphibious operation was unprecedented in world history. With gunpowder bombs and phalanxes of

archers protected by a forward wall of soldiers carrying overlapping shields, the Mongol forces were formidable.

Although the Japanese strategy of fierce individual combat was not very effective against the Monguls' tactics, the Japanese held out for two months until *kamikaze* ("divine winds") sank a portion of the Mongols' fleet and forced the rest to retreat. Preparations for a third invasion ended with Kublai's death in 1294. The defensive campaign yielded no new lands or booty to be distributed among the soldiers, and this caused considerable complaint.

THE QUESTION OF FEUDALISM

Scholars often contend that Yoritomo's rule marks the start of feudalism in Japan. Feudalism may be defined in terms of three criteria: lord-vassal relationships, fiefs given in return for military service, and a warrior ethic. It can be asked, however, whether these criteria truly apply to Kamakura Japan.

Certainly, the mounted warriors who made up the armies of Yoritomo were predominantly his vassals, not his kin. As for fiefs, the situation is ambiguous. Kamakura vassals received rights to income from land in exchange for military service, but fiefs, as such, did not appear until the late 15th century. The warrior ethic, however, is beyond doubt. It had been developing among regional military bands for several centuries before 1185. The samurai prized bravery, cunning, physical strength, and endurance. They gave their swords names. Their sports were hunting, hawking, and archery. Warriors thought of themselves as a military aristocracy that practiced "the way of the bow and arrow," "the way of the bow and horse," "the way of the warriors," and so on.

The common definition of feudalism describes the Kamakura military band, but warrior bands were only one part of society. Kamakura Japan had two political centers. The bakufu had military authority, but the Kyoto court continued the late Heian pattern of civil rule by appointing civil governors, collecting tax revenues, and controlling the region about Kyoto. Noble families, retired emperors, and the great Buddhist temples also contributed to Kyoto's influence. It also remained the fount of rank and honors. After his victory in 1185, Yoritomo asked the emperor for the title of "barbarian-quelling generalissimo" (*Sei i tai shōgun*, shortened to *shōgun*). He was refused, but in 1192 he finally got the title. Even then, the award had to be justified by the argument that Yoritomo was a Minamoto offshoot of the imperial line.

The small size of Yoritomo's vassal band is an even more telling argument against viewing Kamakura Japan as fully feudal. Numbering about 2,000 before 1221 and 3,000 thereafter, most of the band were concentrated in eastern Japan. But even if as many as half were distributed about the rest of the country as military governors and stewards, there would have been only 100 in a region the size of Massachusetts. (Japan in 1180 was about 15 times larger than that state.) How could so few control such a large area? The answer is that they did not have to.

The local social order of the late Heian era continued into the Kamakura period. The Kyoto court, governors, district magistrates, and local notables functioned more or

kamikaze "Divine winds" that sank a portion of the invading Mongol fleet in Japan in 1281.

Government by Military Houses

1160–1180	Taira rule in Kyoto
1185–1333	Kamakura bakufu
1185	Founded by Minamoto Yoritomo
1219	Usurped by Hōjō
1221	Armed uprising by Kyoto court
1232	Formation of Jōei Code
1274 and 1281	Invasion by Mongols
1336–1467	Ashikaga bakufu
1336	Begun by Ashikaga Takauji
1392	End of Southern Court
1467	Start of warring states period

less as they had earlier. To influence the local scene, the newly appointed Kamakura vassals had to win the cooperation of the existing local power-holders. In short, even if the Kamakura vassals themselves could be called feudal, they were only a thin skin on the surface of a society still constructed on older principles.

THE ASHIKAGA ERA

By 1331, various tensions had developed within Kamakura society. Because the patrimony of a warrior was divided among his children, vassals became poorer over time and often fell into debt. High-ranking vassals of Kamakura were also dissatisfied with the Hōjō monopolization of key bakufu posts. While the ties of vassals to Kamakura weakened, the ties to other warriors within their region grew stronger until new regional bands were ready to emerge. The precipitating event was a revolt in 1331 by an emperor who thought emperors should actually rule. Kamakura sent Ashikaga Takauji (1305–1358), the head of a branch family of the Minamoto line, to put down the revolt; instead he joined it. Other regional lords then rose up and destroyed the Hōjō bakufu in Kamakura.

What emerged from the turmoil of the years from 1331 to 1336 was a regional multistate system centering on Kyoto. Each region was based on a warrior band. In the central Kyoto region, Ashikaga Takauji established his bakufu. Its offices were simple and functional: a samurai office for police and military matters, an administrative office for financial matters, a documents office for land records, and a judicial board to settle disputes. The offices were staffed by Takauji's vassals. They became lords (called *daimyo*) in their own right and usually held appointments as military governors in the provinces surrounding Kyoto. The bakufu also appointed vassals to watch over its interests in the far north, in eastern Japan, and in Kyushu.

Government in the outlying regions was more diverse. Some lords held several provinces, some only one. Some had integrated most of the warriors in their areas into their bands. Others had several unassimilated military bands in their territories, forcing them to rely more on the authority of Kyoto. Formally, all regional lords or daimyo were the vassals of the shōgun, but the relationship was often nominal. Sometimes the regional lords lived on their lands; sometimes they lived in Kyoto.

The relationship between the Kyoto bakufu and the regional lords fluctuated from 1336 to 1467. At times, able lords turned their regions into virtually independent states. At other times, the power of the Kyoto bakufu grew. In 1394, the third shōgun strengthened its power by relinquishing his military post as shōgun to his son and taking the highest civil post, grand minister of state. He improved relations with the great Buddhist temples and Shintō shrines and established ties with Ming China. His military campaigns dented the autonomy of regional lords outside of the inner Kyoto circle.

Even the third shōgun, however, depended heavily on his vassals. He gave them the authority to levy taxes; to pull into their own hands all judicial, administrative, and military authority in their regions; and to take on unaffiliated warriors as their own vassals. This created problems for his successors. As ties of personal loyalty wore thin, new local warrior bands formed.

WOMEN IN WARRIOR SOCIETY

The Nun Shōgun was one of a long line of important women in Japan. The central figure of Japanese mythology was the sun goddess, who ruled the Plain of High Heaven. The empresses of the Yamato and Nara courts were followed by the great women writers of the Heian period. Under the Kamakura bakufu, daughters of warrior families often trained in archery and other military arts. Women also occasionally inherited the position of military steward. But as fighting became more common in the 14th century, their position declined, and as warfare became endemic in the 15th, their status plummeted. To protect the integrity of the military fief—the warrior's reward for serving his lord in battle and the lord's guarantee that his warriors would continue their service—multigeniture, the custom by which daughters as well as sons inherited property, gave way to inheritance of an undivided patrimony by a man's most able son.

AGRICULTURE, COMMERCE, AND MEDIEVAL GUILDS

Population figures for medieval Japan were about 6 million for the year 1200 and 12 million for 1600. The increase was brought about by land reclamation and improvements in agricultural technology. Iron-edged tools became available to all. New strains of rice were developed. Irrigation and diking improved. Vegetables were planted during the fall and winter in dry fields, which were flooded and planted with rice during the spring and summer.

In the Nara and early Heian periods, the economy was almost exclusively agricultural. The government had established a mint, but little money actually circulated. Taxes were paid in grain and labor. Commercial transactions were largely barter, with silk or grain as the medium of exchange. Artisans produced for the noble households or temples to which they were attached. Peasants were self-sufficient.

From the late Heian period, more of the growing agricultural surplus stayed in local hands. During the Kamakura and Ashikaga periods, income was transfered from the court aristocrats to the warrior class. As this took place, artisans began to produce for new consumers. Military equipment was an early staple of commerce, but gradually *sake*, lumber, paper, vegetable oils, salt, and products of the sea were also commercialized. A demand for copper coins developed, and they were imported in huge quantities from China.

During the Kamakura period, a class of merchants emerged to market the products of artisans. Trade networks spread throughout Japan. Artisan and merchant guilds, not unlike those of medieval Europe, paid a fee in exchange for monopoly rights in a given area. From the Kamakura period onward, markets were held periodically in many parts of Japan. During the 14th and 15th centuries, markets were held with increasing frequency until they evolved into permanent towns.

BUDDHISM AND MEDIEVAL CULTURE

WHAT VARIETIES of Buddhism emerged in medieval Japan?

The Nara and Heian periods are often referred to as Japan's Classical Age, and the period that followed (approximately 1200 to 1600) is characterized as its Middle Ages. It was medieval in the root sense of the word in that it lay between two major spans of premodern Japanese history. It was also medieval in that it shared some of the characteristics of societies that are labeled medieval in Europe and China. However, there was an important difference. Medieval Japan transitioned from its classical era without interruption. The two periods even overlapped during the early Kamakura, whereas in Europe, a millennium of recovery from barbarian incursions separated classical

Kūja Invoking Buddha. The mid-Heian monk Kūja (903–972) preached Pure Land doctrines in Kyoto and throughout Japan. Little Buddhas emerge from his mouth.

PPS/Pacific Press Service.

Pure Land Buddhism Variety of Japanese Buddhism that maintained that only faith was necessary for salvation.

Rome from the high medieval era. Similarly, China endured 400 years of political disunity and barbarian invasions.

The continuity of Japanese culture is visible throughout its history. The earlier poetic tradition continued with vigor. The style of painting that had reached a peak in the *Genji Scrolls* continued into the medieval era with scrolls dealing with historical and religious themes or fairy-tale adventures. Artisanal production was never interrupted. In short, Heian culture bridged smoothly into medieval Japanese culture. The latter, however, added some new characteristics. First, as the leadership of society shifted from court aristocrats to military aristocrats, new forms of literature appeared. The medieval military tales were as different from the *Tale of Genji* as the elaborate armor of the mounted warrior was from the colorful silken robes of the court nobility. Second, a new wave of culture influence entered from Sung China. Third, and most important, the medieval centuries were Japan's age of Buddhist faith. A religious revolution took place and deeply influenced the arts of Japan.

JAPANESE PIETISM: PURE LAND AND NICHIREN BUDDHISM

Among the doctrines of the Heian Tendai sect was the belief that the true teachings of the historical Buddha had been lost and that salvation could be had only by calling on the name of Amida, the Buddha who ruled over the Western Paradise (or **Pure Land**). During the 10th and 11th centuries, itinerant preachers began to spread Pure Land doctrines and practices beyond Kyoto and into remote provinces. The doctrine that the world had fallen on evil times and that only faith would suffice was given credence by earthquakes, epidemics, fires, banditry, and wars.

Two early Kamakura religious geniuses were behind the surge of interest in Buddhism. Hōnen (1133–1212) was perhaps the first to say that the invocation of the name of Amida alone was enough for salvation and that only faith counted. These claims brought Hōnen into conflict with the older Buddhist establishment and marked the emergence of Pure Land as a separate sect. Shinran (1173–1262) taught that even a single invocation in praise of Amida, if done with perfect faith, was sufficient for salvation. But perfect faith was a gift from Amida. Shinran taught that pride was an obstacle to purity of heart. He famously said: "If even a good man can be reborn in the Pure Land, how much more so a wicked man." In other words, the evil man is less inclined to assume that he is the source of his own salvation and is, therefore, more inclined to trust in Amida.

Shinran's emphasis on faith alone led him to break many of the monastic rules of earlier Buddhism: He ate meat and married a nun, thus authorizing a married clergy for the Pure Land sect. He taught that all occupations were equally "heavenly" if performed with a pure heart, and he traveled about Japan establishing "True Pure Land" congregations. These often developed political and military power. The sect believed that a strong "church" was needed to protect the saved while they were still in this world. During the 15th century, some Pure Land village congregations established self-defense forces. At times they rebelled against feudal lords. Although their power was destroyed in the late 16th century and their sect was depoliticized, a line of distinguished teachers kept them true to their original doctrinal simplicity and reliance on piety. Pure Land Buddhism remains the dominant form of Buddhism in Japan today.

HISTORY'S VOICES

HAKUIN'S ENLIGHTENMENT

Hakuin (1686–1769) was a poet, painter, and Zen master. He wrote in colloquial Japanese as well as in Chinese. He illustrated the continuing power of the Zen tradition in postmedieval times. The following passages are from an autobiographical account of his spiritual quest. The first follows a recounting of his disappointments and failures and tells of his initial enlightenment. His teacher did not accept this as adequate, however. The second passage tells of his experience eight years later.

1

In the spring of my twenty-fourth year, I was painfully struggling at the Eiganji in the province of Echigo. I slept neither day nor night, forgetting either to eat or sleep. A great doubt suddenly possessed me, and I felt as if frozen to death in the midst of an icy field extending thousands of *li*. A sense of an extraordinary purity permeated my bosom. I could not move. I was virtually senseless. What remained was only "*Mu.*" Although I heard the master's lectures in the Lecture Hall, it was as though I were listening to his disclosure from some sixty or seventy steps outside the Hall, or as if I were floating in the air. This condition lasted for several days until one night I heard the striking of a temple bell. All at once a transformation came over me, as though a layer of ice were smashed or a tower of jade pulled down. Instantly I came to my senses. Former doubts were completely dissolved, like ice which had melted away. "How marvelous! How marvelous!" I cried out aloud. There was no cycle of birth and death from which I had to escape, no enlightenment for which I had to seek.

2

At the age of thirty-two I settled in this dilapidated temple [Shoinji]. In a dream one night my mother handed me a purple silk robe. When I lifted it I felt great weights in both sleeves. Examining it, I found in each sleeve an old mirror about five or six inches in diameter. The reflection of the right-hand mirror penetrated deep into my heart. My own mind, as well as mountains and rivers, the entire earth, became serene and bottomless. The left-hand mirror had no luster on its entire surface. Its face was like that of a new iron pan not yet touched by fire. Suddenly I became aware that the luster on the left-hand mirror surpassed that of the right by a million times. After this incident, the vision of all things was like looking at my own face. For the first time I realized the meaning of the words, "The eyes of the Tatha-gata behold the Buddha-nature."

Source: *The Buddhist Tradition in India, China, and Japan* by William Theodore de Bary. Copyright © 1969 by William Theodore de Bary. Reprinted by permission of Modern Library, a division of Random House Inc.

A second devotional sect was founded by Nichiren (1222–1282), who believed that the Lotus Sutra perfectly embodied the teachings of the Buddha. He instructed his adherents repeatedly to chant, "Praise to the Lotus Sutra of the Wondrous Law," usually to the accompaniment of rapid drumbeats. The chanting optimally induced a state of religious rapture. Nichiren was remarkable for a Buddhist in being both intolerant and nationalistic. He blamed the ills of his age on rival sects and asserted that only his sect could protect Japan. Even his adopted Buddhist name, the Sun Lotus, combined the term for the rising sun of Japan with that of the flower that had become the symbol of Buddhism.

ZEN BUDDHISM

Meditation had long been a part of Japanese monastic practice. Zen meditation and doctrines were introduced by monks returning from study in Sung China. Zen in Japan was a religion of paradox. Its monks were learned, yet it stressed a return to the uncluttered "original mind," a state attained in a flash of intuitive understanding (see "Hakuin's Enlightenment"). Zen was punctiliously traditional and the most Chinese of Japan's medieval sects. The authority of the Zen master over his pupil-monks was absolute. Yet Zen was also iconoclastic. Its sages were depicted tearing up sutras to make the point that it is religious experience and not words that count. Within a rigidly structured monastic regimen, monks tested their understanding, gained through long hours of meditation, in encounters with their master. Buddhism stressed compassion for all sentient beings, yet in Japan the Zen sect included many samurai whose duty it was to fight and kill. A few military leaders encouraged the practice of Zen among their retainers in the hope of instilling a single-minded attention to duty.

The most remarkable aspect of Zen was its influence on the arts of medieval Japan. The most beautiful gardens, for example, were in Zen temples. Zen monks, such as Josetsu, Shūbun (ca. 1415), and Sesshū (1420–1506) are among the masters of ink painting in East Asia. Because the artist's creativity itself was seen as grounded in his experience of meditation, a painting of a waterfall or of a crow on a leafless branch in late fall was viewed as no less religious than a painting of the mythic Zen founder Bodhidharma.

Nō Plays

Another fascinating product of medieval culture was the Nō play, a kind of mystery drama without parallels in East Asia. The play was performed on an almost square, bare wooden stage (often outdoors) by male actors wearing robes of great beauty and carved, painted masks with enigmatic expressions. Many such masks and robes are regarded as Japan's national treasures. The chorus was chanted to the accompaniment of flute and drums. The language was poetic. The action was slow and highly stylized. At a critical juncture in most plays, the protagonist was possessed by the spirit of another and performed a dance. Spirit possession was common in Japanese folk religion and also occurred in the *Tale of Genji*.

SUMMARY

Yamato Japan Early Japanese history has two main turning points. The first occurred in the third century B.C.E. when an Old Stone Age Japan became an agricultural, metal-working society. The new technologies came to Japan from Korea. By the fifth century C.E., the Yamato court ruled most of Japan. It was heavily influenced by Korea until the seventh century when, in the second main turning point of their history, the Japanese began to adopt and adapt many features of Chinese culture, including Buddhism and Chinese writing, literature, and political institutions.

Nara and Heian Japan In this period, Japan was ruled by a civil aristocracy under an emperor. An enormous gap existed between aristocrats and commoners. Japanese government was heavily influenced by the Chinese imperial system. Japanese culture, however, grew increasingly self-confident and aristocratic in its tastes and forms of expression. Noblewomen wrote many of the great works of Japanese literature during this age. Buddhism, heavily influenced by Shintōism, was increasingly assimilated.

IMAGE KEY
for pages 204–205

a. Ishiyama-Gire (Fragment)
b. Naran tomb paining in Japan
c. Antique Japanese No mask
d. Horyuji temple
e. A clay statue of a warrior in armor from an ancient tomb
f. The Prince Shotoku (574–622)
g. Fan-shaped sutra, Heian period
h. Scroll with depictions of the13th century attack on the Sanjo Palace
i. Mid-Heian monk

The Early Feudal Age In the eighth century, mounted warriors called *samurai* began to dominate local government. By the late 1100s, power passed from the civil bureaucracy to military aristocrats, and a series of shōguns, military officials, ruled in the emperor's name. The shōguns' power was based on their ability to command the loyalty of military vassals. Minamoto Yoritomo's seizure of power in 1185 marked the beginning of Japan's feudal age. He established bakufu, or "tent government," which endured in Japan until the mid-19th century. In 1274 and 1281, the Japanese, with the help of storms that destroyed the Mongol fleet, managed to defeat Mongol invaders sent by Kublai Khan.

REVIEW QUESTIONS

1. How did Chinese culture influence Japan's government and religion? How did the Japanese change what they borrowed?

2. How did the Buddhism of the Nara and Heian periods differ from that of the early medieval era?

3. How did Japan become a society dominated by military lords and their vassals?

4. How and why did the role of women change from the Heian to the Ashikaga eras?

KEY TERMS

bakufu (p. 215)   **samurai** (p. 211)   **Shōgun** (p. 215)
kamikaze (p. 217)   **Shintō** (p. 207)   **tennō** (p. 209)
Pure Land Buddhism (p. 220)

 For additional study resources for this chapter, go to: www.prenhall.com/craig/chapter9

BUDDHISM

Hinduism, Buddhism. and Jainism all arose out of the spiritual ferment of Vedic India after 700 B.C.E. Buddhism shares a kinship with these other religions much as Judaism, Christianity, and Islam have a relationship.

The founder of Buddhism, Siddhartha Gautama, was born about 563 B.C.E. A prince in a petty kingdom near what is now the border of India and Nepal, Gautama was reared amid luxury and comforts, married at 16, and had a child. According to legend, at age 29 he saw a decrepit old man, sick and suffering, and a corpse. He suddenly realized that all humans would suffer the same fate. Gautama renounced his wealth and family and entered the life of a wandering ascetic. He visited famous teachers, for almost six years practiced extremes of ascetic self-deprivation, and finally discovered the Middle Path between self-indulgence and self-mortification. At the age of 35 he attained *nirvana*, becoming the *Buddha*, or the Enlightened One. The Buddha spent the rest of his 80 years teaching others the truths he had learned.

Basic to the Buddha's understanding of the human condition were the "Four Noble Truths:"

1. All life is suffering—an endless chain of births and rebirths (karma).

2. The cause of the suffering is desire. It is desire that binds humans to the wheel of karma.

3. Escape from suffering and endless rebirths can come only by the cessation of desire and the attainment of nirvana.

4. The path to nirvana is eightfold, requiring right views, thought, speech, actions, living, efforts, mindfulness, and meditation. Buddhists say that nirvana cannot be described: It is the ground of all existence, ineffable, and beyond time and space—an ultimate reality that may be experienced, but not grasped intellectually.

The Buddha was a religious teacher, not a social reformer, yet his religious understanding led to ethical conclusions. He condemned the caste system that flourished in the India of his day. He denounced war, slavery, and the taking of life. He opposed appeals to miracles. He did not demand a blind faith in his doctrines: He told his followers to accept his teachings only after they had tested them against their own experience. He taught that poverty was a cause of immorality, and that it was futile to attempt to suppress crime with punishments. He identified with all humanity, saying, "He who attends on the sick attends on me." Because the goal of Buddhism is for all humans to become Buddhas, some have called Buddhism the most contemplative and otherworldly of the great world religions. For the spiritually unprepared, and even for the historical Buddha, the way was not easy, and one lifetime was not enough.

Monks and nuns might practice the Eightfold Path, meditate for months and years, and experience an inner spiritual awakening, but only a few would gain enlightenment,

Two seated Buddhas. This fifth- to sixth-century painting adorns a wall of a cave in Ajanta, India.
Borromeo/Art Resource, N.Y.

Tibetan Buddhist nuns. They belong to a Tibetan sect of the Mahayana (Greater Vehicle) Buddhism that swept north to Central Asia and Tibet, and then East to China, Korea and Japan. Behind them, prayer flags blow in the wind.
Patrick Feld/Eye Ubiquitous/Corbis.

the release from karmic causation. Most could only hope for a rebirth in a higher spiritual state—to begin again closer, to the goal. For laypeople the emphasis of Buddhism was on ethical living in human society as a preparation for a more dedicated religious quest in a future life.

Buddhism spread rapidly along the Ganges River and through northern India. In the time of King Ashoka (272–232 B.C.E.) of the Mauryas, it spread to southern India, Ceylon, and beyond. This was its great missionary age. As it spread throughout India its influence on religious practice at the village level was enormous, and its meditative techniques helped reshape Hindu yogic exercises. Eventually, however, Buddhism in India was re-Hinduized. It developed competing schools of metaphysics, a pantheon of gods and cosmic Buddhas, and devotional sects focusing on one or another of these cosmic figures. Its original character as a reform movement of Hinduism was lost, and between 500 and 1500 C.E. it was largely reabsorbed into Hinduism.

Beyond India, two major currents of Buddhism spread over Asia. One, known as the "Way of the Elders" (*Theravada*), swept through continental Southeast Asia and the islands that are today Indonesia. The Theravada teaching was close to early Indian Buddhism and, as it spread, it carried with it other strands of Indian culture as well.

Buddhism remains the predominant religion of Burma, Thailand, Cambodia, and Laos, although it must contend with more recent secular ideologies. In Thailand, it remains the state religion: Thai kings rule as Buddhist monarchs; Thai boys spend short periods as Buddhist monks; and Thai temples (*wats*) continue as one center of village life. Before the spread of Islam, Buddhism also once flourished in Malaya, Sumatra, and Java.

The second major current, known as the "Greater Vehicle" (*Mahayana*), spread through northwest India to Afghanistan and Central Asia, and then to China, Tibet and Mongolia, Vietnam, Korea, and Japan. In each region the pattern that unfolded was different. In what is today Pakistan, Afghanistan, and Central Asia, Buddhism was overtaken and replaced by Islam. Mahayana doctrines entered Tibet during the sixth century C.E. and became firmly established several centuries later.

Today Tibetan Buddhism is the predominant religion of Tibet, Nepal, Sikkim, Bhutan, and Mongolia (although there it is severely curtailed by Chinese authorities). In China, and then spreading from China to Korea, Vietnam, and Japan, Mahayana Buddhism saw its fullest development. One key doctrine in this current was the ideal of the *bodhisattva*, a being who had gone all the way to nirvana, but held back to help others attain salvation.

Another Mahayana doctrine, that of the Chan (in China) or Zen (in Japan) sect, stressed meditation and perhaps was closer to the teachings of the historical Buddha.

In China, the Tang dynasty (618–907) was the great Buddhist age, a time of unparalleled creativity in religious art, sculpture, and music. After that, although Buddhism continued to flourish at the village level, the governing scholar-gentry class shifted to the more worldly doctrines of Neo-Confucianism. In Vietnam, Korea, and Japan, the overall process replicated that of China, but the shift occurred later and with many local variations.

During modern times Buddhism—like all structures of faith—has struggled, with the secular doctrines of the scientific, and industrial, and communist revolutions exerting a powerful influence in the 19th and 20th centuries. The future is unclear, but undoubtedly Buddhism will be powerfully affected by the ongoing transformations of Asian societies.

- In what way is Buddhism's relation to Hinduism parallel to Christianity's relation to Judaism?

- How can the teachings of a religion be tested against an individual's experience? If you were a Buddhist, how would you define a fair test?

10 Iran and India Before Islam

CHAPTER HIGHLIGHTS

Iran Under the Parthians (247 B.C.E.–223 C.E.) and the Sasanids (224–651 C.E.), Iran was a rival to Roman and Byzantine power in the Near East. The Sasanids, in particular, sought to restore the glory of the ancient Achaemenid Empire and promoted native Persian culture. They also based their rule on orthodox Zoroastrianism and suppressed the Manichaeans as heretics. Although foreign trade flourished, the Parthian and Sasanid rulers favored the landed aristocracy at the expense of the peasantry, who were heavily taxed. The long wars with Rome and Byzantium ultimately sapped Sasanid strength and left the empire vulnerable to Islamic Arab invasion in the seventh century.

India The Gupta period (320–467 C.E.) is considered one of the high points of Indian civilization. Art, especially architecture and sculpture, flourished, and Indian civilization took on its enduring "Hindu" social, religious, and cultural shape. In society the fundamentally hierarchic nature of the caste system solidified. Hindu piety emphasized devotional cults to deities, especially Vishnu and Shiva. Indian Buddhism developed two main schools, the Mahayana and the Theravada, and spread to other parts of Asia.

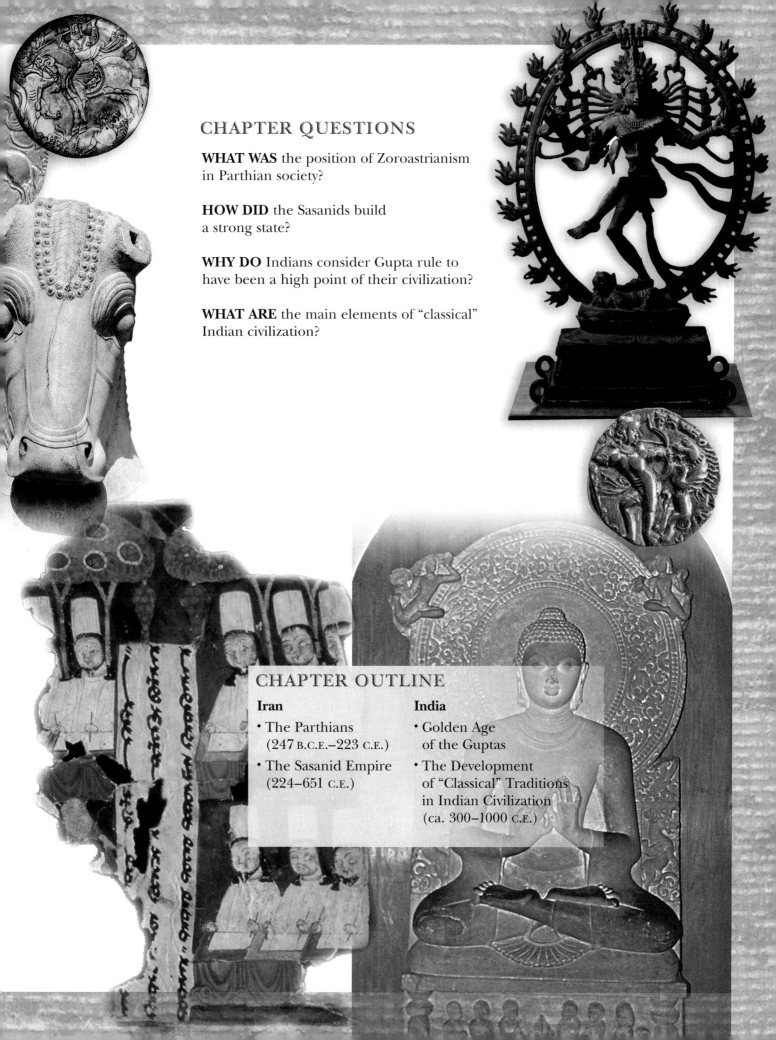

CHAPTER QUESTIONS

WHAT WAS the position of Zoroastrianism in Parthian society?

HOW DID the Sasanids build a strong state?

WHY DO Indians consider Gupta rule to have been a high point of their civilization?

WHAT ARE the main elements of "classical" Indian civilization?

CHAPTER OUTLINE

Iran
- The Parthians (247 B.C.E.–223 C.E.)
- The Sasanid Empire (224–651 C.E.)

India
- Golden Age of the Guptas
- The Development of "Classical" Traditions in Indian Civilization (ca. 300–1000 C.E.)

In this chapter we look at Southwest and South Asia before the spread of Islam. In Iran the Sasanids, a dynasty of Persian imperial rulers, reigned from the breakdown of Parthian rule in the early third century C.E. to the coming of Islam in the seventh. Although Zoroastrian traditions regained their vitality, a small ruling nobility dominated the social and political system, and there was constant competition with the Byzantine Empire. This competition finally exhausted both Sasanid and Byzantine resources. Both empires were defeated by the Arabs under the banner of Islam in the mid-seventh century.

In India the imperial Gupta kings presided also over a cultural flowering of unprecedented magnificence until new incursions of steppe peoples from about 500 C.E. led to political fragmentation. Nevertheless, regional empires lasted until the 13th century, when Islamic power under the Delhi sultans began to forge new patterns of power and culture north and south.

The coming of Islamic civilization—with Muslim conquerors or, more often, with Muslim traders and religious brotherhoods—took place at different times and with differing consequences in Iran and India.

In Iran, Islam was prominent in government and public life from the early years of the Arab conquests in the mid-seventh century, although the populace in the regions of the traditional Iranian cultural sphere did not convert until much later.

In India, Arab armies penetrated the Indus region as early as 711, and Muslim rulers of Central Asian extraction controlled the Panjab from around 1000. The establishment of the so-called Delhi Sultanate in 1205 marked the entrenchment of Muslim ruling dynasties in the Indian heartlands. Similarly, Sufi brotherhoods made significant converts in India from about the 13th century onward. Even earlier, in trading communities on the coasts of Gujarat and South India, Muslim settlers and converts had already provided the nuclei of smaller, often scattered Muslim communities that grew up within the larger Hindu society.

IRAN

THE PARTHIANS

WHAT WAS the position of Zoroastrianism in Parthian society?

Parthian Arsacid rule (ca. 247 B.C.E.–223 C.E.) began in the eastern Iranian province of Parthia in Seleucid times and eventually dominated the Iranian heartlands of the Achaemenids (see Chapter 4). The Parthians even managed by 129 B.C.E. to extinguish Seleucid power east of the Euphrates. They also continued the Iranian imperial and cultural traditions of the Achaemenids. The relative Parthian tolerance of religious diversity was paralleled by the growth of regionalism in political and cultural affairs. A growing nobility built strong local power bases and became the backbone of Parthian military power. Aramaic, the common language of the empire, gradually lost ground to regional Iranian tongues after the second century B.C.E., although Greek was widely spoken.

Despite their general religious tolerance, the Parthians upheld such Zoroastrian traditions as maintenance of a royal sacred fire at a shrine in their Parthian homeland and included priestly advisers on the emperor's council. The last century of their rule saw increased emphasis on Iranian as opposed to foreign traditions in religious and cultural affairs, perhaps in reaction to the almost constant warfare with the Romans on their west flank and the Graeco-Bactrian Kushan threat to the east. By this time Christianity and Buddhism were making sufficient converts in border areas to threaten Zoroastrian tradition. These threats may have stimulated Parthian attempts to collect the largely oral

Zoroastrian textual heritage. In such ways, Parthian rule laid the groundwork for the nationalistic emphases of subsequent centuries.

THE SASANID EMPIRE (224–651 C.E.)

The Sasanids were a Persian dynasty and claimed to be the rightful Achaemenid heirs. They championed Iranian legitimacy and tried to brand the Parthians as outside invaders from the northeast who followed Greek and other foreign ways. The first Sasanid king, Ardashir (r. 224–ca. 239 C.E.), was a Persian warrior noble from a priestly family. The Sasanid name came from his grandfather, Sasan. Ardashir and his son, Shapur I (r. ca. 239–272), built a strong internal administration in Persia (Fars), extended their sway to Ctesiphon, and took Bactria from the Kushans. Under Shapur's long rule, the empire grew in the east, beyond the Caucasus, and into Syria, Armenia, and parts of Anatolia. Shapur defeated three Roman emperors, even capturing one of them, Valerian (r. 253–260). Thus he could justifiably claim to be a restorer of Iranian glory and a "king of kings," or *shahanshah*. He also centralized and rationalized taxation, the civil ministries, and the military, although neither he nor his successors could fully contain the growing power of the nobility.

With the shift of the Roman Empire east to Byzantium in the early fourth century C.E., the stage of imperial conflict was set for the next 350 years. Byzantium (Constantinople) on the Bosphorus and Ctesiphon on the Tigris were home to the two mightiest thrones of Eurasia until the coming of the Arabs. Each won victories over the other and championed a different religious orthodoxy, but neither could ever completely conquer the other. In the sixth century, each produced its greatest emperor: the Byzantine Justinian (r. 527–565) and the Sasanid Chosroes Anosharvan ("Chosroes of the Immortal Soul," r. 531–579). Yet, less than a century after their deaths, the new Arab power reduced one empire dramatically and destroyed the other. Byzantium survived with the loss of most of its territory for another 800 years, but the Sasanid imperial order was swept away in 651. Memory of the Sasanids did not, however, entirely die. Chosroes, for example, became a legendary model of greatness for Persians and a symbol of imperial splendor among the Arabs. The Pahlavi monarchy in 20th-century Iran also utilized the historical memory of the Sasanid to legitimize their own rule and persuade modern-day Iranians of their cultural distinctiveness.

SOCIETY AND ECONOMY

Sasanid society was largely like that of earlier times. The extended family was the basic social unit. Zoroastrian orthodoxy recognized four classes: priests, warriors, scribes, and peasants. However, a great divide separated the royal house, the priesthood, and the warrior nobility from the common people (artisans, traders, and the rural peasantry).

The basis of the economy remained agriculture, but land became increasingly concentrated in the hands of an ever-richer minority of the royalty, nobility, and priesthood. As in Roman domains, the growth of great estates was responsible for a growing imbalance between the rich few and the impoverished many. Many small farmers were reduced to serfdom. The burden of land taxation, like

HOW DID the Sasanids build a strong state?

Shapur I. A cameo depicts the capture of the Emperor Valerian by Shapur I, following the great Persian victory against the Romans near Edessa in 259 C.E.

Bibliotheque Nationale. Paris, France.

that of conscript labor work and army duty, hit hardest those least able to afford it. This produced a popular reaction, as the Mazdakite movement, discussed below, shows.

The Sasanids also closely oversaw and heavily taxed the lucrative caravan and sea trade in their territory. Silk and glass production increased under government monopoly, and the state also controlled mining. The empire's many urban centers and its foreign trade relied on a money system. It was from Jewish bankers in Babylonia and their Persian counterparts that Europe and the rest of the world got the use of bills of exchange (the term *check* comes from a Pahlavi word).[1]

Sasanid aristocratic culture drew on diverse traditions, from Roman, Hellenistic, and Bactrian-Indian to Achaemenid and other native Iranian ones. Its heyday was the reign of Chosroes. Indian influences—not only religious ones, as in the case of Buddhist ideas, but also artistic and scientific ones—were especially strong. Indian medicine and mathematics were notably in demand. Hellenistic culture was also revived in the academy at Jundishapur in Khuzistan, where refugee scholars from Byzantium came to teach medicine and philosophy after Justinian closed the Greek academies in the West.

RELIGION

Zoroastrian Revival   The Sasanids institutionalized Zoroastrian ritual and theology as state orthodoxy. Although they were continuing the Arsacid patronage of Zoroastrian worship, the Sasanids claimed to be restoring the true faith after centuries of neglect. The initial architect of this propaganda and the Zoroastrian revival was the first chief priest (Mobad) of the empire, Tosar (or Tansar). Under Ardashir, Tosar instituted a state church and began to compile an authoritative, written canon of the Avesta, the scriptural texts that include the hymns of Zarathushtra (see Chapter 4). He may also have instituted a calendar reform and replaced all images in the temples with the sacred altar fires of Zoroastrian tradition.

The most influential figure in Sasanid religious history was Tosar's successor, Kartir (or Kirdir), who served as chief priest to Shapur I and three successors (ca. 239–293). Although his zealotry was initially restrained by the religiously tolerant Shapur, Kirdir gained greater power and influence after Shapur's death. He seems to have tried to convert not only pagans, but also Christians, Buddhists, and others. His chief opponents were the Manichaeans, whom he considered Zoroastrian heretics, much as Christian groups saw them as Christian heretics.

Manichaeism   Mani (216–277 C.E.) was born of a noble Parthian family but raised in Babylonia. A cosmopolitan who spoke Aramaic, Persian, and Greek and traveled to India, Mani preached a message both similar to and sharply divergent from its Zoroastrian, Judaic, and Christian forerunners. **Manichaeism**

Manichaeism   A dualistic and moralistic view of reality in which good and evil, spirit and matter warred with each other.

Manichaean Priests.   This leaf from a Manichaean book (ca. eighth–ninth century C.E.) shows priests in white robes and tall hats kneeling in front of low desks. Each has a sheet of white paper and some hold pens. Works such as this are an important source for our knowledge of Manichaean communities.

A leaf from a Manchurian book, Roko, Templek (MIK III 6368), 8th-9th century, a manuscript painting 17.2 × 11.2 cm. Museum fur Indische Kunst, Staatliche Museen Preussischer Kulturbesitz, Berlin.

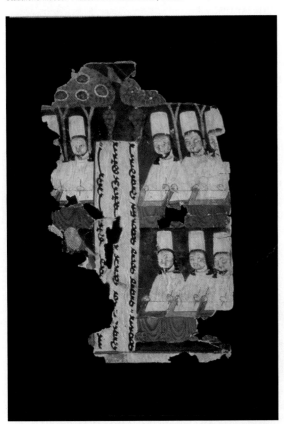

[1]R. Girshman, *Iran* (Harmondsworth, U.K.: Penguin Books, 1954), pp. 341–346. "Pahlavi" is the name of the Middle Persian language.

centered on a radically dualistic and moralistic view of reality in which good and evil, spirit and matter, were constantly at war with one another. Mani sought to convert others to his views which he presented as the culmination and restoration of the original unity of Zoroastrian, Christian, and Buddhist teachings. He may have been the first person in history whose conscious intent was to "found" a new religious tradition or to seek to create a "scripture" for his followers. He called his new system "Justice," although outsiders called it *Manichaeism*. The popularity of Mani's movement probably contributed to Kirdir's and later attempts to establish a Zoroastrian "orthodoxy" and scriptural canon.[2]

Kirdir eventually had Mani executed as a heretic in 277, but Mani's movement had great consequences. It spread westward to challenge the Christian church (Saint Augustine was once a Manichaean) and eastward along the Silk Route to Central Asia. The movement's ideas figured even centuries later in both Christian and Islamic heresies. Its adherents probably carried the Western planetary calendar to China, where in some areas it was used for centuries.

Zoroastrian Orthodoxy Kartir had firmly grounded Zoroastrian orthodoxy despite the persistence of challenges to it, such as Mani's. This orthodoxy became the backbone of Sasanid culture. When the Sasanids' Persian dialect, *Pahlavi*, became the official imperial language, the Zoroastrian sacred texts were written in Pahlavi. Throughout Sasanid times, the priesthood increased its power. Priests served as the empire's jurists and legal interpreters as well as its liturgists and scholars. With increasing endowments for new fire temples, the church establishment also came to control much of Iran's wealth.

LATER SASANID DEVELOPMENTS

Despite the Zoroastrian moral idealism of many of their rulers, the Sasanid concept of justice did not include equal distribution of the empire's bounty. The radical inequality of wealth between the aristocracy and the masses sparked a conflict with what is called the Mazdakite movement at the end of the fifth century. The movement's leader, Mazdak, preached asceticism, pessimism about the evil state of the material world, the virtues of vegetarianism, tolerance, and brotherly love—all ideas apparently drawn ultimately from Manichaeism—and the need for a more equal distribution of society's goods. This appealed to the oppressed classes, although even one Sasanid ruler, Kavad I (r. 488–531), was sympathetic for a time to Mazdak's ideas of social justice. However, in 528 Kavad's third son, the later Chosroes Anosharvan, massacred Mazdak and his most important followers. Although this finished the Mazdakites, their name was used later, in Islamic times, for various Iranian popular revolts.

Sasanid Iran

223–224 C.E.	Ardashir (r. 224–ca. 239) defeats the last Arsacid ruler, becomes *shahanshah* of Iran
ca. 225–ca. 239	Tosar chief priest (Mobad) of realm
239–272	Reign of Shapur I; expansion of the empire east and west
ca. 239–293	Kirdir chief priest (Mobad) of the realm
216–277	Mani
ca. 307–379	Reign of Shapur II
488–531	Reign of Kavad I; height of Mazdakite movement
528	Mazdak and many of his followers massacred
531–579	Reign of Chosroes Anosharvan at Ctesiphon
651	Death of last Sasanid; Arabs conquer Persian Empire

[2]W. C. Smith, *The Meaning and End of Religion* (New York: Harper & Row, 1962), pp. 92–98.

INDIA

GOLDEN AGE OF THE GUPTAS

Indians have always considered the Gupta era a high point of their civilization. Historians have seen in it the source of "classical" norms for Hindu religion and Indian culture—the symbolic equivalent of Periclean Athens, Augustan Rome, or Han China. The Guptas ruled when the various facets of Indian life came together to create the recognizable patterns of a single civilization that extended over the whole subcontinent. A major factor in this development was the relative peace and stability that marked most of the Guptas' reign.

GUPTA RULE

The first Gupta king was Chandragupta (r. 320–ca. 330 C.E.). He ruled first in Magadha and then became prominent in the whole Ganges basin after he married Princess Kumaradevi, daughter of a powerful tribal leader north of the Ganges. Although their reign inaugurated Gupta power, it was their son, Samudragupta (r. ca. 330–375), and especially their grandson, Chandragupta II (r. ca. 375–415), who turned kingdom into empire and presided over the Gupta "golden age."

The Gupta realm extended from the Panjab and Kashmir south to the Narbada River in the western Deccan and east to modern Assam (see Map 10–1), and their sphere of influence included some of the Kushan and Saka kingdoms of the northwest and much of the eastern coast of India and possibly Ceylon (Sri Lanka). Unlike the Mauryans, the Guptas usually made a defeated ruler into a vassal prince rather than attempting to take direct control of his kingdom. Seated at the old Mauryan capital, Pataliputra, Gupta splendor and power had no rival. Under Chandragupta II, India was arguably the most civilized and peaceful country in the world (see "A Chinese Traveler's Report on the Gupta Realm").

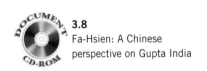

3.8 Fa-Hsien: A Chinese perspective on Gupta India

Two further Gupta kings sustained this prosperity for another half century, despite invasions by a new wave of steppe nomads, the Huns, after about 440. By about 500 the Huns had overrun western India, and the Gupta Empire collapsed about 550. Harsha, a descendant of the Guptas through his grandmother, did revive a semblance of former Gupta splendor between 616 and 657. His loosely held dominions again spanned North India, but when he died without heirs, the empire broke up again.

The succeeding centuries before the arrival of Muslim invaders about 1000 C.E. saw several dynasties in North India share power, but no unified rule of any duration. Outside the north, several long-lived dynasties built regional empires in the western Deccan and Tamilnad (the extreme south) after Gupta times, and the main centers of Indian civilization shifted to those areas.

GUPTA CULTURE

With the decline of Rome in the West, Indian culture experienced little new outside influence from the Gupta

India from the Gupta Age to ca. 1000 C.E.

320 C.E.–ca. 467	Gupta period
320–330	Reign of Chandragupta, first Gupta king
375–454	Reigns of Chandragupta II and Kumaragupta: Kalidasa flourishes; heyday of Gupta culture
399–414	Chinese Buddhist monk, Fa-Hsien, travels in India
ca. 440	Beginning of Hun invasions from Central Asia
616–657	Reign of Harsha; revival of Gupta splendor and power
820	Death of Vedantin philosopher-theologian, Shankara
550–ca. 1000	Regional Indian kingdoms in north and south; major Puranas composed; age of first great Vaishnava and Shaivite devotional poets in southern India

MAP EXPLORATION

Interactive map: To explore this map further, go to **http://www.prenhall.com/craig/map10.1**

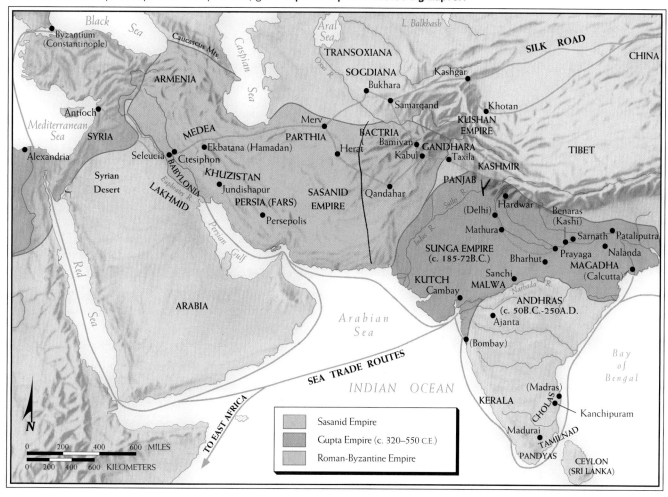

MAP 10-1

International Trade Routes in Gupta and Sasanid Times. This map shows the Gupta and Sasanid Empires and the trade routes that linked them to each other and to other areas of the world.

HOW DID the Indian Ocean facilitate trade between different regions?

era until Muslim times. India's chief contacts were now with Southeast Asia and China, and most of the cultural transmission was from India eastward, not vice versa.

The claim of the Gupta era to being India's golden age of culture could be sustained solely by its magnificent architecture and sculpture, the wall paintings of the Ajanta caves, and Kalidasa's matchless drama and verse. Kalidasa, the "Shakespeare" of Sanskrit letters, flourished in the time of Chandragupta II and his successor.

The depth of Gupta culture is indicated by the era's strong emphasis on education, whether in Jain and Buddhist monasteries or in Brahmanical schools. In addition to religious texts, typical subjects included rhetoric, prose and poetic composition, grammar, logic, medicine, and metaphysics. Using an older Indian

HISTORY'S VOICES

A CHINESE TRAVELER'S REPORT ON THE GUPTA REALM

*F*a-Hsien, a Chinese Buddhist monk, was the first of several Chinese known for traveling to India to study and bring back Buddhist scriptures from the intellectual centers of Buddhist thought there. He wrote an account of his travels, first through Central Asia, then all over India, and finally through Ceylon and Indonesia again to China (399–414 C.E.).

WHAT THINGS about India seem most to surprise Fa-Hsien? Is his image of Indian rule a positive one? What do his remarks say about the prestige of the Buddhist tradition and its monks in the Indian state? What does he tell us about Indian society?

On the sides of the river, both right and left, are twenty san ghârâmas [monasteries], with perhaps 3,000 priests. The law of the Buddha is progressing and flourishing. Beyond the deserts are the countries of Western India. The kings of these countries are all firm believers in the law of Buddha. They remove their caps of state when they make offerings to the priests. The members of the royal household and the chief ministers personally direct the food-giving; when the distribution of food is over, they spread a carpet on the ground opposite the chief seat (the president's seat) and sit down before it. They dare not sit on couches in the presence of the priests. The rules relating to the almsgiving of kings have been handed down from the time of Buddha till now. Southward from this is the so-called middle-country (Mâdhyade´sa). The climate of this country is warm and equable, without frost or snow. The people are very well off, without poll tax or official restrictions. Only those who till the royal lands return a portion of profit of the land. If they desire to go, they go; if they like to stop, they stop. The kings govern without corporal punishment; criminals are fined, according to circumstances, lightly or heavily. Even in cases of repeated rebellion they only cut off the right hand. The king's personal attendants, who guard him on the right and left, have fixed salaries. Throughout the country the people kill no living thing nor drink wine, nor do they eat garlic or onions, with the exception of Chandâlas [outcasts] only. The Chandâlas are named "evil men" and dwell apart from others; if they enter a town or market, they sound a piece of wood in order to separate themselves; then men, knowing who they are, avoid coming in contact with them. In this country they do not keep swine nor fowls, and do not deal in cattle; they have no shambles or wine-shops in their market places. In selling they use cowrie shells. The Chandâlas only hunt and sell flesh. Down from the time of Buddha's Nirvâna, the kings of these countries, the chief men and householders, have raised vihâras [monasteries] for the priests, and provided for their support by bestowing on them fields, houses, and gardens, with men and oxen. Engraved title-deeds were prepared and handed down from one reign to another; no one has ventured to withdraw them, so that till now there has been no interruption. All the resident priests having chambers (in these vihâras) have their beds, mats, food, drink, and clothes provided without stint; in all places this is the case. The priests ever engage themselves in doing meritorious works for the purpose of religious advancement (karma—building up their religious character), or in reciting the scriptures, or in meditation.

Source: "Buddhist Country Records," in Si-Yu-Ki, *Buddhist Records of the Western World*, trans. by Samuel Beal (London, 1884; reprint, Delhi: Oriental Books Reprint Corporation, 1969), pp. xxxvii–xxxviii. Reprinted by permission of Motilal Banarsidass Publishers Pvt. Ltd., Delhi, India.

number system that the Arabs transmitted to the West as "Arabic numerals," Gupta scholars were especially adept at mathematics.

In sculpture, the monastic complex at Sarnath was a great center of activity. The superb technique and expressive serenity of Gupta style grew out of native Mathura and Greco-Roman schools. Hindu, Jain, and Buddhist works all shared the same style and conventions. Even in handwork and luxury crafts (silks, muslin, linen, ivory and other carvings, bronze metalwork, gold and silver work, and cut stones), Gupta products achieved new levels of quality and were in great demand abroad. In architecture, Gupta splendor is less evident, except in the culmination of cave-shrine (Chaitya-hall) development at Ajanta and in the erection of the earliest surviving free-standing temples in India. The Hindu temple, however, underwent its most important development in post-Gupta times, beginning in the eighth century.

MAP 10–2

Indian influence in Southeast Asia, ca. 650 C.E.   By the middle of the seventh century C.E., Indian traditions, art, and music had a pervasive influence throughout Southeast Asia, even though the number of Indians who traded and migrated there was not great.

HOW DOES the influence of India on Southeast Asian civilization demonstrate the role of trade in spreading ideas and customs?

jatis The many subgroups that make up the Hindu caste system.

varnas The four main classes that form the basis for Hindu caste relations.

Gupta Sculpture. Fifth-century C.E. statue of Lokanatha from Sarnath, which despite damage, shows the fine sculptural work of the important school of Gupta artists at Sarnath and the influence on them of both Graeco-Roman antecedents and native Indian traditions and conventions.

Scala/Art Resource, N.Y.

THE DEVELOPMENT OF "CLASSICAL" TRADITIONS IN INDIAN CIVILIZATION (CA. 300–1000 C.E.)

The Guptas' support of Brahmanic traditions and Vaishnava[3] devotionalism reflected the waning of Buddhist traditions in the mainstream of Indian religious life. In Gupta times and subsequently, down to the advent of Muslim rule, Indian civilization assumed its classical shape, its enduring "Hindu" forms of social, religious, and cultural life.

SOCIETY

In these centuries, the fundamentally hierarchical character of Hindu/Indian society solidified. The oldest manual of legal and ethical theory, the *Dharmashastra* of Manu, dates from about 200 C.E. Based on Vedic tradition, it treats the *dharma* (duties) appropriate to one's class and stage of life, rules for rites and for the study of the Veda, pollution and purification measures, dietary restrictions, royal duties and prerogatives, and other legal and moral questions.

The manual presents a classic statement of the four-class theory of social hierarchy. This ideal construct rests on the principle that every person is born into a particular station in life as a result of *karma* from earlier lives. Every station has its particular *dharma*, or appropriate duties and responsibilities, from the lowest servant to the highest prince or Brahman. The Brahmans' ancient division of Aryans into the four *varnas* or classes—*Brahman* (priest), *Kshatriya* (noble/warrior), *Vaishya* (tradesperson), and *Shudra* (servant)—provided a schematic structure designed to assure the status and power of the upper three groups, especially the Brahmans, at the expense of the Shudras and the "fifth estate," the non-Aryan "outcasts" who performed the jobs society regarded as most polluting. Although class distinctions had already hardened before 500 B.C.E., the classes were, in practice, somewhat fluid. If the traditional occupation of a varna was unavailable to one of its members, he could often take up another, despite theory to the contrary. When Brahmans, Vaishyas, or even Shudras gained political power as rulers (as was evidently the case with the Mauryas, for example), their family gradually came to be viewed as *Kshatriyas*, the appropriate class for princes.

Although the four classes, or ***varnas*** (see "Overview"), are the theoretical basis for *caste* relations, much smaller and far more numerous subgroups, or ***jatis***, are the units closest to what "caste" means in English. (*Caste* comes from *casta*, Portuguese for *jati*.) These divisions (most representing occupational groups) were already the primary units of social distinction in Gupta times. *Jati* groupings are hereditary and distinguished essentially by concerns for purity and pollution. These are determined by three kinds of regulations: (1) commensality (one may take food only from or with persons of the same or a higher group); (2) endogamy (one may marry only within one's own group); and (3) trade or craft limitation (one must practice only the trade of one's group).[4]

The caste system has been the basis of Indian social organization for at least two millennia. It enabled Hindus to accommodate foreign cultural, racial, and religious communities within Indian society by treating them as new caste

---

[3] *Vaishnava* or *Vaishnavite* means "related to Vishnu"; similarly, *Shaiva* or *Shaivite* refers to Shiva worship.
[4] A. L. Basham, *The Wonder that was India* (New York: 1963), pp. 148–149.

groups. The caste system promoted social stability and individual security by permitting everyone to tell by dress and other marks how to relate to others. It was also the logical extension of the religious doctrine of karma into society—whether as justification, result, or partial cause of the system itself (see Chapter 2).

RELIGION

Hindu Religious Life   Gupta and later times saw the growth of devotional cults of deities, preeminently Vishnu and Shiva, who were unknown or unimportant in Vedic religion. The temple worship of a particular deity has ever since been a basic form of Hindu piety. After Vishnu (especially in his form as the hero-savior Krishna) and Shiva (originally a fertility god), the chief focus of devotion came to be the Goddess in one of her many forms, such as Parvati, Shakti, Durga, or Kali. Vishnu and Shiva, like Parvati, have many forms and names and have always been easily identified with other deities, who are then worshipped as one form of the Supreme Lord or Goddess. Animal or nature deities were presumably part of popular piety from Indus Valley days forward. Indian reverence for all forms of life and stress on *ahimsa*, or "noninjury" to living beings (see Chapter 2), are most vivid in the sacredness of the cow, which has always been a mainstay of life in India.

In the development of Hindu piety and practice, a major strand was the tradition of ardent theism known as *bhakti*, or "loving devotion." *Bhakti* was already evident, at the latest by 200 C.E., in the Bhagavad Gita's treatment of Krishna. Gupta and later times saw the rise, especially in the Tamil-speaking south, of schools of bhakti poetry and worship. The central bhakti strand in Hindu life

The Bodhisattva Avalokiteshvara. Detail of a Buddhist wall painting from the cave shrines at Ajanta (Maharashtra, India), Gupta period, ca. 475 C.E. Avalokiteshvara (known in China as Kwan-yin and in Japan as Kannon) is the supreme figure of infinite mercy.

Art Resource, N.Y.

OVERVIEW   THE FOUR MAIN HINDU CASTES

Traditional Hindu/Indian society is fundamentally hierarchic in character. There are four main classes (*varnas*) into which a person is born according to how he or she lived in a previous life. Every class has its appropriate duties and responsibilities. In addition, there are numerous subgroups (*jatis*) based on a person's occupation. The English word "caste" is used to refer to all of these groups.

Brahman	Priest. This is the highest caste.
Kshatriya	Warrior or aristocrat. This is considered the appropriate caste for rulers.
Vaishya	Tradespeople and merchants.
Shudra	Servant. This caste includes peasants and manual laborers as well as domestic servants.

In addition, there is a fifth group of "outcastes" who performed the necessary but most polluting tasks in society, such as removing human waste. Persons in this category were considered "untouchable," and contact with them was considered morally and spiritually unclean.

Vishnu. A bronze statue of Hindu deity Vishnu from Thailand reflects the impact of Indian civilization on Southeast Asia.

Luca I. Tettoni/Corbis N.Y.

QUICK REVIEW

Bhakti

- *Bhakti*, or loving devotion, evident in the Bhagavad Gita's treatment or Krishna
- Derives in part from Tamil and other vernacular poets
- Through bhakti, pre-Aryan religious sensibilities reasserted themselves

Mahayana The "Great Vehicle" for salvation in Buddhism. It emphasized the Buddha's infinite compassion for all beings.

Theravada The "Way of the Elders." A school of Buddhism that emphasized the monastic ideal.

bodhisattva A "Buddha to be" who postpones his own nirvana until he has helped all other beings become enlightened.

---

derives in good part from Tamil and other vernacular poets who first sang the praises of Shiva or Vishnu as Supreme Lord. Here, pre-Aryan religious sensibilities apparently reasserted themselves through the non-Aryan Dravidian peoples of the south. The great theologian of devotional Hinduism, Ramanuja (d. ca. 1137), would later come from this same Dravidian tradition. Of major importance also to devotional piety was the development in this era of the Puranas—epic, mythological, and devotional texts. They are still today the functional sacred scriptures of grassroots Hindu religious life (the Vedic texts remaining the special preserve of the Brahmans).

Whatever god or goddess a Hindu worships, it is usual to pay homage on proper occasions also to other appropriate deities. Most Hindus view one deity as Supreme Lord but see others as manifestations of the Ultimate at lower levels. Hindu polytheism is not "idolatry" but a vivid affirmation of the infinite forms that transcendence takes in this world. The sense of the presence of the Divine everywhere is evident in the importance attached to sacred places. India is the land of religious pilgrimage *par excellence.* Sacred mountains, rivers, trees, and groves are all *tirthas,* or "river fords" to the Divine.

The intellectual articulation of Hindu polytheism and relativism found its finest expression in post-Gupta formulations of Vedanta ("the end of the Veda"). The major Vedantin thinker, Shankara (d. 820), stressed a strict "nonduality" of the Ultimate, teaching that Brahman was the only Reality behind the "illusion" (*maya*) of the world of sense experience. Yet he accepted the worship of a lesser deity as appropriate for those who could not follow his extraordinary norm—the intellectual realization of the formless Absolute beyond all "name and form."

Buddhist Religious Life The major developments of these centuries were: (1) the solidification of the two main strands of Buddhist tradition, the **Mahayana** and the **Theravada**, and (2) the spread of Buddhism abroad from its Indian homeland. The Mahayana ("Great Vehicle [of salvation]") arose in the first century B.C.E, Its proponents differentiated it sharply from the older, more conservative traditions of monk-oriented piety and thought, which they labeled the Hinayana ("Little Vehicle"). In Mahayana speculation Buddhas were seen as manifestations of a single principle of "Ultimate" Reality, and Siddhartha Gautama was held to be only one Buddha among many. The Mahayana stressed the example of the Buddha's infinite compassion for all beings. The highest goal was not a *nirvana* of "selfish" extinction but the status of a **bodhisattva**, or "Buddha-to-be," the one who postpones his own nirvana to help all other beings become enlightened.

The *bodhisattva* can offer this aid because his long career of self-sacrifice has gained him infinite merit. Salvation becomes possible not only through individual effort, but also through devotion to the Buddhas and *bodhisattvas*. At the popular level, this idea translated into devotional cults focusing on transcendent Buddhas and *bodhisattvas* conceived of as cosmic beings. One of the most important was that of the Buddha Amitabha, the personification of infinite compassion. Amitabha presides over a Western Paradise, or Pure Land, to which (through his infinite compassion) all who have faith in him have access (see Chapter 9 for a discussion of Pure Land Buddhism in Japan).

The older, more conservative "Way of the Elders" (Theravada) always focused on the monastic community, but taught that service and gifts to the monks were a major source of merit for the laity. It emphasized gaining merit for a better rebirth through high standards of conduct, lay devotion to the Buddha, and pilgrimage to his relics at various **stupas**. The Mahayana also held monastic life as the ideal, but some of its greatest attractions were its strong devotionalism and virtually polytheistic delight in divine Buddhas and *bodhisattvas* to whom one could pray for mercy, help, and rebirth in paradise. The basis of Theravada piety and practice was the scriptural collection of the traditional teachings ascribed to the Buddha, as reported by his disciples. Theravadins rejected the Mahayana claim that later texts (e.g., the Lotus Sutra) contained the highest teachings of the Buddha.

stupa   A Buddhist shrine.

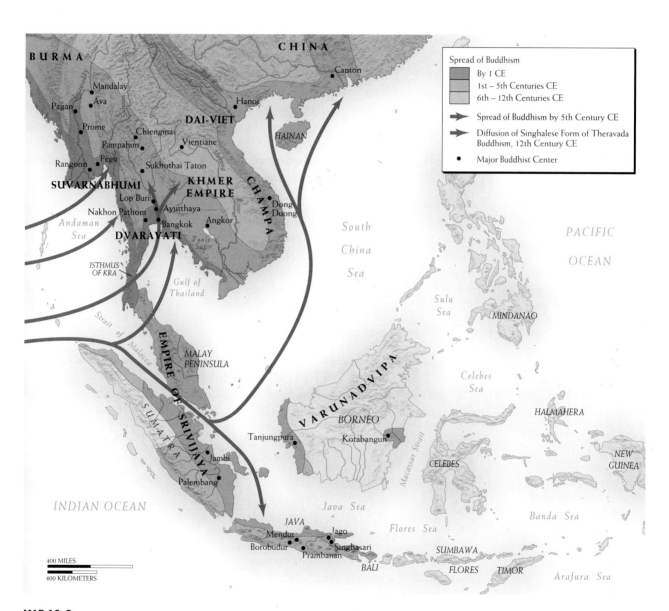

MAP 10–3

Spread of Buddhism throughout Southeast Asia.   By the 12th century C.E., Buddhism had taken root in many parts of Southeast Asia, often blending with local customs, as well as Hindu traditions that had been introduced earlier.

HOW DID the spread of Buddhism in Southeast Asia replicate the spread of Hindu traditions earlier?

India gave Theravada Buddhism to Ceylon, Burma, and parts of Southeast Asia. Mahayana Buddhism predominated in Central Asia and China, from which it spread in the fifth to eighth centuries to Korea and Japan. Tantric Buddhism, an esoteric Mahayana tradition heavily influenced by Hinduism, entered Tibet from North India in the seventh century and became the dominant tradition there.

IMAGE KEY

for pages 226–227

a. Four-armed Ganesa
b. Relief carving of the Hindu deity Vishnu reclining on the serpent Sesa at the Temple of Vishnu in Rajasthan, India.
c. Gupta coin with horse on it
d. Gupta coin with horseman on it
e. Statue of Lokanatha from Sarnath
f. The ruins of the Great Hall in the Palace of the Parthian Kings
g. Bottom of a silver bowl with Sassanid relief work
h. Seated Buddha
i. Shiva Nataraja
j. Bull from Persian ruin
k. Manichaean book leaf showing priests in white robes

SUMMARY

Iran Under the Parthians (247 B.C.E.–223 C.E.) and the Sasanids (224–651 C.E.), Iran was a rival to Roman and Byzantine power in the Middle East. The Sasanids, in particular, sought to restore the glory of the ancient Achaemenid Persian Empire and promoted native Persian culture. They also based their rule on orthodox Zoroastrianism and suppressed the Manichaeans as heretics. The Parthian and Sasanid rulers favored the landed aristocracy at the expense of the peasantry, who were heavily taxed. The long wars with Rome and Byzantium ultimately sapped Sasanid strength and left the empire vulnerable to Islamic Arab invasion in the seventh century.

India The Gupta period (320–467 C.E.) is considered one of the highlights of Indian civilization. Art, especially architecture and sculpture, flourished, and Indian civilization took on its enduring "Hindu" social, religious, and cultural shape. In society the fundamentally hierarchic nature of the caste system solidified. Hindu piety emphasized devotional cults to deities, especially Vishnu and Shiva. Indian Buddhism developed two main schools, the Mahayana and the Theravada, and spread to other parts of Asia.

REVIEW QUESTIONS

1. How did the Sasanid Empire develop after the fall of the Parthians?

2. What were the major religious issues in the Sasanid empire?

3. Why is the high Gupta period (ca. 320–450) considered a "golden age"?

4. What are some similarities and differences between the classical Buddhist and Hindu traditions that crystallized in the first half of the first millennium?

5. What might have contributed to the fact that Persia and India fell to Arab invaders?

KEY TERMS

bodhisattva (p. 238)   *Manichaeism* (p. 230)   **Theravada** (p. 238)
jatis (p. 236)   **stupa** (p. 239)   *varnas* (p. 236)
Mahayana (p. 238)

  For additional study resources for this chapter, go to:
www.prenhall.com/craig/chapter10

HINDUISM

The term *Hinduism* is our modern word for the whole of the diverse religious traditions of India. Until the word was coined in the 19th century, Hinduism (like *Buddhism*) was not even a concept in the West, let alone in India. In contemporary usage, it has become a catchall term for all the Indian religious communities that look upon the texts of the Vedas (see Chapter 1) as eternal, perfect truth.

The historical beginnings of the varied Hindu traditions can be traced to the ancient Aryan migrations into southern Asia in the second millennium B.C.E. During this era the Vedic hymns were composed. They describe a pantheon of gods not unlike that among the Greeks, the Romans, and other Indo-European peoples. Centered on a sacrificial cult of these gods, Vedic religion increasingly became the preserve of the Brahman priestly class of early Indian society. The Brahmans gradually elaborated a cult characterized by sacrificial rituals, purificatory rules, and fixed distinctions of birth on which India's later caste system was based.

▲ **Shiva.** This exquisitely crafted bronze figure of Shiva dating from the 11th century C.E. depicts him as Lord of the Dance. He is surrounded by a circle of fire, which symbolizes both death and rebirth.

The Cleveland Museum of Art, 2002, Purchase from the J.H. Wade Fund 1930.331.

These developments are mirrored in the later Vedic, or Brahmanical, texts (ca. 1000–500 B.C.E.) that provide commentary on and instructions for ritual use of the Vedic hymns.

After about 700 B.C.E. new developments emerged. North India produced a series of religious reformers, some of whom broke with Vedic tradition and championed knowledge and ascetic discipline over purity and ritual action. Of these, the most famous were Siddhartha Gautama (the Buddha, b. ca. 563 B.C.E.) and Mahavira Vardhamana (founder of the Jain tradition, b. ca. 550 B.C.E.). Other religious leaders reinterpreted the older sacrifice as an inner activity and deepened its spiritual dimensions. Their thinking is represented especially in the Upanishads, which many Hindus consider the most sublime philosophical texts in the Indian tradition.

Developed so long ago, such notions have been part of the complex vision of existence that lies behind the myriad forms of religious life known to us as Hinduism. In this vision the immortal part of each human being, the *atman*, is enmeshed in existence, but not ultimately of it. The nature of existence is *samsara*, a ceaseless round of cause and effect determined by the inescapable consequences of *karma*, or "action." The doctrine of *karma* is a moral as well as physical economy in which every act has unavoidable results; so long as mental or physical action occurs, life and change go on repeatedly. Birth determines one's place and duties in the traditional Indian caste system. Caste is the most visible and concrete reminder of the pervasiveness of the Hindu concept of absolute causality. The final goal is to transcend this cycle, or *samsara*, in which we are all caught. The only way out of this otherwise endless becoming and rebirth is *moksha*, which may be gained through knowledge, action, or devotion.

On the popular level, the period after about 500 B.C.E. is most notable in Indian religious life for two developments. Both took place alongside the ever deeper entrenchment in society of caste distinctions and a supporting ethic of obligations and privileges. The first was

▲ **Purification rituals in the waters of the holy Ganges.** Purification rituals are part of the obligatory daily rituals of all "twice-born" Hindus. The morning rituals performed by the women here in the Ganges include greeting the sun with recitation and prayer and purification by bathing.

Ian Berry/Magnum Photos, Inc.

the elaboration of ascetic traditions of inner quest and self-realization, such as that of yoga. The second was the rise of devotional worship of specific gods and goddesses who were seen by their worshippers as identical with the Ultimate—in other words, as supreme deities for those who served them. The latter development was of particular importance for popular religion in India. Evident in the famous and beloved Hindu devotional text, the Bhagavad Gita, it reached its highest level after 500 B.C.E. in the myriad movements of fervent, loving devotionalism, or *bhakti*, many of which remain important today. A striking aspect of Hindu piety has been its willingness to accommodate the focus on one "chosen deity" who is worshipped as supreme to a worldview that holds that the Divine can and does take many forms. Thus most Hindus

worship one deity, but they do so in the awareness that faith in other deities can also lead one to the Ultimate.

The period between about 500 B.C.E. and 1000 C.E. saw the rise to special prominence of two gods, Vishnu and Shiva, as the primary forms in which the Supreme Lord was worshipped. Along with the mother-goddess figure, who takes various names and forms (Kali and Durga, for example), Vishnu and Shiva have remained the most important manifestations of the Divine in India. Their followers are known as Vaishnavas and Shaivas, respectively. A few recurring phenomena and ideas can suggest something of Indian religiousness in practice.

Hindu practice is characterized especially by temple worship (*puja*), in which *worshippers bring* offerings of flowers, food, and the like. They especially seek out temple images for the blessing that the sight of these images brings. Another important part of Hindu devotionalism is the recitation of sacred texts, many of which are vernacular hymns of praise to a particular deity. *Mantras*, or special recitative texts from the Vedas, are thought to have extraordinary power and are used by many Hindus in their original Sanskrit form. Pilgrimage to sacred sites, especially rivers, mountains, and famous shrines, is a prominent part of Hindu religious life. India's landscape is filled with sacred sites and sacred pilgrim routes, both local and national in reputation. A prominent feature of Hindu life is preoccupation with purity and pollution, most evident in the food taboos associated with caste groupings.

The ascetic tendency in India is also highly developed. Although only a tiny minority of Indians take up a life of full renunciation, they are influential. Ascetic worshippers do not settle in one place, acquire possessions, or perform regular worship. Rather, they wander about in search of teachers and devote themselves to meditation and self-realization. Even though most Hindus have families and work at their salvation through *puja* and moral living, the ascetic ideal has an important place in the overall Indian worldview. It stands as a constant reminder of the deeper reality beyond the everyday world and any individual, life.

- Compared to other faiths that have expanded globally, such as Christianity and Islam, why has Hinduism been largely confined to India?

- How has Hinduism accomodated and absorbed different beliefs and value systems?

11 The Formation of Islamic Civilization 622–945

CHAPTER HIGHLIGHTS

Muhammad The Prophet Muhammad (570-632) was the founder of Islam. At about age 40, he had a religious experience during which, Muslims believe, the angel Gabriel repeatedly recited *(qur'an)* God's word to him. The message of the Qur'an was that social justice and worship of the one true God are required of every person. The proper response to God is submission *(islam)* to his will by becoming a Muslim (one who submits).

Islamic Conquest By the time of Muhammad's death, his followers had conquered all of Arabia. Under his successors, the caliphs, Muslim Arab armies conquered most of the Middle East, North Africa, Spain, Iran, and northwest India. Many of the peoples of these territories welcomed Islamic rule and eventually converted to Islam and became part of the *(umma)*, the community of Islamic believers.

The High Caliphate Under the Abbasid caliphs, Islamic culture enjoyed its "classical" phase. Arabic translations of Greek and Sanskrit works stimulated progress in astronomy and medicine. Arabic literature and poetry flourished and Arabic language spread throughout the Islamic world. Arabic artists and architects built on earlier traditions to develop a distinctive Islamic style in decoration, painting, and architecture. The *ulama*, Islamic religious and legal scholars, played a prominent part in Islamic society as interpreters of Islamic tradition and law.

Decline of the Caliphate The Islamic empire began to splinter early. Disputes over the succession to the Prophet divided Muslims. Large parts of the Empire–Spain, North Africa, Iran–seceded. Military commanders reduced the caliphs to mere figureheads. The last Abbasid caliph was killed by the Mongols when they sacked Baghdad in 1258.

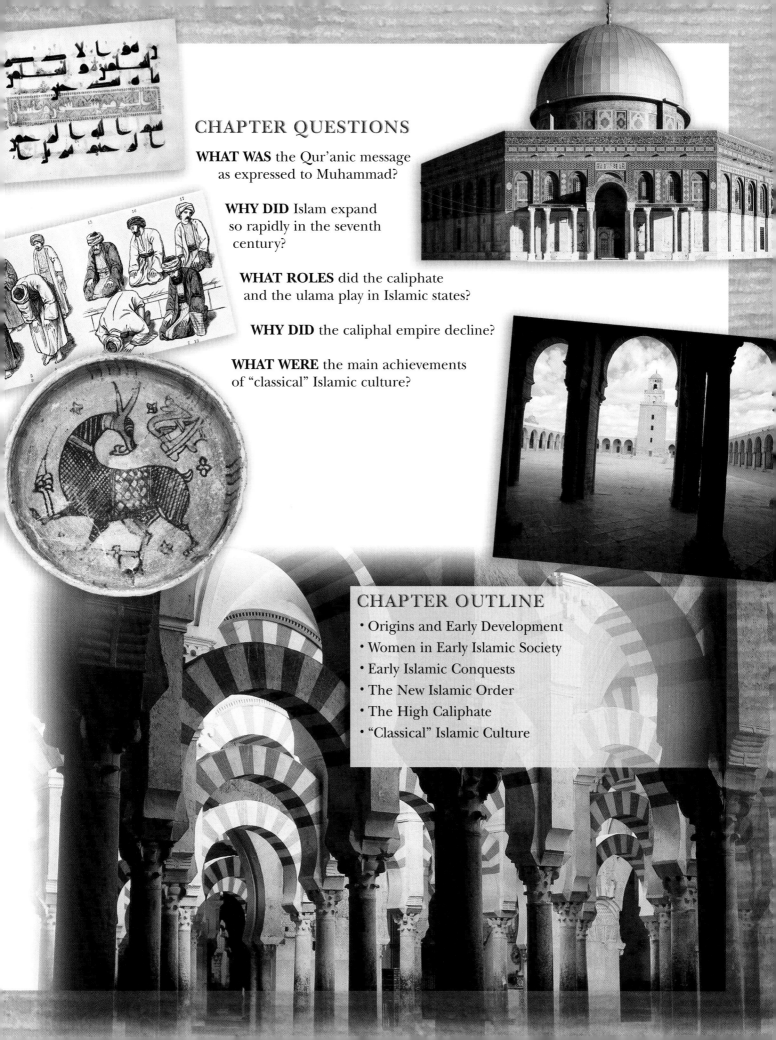

CHAPTER QUESTIONS

WHAT WAS the Qur'anic message as expressed to Muhammad?

WHY DID Islam expand so rapidly in the seventh century?

WHAT ROLES did the caliphate and the ulama play in Islamic states?

WHY DID the caliphal empire decline?

WHAT WERE the main achievements of "classical" Islamic culture?

CHAPTER OUTLINE

- Origins and Early Development
- Women in Early Islamic Society
- Early Islamic Conquests
- The New Islamic Order
- The High Caliphate
- "Classical" Islamic Culture

Islamic civilization has been the last great world civilization to appear to date, if one excepts the post-Enlightenment modern West. The basic ideas and ideals of the Islamic worldview derived from a single, prophetic-revelatory event, Muhammad's proclamation of the Qur'an. This event galvanized the Arabs into a new kind of unity—that of the community of Muslims, or "submitters" to God. This community subsequently spread far beyond Arabia, and Persians, Indians, and others raised it to new heights. Their acceptance of a new vision of society (and also of reality) as more compelling than any older vision— Jewish, Greek, Iranian, Christian, Buddhist—brought an Islamic civilization into being.

ORIGINS AND EARLY DEVELOPMENT

THE SETTING

WHAT WAS the Qur'anic message as expressed to Muhammad?

By 600 C.E., the dominant Eurasian political powers, Christian Byzantium and Sasanid Iran, had confronted one another for centuries. This rivalry did not, however, continue much longer. In the wake of one final, mutually exhausting conflict (608–627), a new Arab power humbled one and destroyed the other.

Pre-Islamic Arabia was not just a land of desert nomads. In the Fertile Crescent, Byzantium and Iran had kept the nomads of the Syrian and northern Arabian steppe at bay by enlisting small Arab client kingdoms on the edge of the desert as buffer states. One of the biggest of these was Christian. There had long been settled Arab kingdoms in the highlands of southern Arabia, which had direct access to the international trade that moved along the peninsula's coasts (see Chapter 4). Some of these kingdoms, including a Jewish one, had been independent; others had been under Persian or Abyssinian control. In the western Arabian highland of the Hijaz, the town of Mecca was a center of the caravan trade. It was also a pilgrimage center because of its famous sanctuary, the **Ka'ba** (or Kaaba), where many pagan Arab tribes had gods enshrined. Mecca was a merchant republic in which older tribal values were breaking down under the strains of urban and commercial life. But neither the Meccans nor other settled Arabs were wholly cut off from the nomads. The Arabic language defined and linked the Arab peoples, however divided they were by religion, blood feuds, rivalry, and conflict.

QUICK REVIEW

Mecca
- Center of caravan trade
- Pilgrimage center because of presence of Ka'ba
- A merchant republic

The popular notion of Islam as a "religion of the desert" is largely untrue. Islam began in a commercial center and first flourished in an agricultural oasis. Its first converts were settled Meccan townsfolk and date farmers of Yathrib (Medina). Before becoming Muslims, most of these Arabs were pagans, but some were Jews or Christians, or influenced by them. Caravans passed north and south through Mecca, and no merchant involved in this traffic, as Muhammad himself was, could have been ignorant of diverse cultures. Early Muslim leaders used the Arabs as warriors and looked to Arab culture for roots long after the locus of Islamic power had left Arabia. But the empire and civilization they built were centered in the heartlands of Eurasian urban culture and based on settled communal life rather than desert tribal anarchy.

MUHAMMAD AND THE QUR'AN

8.1
Koran
CD-ROM

Muhammad (ca. 570–632) was raised an orphan in one of the commercial families of the old Meccan tribe of Quraysh. Later, in the midst of a successful business career made possible by his marriage to Khadija (d. ca. 619), a wealthy Meccan widow and entrepreneur, he grew troubled by the idolatry, worldliness, and lack of social conscience around him. These traits would have offended Jewish or Christian morality, about which he knew something. But for most

Ka'ba A black meteorite in the city of Mecca that became Islam's holiest shrine.

Arabs, these religious traditions were foreign, even though some Arab tribes were Jewish or Christian.

Muhammad's discontent paved the way for a religious experience that changed his life when he was about 40 years old. He felt himself called by the one true God to "rise and warn" his fellow Arabs about their disregard for morality and neglect of the worship of their creator. On repeated occasions, revelation came to him through God's messenger angel, Gabriel. It took the form of a "reciting" (*qur'an*) of God's word—now rendered in "clear Arabic" for the Arabs, just as it had been given in other languages to previous prophets for their people.

The message of the Qur'an was clear: The Prophet is to warn his people against false gods and immorality, especially injustice to the poor, orphans, widows, and women in general. At the end of time, on judgment day, every person will be bodily resurrected to face eternal punishment in hellfire or joy in paradise, according to how he or she lived. The way to paradise lies in gratitude to God for the bounties of creation, His prophetic and revelatory guidance, and His readiness to forgive. Social justice and worship of the one Lord are required of every person. Each is to recognize his or her creatureliness and God's transcendence. The proper response is "submission" (*islam*) to God's will, becoming *muslim* ("submissive" or "surrendering") in one's worship and morality. All of creation praises and serves God by nature except humans, who can choose to obey or to reject him (see "The Qur'an, or 'Recitation,' of God's Word").

In this Qur'anic message, the ethical monotheism of Judaic and Christian tradition (probably reinforced by Zoroastrian and Manichaean ideas) reached its logical conclusion—it demanded absolute obedience to the one Lord of the universe. The Qur'anic revelations state that Muhammad is the last in a line of prophets chosen to bring God's word. Noah, Abraham, Moses, Jesus, and non-biblical Arabian figures such as Salih had been sent on similar missions. But because the followers of these earlier prophets had strayed from their teachings or altered them, Muhammad was given one final iteration of God's message. Jews and Christians, like pagans, were summoned to respond to the moral imperatives of the Qur'an.

The Prophet's preaching fell largely on deaf ears in the first years after his calling. A few followed the lead of his wife, Khadija, in recognizing him as a divinely chosen reformer, but the merchant aristocracy as a whole resisted. His preaching against their traditional gods and goddesses threatened both their ancestral ways and also the Meccan pilgrimage shrine and the lucrative trade it attracted. The Meccans began to persecute Muhammad's followers. After the deaths of Khadija and Muhammad's uncle and protector, Abu Talib, the situation worsened. Then, as a result of his growing reputation as a moral and holy man, Muhammad was called to Yathrib (an agricultural oasis about 240 miles north of Mecca) as a neutral arbitrator among its five quarrelsome tribes, three of which were Jewish. Having sent his Meccan followers ahead, Muhammad fled Mecca in July 622 for Yathrib, afterward to be known as Medina (al-Madina, "the City [of the Prophet]"). Some dozen years later, this "emigration," or **Hegira**, became the starting point for the Islamic calendar, the event marking the creation of a distinctive Islamic community, or *Umma*.[1]

Qur'an "A reciting." Islamic bible, which Muslims believe God revealed to the prophet Muhammad.

Islam "Submission." Religion founded by the prophet Muhammad.

Hegira Flight of Muhammad and his followers from Mecca to Medina in 622 C.E. It marks the beginning of the Islamic calendar.

Umma Islamic community.

[1]The 12-month Muslim lunar year is shorter than the Christian solar year by about 11 days, giving a difference of about three years per century. Muslim dates are reckoned from the month in 622 in which Muhammad began his Hegira (Arabic: *Hijra*). Thus Muslims celebrated the start of their lunar year 1401 in November 1980 (1979–1980 C.E. = A.H. [Anno Hegirae] 1400), whereas it was only 1,358 solar years from 622 to 1980.

HISTORY'S VOICES

THE QUR'AN, OR "RECITATION," OF GOD'S WORD

The Qur'an has many themes, from moral admonition, social justice, eternal punishment for the ungodly, and exemplary stories of past peoples and their prophets, to God's majesty and uniqueness, his bountiful natural world and compassion for humankind, and the joys of paradise.

CAN YOU identify at least four major Qur'anic themes in the selections that follow? To what end are the bounties of creation cited? What is the image of God conveyed in these selections? What can you infer about the Qur'anic conception of prophethood? Of the Judgment Day?

The revelation of the Book is from God who is mighty and wise. There are signs for men of faith, in the heavens and in the earth, in your being created and in God's scattered throng of creatures—signs for people with a grasp of truth.

There are signs, too—for those with a mind to understand—in the alternation of night and day, and in the gracious rain God sends from heaven to renew the face of the parched earth, and in the veering of the winds.

These are the signs of God which truly We recite to you. Having God and His signs, in what else after that will you believe as a message?

—Sura 45:1–6

Were you set to count up the mercies of God you would not be able to number them. God is truly forgiving and merciful.

—Sura 16:18

Such is God your Lord. There is no god but He, creator of all things. Then worship Him who is guardian over all there is. No human perception comprehends Him, while He comprehends all perception. He is beyond all conceiving, the One who is infinitely aware.

—Sura 6:102–103

To God belong the east and the west, and wheresoever you turn there is the face of God. Truly God is all-pervading, all-knowing.

—Sura 2:115

You people of the Book, why are you so argumentative about Abraham, seeing that the Torah and the Gospel were only sent down after his time? Will you not use your reason? You are people much given to disputing about things within your comprehension: why insist on disputing about things of which you have no knowledge? Knowledge belongs to God and you lack it!

Abraham was not a Jew, nor was he a Christian. He was a man of pure worship (a hanif) and a Muslim: he was not one of those pagan idolaters . . . .

—Sura 3:65–67

Yet you [people] deny the reality of the judgement. There are guardians keeping watch over you, noble beings keeping record, who know your every deed. The righteous will dwell in bliss. The evil-doers will be in *Jahim*, in the burning on Judgement Day, and there will be no absconding for them.

What can make you realize the Day of judgement as it is? . . . the Day when there is no soul that can avail another soul. For the authority on that Day is God's alone.

—Sura 82.1–5, 9, 19

8.3
Orations: The Words of the Prophet Through His Speeches

Muhammad quickly cemented ties between the Meccan emigrants and the Medinans, many of whom became converts. Raids on his Meccan enemies' caravans established his leadership. The Arab Jews of Medina largely rejected his religious message. And when they made contact with his Meccan enemies, he turned on them and took their lands. Many of the revelations of the Qur'an from this period pertain to communal order and to the Jews and Christians who rejected Islam.

The Ka'ba in Mecca. The Ka'ba is viewed in Muslim tradition as the site of the first "house of God" built by Abraham and his son Ishmael at God's command. It is held to have fallen later into idolatrous use until Muhammad's victory over the Meccans and his cleansing of the holy cubical structure (*Ka'ba* means "cube"). The Ka'ba is the geographical point toward which all Muslims face when performing ritual prayer. It and the plain of Arafat outside Mecca are the two foci of the pilgrimage of Hajj that each Muslim aspires to make at least once in a lifetime.

Mehmet Biber/Photo Researchers, Inc.

The basic Muslim norms took shape in Medina: allegiance to the *Umma*; honesty; modesty; abstention from alcohol and pork; fair division of inheritances; improved treatment of women, especially as to property and other rights in marriage; regulation of marriage and divorce; ritual ablution before worship (Qur'an reciting or prayer); three—later five—daily prayers facing the Meccan shrine of the Ka'ba; payment to support less fortunate Muslims; daytime fasting for one month each year; and, eventually, pilgrimage to Mecca at least once in a lifetime, if one can. These constitute the five pillars of Islam: (1) *Shahada*, the creed, "There is no god but God and Muhammad is God's prophet"; (2) *Salat*, prayer; (3) *Sawm*, fasting during the month of Ramadan; (4) *Zakat*, alms; and (5) *Hajj*, pilgrimage.

Groups that accepted the political authority of Islam were granted religious tolerance. A Jewish oasis that yielded to Muhammad was allowed, unlike the resistant Medinan Jews, to keep its lands, practice its faith, and receive protection in return for the payment of a head tax. This set a precedent that was followed ever after by Jews, Christians, and other "people of Scripture" who accepted Islamic rule. After long conflict, the Meccans surrendered to Muhammad, and his generosity in receiving them into the *Umma* set the pattern for the later Islamic conquests. Muhammad cemented many of his alliances with marriages. In the last years of the Prophet's life, his once tiny band of Muslims became the heart of a pan-Arabian tribal confederation, bound together by personal allegiance to Muhammad, submission (*islam*) to God, and membership in the *Umma* of "submitters."

Hajj Pilgrimage to Mecca that all Muslims are enjoined to perform at least once in their lifetime.

WOMEN IN EARLY ISLAMIC SOCIETY

HOW DID the status of women improve under Islam?

The Qur'an introduced the Arabs to ideas that drastically improved the status of women. It prohibited the common practice of female infanticide, and guaranteed a woman the right to inherit, own, and manage property.

The Qur'an recognized a woman's right to contract her own marriage, and stipulated that she, not a male relative, receive the dowry provided by her husband. In effect, it declared that a bride was not an object to be sold by one man to another, but a party to a negotiated contract.

The Qur'an, however, did not envision the kind of gender equality that is expected by many in the modern world. Islamic law stipulates that a senior male control and guide the family unit. He is to receive a larger share in an inheritance. He is freer to initiate divorce, and in court his eye-witness testimony is weighted more heavily than that of a woman.

The Qur'an presupposes and legitimizes patriarchal authority and it does not outlaw customs that have prevented women from reaching full equality. It tolerates, but seeks to control, polygamy. The Qur'an permits a man to have as many as four wives on condition that he treat each equally and fairly. (Some Muslims claim that this is a prohibition of polygamy, for absolutely equal treatment is impossible.) The veiling of women is associated with Islam, but Muslims did not invent the custom. It was a common practice among upperclass women in the Byzantine and Sasanid Empires. The Qur'an, however, does stipulate that both men and women conduct themselves with modesty and that women "should draw their veils over their bosom and display their beauty only to their husbands and their fathers." (Q. 24:31). Rigid implementation of this rule has led, at some times and in some places, to practices of extreme veiling, seclusion of women in their homes, and their exclusion from all roles in public life. Some modern Muslim women have, however, interpreted these verses in ways that bring them more in line with modern ideas of gender equality. They can point to history for support, for many women—among them some of Muhammad's wives—played influential roles in the development of Islam.

Veiled Women. Women mourning the death of martyrs in combat. Safavid fresco, 17th century.

Art Resource, N.Y.

EARLY ISLAMIC CONQUESTS

WHY DID Islam expand so rapidly in the seventh century?

In 632, Muhammad died. Because he left no son and did not designate a successor, the new *Umma* faced its first major crisis. A political struggle erupted between Meccan and Medinan factions, which ended in a pledge of allegiance to Abu Bakr, the most senior of the early Meccan converts. Many tribes assumed that their allegiance had been to the Prophet and ended at his death. But Abu Bakr's rule (632–634) as Muhammad's successor, or "caliph" (Arabic: *khalifa*), reestablished at least nominal religious unity among the Arabs. They were forced to recognize in the *Umma* a new kind of supra-tribal community that demanded more than fidelity to a particular leader.

COURSE OF CONQUEST

Under the next two caliphs, Umar (634–644) and Uthman (644–656), Arab armies burst out of the peninsula. By 643, they had conquered the Byzantine and Sasanid territories of the Fertile Crescent, Egypt, and most of Iran. For the first time in centuries, the lands from Egypt to Iran came under one rule. Finally, Arab armies swept west over the Byzantine-controlled Libyan coast, and in the east in 651, they defeated the last Sasanid ruler.

An interlude of civil war followed during the disputed caliphate of Ali (656–661). Then expansion resumed under the fifth caliph, Mu'awiya (661–680). An Islamic fleet conquered Cyprus, plundered Sicily and Rhodes, and crippled Byzantine sea power. By 680, control of greater Iran was solidified by permanent Arab garrisoning of Khorasan, much of Anatolia was raided, Constantinople was besieged (but not taken), and Armenia was under Islamic rule.

Succeeding decades saw the eastern Berbers of Libyan North Africa defeated and converted to Islam. With their help, "the West" (*al-Maghrib*, modern Morocco and Algeria) was quickly overrun. By 716, the disunited Spanish Visigoth kingdoms had fallen, and much of Iberia had come under Islamic control. Pushing north into France, the Arabs were finally checked by the Frankish leader, Charles Martel, south of Tours (732). In 710, when Arab armies reached the Indus region, Islamic power stretched from the Atlantic to central Asia (see Map 11–1).

FACTORS OF SUCCESS

A combination of factors underlay this rapid expansion. The basic one was the weakened military and economic condition of the Byzantines and Sasanids—the result of their chronic warfare with one another. Also important was the power of

QUICK REVIEW

Islamic Conquest
- By 643, Arab armies had conquered the Byzantine and Sasanid territories of the Fertile Crescent, Egypt, and most of Iran
- Arab armies defeated the last Sasanid ruler in 651
- Over the rest of the seventh century, Arab armies extended the territory under their control

OVERVIEW **THE BASIC TENETS OF ISLAM**

Islam, meaning "submission to God's will," is a monotheistic religion without an ordained clergy or elaborate ritual. From its earliest days, Islam has required or enjoined all Muslims (those who submit or surrender themselves to God) to adhere to a few relatively simple norms.

Allegiance to the *Umma*, the community of Islamic believers

Honesty

Modesty in dress and demeanor

Abstention from alcohol or pork

Benevolence and fair treatment to women, especially in regard to property and marriage rights

Ritual washing before worship

Prayer five times a day facing Mecca

Giving alms

Daytime fasting once a year during the month of Ramadan

Pilgrimage to Mecca at least once in a person's lifetime if possible

MAP EXPLORATION

Interactive map: To explore this map further, go to **http://www.prenhall.com/craig/map11.1**

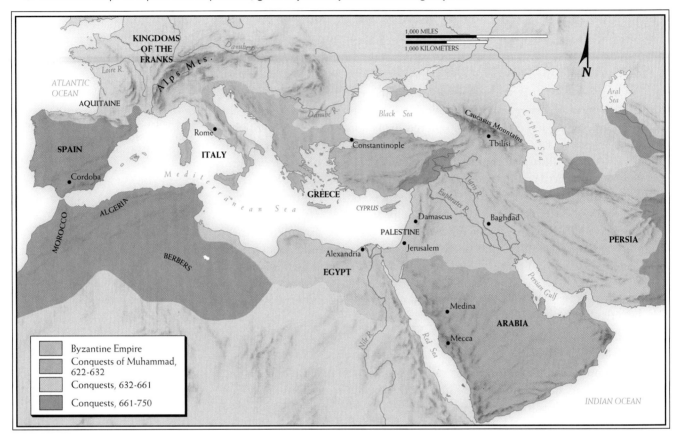

	Byzantine Empire
	Conquests of Muhammad, 622-632
	Conquests, 632-661
	Conquests, 661-750

MAP 11–1

Muslim Conquests and Domination of the Mediterranean to about 750 c.e. The rapid spread of Islam (both religion and political-military power) is shown here. Within 125 years of Muhammad's rise, Muslims came to dominate Spain and all areas south and east of the Mediterranean.

WHY DID so many subject peoples welcome Islamic rule?

jihad "Struggle in the path of God." Although not necessarily implying violence, it is often interpreted to mean holy war in the name of Islam.

the new Islamic vision of society and life to unite the Arabs and attract converts from other peoples. An implication of the vision was a duty to support campaigns to extend "the abode of submission" (*Dar al-Islam*) abroad. Paradise was assured for those who engaged in **jihad**, or "struggle (in the path of God)," but it is less likely to have motivated the average Arab tribesman than booty. The marginal life in the peninsula was such that the hope of greater prosperity must have been compelling. Still, religious zeal cannot be discounted.

Another major factor was the excellent leadership of the first caliphs and generals, which, combined with Byzantine and Iranian exhaustion, gave Arab armies an advantage. Also important was the readiness of many subject populations to welcome Islamic rule as a relief from Byzantine or Persian oppression. Crucial here was the Muslim willingness to allow Christian, Jewish, and even Zoroastrian groups to continue as minorities (with their own legal systems and no military obligations) under the protection of Islamic governments. These religious communities had to recognize Islamic political authority, pay a non-Muslim head tax (*jizya*), and refrain from proselytizing or interfering with Muslim religious practice. As time went on, the head tax and other strictures on non-Muslims encouraged Christians and Jews to convert.

Finally, the astute policies of the early leaders led to the permanence of the conquests: relatively little bloodshed, destruction, or disruption in conquest; adoption of existing administrative systems (and personnel) with minimal changes; adjustment of unequal taxation; appointment of capable governors; and strategic siting of new garrison towns such as Basra, Kufa, and Fustat (later Cairo).

THE NEW ISLAMIC ORDER

lthough they were quick to adopt and adapt existing traditions, the Muslims brought with them a new worldview that demanded a new political, social, and cultural reality. Beyond military and administrative problems loomed the question of the nature of Islamic society. Under the Prophet, the new community of the *Umma* had replaced, at least in theory, the tribal, blood-based sociopolitical order in Arabia. Yet once the Arabs (most of whom became Muslims) had to rule non-Arabs and non-Muslims, new problems tested the ideal of an Islamic polity. Chief among these were leadership and membership qualifications, social order, and religious and cultural identity.

THE CALIPHATE

Allegiance to Muhammad had rested on his authority as a divine spokesperson and gifted leader. His first successors were chosen much as were Arab *shaykhs* ("sheiks"), or tribal chieftains. Leaders, or elders, of the new religious "tribe" of

WHAT ROLES did the caliphate and the ulama play in Islamic states?

The Dome of the Rock, Jerusalem. An early example of Islamic architecture, it dates from the seventh century and the first wave of Arab expansion. It is built on the rock from which Muslims believe Muhammad ascended into heaven and on which Jews believe Abraham prepared to sacrifice Isaac. The Dome of the Rock has special symbolic significance for Muslims because the site is associated with the life and story of the Prophet. For a few years of Muhammad's time in Medina, Muslims faced Jerusalem when they prayed, before a new Qur'anic revelation changed the direction to Mecca.

Scala/Art Resource, N.Y.

Muslims came to agreement on the choice of an individual on the basis of his superior personal qualities. In addition to these attributes, precedence in the faith deriving from a reputation for piety and a history of association with the Prophet were also important. The men chosen bore several titles: "successor" (*khalifa*, or caliph), "leader" (**imam**—literally, the one who stands in front to lead the ritual prayer), and "commander (**amir**) of the faithful." These terms underscored the caliph's function as the guardian of the *Umma*. Most Muslims agreed that the necessary qualities were to be found in the caliphs Abu Bakr and Umar, and potentially in Uthman and Ali. But by the time of Uthman and Ali, dissension arose and led to civil war. The first four caliphs had all been close to Muhammad, and this closeness gave their reigns a nostalgic aura of pristine purity, especially as the later **caliphate** institution was based largely on sheer power legitimized by hereditary succession.

The nature of Islamic leadership became an issue with the first civil war (656–661) and the recognition of Mu'awiya, a kinsman of Uthman, as caliph. He founded the first dynastic caliphate, that of his Meccan clan of Umayya (661–750). Umayyad descendants held power until they were ousted in 750 by the Abbasid clan, which based its legitimacy on descent from Abbas, an uncle of the Prophet. The Umayyads had the prestige of an office held by the first four, "rightly guided" caliphs. Many, however, considered them to be worldly kings in comparison to the first four, who were seen as true Muslim successors to Muhammad.

The Abbasids launched a rebellion in 750 that won them the caliphate. Their followers were inspired by pious dissatisfaction with Umayyad worldliness, non-Arab Muslim resentment (primarily in Iran) of preferential treatment given Arabs, and ongoing dissension among Arab tribal factions in the garrison towns. The Abbasids, however, proved to be scarcely less worldly than the Umayyads and continued the custom of hereditary succession to the caliphate begun by the Umayyads. They retained control of most of the Islamic territories until 945. Thereafter, although their line continued until 1258, the caliphate was primarily a titular office representing an Islamic unity that existed, in the political realm, in name only.

THE ULAMA

The caliph was never "emperor and pope combined." Religious leadership in the *Umma* devolved on another group, those Muslims whose reputations for piety and learning led them to be regarded as authorities. Initially, they were the "Companions" (male and female) of Muhammad. This generation was succeeded by younger believers who were concerned with preserving, interpreting, and applying the Qur'an, and maintaining the norms of the Prophet's original *Umma*. Because the Qur'an contained few actual legal prescriptions, they had to draw on precedents from Meccan and Medinan practice, as well as on oral traditions from and about the Prophet and his Companions. They also had to develop and standardize grammatical rules for a common Arabic language based on the Qur'an and pre-Islamic poetry. Furthermore, they had to improve the phonetic, cursive Arabic script, a task done so well that the script gradually became the standard written medium for languages wherever Islamic religion and culture was dominant: among Iranians, Turks, Indians, Indonesians, Malays, East Africans, and others. They also developed an enduring pattern of education based on study under persons who could claim high rank in an unbroken succession of trustworthy Muslims stretching back to the earliest *Umma*.

imam Islamic prayer leader.

amir/emir Islamic military commander.

caliphate Spiritual and temporal rule of the Muslim community.

These scholars came to be known as *ulama* ("persons of right knowledge"). Their legal opinions and collective discussions of issues, from theological doctrine to criminal punishments, established a basis for religious and social order. By the ninth century, they had largely defined the understanding of the divine law, or *Shari'a*, that Muslims ever after have held to be the definitive guide for legal, social, commercial, political, ritual, and moral concerns. This understanding and the methods by which it was derived together form the Muslim science of jurisprudence, the core discipline of Islamic learning.

In Umayyad time, the *ulama* became a new elite. Caliphs and their governors regularly sought their advice, but often only for moral or legal (the two are, in Muslim view, the same) sanction of a contemplated (or accomplished) action. Some *ulama* compromised themselves. Yet, incorruptible *ulama* were seldom persecuted for their opinions, mostly because of the respect they enjoyed in the Muslim community.

Thus, without building a formal clergy, Muslims developed a workable moral-legal system based on a formally trained scholarly elite and a tradition of concern with religious ideals in public affairs and social order. Because the caliphs and their deputies had at least to act with circumspection and support for pious standards in public, the *ulama* enjoyed de facto leadership in Muslim societies with the rulers—a pattern that has endured in Islamic states.

THE UMMA

A strength of the Qur'anic message was its universalism, the acceptance into the *Umma* of anyone who would submit to God and follow Muslim precepts. Non-Arab converts had to be accepted, even if it meant loss of tax revenue. The social and political status of new converts was, however, clearly second to that of Arabs. Umar had organized the army register, or *diwan*, according to tribal precedence in converting to Islam. Because the diwan served as the basis for distribution and taxation of the new wealth, this perpetuated Arab precedence. The garrisons the Arabs planted in conquered lands became centers of Islamic culture, and they kept the Arabs sufficiently separate from native populations that they were not simply absorbed into the cultures of their new subjects. The dominance of the Arabic language was ensured by the centrality of the Qur'an in Muslim life and the notion of its perfect Arabic form, together with the increasing administrative use of Arabic to replace Aramaic, Greek, Middle Persian, or Coptic languages.

Non-Arab converts routinely attached themselves to Arab tribes as "clients," which assured a place in the diwan. This attachment, however, still meant second-class citizenship alongside the Arabs. Dissatisfaction among client Muslims was widespread and led to uprisings. Persian-Arab tensions were strong in Umayyad and early Abbasid times. Nevertheless, a Persian cultural renaissance raised the Islamicized modern Persian language to high status in Islamic culture. Consequently, it affected religion, art, and literature in much of the Islamic world.

Caliphal administration joined with the evolution of legal theory and practice and the consolidation of religious norms to give stability to the emerging Islamic society. So powerful was the Muslim vision of society that, upon the demise of a caliph, or even a dynasty such as the Umayyads, the *Umma* and the caliphal office continued. There were, however, conflicting notions of that vision. In the first three Islamic centuries, two major interpretations crystallized that reflected idealistic interpretations of the *Umma*—its

ulama "Persons with correct knowledge." Islamic scholarly elite who served a social function similar to the Christian clergy.

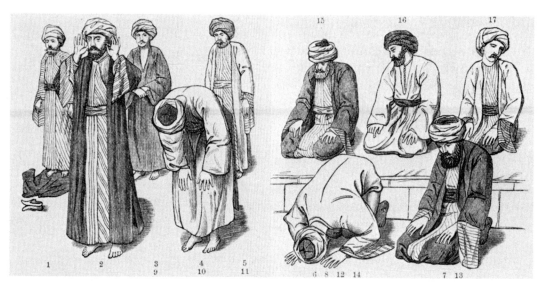

The Ritual Worship, or Prayer. These illustrations show the sequence of movement prescribed for the ritual prayers that each Muslim should perform five times a day. Various words of praise, prayer, and recitation from the Qur'an accompany each position and movement. The ritual symbolizes the Muslim's complete obedience to God and recognition of God as the one, eternal, omnipotent Lord of the universe.

Library of Congress.

leadership and membership. When neither proved viable in the practical world, they failed to win broad-based support. A third, "centrist," vision found favor with the majority because it accommodated inevitable compromises in the higher cause of Islamic unity.

The Kharijites The most radical idealists traced their political origin to the first civil war (656–661). They were the Kharijites, or "seceders" — those who left Ali's camp because, in their view, he compromised with his enemies. The Kharijites' position was that the Muslim polity must be based on strict Qur'anic principles. They espoused total equality of the faithful and held that the leader of the *Umma* should be the best Muslim, whoever that might be. They took a moralistic view of membership in the *Umma*: Anyone who committed a major sin was no longer a Muslim. Extreme Kharijites were rallying points for opposition to the Umayyads and the Abbasids. Although the movement declined, Kharijite groups survive today in Oman and North Africa.

The Shi'a A second position was defined largely in terms of a dispute over qualitifications for leadership of the *Umma*. Muhammad had no surviving sons, and his son-in-law and cousin Ali claimed the caliphate in 656, partly on the basis of his blood tie to the Prophet. His claim was contested by Mu'awiya in the first Islamic civil war. After a Kharijite murdered Ali in 661, Mu'awiya took over. The "partisans of Ali" (*Shi'at Ali*, or simply the **Shi'a**, or *Shi'ites*) originated with Ali's murder and the death of his son Husayn at Karbala, in Iraq, at the hands of Umayyad troops (680).

Whereas all Muslims esteem Ali for his closeness to Muhammad, Shi'ites believe him to be the Prophet's appointed successor. Ali's blood tie with Muhammad was augmented in Shi'ite thinking by belief in the Prophet's designation of him as the true imam, or Muslim leader, after him. Numerous rebellions in Umayyad times rallied around persons claiming to be such a true successor, whether as an Alid or merely a member of Muhammad's clan, the Hashim. Even the Abbasids based their right to the caliphate on their Hashimite ancestry. The major Shi'ite pretenders who emerged in the 9th and 10th centuries based their claims on both the Prophet's designation and their descent from Ali and Fatima, Muhammad's daughter. They also stressed the idea of a

Shi'a Muslims who trace their beliefs to the caliph Ali, who was assassinated in 661 C.E.

divinely inspired knowledge passed on by Muhammad to his designated heirs. Thus, the true Muslim was the faithful follower of the imams, who carried Muhammad's blood and spiritual authority.

Shi'ites saw Ali's assassination by a Kharijite and the massacre of Husayn and his family as proofs of the evil nature of this world's rulers, and as rallying points for true Muslims. True Muslims, like their imams, must suffer. But they would ultimately be vindicated by a *mahdi*, or "guided one," who would usher in a messianic age and a judgment day when the faithful would be rewarded.

On several occasions, Shi'ite rulers headed Islamic states. But only after 1500, in Iran, did Shi'ism prevail as the majority faith in a major Muslim state. The Shi'ite vision of the true *Umma* has not been able to dominate the larger Islamic world.

The Centrists   It was a third, less sharply defined position on the nature of leadership and membership in the *Umma* that most Muslims accepted. It proved acceptable not only to lukewarm Muslims or pragmatists but also to persons of piety as intense as that of any Kharijite or Shi'ite. We may term the proponents of this position *centrists*. They called themselves *Sunnis*—followers of the tradition (*sunna*) established by the Prophet and the Qur'an. Neither they, nor the Shi'ites, nor the Kharijites, have ever been a single sect, but have always encompassed a wide range of ideas and groups. They have made up the broad middle spectrum of Muslims who tend to put communal solidarity and maintenance of the Islamic polity above purist adherence to particular theological tenets. They have been inclusivist rather than exclusivist, a trait that has typified the Islamic (unlike the Jewish or Christian) community.

The centrist position was the most workable framework for the new Islamic state. Its basic ideas were:

1. The *Umma* is a theocratic entity, a state under the authority of God's law, the Shari'a. The sources of guidance are, first, the Qur'an; second, Muhammad's precedent; and, third and fourth, the interpretive efforts and consensus of the Muslims (that is, of the *ulama*).

2. The caliph is the absolute temporal ruler, charged with administering and defending the Abode of Islam and protecting Muslim norms and practice; he possesses no greater authority than other Muslims in matters of faith.

3. A person who professes to be Muslim by witnessing that "There is no god but God, and Muhammad is His Messenger" should be considered a Muslim (because "only God knows what is in the heart"), and not even a mortal sin excludes such a person from the *Umma*.

These and other basic premises of Muslim community came to be the theological underpinnings of both the caliphal state and the international Islamic social order.

Origins and Early Development of Islam

ca. 570	Birth of Muhammad
622	The Hegira ("emigration") of Muslims to Yathrib (henceforward *al-Madina*, "The City [of the Prophet]"); beginning of Muslim calendar
632	Death of Muhammad; Abu Bakr becomes first "successor" (*khalifa*, caliph) to leadership, reigns 632–634
634–644	Caliphate of Umar; rapid conquests in Egypt and Iran
644–656	Caliphate of Uthman (member of Umayyad clan); more conquests; Qur'an text established; growth of sea power
656–661	Contested Caliphate of Ali; first civil war
661–680	Caliphate of Mu'awiya; founding of Umayyad dynasty (661–750); capital moved to Damascus; more expansion
680	Second civil war (680–692) begins with death of al-Husayn at Karbala

Sunna "Tradition." Dominant Islamic group.

THE HIGH CALIPHATE

WHY DID the caliphal empire decline?

The consolidation of the caliphal institution began with the victory of the Umayyad caliph Abd al-Malik in 692, in the second civil war. The ensuing century and a half mark the era of the "high caliphate" that flourished first under the Umayyads in Damascus and then in the Abbasid capital of Baghdad. The height of caliphal power and splendor came in the first century of Abbasid rule, notably during the caliphates of the fabled Harun al-Rashid (786–809) and his third son, al-Ma'mun (813–833; see Map 11–2).

THE ABBASID STATE

The Abbasids' victory effectively ended Arab dominance as well as Umayyad ascendancy (except in Spain). The shift of the imperial capital from Damascus to Baghdad on the Tigris (762–766) was indicative of the influence the eastern cultures had on the new regime as more and more Persians entered its bureaucracy. Although the Abbasids stressed their descent from al-Abbas (ca. 565–653), uncle of both Muhammad and Ali, their religious policy was to disavowal support for Shi'ite hopes for a divinely inspired imamate. This made their rule attractive to a broad spectrum of Muslims.

Whereas the Umayyads had relied on Syrian Arab forces, the Abbasids used Khorasanian Arabs and Iranians. Beginning in the ninth century, however, they began to enlist slave soldiers (*mamluks*), mostly Turks from the northern steppes, as their personal troops. The officers of these forces, who were also mamluks,

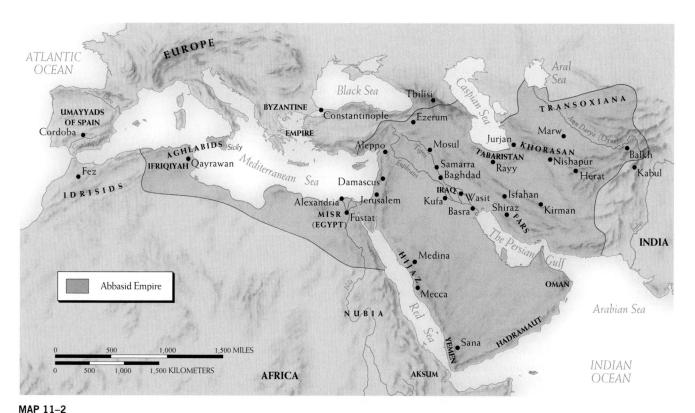

MAP 11–2

The Abbasid Empire, ca. 900 C.E.   A great diversity of peoples and nations were united by the Abbasids. Their capital at Baghdad became the center of a trading network that linked India, Africa, and China.

WHICH MUSLIM regions were not part of the Abbasid Empire?

soon seized the positions of power in the bureau-cracies and the army and dominated the caliphs. This increasingly alienated the Muslim populace from their own rulers.

SOCIETY

A deep division between rulers and populace became typical of Islamic societies. However, even while Abbasid central power declined (after the mid-ninth century) as more provincial rulers asserted indepdencence, these rulers generally chose to recognize nominal caliphal authority. This underscored their role as guardians of the Islamic order, which found its real cohesiveness in the Muslim ideals propagated by the *ulama.*

Conversion of the diverse populace of the Islamic Empire lagged behind centralization of political power and development of Islamic institu-tions. Prior to the mid-12th century, Iraq and Iran (especially Khorasan, which had substantial early Arab Muslim immigration) experienced the most complete Islamization of local elites. They were fol-lowed by Spain, North Africa, and Syria. As conversion and Islamization pro-gressed, a more self-confident Muslim community appeared that had less need for centralized caliphal power.[2]

DECLINE

The eclipse of the caliphal empire was foreshadowed at the outset of Abbasid rule, when one of the last Umayyads founded the Islamic state (756–1030) on the Iberian peninsula that produced the spectacular Moorish culture of Spain. In 929, the Spanish Umayyads claimed the title of caliph. In all the Abbasid provinces, regional governments always had the potential to become independent states. Harun al-Rashid's governor of what is today Tunisia set up a separate state in North Africa in 801. A later North African dynasty, the Fatimids, conquered Egypt in 969 and established a Shi'ite dynasty that claimed to be the only true caliphate.

In the East, Baghdad had a difficult time control-ling Iran. For two centuries, beginning in 821 in Khorasan, Abbasid governors or rebel groups founded independent dynasties, and the caliph usually had to rec-ognize their rule. The Samanids of Khorasan and Transoxiana ruled at Bukhara as nominal Abbasid vassals from 875 until 999. They gave northeastern Iran a long period of economic and political security from Turkish steppe invaders. Under their aegis, Persian poetry and Arabic scientific studies began a Persian Islamic cultural renaissance and influential scientific tradition.

The Great Mosque of Samarra. Built in the middle of the ninth century by the Abbasid caliph al Mutaanakkil, this Friday, or congregational Mosque has a prayer space larger than nine football fields, making it the largest enclosed such space in the Islamic world. The style of the Minaret recalls the ziggu-rats of ancient Babylon.

Aerofilms.

Early Period of the High Caliphate

680–692	Second civil war
685–705	Caliphate of Abd al-Malik; consolidation, Arabization of administration
705–715	Caliphate of al-Walid; Morocco conquered, Spain invaded; Arab armies reach the Indus
ca. 750	Introduction of paper manufacture from China through Samarqand to Islamic world
750	Abbasids seize caliphate from Umayyads, begin new dynasty (750–1258)
756	Some Umayyads escape to Spain, found new dynasty (756–1030)
762–766	New Abbasid capital built at Baghdad

[2]Richard W. Bulliet, *Conversion to Islam in the Medieval Period* (Cambridge: Harvard University Press, 1979), especially pp. 7–15, 128–138.

Of greatest consequence for the Abbasid caliphate, however, was the rise of a Shi'ite clan, the Buyids. In 945, they brought the Abbasid caliphs under their control, and henceforth the caliph was a puppet in the hands of Buyid "commanders" (*amirs* or *emirs*; later, *sultans*). In 1055, the Buyids were replaced by the more famous Seljuk *sultans*. Abbasid caliphs continued as figureheads of Muslim unity until Mongol invaders killed the last of them in 1258.

"CLASSICAL" ISLAMIC CULTURE

WHAT WERE the main achievements of "classical" Islamic culture?

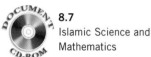

8.7
Islamic Science and Mathematics

An illustration from The Maqamat of al Hariri (d.1122), one of the great masterpieces of Arabic literature of the later Middle Ages. It is a narrative written in rhymed prose for the purposes of entertainment.

Maquamat of al Hariri, Library in a mosque, Arab manuscript, 13th century (1237). Paris, France Bibliotheque Nationale (National Library), Photos 12.com-ARS.

The splendor of the Abbasid court became the stuff of Islamic legends, such as those in *The Thousand and One Nights*. Its rich cultural legacy outlived the Abbasids themselves. Their achievements had been made possible by a strong army and central government and vigorous internal and external trade. The latter may have been stimulated by the Tang Empire of China, with which the Islamic world had overland and sea contact. Material factors, such as the introduction of paper manufacture (from China about 750) or the flight of Byzantine scholars east to new Abbasid centers of learning, also contributed to making the early Abbasid Era special.

INTELLECTUAL TRADITIONS

The Abbasid heyday was marked by sophisticated tastes and an insatiable thirst for knowledge—*any* knowledge. Contacts (primarily among intellectuals) between Muslims and Christian, Jewish, Zoroastrian, and other "protected" religious communities contributed to the cosmopolitanism of the age. Some older intellectual traditions experienced a revival in early Abbasid times, as with Hellenistic learning. Philosophy, astronomy, mathematics, medicine, and other natural sciences enjoyed patronage. Islamic culture took over the tradition of rational inquiry from the Hellenistic world and developed and preserved it at a time when Europe was by comparison a cultural wasteland.

Arabic translations of Greek and Sanskrit works stimulated progress in astronomy and medicine. Translation reached its peak in al-Ma'mun's new academy headed by a Nestorian Christian, Hunayn ibn Ishaq (d. 873), noted for his medical and Greek learning. There were Arabic translations of everything from the Greek authors Galen, Ptolemy, Euclid, Aristotle, Plato, and the Neo-Platonists to the Indian fables that had been rendered into Middle Persian under the Sasanids. Such translations stimulated not only Arabic learning, but that of the less advanced European world, especially in the 12th and 13th centuries.

LANGUAGE AND LITERATURE

Arabic language and literature developed greatly in the expanded cultural sphere of the new empire. In *belles lettres* there arose a significant genre of Arabic writing known as *adab*, or "manners" literature. It included essays and didactic literature influenced by earlier Persian examples. While translations of different literary genres increased the range of the Arabs' original bedouin idiom, poetry flourished by building on the sophisticated tradition of the Arabic ode, or *qasida*. Grammar was central to the interpretation of the Qur'an that occupied the *ulama*, and this linguistic concern undergirded an emerging curriculum of Muslim learning. Historical and biographical writings became major genres of Arabic writing. They arose primarily to record first the lives and times of the Prophet and his earliest companions, then those of subsequent generations of Muslims. This information was crucial to judging the reliability of the "chains" of transmitters attached to each traditional report, or **hadith**. A *hadith* consisted of words or actions ascribed to Muhammad and the Companions; it became the chief source of Muslim legal and religious norms alongside the Qur'an, as well as the basic unit of most prose genres, from history to Qur'an exegesis. Collections of the *hadith* also formed a separate genre that was mined by preachers and by the developing schools of legal interpretation, whose crowning glory was al-Shafi'i's (d. 820) work on legal reasoning.

ART AND ARCHITECTURE

In art and architecture the Abbasid Era saw the crystallization of a "classical" Islamic style by about 1000 C.E. Except for ceramics and Arabic calligraphy, most of the discrete elements of Islamic art and architecture had antecedents in Greco-Roman, Byzantine, or Iranian art. What was new was the use of older forms and motifs for new purposes and combinations, and also the spread of such elements to new locales, generally from east (especially the Fertile Crescent) to west (Syria, Egypt, North Africa, and Spain). The combination and elaboration of discrete forms, as in the case of the colonnade (or hypostyle) mosque or complex arabesque designs, were also introduced.

The Muslims had good reason for confidence in their faith and culture and to want to distinguish themselves from others. Particular formal items, such as calligraphic motifs and inscriptions on buildings, characterize Islamic architecture and define its functions. Most striking was the avoidance of pictures or icons in public art. This was, of course, in line with the Muslim aversion to idolatry and to Byzantine Christian art. Although this iconoclasm later diminished, it was a telling proclamation of the general thrust of Muslim faith.

Decorated Ceramic Bowl. A glazed ceramic bowl decorated with a gazelle or antelope, a symbolic figure of beauty and grace. From North Africa, Tunisian area, Fatimid (10th–12th centuries).

Werner Forman/Art Resource, N.Y.

hadith Saying or action ascribed to Muhammad.

"Classical" Period of the High Caliphate

786–809	Caliphate of Harun al-Rashid; apogee of caliphal power
813–833	Caliphate of al-Ma'mun; strong patronage of translations of Greek, Sanskrit, and other works into Arabic; first heavy reliance on slave soldiers (*mamluks*)
875	Rise of Sasanid power at Bukhara; patronage of Persian poetry paves way for Persian literary renaissance
945–1055	Buyid amirs rule the eastern empire at Baghdad; the Abbasid caliphs continue largely as figureheads
969	Rise of Shi'ite Fatimid dynasty in North Africa
1055	Buyid amirs replaced by Seljuk sultans as effective rulers at Baghdad and custodians of the caliphate

A

B

The Congregational Mosque. Two examples of the finest great mosques of the classical Islamic world. Such buildings were designed not only for worship; their large courtyards and pillared halls were also intended to hold the population of a given city and could be used for governmental purposes or for mustering troops in time of war. Their splendor also announced the power and wealth of Islamic rule. Figure A is the Great Mosque at Qayrawan in modern Tunisia, built between the 8th and 9th centuries. Figure B shows the Spanish Umayyad mosque in Cordoba, built and added to from the 8th to the 10th centuries, in a series of roofed extensions—unlike that in Qayrawan, which has only covered colonnades and one great hall (behind the photographer in this picture).

(A) Werner Forman Archive, Art Resource, N.Y.; (B) Adam Lubroth, Art Resource, N.Y.

SUMMARY

Muhammad The Prophet Muhammad (570–632) was the founder of Islam. Born in the Arabian commercial city of Mecca, he was influenced by contact with Arab Christians and with Jews. At about age 40, he had a religious experience during which, Muslims believe, God's messenger angel Gabriel repeatedly recited (*qur'an*) God's word to him. The message of the Qur'an was that social justice and worship of the one true God are required of every person. At the end of time, people will be resurrected and judged by God to be rewarded or punished according to how they lived. The proper response to God is submission (*islam*) to His will by becoming a Muslim (one who submits).

Islamic Conquest By the time of Muhammad's death, his followers had conqured all of Arabia. Under his successors, the caliphs, Muslim Arab armies conquered most of the Middle East, North Africa, Spain, Iran, and northwest India. Many of the peoples of these territories converted to Islam.

The High Caliphate Under the Abbasid caliphs who ruled from the city of Baghdad, Islamic culture enjoyed its "classical" phase. As the sacred medium of God's final revelation, the Arabic language spread throughout the Islamic world. Arabic artists and architects developed a distinctive Islamic style. The *ulama*, Islamic religious and legal scholars, played a prominent part in Islamic society as interpreters of Islamic tradition and law.

Decline of the Caliphate The Islamic empire began to splinter early. Disputes over the succession to the Prophet divided Muslims. Large parts of the Empire seceded. Military commanders (*amirs*) reduced the caliphs to figureheads. The last Abbasid caliph was when the Mongols sacked Baghdad in 1258.

IMAGE KEY
for pages 244–245

a. Mohammed, Abu Bakr and Ali travel to the Ukaz Fair, from Siyar-i-Nabi (Life of the Prophet) IV. 2, f. 132v. Ink, color, gold on paper, 1594–95. Spencer Collection, Astor, Lenox and Tilden Foundations.
b. Tenth century, earthenware bowl
c. The Ka'ba in Mecca
d. Recitation of the Muslim religion, written in black Sanskrit
e. Page from a Koran, 8th–9th century Kufic script.
f. The Great Mosque at Kairouan
g. Ritual worship, or prayer
h. Dome of the Rock
i. Spanish Umayyad mosque in Cordoba

REVIEW QUESTIONS

1. What was Arabian society like before the coming of Islam?
2. How do Islamic ideas about history, salvation, law, social justice, and other key issues compare with those of Christianity and Judaism?
3. To what extent were political and religious leadership separated in early Islam?
4. What explains the initial rapid conquests of the Arab armies?
5. What role did foreign traditions play during the high caliphate?

KEY TERMS

caliphate (p. 254) imam (p. 254) Shi'a (p. 256)
emir (p. 254) islam (p. 247) Sunna (p. 257)
hadith (p. 261) jihad (p. 252) ulama (p. 255)
Hajj (p. 249) Ka'ba (p. 246) Umma (p. 247)
Hegira (p. 247) Qur'an (p. 247)

 For additional study resources for this chapter, go to:
www.prenhall.com/craig/chapter11

12 The Byzantine Empire and Western Europe to 1000

CHAPTER HIGHLIGHTS

The Byzantine Empire In the fifth century, Roman authority in the west collapsed under the impact of Germanic invasions. However, imperial power shifted to the eastern part of the Roman Empire, known as the Byzantine Empire. The Byzantine Empire would endure until 1453. The Byzantine Empire provided a model of civilized society to medieval Europe, helped protect it from Muslim invaders, and preserved much of classical learning.

The Islamic world also acted as a conduit for classical learning to the West, particularly in medicine, astronomy, and mathematics.

The Roman Church The church was the strongest and most prestigious institution in early medieval Europe where it filled the vacuum created by the collapse of Roman authority. Monasteries were an economic, political, and spiritual force throughout the West.

With the collapse of imperial authority in the West, the bishops of Rome, the popes, developed the doctrine of papal primacy by which they claimed supreme authority over church doctrine and the clergy. These claims were unacceptable in the East, where a separate Greek Orthodox Church developed under the control of the Byzantine emperors.

Charlemagne's Empire

The Frankish ruler Charlemagne (r. 768–814) sought to re-create a universal Western empire and was crowned emperor by the pope in 800. Charlemagne formed a close alliance with the church and relied on churchmen as royal agents and administrators. His palace school at Aachen was the center of a modest renaissance of classical learning. After Charlemagne's death, his empire dissolved amid quarrels among his heirs, the revolts of powerful nobles, and invasions by Vikings, Magyars, and Muslims.

Feudal Society The Middle Ages were characterized by a chronic absence of central government and the constant threat of famine, disease, and invasion. Feudal society was one in which local lords offered security in return for allegiance from his dependents or vassals.

The feudal economy was organized and controlled through agrarian villages known as manors, worked by free peasants or by serfs.

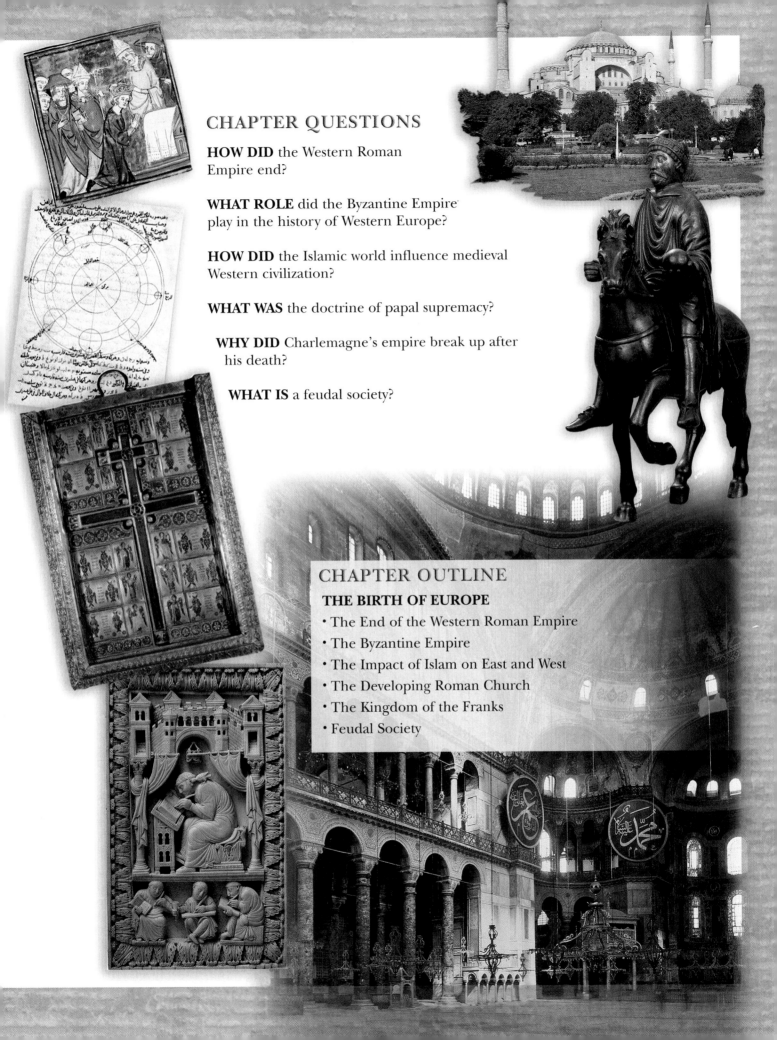

CHAPTER QUESTIONS

HOW DID the Western Roman Empire end?

WHAT ROLE did the Byzantine Empire play in the history of Western Europe?

HOW DID the Islamic world influence medieval Western civilization?

WHAT WAS the doctrine of papal supremacy?

WHY DID Charlemagne's empire break up after his death?

WHAT IS a feudal society?

CHAPTER OUTLINE

THE BIRTH OF EUROPE

- The End of the Western Roman Empire
- The Byzantine Empire
- The Impact of Islam on East and West
- The Developing Roman Church
- The Kingdom of the Franks
- Feudal Society

The early Middle Ages marks the birth of Europe. Within what had been the northern and western provinces of the Roman Empire, Greco-Roman culture combined with Germanic culture and Christianity to create distinctive political and cultural forms. In government, religion, and language, as well as geography, these regions grew separate from the eastern Byzantine world and the Islamic Arab world that extended across North Africa from Spain to the eastern Mediterranean.

Surrounded and assailed from north, east, and south, western Europe became insular and stagnant, its people losing touch with classical, especially Greek, learning and science. They worked hard to develop their native resources, and the reign of Charlemagne saw a modest renaissance of antiquity. The social and political forms that emerged during this period—manorialism and feudalism—proved to be fertile seedbeds for the growth of distinctively Western institutions.

THE END OF THE WESTERN ROMAN EMPIRE

HOW DID the Western Roman Empire end?

In the early fifth century, Italy and Rome suffered devastating blows. In 410, the Visigoths sacked the city of Rome. In 452, the Huns, led by Attila, invaded Italy. In 455, Rome was overrun by the Vandals.

By the mid-fifth century, power in western Europe had passed to barbarian chieftains. In 476, the barbarian Odovacer (ca. 434–493) deposed the last western emperor Romulus Augustulus. The eastern emperor Zeno (r. 474–491) recognized Odovacer as his western viceroy. But Zeno had little power to command in what had been the western empire, which by the end of the fifth century, was completely overrun by German barbarians (see Map 12-1).

The barbarians admired Roman culture and had no desire to destroy it. Except in Britain and northern Gaul, Roman law and government and Latin coexisted with the new Germanic institutions. Only the Vandals and the Anglo-Saxons refused to profess titular obedience to the emperor in Constantinople.

The Visigoths, the Ostrogoths, and the Vandals were followers of the Arian creed, which had been condemned at the Council of Nicea in 325 and was considered heretical in the west (see Chapter 6). Later, around 500, the Franks, who had settled in Gaul, would convert to the orthodox, or "Catholic," form of Christianity supported by the bishops of Rome. The Franks ultimately helped convert the other barbarians to Roman Christianity.

A gradual interpenetration of two strong cultures marked the period of the Germanic migrations. Despite western military defeat, the Goths and the Franks became far more romanized than the Romans were germanized. Latin, Nicene Christianity, and Roman law and government were to triumph in the west during the Middle Ages.

THE BYZANTINE EMPIRE

WHAT ROLE did the Byzantine Empire play in the history of Western Europe?

As barbarian invaders overran the western half of the Roman Empire, its eastern half thrived under the rule of emperors who ruled from the city of Byzantium (modern Istanbul). Between 324 and 330, the emperor Constantine the Great rebuilt the city and renamed it Constantinople. It was regarded as the capital of the old Roman Empire, but its future was as the capital of a new Byzantine Empire. The term Byzantine indicates the Greek, Hellenistic Roman, and Judaic monotheistic elements that came, during the Middle Ages, to distinguish the culture of the East from the Latin West.

MAP EXPLORATION

Interactive map: To explore this map further, go to **http://www.prenhall.com/craig/map12.1**

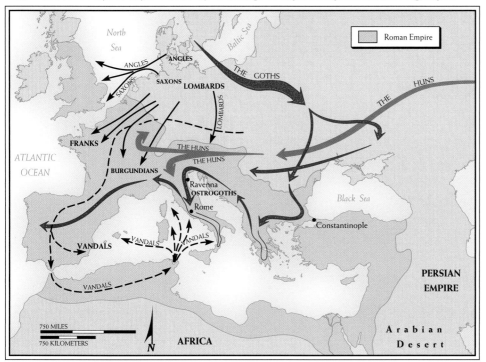

MAP 12–1

Barbarian Migrations into the West in the Fourth and Fifth Centuries. The forceful intrusion of Germanic and non-Germanic tribes into the Empire from the last quarter of the fourth century through the fifth century made for a constantly changing pattern of movement and relations. The map shows the major routes taken by the usually unwelcome newcomers and the areas most deeply affected by the main groups.

WHICH PART of the Roman Empire was least affected by barbarian migrations?

The history of the Byzantine Empire divides into three periods:

1. From the founding of Constantinople in 324 to the spread of Islam in 632;

2. From 632 to the loss of Asia Minor to the Seljuk Turks in 1071 and the sack of Constantinople by Latin Cusaders in 1204; and

3. to the conquest of Constantinople and the Byzantine Empire by the Ottoman Turks in 1453.

THE REIGN OF JUSTINIAN

The first period of Byzantine history (324–632) was by far its greatest, and its pinacle was the reign of the emperor Justinian (r. 527–565). He ruled with the assistance of his remarkable wife, Theodora. Born a commoner, Theodora had allegedly been a circus entertainer and a prostitute before attracting the emperor's eye. She equaled her husband in intelligence and may have exceeded him in toughness. In 532, when a riot threatened to overthrow their administration, she dissuaded him from flight and urged him to put down the rebellion by ordering the slaughter of tens of thousands of protesters.

Hagia Sophia. One of the greatest achievements of Byzantine civilization, Hagia Sophia (the church of Holy wisdom) was completed in 537 by Anthemius of Tralles and Isidone of Miletus. Circled with numerous windows, the great dome floods the hall with light and, together with the church's many other windows, mosaics, and open spaces, gives the interior a remarkable airiness and luminosity. With the Turkish conquest of Constantinople in 1453, Hagia Sophia was transformed into a mosque.

Hagia Sophia, Istanbul. Erich Lessing/Art Resource. N.Y.

Cities The strength of Justinian's empire was its more than 1,500 cities. The largest, Constantinople, was the crossroad of Asian and European cultures. It had about 350,000 inhabitants, and the larger provincial cities of its empire numbered approximately 50,000. These towns were administered at first by councils of wealthy local landowners, the *Decurions*. But being heavily taxed, they were prone to rebellion. Consequently, by the sixth century the emperor had replaced them with governors chosen for their loyalty to his person. Tighter central control was encouraged by the need to resist barbarian pressures on the empire from the north and east (see Map 12-2).

Law Justinian's policy—"one God, one empire, one religion"—was to centralize government by imposing legal and doctrinal conformity throughout his domain. To this end he ordered a codification of the mass of legal materials he had inherited from his predecessors. The result was the *Corpus Juris Civilis*, or "Body of Civil Law." It was organized in four parts. The *Code* revised imperial edicts issued by emperors since the reign of Hadrian (r. 117–138). The *Novellae*, or "New Things," dealt with decrees issued by emperors since 534, including Justinian. The *Digest* organized opinions penned by famous jurists, and the *Institutes* was a kind of text-book for young scholars. Because Roman law emphasized the authority of a single sovereign, rulers who struggled to centralize governments found Justinian's collection useful. Between the Renaissance and the 19th century, his code powerfully influenced the development of governments throughout Europe.

Avars, Slavs, and Bulgars Justinian attempted to regain control of the western Roman Empire, but his success was partial and temporary. He reoccupied Italy, North Africa, and parts of Spain, but at a cost that his beleaguered empire could ill afford.

Avars, Slavs, and Bulgars, nomadic barbarian tribes, invaded the lands north and west of Constantinople in the sixth and seventh centuries. The Slavs were converted to Eastern Orthodoxy (Byzantine Christianity) by two learned missionaries sent from Constantinople: the future Saints Cyril and Methodius. They created a Greek-based alphabet adapted to writing the Slavic language.

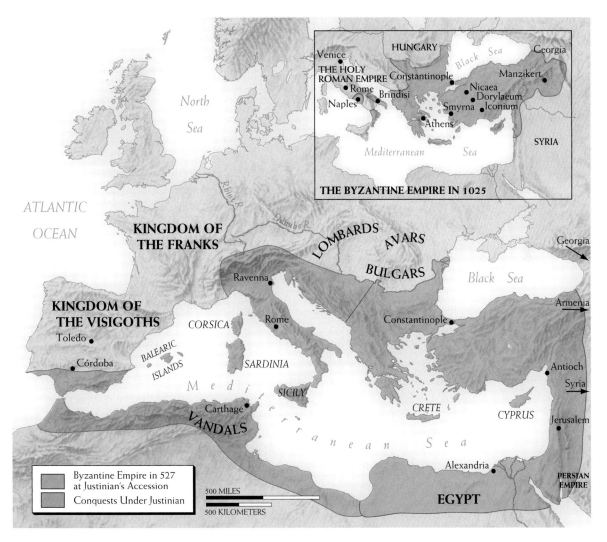

MAP 12–2
The Byzantine Empire at the Death of Justinian.   The inset shows the Empire in 1025, before its losses to the Seljuq Turks.

WHY DID the Byzantine Empire suffer major territorial losses between the death of Justinian and the 11th century?

Emperor Justinian and His Attendants.
Mosaic in the Church of San Vitale,
Ravenna, Italy, ca 547.

Scala/Art Resource, N.Y.

When the Bulgars conquered and absorbed the Slavs, this script was revised and is now known as Cyrillic or Old Church Slavonic. It facilitated the spread of Byzantine Christianity and culture in eastern Europe and Russia.

Persians and Muslims   During the reign of the emperor Heraclius (r 610–641), Constantinople decidedly oriented itself toward the East. Heraclius spoke Greek, not Latin, and spent his reign combating Persian and Islamic invaders. The Persians were repulsed, but Heraclius suffered a defeat by the Muslims in 632 that cleared the way for them to overrun much of his empire. Not until the reign of Leo III (r. 717–740), founder of the Isaurian dynasty, did the Byzantines drive the Arab armies back and regain most of Asia Minor. Their larger Mediterranean empire, however, was gone forever.

The loss of territory required a restructuring of Constantinople's empire. The older hierarchical administration gave way to locally governed and garrisoned provincial strongholds headed by generals appointed by the emperor. This created a stronger, more flexible military defense for the remaining Byzantine lands.

In the 11th century, Constantinople again suffered major losses. The Muslim Seljuk Turks destroyed the imperial army at the battle of Manzikert in 1071 and then overran Asia Minor, the heartland from which Constantinople recruited its soldiers. This foreshadowed the inevitable fall of Constantinople, but in the interim the Byzantines and Muslims were distracted by the intervention in their affairs of Latin crusaders.

The Religious Diversity of Christendom   Religious belief encouraged the unity of the Byzantine Empire, and religious controversy undermined it. Christianity was declared the empire's official faith in 391 and all other religions dismissed as "demented and insane." Emperors were crowned by the patriarch of Constantinople. Lavish endowments were provided for the church. It acted as the state's welfare agency, and its clergy were tightly bound to state service.

Although Christianity in one form or another was the dominant faith, large numbers of Jews lived within the Byzantine Empire. Roman law had protected them, so long as they did not proselytize Christians, but some Byzantine emperors tried to induce or to compel their conversion to Christianity. Neither approach was successful.

Despite the fact that the state religion was Orthodox Christianity, some Christian heresies attracted large followings and occasionally received imperial support. Justinian, for instance, was passionately orthodox, but his wife, the empress Theodora, was a Monophysite, a popular eastern variant of the faith, which the West regarded as a heresy. The Monophysites taught that Christ had a single, immortal nature and was not a union of eternal God and mortal man. The modern Coptic, Syrian, and Armenian churches endorse this belief.

The theological debates that thrived in the East were regarded with suspicion in the West. The West, for instance, rejected the Monophysites' view of Christ as incompatible with its understanding of the doctrine of the Trinity. It also disagreed with the east on interpretations of the Holy Spirit. To oppose Arian Christianity, which had spread among some German tribes, the western church insisted that the Holy Spirit proceeded from both the Father and the Son. This made it clear that the Son was not, as the Arians claimed, subordinate to the Father.

A dispute over the use of sacred images (icons) in worship, which erupted in the eighth century, further divided the east and west. In 726, Emperor Leo III (r. 717–741) forbade the use of images and icons by all Christians. His intention may have been to weaken the monastic owners of popular icons and to court populations influenced by Muslim and Jewish contempt for image worshipers. At any rate, his attack on traditional practices shocked the West and helped drive the Roman popes into an alliance with Europe's strongest emerging rulers, the Frankish kings. Constantinople underwent a spate of iconoclasm (destruction of icons) but reversed itself in the mid-ninth century and restored respect for sacred images.

If the Western church rejected eastern ideas, the Eastern church also dismissed beliefs that were winning popular support in the West. It denied the existence of Purgatory. It permitted the laity to divorce and to remarry. It allowed its priests, but not its bishops, to marry. It endorsed liturgies in vernacular languages. It also embraced Caesaropapism–an elevation of the emperor to sovereignty over the church as well as the state.

In 1054, these accumulating differences finally precipitated the formal separation of the western Catholic and the eastern Orthodox churches. The pope's

OVERVIEW   BARBARIAN INVASIONS OF THE WESTERN ROMAN EMPIRE

The Germanic tribes—the barbarians—who overran the Western Roman Empire had coexisted with the Romans for centuries in a relationship marked more by the commingling of cultures and by trade than by warfare. The arrival of the Huns from the east in the late fourth century, however, caused many of the tribes, beginning with the Visigoths in 376, to flee westward and seek refuge within the empire. They found the western half of the empire weakened by famine, disease, overtaxation, and an enfeebled military. The Romans lost control of their frontiers, and in the fifth century, the tribes overran the West and set up their own domains. The following is a list of the most important tribes and the areas they controlled by the year 500.

Tribes	Area of Control
Anglo-Saxons	most of England
Franks	northeast France
Burgundians	eastern-central France
Alemani	Switzerland
Visigoths	most of Spain and southern France
Suevi	northwest Spain
Vandals	North Africa
Ostrogoths	Italy, Austria, Croatia, Slovenia

Religious Diversity. A Muslim and a Christian play the *ud* or lute together, from a 13th-century *Book of Chants* in the Escorial Monastery of Madrid. Medieval Europe was deeply influenced by Arab-Islamic culture, transmitted particularly through Spain. In music some of the many works in Arabic on musical theory were translated into Latin and Hebrew, but the main influence came from the actual arts of singing and playing spread by minstrels.

A Moor and a Christian playing the lute, miniature in a book of music from the 'Cantigas' of Alfonso X 'the Wise' (1221–84). Thirteenth century (manuscript). Monastero de El Escorial, El Escorial, Spain/Index/ Bridgeman Art Library.

envoy, Cardinal Humbertus, who was sent to Constantinople to try to resolve some of the points in contention, excommunicated his Eastern colleagues, and they in turn condemned the West. The result was a breach that remained until 1965, when a Roman pope met with the patriarch of Constantinople to revoke the mutual medieval condemnations.

THE IMPACT OF ISLAM ON EAST AND WEST

A new drama began to unfold for the West in the seventh century with the rise of Islam (see Chapter 11). By the middle of the eighth century, Arabs had conquered the southern and eastern Mediterranean coastline and occupied parts of Spain. Assaulted from east and west, Christian Europe developed a lasting fear of the Muslims. In 718, the Byzantine Emperor Leo III halted the Muslim advance on Constantinople and began a counteroffensive that, during the next several centuries, pushed the Arabs back. In 732, the Franks defeated the Arabs near Tours (in central France), but Muslims preserved their hold on Andalusia, which they had taken from the Visigoths in 711, for another 700 years. Although the momentum of the Muslim advance was broken, the Mediterranean had become (and until the mid-11th century remained) something of a Muslim lake. The center of evolving European civilization shifted north away from the sea, but positive contacts between Muslims and Christians did not end. Western trade with the East continued to be important.

THE WESTERN DEBT TO ISLAM

The Arab invasions during the early Middle Ages helped western Europe develop a unique civilization of its own. Arab belligerence forced western Europeans to fall back on and exploit the cultural potential of their own resources: their Germanic tribal, Judeo-Christian, and Greco-Roman heritages. By diverting the energies of the Byzantine Empire, the Arabs also prevented Constantinople from expanding into western Europe. This gave the Frankish and the Lombard kingdoms an opportunity to establish themselves.

Despite hostilities, a creative interchange developed between the Christian West and the Muslim world. The backward West stood to gain most from this, for Arab civilization was enjoying its golden age. Moorish Cordoba was a model multicultural city and a conduit through which Arab products and ideas reached Europe. The Arabs taught Western farmers how to irrigate fields and Western artisans how to tan leather and refine silk. Arabic scholars passed on knowledge of ancient Greek works on astronomy, mathematics, and medicine. Jewish scholars also thrived. The era produced numerous major researchers, thinkers, and poets whose influence was far-reaching.

THE DEVELOPING ROMAN CHURCH

Throughout this period in which most of the institutions of the old Roman Empire decline, one gained in strength: the Christian church. As the Western empire crumbled, local bishops and cathedral chapters (ruling bodies of clergy) filled the resulting vacuum of leadership. The local cathedral became the center of urban life and the local bishop the highest authority for those who remained in Europe's shrinking cities. German leaders, who struggled to found new kingdoms amid the ruins of the empire, discovered that the Christian church was a valuable repository of Roman administrative skills and classical culture. The church also had a religious message of providential purpose and individual worth that could give solace and meaning to life at a time when encouragement was desperately needed. The church's ritual of baptism and creed united people across traditional barriers of class, education, and gender. And alone in the West, the church retained an effective, if somewhat scattered, hierarchical administration. It was staffed by the best-educated minds in Europe, and it centered on Rome, whose bishop had stepped into the vacancy created by the departure of emperors.

MONASTIC CULTURE

Monasticism provided a major support for Europe's Christian faith throughout the early medieval period. The first monks were hermits, such as Anthony of Egypt (ca. 251–356), who felt compelled to withdraw from society and give up all worldly attachments to pursue a purely spiritual life. So many people were attracted to the movement the hermits began that communal organizations had to be devised to serve them. Pachomius (ca. 286–436), another Egyptian, founded some of the earliest of these. The monastic life, which was guided by the biblical "counsels of perfection" (chastity, poverty, and obedience), came to be regarded as the purest form of religious practice.

The extreme asceticism of the early hermits was soon tempered by men who had a different vision of what was required to live a life in imitation of Christ. Basil the Great (329–379), whose rule (regulations to govern a monastery) spread widely throughout the East, urged monks to leave their protected enclaves and serve the needs of others by caring for orphans, widows, and the infirm.

Benedict of Nursia (ca. 480–547) devised the rule that became popular in western Europe. In 529, he established a monastery at Monte Cassino, in Italy. It became the mother-house of the Benedictine order of monks. His *Rule for Monasteries* defined a regimented but humane way of life for monks. Benedictine monasteries were hierarchically organized under an abbot. His command was beyond question, but he was to care for his subordinates—discouraging extreme asceticism and making sure that they had adequate, if simple, food and clothing. The Benedictine Rule also deceed that monks should do manual labor to support themselves and set aside time for study. The pattern of life in Benedictine houses followed a cycle of periods for prayer, study, and labor. Monasteries were organized for self-sufficiency. Therefore, they did a better job than most late Roman institutions of surviving the decline of the empire. In the wake of the barbarian invasions, Benedictine missionaries were equipped to begin the process of Christianizing England and Germany. Their disciplined organization and devotion to hard work made the Benedictines an economic and political power as well as a spiritual force. The

WHAT WAS the doctrine of papal supremacy?

6.8
St. Benedict

Major Political and Religious Developments of the Early Middle Ages

313	Emperor Constantine issues the Edict of Milan
325	Council of Nicea defines Christian doctrine
410	Rome invaded by Visigoths under Alaric
413–426	St. Augustine writes *The City of God*
451–453	Europe invaded by the Huns under Attila
476	Barbarian Odovacer deposes western emperor and rules as king of the Romans
488	Theodoric establishes kingdom of Ostrogoths in Italy
529	St. Benedict founds monastery at Monte Cassino
533	Justinian codifies Roman law
732	Charles Martel defeats Arabs at Tours
754	Pope Stephen II and Pepin III ally

apostolic primacy Doctrine that the popes are the direct successors to the Apostle Peter and as such heads of the church.

plenitude of power Teaching that the popes have power over all other bishops of the church.

schools and libraries that survived within the shelter of their walls played a major role in the rescue and revival of medieval Europe's literary culture.

THE DOCTRINE OF PAPAL PRIMACY

The Eastern emperors treated the Byzantine church like a department of the state, but their power did not reach to Rome, whose bishops resisted royal intervention. Their doctrine of "papal primacy," which declared the Roman pontiff supreme within the church, gave him the power to define doctrine and command the clergy. This doctrine also enabled the pope to make important secular claims, leading to repeated conflicts between church and state, pope and emperor, throughout the Middle Ages.

Pope Damasus I (366–384) laid the foundation for papal claims to absolute authority by asserting Rome's **apostolic primacy**. He pointed to Jesus' words to Peter in the Gospel of Matthew (16:18): "Thou art Peter, and upon this rock I will build my church." Because tradition maintained that Peter was the first bishop of Rome and that he died there, Damasus insisted that Rome's popes, Peter's successors, were heirs to the role Jesus had decreed for Peter. Pope Leo I (440–461) assumed the title *pontifex maximus*—"supreme priest" and laid claim to a "**plenitude of power**," supremacy over all other bishops in the church. Pope Gelasius I (492–496) stated that the authority of the clergy was "more weighty" than the power of kings, for priests were given charge over divine affairs.

DIVISION OF CHRISTENDOM

The division of Christendom into Eastern (Byzantine) and Western (Roman Catholic) churches arose in the early Middle Ages in response in part to linguistic and cultural differences between the Greek East and the Roman West. In both regions, church organization closely followed the structure of the secular state. A "patriarch" ruled over "metropolitans" and "archbishops" in the cities and provinces, and they in turn ruled over bishops, who ruled the local clergy. A novel combination of Greek, Roman, and Asian elements, however, shaped Byzantine culture, giving Eastern Christianity more of a mystical orientation and a greater preoccupation with the hereafter than Western Christianity. This difference in outlook may have predisposed Eastern patriarchs to submit more readily to royal intervention in their affairs than Western popes ever would.

Three major factors lay behind the religious break that separated the Eastern and Western churches in 1054. The first revolved around questions of doctrinal authority. The Eastern church put more stress on the authority of the Bible and ecumenical councils of the church to define Christian doctrine than on the decrees of the bishop of Rome. The claims of Roman popes were unacceptable to the East. A second factor was the western addition of the *filioque* clause to the Nicene Creed. According to this anti-Arian clause, the Holy Spirit proceeds "also from the Son" (*filioque*) as well as from the Father, making clear the western belief that Christ was fully one essence with God the Father and not a lesser being. The third factor dividing the Eastern and Western churches was the iconoclastic controversy of the eighth century. As noted earlier, when the Byzantine Emperor Leo III (r. 717–741) ordered western popes to abolish the use of images in their churches, he met fierce resistance. In 754, Pope Stephen II (752–757) solved two problems at one time. He enlisted the aid of the Franks and their ruler, Pepin III, against his Italian enemies, the Lombards, and used this alliance with the Franks as a counterweight to the influence of the Eastern emperor. Cooperation between Roman pope and Frankish king chartered a new course for Western history.

THE KINGDOM OF THE FRANKS

MEROVINGIANS AND CAROLINGIANS: FROM CLOVIS TO CHARLEMAGNE

Clovis (ca. 466–511), a chieftain who converted to orthodox Christianity around 496, founded the first Frankish dynasty, the Merovingians. Clovis and his successors gave the Franks a major role in the recovery of western Europe. The territory under their control included modern France, Belgium, the Netherlands, and western Germany. In attempting to govern this extensive kingdom, the Merovingians encountered the most persistent problem of medieval political history—the competing claims of the "one" and the "many," the struggle of a lone king to impose centralized government on local magnates.

The Merovingian kings addressed this problem by making pacts with the landed nobility and creating officials called *counts*. The men they appointed as counts had no personal powerbases in the regions they governed and were, therefore, presumed to be dependent on and loyal to the king. But like local landed aristocrats, the Merovingian counts soon laid claim to authority in their own names, and the Frankish kingdom fragmented into independent, tiny principalities. This tendency was aggravated by the Frankish custom of dividing the kingdom among the king's legitimate male heirs.

By the seventh century, the Frankish king had no effective authority left. Real power was concentrated in the office of the mayor of the palace, who was the spokesman at the king's court for the great landowners. The Carolingian dynasty used this office to rise to power and unseat the Merovingians.

The Carolingians (named for the dynasty's greatest ruler, Carolus, later known as Charlemagne, or Charles the Great) controlled the office of the mayor of the palace from the ascent to that post of Pepin I (d. 639) until 751, when, with the connivance of the pope, they expropriated the Frankish crown. Pepin II (d. 714) was king in fact if not in title over the Frankish realm. His son, Charles Martel ("the Hammer," d. 741), created a great cavalry by bestowing lands (*benefices* or *fiefs*) on nobles in exchange for their military service. The army he created checked the Arabs at Tours in 732.

The fiefs bestowed by Charles Martel came in large part from land usurped from the church. The Carolingians chose their counts almost entirely from the

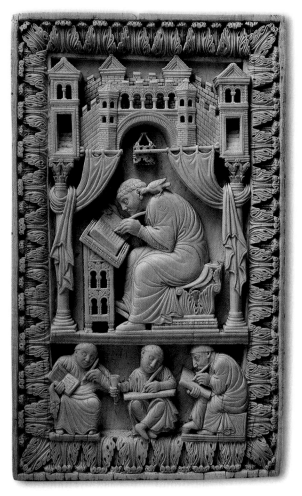

Scribes at work. During the Carolingian Renaissance, scholars made editions of the works of Gregory the Great, shown here in a monastic scriptorium (an area devoted to copying and preserving books) receiving the divine word from a dove perched on his shoulder. Below St. Gregory three monks are shown writing. Note the inkwell held by the middle monk. Before the invention of the printing press in about 1450, manuscripts could only be duplicated by laborious hand copying. Much of this painstaking work was done by monks.
Kunsthistorisches Museum, Vienna.

WHY DID Charlemagne's Empire break up after his death?

fief Land granted to a vassal in exchange for services, usually military.

ranks of the landed nobility. The Merovingians had tried to compete with these great aristocrats by raising landless men to power, but this strategy had failed. By playing to strength rather than challenging it, the Carolingians empowered themselves, at least for the short term. The church had little choice but to tolerate the seizure of its lands to support the army that defended Christian Europe from Muslim attack.

Frankish Church   The church, particularly its monasteries, played a large role in the Frankish government. Many monasteries had rich landed estates, and their abbots were wealthy, powerful magnates. The higher clergy were employed as royal agents, and the Carolingians used the missionary clergy to pacify the tribes whose lands they conquered. Christian bishops became lords, appointed by and subject to the king.

In 751 Pope Zacharias (741–752) sanctioned the deposition of the last of the Merovingians, and Pepin III was proclaimed king by the nobility in council Zacharias's successor, When Pope Stephen II (752–757) was driven from Rome in 753 by the Lombards, he appealed to Pepin to cast out the invaders and guarantee papal claims to rule central Italy, a region then under the jurisdiction of the eastern emperor. In 754, the Franks and the church allied against the Lombards and the eastern emperor. Carolingian kings officially became the protectors of the Catholic Church. Pepin was proclaimed *patricius Romanorum*, "father-protector of the Romans," a title heretofore borne by the representative of the Eastern emperor. In 755, the Franks defeated the Lombards and gave the pope the lands surrounding Rome. This created a political entity called the **Papal States**. During this time the papacy began to circulate a fraudulent document, *Donation of Constantine*, which was intended to prove to the Franks that the church was the heir to the legacy of Rome's empire. It was exposed as a forgery in the 15th century.

The papacy had looked to the Franks to protect it from the Eastern emperors. But the Carolingian dynasty drew almost as slight a boundary between state and church as did Eastern emperors. Although preferable to Eastern domination, Carolingian patronage of the church proved to be no less constraining.

REIGN OF CHARLEMAGNE (768–814)

Charlemagne, son of Pepin the Short, continued his father's policies. He served as papal protector in Italy and pursued the conquest of additional territory in the north. In 774 Charlemagne defeated the Lombards of northern Italy and assumed their crown The subjugation of neighboring pagan tribes, especially the Saxons whom the Franks Christianized and dispersed, brought more of Europe under his control. The Danubian plains were drawn into the Frankish orbit by a war that routed the Avars. The Arabs were chased beyond the Pyrenees. By the time of his death on January 28, 814, Charlemagne's kingdom embraced modern France, Belgium, Holland, Switzerland, almost all of Germany, much of Italy, and part of Spain (see Map 12–3).

The New Empire   Charlemagne aspired to recognition as emperor. To support his case, he constructed a palace city, Aachen, in imitation of the courts of the ancient Roman and the Eastern emperors. He treated the church with a paternalism almost as great as that of any Eastern emperor and used it to help build his empire. Frankish Christians professed the Nicene Creed (with the

Papal States   Territory in central Italy ruled by the pope until 1870.

MAP 12–3
The Empire of Charlemagne to 814.   Building on the successes of his predecessors, Charlemagne greatly increased the Frankish domains. Such traditional enemies as the Saxons and the Lombards fell under his sway.

HOW DOES the extent of Charlemagne's Empire compare with that of the Roman Empire in the west?

filioque clause the emperor endorsed) and were taught by their clergy to revere Charlemagne.

On Christmas Day 800, Pope Leo III (795–816) crowned Charlemagne emperor. This event created what would later be called the Holy Roman Empire, a revival (confined after 870 largely to Germany) of the old Roman Empire in the West. The coronation benefited both the church and Charlemagne. Before his coronation, Charlemagne had been a minor Western potentate in the eyes of

Eastern emperors. After the coronation, Eastern emperors reluctantly recognized his new imperial dignity.

The New Emperor   Charlemagne was a physically daunting man. An examination of his remains conducted in 1861 verified that he was six feet, three and one half inches tall. Contemporary witnesses describe him as athletic, energetic, restless, and ever ready for a hunt or a swim in Aachen's hot springs. Informal and gregarious, he was known for his humor and hospitality. Aachen was a festive palace city to which people and gifts came from all over the world. Baghdad's famous caliph, Harun-al-Rashid once honored him with a truly imperial present—a white elephant.

Charlemagne had a series of five official wives by whom he sired numerous children. This created problems. His oldest son, Pepin grew jealous of the attention he gave to the sons of his second wife and joined in a conspiracy against him. The plot was exposed, and Pepin was confined to a monastery for the rest of his life.

Problems of Government   Charlemagne governed his kingdom through counts, strategically located within the administrative districts into which the kingdom was divided. Carolingian counts tended to be local magnates who already had armed followings and the self-interest to enforce the will of the king. Their three main duties were to maintain a local army loyal to the king, to collect tribute and dues, and to administer justice. They discharged this last responsibility through a district law court known as the *mallus*. The court heard testimony, passed judgment, and assessed a monetary compensation to be paid to injured parties.

Many counts used their official position and judicial powers to their own advantage. They set themselves up as local despots and claimed the land grants with which they were paid as hereditary possessions, not loans that the emperor could cancel. Charlemagne tried to supervise his officials by dispatching royal envoys, the *missi dominici*, to visit their counties and report on how they were discharging their duties. But this policy had minimal effect. The king appointed various kinds of provincial governors with titles like prefect, duke, or margrave, but none of them was incorruptible.

Charlemagne never solved the problem of creating a loyal bureaucracy. His ecclesiastical agents had the same responsibilities, secular lifestyles, and aspirations as his counts. Except for duties involving liturgy and prayers, they were indistinguishable from the lay nobility. Capitularies, or royal decrees, discouraged the more outrageous behavior of the clergy. But Charlemagne also sensed that reform-minded ecclesiastical landowners could, for different reasons, undercut royal authority. Charlemagne treated his bishops as vassals who served at his pleasure.

Alcuin and the Carolingian Renaissance   Charlemagne used some of his wealth to encourage a revival of literacy and learning. His generous patronage brought notable scholars, such as his biographer Einhard (ca. 770–840) and

Charlemagne. An equestrian figure of Charlemagne (or possibly one of his sons) from the early ninth century.

Bronze equestrian statuette of Charlemagne, from Metz Cathedral, 9th–10th century 3/4 view. Louvre, Paris, France. Copyright Bridgeman-Giraudon/Art Resource, N.Y.

7.5
The Missi Domenici

Alcuin of York (735–804), director of his palace school, to Aachen. There, they set about developing a court culture and a new educational program. Their labors were richly rewarded. Alcuin's classical and Christian learning earned him the income from several wealthy monasteries.

Although Charlemagne appreciated learning for its own sake, his palace school was intended to upgrade the administrative skills of his officials by providing training in the basic tools of bureaucrats: reading, writing, speaking, logic, and counting. To this end Charlemagne's scholars created a new, clear, standardized style of handwriting—Carolingian minuscule—and fostered the use of accurate Latin in official documents. These developments helped increase lay literacy. Alcuin created a genuine community of scholars and clerics at court and infused the highest administrative levels with a sense of comradeship and common purpose.

The result was a modest renaissance, or rebirth, of interest in antiquity at the palace school. Its scholars collected and preserved ancient manuscripts and attempted to immitate the styles and forms employed by classic authors. These scholarly activities served official efforts to bring uniformity to church law and liturgy, educate the clergy, and elevate spiritual life.

The Manor and Serfdom   The agrarian economy of the Middle Ages was organized and controlled through village farms known as **manors**. Here peasants labored as farmers in subordination to a lord, that is, a more powerful landowner who gave them land and a dwelling in exchange for their services and a portion of their crops. The land farmed by the peasants for the lord was the **demesne**, about one-quarter to one-third of the arable land. All crops grown there belonged to the lord.

manors Village farms owned by a lord.

demesne Part of a manor that was cultivated directly for the lord of the manor.

Moldboard plow. The invention of the moldboard plow greatly improved farming. The heavy plow cut deeply into the ground and furrowed it. This illustration from the Luttrell Psalter (ca. 1340) also shows that the traction harness, which lessened the strangulation effect of the yoke on the animals, had not yet been adopted. Indeed, one of the oxen seems to be on the verge of choking.

The British Library/The Art Archive.

Peasants were treated according to their social status and the size of their land holdings. A freeman—that is, a peasant with his own modest property—became a **serf** by surrendering his property to a lord in exchange for protection and assistance. The freeman received his land back from the lord with a clear definition of his economic and legal rights. Although the land was no longer his property, he had full possession and use of it and could not be separated from it. The services and goods he was to supply to the lord were also spelled out. Peasants who had little real property to bargain with ended up as unfree serfs and were more vulnerable to the lord's demands. Impoverished peasants were the most vulnerable to abuse.

Serfs were subject to dues in kind. They owed firewood for cutting wood in the lord's forests, sheep for grazing their sheep on the lord's land, and the like. The lord, who furnished shacks and small plots of land from his vast domain, had an army of servants who provided him with everything from eggs to boots. Many serfs were discontented and fled their lords hoping to find better deals under new masters.

By the time of Charlemagne, the moldboard plow, which was needed in northern Europe where the soil was heavy, and the **three-field system** were coming into use. These developments improved agricultural productivity. The moldboard cut deep into the soil and turned it to form a ridge, providing a natural drainage system as well as permitting deep planting. Unlike the earlier two-field system, which alternated fallow with planted fields each year, the three-field system increased the amount of cultivated land by leaving only one-third fallow.

Religion and the Clergy   As owners of the churches on their lands, the lords had the right to chose serfs to serve as priests for the parishes on their estates. Church law directed the lord to set a serf free before he entered the clergy, but lords preferred a "serf priest," one who not only said Mass but continued to serve his lord. Frankish lords cultivated a docile parish clergy.

Ordinary people baptized themselves and their children, confessed the Creed at mass, tried to learn the Lord's Prayer, and hoped to receive last rites from the priest at death. Local priests were no better educated than their congregations, and instruction in Christian doctrine remained at a minimum.

BREAKUP OF THE CAROLINGIAN KINGDOM

In his last years, Charlemagne knew that his empire was becoming ungovernable. The seeds of dissolution lay in the determination of each locality to protect its self-interests. In medieval society, a direct relationship existed between physical proximity to authority and loyalty. Local people obeyed local lords more than a distant king, and Charlemagne had courted the support of regional magnates by enhancing their power.

Louis the Pious   Charlemagne's successor, Louis the Pious (r. 814–840), had three sons by his first wife; according to Salic or Germanic law, a ruler partitioned his kingdom equally among his surviving sons. Louis tried to break this tradition by making his eldest son, Lothar (d. 855), coregent and sole imperial heir in 817. To Lothar's brothers he gave lesser appanages, or hereditary lands.

serfs Peasants tied to the land they tilled.

three-field system Medieval innovation that increased the amount of land under cultivation by leaving only one-third fallow in a given year.

Pepin (d. 838) became king of Aquitaine, and Louis "the German" (d. 876) became king of Bavaria over the eastern Franks.

In 823, Louis's second wife, Judith of Bavaria, bore him a fourth son, Charles (d. 877). Determined that her son should receive more than just a nominal inheritance, the queen incited Pepin and Louis to war against Lothar, and persuaded Louis to divide the kingdom equally among his four living sons. The pope had an important stake in the preservation of the revived Western empire and the imperial title, which Louis's partition of his kingdom threatened to undo. The pope, therefore, restored Lothar to his inheritance, but he could not prevent Lothar's brothers from renewing war against him.

The Treaty of Verdun and Its Aftermath   In 843, with the Treaty of Verdun, the Carolingian Empire was partitioned into three equal parts. Lothar received a middle section, which embraced modern Holland, Belgium, Switzerland, Alsace-Lorraine, and Italy; Charles the Bald received roughly modern France; and Louis the German got territory approximating modern Germany (see Map 12–4). This terminated the universal empire to which Charlemagne and Louis the Pious aspired.

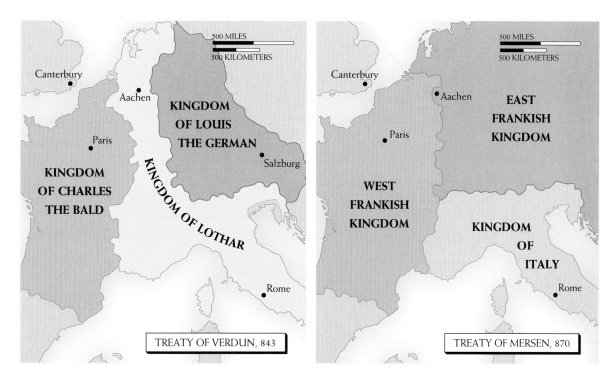

MAP 12–4
The Treaty of Verdun (843) and the Treaty of Mersen (870).   The Treaty of Verdun divided the kingdom of Louis the Pious among his three feuding children: Charles the Bald, Lothar, and Louis the German. After Lothar's death in 855, the middle kingdom was so weakened by division among his three sons that Charles the Bald and Louis the German divided it between themselves in the Treaty of Mersen.

HOW DID the division of the Carolingian Empire lay the basis for modern nation states?

The Treaty of Verdun proved to be only the beginning of Carolingian fragmentation. When Lothar died in 855, his kingdom was divided among his three surviving sons. Henceforth, Western Europe would be split between eastern and western Frankish kingdoms—roughly Germany and France—perpetually at war to claim portions of the fractionalized middle kingdom. The contest continued into modern times.

Vikings, Magyars, and Muslims   The political breakdown of the Carolingian Empire coincided with new external threats. In the late 9th and 10th centuries, waves of Normans (North men), better known as Vikings, swept into Europe from Scandinavia. *Vikings* was a catchall term for Scandinavians who visited Europe to trade and raid. Their rugged ocean-going longboats enabled them to threaten the coastal and river towns of the continent and British Isles. Danes penetrated as far as Paris in the ninth century. Other Vikings established themselves in northern England and Ireland. They colonized Greenland and appear to have explored the shores of New England 500 years before Columbus sailed. Their foreign adventures continued into the 11th century.

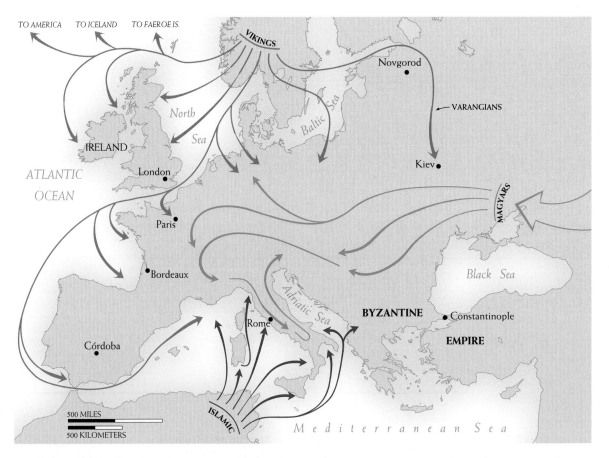

MAP 12–5
Viking, Muslim, and Magyar Invasions to the 11th Century.   Western Europe was sorely beset by new waves of outsiders from the 9th to the 11th century. From north, east, and south, a stream of invading Vikings, Magyars, and Muslims brought the West at times to near collapse and of course gravely affected institutions within Europe.

HOW DID early medieval Europe respond to invasions?

Magyars, or Hungarians, likewise swept in from the eastern plains, while Muslims made incursions from North Africa (see Map 12–5). The Franks built fortified towns and castles as refuges or bought off the invaders with land and silver. In this turmoil, local populations became more dependent on local strongmen, creating the precondition for feudal society.

Magyars Majority ethnic group in Hungary.

FEUDAL SOCIETY

WHAT IS a feudal society?

*T*he Middle Ages were characterized by a chronic absence of effective central government and the constant threat of famine, disease, and invasion. The true lords were those who could guarantee protection from rapine and starvation. *Feudal society* refers to the social, political, military, and economic system that emerged in these circumstances. It is a social order in which a regional prince or a local lord is dominant, and society is held together by trust in pledges of fidelity. In a feudal society, people require the assurance that others can be depended on in time of need. It is a system of mutually recognized rights and responsibilities.

During the early Middle Ages, the landed nobility ruled over their domains as miniature kingdoms. They maintained their own armies and courts, regulated local tolls, and even minted their own coins. Large groups of warrior **vassals** were created by bestowals of land, and these constituted a professional military class with its own code of conduct. In feudal society, serfs worked the land, the clergy prayed and gave counsel, and lords and knights maintained law and order.

ORIGINS

The origins of feudal government can be found in the divisions and conflicts of Merovingian society when freemen began placing themselves under the protection of more powerful men. The latter became local magnates, and the former solved the problem of survival. Freeman who so entrusted themselves to others or gave themselves to the king came to be described as *vassi* ("those who serve"), from which evolved the term *vassalage*, meaning to pledge oneself to the personal service of someone who promises protection.

Landed nobles, like kings, tried to acquire as many vassals as they could, because military strength lay in numbers. To maintain these growing armies, they were granted land, which came to be known as a *benefice*, or a *fief*. Vassals were expected to dwell on it and maintain their accouterments of war in good order.

VASSALAGE AND THE FIEF

Vassalage involved **fealty** to the lord. To swear fealty was to promise not to act against the lord's well-being and to perform personal services for him whenever requested. Chief among the expected services was military duty as a mounted knight. Continuous bargaining and bickering occurred over the terms of service.

Limitations were placed on the number of days a lord could require services from a vassal. In France in the 11th century, about 40 days of service per year were considered sufficient. Vassals could also buy their way out of military service by a monetary payment known as *scutage*. The lord, in turn, used this payment to hire mercenaries. The vassal was also expected to give the lord advice and to sit as a member of his court.

feudal society Social, political, military, and economic system that prevailed in the Middle Ages and beyond in some parts of Europe.

vassal Person granted an estate or cash payments in return for accepting the obligation to render services to a lord.

fealty Oath of loyalty by a vassal to a lord, promising to perform specified services.

The lord's obligations to his vassals were specific. He was obligated to protect the vassal from physical harm and to stand as his advocate. After fealty was sworn and homage paid, the lord bestowed a benefice, or fief. The fief was the physical or material wherewithal to meet the vassal's obligations. It could take the form of liquid wealth. Money fiefs empowered a vassal to receive regular payments from the lord's treasury. Normally, however, the fief consisted of a landed estate or a castle.

In Carolingian times, a benefice varied in size from one or more small villas to several *mansi* of 25 to 48 acres. The king's vassals received benefices of at least 30 and as many as 200 such mansi. Royal vassalage with a benefice was widely sought by the highest classes of Carolingian society; however, it proved deadly to the king. Although Carolingian kings guarded their rights over property granted in benefice to vassals, vassals were still free to dispose of their benefices as they pleased. Vassals of the king, in turn, created their own vassals. These vassals created still further vassals of their own—vassals of vassals of vassals—in a reverse pyramiding effect that by the late ninth century fragmented both land and authority from the highest to the lowest levels.

Beginning with the reign of Louis the Pious (r. 814–840), bishops and abbots swore fealty and received their offices from the king as a benefice. The king invested these clerics with a ring and a staff, the symbols of high spiritual office. Lay investiture would eventually provoke a great confrontation between church and state (see "Bishop Fulbert Describes Obligations of Vassals and Lords").

FRAGMENTATION AND DIVIDED LOYALTY

Occupation of the land led to claims of hereditary possession. Hereditary possession became legally recognized in the ninth century and laid the basis for claims to real ownership. Further, to accumulate as much land as possible, one man could become a vassal to several different lords. This led in the ninth century to the concept of a "liege lord"—one master whom the vassal must obey even to the harm of the others, should a direct conflict among them arise.

The problem of loyalty was reflected in the ceremonial development of the act by which a freeman became a vassal. In the mid-eighth century, an "oath of fealty" highlighted the ceremony. A vassal reinforced his promise of fidelity to the lord by swearing a special oath with his hand on a sacred relic or the Bible. In the 10th and 11th centuries, paying homage also involved placing the vassal's hands between the lord's and sealing the ceremony with a kiss.

Despite their limitations and risks, feudal arrangements provided stability in the early Middle Ages and aided the process of political centralization during the High Middle Ages. Feudal government was adaptable. The foundations of the modern nation-state would emerge in France and England from fine-tuning feudal arrangements as kings sought to adapt their goal of centralized government to local power and control.

Carolingian Dynasty (751–987)

751	Pepin III "the Short" becomes king of the Franks
755	Franks drive Lombards out of central Italy; creation of Papal States
768–814	Charlemagne rules as king of the Franks
774	Charlemagne defeats Lombards in northern Italy
750–800	Fraudulent *Donation of Constantine* created in an effort to counter Frankish domination of church
800	Pope Leo III crowns Charlemagne
814–840	Louis the Pious succeeds Charlemagne as "Emperor"
843	Treaty of Verdun partitions the Carolingian Empire
870	Treaty of Mersen further divides Carolingian Empire
875–950	Invasions by Vikings, Muslims, and Magyars
962	Ottonian dynasty succeeds Carolingian in Germany
987	Capetian dynasty succeeds Carolingian in France

HISTORY'S VOICES

BISHOP FULBERT DESCRIBES OBLIGATIONS OF VASSALS AND LORDS

Trust held the lord and vassal together. Their duties in this regard were carefully defined. Here are six general rules for vassal and lord, laid down by Bishop Fulbert of Chartres in a letter to William, Duke of Aquitaine, in 1020.

WHAT ARE the respective obligations of vassal and lord? Do they seem fair for each side? Why might a vassal have more responsibilities and a lord fewer?

He who swears fealty to his lord ought always to have these six things in memory: what is harmless, safe, honorable, useful, easy, practicable. Harmless, that is to say, that he should not injure his lord in his body; safe, that he should not injure him by betraying his secrets or the defenses upon which he relies for his safety; honorable, that he should not injure him in his possessions; easy and practicable, that that good which his lord is able to do easily he make not

difficult, nor that which is practicable he make not impossible to him.

That the faithful vassal should avoid these injuries is certainly proper, but not for this alone does he deserve his holding; for it is not sufficient to abstain from evil, unless what is good is done also. It remains, therefore, that in the same six things mentioned above he should faithfully counsel and aid his lord, if he wishes to be looked upon as worthy of this benefice and to be safe concerning the fealty which he has sworn.

The lord also ought to act toward his faithful vassal reciprocally in all these things. And if he does not do this, he will be justly considered guilty of bad faith, just as the former, if he should be detected in avoiding or consenting to the avoidance of his duties, would be perfidious and perjured.

Source: James Harvey Robinson, ed., *Readings in European History*, Vol. 1 (Boston: Athenaeum, 1904), p. 184.

SUMMARY

The Byzantine Empire In the fifth century, Roman authority in the west collapsed under the impact of Germanic invasions. However, imperial power shifted to the eastern part of the Roman Empire—known as the Byzantine Empire—with its capital at Constantinople. The Byzantine Empire would endure until the Ottoman Turks captured Constantinople in 1453. The peak of Byzantine power occurred during the reign of Justinian (527–565), one of whose major achievements was the *Corpus Juris Civilis*, a codification of Roman law on which most European law was based until the 19th century. The Byzantine Empire provided a model of civilized society to medieval Europe, helped protect it from Muslim invaders, and preserved much of classical learning.

The Islamic world also acted as a conduit for classical learning to West, particularly in medicine, astronomy, and mathematics.

The Roman Church The church was the strongest and most prestigious institution in early medieval Europe where it filled the vacuum created by the collapse of Roman authority. Monastic culture was especially strong. The greatest organizer of Western monasticism was St. Benedict of Nursia (480–547). Benedictine monasteries were an economic, political, and spiritual force throughout the West.

IMAGE KEY
for pages 264–265

a. An illustration from the Luttrell Psalter (ca.1340)

b. A vassal

c. Book of Kells: St. Matthew, Chi Rho initial.

d. Reliquary of the True Cross, Constantinople, c.960

e. Byzantine empress Theodora with ladies of the court

f. Non-Ptolemaic model for the motions of sun, moon and planets

g. The coronation of Charlemagne by Pope Leo III in Rome

h. Bronze equestrian statuette of Charlemagne

i. The Hagia Sophia, exterior

j. The Hagia Sophia, interior

k. Relief of a monastic scriptorium

With the collapse of imperial authority in the West, the bishops of Rome, the popes, developed the doctrine of papal primacy by which they claimed supreme authority over church doctrine and the clergy. These claims were unacceptable in the East, where a separate Greek Orthodox Church developed under the control of the Byzantine emperors.

Charlemagne's Empire The Frankish ruler Charlemagne (r. 768–814) sought to recreate a universal Western empire and was crowned emperor by the pope in 800. Charlemagne's realm embraced modern France, Belgium, Holland, and Switzerland, most of Germany, and parts of Italy and Spain. He formed a close alliance with the church and relied on churchmen as royal agents and administrators. His palace school at Aachen was the center of a modest renaissance of classical learning under scholars such as Alcuin of York (735–804).

Yet, despite his efforts at administrative control, Charlemagne's empire proved to be ungovernable. Charlemagne had increased the power of local lords whose support he needed to rule, but their power and wealth became so great that they were able to put their self-interests above royal authority. After Charlemagne's death, his empire dissolved amid quarrels among his heirs, revolts of powerful nobles, and invasions by Vikings, Magyars, and Muslims.

Feudal Society The Middle Ages were characterized by a chronic absence of central government and the constant threat of famine, disease, and invasion. Lords were those who could guarantee protection under these conditions. Feudal society was one in which a local lord is dominant and offers security in return for allegiance from his dependents or vassals. It was a system of mutual rights and responsibilities. Medieval vassals pledged fealty to their lord in return for a fief, or grant of land. They promised to support their "liege lord" with troops or money when he called upon them for aid.

The feudal economy was organized and controlled through agrarian villages known as manors, worked by free peasants, who had their own modest property and economic and legal rights, or by serfs, impoverished peasants who were bound to the land and obliged to provide their lords with an array of services, dues in kind, and products.

REVIEW QUESTIONS

1. How did the situation that faced the church in the western Roman Empire differ from that it confronted in the east at the start of the Middle Ages?

2. How did the Franks become the dominant force in western Europe? Why did Charlemagne's empire break apart?

3. How and why was the history of the eastern or Byzantine half of the Roman Empire so different from the western half?

4. What were the defining features of feudalism? Is a feudal society a "backward" society?

KEY TERMS

apostolic primacy (p. 274)	*fief* (p. 275)	**plenitude of power** (p. 274)
demesne (p. 279)	**Magyars** (p. 283)	**serf** (p. 280)
fealty (p. 283)	**manor** (p. 279)	**three-field system** (p. 280)
feudal society (p. 283)	**Papal States** (p. 276)	**vassal** (p. 283)

 For additional study resources for this chapter, go to:
www.prenhall.com/craig/chapter12

13 Islam in the Heartlands and Beyond, ca. 1000–1600

CHAPTER HIGHLIGHTS

Religion Between 1000 and 1500, Sunnism was the dominant tradition across the Islamic world, but in both main branches of Islam, the *ulama* joined the religious, social, and political elites and discouraged religious innovation. Shiism flourished in Iran under the Savafid rulers. Sufi fraternal orders, whether Sunni or Shi'ite, became the chief instruments for the spread of Muslim faith in most Islamic societies.

Regional Developments Muslims were gradually pushed out of Spain by the Spanish Christian states between 1000 and 1492. In Egypt, the Shi'ite Fatamids established a separate caliphate from 969 to 1171. The Mamluks, whose rule in Egypt lasted from 1260 to 1517, were the only Muslim dynasty to withstand the Mongol invasions. The Seljuks were the first major Turkish dynasty of Islam.

Mongol Invasions In 1255, the Mongols invaded the Muslim world and swept all before them, conquering Transoxiana, Iran, and Iraq, before being defeated by the Mamluks in Syria in 1260. Thereafter, the Mongols established the Ilkhanid dynasty in Iran and converted to Islam. Another wave of Turko-Mongol conquest under Timur-I Lang further devastated much of the Middle East between 1379 and 1405.

India Muslim invaders and rulers spread Islam in India, where it became an enduring and influential part of Indian civilization. There was reciprocal influence between Muslims and Hindus, and Hindu religion and culture flourished, even under Muslim control.

CHAPTER QUESTIONS

HOW DID the Sunni, Shi'ite, and Sufi traditions develop between the years 1000 and 1500?

WHO WERE the Mamluks and why were they able to withstand the Mongols?

HOW DID Islam become an enduring part of Indian civilization?

CHAPTER OUTLINE

THE ISLAMIC HEARTLANDS
- Religion and Society
- Regional Developments
- The Spread of Islam Beyond the Heartlands

INDIA AND SOUTHEAST ASIA
- The Spread of Islam to South Asia
- Muslim-Hindu Encounter
- Islamic States and Dynasties
- Religious and Cultural Accomodation
- Hindu and Other Indian Traditions

The centralized power of the caliphate in the Islamic world had broken down by the mid-10th century. Regional Islamic states with distinctive political and cultural identities took its place—a pattern that endured into modern times (see Map 13–1). Yet the diverse Islamic lands remained part of a larger civilization.

Socially and religiously, the next 500 years saw the growth of a truly international Islamic community, united by shared norms of communal order represented and maintained by the Muslim religious scholars (the ulama). Sufism, a strand of Islam stressing piety and allegiance to a spiritual master, gained widespread popularity, especially after 1200, through the growth of Sufi affiliations or brotherhoods. Shi'ite ideas also offered an alternative vision of society for many. Movements loyal to Ali and his heirs challenged but failed to reverse centrist, Sunni predominance, even though Shi'ite dynasties ruled much of the Islamic heartlands in the 10th and 11th centuries.

Culturally, the rise of the New Persian language in the 10th century resulted in a rich new Islamic literature. A cultural renaissance fueled the spread of Persian as the major language of Islam alongside Arabic. The Persian-dominated Iranian and Indian Islamic world became increasingly distinct from the western Islamic lands.

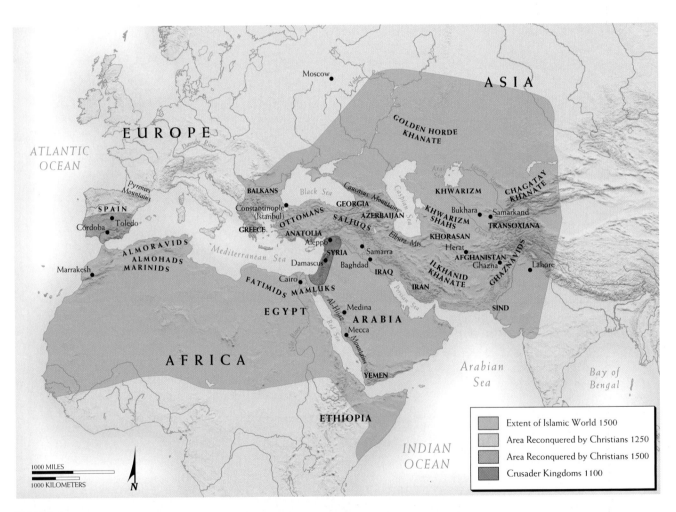

MAP 13–1

The Islamic World, 1000 ca. 1500. Compare this with Map 11–1 on page 252. Though the Muslim world had expanded deep into Africa, India, and Central Asia, it had also lost Spain to Christian reconquest.

GIVEN THE many Muslim states shown on this map, to what extent is it correct to speak of a single Islamic civilization?

Two Asian steppe peoples, the Mongols and the Turks, came to rule much of the Islamic world in these centuries, while Islam impinged more and more on the Indian subcontinent, Southeast Asia, and sub-Saharan Africa. Although Muslims remained a minority in these regions, Islam became the major new influence in all of them.

THE ISLAMIC HEARTLANDS

RELIGION AND SOCIETY

uring this period Islamic society was shaped by consolidation of Sunni orthodoxy, Sufi piety and organization, and Shi'ite traditions.

CONSOLIDATION OF SUNNI ORTHODOXY

The *ulama* (both Sunni and Shi'ite) gradually became entrenched religious, social, and political elites throughout the Islamic world, especially after the breakdown of the caliphate's centralized power in the 10th century. Their integration into local merchant, landowning, and bureaucratic classes led to stronger identification of these economic and political groups with Islam.

From the 11th century onward, the *ulama's* power and continuity as a class were expressed in the institution of the **madrasa**, or college of higher learning. In contrast to the university, with its corporate organization and institutional degrees, the *madrasa* was a support institution for individual teachers, who personally certified students' mastery of particular subjects. It gave an institutional base (often providing not only teaching space but stipends and student living quarters) to Islam's long-developed system of students seeking out the best

HOW DID the Sunni, Shi'ite, and Sufi traditions develop between the years 1000 and 1500?

 12.1
Sunni versus Shi'ite: "We Exhort You to Embrace the True Faith!"

madrasa Islamic college of higher learning.

The Sultan Hasan Madrasa and Tomb-Mosque. This imposing Mamluk building (1356–1363) was built to house teachers and students studying all four of the major traditions or "schools" of Islamic law. Living and teaching spaces are combined here in a building with a mosque and the Sultan's tomb enclosure.

SuperStock, Inc.

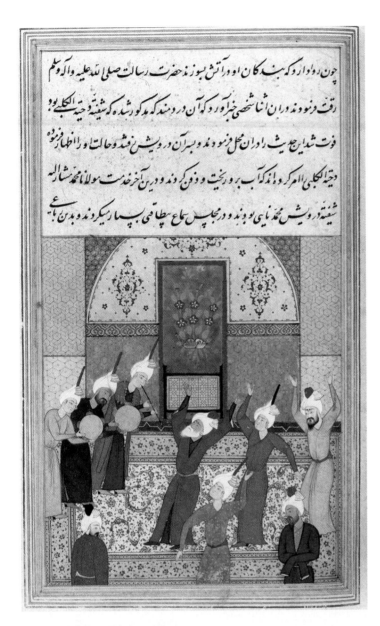

Dancing Dervishes. This image from a 1552 Persian manuscript depicts a Sufi master dancing with his disciples. Sufis often use music and bodily movement to induce a feeling of ecstacy which they feel brings them closer to God.

Bodleian Library, University of Oxford.

Ramadan Month when Muslims must fast during daylight hours.

orthopraxy Correct practice of a religion.

Sufi Movement within Islam that emphasizes the spiritual and mystical.

teachers and studying texts with them until they received the teachers' formal certification, or "permission" to transmit and teach those same texts themselves.

Popular "unofficial" piety flourished in pilgrimages to saints' tombs, in folk celebrations of Muhammad's birthday, in veneration of him in poetry, and in ecstatic chant and dance among Sufi groups. But the shared traditions that directed family and civil law, the daily worship rituals, fasting in the month of **Ramadan**, and the yearly Meccan pilgrimage remained the public bond uniting almost all Muslims. The tendency among Muslims, despite their theological disputes, was to define Islam in terms of what Muslims do—namely by **orthopraxy** (practice) rather than by ortho*doxy* (beliefs). The chief arbiters of "normative" Sunni and Shi'i Islam among the ulama were the legal scholars, not the theologians.

A basic Sunni orthopraxy, discouraging religious or social innovation, was well established by the year 1000 as the dominant tradition. Further, a growing social conservatism among the ulama reflected their integration in regional social aristocracies. The ulama were often committed to the status quo, as were the rulers.

SUFI PIETY AND ORGANIZATION

Sufi piety stresses the spiritual and mystical dimensions of Islam. The term *Sufi* apparently came from the Arabic *suf* ("wool"), recalling an old ascetic practice of wearing only a coarse woolen garment. Sufi simplicity and humility developed as a distinctive tendency when, after about 700 C.E., male and female pietists emphasized a godly life over and above mere observance of Muslim duties. Some stressed ascetic avoidance of temptations, others loving devotion to God. Sufi piety mystically bridged the abyss between the human and the divine that is implied in the exalted Muslim concept of the omnipotent God of creation. Sufi piety merged with folk piety in saint veneration, shrine pilgrimage, ecstatic worship, and seasonal festivals. Sufi writers composed some of the world's finest mystical poetry.

Some Sufis were revered as spiritual masters and saints. Their disciples formed brotherhoods that, from about the 11th century on, became both regional and international organizations. Each had its distinctive mystical teaching, Qur'anic interpretation, and devotional practice. These fraternal orders became the chief instruments for spreading Muslim faith in almost all Islamic societies. Indeed, Sufi orders became in this age one of the typical social institutions of everyday Muslim life. Whether Sunni or Shi'ite, casually or seriously pious, many Muslims have ever since identified in some degree with one or another Sufi order.

CONSOLIDATION OF SHI'ITE TRADITIONS

Shi'ite traditions crystallized between the 10th and 12th centuries. Numerous states came under Shi'ite rulers despite the fact that substantial Shi'ite populations developed only in Iran, Iraq, and the lower Indus (Sind).

Two Shi'ite groups emerged as the most influential. The first were the "Seveners," or "Isma'ilis," who recognized Isma'il (d. ca. 760), first son of the sixth Alid *imam*, as the seventh *imam*. Isma'ili groups were often revolutionary, and one Isma'ili group, the Qarmatians of eastern Arabia, ruled or agitated in Iraq, Syria, and Arabia through much of the 10th century.

By the 11th century, however, most Shi'ites accepted a line of 12 *imams* descended through another son of the sixth *imam*. The last of these is said to have disappeared in Samarra (Iraq) in 873 and to have been cosmically concealed until the time comes for him to emerge as the Mahdi, or "Guided One." His return is to usher in the messianic age and final judgment. The "Twelvers," the Shi'ite majority, focus their faith on the martyrdom of the 12 *imams* and look for their intercession on the Day of Judgment. The "Twelvers" have flourished best in Iran, where most Shi'ite doctrines have originated, no matter the sect. The Safavids of Iran made Twelver theology the "state religion" in the 16th century (see Chapter 23).

REGIONAL DEVELOPMENTS

Beginning in the 10th century, the western half of the Islamic world evolved two regional foci: (1) Spain, Moroccan North Africa, and to a lesser extent, West Africa; and (2) Egypt, Syria-Palestine, Anatolia, along with Arabia and Libyan North Africa. The eastern half of the Islamic world, in the period between 1000 and 1500, was profoundly affected by the incursion of the Mongols in the 13th century.

THE ISLAMIC WEST: SPAIN AND NORTH AFRICA

The grandeur of Spanish Islamic ("Moorish") culture can still be seen in Córdoba's great mosque and the remnants of the legendary Alhambra castle. Abd al-Rahman I (r. 756–788) established the Umayyad dynasty at Córdoba, the cultural center of the western world for the next two centuries. Renowned for its intellectual life, commercial activity, public baths and gardens, and elegance, Córdoba reached its zenith under Abd al-Rahman III (r. 912–961). He took the title of caliph in 929, and as an absolute but benevolent ruler, he presided over a largely unified, peaceful Islamic Spain. The mosque-university of Córdoba that he founded was the earliest of its kind. It attracted students from Europe as well as the Islamic world. A sad irony of this cosmopolitan culture was recurring religious exclusivism in both the Muslim and Christian camps, which sparked conflict between them.

Western Islamic Lands

756–1021	Spanish Umayyad dynasty
912–961	Rule of Abd al-Rahman III; height of Umayyad power and civilization
969–1171	Fatimid Shi'ite dynasty in Egypt
ca. 1020	Origin of Druze community (Egypt/Syria)
1171	Fatimids fall to Salah al-Din (Saladin), Ayyubid lieutenant of the ruler of Aleppo
1056–1275	Almoravid and Almohad dynasties in North Africa, West Africa, and Spain
1096–1291	Major European Christian crusades into Islamic lands; some European presence in Syria-Palestine
1198	Death of Ibn Rushd (Averroës), philosopher
1204	Death of Ibn Maymun (Maimonides), philosopher and Jewish savant
1240	Death of Ibn al-Arabi, theosophical mystic
1250–1517	Mamluk sultanate in Egypt and (from late 1200s) Syria; claim laid to Abbasid caliphate
1260	Mamluk victory at Ain Jalut halts Mongol advance into Syria
1406	Death of Ibn Khaldun, historian and social philosopher
ca. 1300	Rise of Ottoman state in western Anatolia

Eastern Islamic Lands

875–999	Samanid dynasty, centered at Bukhara
945–1055	Buyid Shi'ite dynasty in Baghdad, controls caliphs
994–1186	Ghaznavid dynasty in Ghazna (modern Afghanistan) and Lahore (modern Pakistan), founded by Subuktigin (r. 976–997) and his son, Mahmud of Ghazna (r. 998–1030)
ca. 1020	Death of Firdawsi, compiler of *Shahnama*
ca. 1048	Death of al-Biruni, scientist and polyglot
1055–1194	Seljuk rule in Baghdad
1063–1092	Viziership of Nizam al-Mulk
1111	Death of al-Ghazzali, theologian and scholar
1219–1222	Genghis Khan plunders eastern Iran to Indus region
1258	Hulagu Khan conquers Baghdad
1261	Mamluk-Mongol treaty halts westward Mongol movement
1260–1335	Hulagu and his Il-Khanid successors rule Iran
1379–1405	Campaigns of Timur-i Lang (Tamerlane) devastate entire Islamic East
1405–1494	Timurids, successors of Tamerlane, rule in Transoxiana and Iran
1405–1447	Shahrukh, Timurid ruler at Herat; great patronage of the arts and philosophy

Reconquista Christian reconquest of Spain from the Muslims from 1000 to 1492.

Abd al-Rahman III checked both the new Fatimid power in North Africa and the Christian kingdoms in northern Spain, making possible a golden era of Moorish power and culture. But after his death, his realm broke up into warring Muslim principalities. This made them vulnerable to attack by Spain's Christian states. Between 1000 and 1085, when Christians took the key city of Toledo, these states won control of the northern half of the Iberian peninsula.

Brief Islamic revivals in Spain and North Africa were sparked by religious reform movements led by the Almoravids and Almohads. The Almoravids originated as a religious-warrior brotherhood among Berber nomads in West Africa. In 1086, they carried their zealotry into Spain and reunited its Islamic kingdoms. Under their rule, arabized Christians (Mozarabs) were persecuted, as were some Moorish Jews. The subsequent wars began the last major phase of the Spanish "Reconquest" (*Reconquista*) in which Christian rulers sought to regain and Christianize the peninsula.

The Almohads ended Almoravid rule in Morocco in 1147 and then conquered much of southern Spain. Before their demise (1225 in Spain; 1275 in Africa), they stimulated a brilliant revival of Moorish culture. During this era, paper manufacture reached Spain and then the rest of western Europe. Fables originating in India also completed a long westward journey at this time and were circulated in Spanish and Latin translations. The greatest of Spain's Islamic intellectuals were the philosopher and physician, Ibn Rushd (Averroës, d. 1198); the Muslim mystical thinker, Ibn al-Arabi (d. 1240); and the Arab-Jewish philosopher, Ibn Maymun, or Maimonides (d. 1204).

THE ISLAMIC WEST: EGYPT AND THE EASTERN MEDITERRANEAN WORLD

The Fatimids The Shi'ite Fatimids were the strongest Islamic power in the Mediterranean region from the 10th to the 12th century. Their name advertized their claim to descent from Muhammad's daughter, Fatima. They began as a Tunisian dynasty, then conquered Morocco, Sicily, and Egypt (969). They founded a new city in Egypt to serve as their capital, Cairo (*al-Qahira*, "the Victorious"). It was located near the first garrison town that the early Muslims had established when they occupied Egypt. Because the Fatimids assumed the title of caliph, for a time there were three "caliphates"—headquartered in Baghdad, Córdoba, and Cairo. The Fatimids were Isma'ilis (see above). They won the allegiance of a Yemeni Shi'ite state and were able, for a time, to take western Arabia and most of Syria.

Fatimid rule spawned two splinter groups. The Druze of modern Lebanon and Syria originated around 1020. They were founded by members of the Fatimid court who professed belief in the divinity of one of the Fatimid caliphs. Their beliefs range too far from Islam for them to be considered a

Muslim sect. The Isma'ili Assassins, on the other hand, were a radical Muslim movement founded in Iran by a Fatimid defector around 1100. The name "Assassins" comes not from the political assassinations that made them infamous but from the Arabic *Hashishiyyin* ("users of hashish"). It was possibly connected with the story that drugs were used to induce their assassins to undertake suicidal missions. The Assassins were destroyed by the Mongols in the 13th century.

Fatimid rulers treated Egypt's Coptic Christians and Jews generally as well as they did their Sunni majority. Many Copts held high offices. After 1100 the Fatimids weakened, falling in 1171 to Salah al-Din (Saladin, 1137–1193), a general serving the Turkish ruler of Syria, Nur al-Din (1118–1174). After Nur al-Din's death, Saladin, a Sunni Kurd, struck out on his own. He added Syria-Palestine and Mesopotamia to his Egyptian dominions and founded the Ayyubid dynasty. It controlled these areas until 1250, when Egypt fell to the Mamluks, and 1260, when the Mongols overran most of Syria and Mesopotamia.

Like Nur al-Din, and on the model of the Seljuks (see Chapter 11), Saladin founded madrasas to teach and promote Sunni law. A self-conscious Sunnism entrenched itself in Egypt under his dynasty, and Shi'ite Islam disappeared.

The Mamluks   The heirs of the Fatimids and Saladin in the eastern Mediterranean were the redoubtable sultans of the Mamluk dynasty. The Mamluks were the only Islamic dynasty to withstand the Mongol invasions. Their victory at Ain Jalut in Palestine in 1260 halted the Mongols' westward movement. The first Mamluk **sultan**, Aybak (r. 1250–1257), and his successors were elite Turkish and Mongol slave officers. Whereas the early Mamluk sultans passed down their office within their families, after the 1390s succession was vigorously contested. No sultan reigned more than a few years. The Mamluk state consisted of military fiefs and was totally controlled by its slave-officer elite.

The Mamluk sultan Baybars (r. 1260–1277), who took the last Crusader fortresses, is a larger-than-life figure in Arab legend. To legitimize his rule, he installed an uncle of Baghdad's last Abbasid caliph as caliph at Cairo. This, nominally at least, revived the Abbasid caliphate after its extinction by the Mongols who sacked Baghdad in 1258 (discussed later). He extended Mamluk rule south to Nubia and west among the Berbers.

As trade relations with the Mongol domains improved after 1300, the Mamluks enjoyed prosperity. At their zenith, they commanded an empire worthy of the early Abbasids or the later Ottomans. The prosperity and peace of the reign of Ibn Qala'un (1310–1340) marked the heyday of Mamluk rule. The Black Death epidemic of 1347–1348 in the Arab Middle East hurt the Mamluk and other regional states. However, the Mamluks survived this and even the Ottoman conquest of Egypt in 1517. Mamluks continued to rule Egypt as Ottoman governors into the 19th century.

Architecture, especially from the reigns of Baybars and al-Nasir (r. 1293–1340), much of which still graces Cairo, is the most magnificent Mamluk bequest to posterity. Mosaics, calligraphy, and metalwork from their era

Military Banner. Made in southern Spain in the early 13th century, the banner of Las Navas de Tolosa, of silk tapestry with gold parchment (3.3 × 2.2 m), reflects the emphasis on architectural designs that emerged at this time among Spanish weavers. The central section of the banner, bordered with Qur'anic inscriptions, resembles a Spanish courtyard garden. The banner was captured in battle by Christians not long after it was made.

Banner of Las Navas de Tolosa, from southern Spain. First half of 13th century. Silk tapestry-weave w/gilt parchment, 10'9 7/8" × 7'2 5/8" (3.3 × 2.2 m) Museo de Telas Medievales, Monasterio de Santa Maria la Real de Las Huelgas, Burgos, Spain. Patrimonio Nacional. Arxiu Mas.

sultan Muslim royal title that means "authority."

Mamluk Trade. Trade in spices and other precious commodities between the Mamuluks and western Europe was of great importance. In this painting from about 1500 we see Venetian ambassadors being received by the governor of Damascus, who sits on a low platform and wears a distinctively-shaped turban.

Erich Lessing/Art Resource, N.Y.

are also worthy of note. The Mamluks were great patrons of scholars as well as artists. The most important of these was Ibn Khaldun (d. 1406), a great social historian and philosopher (see "Ibn Khaldun 'The Muqaddimah'").

THE ISLAMIC EAST: BEFORE THE MONGOL CONQUESTS

The Iranian dynasties of the Samanids at Bukhara (875–999) and the Buyids at Baghdad (945–1055) were the major usurpers of the eastern Abbasid dominions. Their successes epitomized the rise of regional states that had begun to undermine the caliphate by the ninth century. Their demises reflected a second pattern: the ascendancy of Turkish slave-rulers (like the Mamluks in the west) and of Oghuz Turkish peoples (called Turkomans). With the Seljuks (successors of the Buyids), the process begun by the use of Turkish slave troops in ninth-century Baghdad ended with the establishment in the Islamic world of Turkish ruling dynasties. As is typical of late converts, they became the most zealous of Sunni Muslims.

The Ghaznavids The rule of the Samanids in Transoxiana was ended by a Turkoman group in 999. Previously, by 994, the Samanids had lost all of eastern Iran south of the Oxus to one of their slave governors, Subuktigin (r. 976–997). He set up his own state in modern Afghanistan, at Ghazna, whence he and his son and successor, Mahmud of Ghazna (r. 998–1030), launched campaigns against his former masters. The Ghaznavids are notable for their patronage of Persian culture and for their conquests in northwestern India, which established a lasting Muslim presence in India. Mahmud was their greatest ruler. His empire stretched from western Iran to the Oxus and the Indus.

HISTORY'S VOICES

IBN KHALDUN "THE MUQADDIMAH"

bd al-Rahman Ibn Khaldun (1336–1406) of
Tunisia was a brilliant thinker who has sometimes been called the first modern social scientist. He studied and held important positions
in Granada, Cairo, and Fez. His most famous work, the
Muqaddima, or Introduction to Universal History, was a
major intellectual contribution. In this text, a portion of
which follows, he presented his philosophy of history. Like
many Roman and Greek historians before him, he considered
history to be cyclical. He considered culture, geography, climate, and economic trends to be the major forces behind historical changes. In the following chapter, Ibn Khaldun
examines how dynasties rise and fall.

WHAT MAKES Ibn Khaldun a "modern" thinker?
Does this description seem applicable today?

We have stated that the life of a dynasty does not as a
rule extend beyond three generations. The first generation retains the desert qualities, desert toughness,
and desert savagery. (Its members are used to) privation and to sharing their glory (with each other); they
are brave and rapacious. Therefore, the strength of
group feeling continues to be preserved among
them. They are sharp and greatly feared. People submit to them.

Under the influence of royal authority and a life
of ease, the second generation changes from the
desert attitude to sedentary culture, from privation
to luxury and plenty, from a state in which every-
body shared in the glory to one in which one man
claims all the glory for himself while the others are
too lazy to strive for glory, and from proud superiority to humble subservience. Thus, the vigour of
group feeling is broken to some extent. People
become used to lowliness and obedience. But many
of the old virtues remain in them, because they
had had direct personal contact with the first generation and its conditions, and had observed with
their own eyes its prowess and striving for glory and

its intention to protect and defend (itself). They
cannot give all of it up at once, although a good
deal of it may go. They live in hope that the conditions that existed in the first generation may come
back, or they live under the illusion that those conditions still exist.

The third generation, then, has (completely) forgotten the period of desert life and toughness, as if it
had never existed. They have lost (the taste for) the
sweetness of fame and for group feeling, because they
are dominated by force. Luxury reaches its peak
among them, because they are so much given to a life
of prosperity and ease. They become dependent on
the dynasty and are like women and children who
need to be defended. Group feeling disappears completely. People forget to protect and defend themselves and to press their claims. With their emblems,
apparel, horseback-riding, and (fighting) skill, they
deceive people and give them the wrong impression.
For the most part, they are more cowardly than
women upon their backs. When someone comes and
demands something from them, they cannot repel
him. The ruler, then, has need of other, brave people
to support him. He takes many clients and followers.
They help the dynasty to some degree, until God permits it to be destroyed, and it goes with everything it
stands for.

As one can see, we have there three generations. In the course of these three generations, the
dynasty grows senile and is worn out. Therefore, it is
in the fourth generation that (ancestral) prestige is
destroyed. . . .

In this way, the life span of a dynasty corresponds
to the life span of an individual; it grows up and
passes into an age of stagnation and thence into retro-
gression. Therefore, people commonly say that the
life span of a dynasty is one hundred years. . . .

Source: Ibn Khaldun, *The Muqaddimah: An Introduction to History*,
ed. N.J. Dawood, trans. Franz Rosenthal (Princeton NJ: Princeton
University Press, 1967) pp. 137–138.

11.5
William of Rubrick:
Impressions of the
Medieval Mongols

Mamluk Bottle This elegant glass bottle was made in Mamluk workshops in Syria in the mid–14th century for the rulers of the Yemen in southern Arabia.

John Tsantes/Courtesy of the Freer Gallery of Art, Smithsonian Institution, Washington, D.C.

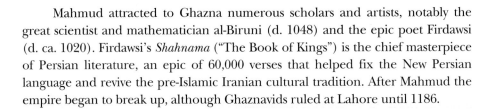

Mahmud attracted to Ghazna numerous scholars and artists, notably the great scientist and mathematician al-Biruni (d. 1048) and the epic poet Firdawsi (d. ca. 1020). Firdawsi's *Shahnama* ("The Book of Kings") is the chief masterpiece of Persian literature, an epic of 60,000 verses that helped fix the New Persian language and revive the pre-Islamic Iranian cultural tradition. After Mahmud the empire began to break up, although Ghaznavids ruled at Lahore until 1186.

The Seljuks The Seljuks, a steppe clan who became avid Sunnis, were the first major Turkish dynasty of Islam. In 1055 they took Baghdad. As the new guardian of the caliphate and master of an Islamic empire, the Seljuk leader Tughril Beg (r. 1037–1063) took the title of *sultan* ("authority") to signify his power. He was invested by the caliph as "king of east and west."

As new Turkish tribes joined their ranks, the Seljuks extended Islamic rule into the central Anatolian plateau at Byzantine expense, even capturing the Byzantine emperor in 1071. They also conquered much of Syria and wrested Mecca and Medina from the Shi'ite Fatimids. Turkish rule in Anatolia dates from 1077, when the Seljuk governor there formed a sultanate. Known as the Seljuks of Rum ("Rome," i.e., Byzantium), these Seljuks were displaced after 1300 by the Ottomans (see Chapter 21).

The most notable figure of Seljuk rule was the vizier Nizam al-Mulk from 1063 to 1092. In his time, new roads and inns (caravanserais) for trade and pilgrimage were built, canals were dug, mosques and other public buildings were founded, and science and culture were patronized. He appointed as professor in his Baghdad madrasa Muhammad al-Ghazzali (d. 1111), probably the greatest of Muslim religious thinkers. He also patronized the mathematician and astronomer Umar Khayyam (d. 1123), whose Western fame rests on the poetry of his "Quatrains," or *Ruba'iyat*.

By 1194, Iranian Seljuk rule was erased by another Turkish slave dynasty from Khwarizm in the lower Oxus basin. By 1200, these Khwarizm Shahs had built a large but shaky empire covering Iran and Transoxiana. In the same era, the Abbasid caliph at Baghdad, al-Nasir (r. 1180–1225), established an independent caliphal state in Iraq. But neither his heirs nor the Khwarizm Shahs survived for long.

THE ISLAMIC EAST: THE MONGOL AGE

Mongols and Ilkhanids The building of a vast Mongol empire (see Chapter 8) proved momentous for Islamic Eurasia and India. The Great Khan, Genghis (ca. 1162–1227) plundered mercilessly (1219–1222) from Transoxiana and Khorasan to the Indus, razing entire cities. After his death, a division of his empire into four khanates under his four sons gave the Islamic world a respite. Then in 1255 Hulagu Khan (r. 1256–1265), a grandson of Genghis, again led a massive army across the Oxus. He went from victory to victory, destroying every Iranian state. In 1258, Hulagu's troops smashed Baghdad's defenses and plundered the city, killing at least 80,000 inhabitants, including the caliph and his sons.

At the urging of his wife and of Nestorian Christians and Buddhists in his inner circle, Hulagu spared the Christians of Baghdad and followed this policy in his other conquests. When Damascus surrendered, Western Christians hoped (in vain, as it turned out) that Mamluk Cairo and Islamic power would collapse. But Hulagu's drive west was slowed by

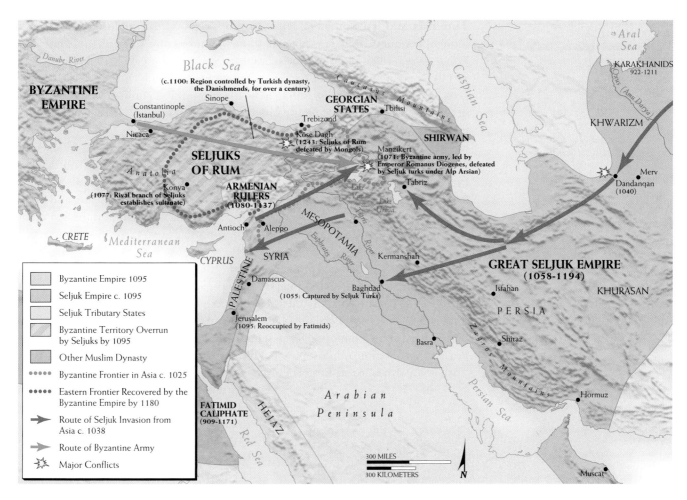

MAP 13–2

The Seljuk Empire, ca. 1095.   By the end of the 11th century, the Seljuks had conquered Persia, Mesopotamia, and Syria, and had inflicted a devasting blow against the Byzantine Empire at the battle of Manzikert in 1071, altering the balance of power in the eastern Mediterranean and the Near East.

HOW DO the Seljuk conquests reveal the power of steppe peoples to overturn settled societies?

rivalry with his kinsman Berke. A Muslim convert, Berke ruled the khanate of the Golden Horde, the Mongol state centered in southern Russia. He was in contact with the Mamluks, and some of his Mongol troops even fought with them when they won a victory over Hulagu in Palestine (1260), which prevented his advance into Egypt. A treaty in 1261 between the Mamluk sultan and Berke established a formal alliance that confirmed the breakup of Mongol unity and the autonomy of the four khanates: in China (the Yuan dynasty), in Iran (the Ilkhans), in Russia (the Golden Horde), and in Transoxiana (the Chagatays).

Hulagu pledged allegiance to the new Great Khan of China, and he and his heirs ruled the old Persian Empire from Azerbaijan for some 75 years as the Great Khan's viceroys (or *Il-Khans*; the title from which Hulagu's line takes its name *Ilkhanid*). Here, as elsewhere, the Mongols did not eradicate the society they inherited. Instead, both their native paganism and their Buddhist and Christian leanings yielded to Muslim faith and practice. Religious tolerance, however, remained the norm under their rule. After 1335, Ilkhanid rule fell prey to the familiar pattern of a gradual breaking away of provinces, and for 50 years, Iran was again fragmented.

Genghis Khan.

The Granger Collection, N.Y.

HOW DID Islam become an enduring part of Indian civilization?

Tamerlane's Army. A miniature painting of the Army of Tamerlane storming the walls of the Rajput city of Bhatnair in 1398. Bhatnair was one of the many North Indian cities and fortresses that fell to the relentless onslaught of Tamerlane's armies.

Art Resource/Bildarchiv Preussischer Kulturbesitz.

Timurids and Turkomans This situation prepared the way for a new Turko-Mongol conquest from Transoxiana, under Timur-i Lang ("Timur the Lame," or "Tamerlane," 1336–1405). Timur's savage campaigns, between 1379 and his death in 1405, were aimed at sheer conquest. Timur was a Muslim convert who evidently possessed a strong sense of a calling to be the protector of commerce and punisher of the injustices of regional petty tyrants and extremist groups. His means were brutal. His campaign spread a wave of devastation through eastern Iran (1379–1385); western Iran, Armenia, the Caucasus, and upper Mesopotamia (1385–1387); southwestern Iran, Mesopotamia, and Syria (1391–1393); Central Asia from Transoxiana to the Volga and as far as Moscow (1391–1395); North India (1398); and northern Syria and Anatolia (1400–1402). In his wake he left ruins, death, disease, and political chaos across the entire eastern Islamic world. His was, however, the last great steppe invasion, for firearms soon ended the advantage that the steppe's horsemen had long enjoyed.

Timur's sons, the Timurids, ruled after him with varying results in Transoxiana and Iran (1405–1494). The most successful of them was Shahrukh (r. 1405–1447), who ruled a united Iran for a time. His capital, Herat, became an important center of Persian Islamic culture and Sunni piety. He provided patronage for the famous Herat school of miniature painting as well as for Persian authors and philosophers. The Timurids had to share Iran itself with Turkoman dynasties in western Iran, once even losing Herat to one of them. They and the Turkomans were the last Sunnis to rule Iran. Both were eclipsed at the end of the 15th century by the militant Shi'ite dynasty of the Safavids, who ushered in a new, Shi'ite era in the Iranian world (see Chapter 21).

THE SPREAD OF ISLAM BEYOND THE HEARTLANDS

The period from roughly 1000 to 1500 saw the spread of Islam as a lasting religious, cultural, and political force into new areas. India, Malaysia, and Indonesia became major spheres of Islamic political or commercial power even though large numbers, often the majority, of their inhabitants continued the practice of their traditional religions.

Islamic civilization in India was formed by creative interaction between invading foreigners and indigenous peoples. The early Arab and Turkish invaders were a foreign Muslim minority, but their heirs became truly "Indian" as well as Muslim. From then on, Indian civilization both included and enriched Islamic traditions.

INDIA AND SOUTHEAST ASIA

The port cities of Gujarat and southern India attracted Muslim merchants who hoped to profit from internal Indian trade as well as from trade with the Indies and China (see Map 13–2). Wherever Muslim traders went, converts to Islam followed. Sufi orders also drew converts.

India

ca. 900–1300	Chola dynasty in southern India
1137	Death of Ramanuja
1206–1290	Slave Sultans of Delhi
1290–1320	Khalji sultans of Delhi
1320–1413	Tughluqid sultans of Delhi
1414–1526	Sayyid sultans of Delhi
1336–1565	Hindu dynasty of Vijayanagar
1347–1527	Muslim Bahmanid dynasty in the Deccan
1398	Timur's sack of Delhi

MUSLIM-HINDU ENCOUNTER

From the outset, Muslim leaders faced the problem of ruling a country dominated by utterly different cultural and religious traditions. The first Arab conquerors in Sind (711) had treated Hindus as "protected peoples" under Muslim sovereignty. These precedents gave later Indian Muslim rulers a legal basis for coexistence with their Hindu subjects, but they did not eliminate Hindu resistance to Muslim rule.

The chief obstacle to Islamic expansion in India was the military prowess of the Hindu warrior class, known from about the mid-seventh century as *Rajputs*. The Rajputs were a large group of clans bound together by a fierce warrior ethic and strong Hindu cultural and religious traditionalism. They fought the Muslims with tenacity, but their inability to form a common front against their enemy resulted, in the 16th century, in their dominance by the Muslims (see Chapter 21).

The Qutub Minar (Victory Tower) in Delhi in India is an example of classic Indo-Muslim art and architecture. Constructed in the 12th century, this soaring tower made from red sandstone commemorated a decisive Muslim military victory.

Getty Images, Inc.-Taxi.

ISLAMIC STATES AND DYNASTIES

After the Ghaznavids and a brief period of Afghan rule, Turkish-Afghan rulers (the "Slave Sultans of Delhi") extended Islamic power over North India (1206–1290). Four later Muslim dynasties—the Khaljis, Tughluqs, Sayyids, and Lodis—continued the Delhi sultanate through the 15th century. Their reigns were interrupted by several years of chaos following the Mongol-Turkish invasion and Timur's sack of Delhi in 1398, from which the city took decades to recover. Throughout its history the Delhi sultanate's authority over its provincial governors fluctuated, even in the heart of North India. Before the advent of the Mughals in the mid-16th century, many regions split off from the sultanate and became independent. Regional rule predominated across the subcontinent.

MAP EXPLORATION

Interactive map: To explore this map further, go to **http://www.prenhall.com/craig/map13.3**

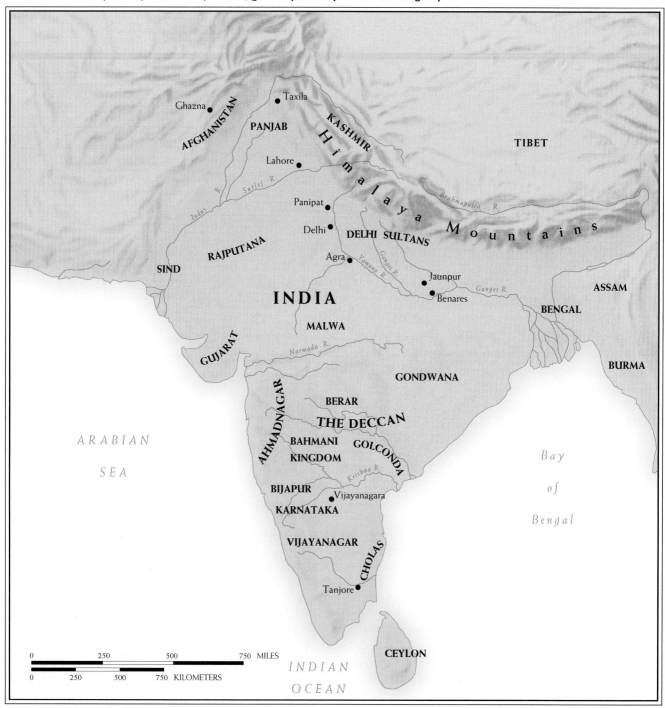

MAP 13–3

The Indian Subcontinent, 1000–1500.   Shown are major kingdoms and regions.

WHERE IN India were the principle Islamic states located during this period?

OVERVIEW   MAJOR ISLAMIC DYNASTIES, 1000–1500

The years between 1000 and 1500 were marked by political fragmentation in the Islamic world. While the Muslims eventually defeated the Crusader states in Palestine and Syria, in Spain the Christians gradually conquered every Islamic state. The Mongol invasions of the mid-13th century and the campaigns of Timur-i Lang in the 14th century devastated much of the eastern Islamic world. Yet, despite these reverses and the rise and fall of dynasties, Islamic civilization endured, and the Muslim faith spread to new areas in Africa, India, and East Asia.

Dynasty	Location
Umayyads	Spain
Almoravids	West Africa, North Africa, Spain
Almohads	Morocco, Spain
Fatimids	Tunisia, Egypt
Ayyubids	Egypt, Syria
Mamluks	Egypt, Syria
Samanids	Transoxiana
Buyids	Iraq
Seljuks	Anatolia, Iraq
Abbasids	Iraq
Ghaznavids	Transoxiana, Pakistan
Khwarzims	Iran
Ilkhanids	Iran
Timurids	Transoxiana, Iran
Delhi Sultans	Northern India
Bahmanids	Deccan

SOUTHEAST ASIA

The most important independent Islamic state was that of the Bahmanids in the Deccan (1347–1527). Bahmanid rulers were famous for their architecture and the intellectual life of their court, as well as for their role in containing the powerful South Indian Hindu state of Vijayanagar (1336–1565). Most regional capitals boasted rich cultures. After Timur's sack of Delhi in 1398, its artists and intellectuals found refuge in Jaunpur, which developed an impressive tradition of Islamic architecture. Many Indian texts were translated into Persian in the Kashmir, which, from 1346 to 1589, was an independent sultanate.

Geographically, the islands in Southeast Asia linked India and China, and by the 15th century they had developed as an important trade route. Islam's

HOW DID local traditions influence the spread of Islam in Southeast Asia?

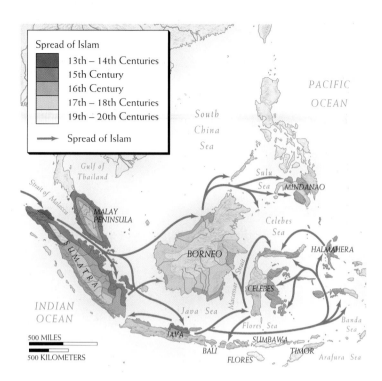

MAP 13–4
The Spread of Islam in Southeast Asia.

WHAT WERE the main reasons for the spread of Islam in Southeast Asia?

spread in the region was, however, not steady and progressive, but idiosyncratic. The result was the emergence of a number of distinct Islamic traditions clustering in five areas: Java, Samudra, Melaka, Acheh, and Moluccas (see Map 13–3). In some places Islam coexisted with worship of ancestors, sorcery, and magic. Some significant Islamic rites (the *hajj*, for example) were viewed as Arab customs and, therefore, not regarded as integral to the true practice of the faith for all Muslims. Islam's support for centralization and consolidation of power, however, encouraged many political leaders to adopt a more stringent version of Islam.

Major tensions in the region derived not from religion but from a struggle between the coastal districts and the interior. Urban (mostly port) rulers, who profited most from the era's growing trade, tried to assert their authority over hereditary chiefs of rural areas. They invoked Islam's vision of a perfect society to justify this, but local traditions proved durable. Muslims in Southeast Asia adapted Islam to their needs and customs rather than substituting it for their indigenous practices.

HOW DID India accomodate Hinduism and Islam?

RELIGIOUS AND CULTURAL ACCOMMODATION

Despite the enduring division of the subcontinent into multiple and diverse units, the five centuries after Mahmud of Ghazna's (r. 998–1030) planting of Islam in India saw the faith become an enduring, influential, and transregional, if still minority, element in Indian culture. Its greatest strength was in the north and in the Deccan. The Delhi sultans provided a basic political and social framework within which Islam could take root. Although the ruling class remained a Muslim minority of Persianized Turks and Afghans governing a Hindu majority, converts were to be found at various levels of society.

Ghazis ("warriors") spread Islam by force of arms to pagan groups in eastern Bengal and Assam. More significantly, Sufi orders converted numerous Hindus among the lower classes across the North. The Muslim aristocracy was usually treated in Indian society as a separate caste group or groups. When lower class or other Hindus converted, they were assimilated into lower "Muslim castes," often identified by occupation.

Sanskrit had long been the Indian scholarly language and lingua franca, but in this period regional languages, such as Tamil in the south, gained status, and Persian became the language of intellectual and cultural life for the ruling elites of North India. However, a new language with both Perso-Arabic and indigenous Indian elements, **Urdu-Hindi**, grew in popularity until it gained wide

ghazis Warriors who carried Islam by force of arms to pagan groups.

Urdu-Hindi Language that combines Persian-Arabic and native Indian elements. Urdu is the Muslim version of the language; Hindi is the Hindu version.

use in the subcontinent by modern times. It began to take shape not long after the initial Muslim influx in the 11th century and developed in response to the increasing need of Hindus and Muslims for a shared medium of communication. The name *Urdu* designated the Muslim version that continued to draw on its Perso-Arabic heritage, whereas Hindi ("Indian") was used for the version associated with Hindu culture and Sanskritic heritage. Each would later become an official national language: Urdu for modern Pakistan and Hindi for modern India.

Indian Muslims were always susceptible to Hindu influence (in language, marriage customs, and caste consciousness), but they were never completely absorbed into Hindu culture. Consciousness of their uniqueness in the Hindu world made them proud of their distinctness. Nevertheless, Muslims and Hindus inevitably influenced one another, especially in popular piety. Sufi devotion had an appeal similar to that of Hindu devotional, or **bhakti**, movements (see Chapter 10), and each influenced the other. Various theistic mystics preached devotion to a God who saves His worshipers without regard either to Hindu caste obligations or to the legalistic observance of Muslim orthopraxy. The poet-saints Ramananda (d. after 1400) and Kabir (d. ca. 1518) were the two most famous such reformers.

bhakti Hindu devotional movements.

HINDU AND OTHER INDIAN TRADITIONS

The Jain tradition continued to flourish, but in the north by the 11th century the Muslim conquests had effectively ended India's Buddhist monastic and lay traditions. Buddhism was already waning long before Islam came to India, and the coming of Islam either dealt it a death blow or coincided with its reduction to small-minority status.

Hindu religion and culture continued to flourish, even under Muslim control. *Bhakti* was especially creative. The great Hindu Vaishnava Brahman, Ramanuja (d. 1137), provided a theological basis for bhakti, reconciling its ideas with the classical Upanishadic Hindu worldview in the Vedantin tradition. Important examples of bhakti movements are the Shaivite and Vaishnavite traditions. Bhakti piety underlies the masterpiece of Hindu mystical love poetry, Jayadeva's *Gita Govinda* (12th century), which is devoted to Krishna, the most important of Vishnu's incarnations.

The south continued to be the center of Hindu cultural, political, and religious activity. Of several important dynastic states in the south during this age, the foremost was that of the Cholas, which flourished from about 900–1300. Their mightiest successor, the kingdom of Vijayanagar (1336–1565), subjugated the entire south in the 14th century and resisted its Muslim foes longer than any other kingdom. Vijayanagar itself was one of India's most lavishly developed cities and a center of the cult of Shiva.

SUMMARY

Religion   Between 1000 and 1500, the most important developments for shaping of Islamic society were of Sunni and Shi'ite legal and religious norms and of Sufi traditions and personal piety. Sunnism was the dominant tradition across the Islamic world, but in both main branches of Islam, the ulama joined the religious, social, and political elites and discouraged religious innovation.

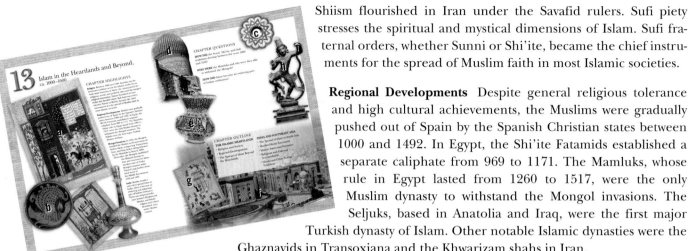

Shiism flourished in Iran under the Savafid rulers. Sufi piety stresses the spiritual and mystical dimensions of Islam. Sufi fraternal orders, whether Sunni or Shi'ite, became the chief instruments for the spread of Muslim faith in most Islamic societies.

Regional Developments Despite general religious tolerance and high cultural achievements, the Muslims were gradually pushed out of Spain by the Spanish Christian states between 1000 and 1492. In Egypt, the Shi'ite Fatamids established a separate caliphate from 969 to 1171. The Mamluks, whose rule in Egypt lasted from 1260 to 1517, were the only Muslim dynasty to withstand the Mongol invasions. The Seljuks, based in Anatolia and Iraq, were the first major Turkish dynasty of Islam. Other notable Islamic dynasties were the Ghaznavids in Transoxiana and the Khwarizam shahs in Iran.

Mongol Invasions In 1255, the Mongols invaded the Muslim world and swept all before them, conquering Transoxiana, Iran, and Iraq, where they captured Baghdad and killed the last Abbasid caliph in 1258, before being defeated by the Mamluks in Syria in 1260. Thereafter, the Mongols established the Ilkhanid dynasty in Iran and converted to Islam. Another wave of Turko-Mongol conquest under Timur-I Lang further devastated much of the Middle East between 1379 and 1405.

India Muslim invaders and rulers spread Islam in India, where it became an enduring and influential part of Indian civilization. There was reciprocal influence between Muslims and Hindus, and a new language, Urdu-Hindi, combined Persian-Arabic and indigenous Indian elements. Buddhism all but disappeared from India during these years, but Hindu religion and culture flourished, even under Muslim control. Hindu devotional, or Bhakti, movements were especially creative.

IMAGE KEY

for pages 288–289

a. Folio from a manuscript of "Khusraw and Shirin" by Nizami.

b. Bowl. Iran, late 12th century

c. Mosaic from the Alhambra Palace, Granada, Spain

d. The Sultan Hasan Madrasa and tomb-mosque

e. A mamluk lamp covered in arabic

f. The Gur-i-mir, the tomb of Timur in Samarkand

g. A picture from a Hebrew Haggada, Spain, fourteenth century

h. South Indian bronze figure of Krishna

REVIEW QUESTIONS

1. In the period 1000–1500, why did no Muslim leader build a large-scale Islamic empire of the extent of the early Abbasids?

2. Who were the ulama? What was their relationship to political leadership? What social roles did they play?

3. How did Córdoba become a model of civilized culture?

4. Why was Islam able to survive the invasions by steppe peoples from 945 on? What were the lasting results of these "invasions" for the Islamic world?

5. How did Islam affect India? What happened to Islam as it spread through Southeast Asia?

KEY TERMS

bhakti (p. 305)
ghazis (p. 304)
madrasa (p. 291)

orthopraxy (p. 292)
Ramadan (p. 292)
Reconquista (p. 294)

Sufi (p. 292)
sultan (p. 295)
Urdu-Hindi (p. 304)

  For additional study resources for this chapter, go to:
www.prenhall.com/craig/chapter13

Visualizing The Past

The Divine in the Middle Ages

HOW DID artists of different religions depict the divine? How did their differing conceptions of the divine, and rules within religions about how and whether, the divine should be depicted, shape religious art?

The Middle Ages (500 C.E.–1300 C.E.) witnessed the creation of a new world religion, Islam, and the expansion and consolidation of others, including Christianity, Buddhism, and Hinduism. Each of these religions fostered forms of religious art suited to its conception of the divine. Religious and secular leaders alike commissioned the art as objects or focuses of worship, teaching tools, and decorations. Secular leaders enhanced their status by associating themselves with the divine through patronage of religious art.

Hinduism. "Standing Parvati," India, Chola Period (880–1279), circa first quarter of the 10th century. This statue of the Hindu goddess Parvati hails from the Chola-ruled region of South India. Chola art, known for its exceptional grace and beauty, influenced Hindu art throughout south Asia. Hinduism is the only major polytheistic world religion of the medieval period and it also was the only one to retain female as well as male gods.

Indian, Tamil Nadu, Standing Parvati, Chola period (ca. 860–1279), ca. first quarter of 10th century, Copper alloy. H. 27 3/8 in. (69.5 cm). "The Metropolitan Museum of Art, Bequest of Cora Timken Burnett, 1956. (57.5.3). Photograph by Bruce White. © 1994 The Metropolitan Museum of Art."

▼

▲

Islam. This is a page from a vellum medieval Koran with a rosette in the margin, by the medieval Islamic School. Islam follows the Jewish tradition in prohibiting images of God (Allah). Because Islam also prohibits depicting the human form (although some Islamic artists did produce images of people and animals), as this picture shows, Islamic art tended to be highly abstract, and Islamic writing itself became an art form of great beauty and refinement.

Page from the Koran with a rosette in the margin by Islamic School Musee Conde, Chantilly, France, France/Bridgeman Art Library.

◀**Christianity.** This cloisonné and gold medallion crafted by Georgian artisans for a Byzantine icon frame, circa 1100 C.E., shows Jesus Christ, his divinity communicated by his halo, and his wisdom as a human teacher by the book he carries. By the Middle Ages, the Byzantine world had produced many icons, and the defeat of the iconoclasts, who opposed the creation of religious images for fear that ordinary people would worship them, in the ninth century ensured that religious art replete with images of God, Jesus, and the saints would dominate medieval Christian art throughout Europe.

Giraudon/Art Resource, N.Y.

Buddhism. This seated porcelain *bodhisattva* from the Chinese ▶ Yuan dynasty (1279–1368) symbolizes the spirituality of medieval Mahayana Buddhism. Siddhartha Gautama (563–483 B.C.E.) was a wealthy nobleman from India whose search for enlightenment led him to found a new religion, the goal of which was not salvation but, rather, attainment of *nirvana*. By the medieval period, however, some Buddhist theologians had begun to worship the Buddha as divine, and also had developed the concept of bodhisattvas, enlightened individuals who, like Christian saints, spent the afterlife assisting humans to reach nirvana, and also served as role models of spiritual excellence for the living.

Thierry Ollivier/Art Resource, N.Y.

14 Ancient Civilizations of the Americas

CHAPTER HIGHLIGHTS

Mesoamerica Although there was no single Mesoamerican civilization, the civilizations of the Olmecs, the people of Monte Alban and Teotihuacan, the Maya, the Toltecs, and the Aztecs shared many features: urban centers with monumental buildings arranged around large plazas, writing, a sophisticated calendrical system, religions that included human sacrifice, and the cultivation of certain crops, especially maize and beans.

The Aztecs established the largest Mesoamerican state before the coming of the Spanish in the sixteenth century. The Aztec Empire depended on tribute from conquered peoples. It was a society organized for war. Women could own property and participate in trade, but were subordinate to men and excluded from high authority.

Andean South America Monumental architecture and public buildings in Peru date from the third millenium B.C.E. Over the next 3,000 years, the Andean peoples developed pottery, urban centers, intricate cotton weaving, and sophisticated agriculture.

The Incas built the most extensive Andean empire. It spanned 2,600 miles from Ecuador to Chile between the Pacific and the Amazon basin, with over 14,000 miles of roads and numerous rope bridges. Although the Inca lacked writing, they kept detailed accounts using a system of knotted strings.

CHAPTER QUESTIONS

WHAT PROBLEMS do scholars face in reconstructing the history of native American civilization?

WHAT GROUPS dominated Olmec society?

WHAT WERE some of the main achievements of the Classic period civilizations in Mesoamerica?

WHAT ROLE did human sacrifice play in the Aztec Empire?

WHEN DID Andean people first become dependent on agriculture?

HOW DID the Inca enlarge and organize their empire?

CHAPTER OUTLINE

Humans first settled the American continents between 12,000 and 40,000 years ago. At that time, glaciers locked up much of the world's water, lowering the sea level and opening a bridge of dry land between Siberia and Alaska. When the glaciers receded, the oceans rose, severing Asia from America. The inhabitants of the Americas were isolated from the inhabitants of Africa and Eurasia and remained so until 1492.

Although separated from one another, the peoples of the Americas, Africa, and Eurasia experienced similar cultural changes at the end of the Paleolithic period. People in some regions shifted from hunting and gathering to a settled, agricultural way of life. And in some places civilization emerged.

Mesoamerica (modern Mexico and Central America) and the Andean region of South America have histories of civilization reaching back thousands of years. At the time of the European conquest of the Americas in the 16th century, both regions were dominated by powerful empires—the Aztecs, or Mexica, in Mesoamerica and the Inca in the Andes. Spanish conquerors obliterated both empires. But Native American traditions have endured, overlaid, and combined with Hispanic culture to provide clues to the pre-Hispanic past.

WHAT PROBLEMS do scholars face in reconstructing the history of Native American civilization?

RECONSTRUCTING THE HISTORY OF NATIVE AMERICAN CIVILIZATION

Andean civilizations never developed writing, and in Mesoamerica much of the written record was destroyed by time and conquest. Archaeologists have been able to create a picture of the economic and social organization of ancient American civilizations, but archaeology alone cannot produce the kind of narrative history that thousands of years of written records have made possible for Eurasian civilizations. From one ancient Mesoamerican people, however—the Maya—specimens of writing survive, and scholars have deciphered their script and attached names, dates, and events to silent ruins.

We also have information about the history and culture of the Aztecs and Inca that was told to the Spanish in the wake of their conquests of these peoples. But these accounts are colored by the interests and prejudices of the conquerors. Scholars seeking to understand Native American civilization have had to rely on the language and categories of European thought to investigate peoples and culturals that had nothing to do with Europe. Cultural blinders and arrogance exacerbate this situation.

MESOAMERICA

Mesoamerica, which means "middle America," extends from central Mexico into Central America. It also designates a distinctive and enduring cultural tradition that emerged between 1000 and 2000 B.C.E. and manifested itself in a succession of impressive states that flourished prior to the arrival of European conquerors in the 16th century. The peoples of Mesoamerica were and are ethnically and linguistically diverse. There was no single Mesoamerican civilization or linear development of civilization in the region. Nonetheless, Mesoamerican civilizations shared many traits, including writing, a sophisticated calendrical system, religious ideas, a ritual ball game, and urban centers with buildings arranged around large plazas.

Throughout their history, the peoples of the region were linked by trade. Metallurgy came late to Mesoamerica and was used primarily for ceremonial

OVERVIEW   PERIODS OF MESOAMERICAN AND ANDEAN CIVILIZATIONS

Scholars divide the history of the Mesoamerican and Andean peoples into several distict periods.

MESOAMERICA

Period	Civilization
Archaic, 8000–2000 B.C.E.	agricultural villages; maize cultivation
Formative, 2000 B.C.E.–150 C.E.	Olmecs, Monte Alban; urban centers, writing, calendar
Classic, 150–900 C.E.	Maya, Teotihuacán; sophisticated mathematics, astronomy, and calendar
Post-Classic, 900–1521 C.E.	Toltecs, Aztecs

ANDES

Period	Civilization
Preceramic and Initial, ca. 3000–800 B.C.E.	coastal peoples; monumental architecture, pottery
Early Horizon, ca. 800–200 B.C.E.	Chavin; innovations in ceramics, weaving, and metallurgy
Early Intermediate, ca. 200 B.C.E.–600 C.E.	Nazca, Moche; political centralization, monumental earthworks, advanced pottery and metallurgy
Middle Horizon and Late Interemediate, ca. 600 C.E.–1475	Tiwanaku, Huari, Chimu; expansionist empires, sophisticated agriculture
Inca Empire, ca. 1475–1532	extensive network of roads and bridges, sophisticated record keeping, advanced architecture

objects. In place of metal, Mesoamericans made weapons and tools from **obsidian**, a volcanic glass highly valued for its ability to hold a razor-sharp edge.

Mesoamerican history before the Spanish conquest is conventionally divided into four major periods: the Archaic, Formative (Olmecs), Classic (Maya), and Post-Classic (Toltecs and Aztecs). The term "Classic" reflects the view of many early Mesoamericanists that the era during which the Maya civilizations of the southern Yucatán erected dated stone monuments was the high point of Mesoamerican civilization. Although that view is no longer so prevalent, the terminology has endured, and the four periods still provide a useful framework for understanding Mesoamerican history.

During the Archaic period some people in Mesoamerica made the transition from hunting and gathering to settled village life. The key to this development was the domestication of maize (corn) and other staple crops, including beans, squash, tomatoes, chili peppers, and avocado. Maize and beans together provide a superior source of protein to the grains that were the basis of the Neolithic revolution in the Ancient Middle East and China. Eurasians relied to some extent on domesticated animals for protein, but Mesoamerica had few domesticated species—among them dogs and turkeys—and no large herd animals like the cattle, sheep, and goats of the Old World.

Probably because they had no large draft animals, the people of the Americas, including Mesoamerica, utilized the wheel only for toys. In Mesoamerica, humans did the carrying, and armies were composed of foot soldiers.

QUICK REVIEW

Transition to Settled Village Life
- Occurred during Archaic period
- Cornerstone of process was domestication of maize
- Mesoamerica had few domesticated animals

obsidian Hard volcanic glass that was widely used in Mesoamerica.

WHAT GROUPS dominated

Olmec society?

THE FORMATIVE PERIOD AND THE EMERGENCE OF MESOAMERICAN CIVILIZATION

By about 1500 B.C.E., Mesoamerica's agricultural villages were beginning to coalesce into more complicated societies, with towns and monumental architecture, social classes, trade among regions, and sophisticated artistic traditions.

THE OLMEC

The most prominent of the early Formative period cultures is that of the Olmec, centered on the lowlands of Mexico's Gulf Coast. Most of what is known about the Olmecs comes from the archaeological sites of San Lorenzo and La Venta (see Map 14–1). San Lorenzo had developed into a prominent center by about 1200 B.C.E. It included public buildings, a drainage system linked to artificial ponds, and what was probably the earliest court for the unique Mesoamerican ball game. The settlement flourished until about 900 B.C.E., then went into decline and was abandoned by about 400 B.C.E. La Venta thrived during the era in which San Lorenzo faded. Its most conspicuous feature is a 110-foot scalloped pyramid, known as the Great Pyramid, which stands at one end of a group of platforms and plazas aligned along a north–south axis.

Olmec Monument. A large carved monument from the Olmec site of La Venta with a naturalistically rendered human figure.

Robert and Linda Mitchell Photography.

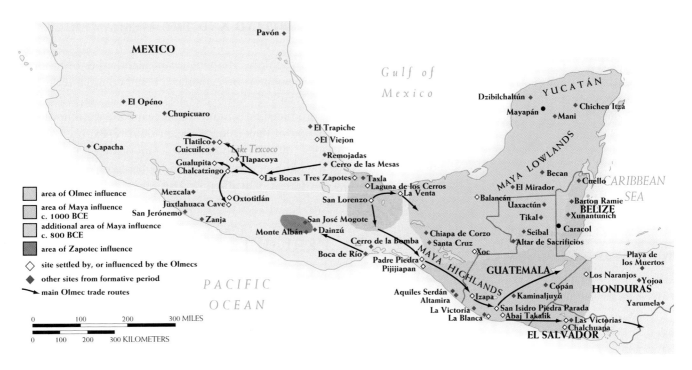

MAP 14–1
Mesoamerica in the Formative Periods.

WHAT ROLE did trade play in the formation of Mesoamerican civilizations?

San Lorenzo and La Venta probably had fewer than 1,000 inhabitants. They were, in all likelihood, a powerful elite who were supported by farmers in outlying villages. The monumental architecture and sculpture at these sites suggests that Olmec society was dominated by a class of ruler-priests who could mobilize large gangs of laborers.

The raw material for many Olmec artifacts, such as jade and obsidian, comes from other regions of Mesoamerica. Likewise, Olmec goods and iconography are found in other regions. This suggests that from an early time, the parts of Mesoamerica were linked in a web of trade. Trade contacts would have contributed to the formation of common Mesoamerican traditions.

THE VALLEY OF OAXACA AND THE RISE OF MONTE ALBAN

Olmec civilization had disappeared by about 200 B.C.E., but by then important developments were taking place elsewhere. Some of the most significant settlements in the Late Formative period were in the Valley of Oaxaca. Around 500 B.C.E., Monte Alban was built on a hill where three branches of the valley meet. Its population grew to about 5,000, and it emerged as the capital of a state that dominated the Oaxaca region. Carved images of bound prisoners imply that warfare played a role in establishing its authority. These images also suggest an early origin for the ritual human sacrifice that characterized most Mesoamerican cultures. Monte Alban maintained its independence against the growing power of the greatest Classic period city, Teotihuacán.

Major Periods in Ancient Mesoamerican Civilization

Archaic	8000–2000 B.C.E.
Formative (or Pre-Classic)	2000 B.C.E.–150 C.E.
Classic	150–900 C.E.
Post-Classic	900–1521 C.E.

WHAT WERE some of the main achievements of the Classic period civilizations in Mesoamerica?

THE EMERGENCE OF WRITING AND THE MESOAMERICAN CALENDAR

The earliest evidence of writing and the Mesoamerican calendar has been found in the Valley of Oaxaca. The Mesoamerican calendar is based on two interlocking cycles. One cycle, tied to the solar year, was of 365 days; the other was of 260 days. Combining the two cycles produced a "century" of 52 years, the amount of time required before a combination of days in each cycle would repeat itself. At the time of the Spanish conquest, all the peoples of Mesoamerica used this 52-year calendrical system. Only the Maya developed a calendar based on a longer time period, anchored—like the Jewish, Christian, or Muslim calendars—to a fixed starting point in the past.

THE CLASSIC PERIOD IN MESOAMERICA

*T*he Classic period was a time of cultural florescence. The Maya, who built densely populated cities in the rain forests of the southern Yucatán, developed a sophisticated system of mathematics and Mesoamerica's most advanced hieroglyphic writing. Indeed, Classic period urban life in Mesoamerica was richer and on a larger scale than in Europe north of the Alps at the same time.

Classic period cities were religious and administrative centers whose rulers combined secular and religious authority. Warfare was common and rulers used force to expand and maintain their power. The ritual sacrifice of captive enemies was a feature of Classic period societies.

TEOTIHUACÁN

In the late Formative period, two centers competed for dominance over the growing population of the Valley of Mexico. One of these, Cuicuilco, was at the southern end of the valley. The other, Teotihuacán, was about 30 miles northeast of Mexico City. When a volcano destroyed Cuicuilco in the first century C.E., Teotihuacán grew into a great city, perhaps Mesoamerica's first true city-state. It dominated central Mexico for centuries and influenced the rest of Mesoamerica.

Natural advantages contributed to Teotihuacán's rise. A network of caves recently discovered under its most prominent monument, the Pyramid of the Sun (the name by which the Aztecs knew it), may have been considered an entrance to the underworld. Stone quarried from the caves was used to construct the city, creating a symbolic link between the city's buildings and its sacred origins. Teotihuacán is also near a source of obsidian, and it straddled a trade route to the Gulf Coast and southern Mesoamerica. The quarrying of obsidian and the manufacture and trade of obsidian goods were apparently major sources of the city's wealth and influence, but it was also surrounded by fertile farmland.

At its height in about 500 C.E., Teotihuacán extended over almost 9 square miles and had a population of more than 150,000, making it, at that time, one of the largest cities in the world. Its size and organization suggest that it was ruled by a powerful, centralized authority. Teotihuacán is laid out on a rigid grid plan dominated by a broad, 3-mile-long thoroughfare known as the Avenue of the Dead. Religious and administrative structures and a market occupy the center of the city. At one end of the Avenue of the Dead is the 210-foot-high Pyramid of the Sun. More than 2,000 residences surround the city center. The lavish homes of the city's elite lie nearest its center. Most residents lived in walled apartment compounds located farther out. In addition to being residences,

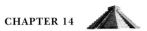

The Pyramid of the Sun. This monumental structure stands near the southern end of Teotihuacán's great central thoroughfare, the Avenue of the Dead.

Kal Muller/Woodfin Camp & Associates.

these compounds housed craft manufacture. Neighborhoods specialized in different products, such as pottery or obsidian work. Parts of the city were reserved for foreign traders. Murals adorned the interiors of many buildings. The humble dwellings of poor farmers occupied the city's periphery. As the city grew, local farmers were forced to move to Teotihuacán, which is another indication of the power of its rulers.

Teotihuacán's influence extended throughout Mesoamerica. In the central highlands, dispersed settlements were consolidated into larger centers laid out similarly to Teotihuacán, suggesting conquest and direct control—a Teotihuacán empire. The city's influence in more distant regions may reflect close trading ties rather than conquest. The city's obsidian and pottery were exchanged widely for items like the green feathers of the quetzal bird and jaguar skins, materials used to make ritual garments.

Many of the buildings in Teotihuacán were decorated with sculptures and murals depicting the city's gods and ritual practices. Among the deities of Teotihuacán are a storm god and his goddess counterpart, who may be linked to the Aztecs' rain god and his consort. The people of Teotihuacán also worshipped a feathered serpent who is recognizable as the antecedent of the deity the Aztecs worshipped as Quetzalcoatl and the Maya as Kukulcan. Murals also suggest that the Teotihuacán elite, like the Maya and later Mesoamerican peoples, drew their own blood as a form of sacrifice to the gods. They also practiced human sacrifice.

After 500 C.E., Teotihuacán's influence began to decline, and in the eighth century its authority collapsed. The ritual center and the residences of the elite were destroyed by fire, perhaps as a consequence of a popular uprising. The city never regained its former status, but it retained its hold on the imaginations of

QUICK REVIEW

Teotihuacàn
- Population of more than 150,000 at its height
- Dominated by Avenue of the Dead
- Influence of city extended throughout Mesoamerica

succeeding generations of Mesoamericans—much like the appeal the ruins of ancient Greece and Rome had for Europeans. Teotihuacán is an Aztec word meaning "City of the Gods," and it was still a revered pilgrimage site at the time of the Spanish conquest.

THE MAYA

Maya civilization arose in southern Mesoamerica. During the Classic period, it experienced a remarkable florescence in the lowland jungles of the southern Yucatán.

All the pre-Spanish societies of Mesoamerica were literate. They recorded historical and religious information on scrolled or screenfold books made with deerhide or bark paper, but only a handful of these documents have survived. The Maya of the Classic period developed Mesoamerica's most advanced writing system, and they were unique in the extent to which they inscribed words and calendrical symbols on stone, pottery, and other imperishable materials.

The largest Maya city, Tikal, probably had a population of between 50,000 and 70,000 at its height. Powerful ruling families and their elite retainers dominated Maya cities, supported by a large class of farmer-commoners. Maya inscriptions are almost entirely devoted to recounting important events in the lives of these rulers. Warfare between cities was chronic, and as murals and sculptures document, captured prisoners were sacrificed to appease the gods and glorify victorious leaders.

Religion profoundly influenced the social and political lives of the Maya, for they recognized no clear distinction between a natural and a supernatural

Mayan Mural. This reproduction of one of the remarkable murals found at the Maya site of Bonampak shows the presentation of captives to the city's ruler, Chan Muan.

world. As had probably been true in Teotihuacán, rulers and an elite exercised a combination of religious and political authority. Rulers claimed association with the gods and mediated between humans and gods by means of elaborate rituals. They wore special regalia to symbolize their power, and the ceremonies over which they presided were believed to be essential to sustaining the gods and the cosmic order. Religious rituals included bloodletting ceremonies, the sacrifice of captives, and ball games.

Maya believed that the world had gone through several cycles of creation, and a creation myth explains why all Maya cities had courts on which a unique sacrificial ball game was played. The myth tells how the Hero Twins defeated the gods of the underworld in the ball game and returned to life after being sacrificed. One became the sun and the other Venus. The regular rising and setting of these heavenly bodies represented the Twins' descent into the underworld and their subsequent rebirth. The games were ritual reinactments of the confrontation between the Hero Twins and the lords of the underworld. The losing team was sometimes sacrificed.[1]

During the Classic period, Maya developed a sophisticated mathematics and were among the first peoples in the world to invent the concept of zero. In addition to the 52-year calendar based on interlocking 260- and 365-day cycles they shared with other Mesoamerican societies, the Maya developed an absolute calendar. It was known as the **Long Count**, for it was reckoned from a fixed point in the past. The calendar had great religious as well as practical significance for the Maya, because it was determined by the movements of certain celestial bodies that were worshipped as deities. Great skill in astronomical observation was required to achieve the complexity and accuracy of the Maya calendar. The lunar calendar was adjusted to remain in sync with the actual length of the lunar cycle (29.53 days), and it may have had provisions like our leap years to coordinate with the solar year. Maya also made accurate observations of Venus and recognized before other peoples that it is both the morning and the evening star. The importance of the calendar, its association with divine forces, and the esoteric knowledge required to maintain it go a long way toward explaining the prestige and power of the elite who were its guardians.

During the Classic period, no single center dominated the Maya region. Many independent units, consisting of a capital city and smaller subject towns and villages, rose and fell in prominence. Tikal, which emerged as an important center in the Late Formative period, is a good example. At its height, it was the largest Classic Maya city, having a residential center covering more than 14 square miles and containing about 3,000 structures. The city follows the uneven terrain of the rain forest. It is not, like Teotihuacán, laid out on a grid, but monumental causeways link its major structures. Tikal benefited from its strategic location near a source of flint, a valued raw material for stone tools. Nearby swamps, with modification, might have been agriculturally productive. River systems connect the city to the coasts.

A single dynasty of 39 rulers reigned in Tikal from the Early Classic period until the eighth century. Early rulers in this Jaguar Paw line were buried in a structure known as the North Acropolis. Inscriptions associated with their tombs provide details about them, including in many cases their names and the dates of their reigns and military victories.

Long Count Mayan calendar that dated from a fixed point in the past.

---

[1]Robert J. Sharer, *The Ancient Maya*, 5th ed. (Stanford, CA: Stanford University Press, 1994), p. 522.

For about 100 years beginning in the mid-sixth century, Tikal and most other lowland Maya sites undertook little new construction. Tikal may have suffered a serious defeat at the hands of the city of Caracol, but in 682, the ruler Ah Cacau (r. 682–723?) initiated a new period of vigor and prosperity for Tikal. He extended its influence through conquests and strategic marriage alliances, and he and his two immediate successors began an ambitious building program. They created most of Tikal's surviving monumental structures, including the dramatic, soaring temples that dominate the site. After the death of Chitam (r. 769–?), the last ruler in the Jaguar Paw dynasty, Tikal declined and never recovered.

Similar dynastic histories are being recovered at other Classic Maya sites. Inscriptions above the tomb of Lord Pacal (r. 615–683), the greatest ruler of the city of Palenque, located in the western Mayan region, trace the city's entire dynastic history back to mythic ancestors. Two of its rulers were women, one of them Pacal's mother, Lady Zac Kuk (r. 612–640), and another predecessor, Lady Kanal Ikal (r. 583–604).

Between 800 and 900 C.E., Classic period civilization collapsed in the southern lowlands. The ruling dynasties came to an end, and the great cities were virtually abandoned. The cause of the collapse is not known with certainty, but it is clear that the Maya exceeded their resources. Intensifying warfare, population growth and concentration, and attempts to increase agricultural production that ultimately backfired may all have worked to bring down the civilization. As the urban areas around the ceremonial centers grew, so did the demand for food. But because ambitious building projects continued right up to the collapse, a growing proportion of the population must have been employed on these projects, leaving fewer to produce food. Overfarming may then have led to soil exhaustion, and a major drought may also have occurred.

The focus of Maya civilization next shifted to the northern Yucatán. There the site of Chichén Itzá, located next to a sacred well, flourished from the 9th to the 13th centuries. Stylistic resemblances between Chichén Itzá and Tula, the capital of the Post-Classic Toltec Empire in central Mexico (see the next section), suggest ties between the two cities. After Chichén Itzá fell, Mayapan became the main Maya center. But by the time of the Spanish conquest, only small, competing Maya settlements remained.

THE POST-CLASSIC PERIOD

WHAT ROLE did human sacrifice play in the Aztec Empire?

After Teotihuacán's collapse in the eighth century, smaller, militaristic states emerged. Many centered on fortified hilltop cities. Interregional trade and market systems became increasingly important, and secular and religious authorities began to diverge.

THE TOLTECS

About 900 C.E., a people known as the Toltecs rose to prominence. Their capital, Tula, is near the northern periphery of Mesoamerica. Like Teotihuacán, it lay close to an important source of obsidian. The Toltecs themselves were apparently descendants of one of many "barbarian" northern peoples (like the later Aztecs) who began migrating into Mesoamerica during the Late Classic.

Aztec mythology glorified the Toltecs as the fount of civilization, attributing to them a vast empire to which the Aztecs were the heirs. Other Mesoamerican peoples also attributed legendary status to the Toltecs. However, Tula, although a substantial city with a population of between 35,000 and 60,000 people, was never as large or as organized as Teotihuacán. Toltec influence reached many regions of Mesoamerica, but archaeologists are uncertain whether that influence translated into political control.

Toltec iconography, which stresses human sacrifice, death, blood, and military symbolism, supports their warlike reputation. But Toltec power was short-lived. By about 1100, Tula was in decline and its influence gone.

THE AZTECS

The people commonly known as the Aztecs referred to themselves as the **Mexica**. When the Spanish arrived in 1519, the Aztecs dominated much of Mesoamerica. Their capital city, Tenochtitlán, was the most populous in Mesoamerica up to that time. Built on islands in the southern part of Lake Texcoco in the Valley of Mexico, it was home to between 200,000 and 300,000 people. Tenochtitlán had great temples and palaces. Traders brought goods from distant regions, and vast wealth flowed to the city from subject territories. Yet the Aztecs were relative newcomers, having begun their rise to power only about 200 years before the Spaniards arrived.

According to their legends, the Aztecs were originally a nomadic people from somewhere to the northwest of the Valley of Mexico. At the urging of their patron god Huitzilopochtli, they began to migrate, arriving in the Valley of Mexico early in the 13th century. Scorned by the people already living there, they settled in 1325 on the island that became Tenochtitlán. The site was indicated to them by an omen from Huitzilopochtli: an eagle perched on a prickly pear cactus.

At first the Aztecs paid tribute to and served as mercenaries for Azcazpotzalco, the most powerful state in the valley. Soon, however, they became independent allies with their own tribute-paying territories. They consolidated their position by marriage alliances with ruling families of other cities. These marriages gave their rulers claim to descent from the Toltecs. In 1428, under their fourth ruler, Itzcoatl (r. 1427–1440), the Aztecs formed a triple alliance with Texcoco and Tlacopan and became the dominant power in the Valley of Mexico. Less than 100 years before the arrival of Cortés, the Aztecs, at the head of this Triple Alliance, began the aggressive expansion that brought them their vast tribute-paying empire (see Map 14–2).

Itzcoatl inaugurated the official Aztec imperial ideology by burning all the ancient books in the valley, expunging any histories that conflicted with Aztec pretensions, and restructuring Aztec religion to support Aztec preeminence. The Aztecs wished to present themselves as the divinely ordained successors to the Toltecs.

Aztec conquests ultimately included almost all of central Mexico. To the west,

Mexica Aztecs' name for themselves.

Human Sacrifice. Illustration from a colonial era manuscript volume, known as the Codex Magliabecchiano, presenting Aztec ritual sacrifice on a temple altar.

Scala/Art Resource.

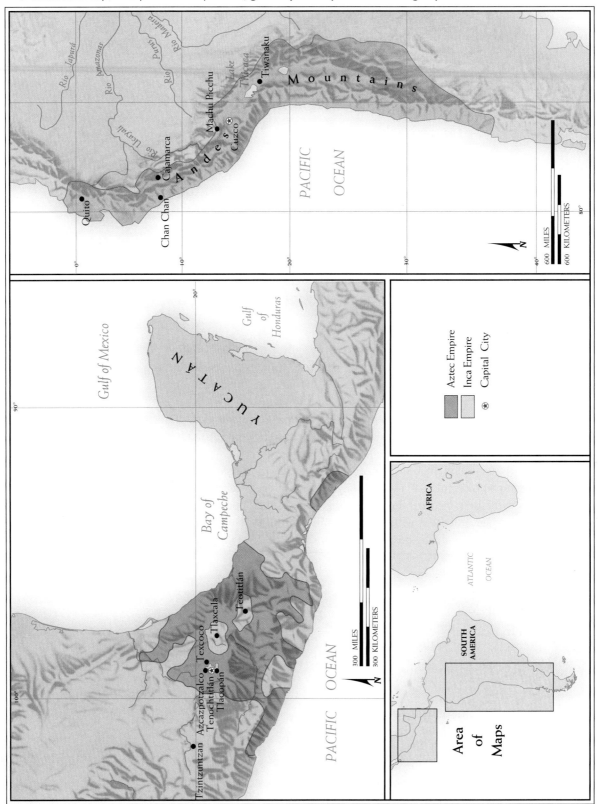

MAP 14–2
The Aztec and Inca Empires on the Eve of the Spanish Conquest.

WHAT WERE the chief differences between the Aztec and Inca Empires?

however, they were unable to conquer the rival Tarascan Empire. And within their realm, several pockets of resistance (notably, Tlaxcala) remained at war with the Aztecs.

The Aztec Extractive Empire   The Aztec Empire was extractive; meaning that after a conquest, the Aztecs usually left the local elite in power but extracted heavy tribute in goods and labor from their people. Tribute included agricultural products, fine craft goods, gold and jade, textiles, and feathers. The volume was considerable. For instance, up to 7,000 tons of maize and two million cotton cloaks flowed into Tenochtitlán's coffers annually. This wealth underwrote the grandeur of Tenochtitlán (see "A Spaniard Describes the Glory of the Aztec Capital").

Aztec Religion and Human Sacrifice   Aztec imperial exploitation did not end with valued craft goods. Human sacrifice on a prodigious scale was central to Aztec ideology. The Aztecs believed that Huitzilopochtli, the sun god, required human blood to rise again each day, and that it was their responsibility to provide the victims. The prime candidates for sacrifice were war captives, and the Aztecs often engaged in "flowery wars" with traditional enemies like Tlaxcala just to obtain captives. On major festivals, thousands of victims might perish. Led up the steps of the temple of Huitzilopochtli, a victim was thrown backward over a stone, his arms and legs pinned, while a priest cut out his heart. He would then be rolled down the steps of the temple, his head placed on a skull rack, and his limbs butchered and distributed to be eaten. Small children were sacrificed to the rain god Tlaloc, who, it was believed, was pleased by their tears.

Victims were also selected as stand-ins for particular gods and were sacrificed after a series of rituals. In ceremonies honoring the powerful god Tezcatlipoca, a beautiful male youth was chosen to represent the god for a year, during which he was treated with reverence. He wandered through the city dressed as the god and playing the flute. A month before the end of his reign he was given four wives. Twenty days before his death he was dressed as a warrior, and for a few days he was virtual ruler of the city. Then he was sacrificed.

No other Mesoamerican people practiced human sacrifice on the scale of the Aztecs. The slaughter doubtless served a variety of spiritual functions, but on a practical level it intimidated subject peoples and, by reducing their population of fighting-age men, headed off rebellions. But human sacrifice and the heavy burden of tribute also fed resentment and fear that may explain why so many subject peoples were willing to support Cortés when he challenged the Aztecs.

Tenochtitlán   Three great causeways linked Tenochtitlán to the mainland. They met at the ceremonial core of the city, which was dominated by the temple to Huitzilopochtli and Tlaloc where most of the Aztecs' sacrificial victims met their fates. The palaces of the ruler and high nobles lay just outside the central precinct. The ruler's palace was the empire's administrative center, with government officials, artisans and laborers, gardens, and a zoo. The rest of the city was divided into wards (*calpulli*). Some *calpulli* were reserved for merchants (*pochteca*) or artisans. The city was laid out on a grid formed of streets and canals. Agricultural plots of great fertility bordered the canals and the lake. Aqueducts

calpulli Wards into which the Aztec capital, Tenochtitlan, was divided.

HISTORY'S VOICES

A Spaniard Describes the Glory of the Aztec Capital

On November 8, 1519, a group of approximately 400 Spaniards under the command of Hernán Cortés entered the Aztec capital of Tenochtitlán. One of them was Bernal Díaz del Castillo (b. 1492) who later wrote The Conquest of New Spain, a chronicle of his experience. This gives some sense of the magnificence of the Aztec capital.

WHICH ELEMENTS of Aztec life especially astonished Díaz? What can one conclude about the social and political life of the Aztec elite from the manner in which Montezuma was attended? Which forms of wealth were most apparent?

Early next day we left Iztapalapa [where Cortés forces had been camped] with a large escort of these great Caciques [Aztec nobles], and followed the causeway, which is eight yards wide and goes so straight to the city of Mexico [Tenochtitlán] that I do not think it curves at all. Wide though it was, it was so crowded with people that there was hardly room for them all. Some were going to Mexico and others coming away, besides those who had come out to see us, and we could hardly get through the crowds that were there. For the towers and the cues [temples] were full, and they came in canoes from all parts of the lake. No wonder, since they had never seen horses or men like us before.

With such wonderful sights to gaze on we did not know what to say, or if this was real that we saw before our eyes. On the land side there were great cities, and on the lake many more. The lake was crowded with canoes. At intervals along the causeway there were many bridges, and before us was the great city of Mexico . . . .

We marched along our causeway to a point where another small causeway branches off to another city . . . and there, beside some towerlike buildings, which were their shrines, we were met by many more Caciques and dignitaries in very rich cloaks. The different chieftains wore different brilliant liveries, and the causeways were full of them. . . .

. . . When we came near to Mexico, at the place where there were some other small towers, the great Montezuma descended from his litter, and these other great Caciques supported him beneath a marvelously rich canopy of green feathers, decorated with gold work, silver, pearls . . . which hung from a sort of border. It was a marvelous sight. The great Montezuma was magnificently clad, in their fashion and wore sandals . . . the soles of which are of gold and the upper parts ornamented with precious stones. And the four lords who supported him were richly clad also in garments that seem to have been kept ready for them on the road so they could accompany their master . . . and many more lords . . . walked before the great Montezuma, sweeping the ground on which he was to tread, and laying down cloaks so that his feet should not touch the earth. Not one of these chieftains dared to look him in the face. All kept their eyes lowered most reverently except those four lords, his nephews, who were supporting him.

. . . Who could now count the multitude of men, women, and boys in the streets, on the roof-tops and in canoes on the waterways, who had come out to see us? . . .

They led us to our quarters, which were in some large houses capable of accommodating us all and had formerly belonged to the great Montezuma's father . . . . Here Montezuma now kept the great shrines of his gods, and a secret chamber containing gold bars and jewels. This was the treasure he had inherited from his father, which he never touched.

Source: *The Conquest of New Spain*, by Bernal Díaz, trans. by J. M. Cohen (New York: Penguin Books, 1963), copyright © J. M. Cohen, 1963, pp. 216–218.

carried water into the city. A dike kept the briny water of the northern part of Lake Texcoco from contaminating the waters around Tenochtitlán.

Society   Aztec society was hierarchical, authoritarian, and militaristic. It was divided into two broad classes, noble and commoner, with merchants and certain artisans forming an intermediate category. The nobility enjoyed wealth and luxury. Laws and regulations relating to dress reinforced social divisions. Elaborate and brilliantly colored regalia distinguished nobles from commoners, who were required to wear rough, simple garments.

The Aztecs were morally austere. They valued obedience, respectfulness, discipline, and moderation. Laws were strict and punishment severe. Standards for the nobility were higher than for commoners and punishments for sexual and social offenses were more strictly enforced for them. Drunkenness was harshly punished among the elite.

The most exalted rank in the nobility was that of *tlatoani* (plural *tlatoque*), or ruler of a major political unit. Of these, the chiefs were the rulers of the three cities of the Triple Alliance, and of them, the highest was the *tlatoani* of Tenochtitlán. Below these rulers were the *tetcutin*, the lords of subordinate units, and below them were the *pipiltin*, the bureaucrats and priests.

The bulk of the population, the commoners, farmed, harvested fish from the lake, and provided labor for public projects. All commoners belonged to a *calpulli*, each of which had its own temple. Children received training in the song houses attached to these temples. *Calpulli* officials assured that the *calpulli* fulfilled its tribute obligations. Commoners who could not pay their debts or the tribute they owed could be enslaved. Slavery was also the punishment for some criminal offenses. Serfs worked the estates of noblemen.

Traders and merchants (*pochteca*) were important figures in Aztec society. Together with the Aztec armies, they helped spread Aztec influence, and their far-reaching expeditions obtained luxury goods for the lords of Tenochtitlán. The pochteca organized guilds and established laws and customs for doing business. Their wealth gave them a somewhat ambiguous position in Aztec society, and they usually avoided ostentatious display so as not to attract unwanted attention. Artisans who made luxury goods, like the merchants who sold them, also enjoyed special status.

Markets were central to Aztec economic life. More than 60,000 people bought and sold in the great market at Tlatelolco each day. Market administrators, some of whom were women, regulated transactions. Cacao beans and cotton cloaks served as mediums of exchange.

Above all, Aztec society was structured and constantly mobilized for war. All young men received military training. Battles were fought to capture new territory, punish rebellious tributaries, protect trading expeditions, secure natural resources, and replenish the supply of sacrificial victims. Battles were not coordinated confrontations of massed infantry units, but fields on which a myriad of simultaneous individual combats took place. A warrior's goal was to subdue and capture prisoners for sacrifice. Prowess in battle was key to social advancement and to rewards for both commoners and nobles. On the other hand, failure in battle entailed social disgrace.

Women in Aztec society could inherit and own property. They traded in the marketplace and served as market officials. Their craft work provided their

14.6
Bernal Díaz del Castillo

tlatoani   An Aztec ruler.

tetcutin   Subordinate Aztec lords.

pipiltin   Aztec bureaucrats and priests.

pochteca   Aztec merchants.

families with income. Girls and boys alike were educated in the song houses, and women had access to priestly roles, although they were barred from the higher religious positions. In general, however, Aztec society's fixation on war relegated women to subordinate status and excluded them from major leadership roles. A man's function was to wage war, and a woman's purpose was to bear children. Childbirth was compared to battle, and death in childbirth, like death in battle, guaranteed rewards in the afterlife.

ANDEAN SOUTH AMERICA

HOW HAVE the Andes affected the development of civilization in South America?

The Andean region of South America—primarily modern Peru and Bolivia—had, like Mesoamerica, a long history of civilization before the Spanish conquerors arrived in the 16th century. Andean civilization is conventionally divided into seven periods: Preceramic, Initial, Early Horizon, Early Intermediate, Middle Horizon, Late Intermediate, and Late Horizon (Inca Empire). During the Early, Middle, and Late Horizon periods, a homogeneous art style spread over a wide area. The intermediate periods are characterized by regional stylistic diversity.

THE PRECERAMIC AND THE INITIAL PERIOD

WHEN DID Andean people first become dependent on agriculture?

The earliest monumental architecture in Peru dates to the early third millennium B.C.E., roughly contemporary with the Great Pyramids of Egypt. Located on the coast mostly near the shore, these earliest centers, which predate the introduction of pottery to Peru, feature ceremonial mounds and plazas. Coastal people at this time subsisted primarily on the bounties of the sea, supplemented by squash, beans, and chili peppers. They also cultivated cotton. Their cotton fishing nets and textiles mark the start of a sophisticated Andean textile tradition.

The earliest public buildings in the highlands date to before 2500 B.C.E. Highland people were more dependent on agriculture than coastal people during the late Preceramic, cultivating maize as well as potatoes and other tubers. Llamas and alpacas were fully domesticated by about 2500 B.C.E.

There is little evidence of social stratification for the late Preceramic. Public structures of both the coast and the highlands appear to have been centers of community ritual for relatively egalitarian societies.

The introduction of pottery to Peru around 2000 B.C.E. marks the beginning of the Initial period and corresponds to a major shift in settlement and subsistence patterns on the coast. People became dependent on agriculture as well as on maritime resources. They moved their settlements inland, constructed irrigation systems, began cultivating maize, and built large ceremonial centers adorned with sculpture and brightly painted façades. Population grew, society became stratified, and incised carvings of bodies with severed heads suggest

MAP 14–3
Pre-Inca Sites.

WHAT WERE the differences between highland and coastal cultures in early South American history?

that conflicts were increasing. Centers appear, however, to have maintained their independence of any overarching political authority.

CHAVÍN DE HUANTAR AND THE EARLY HORIZON

The large coastal centers of the Initial period declined early in the first millennium B.C.E. At about the same time, beginning around 800 B.C.E., a site in the highlands, Chavín de Huantar, was growing in influence. Located on a trade route between the coast and the lowland tropical rain forest and boasting a powerful religious cult, Chavín had a population of perhaps 3,000 at its height. Between about 400 and 200 B.C.E., Chavín influence spread widely throughout Peru, due probably to the prestige of its cult and not to political or military expansion.

The flowering of the Chavín culture was marked by innovations in ceramics, weaving, and metallurgy. Excavations also point to increasing social stratification. Skeletal remains at Chavín, for example, suggest that people who lived closer to the ceremonial center ate better than people living on the margins of the site.

The Periods of Andean Civilization

Preceramic	ca. 3000–ca. 2000 B.C.E.
Initial Period	ca. 2000–ca. 800 B.C.E.
Early Horizon	ca. 800–ca. 200 B.C.E.
Early Intermediate Period	ca. 200 B.C.E.–ca. 600 C.E.
Middle Horizon	ca. 600 C.E.–ca. 800/1000 C.E.
Late Intermediate Period	ca. 800/1000–ca. 1475
Late Horizon (Inca Empire)	ca. 1475–1532

THE EARLY INTERMEDIATE PERIOD

Signs of increasing warfare accompany the collapse of the Chavín culture and the ideological unity it had brought to the Andes. During the Early Intermediate period that followed, both regional diversity and political centralization developed as the first territorial states appeared in the Andes.

WHICH CULTURES followed in the wake of Chavín?

NAZCA

The Nazca culture, which flourished from about 100 B.C.E. to about 700 C.E., was centered in the Ica and Nazca valleys. The people of the Nazca valley built underground aqueducts to divert ground water from the middle of the valley to supply their irrigation canals. Cahuachi, the largest Nazca site, may have been the capital of a Nazca confederation. It was, however, empty most of the year and filled only when pilgrims arrived to celebrate religious festivals.

The Nazca are renowned for their textiles and fine pottery, decorated with images of Andean plants and animals. They are most famous, however, for their colossal earthworks, or geoglyphs, the so-called Nazca lines. These massive designs were created by brushing away the dark gravel of the desert to reveal the lighter-colored subsurface. Some geoglyphs are located on hillsides and visible from ground level, but others can be seen only from the air.

MOCHE

The Moche culture, named for the Moche valley on the north coast of Peru, flourished from about 200 to 700 C.E. Two huge structures, the Pyramid of the Sun and the Pyramid of the Moon, overlook this site. The cross-shaped Pyramid

The Nazca Geoglyph. Located in the Peruvian desert, the geoglyph depicts a vast hummingbird. The lines were constructed by the Nazca people probably sometime between 250 C.E. and 600 C.E. They appear to have been sacred paths walked by Nazca people perhaps somewhat as medieval Europeans walked a labyrinth. At the summer solstice the final parallel line points to the sun. Features of this and other geoglyphs can only be discerned from the air, and their exact purpose remains a matter of speculation.

Marilyn Bridges/Corbis Bettman.

HOW DO Tiwanaku and Huari foreshadow the achievements of the Inca?

of the Sun is the largest adobe structure in the Americas. It was some 1,200 feet long by 500 feet wide and rose in steps to a height of 60 feet. Its construction required more than 143 million adobe bricks.

The Moche were skilled potters. They sculpted realistic portrait vessels that may depict actual people. Ceremonial scenes feature elaborately dressed figures drinking the blood of sacrificed prisoners. The Moche were also the most sophisticated smiths in the Andes. They developed innovative alloys, cast weapons and agricultural tools, and used the lost-wax process to create small, intricate works.

THE MIDDLE HORIZON THROUGH THE LATE INTERMEDIATE PERIOD

TIWANAKU AND HUARI

In the fifth century C.E., as the Roman Empire was crumbling under the pressure of Germanic invasions and as Teotihuacán was reaching its height in Mesoamerica, the first expansionist empires were emerging in the Andean highlands. One of these was centered at Tiwanaku in Bolivia and the other at Huari in Peru. Both are associated with new agricultural technologies and show signs of statecraft that foreshadow the administrative practices of the later Inca

Empire. The artistic symbols used by both peoples also suggest that they shared a religious ideology.

Tiwanaku lies more than 12,600 feet above sea level, making it the highest capital in the ancient world. Construction apparently began at the site about 200 C.E., and it experienced its greatest growth from about 500 to 600 C.E. It collapsed some 500 years later. The city occupied one to two square miles, and may have had a population of 20,000 to 40,000 people at its height. Laid out on a grid, Tiwanaku is dominated by large public structures and ceremonial gateways. The effort expended to transport the stone for these monuments was enormous, and their existence is evidence of the power of Tiwanaku's rulers.

An economy based on raised-field agriculture on the shores of Lake Titicaca sustained Tiwanaku. This system involved farming on artificial platforms capped with rich topsoil and separated by basins of water. Experimental reconstructions have shown it to be extremely productive.

Tiwanaku dominated the Titicaca basin and neighboring regions. It probably owed its influence to its religious prestige and to a policy of establishing colonies and religious-administrative structures in distant territories.

The Huari Empire, which flourished from about 600 to 800 C.E., dominated the highlands from near Cuzco in the south to Cajamarca in the north. Its capital city, Huari, covers about 1.5 square miles and had a population of 20,000 to 30,000 people.

Huari is located in a valley, and its origin is associated with development of techniques for terracing and irrigating hillsides to increase productivity. Huari administrative centers were undefended and built in accessible places. Many archaeologists think they may have functioned like later Inca administrative centers; that is, they housed a small Huari elite that organized local labor for state projects. Also like the Inca, Huari administrators used *quipu*, record-keeping devices made of string.

THE CHIMU EMPIRE

After the demise of the Moche, two new states emerged on the north coast. One is named for the site of Sican and was centered in the Lambayeque Valley. The other, known as Chimu, was centered in the Moche valley. In two waves of expansion, the Chimu built an empire that took over the Lambayeque valley and stretched for 800 miles along the coast. Its administrative capital, Chan Chan, was a vast walled city covering 8 square miles. The city's focal points are some 10 immense adobe-walled enclosures that probably housed the empire's ruling elite. Smaller compounds probably belonged to lesser nobility. Surrounding these were the homes and workshops of the artisans and

quipu Knotted string used by Andean peoples for recordkeeping.

The Inca *Quipumayoc*. The Inca Guipumayoc grand treasurer, is shown holding a *quipu*, a device made of knotted strings, used to record administrative matters and sacred histories. Information was encoded in the colors of the strings and the style of the knots.

The Granger Collection.

workers who served the upperclasses. Two areas were apparently transport centers, where llama caravans brought raw materials to the capital from the empire's territories. The total population of the city was between 30,000 and 40,000. All of this was swept away about 1470 by the rising Inca Empire.

THE INCA EMPIRE

HOW DID the Inca enlarge and organize their empire?

*I*n 1532, when Francisco Pizarro and his companions happened on it, the Inca Empire was one of the largest states in the world. It spanned the region between the Pacific Coast and the Amazon basin and stretched some 2,600 miles from Ecuador to northern Chile (see Map 14–2). Its population numbered in the millions.

The Inca called their domain the Land of the Four Quarters. Their capital, Cuzco, lay at the intersection of these divisions. Home to the ruler (Inca) and the ruling elite, the city enjoyed great splendor. Its principal temples, dedicated to the sun and moon, gleamed with gold and silver.

The origins of the Inca are obscure. According to their own traditions, Inca expansion began only in the 15th century in the wake of a revolt by the Chanca people that nearly destroyed Cuzco. Inca Yupanqui, son of the city's aging ruler, crushed the revolt, and he and his successors expanded their domains, spreading civilization through the Andean region. There is an element of imperial propaganda in this legend, for archaeological evidence suggests that the Inca had been expanding for decades—perhaps centuries—before the Chanca revolt.

The Inca enlarged their empire through alliance, intimidation, and conquest. They ruled their realm through a hierarchical administrative system and imposed their language, **Quechua**, as the official tongue. Quechua is still widely spoken in the Peruvian Andes.

The Inca relied on various forms of labor taxation. They divided agricultural lands into categories, allowing local populations to retain some for their own support and reserving the rest for the state and the gods. In a system known as the *mita*, local people worked for the state on a regular basis, receiving in return gifts and ritual entertainments. Men also owed military service and labor on public works projects. The Inca designated entire communities as *Mitimaqs* and relocated them at will to exploit various resources of their empire. They sometime pacified territories by settling loyal people in hostile regions and moving hostile people to loyal regions.

Several groups of people were employed in full-time state service. The *mamakuna*, the so-called Virgins of the Sun, formed one of these groups. These women lived privileged but celibate, regulated lives in cities and towns scattered throughout the empire. They could be given in marriage by Inca rulers to cement alliances, and they had important economic as well as religious roles. They wove cloth and brewed the maize beer known as *chicha*, which was consumed at state religious festivals. Another group of full-time state workers were men whose duties included tending the royal llama herds.

Cloth and clothing were means of communication. Inca warehouses were filled with textiles as well as with food and other craft goods. Complex textile patterns indicated a person's rank and ethnic affiliation. The Incas controlled their empire through regional administrative centers and warehouses linked

Quechua Inca language.

mita Inca system of forced labor in return for gifts and ritual entertainments.

Mitimaqs Communities whom the Incas forced to settle in designated regions for strategic purposes.

mamakuna Inca women who lived privileged but celibate lives and had important economic and cultural roles.

chicha Maize beer brewed by the mamakuna for the Inca elite.

Machu Picchu. The Inca city of Machu Picchu perches on a saddle between two peaks on the eastern slopes of the Andes.

Robert Frerk/Odyssey Productions.

by roads. These facilities organized, housed, and fed people engaged in mita labor service and staged feasts and rituals to impress them with the power and beneficence of the state. The wealth of the empire, collected in storehouses, sustained the mita laborers, fed and clothed the army, and enriched the Inca elite. Although the Inca lacked writing, they kept detailed administrative records on quipu, accounting devices made from knotted strings. The Inca also built more than 14,000 miles of road, ranging from narrow paths to wide thoroughfares. Rope bridges crossed gorges and rivers, and stairways made ascent of steep slopes easier. A system of relay runners sped messages to Cuzco from the far reaches of the empire.

Over their long history, the people of the Andes developed an adaptation to their challenging environment that allowed them to prosper and grow. They brought more land under cultivation than is farmed in that part of the world today, and they engineered an economy that brought them a measure of well-being superior to that which followed the destruction of the Inca Empire by the Spanish invaders.

IMAGE KEY

for pages 310–311

a. Mayan numbers on terra-cotta, 100 C.E.

b. Corn seeds

c. Separated head, limbs, and torso of the Aztec goddess Coyolxauhqui

d. Sipan earspool

e. Aztec sun stone

f. A ball game player, Mayan funerary gift

g. Chichen Itza, Mexico, El Castillo/ Pyramid of Kukulcan

h. Tula statuary

i. El Castillo, Mayan castle at Tulum, on the Yucatan peninsula, Mexico

j. Olmec Monument

k. Machu Picchu

SUMMARY

Mesoamerica Mesoamerica means "middle America." It extends from central Mexico through Central America. Although there was no single Mesoamerican civilization, the civilizations of the Olmecs, the peoples of Monte Alban and Teotihunacán, the Maya, the Toltecs, and the Aztecs shared many features: urban centers with monumental buildings arranged on large plazas, writing, a sophisticated calendrical system, religions that included human sacrifice, and the cultivation of certain crops, especially maize and beans. Throughout its history, the cities of Mesoamerica also were linked by trade.

The Aztecs established the largest Mesoamerican state before the coming of the Spanish in the 16th century. The Aztec Empire depended on tribute from conquered peoples. Aztec society was organized for war and was divided into nobles and commoners, with merchants and certain artisans forming intermediate categories. The Aztecs practiced widescale human sacrifice. Most of the victims were captured warriors. Women could own property and participate in trade, but were subordinate to men and excluded from high authority.

Andean South America Monumental architecture and public buildings in Peru date from the third millennium B.C.E. Over the next 3,000 years, the Andean peoples developed pottery, urban centers, intricate cotton weaving, and sophisticated agriculture. The first expansionist empires emerged in the Andean highlands in the fifth century C.E..

The Incas built the most extensive Andean empire. It spanned 2,600 miles from Ecuador to Chile between the Pacific and the Amazon basin. Inca rule relied on conquest, intimidation, and alliances with other peoples. The Inca exacted taxation in terms of forced labor and constructed more than 14,000 miles of roads and numerous rope bridges. Although the Inca lacked writing, they kept detailed accounts using knotted strings.

REVIEW QUESTIONS

1. What did the rise of civilization in Mesoamerica and Andean South America have in common with the rise of civilization in Africa and Eurasia? How did these regions differ?

2. What were the distinguishing characteristics of the Classic period civilizations of Mesoamerica?

3. How was the Aztec Empire organized? The Inca Empire?

4. Both the Aztec and Inca Empires fell in the early 16th century when confronted with Spanish forces of a few hundred men. What might explain this?

KEY TERMS

calpulli (p. 323)

chicha (p. 330)

Long Count (p. 319)

Mexica (p. 321)

mita (p. 330)

Mitimaqs (p. 330)

manakuna (p. 330)

obsidian (p. 313)

pipiltin (p. 325)

pochteca (p. 325)

quipu (p. 329)

Quechua (p. 330)

tlatoani (p. 325)

tetcutin (p. 325)

  For additional study resources for this chapter, go to:
www.prenhall.com/craig/chapter14

Visualizing The Past
Mapping the World before 1500

HOW DO world maps convey a culture's understanding of its place in the cosmos? Is it possible for any map of the world to be objective?

Long before explorers knitted the globe into a single planet, humans mapped their world. Environmental factors and cultural values influenced the way mapmakers executed their craft. Despite these differences, the maps below share a technical proficiency matched only by their intrinsic beauty.

Arabia. The Arab scholar al-Idrisi created this world map in 1154. In keeping with Arab cartographic traditions, the map is oriented with south on top. Europe appears as a fairly insignificant appendage of Asia while Africa is depicted as a huge landmass turning all the way east towards China. The entire world is surrounded by an "All-Encompassing Ocean."

Map of World by Islamic scholar, Al Idrisi, copy made in 1553 (960 AH or Anno Hegirae) of original of 1154, Arabic. Pococke 375 folio 3v-4r. Bodleian Library Oxford.

Africa. This is a late 15th-century map of ▶ the world based on a description by the second century CE scholar Claudius Ptolemaeus of Alexandria, more commonly known as Ptolemy. The Ptolemaic view of the world held sway in western Europe until the great age of discovery. Note how, in contrast to the map of al-Idrisi, Africa curves eastward to connect with China on the far right, making the Indian Ocean an enclosed sea—which for Europeans it practically was until Vasco da Gama sailed to the Indian Ocean in 1497–1499.

Courtesy of the Library of Congress.

◀ **The New World.** More a cosmic diagram than a map, this startling image, painted on animal hide sometime between 1400 and 1500 by either the Mixtec or Aztec peoples of present-day Mexico, illuminates a native American worldview before the arrival of Europeans. At the center is the fire god Xiuhtecutli. Radiating out from him are the four directions—each represented by a specific color, deity, and tree with a bird in its branches. In each corner, to the right of a U-shape, is one of the attributes of Tezcatlipoca, the Smoking Mirror, a primal god who could see humankind's thoughts and deeds. Intense symbolism, such as the kind depicted here, played a central role in the cultures of pre-Colombian America.

Liverpool Museum, Liverpool, Great Britain.

Polynesia. Polynesians were among the world's greatest explorers ▶ in the pre-modern era. Starting out from their ancestral homeland in New Guinea, by 1000 CE they had discovered almost every island in the Pacific. Expert navigators, they sailed in twin-hulled canoes and used the sun, stars, and the direction of prevailing winds and ocean currents to cross vast stretches of ocean. Stick charts, like the one depicted here, were used to record patterns of ocean swells. The shells indicate islands.

Courtesy of the Library of Congress.

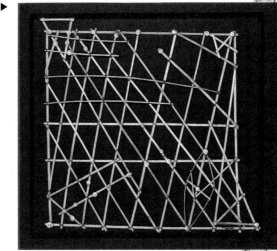

15 Europe to the Early 1500s
Revival, Decline, and Renaissance

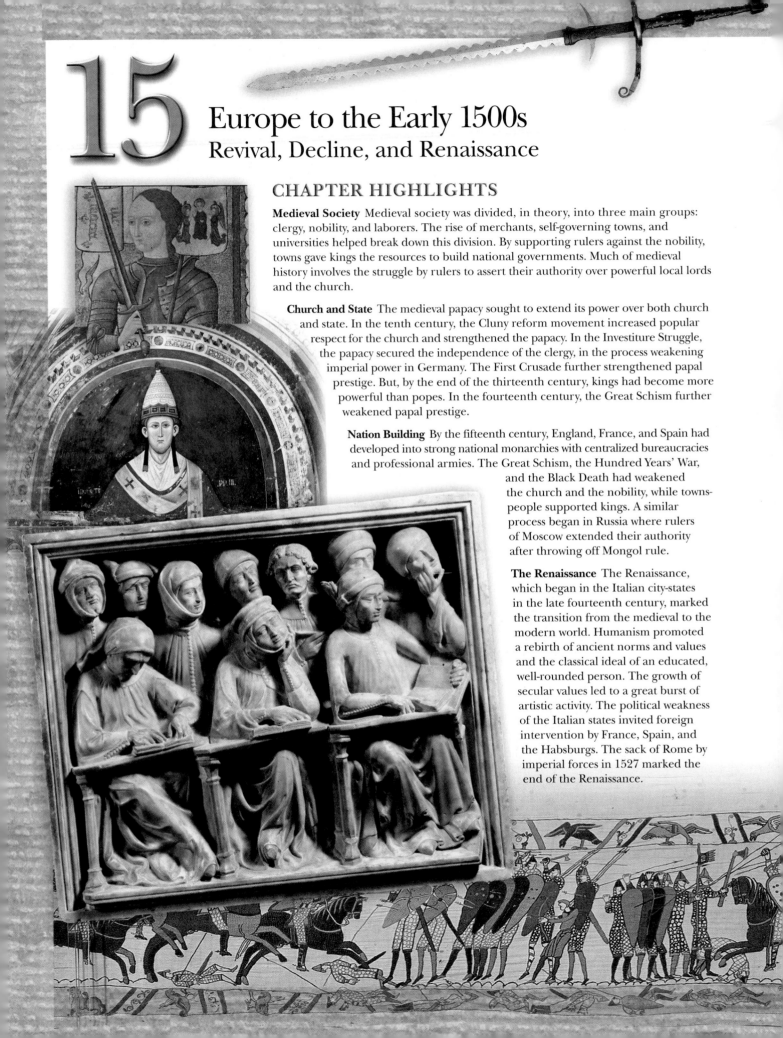

CHAPTER HIGHLIGHTS

Medieval Society Medieval society was divided, in theory, into three main groups: clergy, nobility, and laborers. The rise of merchants, self-governing towns, and universities helped break down this division. By supporting rulers against the nobility, towns gave kings the resources to build national governments. Much of medieval history involves the struggle by rulers to assert their authority over powerful local lords and the church.

Church and State The medieval papacy sought to extend its power over both church and state. In the tenth century, the Cluny reform movement increased popular respect for the church and strengthened the papacy. In the Investiture Struggle, the papacy secured the independence of the clergy, in the process weakening imperial power in Germany. The First Crusade further strengthened papal prestige. But, by the end of the thirteenth century, kings had become more powerful than popes. In the fourteenth century, the Great Schism further weakened papal prestige.

Nation Building By the fifteenth century, England, France, and Spain had developed into strong national monarchies with centralized bureaucracies and professional armies. The Great Schism, the Hundred Years' War, and the Black Death had weakened the church and the nobility, while towns-people supported kings. A similar process began in Russia where rulers of Moscow extended their authority after throwing off Mongol rule.

The Renaissance The Renaissance, which began in the Italian city-states in the late fourteenth century, marked the transition from the medieval to the modern world. Humanism promoted a rebirth of ancient norms and values and the classical ideal of an educated, well-rounded person. The growth of secular values led to a great burst of artistic activity. The political weakness of the Italian states invited foreign intervention by France, Spain, and the Habsburgs. The sack of Rome by imperial forces in 1527 marked the end of the Renaissance.

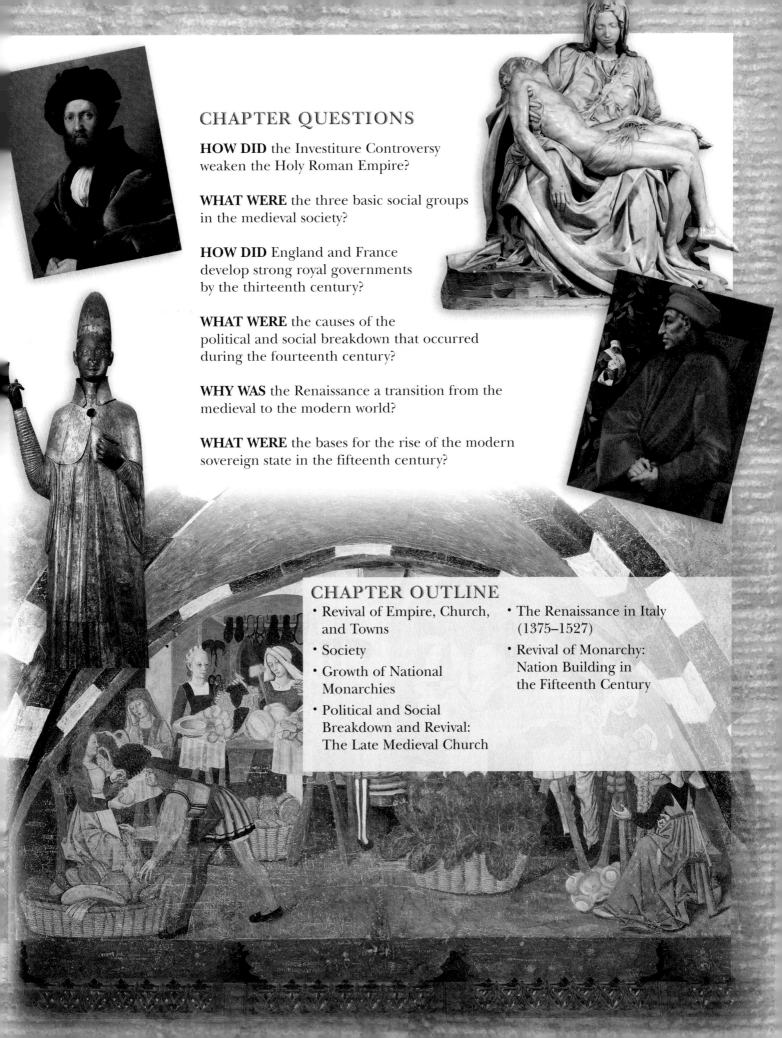

CHAPTER QUESTIONS

HOW DID the Investiture Controversy weaken the Holy Roman Empire?

WHAT WERE the three basic social groups in the medieval society?

HOW DID England and France develop strong royal governments by the thirteenth century?

WHAT WERE the causes of the political and social breakdown that occurred during the fourteenth century?

WHY WAS the Renaissance a transition from the medieval to the modern world?

WHAT WERE the bases for the rise of the modern sovereign state in the fifteenth century?

CHAPTER OUTLINE

- Revival of Empire, Church, and Towns
- Society
- Growth of National Monarchies
- Political and Social Breakdown and Revival: The Late Medieval Church
- The Renaissance in Italy (1375–1527)
- Revival of Monarchy: Nation Building in the Fifteenth Century

The High Middle Ages (from the eleventh through the thirteenth centuries) were a period of both political expansion and consolidation and intellectual flowering and synthesis. The Latin, or Western, church established itself as a spiritual authority independent of secular monarchies, which themselves became more powerful and self-aggrandizing. The parliaments and popular assemblies that accompanied the rise of these monarchies pioneered modern representative institutions.

The High Middle Ages saw a revolution in agriculture that increased food supplies and populations. Trade and commerce revived, towns expanded, protomodern forms of banking and credit developed, and a "new rich" merchant class rose to power in Europe's cities. Universities were established, and contact with the Arab world led to the beginning of the recovery of the works of the ancient Greek philosophers. This helped to stimulate the great expansion of Western education and culture that was achieved during the late Middle Ages and the Renaissance.

The late Middle Ages and the Renaissance (the fourteenth, fifteenth, and early sixteenth centuries) were a time of unprecedented calamity and of bold new beginnings in Europe. France and England grappled with each other in a bitter conflict, the Hundred Years' War (1337–1453). Between 1348 and 1350, Bubonic plague, which contemporaries called the Black Death, reduced the population in many regions by approximately one-third. A schism divided the papacy and the church (1378–1417), and in 1453 the Turks captured Constantinople and expanded into Europe. From this perspective, Western civilization seemed to be collapsing.

But the late Middle Ages also witnessed an intellectual and artistitic renaissance that continued into the seventeenth century. Scholars criticized medieval assumptions about the nature of God, humankind, and society. Italian and northern humanists made a full recovery of classical learning and languages and conceived of ideas that would spread and transform life in Europe. The "divine art" of printing was invented. The vernaculars, the languages of ordinary people, began to take their place alongside Latin as vehicles for art and serious discourse, and patriotism and incipient nationalism became important factors in the politics of Europe's independent nation-states.

HOW DID the Investiture Controversy weaken the Holy Roman Empire?

REVIVAL OF EMPIRE, CHURCH, AND TOWNS

OTTO I AND THE REVIVAL OF THE EMPIRE

The fortunes of both the old empire and the papacy began to revive in 918, when the Saxon Henry I ("the Fowler"; d. 936) became the first non-Frankish king of Germany. Henry rebuilt royal power and left his son and successor Otto I (r. 936–973) in a strong territorial position. Otto maneuvered his own kin to dominate Bavaria, Swabia, and Franconia. Then, in 951, he invaded Italy and proclaimed himself its king. In 955, he defeated the Hungarians at Lechfeld, which secured German borders against barbarian attacks. All this earned Otto the title "the Great."

Otto enlisted the help of the church in rebuilding his realm. As agents to administer his lands, he preferred to appoint bishops and abbots. These men possessed a sense of universal empire but they could not marry and found families to compete with his own. In 961, Otto responded to a call for help from Pope John XII (955–964), and on February 2, 962, Otto received from the pope in return the imperial coronation he had long desired. The church was brought ever more under royal control, but it was increasingly determined to assert its independence.

THE REVIVING CATHOLIC CHURCH

Otto's successors became so preoccupied with Italy that they allowed their German base to disintegrate. As the revived empire began to crumble in the 11th century, the church, long unhappy with imperial domination, declared its independence by embracing a reform movement pioneered by a monastic order.

Cluny Reform Movement   In 910, a monastery was founded at Cluny in east-central France, and the Cluniac monks launched a campaign to free the church from lay control. Their cause was aided by the popular respect the church commanded. The church was medieval society's most democratic institution. Theoretically, any man could become pope, for the pope was usually elected by the people and the clergy of Rome. The grace and salvation the church dispensed were available to everyone, and the church promised a better life to come to the great mass of ordinary people, who found their earthly circumstances brutish and hopeless.

The Cluny reformers maintained that clergy should not be subservient to kings, and that all clergy should come directly under the authority of the pope. They denounced "secular" parish clergy, who by living with concubines in a relationship akin to marriage, fell short of Cluny's ascetic ideals. Distinctive features of Western religion—separation of church and state and the celibacy of the Catholic clergy—had their definitive origins in the Cluny reform movement. From Cluny, reformers were dispatched throughout France and Italy, and in the late 11th century the papacy embraced their reforms.

Investiture Struggle: Gregory VII and Henry IV   In 1075, Pope Gregory VII (r. 1073–1085), a fierce advocate of church reform, condemned under penalty of excommunication the well-established custom of king's appointing bishops to administer their estates and "investing" them with the ring and staff that symbolized their ecclesiastical office. The emperor Henry IV of Germany considered Gregory's action a direct challenge to his authority. Germany's territorial princes, on the other hand, were inclined to support the pope, for they believed that anything that weakened the emperor strengthened them.

The lines of battle were quickly drawn. Henry assembled his loyal German bishops at Worms in January 1076 and had them declare their independence from Gregory. Gregory promptly excommunicated Henry and absolved all Henry's subjects from loyalty to him. The German princes were delighted. Henry, facing a general revolt, had to come to terms with Gregory. In a famous scene, he prostrated himself outside Gregory's castle retreat at Canossa in northern Italy. Reportedly he stood barefoot in the snow off and on for three days before the pope absolved him. Papal power seemed to triumph, but the struggle was not yet over.

The investiture controversy was not settled until 1122. In the Concordat of Worms, Emperor Henry V (r. 1106–1125) agreed not to invest bishops with the ring and staff that signified their spiritual authority, and Pope Calixtus II (r. 1119–1124) recognized the emperor's right to be present at episcopal consercations and to grant bishops their secular fiefs before or after their investment

Otto I and the Church. Otto I presents the Magdeburg Cathedral to Christ, as the pope (holding the keys to the kingdom of heaven) watches, a testimony to Otto's guardianship of the Church.

"Christ Enthroned with Saints and Emperor Otto I" (r. 962–973). One from a series of 19 known as the Magdeburg Ivories. Ivory H 5" × W 41/2" (12.7 × 11.4 cm).

QUICK REVIEW

Church and State
- Investiture crisis centered on authority to appoint and control clergy
- Pope Gregory excommunicated Henry IV when he proclaimed his independence from papacy
- Crisis settled in 1122 with Concordat of Worms

Struggle Between Emperor and Pope. A 12th-century German manuscript portrays the struggle between Emperor Henry IV and Pope Gregory VII. In the top panel, Henry installs the puppet pope Clement III and drives Gregory from Rome. Below, Gregory dies in exile. The artist was a monk, whose sympathies were with Gregory, not Henry.

Thuringer Universities and Landesbibliothek, Jena: Bos. q. 6, Blatt 79r.

Crusades Religious wars directed by the church against infidels and heretics.

with the spiritual symbols by the church. The emperor effectively retained the right to nominate or veto a candidate. The settlement had the effect of separating spheres of ecclesiastical and secular authority and setting the stage for future and greater conflicts between church and state.

THE CRUSADES

If evidence of a surge of popular piety and support for the pope in the High Middle Ages is needed, the **Crusades** provide it. What the Cluniac reform was to the clergy, the First Crusade to the Holy Land was to the laity: an outlet for heightened religious zeal.

Late in the 11th century, the Byzantine Empire was under severe pressure from the Seljuk Turks, and Emperor Alexius I Comnenus (r. 1081–1118) appealed for Western aid. At the Council of Clermont in 1095, Pope Urban II (r. 1088–1099) responded by launching the First Crusade. Scholars debate the motives of the Crusaders. Genuine religious piety played a major part. The papacy promised crusaders forgiveness for all their sins should they die in battle, and a crusade to the Holy Land was the ultimate religious pilgrimage. But the pope and others may also have hoped to stabilize the West by sending large

be reconciled to Latin rule, and in 1261 the man they recognized as their legitimate emperor, Michael Paleologus, recaptured the city. He had help from Venice's rival, Genoa. The Fourth Crusade did nothing to heal the political and religious divisions that separated East and West.

TOWNS AND TOWNSPEOPLE

In the 11th and 12th centuries, most towns were small. Only about 5 percent of western Europe's population lived in an urban context, but they were some of the most creative members of medieval society.

The Chartering of Towns   Towns were originally dominated by the feudal lords who issued charters spelling out terms for their organization. The lords' purpose was to court skilled laborers who could manufacture the finished goods the feudal nobility desired. A charter guaranteed a town's safety and gave its residents a degree of independence unknown to a rural peasant.

As towns grew and their privileges beckoned, many serfs migrated to the new urban centers. There they found the freedom and opportunity to earn the wealth that elevated an industrious craftsperson's social standing. As movement of serfs to towns accelerated, the lords in the countryside were forced to offer serfs more favorable terms of tenure to keep them on the land. The growth of towns thus improved the lot of serfs in several ways.

The Rise of Merchants   Rural society not only provided craftspeople and day laborers for towns, but the first merchants may have been enterprising serfs. Certainly, some of the long-distance traders were people who had nothing to lose and everything to gain from the enormous risks of foreign trade. They traveled together in armed caravans and convoys, buying goods and products as cheaply as possible at the source, and selling them for all they could get.

At first the merchants were disliked because they were outside the traditional social groups of nobility, clergy, and peasantry. Over time, however, the powerful came to respect the merchants and the weak to imitate them. Merchants brought prosperity and a higher standard of living.

As traders established themselves in towns and grew in wealth and numbers, they formed their own protective associations. These soon challenged seigneurial authority over their communities. Merchants especially wanted to end the arbitrary tolls and tariffs that regional magnates imposed on the goods merchants moved through the countryside.

Townspeople needed simple, uniform laws and a government sympathetic to their new forms of business activity. Commerce was incompatible with the defensive, fortress mentality of the lords of the countryside. The result was often a struggle with the old nobility within and outside the towns. This conflict led townspeople in the High and late Middle Ages to form independent communes and to ally themselves with kings against the rural nobility, a development that rearranged the centers of power in medieval Europe and ended classic feudal government.

Foundry in Florence. Skilled workers were an integral component of the commerce of medieval towns. This scene shows the manufacture of cannons in a foundry in Florence.
Scala/Art Resource, N.Y.

MAP EXPLORATION

Interactive map: To explore this map further, go to **http://www.prenhall.com/craig/map15.2**

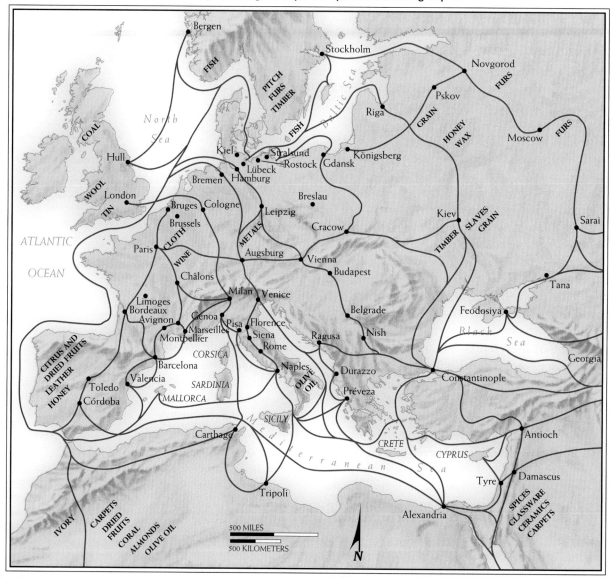

MAP 15–2

Medieval Trade Routes and Regional Products. Trade in Europe varied in intensity and geographical extent in different periods during the Middle Ages. The map shows some of the channels that came to be used in interregional commerce. Labels tell part of what was carried in that commerce.

HOW STRONG were the connections among Europe, the Middle East, and Africa at this time?

Because the merchants were the engine of the urban economy, small shopkeepers and artisans identified far more with them than with the aloof lords and bishops who were medieval society's traditional masters. The lesser nobility (small knights) also recognized the new mercantile economy as the wave of the future. During the 11th and 12th centuries, the burgher upper classes increased their economic strength and successfully challenged the old noble urban lords for control of towns.

New Models of Government   With urban autonomy came new models of self-government. Around 1100 the old urban nobility and the new burgher upper class merged to form an urban patriciate. It was a marriage between those wealthy by birth (inherited property) and those who made their fortunes in long-distance trade. From this new ruling class was born the aristocratic town council, which henceforth governed towns.

Enriching and complicating the situation, small artisans and craftspeople also slowly developed their own protective associations or **guilds** and began to gain a voice in government. The opportunities towns created for the "little people" established a new principle: "Town air brings freedom." Within town walls people thought of themselves as citizens with basic rights, not subjects liable to a master's whim.

Towns and Kings   By providing kings with the resources they needed to curb factious noblemen, towns became a major force in the transition from feudal societies to national governments. Towns were a ready source of educated bureaucrats and lawyers who knew Roman law, an effective tool for building royal government. The money that towns could provide for kings also enabled kings to hire their own armies and free themselves from dependence on the nobility. In turn, towns won political recognition and had their privileges guaranteed by national governments. In France, towns were integrated early into the royal administration. In Germany, they came under ever-tighter control by princes. In Italy, uniquely, they grew into genuine city-states that reached the peak of their power and influence during the Italian Renaissance.

Jews in Christian Society   Towns also attracted Jews who plied trades in small businesses. Many became wealthy as moneylenders to kings, popes, and businesspeople. Jewish intellectual and religious culture both dazzled and threatened Christians. These various factors encouraged suspicion and distrust among Christians, and led to a surge in anti-Jewish sentiment in the late 12th and early 13th centuries.

Schools and Universities   In the 12th century, translations and commentaries by Byzantine and Spanish Islamic scholars introduced western Europeans to the philosophical works of Aristotle, the writings of Euclid and Ptolemy, the texts of Greek physicians and Arab mathematicians, and the corpus of Roman law. The intellectual ferment created by this explosion of information began the development of the modern universities. The first important Western university was established in 1158 in Bologna. It specialized in the study of Roman law and became the model for the universities of Spain, Italy, and southern France. Paris provided a different model for northern European universities, and it was leading school for theologians

At the start of the High Middle Ages, learning involved mastering what was already known. People assumed that all truth had been discovered and only needed to be properly organized, elucidated, and defended. Students wrote commentaries on authoritative texts, especially those of Aristotle and the church fathers. Teachers did not encourage students to strive independently for undiscovered truth. They taught them to organize and harmonize the accepted truths of tradition and drilled these into them.

Under this method of study, called **Scholasticism**, students summarized the opinions of the received authorities in their field, debated their arguments pro

guild Association of merchants or craftsmen that offered protection to its members and set rules for their work and products.

Scholasticism Method of study based on logic and dialectic that dominated the medieval schools. It assumed that truth already existed; students had only to organize, elucidate, and defend knowledge learned from authoritative texts, especially those of Aristotle and the Church Fathers.

and con, and then drew logical conclusions. The arrival of Aristotle's works in the West honed the tools of logic and dialectic they used to discipline their thinking. Dialectic is the art of testing a truth by examining arguments against it. The assumption that truth could be discovered by debating authoritative texts was accepted even in fields such as medicine—to the detriment of practical experience and empirical research.

Abelard Peter Abelard (1079–1142) was the boldest and most controversial of the advocates for the new Aristotelian learning. As the leading philosopher and theologian of his day, he was the first European scholar to attract a large student following. His audacious logical critique of religious doctrine, however, earned him powerful enemies. His thinking was unique in its appreciation of subjectivity. He claimed, for instance, that the motives of an act's agent determined whether that act was good or evil, not the act itself. He also said that an individual's feeling of repentance was a more important factor in receiving God's forgiveness than the church's sacrament of penance.

Abelard, as he laments in his autobiography, played into the hands of his enemies by seducing Heloise, a young woman he was hired to tutor. She was the niece of a powerful canon of Paris's cathedral of Notre Dame. After she became pregnant, Abelard wed her—but kept the marriage secret, for university teachers, like clergy, were required to be celibate. Her chagrined uncle hired men to break into Abelard's rooms and castrate him.

Abelard sought refuge in the monastic life and induced Heloise to enter a convent. They exchanged letters in which he denigrated his love for her as wretched desire. Repentance failed, however, to ingratiate him with the church authorities. In 1121, his works were burned, and in 1140, 19 propositions that he had taught were condemned as heresies. Heloise outlived him by 20 years and won renown for her efforts to improve conditions for cloistered women.

SOCIETY

THE ORDER OF LIFE

WHAT WERE the three basic social groups in the medieval society?

Medieval commentators described society as consisting of only three categories of people: those who fought as mounted knights (the landed nobility), those who prayed (the clergy), and those who labored in fields and shops (the peasantry and village artisans). After the revival of towns in the 11th century, a fourth social group emerged: the long-distance traders and merchants.

Nobles   By the late Middle Ages, separate classes of higher and lower nobility had evolved. The higher were the great landowners and territorial magnates, long the dominant powers in their regions; the lower were petty landlords, the descendants of minor knights, newly rich merchants, or wealthy farmers.

Arms were the nobleman's profession and waging war his sole occupation. In the eighth century, the adoption of stirrups made mounted warriors Europe's most valued military assets. The chief virtues of these knights were physical strength, courage, and beligerancy. For them, warfare was an opportunity to win wealth, honor, and glory. Peace, on the other hand, meant economic stagnation and boredom.

No medieval social group was absolutely uniform. Noblemen formed a broad spectrum—from minor vassals without subordinate vassals to mighty barons, the principal vassals of a king or prince, who had many vassals of their own. Dignity and status within the nobility were directly proportional to how much authority one exercised over others; a chief with many vassals far excelled the small country nobleman who was lord over none but himself.

By the late Middle Ages, several developments were forcing the landed nobility into a steep economic and political decline from which it never recovered. Climatic changes and agricultural failures created large famines, while the great plague (discussed later in this chapter) brought about unprecedented population losses. Changing military tactics and the appearance of heavy artillery during the Hundred Years' War empowered infantry and made the noble cavalry nearly obsolete. The support wealthy towns gave to kings enabled strong royal governments to reduce the power nobles once had over their private domains. After the 14th century, land and wealth counted for far more than noble lineage as qualifications for entrance into the highest social class.

Clergy   Unlike a noble or a peasant, one was not born into the clerical estate. It was acquired by religious training and ordination and was, in theory at least, open to anyone. There were two fundamental categories of clergy. The **regular clergy** were the monks who lived according to a special ascetic rule (*regula*) in cloisters apart from the world. In the 13th century, the papacy authorized a different kind of monastic order. The friars—the Franciscans and the Dominicans—stayed in the world to preach, combat heresy, and provide social services. The **secular clergy** lived and worked among the laity in the world (*saeculum*). They staffed a vast hierarchy. At the top were the wealthy cardinals, archbishops, and bishops who were drawn almost exclusively from the nobility. Below them were the urban priests, cathedral canons, and court clerks. Finally, there was the great mass of poor parish priests, who were neither financially nor intellectually much above the common people they served.

During most of the Middle Ages, the clergy were honored as the first estate, and theology was the queen of the sciences. There was great popular respect and reverence for the clergy's function as mediators between God and humanity. The priest brought the Son of God down to earth when he celebrated the sacrament of the Eucharist, and his absolution released penitents from punishment for sin. Mere laypeople were not to presume to sit in judgment on such a priest.

Peasants   The largest and lowest social group in medieval society was the one on whose labor the welfare of all the others depended: the agrarian peasantry. Many peasants lived and worked on the manors of the nobility, the vital cells of rural social life. The lord of a manor was owed a fixed amount of produce (grain,

regular clergy Monks and nuns who belong to religious orders.

secular clergy Parish clergy who did not belong to a religious order.

OVERVIEW   MEDIEVAL UNIVERSITIES

In the 12th century, Latin translations of of ancient texts in law, astronomy, philosophy, and mathematics, and of learned commentaries on them by Islamic and Byzantine scholars, reached the West. The resulting intellectual ferment gave rise to the medieval universities. The first university was established at Bologna in Italy in 1158. By 1500, there were almost 50 universities across Europe from Scotland to Poland. Universities helped bring wealth and prestige to towns; graduated professionals, such as lawyers, physicians, and theologians; and provided rulers with trained bureaucrats for their increasingly complex administrations. The following is a list of the medieval universities and the dates of their founding:

University	Country	Date of Founding	University	Country	Date of Founding
Bologna	Italy	1158	Erfurt	Germany	1379
Paris	France	ca. 1150–1160	Heidelberg	Germany	1385
Oxford	England	1167	Ferrara	Italy	1391
Vicenza	Italy	1204	Wurzburg	Germany	1402
Cambridge	England	1209	Leipzig	Germany	1409
Salamanca	Spain	1218	St. Andrews	Scotland	1411
Padua	Italy	1222	Turin	Italy	1412
Naples	Italy	1224	Louvain	Belgium	1426
Toulouse	France	1229	Poitiers	France	1431
Rome	Italy	1244	Caen	France	1437
Siena	Italy	1247	Bourdeaux	France	1441
Piacenza	Italy	1248	Barcelona	Spain	1450
Montpellier	France	1289	Trier	Germany	1450
Lisbon	Portugal	1290	Glasgow	Scotland	1451
Avignon	France	1303	Freiburg	Germany	1455
Orleans	France	1305	Ingolstadt	Germany	1459
Perugia	Italy	1308	Basel	Switzerland	1460
Coimbra	Portugal	1308	Nantes	France	1463
Grenoble	France	1339	Bourges	France	1465
Pisa	Italy	1343	Ofen	Germany	1475
Valladolid	Spain	1346	Tubingen	Germany	1477
Prague	Bohemia	1348	Uppsala	Sweden	1477
Pavia	Italy	1361	Copenhagen	Denmark	1479
Vienna	Austria	1364	Aberdeen	Scotland	1494
Cracow	Poland	1364			

eggs, and the like) and services from its peasant families, and he held judicial and police authority over them. He owned and operated the machines that processed their crops into food and drink, and he had the right to subject his tenants to exactions called *banalities*. He could, for example, force them to breed their cows with his bull, to grind their bread grains in his mill, to bake their bread in his oven, and to make their wine in his wine press—all for a fee. He might also compel them to buy their beer from his brewery and even give him the choice parts of all animals slaughtered on his lands. He collected as an inheritance tax a serf's best animal. Without the lord's permission, a serf could neither travel nor marry outside the manor to which he was attached.

However, the serfs' status was not chattel slavery. It was to a lord's advantage to keep his serfs healthy and happy, for his welfare, like theirs, depended on the quality of their work. Serfs had their own dwellings and strips of land that produced their incomes. They organized their own labor and could market for their own profit any surpluses that remained after they met their obligations. Serfs could pass their property (their dwellings, fields, and personal possessions) on to their children.

Two basic changes transformed conditions of life for the peasantry during the course of the Middle Ages. The first was increasing importance of single-family holdings. As families acquired and retained property from generation to generation, family farms replaced manorial units. The second was the conversion of the serf's dues into money payments, a change made possible by the revival of trade, the rise of town markets, and the return of a monetary economy. By the 13th century, many peasants held their land as rent-paying tenants and no longer had servile status.

In the mid-14th century, when the great plague and the Hundred Years' War created a labor shortage, nobles in England and France tried to turn back the clock by increasing taxes on the peasantry and restricting their migration to the cities. Their efforts triggered rebellions. The revolts of the agrarian peasantry, like those of the urban proletariat, were brutally crushed, but they were only one of the stresses that were threatening to destabilize European society at the end of the Middle Ages.

MEDIEVAL WOMEN

The image of women and the reality of their lives were quite different in the Middle Ages. The image was sketched by celibate male clergy who viewed virginity as morally superior to marriage. Drawing on ancient pagan as well as biblical sources, they claimed that women were physically, mentally, and morally inferior to men. They defined only two respectable roles for them: subjugated housewife, or confined nun. Many medieval women were neither.

Image and Status   The clerical view of women was contradicted both within the church itself and in secular society. During the 12th and 13th centuries, the burgeoning popularity of the cult of the Virgin Mary, of chivalric romances, and of courtly love literature celebrated women as natural moral superiors of men. The church also condemned extreme misogyny.

Virgin and Child, surrounded by angels, by Giovanni Cimabue (1240–1302).

SuperStock, Inc.

Medieval Marketplace. A 15th-century rendering of an 11th- or 12th-century marketplace. Medieval women were active in all trades, but especially in the food and clothing industries.

Scala/Art Resource, N.Y.

10.3
The Goodman of Paris

vernacular Everyday language spoken by the people as opposed to Latin.

HOW DID England and France develop strong royal governments by the 13th century?

Peter Lombard (1100–1169), an influential theologian, taught that God created Eve from Adam's rib because God intended woman neither to rule nor be ruled, but to be at man's side as his partner in a mutual relationship.

Germanic customary law also treated women better than Roman law. German women married men of their own age, and a German bride was entitled to a gift of property from her husband that she retained in case of his death. German law gave women the right to inherit, administer, dispose of, and confer property, and it allowed women to take men to court and sue for bodily injury and rape.

Life Choices   The nunnery was an option only for women from the propertied classes, for admission to a cloister was contingent on payment of a substantial dowry. The number of nuns was never very large in the Middle Ages, but the cloister was an appealing refuge for some. Within a nunnery a woman could rise to a position of leadership and exercise a kind of authority often denied her sisters in the outside world. Even cloistered women, however, had to submit to supervision by male clergy.

In the ninth century, the Carolingian monarchs obeyed the church and began to enforce monogamy. This was both a gain and a loss for women. Wives were accorded greater dignity and legal security, but their burdens as household managers and bearers of children multiplied. The mortality rates of Frankish women increased and their longevity decreased in the ninth century.

Working women   The vast majority of medieval women were neither housewives nor nuns, but working women. Evidence suggests that they were respected and loved by their husbands, perhaps because they worked shoulder to shoulder with them. Between the ages of 10 and 15, girls were apprenticed to learn productive trades, much like boys. If they married, they might operate businesses of their own or go to work in their husband's shops. Women appeared in virtually every "blue-collar" trade, but were especially prominent in the food and clothing industries. They belonged to guilds, and they could become craftmasters, but working women were paid less than men who did the same jobs. In the late Middle Ages, townswomen had opportunities to get some schooling and acquire **vernacular** literacy, but they were excluded from the learned professions.

GROWTH OF NATIONAL MONARCHIES

ENGLAND AND FRANCE: HASTINGS (1066) TO BOUVINES (1214)

William the Conqueror   Medieval England's political destiny was determined by the response to the death of the childless Anglo-Saxon ruler Edward the Confessor (r. 1042–1066). Through a connection with Edward's mother, a Norman princess, Duke William of Normandy (d. 1087) laid claim to the vacant English throne. The Anglo-Saxon assembly preferred a native nobleman, Harold Godwinsson (ca. 1022–1066). William reacted by invading England and defeating Harold's army at Hastings on October 14, 1066. William I "the Conqueror" was crowned king of England in Westminster Abbey within weeks of the invasion.

Battle of Hastings. William the Conqueror on horseback urging his troops into combat with the English at the Battle of Hastings (October 14, 1066). From the Bayeux Tapestry, about 1073–1083.

Giraudon/Art Resource, N.Y.

As England's conqueror, William was free to establish a strong monarchy. He kept the Anglo-Saxon tax system and practice of issuing court writs (legal warnings). He continued the Anglo-Saxon quasi-democratic tradition of frequent *parleying*; that is, conferring with the lesser powers who had vested interests in royal decisions. This led eventually to the balance between monarchical and parliamentary elements that remains a characteristic of England's government.

Popular Rebellion and Magna Carta The Duke of Normandy, who after 1066 was master of England, was also a vassal of the French king in Paris. France's Capetian kings understandably watched with alarm as the power of their Norman vassal grew alarmingly during the reign of William's grandson, Henry II (r. 1154–1189). From his mother Henry inherited Normandy. His father left him Maine, Touraine, and Anjou. Marriage to Eleanor of Aquitaine (1122–1204) brought him her huge duchy in southern France and completed the so-called Angevin or English-French empire. Henry used his resources to promote royal power, but this was met by strong resistance from both the nobility and the clergy.

Under Henry's successors, the brothers Richard the Lion-Hearted (r. 1189–1199) and John (r. 1199–1216), burdensome taxes levied to support Crusades and a failing war with France turned resistance into rebellion. With the full support in 1215 of the clergy and the townspeople, England's barons forced King John grudgingly to agree to terms spelled out in the **Magna Carta** ("Great Charter") in 1215. This famous cornerstone of modern English law limited royal power and secured the right of the privileged classes to representation when the government considered important matters like taxation. The Great Charter charted a path between dissolution of the monarchy by the nobility and the abridgment of the rights of the nobility by the monarchy.

Philip II Augustus Powerful feudal princes dominated France from the beginning of the Capetian dynasty (987) until the reign of Philip II Augustus (1180–1223). During this period the Capetian kings wisely concentrated their limited resources on securing the territory surrounding Paris, the Île-de-France. By the time of Philip II, Paris had become the center of French government and culture, and the Capetian dynasty had acquired a secure hereditary right to the throne. Thereafter, the kings of France steadily enhanced their power over the French nobles.

Philip Augustus waged both internal and international campaigns, and he succeeded at both. His armies reclaimed all of England's continental fiefdoms,

Magna Carta The "Great Charter" limiting royal power, which the English nobility forced King John to sign in 1215.

Gothic Cathedral. The portal of Reims Cathedral, where the kings of France were crowned. The cathedral was built in the Gothic style—emblematic of the High and late Middle Ages—that originated in France in the mid–12th century. The earlier Romanesque (Roman-like) style from which it evolved is characterized by fortresslike buildings with thick stone walls, rounded arches and vaults, and few windows. The Gothic style, in contrast, is characterized by soaring structures, their interiors flooded with colored light from vast expanses of stained glass.

Scala/Art Resource, N.Y.

except for Aquitaine. At Bouvines on July 27, 1214, the French won a decisive victory over the English and their German allies. Philip solidly united France behind its king and laid the foundation for French ascendancy in the late Middle Ages.

FRANCE IN THE 13TH CENTURY: REIGN OF LOUIS IX

Louis IX (r. 1226–1270), the grandson of Philip Augustus, embodied the medieval ideal of kingly authority. Louis's greatest achievements were on the domestic front. Under him, the efficient French bureaucracy established order and fair play in local government. He dispatched commissioners to monitor the conduct of the royal officials who were responsible for local administration and enforcing justice. These royal ambassadors were perceived as genuine champions of the people. Louis abolished private wars among nobles and serfdom within the royal domain, gave his subjects the right of appeal from local to higher courts, and made the tax system more equitable. The French people came to associate their king with justice, and their awareness of themselves as possessors of a unifying national identity grew strong during his reign.

French society and culture, during Louis's lifetime, set a standard for all of Europe, a pattern that continued into the modern period. Northern France became the showcase of monastic reform, chivalry, and Gothic art and architecture. Louis's reign also coincided with the golden age of Scholasticism, in which Europe's greatest thinkers converged on Paris, among them the famous Thomas Aquinas.

THE HOHENSTAUFEN EMPIRE (1152–1272)

Frederick I Barbarossa   While different, but stable, monarchies developed in France and England, the Holy Roman Empire fragmented (see Map 15-3). Frederick I Barbarossa (1152–1190), founder of the Hohenstaufen dynasty, reestablished imperial authority but also initiated a new phase in the contest between popes and emperors. Frederick attempted to consolidate an empire uniting Germany and Italy by stressing feudal bonds, but his reign ended with stalemate in Germany and rising tensions in Italy. In 1186 his son—the future Henry VI (r. 1190–1197)—married Constance, heiress to the kingdom of Sicily. This union of the empire with Sicily threatened the papacy by encircling the Papal States, and turned the popes into determined opponents of the German emperor.

When Henry VI died in September 1197, chaos followed. Civil war erupted in Germany. Henry VI's four-year-old son, Frederick, the heir to the imperial crown, had for his own safety been made—fatefully, it would prove—a ward of Pope Innocent III (r. 1198–1215). Innocent had both the will, the means, and the opportunity to challenge the power of the Hohenstaufens.

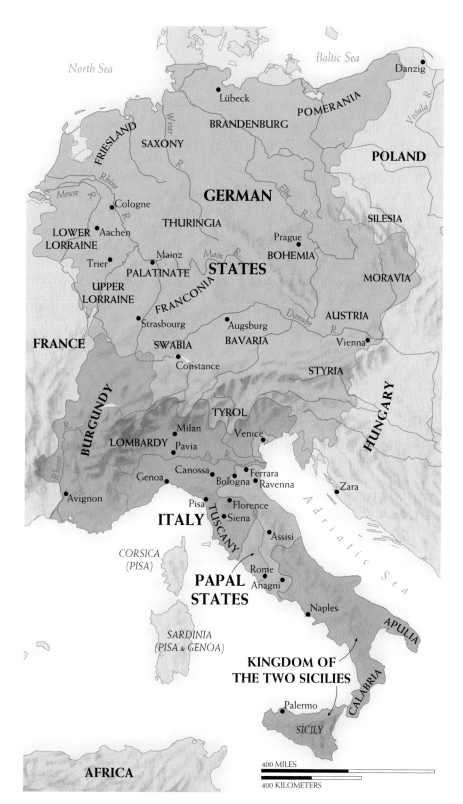

North Sea

Baltic Sea

Danzig

Lübeck

POMERANIA

BRANDENBURG

FRIESLAND

SAXONY

POLAND

Weser R.

Rhine

Meuse R.

GERMAN

Cologne

THURINGIA

SILESIA

LOWER
LORRAINE

Aachen

Prague

Elbe R.

Mainz

BOHEMIA

Trier

STATES

MORAVIA

PALATINATE

UPPER
LORRAINE

FRANCONIA

Main R.

Danube R.

AUSTRIA

FRANCE

Strasbourg

Augsburg

SWABIA

BAVARIA

Vienna

Constance

STYRIA

Rhône R.

BURGUNDY

TYROL

HUNGARY

Milan

Venice

LOMBARDY

Pavia

Po R.

Canossa

Ferrara

Genoa

Bologna

Ravenna

Zara

Avignon

Pisa

Florence

Siena

ITALY

TUSCANY

Assisi

CORSICA
(PISA)

PAPAL
STATES

Rome

Anagni

SARDINIA
(PISA & GENOA)

Naples

APULIA

KINGDOM OF
THE TWO SICILIES

CALABRIA

Palermo

AFRICA

SICILY

Adriatic Sea

400 MILES

400 KILOMETERS

MAP 15–3

Germany and Italy in the Middle Ages.   Medieval Germany and Italy were divided lands. The Holy Roman Empire (Germany) embraced hundreds of independent territories that the emperor ruled only in name. The papacy controlled the Rome area and tried to enforce its will in the Romagna. Under the Hohenstaufens (mid–12th to mid–13th centuries), internal German divisions and papal conflict reached new heights; German rulers sought to extend their power to southern Italy and Sicily.

WHY WERE the emperors unable to unite Germany and Italy in the Middle Ages?

Frederick II In December 1212, shifting alliances in the German war induced the pope to support his ward's coronation as Emperor Frederick II. But Frederick soon disappointed his papal sponsor. He was a Sicilian by upbringing, and he was to spend only 9 of the 38 years of his reign in Germany. To secure the imperial title for himself and his sons, he gave the German princes what they wanted—undisputed authority over their territories. Germany was fragmenting into a gaggle of petty kingdoms.

Frederick had a disastrous relationship with the papacy. Popes excommunicated him four times and roused the German princes against him, launching the church into European politics on a massive scale. Efforts by the papacy to become a formidable political and military power made the church highly vulnerable to criticism from religious reformers and royal apologists.

When Frederick died in 1250, the German monarchy died with him. The princes established an electoral college in 1257 to pick the emperor, and the "king of the Romans" became their puppet. The Hohenstaufen dynasty effectively ended with Frederick.

POLITICAL AND SOCIAL BREAKDOWN

HUNDRED YEARS' WAR

The Causes of the War The Hundred Years' War, which began in May 1337 and lasted until October 1453, started when the English king Edward III (r. 1327–1377), the grandson of Philip the Fair of France (r. 1285–1314), claimed the French throne. But the war was more than a dynastic quarrel. England and France were territorial and economic rivals with a long history of mutual prejudice and animosity This made the Hundred Years' War a struggle for national identity.

Although France had three times the population of England, was far wealthier, and fought on its own soil, most of the major battles were stunning English victories. The primary reason for France's failure was internal disunity caused by endemic social conflict. France lagged behind England in making the transition from a fragmented feudal society to a centralized modern state.

France's defeats also owed much to incompetent leadership and English military superiority. The English infantry was more disciplined than the French feudal cavalry, and English archers could fire six arrows a minute with enough force to pierce an inch of wood or the armor of a knight at 200 yards. Eventually, thanks in part to the inspiring leadership of Joan of Arc (1412–1431), and a sense of national identity and self-confidence, the French were able to expel the English from France. By 1453, all that remained to the English was a coastal enclave at Calais.

Joan was poorly repaid by the king she helped to the throne. When the Burgundians captured her in May 1430, Charles could have secured her release but did not. The Burgundians and the English wanted her publicly discredited, believing this would demoralize French resistance. She was turned over to the Inquisition in English-held Rouen, where, after 10 weeks of interrogation, she was executed on May 30, 1431.

The Hundred Years' War had lasting political and social consequences. It devastated France, but it also awakened French nationalism and hastened the country's transition from a feudal monarchy to a centralized state. In both France and England the burden of the war fell most heavily on the peasantry, who were forced to support it with taxes and services.

WHAT WERE the causes of the political and social breakdown that occurred during the 14th century?

THE BLACK DEATH

Preconditions and Causes   In the late Middle Ages, improvements in agriculture increased the food supply, spurring a growth in population. It is estimated that Europe's population doubled between the years 1000 and 1300, and then began to outstrip food production. Finally, there were more people than food to feed them or jobs to employ them. The average European

10.7
"A Most Terrible Plague:"
Giovanni Boccaccio

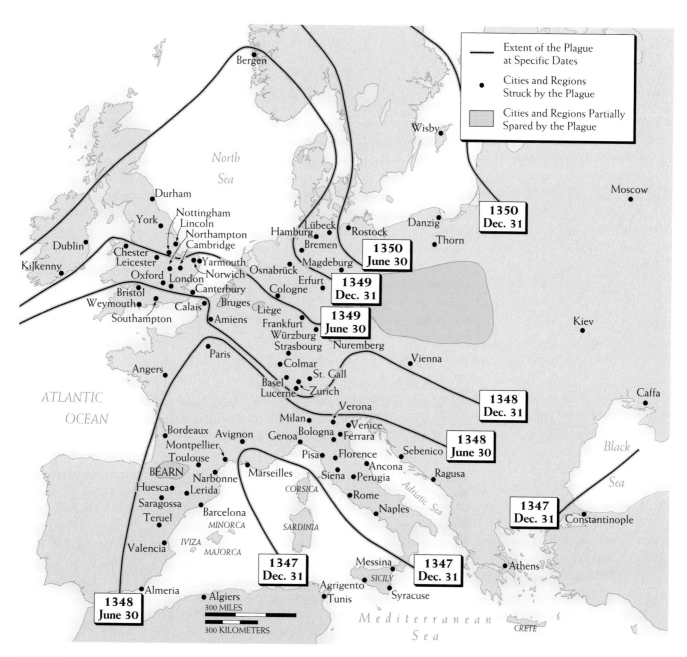

MAP 15–4

Spread of the Black Death.   Apparently introduced by sea-borne rats from areas around the Black Sea where plague-infested rodents have long been known, the Black Death had great human, social, and economic consequences. According to one of the lower estimates, it killed 25 million in Europe. The map charts the spread of the plague in the mid–14th century. Generally following trade routes, it reached Scandinavia by 1350, and some believe it then went on to Iceland and even Greenland. Areas off the main trade routes were largely spared.

WHAT WERE the social and economic consequences of the plague?

faced the probability of famine at least once during his or her average 35-year life-span.

Between 1315 and 1317, crop failures produced the greatest famine of the Middle Ages. Decades of overpopulation, economic depression, famine, and bad health made Europeans vulnerable to a virulent plague that struck with full force in 1348.

This **Black Death**, so called because it discolored the body, travelled the trade routes from Asia into Europe. Appearing in Sicily in late 1347, it entered Europe through Venice, Genoa, and Pisa in 1348, and from there it swept rapidly through Spain and southern France and into northern Europe. Areas outside the major trade routes, like Bohemia, appear to have remained virtually unaffected. The plague made numerous reappearances after its first onslaught, and it is estimated that the population of Europe had been reduced by two-fifths by the early 15th century.

Popular Remedies   The plague was transmitted by fleas and rats, but it also sometimes entered the lungs and was spread by sneezes. Contemporary physicians had little understanding of how diseases worked and no idea how to help people fend off or recover from infection. Popular wisdom held that bad air caused the disease. Some thought that earthquakes had released poisonous fumes. Psychological reactions sometimes went to extremes. Some hoped that moderation and temperance would save them; some wildly indulged their bodily appetites; some fled in panic, and some developed a morbid religiosity. Parades of flagellants whipped themselves, hoping to induce God to show mercy and intervene. Jews were baselessly accused of spreading the disease, and pogroms flared again. The church tried to maintain order, but across Western Europe people developed an obsession with death and dying and a deep pessimism that endured for decades.

Black Death Bubonic plague that killed millions of Europeans in the 14th century.

Social and Economic Consequences   Whole villages vanished in the wake of the plague. With them went much of the labor force that made the estates of the nobility profitable. Demand for farm laborers and skilled artisans drove wages up. Many serfs negotiated substitution of money payment for their traditional servile

Black Death. Men and women carrying plague victims in coffins to the burial ground in Tournai, Belgium, 1349.

The Granger Collection, N. Y.

obligations, or they abandoned the farm altogether and sought jobs in cities. Agricultural prices fell because of lowered demand from a shrunken market, but the price of luxury and manufactured goods—the scarce work of skilled artisans—rose. The standard of living of the nobility was seriously threatened by these developments. Landed aristocrats had to pay more for finished products and for farm labor, but received less for their agricultural produce. Their rents also declined.

Peasants Revolt   To recoup their losses, some landowners converted arable land to sheep pasture. Wool production was less labor-intensive than grain farming. The propertied classes also used their political influence to pass repressive legislation that forced peasants to stay on their farms and froze wages at low levels. The result was the eruption of peasant rebellions in France and England.

Cities Rebound   Although the plague hit urban populations especially hard, the cities and their skilled industries ultimately prospered from its effects. Cities had always protected their interests by regulating competition and immigration from rural areas. After the plague the reach of such laws was extended beyond the cities to include the lands of nobles and landlords, many of whom were now integrated into urban life.

The omnipresence of death whetted the appetite for goods that only skilled urban industries could produce. Expensive cloths, jewelry, furs, and silks were in great demand. Faced with life at its worst, people insisted on having the best. Initially this new demand could not be met, for the first wave of plague transformed an already limited supply of skilled artisans into a shortage almost overnight. As a result, the prices of manufactured and luxury items soared to new heights. This, however, encouraged workers to migrate to the city to become artisans. Urban dwellers enjoyed every advantage. Their products sold at premium prices, but the depressed market for agricultural goods reduced the cost of the things they bought from the countryside.

There was gain and loss for the church as well. As a great landhold, its income and therefore its political influence declined. But it received new revenues from the vastly increased demand for religious services for the dead and the dying and from the multiplication of gifts and bequests.

New Conflicts and Opportunities   The plague contributed to social conflicts within cities. The merchant and patrician classes had long dominated urban government, but they lost ground to the growing economic and political power of artisan and trade guilds. Guilds used their political influence to pass restrictive legislation that protected their markets. Master artisans wanted to keep their numbers low to limit competition, but the journeymen they employed wanted access to the guild so that they could set up shops of their own. To the old conflict between the urban patriciate and the guilds was now added a struggle within the guilds themselves.

In the years following the plague, two groups that had helped to contain the growth of royal power, the landed nobles and the church, were thrust onto the defensive, and kings seized the opportunity to exploit growing national sentiment and work toward the centralization of governments and economies. The nobles lost clout as the new infantry forces that appeared during the Hundred Years' War diminished the importance of the feudal cavalry. The church suffered a reduction in the numbers of clergy—up to one-third in places. To make things worse, the leadership of the church blundered badly.

ECCLESIASTICAL BREAKDOWN AND REVIVAL: THE LATE MEDIEVAL CHURCH

WHAT ISSUES led to the

papal crisis of the late Medieval ages?

BONIFACE VIII AND PHILIP THE FAIR

By the 14th century, popes faced rulers far more powerful than the they were. When Pope Boniface VIII (r. 1294–1303) issued the bull, *Clericis Laicos*, which forbade lay taxation of the clergy without prior papal approval, King Philip the Fair of France (r. 1285–1314) unleashed a ruthless antipapal campaign. On November 18, 1302, Boniface made a last-ditch stand against attempts by states to assert their authority over the churches within their borders. He issued the bull *Unam Sanctam*, which declared that temporal authority was "subject" to the spiritual power of the church. The French, however, responded with force. Philip sent troops into Italy who captured the pope, beat him badly, and might have executed him had not an aroused populace rescued him. No pope ever again seriously tried to threaten a king or emperor. Relations between church and state henceforth were characterized by increasing state control of religion.

THE GREAT SCHISM (1378–1417) AND THE CONCILIAR MOVEMENT TO 1449

After Boniface VIII's death, his successor, Clement V (r. 1305–1314), moved the papal court to Avignon on the southeastern border with France, where it remained until Pope Gregory XI (r. 1370–1378) returned the papacy to Rome in January 1377. His successor, Pope Urban VI (r. 1378–1389), proclaimed his intention to reform the **Curia**. This announcement alarmed the cardinals, most of whom were French. Not wanting to surrender the benefits of a papacy under French influence, the French king, Charles V (r. 1364–1380), supported a schism in the church, and on September 20, 1378, 13 cardinals, all but one of whom was French, elected a cousin of the French king as Pope Clement VII (r. 1378–1397). Clement's papacy was seated in Avignon. This **Great Schism** created two papal courts, and support for them divided along political lines: England and its allies (the **Holy Roman Empire**, Hungary, Bohemia, and Poland) acknowledged Urban VI, whereas France and its allies (Naples, Scotland, Castile, and Aragon) backed Clement VII. Today, only the Roman line of popes is recognized as legitimate by the church.

In 1409, a council at Pisa deposed both the Roman and the Avignon popes and elected its own new pope. But neither Rome nor Avignon accepted its action, so after 1409 there were three contending popes. This intolerable situation ended when Emperor Sigismund (r. 1410–1437) prevailed on the Pisan pope to summon a council of the church in Constance in 1414. The Roman pope Gregory XII (r. 1406–1415) also eventually recognized its legitimacy. After the three contending popes had either resigned or been deposed, the council elected a new pope, Martin V (r. 1417–1431), in November 1417. After nearly 30 years of schism, the church was again reunited

Under Pope Eugenius IV (r. 1431–1447), the papacy regained much of its prestige and authority, and in 1460 the papal bull *Execrabilis* condemned all appeals to councils as "completely null and void." But the conciliar movement had planted deep within the conscience of all western peoples the conviction that the leader of an institution must be responsive to its members and not act against their best interests.

Curia Papal government.

Great Schism Appearance of two and at times three rival popes between 1378 and 1415.

Holy Roman Empire Revival of the old Roman Empire, based mainly in Germany and northern Italy, that endured from 870 to 1806.

THE RENAISSANCE IN ITALY (1375–1527)

*M*ost scholars agree that the **Renaissance** was a transition from the medieval to the modern world. Medieval Europe, especially before the 12th century, had been a fragmented feudal society with an agricultural economy, its thought and culture dominated by the church. Renaissance Europe, especially after the 14th century, was characterized by growing national consciousness and political centralization, an urban economy based on organized commerce and capitalism, and ever greater lay and secular control of thought and culture.

The distinctive features and achievements of the Renaissance are most strikingly revealed in Italy from roughly 1375 to 1527, the year Rome was sacked by imperial soldiers. What was achieved in Italy during these centuries also deeply influenced northern Europe.

THE ITALIAN CITY-STATE: SOCIAL CONFLICT AND DESPOTISM

The Renaissance began in the cities of late medieval Italy. Italy was the natural gateway between East and West. Its vibrant urban societies, such as Venice, Genoa, and Pisa, traded uninterruptedly with the Middle East throughout the Middle Ages. During the 13th and 14th centuries, the trade-rich Italian cities became powerful city-states, dominating the political and economic life of their surrounding countrysides. By the 15th century, the great Italian cities had become the bankers for much of Europe. There were five major and competing states in Italy: the duchy of Milan, the republics of Florence and Venice, the Papal States, and the kingdom of Naples.

Social strife and competition for political power were so intense within the cities that to maintain order and survive, most had, by the 15th century, found it necessary to submit to the control of a despot. Venice, ruled by a successful merchant oligarchy, was the notable exception. Elsewhere, the new social classes and divisions within society produced by rapid urban growth fueled chronic, near-anarchic conflict.

In Florence, divisions created turmoil at every level of society. True stability was not established until the ascent to power in 1434 of Cosimo de' Medici (1389–1464), the wealthiest man in Florence and a most astute statesman. Cosimo controlled the city internally from behind the scenes, skillfully manipulating its constitution and influencing elections. His grandson Lorenzo the Magnificent (1449–1492, r. 1478–1492) exercised near totalitarian authority.

Despotism was less subtle elsewhere in Italy. To prevent internal social conflict and foreign intrigue from paralyzing their cities, the dominant groups in many cities cooperated to install a hired strongman,

WHY WAS the Renaissance a transition from the medieval to the modern world?

Renaissance Revival of ancient learning and the supplanting of traditional religious beliefs by new secular and scientific values that began in Italy in the 14th and 15th centuries.

Cosimo de' Medici (1389–1464). Florentine banker and statesman, in his lifetime the city's wealthiest man and most successful politician. This portrait is by Jacopo da Pontormo (1494–1556).

Jacopo Pontormo (1494–1556), "Cosimo de' Medici the Elder, Pater Patriae," (1389–1464). Oil on wood, 87 × 65 cm. Inv. 3574. Uffize, Florence. Photograph © Erich Lessing/Art Resource, N.Y.

Church and Empire

910	Monastery of Cluny founded
918	Henry I becomes King of Germany
951	Otto I invades Italy
955	Otto I defeats the Hungarians at Lechfeld
962	Otto I crowned emperor by Pope John XII
1077	Gregory VII pardons Henry IV at Canossa
1122	Concordat of Worms settles the investiture controversy
1152–1190	Reign of Frederick Barbarossa
1198–1215	Reign of Innocent III
1214	Collapse of the claims of Otto IV
1220	Frederick II crowned emperor
1232	Frederick II devolves authority to the German princes
1257	The German monarchy becomes elective

humanism Study of the Latin and Greek classics and of the Church Fathers both for their own sake and to promote a rebirth of ancient norms and values.

studia humanitatis During the Renaissance, a liberal arts program of study that embraced grammar, rhetoric, poetry, history, philosophy, and politics.

a *podesta*, to maintain law and order. Because these despots could not depend on the cooperation of a divided populace, they relied on mercenary armies to maintain order.

Political turbulence and warfare motivated the development of diplomacy. Most city-states established resident embassies during the 15th century, and their ambassadors were their watchful eyes and ears at rival courts. They stayed abreast of foreign military developments and, if shrewd enough, gained power and advantage without actually going to war.

HUMANISM

Humanism was the scholarly study of the Latin and Greek classics and the ancient Church Fathers both for their own sake and to promote a rebirth of ancient norms and values. Humanists advocated the *studia humanitatis*, a liberal arts program consisting of rhetoric, poetry, history, politics, and moral philosophy.

The first humanists were orators and poets. They wrote in both the classical and the vernacular languages and drew their inspiration from newly discovered works of the ancients. They taught rhetoric within the universities, and they were sought as secretaries, speech writers, and diplomats in princely and papal courts.

Classical and Christian antiquity had been studied before the Italian Renaissance. However, the Italian Renaissance of the late Middle Ages was more secular and lay dominated, had broader interests, recovered more manuscripts, and possessed far superior technical skills than the earlier medieval rebirths of interest in antiquity.

Unlike their Scholastic rivals, humanists were not content only to summarize and compare the views of recognized authorities on a question, but instead went directly to original sources and drew their own conclusions. Avidly searching out manuscript collections, Italian humanists made the full corpus of Greek and Latin antiquity available to scholars during the 14th and 15th centuries. Mastery of Latin and Greek was their primary instrument. There is a kernel of truth—but only a kernel—in the arrogant boast of the humanists that the period between themselves and classical civilization was a "dark middle age."

Petrarch, Dante, and Boccaccio Francesco Petrarch (1304–1374), the father of humanism, left the legal profession to pursue his love of letters and poetry. Petrarch celebrated ancient Rome in his writings and tirelessly collected ancient manuscripts; among his finds were letters by Cicero. His critical textual studies, elitism, and contempt for the allegedly useless learning of the Scholastics were shared by many later humanists.

Petrarch had a far more secular orientation than Dante Alighieri (1265–1321), whose *Vita Nuova* and *Divine Comedy* form, with Petrarch's sonnets, the cornerstones of Italian vernacular literature. Petrarch's student and friend Giovanni Boccaccio (1313–1375), author of the *Decameron*, 100 bawdy tales told by three men and seven women in a country retreat from the plague that ravaged Florence in 1348, also pioneered humanist studies. An avid

HISTORY'S VOICES

PICO DELLA MIRANDOLA STATES THE RENAISSANCE IMAGE OF MAN

One of the most eloquent Renaissance descriptions of the abilities of humankind comes from the Italian humanist Pico della Mirandola (1463–1494). In his famed Oration on the Dignity of Man (ca. 1486), Pico described humans as free to become whatever they choose.

IN WHAT does the dignity of humankind consist? Does Pico reject the biblical description of Adam and Eve's fall? Does he exaggerate a person's ability to choose freely to be whatever he or she wishes? What inspired such seeming hubris during the Renaissance?

The best of artisans [God] ordained that that creature (man) to whom He [God] had been able to give nothing proper to himself should have joint possession of whatever had been peculiar to each of the different kinds of being. He therefore took man as a creature of indeterminate nature and, assigning him a place in the middle of the world, addressed him thus: "Neither a fixed abode nor a form that is thine alone or any function peculiar to thyself have we given thee, Adam, to the end that according to thy longing and according to thy judgment thou mayest have and possess what abode, what form, and what functions thou thyself shalt desire. The nature of all other beings is limited and constrained within the bounds of laws prescribed by Us. Thou, constrained by no limits, in accordance with thine own free will, in whose hand We have placed thee, shalt ordain for thyself the limits of thy nature. We have set thee at the world's center that thou mayest from thence more easily observe whatever is in the world. We have made thee neither of heaven nor of earth, neither mortal nor immortal, so that with freedom of choice and with honor, as though the maker and molder of thyself, thou mayest fashion thyself in whatever shape thou shalt prefer. Thou shalt have the power to degenerate into the lower forms of life, which are brutish. Thou shalt have the power, out of thy soul's judgment, to be reborn into the higher forms, which are divine." O supreme generosity of God the Father, O highest and most marvelous felicity of man! To him it is granted to have whatever he chooses, to be whatever he wills.

Source: Giovanni Pico della Mirandola, *Oration on the Dignity of Man*, in *The Renaissance Philosophy of Man*, ed. by E. Cassirer et al. Phoenix Books, 1961, pp. 224–225. Reprinted by permission of The University of Chicago Press.

collector of manuscripts, Boccaccio assembled an encyclopedia of Greek and Roman mythology.

Educational Reforms and Goals   The classical ideal of a useful education that produces well-rounded people inspired far-reaching reforms in traditional education. The most influential Italian Renaissance tract on education, Pietro Paolo Vergerio's (1349–1420) *On the Morals That Befit a Free Man*, was derived directly from classical models. Vittorino da Feltre (d. 1446) guided his students through a highly disciplined curriculum that combined the reading of ancient authors with vigorous physical exercise (see "Pico della Mirandola States the Renaissance Image of Man").

Educated and cultured noblewomen also had a prominent place at Renaissance courts, among them Christine de Pisan (1363?–1434). She was an expert in classical, French, and Italian languages and literature and became a well-known woman of letters in the courts of Europe. Her most famous work, *The City of Ladies*, describes the accomplishments of the great women of history.

RENAISSANCE ART

In Renaissance Italy, as later in Reformation Europe, the values and interests of the laity were less subordinated to those of the clergy. In education, culture, and religion, medieval Christian values were adjusting to a more this-worldly spirit. Men and women began again to appreciate and even to glorify the secular world, secular learning, and purely human pursuits as ends in themselves.

This perspective on life is especially prominent in the painting and sculpture of the High Renaissance (late 15th and early 16th centuries), when Renaissance art reached its full maturity. In imitation of Greek and Roman art, painters and sculptors attempted to create harmonious, symmetrical, and properly proportioned figures, portraying the human form with a glorified realism. Whereas Byzantine and Gothic art had been religious and idealized in the extreme, Renaissance art, especially in the 15th century, realistically reproduced nature and human beings as a part of nature.

Renaissance artists took advantage of new technical skills and materials developed during the 15th century: the use of slow-drying oil paints, of contrast of light and shade to enhance realism (**chiaroscuro**), and of linear perspective to give the viewer the illusion of three-dimensional space. Compared with their flat Byzantine and Gothic counterparts, Renaissance paintings seem filled with energy and life. The great masters of the High Renaissance include Leonardo da Vinci (1452–1519), Raphael (1483–1520), and Michelangelo Buonarroti (1475–1564).

chiaroscuro Use of shading to enhance naturalness in painting and drawing.

Aviation Drawings by Leonardo da Vinci (1452–1519). He imagined a possible flying machine with a retractable ladder for boarding.

David Forbert/SuperStock, Inc.

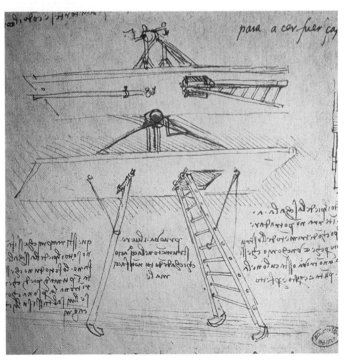

Leonardo da Vinci   Leonardo personified the Renaissance ideal of the universal person, one who is not only a jack-of-all-trades but also a master of many. A military engineer and advocate of scientific experimentation, he dissected corpses to learn anatomy and was a self-taught botanist. He sketched designs for such modern machines as airplanes and submarines. The variety of his interests tended, however, to shorten his attention span, so that he constantly moved from one activity to another. As a painter, his great skill lay in conveying inner moods through complex facial features. This is the intriguing characteristic of his most famous painting, the *Mona Lisa*.

Raphael   Raphael, who died young (37), is reknowned for his tender depictions of the Virgin Mary and the infant Jesus. Art historians also consider his fresco *The School of Athens*, which depicts Plato and Aristotle surrounded by philosophy and science, one of the best examples of Renaissance artistic theory and technique.

Michelangelo   This melancholy genius also excelled in a variety of arts and crafts. His 18-foot statue *David* is a perfect example of the Renaissance artist's devotion to harmony, symmetry, and proportion, and to the extreme glorification of the human form. Four different popes commissioned works by Michelangelo, the best known of which are the frescoes for the Sistine Chapel, which he painted for Pope Julius II (r. 1503–1513).

His later works mark the passing of High Renaissance painting and the advent of a new, experimental style called *mannerism*, which flourished in the late 16th and early 17th centuries. Mannerism derived its name from the "mannered" or "affected" way in which artists expressed their individual perceptions and feelings. Tintoretto (d. 1594) and especially El Greco (d. 1614) are its supreme representatives.

ITALY'S POLITICAL DECLINE: THE FRENCH INVASIONS (1494–1527)

Italy's autonomous city-states had always worked together to oppose foreign invaders. But in 1494, when Naples, backed by Florence and the Borgia pope Alexander VI (1492–1503), prepared to attack Milan, the Milanese despot Ludovico il Moro (r. 1476–1499) invited the French to invade to assert a dynastic claim France had to Naples. France, however, also laid claim to Milan, and the French appetite for territory became insatiable once French armies had crossed the Alps and reestablished themselves in Italy.

The French king Charles VIII (r. 1483–1498) quickly responded to Ludovico's call. Within five months, he had crossed the Alps (August 1495) and raced as conqueror through Florence and the Papal States into Naples. Charles's lightning march through Italy alarmed Ferdinand (r. 1479–1516), king of Aragon and Sicily. He organized a counteralliance (the League of Venice) that forced Charles to retreat.

The French returned to Italy under Charles's successor, Louis XII (r. 1498–1515), this time assisted by the Borgia pope Alexander VI (1492–1503). Alexander, probably the most corrupt pope in history, wanted to carve out a duchy for his son Cesare, in Romagna, officially part of the Papal States. Hoping that a French alliance would allow him to regain control of the region, Alexander abandoned the League of Venice. This made the league too weak to defend Milan, which Louis successfully invaded in August 1499. In 1500, he and Ferdinand of Aragon divided Naples, while the pope and Cesare Borgia conquered the Romagna without opposition.

In 1503, Cardinal Giuliano della Rovere became Pope Julius II (1503–1513). He suppressed the Borgias and placed their newly conquered lands in Romagna under papal jurisdiction. After securing the Papal States with French aid, Julius changed sides and sought to rid Italy of his former allies. Julius, Ferdinand of Aragon, and Venice formed the Holy League in October 1511, which was soon joined by Emperor Maximilian I (r. 1493–1519) and the Swiss. By 1512 the French were in full retreat.

The French invaded Italy again under Louis's successor, Francis I (r. 1515–1547). French armies massacred the Holy League's Swiss army at Marignano in September 1515, and forced the Medici pope Leo X (r. 1513–1521) to agree to the Concordat of Bologna (August 1516). The agreement gave the French king control over the French clergy and the right to collect

mannerism A style of art in the mid to late 16th century that permitted artists to express their own "manner" or feelings in contrast to the symmetry and simplicity of the art of the High Renaissance.

Major Political Events of the Italian Renaissance (1375–1527)

1378–1382	Ciompi revolt in Florence
1434	Medici rule in Florence established by Cosimo de' Medici
1454–1455	Treaty of Lodi allies Milan, Naples, and Florence (in effect until 1494)
1494	Charles VIII of France invades Italy
1495	League of Venice unites Venice, Milan, the Papal States, the Holy Roman Empire, and Spain against France
1499	Louis XII invades Milan (the second French invasion of Italy)
1500	The Borgias conquer Romagna
1512–1513	The Holy League (Pope Julius II, Ferdinand of Aragon, Emperor Maximilian I, and Venice) defeat the French
1513	Machiavelli writes *The Prince*
1515	Francis I leads the third French invasion of Italy
1516	Concordat of Bologna between France and the papacy
1527	Sack of Rome by imperial soldiers

Niccolò Machiavelli. Santi di Tito's portrait of Machiavelli, perhaps the most famous Italian political theorist, who advised Renaissance princes to practice artful deception and inspire fear in their subjects if they wished to succeed.

Scala/Art Resource, N.Y.

taxes from them in exchange for France's recognition of the pope's superiority to church councils. The terms helped keep France Catholic after the outbreak of the Protestant Reformation. But France's thrust into Italy began the first of four major wars with Spain, the Habsburg-Valois wars. These wars stretched over the first half of the 16th century, and France won none of them.

NICCOLÒ MACHIAVELLI

Invasions and wars made a shambles of Italy, and Niccolò Machiavelli (1469–1527) watched as French, Spanish, and German armies wreaked havoc on his country. The more he saw, the more convinced he became that the creation of a unified, independent Italy was an end that justified any means needed to achieve it. Machiavelli admired the heroic acts of ancient Roman rulers, what Renaissance people called their *Virtu*. Romanticizing the old Roman citizenry, he lamented the absence of comparable heroism among his compatriots. His perspective led him to pen distorted interpretations of both ancient and contemporary history.

Machiavelli's comparison of the noble achievements of idealized ancient Romans with the failures of his "Roman" contemporaries led him to conclusions that have made *Machiavellian* synonymous with cynicism. Only an unscrupulous strongman, he argued, using duplicity and terror, could impose order on so divided and selfish a people as his countrymen. Machiavelli was probably in earnest when he advised rulers to consider the advantages of fraud and brutality. He apparently hoped to see a strong ruler emerge from the Medici family. The Medicis, however, were not destined to be Italy's deliverers. The second Medici pope, Clement VII (r. 1523–1534), watched helplessly as Rome was sacked by the army of Emperor Charles V (r. 1519–1556) in 1527, the year of Machiavelli's death.

REVIVAL OF MONARCHY: NATION BUILDING IN THE 15TH CENTURY

*A*fter 1450, unified national monarchies progressively replaced fragmented and divisive feudal governance. The dynastic and chivalric ideals of feudalism did not, however, disappear. Minor territorial princes survived, and representative assemblies even gained influence in some regions. But by the late 15th and early 16th centuries, the old problem of the one and the many was being decided clearly in favor of monarchy.

The feudal monarchies of the High Middle Ages split the basic powers of government between a king and his semiautonomous vassals. The nobility and the towns worked with varying degrees of unity and success through evolving representative bodies, such as the English Parliament, the French Estates General, and the Spanish Cortes, to thwart the centralization of royal power. However, the Hundred Years' War and the schism in the church undercut the

WHAT WERE the bases for the rise of the modern sovereign state in the 15th century?

power of the landed nobility and the clergy respectively in the late Middle Ages, and the increasingly important towns sided with the kings. Loyal, businesswise townspeople, not the nobles and the clergy, staffed offices in royal governments, becoming the king's lawyers, bookkeepers, military tacticians, and diplomats. This alliance between king and town slowly broke the bonds of feudal society and promoted the rise of the modern sovereign state.

In a sovereign state, the powers of taxation, war making, and law enforcement are no longer the right of local semiautonomous vassals but are concentrated at the center in the monarch and exercised by his chosen agents. Taxes, wars, and laws become national rather than merely regional matters. Only as monarchs won free of the nobility and representative assemblies could they overcome the decentralization that was the chief obstacle to nation building.

Monarchies also began to create standing national armies in the 15th century. As the aristocratic cavalry receded in importance and the infantry and the artillery emerged as the primary forces, many kings employed mercenary soldiers recruited from Switzerland and Germany. The growing cost of warfare increased a king's need to develop new sources of income, but expansion of royal revenues was hampered by the upper classes' stubborn belief that they were immune from taxation. The nobility guarded their properties and traditional rights and despised taxation as an insult and a humiliation. Royal revenues accordingly grew at the expense of those least able to resist and least able to pay. Monarchs had several options. As feudal lords they collected rents from their personal domains. They might also levy national taxes on basic food and clothing, such as the *gabelle* or salt tax in France and the *alcabala* or 10 percent sales tax on commercial transactions in Spain. Kings could also levy direct taxes on the peasantry (such as the French *taille*) and on commercial transactions in towns that were under royal protection. They did this with the cooperation of assemblies that represented the privileged classes but not the peasants who paid the taxes. In the 15th century innovative fund-raising devices, such as sale of public offices and issuance of high-interest government bonds, appeared. But kings still did not levy taxes on the powerful aristocrats. Instead, they turned to rich nobles, as they did to the great bankers of Italy and Germany, for loans, bargaining with the privileged classes, who were often as much the kings' creditors and competitors as their subjects.

MEDIEVAL RUSSIA

In the late 10th century, Prince Vladimir of Kiev (r. 972–1015), then Russia's chief city, converted to Greek Orthodoxy. It became the religion of Russia and added a new cultural bond to the long-standing commercial ties the Russians had with the Byzantine Empire.

Vladimir's successor, Yaroslav the Wise (r. 1016–1054), turned Kiev into a magnificent political and cultural center, but after his death, rivalry among princes challenged Kiev's dominance, and it became just one of several national centers.

Mongol Rule (1243–1480)   Mongol (or Tatar) armies (see Chapters 8 and 13) invaded Russia in 1223, and Kiev fell to them in 1240. Russia's cities became tribute-paying principalities of the portion of the Mongol Empire called **Golden Horde**. It had its capital at Sarai, on the lower Volga. Mongol rule drew Russia away from the West but left Russia's traditional political institutions and religion largely intact. Mongolian power and trade contacts also enhanced the peace and prosperity of Russia.

taille   Direct tax on the French peasantry.

Golden Horde   Name given to the Mongol rulers of Russia from 1240 to 1480.

Exterior of a Russian Orthodox Church in Novgorod, Russia.

UNESCO, Ann Ronan/ The Image Works.

11.8
Kuyuk Khan, Letter to
Pope Innocent IV

Russian Liberation The princes of Moscow cooperated with the Mongols, grew wealthy, and gradually expanded their principality through land purchases, colonization, and conquest. In 1380, Grand Duke Dimitri of Moscow (1350–1389) defeated Tatar forces at Kulikov Meadow in a victory that marked the beginning of the decline of Mongolian hegemony. Another century passed before Ivan III, called Ivan the Great (d. 1505), brought all of northern Russia under Moscow's control and ended Mongol rule (1480). By the last quarter of the 15th century, Moscow had replaced Kiev as the political and religious center of Russia. After the fall of Constantinople to the Turks in 1453, Russians laid claim to the legacy of the Byzantine Empire and proclaimed Moscow the "third Rome."

FRANCE

There were two cornerstones of French nation building in the 15th century. The first was England's retreat from the continent following its loss of the Hundred Years' War. The second was the defeat of Charles the Bold (r. 1467–1477) and his duchy of Burgundy. The dukes of Burgundy were probably Europe's strongest rulers in the mid-15th century, and they hoped to build a dominant middle kingdom between France and the Holy Roman Empire. They might have succeeded had not the Continental powers joined forces to oppose them. The dream of Burgundian empire died in 1477, when Charles the Bold was killed in battle at Nancy.

The dissolution of Burgundy removed a serious threat to France and cleared the way for its King Louis XI (r. 1461–1483) to build a powerful monarchy. By annexing and adding Burgundian lands to his own Angevin inheritance, Louis doubled the size of his kingdom. He harnessed the nobility and expanded trade and industry.

Strength does not necessarily ensure a healthy future for a nation. It was because Louis left his successors such a secure and efficient government that they were able to pursue Italian conquests in the 1490s and to fight a long series of losing wars with the Habsburgs in the first half of the 16th century. By the mid-16th century, France was again a defeated nation and almost as divided internally as it had been during the Hundred Years' War.

SPAIN

Spain, too, became a strong country in the late 15th century. Both Castile and Aragon had been poorly ruled, divided kingdoms in the mid-15th century, but the marriage in 1469 of Isabella of Castile (r. 1474–1504) and Ferdinand of Aragon (r. 1479–1516) changed that trend. Their union was strongly protested by their neighbors, Portugal and France, who foresaw the formidable European power it would create. Castile was by far the richer and more populous of the two kingdoms, having an estimated five million inhabitants to Aragon's less than one million. Castile also had a lucrative sheep-farming industry. An example of the growing trend toward centralized economic planning, it was run by a government-backed organization called the *Mesta*. Although the two kingdoms were dynastically united by the marriage of Ferdinand and Isabella in 1469, each retained its own laws, armies, coinage, tax systems, and cultural traditions.

Ferdinand and Isabella could do together what neither could accomplish alone: subdue their realms, secure their borders, and conduct foreign military ventures. Townspeople allied themselves with the crown and progressively replaced nobles within the royal administration. The crown further circumscribed the power of the nobility by extending its authority over the wealthy chivalric orders.

Spain had long been remarkable as a place where three religions—Islam, Judaism, and Christianity—coexisted with a certain degree of toleration. This changed dramatically as Ferdinand and Isabella exerted state control over religion. They totally dominated the Spanish church and made religion serve the cause of national unity. They appointed the higher clergy and the officers of the Inquisition. The Inquisition was a key national agency established in 1479 to monitor the activity of Spain's converted Jews (*conversos*) and Muslims (*Moriscos*). It was run by Isabella's confessor, Tomás de Torquemada (d. 1498). In 1492, Ferdinand and Isabella exiled all Jews from Spain and confiscated their properties. In 1502, nonconverting Moors in Granada were driven into exile. The state imposed regimented, uniform spiritual practices on its subjects. Spain remained a loyal Catholic country through the era of the Reformation and provided a base of operation for the Counter-Reformation resurgence of the Catholic Church.

Ferdinand and Isabella had wide horizons. The anti-French marriage alliances they arranged for their children determined much of European history in the 16th century. In 1496, their eldest daughter, Joanna, later known as "the Mad" (1479–1555), married Archduke Philip (1478–1506), the son of Emperor Maximilian I (r. 1493–1519). Their son, Charles I, the first king of a united Spain, acquired by inheritance and his election as Emperor Charles V in 1519 a European realm almost equal in size to Charlemagne's. A second daughter, Catherine of Aragon (1485–1536), married King Henry VIII of England. The failure of this marriage led to the English Reformation.

Ferdinand and Isabella's vision for Spain's future was also revealed by their sponsorship of overseas exploration. They sent the Genoese adventurer Christopher Columbus (1451–1506) west in search of a shorter route to the spice markets of the Far East. The islands he discovered in the Caribbean began the creation of the Spanish Empire in Mexico and Peru. Gold and silver from their mines helped to make Spain Europe's dominant power in the 16th century.

ENGLAND

The last half of the 15th century was a difficult period for England. Following its loss of the Hundred Years' War, civil war broke out in England between two rival branches of the royal family, the House of York and the House of Lancaster. This conflict, named the Wars of the Roses (York's symbol, according to legend, was a white rose, and Lancaster's a red rose), kept England in turmoil from 1455 to 1485.

The Lancastrian, King Henry VI (r. 1422–1461), was challenged by the Duke of York and his supporters in the prosperous southern towns. In 1461 the Duke of York's son seized power and became King Edward IV (r. 1461–1483). Assisted by loyal and able ministers, he bent Parliament to his will. His brother and successor, Richard III (r. 1483–1485), was confronted by growing support for the exiled Lancastrian leader Henry Tudor. Henry defeated Richard on Bosworth Field in August 1485 to become King Henry VII (r. 1485–1509), founder of a Tudor dynasty that endured until 1603.

To bring the rival royal families together and give his offspring an incontestable hereditary claim to the throne, Henry married Edward IV's daughter, Elizabeth of York. With the aid of a much-feared instrument of royal power, the Court of Star Chamber, he imposed discipline on the English nobility. He shrewdly construed legal precedents to the advantage of the crown and used English law to further his own ends. He confiscated so much noble land and so many fortunes that he was able to govern without depending on Parliament for grants. Henry constructed a powerful monarchy that became one of early modern Europe's most exemplary governments during the reign of his granddaughter, Elizabeth I (r. 1558–1603).

SUMMARY

Medieval Society Medieval society was divided in theory into three main groups: clergy (those who prayed), nobility (those who fought as mounted warriors), and laborers (peasants and artisans). The rise of merchants, self-governing towns, and universities helped break down this division. By supporting rulers against the nobility, towns gave kings the resources—money and university-trained bureaucrats and lawyers—to build national governments. Much of medieval history involves the struggle by rulers to assert their authority over powerful local lords and the church.

Church and State The medieval papacy sought to extend its power over both church and state. In the 10th century, the Cluny reform movement increased popular respect for the church and strengthened the papacy. In the Investiture Struggle, the papacy secured the independence of the clergy by enlisting the support of the German princes against the Holy Roman Emperors, thus weakening imperial power in Germany. The First Crusade further strengthened papal prestige. But, by the end of the 13th century, kings had become more powerful than popes, and the French king, Philip the Fair, was able to defy the papacy. In the 14th century, the Great Schism further weakened papal prestige. Although the papacy was able to fend off a movement to make church councils superior to popes, it never recovered its authority over national rulers.

Nation Building By the 15th century, England, France, and Spain had developed into strong national monarchies with centralized bureaucracies and professional armies. Although medieval institutions, such as the English Parliament, in theory limited royal power, in practice monarchs in these countries held unchallenged authority. The Great Schism, the Hundred Years' War, and the Black Death had weakened the church and the nobility, while townspeople supported kings. A similar process was beginning in Russia where the rulers of Moscow were extending their authority after throwing off Mongol rule. In the empire, however, regional lords had defeated the emperors' attempts to build a strong central state.

The Renaissance The Renaissance, which began in the Italian city-states in the late 14th century, marks the transition from the medieval to the modern world. Humanism, the scholarly study of the Greek and Latin classics and the ancient Church fathers, promoted a rebirth of ancient norms and values and the classical ideal of an educated, well-rounded person. The growth of secular values led to a great burst of artistic activity by artists such as da Vinci, Raphael, and Michelangelo. The political weakness of the Italian states invited foreign intervention by France, Spain, and the Habsburgs. The sack of Rome by imperial forces in 1527 marks the end of the Renaissance.

IMAGE KEY

for pages 336–337

a. Two-handed sword, circa 1600
b. Raphael's portrait (ca.1515) of Baldassare Castiglione (1478–1529)
c. Students attending a lecture, detail of the Tomb of Giovanni da Legnano
d. From the Bayeux Tapestry (ca. 1073–1083), William the Conqueror on horseback
e. An eleventh- or twelfth-century marketplace in a fifteenth-century rendering
f. Pope Innocent III
g. Michelangelo's *Pietà* (ca. 1498–1500)
h. Statue of Pope Boniface VIII
i. Cosimo de' Medici
j. Joan of Arc

REVIEW QUESTIONS

1. What were the objectives of the Cluny reform movement? Why did it succeed?

2. Was the investiture controversy a political or a religious conflict?

3. Why did Germany remain divided while France and England were able to begin forming strong, unified states during the High Middle Ages?

4. How did the Hundred Years' War, the Black Death, and the Great Schism in the church affect the course of history?

5. What gave rise to towns? How did they change medieval society?

6. What was "reborn" in the Renaissance?

KEY TERMS

Black Death (p. 356)
chiaroscuro (p. 362)
Crusades (p. 340)
Curia (p. 358)
Golden Horde (p. 365)
Great Schism (p. 358)

guild (p. 345)
Holy Roman Empire (p. 358)
humanism (p. 360)
Magna Carta (p. 351)
mannerism (p. 363)
regular clergy (p. 347)

Renaissance (p. 359)
Scholasticism (p. 345)
secular clergy (p. 347)
studia humanitatis (p. 360)
taille (p. 365)
vernacular (p. 350)

 For additional study resources for this chapter, go to:
www.prenhall.com/craig/chapter15

PART FOUR THE WORLD IN TRANSITION

EUROPE

1517–1555	Protestant Reformation
1533–1584	Ivan the Terrible of Russia reigns
1540	Jesuit Order founded by Ignatius Loyola
1543–1727	Scientific Revolution
1556–1598	Philip II of Spain reigns
1558–1603	Elizabeth I of England reigns
1562–1598	French Wars of Religion
1581	The Netherlands declares its independence from the Spanish Habsburgs
1588	Defeat of the Spanish Armada
1589–1610	Henry IV, Navarre, founds Bourbon dynasty of France

▲ Queen Elizabeth I

NEAR EAST/ INDIA

1500–1722	Safavid Shi'ite rule in Iran
1512–1520	Ottoman ruler Selim I
1520–1566	Ottoman ruler Suleiman the Magnificent
1525–1527	Babur founds Mughai dynasty in India
1540	Hungary under Ottoman rule
1556–1605	Akbar the Great of India reigns
1571	Battle of Lepanto; Ottomans defeated
ca. 1571–1640	Safavid philosopher-writer Mullah Sadra
1588–1629	Shah Abbas I of Iran reigns

Leaf from "Divan" ▶
by the poet, Hafiz

EAST ASIA

1500–1800	Commercial revolution in Ming-Ch'ing China; trade with Europe; flourishing of the novel
1543	Portuguese arrive in Japan
1568–1600	Era of unification follows end of Warring States Era in Japan
1587	Spanish arrive in Japan
1588	Hideyoshi's sword hunt in Japan
1592–1598	Ming troops battle Hideyoshi's army in Korea

Feluccas ▶
on the Nile

AFRICA

1506	East coast of Africa under Portuguese domination
1507	Mozambique founded by Portuguese
1517	Spanish crown authorizes slave trade to its South American colonies; rapid increase in importation of slaves to the New World
1554–1659	Sa'did Sultanate in Morocco
1575	Union of Bornu and Kanem by Idris Alawma (r. 1575–1610); Kanem-Bornu state the most fully Islamic in West Africa
1591	Moroccan army defeats Songhai army; Songhai Empire collapses

THE AMERICAS

1519	Conquest of the Aztecs by Cortes; Aztec ruler, Montezuma (r. 1502–1519) killed; Tenochtitlán destroyed
1529	Mexico City becomes capital of the viceroyalty of New Spain
1533	Pizarro begins his conquest of the Incas
1536	Spanish under Mendoza arrive in Argentina
1544	Lima becomes capital of the viceroyalty of Peru
1584	Sir Walter Raleigh sends expedition to Roanoke Island (North Carolina)

◀ Aztec drawing of Spanish
conquest of Mexico

▲ Algonquin village of Secotton

1618–1648 Thirty Years' War
1640–1688 Frederick William, the Great Elector, reigns in Brandenburg-Prussia
1642–1646 Puritan Revolution in England
1643–1715 Louis XIV of France reigns
1682–1725 Peter the Great of Russia reigns
1688 Glorious Revolution in England
1690 "Second Treatise of Civil Government," by John Locke

◀ *Louis XIV of France*

1701 Act of Settlement provides for Protestant succession to English throne
1702–1713 War of Spanish Succession
1740–1748 War of Austrian Succession
1756–1763 Seven Years' War
ca. 1750 Industrial Revolution begins in England
1772 First partition of Poland
1789 First French Revolution
1793 and 1795 Last two partitions of Poland

▲ *"Evening" by Francis Wheatley*

1628–1657 Shah Jahan reigns; builds Taj Mahal as mausoleum for his beloved wife
1646 Founding of Maratha Empire
1648 Delhi becomes the capital of Mughal Empire
1658–1707 Shah Aurangzeb, the "World Conqueror," reigns in India; end of religious toleration toward Hindus; beginning Mughal decline
1669–1683 Last military expansion by Ottomans: 1669, seize Crete; 1670s, the Ukraine; 1683, Vienna

▲ *The Taj Mahal*

1700 Sikhs and Marathas bring down Mughal Imperial Power
1708 British East India Company and New East India Company merge
1722 Last Safavid ruler forced to abdicate
1724 Rise in the Deccan of the Islamic state of Hyderabad
1725 Nadir Shah of Afganhistan becomes ruler of Persia
1739 Persian invasion of northern India, by Nadir Shah
1748–1761 Ahmad Shah Durrani of Afghanistan invades India
1757 British victory at Plassey, in Bengal

1600 Tokugawa Ieyasu wins battle of Sekigahara, completes unification of Japan
1600–1868 Tokugawa shogunate in Edo
1630s Seclusion adopted as national policy in Japan
1644–1694 Bashō, Japanese poet
1644–1911 Ch'ing (Manchu) dynasty in China
1661–1722 K'ang Hsi reign in China
1673–1681 Revolt of southern generals in China
1699 British East India Company arrives in China

◀ *"White Heron" castle in Jimeji*

1701 Forty-seven ro-nin incident in Japan
1716–1733 Reforms of Tokugawa Yoshimune in Japan
1737–1795 Reign of Qianlong in China
1742 Christianity banned in China
1784 American traders arrive in China
1787–1793 Matsudaira Sadanobu's reforms in Japan
1798 White Lotus Rebellion in China

Manchu emperor ▶ Ch'ien Lung

1600s English, Dutch, and French enter the slave trade; slaves imported to sugar plantations in the Caribbean
1619 First African slaves in North America land in Virginia
1652 First Cape Colony settlement of Dutch East India Company
1660–1856 Omani domination of East Africa; Omani state centered in Zanzibar; 1698, takes Mozambique from Portuguese

◀ *Slave labor on sugar plantation in Brazil*

1702 Asiento Guinea Trade Company founded for slave trade between Africa and the Americas
1700s Transatlantic slave trade at its height
1741–1856 United Sultanate of Oman and Zanzibar
1754–1817 Usman Dan Fodio, founder of sultanate in northern and central Nigeria; the Fulani become the ruling class in the region
1762 End of Funj Sultanate in eastern Sudanic region

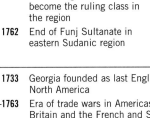
◀ *The Friday Mosque at Shela*

1607 The London Company establishes Jamestown Colony (Virginia)
1608 Champlain founds Quebec
1619 Slave labor introduced at Jamestown (Virginia)

1733 Georgia founded as last English colony in North America
1739–1763 Era of trade wars in Americas between Great Britain and the French and Spanish
1763 Peace of Paris establishes British government in Canada
1776–1781 American Revolution
1783–1830 Simón Bolívar, Latin American soldier, statesman
1789 U.S. Constitution
1791 Negro slave revolt in French Santo Domingo
1791 Canada Constitution Act divides the country into Upper and Lower Canada

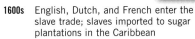

16 Europe 1500–1650: Expansion, Reformation and Religious Wars

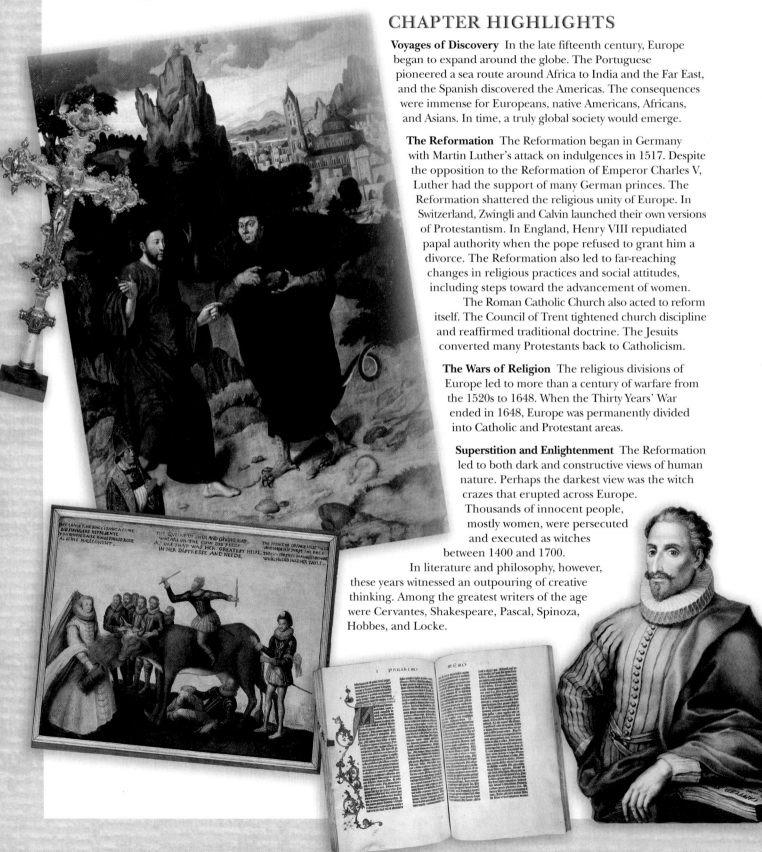

CHAPTER HIGHLIGHTS

Voyages of Discovery In the late fifteenth century, Europe began to expand around the globe. The Portuguese pioneered a sea route around Africa to India and the Far East, and the Spanish discovered the Americas. The consequences were immense for Europeans, native Americans, Africans, and Asians. In time, a truly global society would emerge.

The Reformation The Reformation began in Germany with Martin Luther's attack on indulgences in 1517. Despite the opposition to the Reformation of Emperor Charles V, Luther had the support of many German princes. The Reformation shattered the religious unity of Europe. In Switzerland, Zwingli and Calvin launched their own versions of Protestantism. In England, Henry VIII repudiated papal authority when the pope refused to grant him a divorce. The Reformation also led to far-reaching changes in religious practices and social attitudes, including steps toward the advancement of women.

The Roman Catholic Church also acted to reform itself. The Council of Trent tightened church discipline and reaffirmed traditional doctrine. The Jesuits converted many Protestants back to Catholicism.

The Wars of Religion The religious divisions of Europe led to more than a century of warfare from the 1520s to 1648. When the Thirty Years' War ended in 1648, Europe was permanently divided into Catholic and Protestant areas.

Superstition and Enlightenment The Reformation led to both dark and constructive views of human nature. Perhaps the darkest view was the witch crazes that erupted across Europe. Thousands of innocent people, mostly women, were persecuted and executed as witches between 1400 and 1700.

In literature and philosophy, however, these years witnessed an outpouring of creative thinking. Among the greatest writers of the age were Cervantes, Shakespeare, Pascal, Spinoza, Hobbes, and Locke.

CHAPTER QUESTIONS

WHAT WERE the motives for the European voyages of discovery in the late fifteenth and sixteenth centuries?

WHY DID Martin Luther break with the Roman Catholic Church?

HOW DID the Reformation change religious and social life?

WHAT WAS the final result of the wars of religion in France, the Netherlands, and Germany?

WHY DID witch hunts and panics erupt across Western Europe between 1400 and 1700?

CHAPTER OUTLINE

- The Discovery of a New World
- The Reformation
- The Reformation's Achievements
- The Wars of Religion
- Superstition and Enlightenment: The Battle Within

In the second decade of the 16th century, a powerful religious movement began in Saxony in Germany and rapidly spread throughout northern Europe, deeply affecting society and politics as well as spiritual life. Attacking what they believed to be burdensome superstitions that robbed people of their money and their peace of mind, Protestant reformers led a revolt against the medieval church. In a short time, hundreds of thousands of people from all social classes set aside the beliefs of centuries and adopted a more simplified religious practice.

The Protestant Reformation challenged aspects of the Renaissance, especially its loyalty to traditional religions and humanism's tendency to follow classical sources in glorifying human nature. Protestants were more convinced of the human potential for evil than by any human inclination to do good. This led them to urge parents, teachers, and magistrates to be firm disciplinarians. On the other hand, Protestants also embraced many Renaissance ideas, especially educational reform and the study of ancient languages. These provided the tools they used to interpret Scripture and challenge the papacy.

Protestantism was not the only reform movement to grow out of the religious grievances of the late Middle Ages. Within the Catholic Church itself a reform was emerging that would give birth to new religious orders, rebut Protestantism, and win back a great many of its converts.

As different groups identified their political and social goals with either Protestantism or Catholicism, a hundred years of bloody war between Protestants and Catholics darkened the second half of the 16th century and the first half of the 17th. In the second half of the 16th century, the political conflict that had previously been confined to central Europe and a struggle for Lutheran rights and freedoms shifted to Western Europe—to France, the Netherlands, England, and Scotland—where it became a struggle for Calvinist recognition. In France, Calvinists fought Catholic rulers for the right to form their own communities, to practice their chosen religion openly, and to exclude from their lands those they deemed heretical. During the Thirty Years' War (1618–1648), international armies of varying religious persuasions clashed in central and northern Europe. By 1649 English Puritans had overthrown the Stuart monarchy and the Anglican Church.

For Europe the late 15th and the 16th centuries were also a period of unprecedented territorial expansion. Permanent colonies were established within the Americas, and the exploitation of the New World's human and mineral resources began. Imported American gold and silver spurred scientific invention and a new weapons industry. The new bullion helped fund an international traffic in African slaves as rival tribes sold their captives to the Portuguese. These slaves were brought in ever-increasing numbers to work the mines and the plantations of the New World as replacements for faltering American natives.

THE DISCOVERY OF A NEW WORLD

WHAT WERE the motives for the European voyages of discovery in the late 15th and 16th centuries?

The discovery of the Americas dramatically expanded the geographical and intellectual horizons of Europeans. Knowledge of the New World's inhabitants and exploitation of its vast wealth set new cultural and economic forces in motion throughout Western Europe. Beginning with the successful voyages of Christopher Columbus (1451–1506) in the late 15th century, commercial supremacy started to shift from the Mediterranean and the Baltic to the Atlantic seaboard, and western Europe's global expansion began in earnest (see Map 16–1).

The Portuguese Chart the Course Seventy-seven years before Columbus sailed for Spain, Portugal's Prince Henry the Navigator (1394–1460) began exploration of Africa's Atlantic coast. The Portuguese first sought gold and slaves. During the second half of the 15th century, the Portuguese delivered

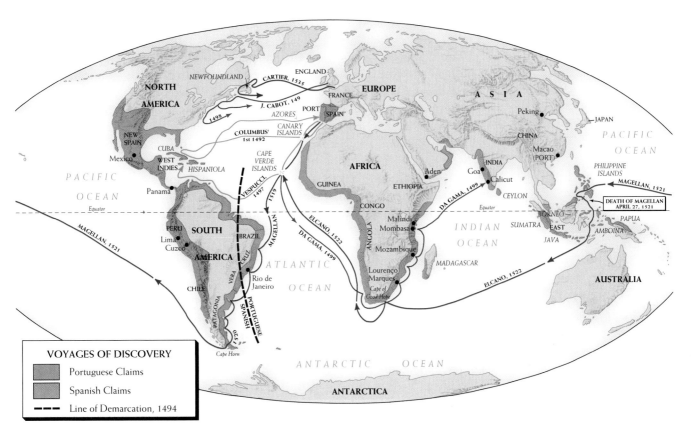

MAP 16–1
European Voyages of Discovery and the Colonial Claims of Spain and Portugal in the 15th and 16th Centuries.   The map dramatizes Europe's global expansion in the 15th and 16th centuries.

WHY DID the Europeans want to find a sea route to Asia?

150,000 slaves to Europe. By the end of that century, however, they were hoping to find a sea route around Africa to Asia's spice markets. Spices, especially pepper and cloves, were in great demand both as preservatives and taste enhancements to food. Overland routes to India and China had long existed, but they were difficult and expensive and monopolized by the Venetians and Turks. The first exploratory voyages were slow and tentative, but the experience they provided taught sailors the skills needed to cross the oceans to the Americas and and Orient.

In 1455, a pope gave the Portuguese rights to all the lands, goods, and slaves they might discover from the coast of Guinea to the Indies. The church hoped that conquests would be followed by mass conversions and the development of allies against the Muslims. Bartholomew Dias (d. 1500) opened the Portuguese Empire in the East when he rounded the Cape of Good Hope at the tip of Africa in 1487. A decade later, in 1498, Vasco da Gama (d. 1524) stood on the shores of India. When he returned to Portugal, his cargo was worth 60 times the cost of the voyage. Later, the Portuguese established colonies in Goa and Calcutta and successfully challenged the Arabs and the Venetians for control of the European spice trade.

While the Portuguese concentrated on the Indian Ocean, the Spanish set sail across the Atlantic, hoping to establish a shorter route to the rich spice markets of the East Indies. Rather than beat the Portuguese at their own game, however, Columbus discovered the Americas—although he did not at first realize that.

14.5
Christopher Columbus

The Spanish Voyages of Christopher Columbus   On October 12, 1492, after a 33-day voyage from the Canary Islands, Columbus landed in San Salvador (Watlings Island) in the eastern Bahamas. He thought San Salvador was an outer island of Japan, for his knowledge of geography was based on Marco Polo's account of his years in China during the 13th century and a global map by Martin Behaim, a Nuremberg map-maker, which showed only ocean between the west coast of Europe and the east coast of Asia.

The friendly naked natives, who greeted Columbus and his crew on the beaches of the New World, were Taino Indians. They spoke a variant of a language known as Arawak. Mistaking the island for the East Indies, Columbus called the people Indians, and the name stuck even after it became known that he had discovered a new continent. The natives' generosity amazed Columbus. They freely gave his men all the corn and yams—and sexual favors—they desired. "They never say no," Columbus marveled and predicted that they could easily be enslaved.

On the heels of Columbus, Amerigo Vespucci (1451–1512), after whom America is named, and Ferdinand Magellan (1480–1521) carefully explored the coastline of South America. Their travels proved that the lands discovered by Columbus were not the outermost territory of the Far East, but a new continent that opened on the still greater Pacific Ocean. Magellan, in search of a westward route to the East Indies, sailed to the Philippines, where he died.

Impact on Europe and America   Columbus's voyage of 1492 marked, unknowingly to those who undertook and financed it, the beginning of more than three centuries of Spanish conquest, exploitation, and administration of a vast American empire. What had begun as voyages of discovery soon became expeditions of conquest. The wars Christian Aragon and Castile waged against the Islamic Moors had just ended in 1492, and they imbued the early Spanish explorers with a zeal for conquering and converting non-Christian peoples.

The voyages to the New World had important consequences for both Europe and America. For Spain, the venture created Europe's largest and longest-surviving trading bloc and yielded the wealth that financed Spain's commanding role in the era's religious and political conflicts. It also fueled European-wide economic expansion, and spurred other European countries to undertake their own colonial ventures.

European expansion had major consequences for ecosystems. Numerous species of fruits, vegetables, and animals were introduced to Europe from America and vice versa. European diseases also devasted America's natives. The imprint that Spain left on the new territories—Roman Catholicism, economic dependence, and a hierarchical society—is visible today.

THE REFORMATION

The **Reformation** was a religious reform movement that began in Germany in the sixteenth Century and led to the establishment of Protestant Christianity.

Religion and Society   The Reformation broke out first in the free imperial cities of Germany and Switzerland. There were about 65 of these, and each was a

QUICK REVIEW

Impact on Europe and America

- Spurred other European nations to colonial expansion
- Financed Spain's role in the age's political and religious conflicts
- For native peoples of the Americas, contact brought disease, war, and destruction

WHY DID Martin Luther break with the Roman Catholic Church?

Reformation Sixteenth-century religious movement that sought to reform the Roman Catholic Church and led to the establishment of Protestantism.

little kingdom unto itself. Most developed Protestant movements, but with mixed success and duration. Some quickly turned Protestant and remained so. Some were Protestant for only a short time. Others developed mixed confessions and let Catholics and Protestants coexist.

The cities not only struggled with higher princely or royal authority, they also suffered deep internal social and political divisions. Certain groups favored the Reformation more than others. In many places, guilds like that of the printers, whose members were prospering both socially and economically and who had a history of conflict with local authority, were in the forefront of the Reformation. Evidence suggests that people who felt pushed around and bullied by either local or distant authority—a guild by an autocratic local government; a city or region by a prince or king—initially perceived an ally in the Protestant movement.

Social and political experience thus coalesced with the larger religious issues in both town and countryside. When Martin Luther and his comrades wrote, preached, and sang about a priesthood of all believers, scorned the authority of ecclesiastical landlords, and ridiculed papal laws as arbitrary human inventions, they touched political as well as religious nerves in German and Swiss cities. This was also true in villages, for the peasants also heard in the Protestant sermon and pamphlet a promise of political liberation and even a degree of social betterment.

Popular Movements and Criticism of the Church The Protestant Reformation could not have occurred without the monumental crises of the late medieval church and the Renaissance papacy. For many people, the church had ceased to provide a viable vehicle for the expression of their piety. Laity and clerics alike began to seek more heartfelt, idealistic, and often—in the eyes of the pope—increasingly heretical religious outlets. The late Middle Ages were marked by independent lay and clerical efforts to reform local religious practice and by widespread experimentation with new religious forms that shared a common goal: the recovery of religious simplicity in imitation of Christ.

A variety of factors contributed to the growth of lay criticism of the church. The laity in the cities were becoming increasingly knowledgeable about the world and those who controlled their lives. They traveled widely—as soldiers, pilgrims, explorers, and traders. New postal systems and the printing press increased the information at their disposal. The new age of books and libraries raised literacy and heightened curiosity. Laypersons were increasingly able to take the initiative in shaping the cultural life of their communities.

Secular Control over Religious Life On the eve of the Reformation, Rome's international network of church offices began to be pulled apart by a growing awareness of regional identity (incipient nationalism) and the increasing competence of local secular administrations. The late medieval church had permitted important ecclesiastical posts ("benefices") to be sold to the highest bidders and had not enforced residency requirements in parishes. Rare was the late medieval German town that did not have complaints about the maladministration, concubinage, or fiscal conduct of its clergy, especially the higher clergy (bishops, abbots, and prelates).

City governments also sought to restrict the growth of ecclesiastical properties and clerical privileges and to improve local religious life by bringing the clergy under the local tax code and by endowing new clerical positions for well-trained and conscientious preachers.

Gutenberg Bible. The printing press made possible the diffusion of Renaissance learning. But no book stimulated thought more at this time than did the Bible. With Gutenberg's publication of a printed Bible in 1454, scholars gained access to a dependable, standardized text, so that Scripture could be discussed and debated as never before.

Huntigton Library.

QUICK REVIEW

Criticism of the Church
- Many people did not see church as a foundation for religious piety
- Laity and clerics interested in alternatives and reform
- Layperson increasingly willing to take the initiative

THE NORTHERN RENAISSANCE

The scholarly works of northern humanists created a climate favorable to religious and educational reforms. Northern humanism was initially stimulated by the importation of Italian learning through such varied intermediaries as students who had studied in Italy, merchants, and a religious organization called the Brothers of the Common Life. The northern humanists tended to come from more diverse social backgrounds and to be more devoted to religious reforms than were their Italian counterparts. They were also more willing to write for lay audiences.

The growth of schools and lay education combined with the invention of cheap paper to create a mass audience for printed books. It was well served when, around 1450, Johann Gutenberg (d. 1468) invented printing with movable type in the German city of Mainz. Thereafter, books were rapidly and handsomely produced on topics both profound and practical. By 1500, printing presses operated in at least 60 German cities and in more than 200 throughout Europe. The provided politicians, humanists, and reformers with a new medium through which to promote their causes.

The most famous of the northern humanists was Desiderius Erasmus (1466–1536), the "prince of the humanists." Idealistic and pacifistic, Erasmus gained fame as both an educational and a religious reformer. He aspired to unite the classical ideals of humanity and civic virtue with the Christian ideals of love and piety. He believed that disciplined study of the classics and the Bible, if begun early enough, was the best way to reform both individuals and society. He summarized his own beliefs with the phrase *philosophia Christi*, a simple, ethical piety in imitation of Christ. He set this ideal against what he believed to be the dogmatic, ceremonial, and factious religious practice of the late Middle Ages. To promote his own religious beliefs, Erasmus edited the works of the Church Fathers and made a Greek edition of the New Testament (1516), which became the basis for a new, more accurate Latin translation (1519). Martin Luther later used both these works as the basis for his famous German translation.

The best known of early English humanists was Sir Thomas More (1478–1535), a close friend of Erasmus. While visiting More, Erasmus wrote his most famous work, *The Praise of Folly* (1511), an amusing and profound exposé of human self-deception. It was quickly translated from the original Latin into many vernacular languages. More's *Utopia* (1516), a criticism of contemporary society, depicts an imaginary society based on reason and tolerance that requires everyone to work and has rid itself of all social and political injustice. Although More remained a staunch Catholic, humanism in England, as in Germany, paved the way for the Reformation. A circle of English humanists, under the direction of Henry VIII's minister Thomas Cromwell, translated and disseminated late medieval criticisms of the papacy and many of Erasmus's satirical writings as well.

Whereas humanism helped the Protestants in Germany, England, and France, in Spain it entered the service of the Catholic Church. Here the key figure was Francisco Jiménez de Cisneros (1437–1517), a confessor to Queen Isabella, and after 1508 Grand Inquisitor—a position from which he was able to enforce the strictest religious orthodoxy. Jiménez was a conduit for humanist scholarship and learning. He founded the University of Alcalá near Madrid in 1509, printed a Greek edition of the New Testament, and translated many religious tracts that aided clerical reform and control of lay religious life. His greatest achievement, taking 15 years to complete, was the Complutensian Polyglot Bible. It is a six-volume work that prints, side by side, Hebrew, Greek, and Latin

QUICK REVIEW

Desiderius Erasmus (1466–1536)

- Prince of the humanists
- Saw study of Bible and classics as best path to reform
- Edited the works of the Church Fathers and made a Greek edition of the New Testament

versions of the Bible. Such scholarly projects and internal church reforms joined with the repressive measures of Ferdinand and Isabella to keep Spain strictly Catholic.

MARTIN LUTHER AND THE GERMAN REFORMATION TO 1525

Late medieval Germany lacked the political unity to enforce "national" religious reforms during the late Middle Ages. What happened on a unified national level in England and France occurred only locally and piecemeal in Germany. As popular resentment of clerical immunities and ecclesiastical abuses spread among German cities and towns—especially regarding the selling of indulgences—an unorganized "national" opposition to Rome formed. German humanists had long voiced such criticism, and by 1517 it provided a solid foundation for Martin Luther's reform.

Luther (1483–1546), the son of a successful Thuringian miner, was educated by teachers who had been influenced by the Northern Renaissance. He received his master of arts degree from the University of Erfurt in 1505 and registered with the law faculty. He never began that course of study, for to the shock and disappointment of his parents, he joined the Order of the Hermits of Saint Augustine in Erfurt on July 17, 1505. This decision had apparently been forming in his mind for some time and was precipitated by a terrifying storm that caused him to promise the saint to whom he prayed that he would enter a monastery if he escaped death.

Luther was ordained in 1507 and was sent to Rome in 1510 on business for his order. There he witnessed the abuses for which the papacy was being criticized. In 1511, he was transferred to the Augustinian monastery in Wittenberg, where he earned his doctorate in theology (1512)—thereafter to become a leader within the monastery, the new university, and the spiritual life of the city.

Justification by Faith Alone

Reformation theology grew out of a problem common to many clergy and laity at this time: the failure of traditional medieval religion to provide full personal or intellectual satisfaction. Luther was especially plagued by the disproportion between his own sense of sinfulness and the perfect righteousness that medieval theology taught that God required for salvation. Traditional church teaching and the sacraments were no consolation. Luther wrote that he came to despise the phrase "righteousness of God," for it seemed to demand of him a perfection he knew neither he nor any other human being could ever achieve. His insight into the meaning of "justification by faith alone" was a gradual process that extended over several years, between 1513 and 1518. The righteousness God demands, he concluded, does not come from religious works but is present in full measure in those who believe and trust in the redemptive life and death of Christ, who alone exhibits the righteousness satisfying to God. To believe in Christ is to stand before God clothed in Christ's righteousness.

13.4
Martin Luther

John Tetzel. A contemporary caricature depicts John Tetzel, the famous indulgence preacher. The last lines of the jingle read: "As soon as gold in the basin rings, right then the soul to heaven springs." It was Tetzel's preaching that spurred Luther to publish his 95 theses.

Courtesy Stiftung Luthergedenkstaten in Sachsen-Anhalt/Lutherhalle, Wittenberg.

The Attack on Indulgences   An **indulgence** was a remission of the temporal penalty imposed by the priest on penitents as a "work of satisfaction" for their sins. According to medieval theology, after the priest had absolved penitents of guilt for their sins, God still imposed on them a temporal penalty, a manageable "work of satisfaction" that the penitent could perform here and now (for example, through prayers, fasting, almsgiving, retreats, and pilgrimages). Penitents who defaulted on such prescribed works of satisfaction could expect to suffer for their sins in purgatory.

Originally, indulgences had been given only for the true self-sacrifice of going on a crusade to the Holy Land. But they came over time to be more commonly issued as a comfort to laity who were genuinely anxious that forgotten or unrepented sins would condemn them to suffering in purgatory. In 1343, Pope Clement VI (r. 1342–1352) proclaimed the existence of a "treasury of merit," on which popes could draw to issue "letters of indulgence" that canceled the works of satisfaction owed by penitents. By Luther's time, they were regularly dispensed for small cash payments (modest sums that were regarded as almsgiving) and were said to remit not only future punishment of the living, but also those of the dead in purgatory for whom they were purchased.

In 1517, a Jubilee indulgence, proclaimed under Pope Julius II (r. 1503–1513) to raise funds for the rebuilding of Saint Peter's in Rome, was revived and preached on the borders of Saxony in the territories of Archbishop Albrecht of Mainz, who had large debts. The selling of the indulgence was a joint venture by Albrecht, the Augsburg banking house of Fugger, and Pope Leo X (r. 1513–1521), half the proceeds going to the pope and half to Albrecht and his creditors. The famous indulgence preacher John Tetzel (d. 1519) exhorted the crowds:

> Don't you hear the voices of your dead parents and other relatives crying out, "Have mercy on us, for we suffer great punishment and pain. From this you could release us with a few alms.... We have created you, fed you, cared for you, and left you our temporal goods. Why do you treat us so cruelly and leave us to suffer in the flames, when it takes only a little to save us?"[1]

When on October 31, 1517, Luther posted his **ninety-five theses** against indulgences on the door of Castle Church in Wittenberg, he especially protested the impression Tetzel gave his customers that indulgences actually remitted sins and released the dead from purgatory. Luther thought that this was excessive and created the impression that salvation could be bought.

Election of Charles V   Luther's theses made him famous overnight. Humanists endorsed them, but the church began official proceedings to discipline him. As sanctions were being prepared against Luther, Emperor Maximilian I died (January 12, 1519), diverting attention from heresy in Saxony to the contest for a new emperor. The pope backed the French king, Francis I. However, Charles I of Spain, then 19, succeeded his grandfather and became Emperor Charles V (r. 1519–1556). Charles was assisted by a long tradition of Habsburg imperial rule and massive Fugger loans, which secured the votes of the seven electors. The electors also won political concessions from Charles that prevented him from taking unilateral action against Germans, something for which Luther eventually had cause to be grateful.

indulgences Remission of the temporal penalty of punishment in purgatory that remained after sins had been forgiven.

ninety-five theses Document posted on the door of Castle Church in Wittenberg, Germany on October 31, 1517 by Martin Luther protesting, among other things, the selling of indulgences.

[1] *Die Reformation in Augenzeugen Berichten*, ed. by Helmar Junghans (Dusseldorf: Karl Rauch Verlag, 1967), p. 44.

A Catholic portrayal of Martin Luther tempting Jesus (1547). Reformation propaganda often portrayed the pope as the Antichrist or the devil. Here Catholic propaganda turns the tables on the Protestant reformers by portraying a figure of Martin Luther as the devil (note the monstrous feet and tail under his academic robes).

Versuchung Christi, 1547, Gemälde, Bonn, Rheinisches Landesmuseum, Inv. Nr. 58.3.

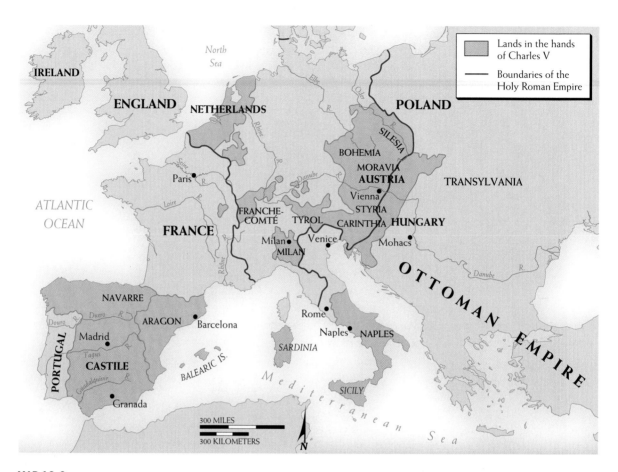

MAP 16–2

The Empire of Charles V. Dynastic marriages and good luck concentrated into Charles's hands rule over the lands shown here, plus Spain's overseas possessions. Crowns and titles rained down on him; election in 1519 as emperor gave him new burdens and responsibilities.

WHAT WERE the geographical advantages and disadvantages of the empire of Charles V?

Diet of Worms Meeting of the representatives (diet) of the Holy Roman Empire, presided over by the Emperor Charles V at the German city of Worms in 1521, at which Martin Luther was ordered to recant his ninety-five theses. Luther refused and was declared an outlaw although he was protected by the Elector of Saxony and other German princes.

Luther's Excommunication and the Diet of Worms In the same month in which Charles was elected emperor, Luther debated the Ingolstadt professor John Eck (1486–1543) in Leipzig (June 27, 1519). Luther challenged the infallibility of the pope and the inerrancy of church councils, and argued for the first time for Scripture as the sole and sovereign authority over faith. He burned all his bridges to the old church when he defended John Huss, a condemned heretic.

In 1520, Luther made his position clear by issuing three famous pamphlets. The *Address to the Christian Nobility of the German Nation* urged the German princes to force reforms on the Roman Church and especially to curtail its political and economic power in Germany. The *Babylonian Captivity of the Church* attacked the traditional seven sacraments and claimed that only two were legitimate. It also exalted the authority of Scripture and the decisions of church councils and secular princes over the judgments of popes. The last pamphlet, *Freedom of a Christian*, eloquently summarized his new teaching: that salvation came by faith alone— that it was the consequence of a "happy union" between the soul and Christ.

In April 1521, Luther presented his views before the imperial **Diet of Worms**, over which Charles V presided. Ordered to recant, Luther refused. On

May 26, 1521, he was placed under the imperial ban and became an "outlaw" within the empire. Friends hid him in Wartburg Castle. There he spent almost a year in seclusion (April 1521 to March 1522), translating Erasmus's new Greek text of the New Testament into German. He also attempted by correspondence to oversee the first stages of the Reformation in Wittenberg.

Imperial Distractions: France and the Turks   The Reformation was greatly assisted at its start by the fact that the emperor was forced to focus his attention on a war with France and the advance of the Ottoman Turks into eastern Europe. Against both adversaries, Charles V, who was also Spain's king and had dynastic responsibilities outside the empire, needed German troops. Consequently, he pursued friendly relations with the German princes. Between 1521 and 1559, Spain (the Habsburg dynasty) and France (the Valois dynasty) fought four major wars. In 1526, the Turks overran Hungary at the Battle of Mohacs, while in western Europe the French-led League of Cognac pushed Charles toward a second Habsburg-Valois war. Thus preoccupied, the emperor agreed at the German Diet of Speyer in 1526 that each German territory could be free to enforce the Edict of Worms (1521) against Luther "so as to be able to answer in good conscience to God and the emperor." That concession, in effect, gave the German princes territorial sovereignty in religious matters while giving the Reformation time to put down deep roots. In 1555, the Peace of Augsburg enshrined this princely privilege as imperial law.

How the Reformation Spread   The Reformation soon passed from the hands of theologians and pamphleteers into those of magistrates and princes. In many cities, Protestant preachers built sizable congregations that pressured urban governments to adopt religious reforms. Many magistrates had long pushed for reform and welcomed the preachers as allies. Reform slogans thus became laws binding on all townspeople.

Religious reform became a territorial political movement as well. It was led by the elector of Saxony and the prince of Hesse. Like the urban magistrates, the princes recognized political and economic opportunities for themselves in the demise of the Roman Catholic Church, and they urged the reform on their neighbors. By the 1530s, there was a powerful Protestant alliance prepared for war with the Catholic emperor.

The Peasants' Revolt   In its first decade, the Protestant movement suffered more from internal division than from imperial interference. By 1525, Luther had become as much an object of protest within Germany as was the pope. Original allies and sympathizers declared their independence from him.

The German peasants had at first believed Luther to be an ally. Since the late 15th century, they had organized to resist efforts by princes to jettison traditional customs and impose new regulations and taxes on them. Peasant leaders saw in Luther's teaching of religious freedom and his criticism of monastic landowners a point of view close to their own. They openly solicited his support of their political and economic rights, including their revolutionary request for release from serfdom.

Luther and his followers sympathized with the peasants, but the Lutherans were no social revolutionaries. Luther believed that Christian freedom was an inner release from guilt and anxiety, not the right to an egalitarian society. When the peasants revolted in 1524–1525, Luther condemned them in the strongest

Execution of a Peasant Leader. The punishment of a peasant leader in a village near Heilbronn. After the defeat of rebellious peasants in and around the city of Heilbronn, Jacob Rorbach, a well-to-do peasant leader from a nearby village, was tied to a stake and slowly roasted to death.

© Badische Landesbibliothek.

possible terms as "unchristian" and urged the princes to crush their revolt without mercy. Tens of thousands of peasants (estimates run between 70,000 and 100,000) had died by the time the revolt was put down.

For Luther, the freedom of the Christian was an inner release from guilt and anxiety, not a right to restructure society by violent revolution. Had Luther supported the Peasants' Revolt, he would have also ended any chance of his reform surviving beyond the 1520s.

Luther and the Jews   Luther's stand toward the Jews has also been controversial. In 1523 he published a pamphlet, "Jesus Christ was Born a Jew," in which he urged Christians to be kind to Germany's Jews in the hope that they might convert to reformed Christianity. But Luther came to regret his pamphlet and decided that the Jews were just another in a long history of foreign predators who threatened German Christians. He expressed these views in a series of pamphlets in the late 1530s and early 1540 in which he urged German princes to forcibly expel Jews who refused to convert. Fortunately, the Jews found a protector in Emperor Charles V, and Luther's colleagues were not inclined to abandon the hope that the Jews would eventually convert. However, in Hesse and Saxony rulers tightened restrictions on Jews, and Luther did not, as he might have, use his influence on their behalf.

ZWINGLI AND THE SWISS REFORMATION

Although Luther's was the first, reform movments occurred in Switzerland and France almost simultaneously with the German Reformation. Switzerland was a loose confederacy of 13 autonomous cantons or states and allied areas. Some became Protestant, some remained Catholic, and a few managed to effect a compromise. The two preconditions of the Swiss Reformation were the growth of national sentiment and a desire for church reform.

The Reformation in Zurich   Ulrich Zwingli (1484–1531), the leader of the Swiss Reformation, was widely known for opposition to the sale of indulgences and religious superstition. As a priest in Zurich, he made the city his base for reform. Zwingli's reform guideline was simple and effective: whatever lacked literal support in Scripture was to be neither believed nor practiced. After a public disputation in January 1523, based on his Scripture test, Zurich became, to all intents and purposes, a Protestant city and the center of the Swiss Reformation. Its rigorous enforcement of its religious ideals made it one of the first examples of a "puritanical" Protestant city.

The Marburg Colloquy   Landgrave Philip of Hesse (1504–1567) sought to unite Swiss and German Protestants in a mutual defense pact, a potentially significant political alliance. His efforts were spoiled, however, by theological disagreements between Luther and Zwingli over the nature of Christ's presence in the Eucharist. Zwingli maintained a symbolic interpretation of Christ's words, "This is my body"; Christ, he argued, was only spiritually, not bodily, present in the bread and wine of the Eucharist. Luther, to the contrary, insisted that Christ's human nature could share the properties of his divine nature. Hence, where Christ was spiritually present, he could also be bodily present, for his was a special nature (***transubstantiation***).

Philip of Hesse brought the two Protestant leaders together in his castle in Marburg in early October 1529, but they were unable to work out their differences

transubstantiation Doctrine that the entire substances of the bread and wine are changed in the Eucharist into the body and blood of Christ.

on this issue. Luther left thinking Zwingli a dangerous fanatic. The disagreement splintered the Protestant movement theologically and politically.

ANABAPTISTS AND RADICAL PROTESTANTS

The moderate pace and seemingly small ethical results of the Lutheran and Zwinglian reformations discontented many people, among them some of the original coworkers of Luther and Zwingli. Many desired a more rapid and thorough implementation of primitive Christianity and accused the major reformers of going only halfway. The most important of these radical groups were the Anabaptists, the 16th-century ancestors of the modern Mennonites and Amish. The Anabaptists take their name from their rejection of infant baptism and their insistence that only baptism as a consenting adult conformed to Scripture and was respectful of human freedom. (*Anabaptism* derives from the Greek word meaning "to rebaptize.")

Anabaptists withdrew from society to form more perfect communities modeled on what they believed to be the example of the first Christians. Due to the close connection between religious and civic life in this period, however, political authorities believed that their separatism was a threat to basic social bonds.

At first, Anabaptism drew adherents from all social classes. But as Lutherans and Zwinglians joined with Catholics in opposing it, a more rural, agrarian class came to make up the great majority of Anabaptists. In 1529, rebaptism became a capital offense throughout the Holy Roman Empire. It has been estimated that between 1525 and 1618 at least 1,000 and perhaps as many as 5,000 men and women were executed for rebaptizing themselves as adults.

A portrait of the young John Calvin.
Bibliotheque Publique et Universitaire, Geneva.

JOHN CALVIN AND THE GENEVAN REFORMATION

Calvinism was the religious ideology that inspired or accompanied massive political resistance in France, the Netherlands, and Scotland. Believing in both divine predestination and the individual's responsibility to create a godly society, Calvinists were zealous reformers. In a famous and controversial study, *The Protestant Ethic and the Spirit of Capitalism* (1904), the German sociologist Max Weber argued that this peculiar combination of religious confidence and self-disciplined activism produced an ethic congenial to emergent capitalism.

Political Revolt and Religious Reform in Geneva

Whereas in Saxony religious reform paved the way for a political revolution against the emperor, in Geneva a political revolution against the local prince-bishop laid the foundation for religious change. In late 1533, the Protestant city of Bern sent Protestant reformers to Geneva and by the summer of 1535, after much internal turmoil, the Protestants triumphed. On May 21, 1536, the city voted officially to adopt the Reformation: "to live according to the Gospel and the Word of God ... without ... any more masses, statues, idols, or other papal abuses."

John Calvin (1509–1564), a reform-minded humanist and lawyer, arrived in Geneva after these events, in July 1536. The local Protestant reformer persuaded him to stay and assist the Reformation. Before a year had passed, Calvin had drawn up articles for the governance of the new church, as well as a catechism to guide and discipline the people. As a result of the strong measures proposed to govern Geneva's moral life, the reformers were accused of trying to create a "new papacy," and in February 1538 they were exiled from the city.

Calvin went to Strasbourg, a model Protestant city, where he became pastor to a group of French exiles. During his two years in Strasbourg, he wrote biblical commentaries and a second edition of his masterful *Institutes of the Christian Religion*, which many consider the definitive theological statement of the Protestant faith. He also married and participated in the ecumenical discussions urged on Protestants and Catholics by Charles V. Most important, he learned from the Strasbourg reformer Martin Bucer (1491–1551) how to implement the Protestant Reformation successfully.

Calvin's Geneva In 1540, Geneva elected officials favorable to Calvin, and he was invited to return. Within months of his arrival, new ecclesiastical ordinances were implemented that allowed the magistrates and the clergy to cooperate in matters of internal discipline.

Calvin and his followers were motivated above all by a desire to make society godly. The "elect," Calvin taught, should live a manifestly God-pleasing life, if they were truly God's elect. The majesty of God demanded nothing less. The *consistory*, a judicial body composed of clergy and laity, was established to enforce the strictest moral discipline. It meted out punishments for a broad range of moral and religious transgressions and became unpopular among many Genevans.

After 1555 the city's magistrates were all devout Calvinists, and Geneva became a refuge for thousands of exiled Protestants driven out of France, England, and Scotland. Refugees (more than 5,000), most of them utterly loyal to Calvin, constituted over one-third of the population of Geneva. From this time until his death in 1564, Calvin's position in the city was greatly strengthened and the magistrates were very cooperative.

POLITICAL CONSOLIDATION OF THE LUTHERAN REFORMATION

By 1530 the Reformation was irreversible, but it would take several decades and major attempts to eradicate it before this was accepted. The political success of Lutheranism in the empire, by the 1550s, gave Protestant movements elsewhere a new lease on life.

Expansion of the Reformation In the 1530s, German Lutherans formed regional consistories, which oversaw and administered the new Protestant churches. These consistories replaced the old Catholic episcopates. Under the leadership of Philip Melanchthon (1497–1560), Luther's most admired colleague, educational reforms were enacted that provided for compulsory primary education, schools for girls, a humanist revision of the traditional curriculum, and catechetical instruction of the laity in the new religion.

The Reformation also dug in elsewhere. Introduced into Denmark by Christian II (r. 1513–1523), Lutheranism became the state religion under Christian III (r. 1536–1559). In Sweden, Gustavus Vasa (r. 1523–1560), supported by a nobility greedy for church lands, confiscated church property and subjected the clergy to royal authority at the Diet of Vesteras (1527). In politically splintered Poland, Lutherans, Calvinists, and others found room to practice their beliefs. The absence of a central political authority made Poland a model of religious pluralism and toleration in the second half of the 16th century.

Reaction Against Protestants: The "Interim" Charles V made abortive efforts in 1540–1541 to enforce a compromise agreement between Protestants and Catholics. When these and other conciliar efforts failed, he sought a military solution. In 1547 imperial armies crushed a Protestant alliance called the Schmalkaldic League.

The emperor established puppet rulers in Saxony and Hesse and issued as imperial law the Augsburg Interim. It ordered Protestants everywhere to readopt Catholic beliefs and practices. The Reformation was, however, too entrenched by 1547 to be ended even by brute force. Confronted by fierce Protestant resistance and weary from three decades of war, the emperor was forced to relent.

The Peace of Augsburg in September 1555 made the division of Christendom permanent. This agreement recognized in law what had already been well established in practice: *cuius regio, eius religio,* meaning that the ruler of a land would determine the religion of the land. Lutherans were permitted to retain all church lands forcibly seized before 1552. Those discontented with the religion of their region were permitted to migrate to another.

Calvinism was not recognized as a legal form of Christian belief and practice by the Peace of Augsburg. Calvinists remained determined not only to secure the right to worship publicly as they pleased, but also to shape society according to their own religious convictions. They organized to lead national revolutions throughout northern Europe.

THE ENGLISH REFORMATION TO 1553

Late medieval England had a well-earned reputation for defending the rights of the crown against the pope. It was, however, the unhappy marriage of King Henry VIII (r. 1509–1547) that precipitated England's break with the papacy.

The King's Affair Henry had married Catherine of Aragon (d. 1536), a daughter of Ferdinand and Isabella of Spain, and the aunt of Emperor Charles V. By 1527, the union had produced only one surviving child, a daughter, Mary Tudor. Henry was justifiably concerned about the political consequences of leaving only a female heir. People in this period believed it unnatural for women to rule over men. At best, a woman ruler meant a contested reign; at worst, turmoil, revolution, and possible foreign invasion. After Henry's queen Catherine had numerous miscarriages and stillbirths, the king concluded

Progress of Protestant Reformation on the Continent

1517	Luther posts 95 theses against indulgences
1519	Charles I of Spain elected Holy Roman emperor (as Charles V)
1519	Luther challenges infallibility of pope and inerrancy of church councils at Leipzig Debate
1521	Papal bull excommunicates Luther for heresy
1521	Diet of Worms condemns Luther
1521–1522	Luther translates the New Testament into German
1524–1525	Peasants' Revolt in Germany
1529	Marburg Colloquy between Luther and Zwingli
1530	Diet of Augsburg fails to settle religious differences
1531	Formation of Protestant Schmalkaldic League
1536	Calvin arrives in Geneva
1540	Jesuits, founded by Ignatius of Loyola, recognized as order by pope
1546	Luther dies
1547	Armies of Charles V crush Schmalkaldic League
1555	Peace of Augsburg recognizes rights of Lutherans to worship as they please
1545–1563	Council of Trent institutes reforms and responds to the Reformation

Main Events of the English Reformation

1529	Reformation Parliament convenes
1532	Parliament passes the Submission of the Clergy, an act placing canon law and the English clergy under royal jurisdiction
1533	Henry VIII weds Anne Boleyn
1534	Act of Succession makes Anne Boleyn's children legitimate heirs to the English throne
1534	Act of Supremacy declares Henry VIII the only supreme head of the Church of England
1535	Thomas More executed for opposition to Acts of Succession and Supremacy
1535	Publication of Coverdale Bible
1539	Henry VIII imposes the Six Articles, condemning Protestantism and reasserting traditional doctrine
1547	Edward VI succeeds to the throne
1549	First Act of Uniformity imposes Book of Common Prayer on English churches
1553–1558	Mary Tudor restores Catholic doctrine
1558–1603	Elizabeth I fashions an Anglican religious settlement

that their union had been cursed by God. Catherine had briefly been the wife of his late brother, Arthur.

By 1527, Henry was thoroughly enamored of Anne Boleyn (ca. 1504–1536), one of Catherine's young ladies in waiting. He decided to put Catherine aside and marry Anne, but this required papal annulment of the marriage— and therein lay a problem. In 1527, the reigning pope, Clement VII (r. 1523–1534), was a prisoner of Charles V, Catherine's nephew. Even if this had not been the case, it would have been virtually impossible for the pope to grant Henry an annulment. Not only had his marriage lasted for 18 years, but it had been made possible in the first place by a special papal dispensation. This had been required because of Catherine's previous marriage to Henry's deceased brother, Arthur.

After Cardinal Wolsey (1475–1530), Lord Chancellor of England since 1515, failed to secure the annulment the king wanted, Henry chose as advisers Thomas Cranmer (1489–1556) and Thomas Cromwell (1485–1540), both of whom harbored Lutheran sympathies. They urged the king to take a different course: Why not simply declare himself supreme in English spiritual affairs as he was in English temporal affairs? The king could then rule on the status of his own marriage.

Reformation Parliament   In 1529 Parliament convened for the seven-year session that earned it the title "Reformation Parliament." It passed a flood of legislation that subjected the clergy to royal authority. In January 1531, the clergy publicly recognized Henry as head of the church in England "as far as the law of Christ allows." In 1532, Parliament passed the Submission of the Clergy, effectively placing canon law under royal control and the clergy under royal jurisdiction.

In January 1533 Henry wed the pregnant Anne Boleyn, with Thomas Cranmer, his newly appointed archbishop of Canterbury, officiating. In 1534, Parliament ended all payments by the English clergy and laity to Rome and gave Henry sole jurisdiction over high ecclesiastical appointments. The Act of Succession in the same year made Anne Boleyn's children legitimate heirs to the throne, and the Act of Supremacy declared Henry "the only supreme head in earth of the church of England."

The Protestant Reformation Under Edward VI   Despite his political break with Rome, Henry remained decidedly conservative in his religious beliefs and continued to endorse Catholic doctrine and practices, despite agitation for Protestant reforms by some of his subjects. Henry forbade the English clergy to marry and threatened to execute clergy caught twice in concubinage. The Six Articles of 1539 reaffirmed belief in transubstantiation, denied the Eucharistic cup to the laity, declared that vows of celibacy could not be voided, provided for private Masses, and ordered the continuation of oral confession to a priest.

Edward VI (r. 1547–1553), Henry's son by his third wife, Jane Seymour, became king at age 10. Under his regents, England enacted much of the

Protestant Reformation. Henry's Six Articles and laws against heresy were repealed, and clerical marriage and Communion with the cup were sanctioned. An Act of Uniformity imposed Thomas Cranmer's Book of Common Prayer on all English churches, which were stripped of their images and altars. His 42-article confession of faith set forth a moderate Protestant doctrine.

These changes were short-lived because in 1553 young Edward died, and his half-sister, Catherine of Aragon's daughter, Mary Tudor (d. 1558), succeeded to the throne. She restored Catholic doctrine and practice with a single-mindedness that rivaled that of her father. It was not until the reign of Anne Boleyn's daughter, Elizabeth I (r. 1558–1603), that a lasting religious settlement was worked out in England.

CATHOLIC REFORM AND COUNTER-REFORMATION

The Protestant Reformation did not take the medieval church completely by surprise. There had been much criticism and many calls for reform before the **Counter-Reformation** began in response to Protestant successes.

Sources of Catholic Reform Before the Reformation began, ambitious proposals had been made for church reform. But 16th-century popes were mindful of how the Councils of Constance and Basel had tried to strip the pope of his traditional powers, and they squelched efforts to bring about basic changes in the laws and institutions of the church. Despite papal foot-dragging, the church was not without reformers. Many new religious orders sprang up in the 16th century to champion renewal within the church.

Ignatius of Loyola and the Society of Jesus Of the various reform groups, none was more instrumental in the success of the Counter-Reformation than the Society of Jesus, the new order of Jesuits. Organized by Ignatius of Loyola in the 1530s, it was officially recognized by the papacy in 1540. Within a century, the society had more than 15,000 members scattered throughout the world and had established thriving missions in India, Japan, and the Americas.

Ignatius of Loyola (1491–1556) was a heroic figure. A dashing courtier and caballero in his youth, he began his spiritual pilgrimage in 1521 while recuperating from a serious battle wound. During a lengthy and painful convalescence, he read Christian classics. So impressed was he with the heroic self-sacrifice of the church's saints and their methods of overcoming mental anguish and pain that he underwent a profound religious conversion. Henceforth, he too would serve the church as a soldier of Christ.

Counter-Reformation
Sixteenth-century reform movement in the Roman Catholic Church in reaction to the Protestant Reformation.

The Ecstasy of Saint Teresa of Avila, by Gianlorenzo Bernini (1598–1680). Catholic mystics like Saint Teresa and Saint John of the Cross helped revive the traditional piety of medieval monasticism.

© Scala/Art Resource, N.Y.

HISTORY'S VOICES

IGNATIUS OF LOYOLA'S "RULES FOR THINKING WITH THE CHURCH"

A s leaders of the Counter-Reformation, the Jesuits attempted to live by and instill in others the strictest obedience to church authority. The following are some of the 18 rules included by Ignatius in his Spiritual Exercises to give Catholics positive direction. These rules also indicate the Catholic reformers' refusal to compromise with Protestants.

WOULD PROTESTANTS find any of Ignatius's "rules" acceptable? Might any of them be controversial among Catholic laity as well as among Protestant laity?

In order to have the proper attitude of mind in the Church Militant we should observe the following rules:

1. Putting aside all private judgment, we should keep our minds prepared and ready to obey promptly and in all things the true spouse of Christ our Lord, our Holy Mother, the hierarchical Church.

2. To praise sacramental confession and the reception of the Most Holy Sacrament once a year, and much better once a month, and better still every week. . . .

3. To praise the frequent hearing of Mass. . . .

4. To praise highly the religious life, virginity, and continence; and also matrimony, but not as highly. . . .

5. To praise the vows of religion, obedience, poverty, chastity, and other works of perfection and supererogation. . . .

6. To praise the relics of the saints . . . [and] the stations, pilgrimages, indulgences, jubilees, Crusade indulgences, and the lighting of candles in the churches.

7. To praise the precepts concerning fasts and abstinences . . . and acts of penance. . . .

8. To praise the adornments and buildings of churches as well as sacred images. . . .

9. To praise all the precepts of the church. . . .

10. To approve and praise the directions and recommendations of our superiors as well as their personal behaviour. . . .

11. To praise both the positive and scholastic theology. . . .

12. We must be on our guard against making comparisons between the living and those who have already gone to their reward, for it is no small error to say, for example: "This man knows more than St. Augustine"; "He is another Saint Francis, or even greater." . . .

13. If we wish to be sure that we are right in all things, we should always be ready to accept this principle: I will believe that the white that I see is black, if the hierarchical Church so defines it. For I believe that between . . . Christ our Lord and . . . His Church, there is but one spirit, which governs and directs us for the salvation of our souls.

Source: *The Spiritual Exercises of St. Ignatius*, trans. by Anthony Mottola. Copyright © 1964 by Doubleday, a division of Bantam, Doubleday, Dell Publishing Group, Inc., pp. 139–141. Used by permission of Doubleday, a division of Random House, Inc.

Ignatius devised a program of religious and moral self-discipline called the *Spiritual Exercises*, which outlined a path to absolute spiritual self-mastery. Ignatius believed that a person could shape his or her own behavior, even create a new religious self, through disciplined study and regular practice (see Ignatius of Loyola's "Rules for Thinking with the Church").

Whereas in Jesuit eyes Protestants had distinguished themselves by disobedience to church authority and by religious innovation, Ignatius's exercises were intended to teach good Catholics to submit without question to higher church authority and spiritual direction. Perfect discipline and self-control were essential for achieving such obedience, as were a passion for traditional spirituality and mystical experience. This potent combination helped counter the Reformation and win many Protestants back to the Catholic fold, especially in Austria and Germany.

The Council of Trent (1545–1563)   The broad success of the Reformation and the insistence of the emperor Charles V forced Pope Paul III (r. 1534–1549) to call a general council of the church to reassert church doctrine. The pope also appointed a reform commission, whose report, presented in February 1537, bluntly criticized the fiscality and simony[2] of the papal Curia (court) as the primary source of the church's loss of esteem. The report was so critical that Pope Paul III attempted unsuccessfully to suppress its publication, and Protestants reprinted and circulated it to justify their criticism.

The long-delayed council met in 1545 in the imperial city of Trent in northern Italy. There were three sessions spread over 18 years with long interruptions due to war, plague, and politics. Unlike the general councils of the 15th century, Trent was strictly under the pope's control, with high Italian prelates prominent in the proceedings.

The council's most important reforms concerned internal church discipline. The selling of church offices and other religious goods was forbidden. Trent strengthened the authority of local bishops so they could effectively discipline popular religious practice. Bishops who resided in Rome were forced to move to their appointed seats of authority. They had to preach regularly and conduct annual visitations. Parish priests were required to be neatly dressed, better educated, strictly celibate, and active among their parishioners. To train better priests, Trent also called for the establishment of a seminary in every diocese.

The Council did not make a single doctrinal concession to the Protestants, however. In the face of Protestant criticism, the Council of Trent reaffirmed the traditional scholastic education of the clergy; the role of good works in salvation; the authority of tradition; the seven sacraments; transubstantiation; the withholding of the Eucharistic cup from the laity; clerical celibacy; the reality of purgatory; the veneration of saints, relics, and sacred images; and the granting of letters of indulgence.

Rulers initially resisted Trent's reform decrees, fearing a revival of papal political power within their lands. But in time the new legislation took hold, and parish life revived under the guidance of a devout and better-trained clergy.

THE REFORMATION'S ACHIEVEMENTS

*A*lthough politically conservative, the Reformation changed traditional religious practices and institutions in many lands. By the end of the 16th century, what had disappeared or was radically altered was often dramatic.

HOW DID the Reformation change religious and social life?

Religion in 15th-Century Life   Prior to the Reformation, the streets of the great cities of central Europe that later turned Protestant (for example, Zurich, Strasbourg, Nuremberg, or Geneva) were filled with people who had clerical vocations. They made up 6 to 8 percent of the total urban population, and they exercised considerable political as well as spiritual power. They legislated and taxed; they tried cases in special church courts; and they enforced their laws with threats of excommunication.

The church calendar regulated daily life. About one-third of the year was devoted to some kind of religious observance or celebration. There were frequent

---

[2]The sin of selling sacred or spiritual things, such as church offices.

periods of fasting. On almost a hundred days out of the year, a pious Christian could not, without special dispensation, eat eggs, butter, fat, or meat.

Monasteries and especially nunneries were prominent, influential institutions. Sons of society's most powerful citizens resided there. Local aristocrats were closely identified with particular churches and chapels, whose walls recorded their lineage and proclaimed their generosity. Friars from near and far worked the streets begging alms. The Mass and liturgy were read entirely in Latin. Images of saints were regularly displayed, and on certain holy days their relics were paraded about and venerated. Pilgrims gathered by the hundreds and thousands at religious shrines, many sick and dying in search of a cure or a miracle, but also "tourists" seeking diversion and entertainment. Several times during the year, special preachers appeared with letters of indulgence to sell. Many clergy lived openly with concubines and had children, although they were sworn to celibacy and forbidden marriage. The church tolerated such relationships if penitential fines were paid.

People everywhere could be heard complaining about the clergy's exemption from taxation and, in many instances, also from the civil criminal code. People also grumbled about having to support local church officials who actually lived and worked elsewhere. Townspeople expressed concern that the church had too much influence over education and culture.

Religion in 16th-Century Life   After the Reformation, few changes in politics and society were evident in these cities. The same aristocratic families governed, and the rich generally got richer and the poor poorer. But overall numbers of clergy fell by two-thirds and religious holidays shrank by one-third. Monasteries and nunneries were almost all gone. Many were turned into hospices for the sick and poor or into educational institutions, their endowments to these new purposes. A few cloisters remained for very devout old monks and nuns, who could not be pensioned off or who lacked families and friends to care for them. But these remaining cloisters died out with their inhabitants.

The number of churchgoers had been reduced by at least a third, and worship was conducted almost completely in the vernacular. In some, particularly those in Zwinglian cities, the walls were stripped bare and white-washed to make sure their congregations meditated only on God's Word. The laity observed no obligatory fasts. Indulgence preachers no longer appeared. Local shrines were closed down, and anyone found openly venerating saints, relics, and images was subject to fine and punishment.

Copies of Luther's translation of the New Testament, or more often excerpts from it, could be found in private homes, and meditation on them was encouraged by the new clergy. The clergy could marry, and most did. They paid taxes and were punished for their crimes in civil courts. Domestic moral life was regulated by committees composed of roughly equal numbers of laity and clergy, over whose decisions secular magistrates had the last word.

Not all Protestant clergy were enthusiastic about the new authority the laity enjoyed in religious affairs, and the laity themselves were ambivalent about some aspects of the Reformation. More than half of the original converts returned to the Catholic fold before the end of the 16th century. Half of Europe could be counted in the Protestant camp in the mid-16th century, but only a fifth were still there by the mid-17th century.[3]

[3]Geoffrey Parker, *Europe in Crisis, 1598–1648* (Ithaca, NY: Cornell University Press, 1979), p. 50.

FAMILY LIFE IN EARLY MODERN EUROPE

Changes in the timing and duration of marriage, family size, and child care suggest that social and economic pressures were altering family life in the 16th and 17th centuries. The Reformation was only one factor—and not the chief—of these changes.

Later Marriages Between 1500 and 1800 men and women married later than in previous centuries: men in their mid-to late 20s and women in their early to mid-20s. The medieval church had recognized marriages made by a private exchange of vows between competent adults, but after the Reformation both Catholics and Protestants required parental consent and public vows for a licit union.

Late marriages reflected the difficulties couples had in accumulating the capital needed to set up independent households. There was a large population of single women: one in five never married, and 15 percent were widowed. Late marriages meant shorter unions, older first-time mothers, and higher mortality in childbirth. That led to more frequent remarriages for men. Delayed marriage also increased incidences of premarital sex and the numbers of children born out of wedlock.

A Young Couple in Love (ca. 1480) by an anonymous artist.

Bildarchiv Preussischer Kulturbesitz.

Arranged Marriages By the 15th century, it was usual for a future bride and groom to have known each other and to have had a prior relationship. Parents did not force strangers to wed, and the law protected children from coercion. Forced marriages where by definition invalid. But marriages were "arranged" in the sense that parents met and discussed terms before the prospective bride and groom began preparations.

Family Size Nuclear families were the rule in Western Europe: a father, a mother, and their children. They might live in larger households with in-laws, servants, and boarders. Children were conceived on the average of every two years. About one-third died by age five, and one-half by their teens.

Birth Control Artificial birth control methods had been known since antiquity. They were, however, not very effective, and the church opposed anything that might be done to prevent conception. St. Thomas Aquinas had argued that acts were moral only when they served nature's ends, and the production of children was the natural purpose of sex.

Wet Nursing The church and physicians both encouraged women to suckle their own newborns rather than hand them off to wet nurses (lactating women who sold their services). Wet nursing increased the risk of infant mortality, for the women who provided this service were not always as healthy, clean, or caring as the well-off women who employed them. Upper-class women, however, tended for reasons of vanity and convenience to employ wet nurses. Because nursing has a contraceptive effect, some women nursed to space out their pregnancies, and those who wanted many children used wet nurses.

Loving Families Some features of family life in this period may seem cold to modern people. Between the ages of 8 and 13, children were usually sent away from home to school or to begin apprenticeships and take up employment. The widowed often remarried within a few months of their bereavement. Marriages between spouses of vastly different ages were common.

In context, these practices made sense. Parents showed love and affection for their children by ensuring that they acquired the skills needed to be self-supporting. The labor involved in maintaining a household pushed people to remarry rapidly, but extreme disparity in age did invite criticism and ridicule.

WHAT WAS the final result of the Wars of Religion in France, the Netherlands, and Germany?

THE WARS OF RELIGION

After the Council of Trent adjourned in 1563, Protestants were met by a Jesuit-led Catholic counteroffensive. At the time of John Calvin's death in 1564, Geneva had become both a refuge for Europe's persecuted Protestants and an international school training Protestant resisters—leaders fully equal to the new Catholic challenge.

Genevan Calvinism and the reformed Catholicism of the Council of Trent were equally dogmatic, aggressive, and unwilling to compromise. Calvinists may have looked like "new papists" to their critics in the cities they dominated, but when they were a minority fighting for civil and religious rights, they could become firebrands and revolutionaries.

Calvinists favored a presbyterian form of church government. Congregations elected boards of *presbyters* (elders) to govern them and represent them at synods and meetings that shaped the policy of the church at large. Calvinism, therefore, encouraged local and regional religious authority. By contrast, the Counter-Reformation affirmed Catholicism's dedication to a centralized episcopal system, a church governed by a clerical hierarchy and owing absolute obedience to the pope. The higher clergy—the pope and bishops—not synods of local churches, ruled supreme. Calvinism attracted proponents of political decentralization who opposed totalitarian rulers, whereas Catholicism was congenial to proponents of absolute monarchy who believed that order required "one king, one church, one law."

The wars of religion that erupted between these camps were both internal national conflicts and international wars. Catholic and Protestant struggled for control of France, the Netherlands, and England. The Catholic governments of France and Spain fought the Protestant regimes in England and the Netherlands. The Thirty Years' War, which began in 1618, illustrated the international nature of religious conflict. Before it ended, it drew in every major European nation.

FRENCH WARS OF RELIGION (1562–1598)

When Henry II (r. 1547–1559) died accidentally during a tournament in 1559, his sickly 15-year-old son, Francis II (d. 1560), came to the throne under the regency of the queen mother, Catherine de Médicis (1519–1589). With the monarchy so weakened, three powerful families competed to control France: the Bourbons based in the south and west, the Montmorency-Châtillons from the center, and the Guises from eastern France. The Guises were by far the strongest, and the name *Guise* was synonymous with militant, ultra-Catholicism. The Bourbon and Montmorency-Châtillon families, by contrast, had strong **Huguenot** sympathies,

Huguenots French Calvinists.

primarily for political reasons. (French Protestants were called Huguenots after Besançon Hughes, the leader of a Genevan political revolt in the late 1520s.) The Bourbon Louis I, prince of Condé (d. 1569), and the Montmorency-Châtillon admiral Gaspard de Coligny (1519–1572) were the leaders of the French Protestant cause.

Ambitious aristocrats and discontented townspeople often joined Calvinist churches to oppose the Guise-dominated French monarchy. By 1561, there were more than 2,000 Huguenot congregations in France. Huguenots made up only about a 1/15 of the population, but they held important geographic areas and were well represented among the leaders of French society. More than 2/5 of the French aristocracy became Huguenots. Many apparently hoped to establish in France a principle of territorial sovereignty akin to the arrangement that the German princes won from the emperor in the Peace of Augsburg (1555). In this sense, Calvinism served the forces of political decentralization.

Catherine de Médicis and the Guises After Francis II's death in 1560, Catherine de Médicis continued as regent for her second son, Charles IX (r. 1560–1574). Fearing the Guises, Catherine, whose first concern was to

The St. Bartholemew's Day Massacre. In this notorious event, here depicted by the contemporary Protestant painter François Dubois, 3,000 Protestants were slaughtered in Paris and an estimated 20,000 others died throughout France. The massacre transformed the religious struggle in France from a contest for political power into an all-out war between Protestants and Catholics.

Le Massacre de la St–Barthelemy, entre 1572 et 1584. Oil on wood, 94 × 154 cm. Musée Cantonal des Beaux Arts, Lausanne. Photo: J.–C. Ducret Musée Cantonal des Beaux–Arts, Lausanne.

preserve the monarchy, sought allies among the Protestants. Early in 1562, she granted Protestants freedom to worship publicly outside towns—although only privately within them—and to hold synods, or church assemblies. In March 1562, the Duke of Guise surprised and massacred a Protestant congregation worshiping illegally at Vassy. This began the French Wars of Religion. Perpetually caught between fanatical Huguenot and Guise extremes, Queen Catherine tried to play one side against the other. She wanted a Catholic France but not under Guise domination.

On August 22, 1572, four days after the Huguenot Henry of Navarre had married Charles IX's sister—a royal alliance based on the queen mother's belief that Protestant power was growing—the Huguenot leader Coligny, who had influence over the king, was wounded by an assassin's bullet. Catherine may have been privy to this Guise plot to eliminate Coligny. After its failure, she feared both the king's response to her complicity and the Huguenots reaction to the attack on their leader. Catherine convinced Charles that a Huguenot coup was afoot and that only the swift execution of Protestant leaders could save the crown from a Protestant attack on Paris. On the eve of Saint Bartholomew's Day, August 24, 1572, Coligny and 3,000 fellow Huguenots were butchered in Paris. Within three days an estimated 20,000 Huguenots were killed in coordinated attacks throughout France.

This event changed the nature of the struggle between Protestants and Catholics throughout Europe. In France, it was no longer an internal political contest between Guise and Bourbon factions, nor was it simply a Huguenot campaign to win basic religious freedoms. Henceforth, Protestants viewed it as an international struggle to the death for survival against an adversary whose cruelty justified any means of resistance.

The Rise to Power of Henry of Navarre   Henry III (r. 1574–1589), who was Catherine's third son and the last Valois king, was caught between a radical Catholic League, formed in 1576 by Henry of Guise, and vengeful Huguenots. Like his mother, he tried to steer a middle course, which won him support from a growing body of neutral Catholics and Huguenots, who put the political survival of France above its religious unity. Such *politiques*, as they were called, were prepared to compromise religious creeds to save the nation.

In the mid-1580s the Catholic League, with Spanish help, totally dominated Paris. Henry III tried to rout the league with a surprise attack in 1588, but he failed and had to flee Paris. Resorting to guerrilla tactics, the king had both the Duke and the Cardinal of Guise assassinated. The Catholic League reacted with a fury that matched the earlier Huguenot response to the Massacre of Saint Bartholomew's Day. In April 1589, the king was forced into an alliance with his Protestant cousin and heir, Henry of Navarre.

However, as the two Henrys prepared to attack Paris, a fanatical Dominican friar murdered Henry III, clearing the way for the Bourbon Huguenot Henry of Navarre to become Henry IV of France (r. 1589–1610).

Henry IV was a *politique*, who valued peace more than religious unity. He believed that a policy of tolerant Catholicism would best achieve his objectives. On July 25, 1593, he abjured the Protestant faith and embraced the majority religion of his subjects. He is reported to have said: "Paris is worth a Mass."

The Edict of Nantes   Five years later, on April 13, 1598, Henry IV issued the Edict of Nantes, a formal religious settlement. In 1591, he had assured the

Huguenots of at least qualified religious freedoms, and the edict fulfilled his promise by sanctioning minority religious rights within what was to remain an officially Catholic country. This religious truce—and it was never more than that—granted the Huguenots, who by this time numbered well over a million, freedom of public worship, the right of assembly, admission to public offices and universities, and permission to maintain fortified towns. Most of these freedoms, however, were confined to specific Huguenot localities. Concession of the right to fortify towns reveals the continuing distrust between French Protestants and Catholics. The edict only transformed a long hot war between enemies into a long cold war. Critics believed the edict created a state within a state.

The Milch Cow. A 16th-century satirical painting depicting the Netherlands as a land all the great powers of Europe wish to exploit. Elizabeth of England is feeding her (England had long-standing commercial ties with Flanders); Philip II of Spain is attempting to ride her (Spain was trying to reassert its control over the entire region); William of Orange is trying to milk her (he was the leader of the anti-Spanish rebellion); and the king of France holds her by the tail (France hoped to profit from the rebellion at Spain's expense).

Rijksmuseum, Amsterdam.

A Catholic fanatic assassinated Henry IV in May 1610. Although Henry is best remembered for the Edict of Nantes, his political and economic policies were equally important. They laid the foundations for the transformation of France into the absolutist state it became in the 17th century. His grandson Louis XIV (r. 1643–1715), renewing the slogan "one king, one church, one law," revoked the Edict of Nantes in 1685 (see Chapter 20). Religion again violently disrupted French society. Rare is the politician who learns from the lessons of history.

IMPERIAL SPAIN AND THE REIGN OF PHILIP II (1556–1598)

Until the English defeated his mighty Armada in 1588, no ruler was greater in the second half of the sixteenth century than Philip II of Spain. During the first half of his reign, Philip II focused attention on the Mediterranean and Turkish expansion. On October 7, 1571, a Holy League of Spain, Venice, and the pope defeated the Turks at Lepanto in the largest naval battle of the 16th century. About 30,000 Turks were killed and more than one-third of the Turkish fleet was sunk or captured.

Revolt in the Netherlands   The spectacular Spanish military success in southern Europe was not repeated in northern Europe, where Philip tried to impose his will within the Netherlands and on England and France. The resistance of the Netherlands was key to undoing Spanish dreams of world empire.

The Netherlands were the richest area in Europe. The merchant towns of the region were, however, Europe's most independent. Many, like the great port of Antwerp, were Calvinist strongholds. Opposition to the Spanish overlords found a leader in a native nobleman, William of Nassau, the Prince of Orange (r. 1533–1584). Like other successful rulers in this period, William of Orange was a politique who valued the Netherlands' political autonomy above religious creeds. He was at various times Catholic, Lutheran, and Calvinist.

In 1564, political and religious opponents to Spain's rule united for the first time under Philip II's unwise insistence that the decrees of the Council of Trent be enforced throughout the Netherlands. They formed a national covenant called the Compromise, a solemn pledge to resist the decrees of Trent and the Inquisition.

Philip ordered the Duke of Alba (1508–1582) to lead an army of 10,000 men into the Netherlands from Milan in 1567, a show of combined Spanish and papal might. Alba put down the revolt and established a tribunal—known to the Spanish as the Council of Troubles and to the Netherlanders as the Council of Blood—to govern the land. Several thousand suspected heretics were publicly executed before Alba's reign of terror ended.

William of Orange, who was an exile in Germany during these turbulent years, emerged as the leader of a broad movement for the Netherlands' independence. In 1576, after a decade of persecution and warfare, the 10 predominantly Catholic southern provinces (roughly modern Belgium) joined the 7 largely Protestant northern provinces (roughly the modern Netherlands) in opposition to Spain. Their union, the Pacification of Ghent, granted each region of the country sovereignty in matters of religion—a Netherlands version of the Peace of Augsburg.

In January 1579, the southern provinces formed the Union of Arras and made peace with Spain. The northern provinces formed the Union of Utrecht and continued the struggle. Spanish preoccupation with France and England in the 1580s gave the northern provinces their chance to evict Spain's armies (1593), and in 1596, France and England formally recognized their independence. However, the northern provinces did not formally conclude peace with Spain until 1609, and Spain did not fully recognize their independence until the Peace of Westphalia in 1648.

ENGLAND AND SPAIN (1558–1603)

Elizabeth I Elizabeth I (r. 1558–1603), daughter of Henry VIII and Anne Boleyn, was perhaps the most astute politician of the 16th century in both domestic and foreign policy. She repealed the anti-Protestant legislation of her predecessor Mary Tudor and guided a religious settlement through Parliament that prevented England from being torn asunder by religious differences in the 16th century, as the Continent was.

Catholic extremists hoped to replace Elizabeth with the Catholic Mary Stuart, Queen of Scots. But Elizabeth fended off Catholic assassination plots and rarely let emotion override her political instincts.

Elizabeth also dealt cautiously with England's Puritans, Protestants who wanted to "purify" the national church of every vestige of "popery" and make its theology purely Protestant. The Puritans had two special grievances: (1) the retention of Catholic ceremony and vestments by the Church of England, and (2) the continuation of the episcopal system of church governance. Sixteenth-century Puritans were not separatists, however. They worked through Parliament to create an alternative national church of semiautonomous congregations governed by representative presbyteries, following the model of Calvin and Geneva. These were the Presbyterians. The more extreme Puritans, who wanted every congregation to be autonomous and a law unto itself, were called Congregationalists. Elizabeth considered their views subversive.

Deterioration of Relations with Spain   A series of events led inexorably to war between England and Spain, despite the sincere desires of both Philip II and Elizabeth to avoid it. Following Spain's victory at Lepanto in 1571, England signed a mutual defense pact with France. Also in the 1570s, Elizabeth's famous seamen, John Hawkins (1532–1595) and Sir Francis Drake (?1545–1596), began to prey on Spanish shipping in the Americas. Drake's circumnavigation of the globe (1577–1580) was one in a series of dramatic demonstrations of England's growing sea power. In 1585, Elizabeth signed a treaty that committed English soldiers to aid the Netherlands. These events pushed England and Spain toward a showdown, and the breakpoint was Elizabeth's reluctant decision to execute Mary, Queen of Scots (1542–1587) for complicity in a plot to assassinate her.

Philip assembled a great armada for an invasion of England, and on May 30, 1588, his fleet of 130 ships bearing 25,000 sailors and soldiers under the command of the Duke of Medina-Sidonia set sail for England. The English, however, ably countered his attack. The barges sent to transport Spanish soldiers from the galleons onto English shores were prevented from leaving Calais and Dunkirk. The swifter English and Netherlands ships, assisted by an "English wind (a storm)", dispersed the Spanish fleet, over a third of which never returned to Spain. The Armada's defeat gave heart to Protestant resistance everywhere, and Spain never fully recovered. By the time of Philip's death on September 13, 1598, his forces had been rebuffed by the French and the Dutch. His 17th-century successors were all inferior leaders, and Spain never again had an era of imperial grandeur comparable to Philip's reign. The French seized the opportunity to dominate the Continent, while the Dutch and the English whittled away at Spain's overseas empire.

Elizabeth died on March 23, 1603, leaving behind her a strong nation poised to expand into a global empire (see Map 16–3).

THE THIRTY YEARS' WAR (1618–1648)

The Thirty Years' War in the Holy Roman Empire was the last and most destructive of the Wars of Religion. Religious and political differences had long set Catholics against Protestants and Calvinists against Lutherans. What made the Thirty Years' War so devastating was the entrenched hatred of the various sides and their seeming determination to sacrifice everything for territorial sovereignty and religion. As conflicts multiplied, virtually every major European land became involved either directly or indirectly. When the hostilities ended in 1648, the peace terms redrew much of the map of northern Europe to conform to the pattern we know today.

Fragmented Germany   During the second half of the 16th century, Germany was an almost ungovernable land of 360 autonomous political entities. The Peace of Augsburg (1555) had given each a significant degree of sovereignty within its own borders. Each levied its own tolls and tariffs and coined its own money, practices that made land travel and trade between the various regions difficult, if not impossible. Many of these little "states" had political ambitions. Unlike France, Spain, and England at the start of the 17th century, Germany was radically decentralized and fragmented (see Map 16–3).

Religious Division   Religious conflict accentuated international and internal political divisions. The Holy Roman Empire was about equally divided between Catholics and Protestants, the latter having perhaps a slight numerical

MAP EXPLORATION

Interactive map: To explore this map further, go to **http://www.prenhall.com/craig/map16.3**

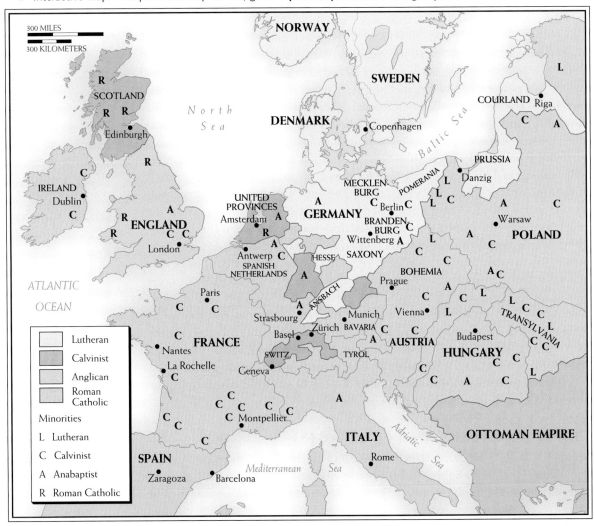

MAP 16–3

Religious Division ca. 1600. By 1600 few could expect Christians to return to a uniform religious allegiance. In Spain and southern Italy, Catholicism remained relatively unchallenged, but note the existence elsewhere of large religious minorities, both Catholic and Protestant.

WHY DID the Wars of Religion fail to reestablish religious uniformity in the Holy Roman Empire?

edge by 1600. The terms of the Peace of Augsburg (1555) had attempted to freeze the amount of territory held by Lutherans and the Catholics. In the intervening years, however, the Lutherans had gained political control in many Catholic areas, and Catholics had taken over a few previously Lutheran areas. There was also religious strife between liberal and conservative Lutherans and between Lutherans and the growing numbers of Calvinists.

As elsewhere in Europe, Calvinism operated as political and religious leaven within the Holy Roman Empire. Calvinism was not recognized as a legal religion by the Peace of Augsburg, but in 1559 it established a strong foothold within the empire when Elector Frederick III (r. 1559–1576) of the Palatinate, a devout convert to Calvinism, made it his domain's official religion. By 1609,

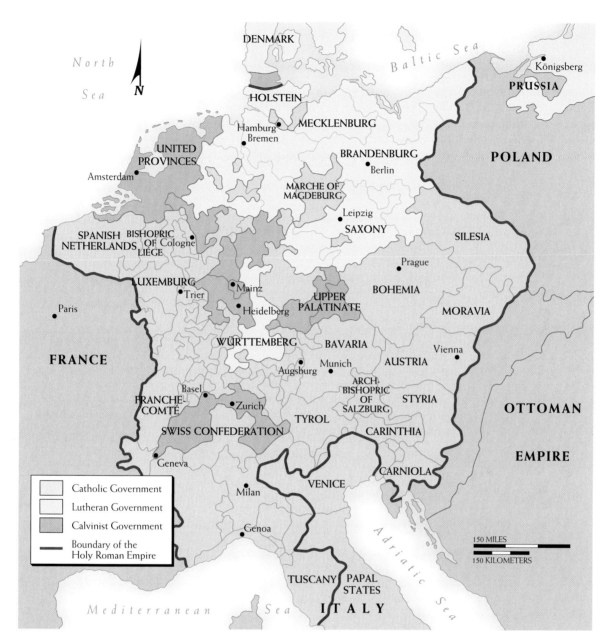

MAP 16–4

The Holy Roman Empire ca. 1618. On the eve of the Thirty Years' War, the empire was politically and religiously fragmented, as this somewhat simplified map reveals. Lutherans dominated the north and Catholics the south, while Calvinists controlled the United Provinces and the Palatinate and also had an important presence in Switzerland and Brandenburg.

DID THE Holy Roman Empire emerge from the Wars of Religion stronger or weaker?

Palatine Calvinists had organized a Protestant defensive alliance supported by Spain's enemies: England, France, and the Netherlands.

If the Calvinists were active within the Holy Roman Empire, so were their Catholic counterparts, the Jesuits. Staunchly Catholic Bavaria, with Spanish backing, was militarily and ideologically for Counter-Reformation Catholicism what the Palatinate was for Protestantism. From Bavaria, the Jesuits launched successful missions throughout the empire. In 1609, Maximilian, Duke of Bavaria (1573–1651), organized a Catholic League to counter a new Protestant

The Reformation permanently shattered the religious unity of Western Europe that had existed since the fifth century C.E. It also gave rise to more than a century of warfare, in which Catholics fought Protestants, and Protestants fought each other all in the name of faith. By 1648, when the Treaty of Westphalia ended the Thirty Years' War, Europe remained divided into mostly Catholic regions, mostly Protestant regions, and those areas with large religious minorities. Most of these divisions have persisted to the present day.

Country	Religion
Austria	Catholic
Belgium	Catholic
Bohemia (modern Czech Republic)	Catholic
Croatia	Catholic
England	Protestant (Anglicans, Calvinists, and Anabaptists); a declining Catholic minority
Estonia	Lutheran
France	Catholic, but with substantial numbers of Calvinists
Germany	North was predominately Protestant (Lutheran, Calvinist, Anabaptist); south and the Rhineland were mostly Catholic; but each area had religious minorities
Hungary	Mostly Catholic, but with a large Calvinist minority
Ireland	Mostly Catholic, but with a Protestant minority (Anglicans and Calvinists) mainly in the north
Italy	Catholic
Latvia	Lutheran
Lithuania	Catholic
Netherlands	Calvinist majority, but with a large Catholic minority
Poland	Catholic
Portugal	Catholic
Scandinavia	Lutheran
Scotland	Calvinist
Slovakia	Catholic
Slovenia	Catholic
Spain	Catholic
Switzerland	Almost evenly divided between Catholics and Protestants (both Calvinists and Lutherans)

alliance that had been formed by the Calvinist Elector Palatine, Frederick IV (r. 1583–1610). When the league fielded a great army under the command of Jean't Senclaes, Count of Tilly (1559–1632), the stage was set for the Thirty Years' War, the worst European catastrophe since the Black Death of the 14th century.

The Treaty of Westphalia In 1648, all hostilities within the Holy Roman Empire were ended by the Treaty of Westphalia. The treaty reasserted the major feature of the religious settlement of the Peace of Augsburg (1555). Rulers were again permitted to determine the religion of their lands. Calvinists were given the legal recognition they had long-sought, but they were denied such status to various sectarians. The independence of the Swiss Confederacy and of the United Provinces of Holland was officially recognized.

By confirming the territorial sovereignty of Germany's many political entities, the Treaty of Westphalia prolonged Germany's division and political weakness into the modern era. However, two German states attained international significance during the 17th century: Austria and Brandenburg-Prussia. The petty regionalism within the empire reflected on a small scale the drift of larger European politics. During the 17th century Europe's distinctive nation-states, each with its own political, cultural, and religious identity, reached maturity and firmly established the competitive nationalism of the modern world.

SUPERSTITION AND ENLIGHTENMENT: THE BATTLE WITHIN

*R*eligious reform and warfare permanently changed religious institutions in major European countries. They also motivated rethinking traditional assumptions about human nature and society. On the one hand, this had dark consequence, for the peak years of religious warfare were also those of the great European witch hunts. On the other hand, however, the era spawned a constructive skepticism that inaugurated a period of significant scientific progress.

WITCH HUNTS AND PANIC

Nowhere is the dark side of the period better seen than in the witch hunts and panics that erupted in almost every western land. Between 1400 and 1700, courts sentenced an estimated 70,000 to 100,000 people to death for harmful magic (*malificium*) and diabolical witchcraft. In addition to threatening their neighbors, witches were said to attend mass meetings known as *sabbats*, to which they were believed to fly. They were accused of indulging in sexual orgies with the devil, who appeared in animal form, most often as a he-goat. They were said to practice cannibalism (having a taste for Christian children) and a variety of ritual acts and practices that denied or perverted Christian beliefs.

Many factors may have contributed to the great witch panics of the second half of the 16th and the early 17th centuries. Religious division and warfare were major influences. The Reformation's rejection of the defenses against the devil and demons that the chuch had traditionally provided forced people to find alternative ways to handle their anxieties. The growing strength of governments intent on weeding out nonconformists also played a part.

WHY DID witch hunts and panics erupt across Western Europe between 1400 and 1700?

Village Origins In village societies, "cunning folk," those who were both revered and feared by their neighbors, played a positive role in helping people cope with calamity. Neighbors turned to them for help in the face of natural disasters or physical disabilities, for they provided consolation and hope that, through magic, something might be done to avert or overcome difficulties.

Possession of magical powers, for good or ill, gave one status in village society. Not surprisingly, therefore, claims to such powers most often were made by the people most in need of security and influence—the old and the impoverished, especially single or widowed women. For villagers, witch beliefs may also have been a way of resisting pressure from urban Christian societies that wanted to impose their laws and institutions on the rural populace. From the perspective of church authorities, entrenched local fertility cults (semipagan practices intended to ensure good harvests) may have looked like diabolical witchcraft.

Influence of the Clergy Had ordinary people not believed that "gifted persons" could help or harm them by magical means and had they not been willing to make accusations against them, witch hunts would not have occurred. But the highly educated also contributed to the witch craze. The Christian clergy believed in and practiced magic—the holy sacraments and exorcism of demons. In the late 13th century the church declared its magic to be the only legitimate magic. Given that magical powers were not human, theologians reasoned that they had to come either from God or the devil. Anyone who practiced magic outside the church obviously derived their power from the devil. From such reasoning grew accusations of "pacts" between non-Christian magicians and Satan.

Attacking witches was one way in which the church brought regions into conformity with its doctrines and established its spiritual hegemony. The clergy viewed the cunning folk as competitors and obstacles. A campaign to root them out was a way to establish moral and policial authority over a village or territory.

Why Women? Roughly 80 percent of the victims of witch hunts were women, most of whom were single and between 45 and 60 years of age, suggesting to some that misogyny fueled the witch hunts. At a time when women threatened to break out from under male control, witch hunts, it has been argued, were simply a conspiracy of males against females.

Older single women may, however, have been vulnerable for more basic social reasons. They were a largely dependent social group in need of public assistance and natural targets for the "social engineering" of the witch hunts. For economic reasons, such women sometimes sought to protect and empower themselves by claiming supernatural powers. They thus found themselves on the front lines in disproportionate numbers when the church declared war against all who practiced magic without its blessing. Also, the practice by many of these women of midwifery

Combating Witchcraft. Three women are burned to death as witches in Baden, Germany. Their alleged crimes are depicted on the right, where they are seen feasting with demons.

"Three witches burned alive from a German Broadside," circa 1555. Courtesy of Stock Montage, Inc.

associated them with the deaths of beloved wives and infants and made them targets of local resentment and accusations. Both the church and their neighbors were prepared to think and say the worst about these women. It was a deadly combination.

End of the Witch Hunts   Many factors helped end the witch hunts. The emergence of a new, more scientific worldview made it difficult to believe in the powers of witches. When, in the 17th century, mind and matter came to be viewed as independent realities, the belief faded that a witch's curse, mere words, could affect things. Advances in medicine and the beginning of insurance companies improved people's ability to cope with calamities and physical affliction and dissuaded them from thoughts of the supernatural. Witch hunts also tended to get out of hand. Accused witches sometimes alleged that important townspeople had attended their sabbats, sometimes even their judges. At this point the trials ceased to serve the purposes of those who were conducting them. They not only became dysfunctional but threatened anarchy as well.

WRITERS AND PHILOSOPHERS

By the end of the 16th century, many could no longer accept either old Catholic or new Protestant absolutes. Intellectually as well as politically, the 17th century was a period of transition for which the humanists and scientists of the Renaissance and post-Renaissance (see Chapter 22) had prepared the way. Writers and philosophers of the era were aware that they lived in a time of change. Some embraced emerging science attitudes wholeheartedly (Hobbes and Locke), some tried to straddle the two ages (Cervantes and Shakespeare), and still others ignored or opposed developments that seemed to threaten traditional values (Pascal).

Miguel de Cervantes Saavedra   Spanish literature of the 16th and 17th centuries was influenced by Spain's peculiar religious and political situation. Spain was dominated by a Catholic Church that enjoyed vigorous state support. The intertwining of Catholic piety and Spanish political power created a preoccupation with medieval chivalric virtues—in particular, honor and loyalty.

Generally acknowledged to be the greatest Spanish writer of all time, Cervantes (1547–1616) explored the strengths and weaknesses of religious idealism. The son of a nomadic physician, he received only a smattering of formal education. Cervantes educated himself by insatiable reading in vernacular literature and immersion in the school of life. As a young man, he worked in Rome for a Spanish cardinal. In 1570, he became a soldier and was decorated for gallantry at Lepanto (1571). He began to write his most famous work, *Don Quixote*, in 1603, while languishing in prison after conviction for theft.

The first part of *Don Quixote* appeared in 1605, and a second part in 1615. If, as many argue, the intent of this work was to satirize the chivalric romances so popular in Spain, Cervantes failed to conceal his deep affection for the character he created as an object of ridicule, Don Quixote. Don Quixote, a none-too-stable middle-aged man, is driven mad by reading too many romances. He comes to believe that he is an aspirant to knighthood and must prove his worthiness. To this end, he acquires a rusty suit of armor, mounts an aged horse, and chooses for his inspiration a quite unworthy peasant girl whom he imagines to be a noble lady to whom he can, with honor, dedicate his life.

Don Quixote's foil in the story—his squire, Sancho Panza, a clever, worldly wise peasant—watches with bemused skepticism and genuine sympathy, as his lord does battle with a windmill (which he mistakes for a dragon) and repeatedly makes a fool of himself. The story ends tragically with Don Quixote's humiliating defeat by a well-meaning friend, who, disguised as a knight, bests Don Quixote in combat and forces him to renounce his quest for knighthood. The humiliated Don Quixote does not, however, come to his senses as a result. He returns sadly to his village to die a shamed and broken-hearted old man.

Throughout *Don Quixote*, Cervantes juxtaposed the down-to-earth realism of Sancho Panza with the old-fashioned religious idealism of Don Quixote. Cervantes admired the one as much as the other. He wanted his readers to realize that to be truly happy, men and women need dreams just as much as a sense of reality.

William Shakespeare   There is much less factual knowledge about William Shakespeare (1564–1616), the greatest playwright in the English language, than one would expect of such an important figure. Shakespeare may have worked as a schoolteacher for a time and in this capacity acquired his broad knowledge of Renaissance learning and literature. His work shows none of the Puritan distress over worldliness. He took the new commercialism and the bawdy pleasures of the Elizabethan Age in stride and with amusement. In politics and religion, he was a man of his time and not inclined to offend his queen.

That Shakespeare was interested in politics is apparent from his historical plays and the references to contemporary political events that fill all his works. He seems to have viewed government simply as a function of the character of a ruler, whether a Richard III or an Elizabeth Tudor, not as the realization of a social ideal. By modern standards he was a political conservative, accepting the social rankings and the power structure of his day and demonstrating unquestioned patriotism.

Shakespeare knew the theater as an insider. A member and principal dramatist of a famous company of actors, the King's Men, he was a playwright, actor, and part owner of a theater. He synthesized the best of the past and current achievements in the dramatic arts. He was particularly skilled at exploring human motivation and passion and had a unique talent for psychological penetration.

Shakespeare wrote histories, comedies, and tragedies. The tragedies are his greatest achievements. Four were written within a three-year period: *Hamlet* (1603), *Othello* (1604), *King Lear* (1605), and *Macbeth* (1606). The most original of the tragedies, *Romeo and Juliet* (1597), transformed an old popular story into a moving drama of "star-cross'd lovers."

In his lifetime and ever since, Shakespeare has been immensely popular with both audiences and readers. As Ben Jonson (1572–1637), a contemporary classical dramatist who created his own school of poets, put it in a tribute affixed to the *First Folio* edition of Shakespeare's plays (1623): "He was not of an age, but for all time."

Blaise Pascal   Blaise Pascal (1623–1662) was a French mathematician and a physical scientist widely acclaimed by his contemporaries. Torn between the continuing dogmatism and the new skepticism of the 17th century, Pascal aspired to write a work that would refute both the Jesuits, whose *casuistry* (confessional tactics designed to minimize or excuse sinful acts) he considered a distortion of Christian teaching, and the skeptics, who either denied religion altogether (atheists) or accepted it only as it conformed to reason (deists). Pascal failed to complete such a definitive work, and his views on these matters exist only in piecemeal form. He opposed the Jesuits in his *Provincial Letters* (1656–1657), and he left behind a provocative collection of reflections on humankind and religion that was published posthumously under the title *Pensées*.

Pascal was early influenced by the Jansenists, 17th-century Catholic opponents of the Jesuits. Although good Catholics, the Jansenists shared with the Calvinists St. Augustine's belief in the total sinfulness of human beings, their eternal predestination by God, and their complete dependence on faith and grace for knowledge of God and salvation.

Pascal believed that reason and science, although attesting to human dignity, remained of no avail in religion. Only the reasons of the heart and a "leap of faith" could found belief. Pascal saw two essential truths in the Christian religion: that a loving God, worthy of human devotion, exists; and that human beings, because they are corrupted in nature, are utterly unworthy of God. Pascal believed that the atheists and deists of the age had spurned the lesson of reason. For him, rational analysis of the human condition attested to humankind's utter mortality and corruption and exposed the inability of reason to resolve the problems of human nature and destiny. Those who truly heed reason should be driven by it to faith and dependence on divine grace.

Pascal made a famous wager with skeptics. It is a better bet, he argued, to believe that God exists and to stake everything on His promised mercy than not to do so; if God does exist, everything will be gained by the believer, whereas the loss incurred by having believed in God should He prove not to exist is, by comparison, slight.

Pascal was convinced that belief in God measurably improved earthly life psychologically and disciplined it morally, regardless of whether God proved in the end to exist. He thought that great danger lay in the surrender of traditional religious values. He urged his contemporaries to seek self-understanding through "learned ignorance" and to discover humankind's greatness by recognizing its misery. This, he hoped, would counter what he believed to be the false optimism of the new rationalism and science.

Baruch Spinoza The most controversial thinker of the 17th century was Baruch Spinoza (1632–1677), the son of a Jewish merchant of Amsterdam. Spinoza's philosophy caused his excommunication by his own synagogue in 1656. In 1670, he published his *Treatise on Religious and Political Philosophy*, a work that criticized the dogmatism of Dutch Calvinists and championed freedom of thought. During his lifetime, both Jews and Protestants attacked him as an atheist.

Spinoza's most influential writing, *Ethics*, appeared after his death in 1677. Religious leaders universally condemned it for its apparent espousal of pantheism. God and nature were so closely identified by Spinoza that little room seemed left either for divine revelation in Scripture or for the personal immortality of the soul, denials equally repugnant to Jews and to Christians.

The most controversial part of *Ethics* deals with the nature of substance and of God. According to Spinoza there is only one substance, which is self-caused, free, and infinite, and God is that substance. From this definition, it follows that everything that exists is in God and cannot even be conceived of apart from him.

Pascal's calculator. Pascal invented this adding machine, the ancestor of mechanical calculators, around 1644. It has eight wheels with ten cogs each, corresponding to the numbers 0 through 9. The wheels move forward for addition, backward for subtraction.

Bildarchiv Preussischer Kulturbesitz

Leviathan. The famous title page from Hobbes's book depicts the ruler as absolute lord of his lands, but note that he incorporates the mass of individuals whose self interests are best served by their willing consent to accept him and cooperate with his rule.

Such a doctrine is not precisely pantheistic, because God is still seen to be more than the created world that he, as primal substance, embraces. Nonetheless, in Spinoza's view, statements about the natural world are also statements about divine nature. Mind and matter are seen to be extensions of the infinite substance of God; what transpires in the world of humankind and nature is a necessary outpouring of the Divine.

Such teaching clearly ran the danger of portraying the world as eternal and human actions as unfree and inevitable, the expression of a divine fatalism. Such points of view had been considered heresies by Jews and Christians because these views deny the creation of the world by God and destroy any voluntary basis for personal reward and punishment.

Thomas Hobbes   Thomas Hobbes (1588–1679) was the most original political philosopher of the 17th century. Although he never broke with the Church of England, he came to share basic Calvinist beliefs, especially the low view of human nature and the ideal of a commonwealth based on a covenant, both of which find eloquent expression in his political philosophy.

Hobbes, an urbane and much-traveled man, was one of the most enthusiastic supporters of the new scientific movement. During the 1630s he visited Paris, where he came to know Descartes. After the outbreak of the Puritan Revolution (see Chapter 20) in 1640, he lived as an exile in Paris until 1651. Hobbes also spent time with Galileo (see Chapter 22) in Italy. He took a special interest in the works of William Harvey, a physiologist famed for the discovery of how blood circulated through the body; Harvey's scientific writings influenced Hobbes's own tracts on bodily motions.

Hobbes was driven to the vocation of political philosophy by the English Civil War (see Chapter 20). In 1651, his *Leviathan* appeared in which he examined the political consequences of human passions. This work's originality lay in (1) its making natural law, rather than common law (i.e., custom or precedent), the basis of all positive law; and (2) its defense of a representative theory of absolute authority against the theory of the divine right of kings. Hobbes maintained that statute law found its justification only as an expression of the law of nature and that rulers derived their authority from the consent of the people.

Hobbes viewed humankind and society in a thoroughly materialistic and mechanical way. Human beings are defined as a collection of material particles in motion. All their psychological processes begin with and are derived from bare sensation, and all their motivations are egotistical, intended to increase pleasure and minimize pain. Despite this seemingly low estimate of human beings, Hobbes believed much could be accomplished by the reasoned use of science. All was contingent, however, on the correct use of that greatest of all human powers, a commonwealth that unites people by their consent as one all-powerful person.

The key to Hobbes's political philosophy is a brilliant myth of the original state of humankind. According to this myth, human beings in the natural state are generally inclined to a "perpetual and restless desire of power after power that ceases only in death."[4] As all people desire—and in the state of nature have a natural right to—everything, their equality breeds enmity, competition, and

---

[4]*Leviathan*, Parts I and II, ed. By H. W. Schneider (Indianapolis, IN: Bobbs-Merrill, 1958), p. 86.

diffidence, and the desire for glory begets perpetual quarreling—"a war of every man against every man."[5]

Whereas earlier and later philosophers saw the original human state as a paradise from which humankind had fallen, Hobbes saw it as a corruption from which social life had delivered people. Contrary to the views of Aristotle and of Christian thinkers like St. Thomas Aquinas, Hobbes saw human beings not as sociable, political animals, but as self-centered beasts, laws unto themselves, utterly without a master unless one is imposed by force.

According to Hobbes, people escape the impossible state of nature only by entering a social contract that creates a commonwealth tightly ruled by law and order. The social contract obliges every person, for the sake of peace and self-defense, to agree to set aside personal rights to all things. We should impose restrictions on the liberty of others only to the degree that we would allow others to restrict our own.

Because words and promises are insufficient to guarantee this state, the social contract also establishes the coercive force necessary to compel compliance with the covenant. Hobbes believed that the dangers of anarchy were far greater than those of tyranny, and he conceived of the ruler's power as absolute and unlimited. There is no room in Hobbes's political philosophy for political protest in the name of individual conscience, nor for resistance to legitimate authority by private individuals—features of *Leviathan* criticized by his contemporaries, Catholics and Puritans alike.

John Locke John Locke (1632–1704) has proved to be the most influential political thinker of the 17th century.[6] His political philosophy came to be embodied in the so-called Glorious Revolution of 1688–1689 (Chapter 20). Although he was not as original as Hobbes, his political writings were a major source of the later Enlightenment Era's criticism of absolutism, and they inspired both the American and French Revolutions.

Locke's two most famous works are the *Essay Concerning Human Understanding* (1690) (discussed in Chapter 22) and *Two Treatises of Government* (1690). He wrote the latter to refute the argument that rulers had absolute power. Rulers, Locke argued, are bound to the law of nature, which is the voice of reason that teaches that "all mankind [are] equal and independent, [and] no one ought to harm another in his life, health, liberty, or possessions,"[7] inasmuch as all human beings are the images and property of God. According to Locke, people enter social contracts, empowering legislatures and monarchs to "umpire" their disputes, precisely to preserve their natural rights and not to surrender them to an absolute authority.

"Whenever that end [namely, the preservation of life, liberty, and property for which power is given to rulers by a commonwealth] is manifestly neglected or opposed, the trust must necessarily be forfeited and the power devolved into the hands of those that gave it, who may place it anew where they think best for their safety and security."[8] From Locke's point of view, absolute monarchy was "inconsistent" with civil society and could be "no form of civil government at all."[9]

18.1
The Mortal God:
Leviathan (1651)

[5] Ibid., p. 106.
[6] Locke's scientific writings are discussed in Chapter 24.
[7] *The Second Treatise of Government*, ed. By P. T. Peardon (Indianapolis, IN: Bobbs-Merrill, 1952), chap. 2, sects. 4–6, pp. 4–6.
[8] Ibid., chap. 13, sect. 149, p. 84.
[9] Ibid.

IMAGE KEY

for pages 370–371

a. Fifteenth century Italian silver cross
b. Martin Luther tempting Jesus
c. *The Milch Cow* a sixteenth-century satirical painting
d. Gutenberg's Bible
e. Miguel de Cervantes Saavedra (1547–1616)
f. *The Ecstacy of Saint Teresa of Avila*, by Bernini
g. *Le Massacre de la St-Barthelemy, entre 1572 et 1584*
h. John Calvin
i. Elizabeth I

SUMMARY

Voyages of Discovery In the late 15th century, Europe began to expand around the globe. Driven by both mercenary and religious motives, the Portuguese pioneered a sea route around Africa to India and the Far East, and the Spanish discovered the Americas. The consequences were immense for Europeans, Native Americans, Africans, and Asians. In time, a truly global society would emerge.

The Reformation The Reformation began in Germany with Martin Luther's attack on indulgences in 1517. Despite the opposition to the Reformation of Emperor Charles V, Luther had the support of many German princes. The Reformation shattered the religious unity of Europe. In Switzerland, Zwingli and Calvin launched their own versions of Protestantism. In England, Henry VIII repudiated papal authority when the pope refused to grant him a divorce. The different Protestant sects were often as hostile to each other as they were to Catholicism. The Reformation also led to far-reaching changes in religious practices and social attitudes, including steps toward the advancement of women.

The Roman Catholic Church also acted to reform itself. The Council of Trent tightened church discipline and reaffirmed traditional doctrine. The Jesuits converted many Protestants back to Catholicism.

The Wars of Religion The religious divisions of Europe led to more than a century of warfare from the 1520s to 1648. The chief battlegrounds were in France, the Netherlands, and Germany. When the Thirty Years' War ended in 1648, Europe was permanently divided into Catholic and Protestant areas.

Superstition and Enlightenment The Reformation led to both dark and constructive views of human nature. Perhaps the darkest view was the witch crazes that erupted across Europe. Thousands of innocent people, mostly women, were persecuted and executed as witches between 1400 and 1700 by both Catholic and Protestant authorities.

In literature and philosophy, however, these years witnessed an outpouring of creative thinking. Among the greatest writers of the age were Cervantes, Shakespeare, Pascal, Spinoza, Hobbes, and Locke.

REVIEW QUESTIONS

1. What were the main problems of the church that contributed to the Protestant Reformation? Why was the church unable to suppress dissent as it had earlier?

2. Why did the Reformation begin in Germany?

3. What was the Catholic Reformation?

4. Why did Henry VIII break with the Catholic Church? Was the "new" religion he established really Protestant?

5. Were the Wars of Religion really over religion?

KEY TERMS

Counter-Reformation (p. 389)   **indulgences** (p. 380)   **Reformation** (p. 376)

Diet of Worms (p. 382)   **ninety-five theses** (p. 380)   **transubstantiation** (p. 384)

Huguenot (p. 394)

For additional study resources for this chapter, go to:
www.prenhall.com/craig/chapter16

CHRISTIANITY

Christianity is based on the teaching of Jesus of Nazareth, a Jew who lived in Palestine during the Roman occupation. His simple message of faith in God and self-sacrificial love of one's neighbor attracted many people. Roman authorities, perceiving his large following as a threat, crucifed him. After Jesus' crucifixion, his followers proclaimed that he had been resurrected from the dead and that he would return in glory, to defeat sin, death, and the devil, and take all true believers with him to heaven—a radical vision of judgment and immortality that has driven Christianity's appeal since its inception. In the teachings of the early church, Jesus became the Christ, the son of God, the long-awaited Messiah of Jewish prophecy. His followers called themselves Christians.

Christianity proclaimed the very incarnation of God in a man, the visible presence of eternity in time. According to early Christian teaching, the power of God's incarnation in Jesus lived on in the preaching and sacraments of the church under the guidance of the Holy Spirit. According to the Christian message, in Jesus, eternity has made itself accessible to every person here and now and forevermore.

The new religion attracted both the poor and powerless and the socially rising and well-to-do. For some, the gospel of Jesus promised a better material life. For others, it imparted a sense of spiritual self-worth regardless of one's place or prospects in society.

In the late second century, the Romans began persecuting Christians as "heretics" (because of their rejection of the traditional Roman gods) and as social revolutionaries (for their loyalty to a lord higher than the emperor of Rome). At the same time, dissenting Christians, particularly sects claiming direct spiritual knowledge of God apart from Scripture, internally divided the young church. To meet these challenges the church established effective weapons against state terrorism and Christian heresy: an ordained clergy, a hierarchical church organization, orthodox creeds, and a biblical canon (the New Testament). Christianity not only gained legal status within the Roman Empire, but also, by the fourth century, most favored religious status thanks to Emperor Constantine's embrace of it.

After the fall of the Western Roman Empire in the fifth century C.E., Christianity became one of history's great success stories. Aided by the enterprise of its popes and the example of its monks, the church cultivated an appealing lay piety centered around the Lord's Prayer, the Apostles' Creed, veneration of the Virgin, and the sacrament of the Eucharist. Clergy became both royal teachers and bureaucrats within the kingdom of the Franks. Despite a growing schism between the Eastern (Byzantine) and Western churches, and a final split in 1054, by 1000 the church held real economic and political power. In the 11th century reform-minded prelates put an end to presumptuous secular interference in its most intimate spiritual affairs by ending the lay investiture of clergy in their spiritual offices. For several centuries thereafter the church remained a formidable international force, able to challenge kings and emperors and inspire crusades to the Holy Land.

Pentecost. This exquisite enamel plaque, from the Mosan school that flourished in France in the 11th and 12th centuries, shows the descent of the Holy Spirit upon the apostles, 50 days after the resurrection of Jesus on the ancient Jewish festival called the "feast of weeks," or Pentecost.
Courtesy Metropolitan Museum of Art.

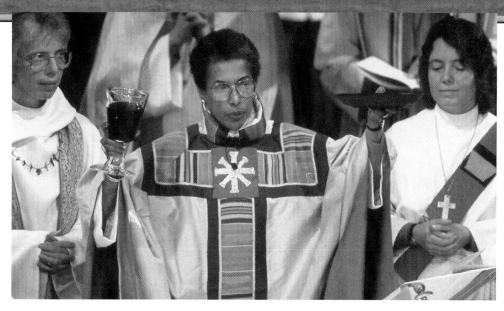

Female Bishop. Women are entering the ministry and priesthood of many Christian denominations. The first woman bishop of the Episcopal Church of North America is here shown consecrating the Eucharist. The Church of England has also voted to admit women to the priesthood.

Ira Wyman/Corbis/Sygma.

By the 15th century the new states of Europe had stripped the church of much of its political power. It was thereafter progressively confined to spiritual and moral authority. Christianity's greatest struggles ever since have been not with kings and emperors over political power, but with materialistic philosophies and worldly ideologies, matters of spiritual and moral hegemony within an increasingly pluralistic and secular world. Since the 16th century a succession of humanists, skeptics, Deists, Rationalists, Marxists, Freudians, Darwinians, and atheists have attempted to explain away some of traditional Christianity's most basic teachings. In addition, the church has endured major internal upheavals. After the Protestant Reformation (1517–1555) made the Bible widely available to the laity, the possibilities for internal criticism of Christianity multiplied exponentially. Beginning with the split between Lutherans and Zwinglians in the 1520s, Protestant Christianity has fragmented into hundreds of sects each claiming to have the true interpretation of Scripture. The Roman Catholic Church, by contrast, has maintained its unity and ministry throughout perilous times, although present-day discontent with papal authority threatens the modern Catholic Church almost as seriously as the Protestant Reformation once did.

Christianity has remained remarkably resilient. It possesses a simple, almost magically appealing gospel of faith and love in and through Jesus. In the present-day world where religious needs and passions still run deep, evangelical Christianity has experienced a remarkable revival. The Roman Catholic Church, still troubled by challenges to papal authority, has become more pluralistic than in earlier periods. The pope has become a world figure, traveling to all continents to represent the church and advance its position on issues of public and private morality. A major ecumenical movement emerging in the 1960s has promoted unprecedented cooperation among evangelical Christian denominations. Everywhere Christians of all sects are politically active, spreading their divine, moral, and social messages. Meanwhile, old hot-button issues, such as the ordination of women, are being overtaken by new ones, particularly the marriage of gay men and women and the removal of clergy who do not maintain the moral discipline of their holy orders.

- Over the century what have been some of the chief factors attracting people to Christianity?

- What forces have led to disunity among Christians in the past? What factors cause tensions among modern Christians?

413

17 Africa
ca. 1000–1800

CHAPTER HIGHLIGHTS

North Africa Developments in African history from 1000 to 1800 varied from region to region. In North Africa, the key new factor was the imperial expansion of the Ottoman Empire as far west as Morocco. But regionalism soon rendered Ottoman authority in North Africa purely nominal.

Empires of the Sudan Several substantial states arose south of the Sahara: Ghana, Mali, Songhai, and Kanem. The ruling elites of these states converted to or were heavily influenced by Islam, although most of their populations clung to their older traditions. Much of the wealth of these states was tied to their control of the trans-Saharan trade routes. Farther south, in Central Africa, another substantial kingdom arose in Benin, famous for its brass sculptures.

East Africa On the east coast, Islam influenced the development of the distinctive Swahili culture and language, and Islamic traders linked the region to India and East Asia.

The Coming of the Europeans The key development of the fifteenth century was the arrival of European traders, missionaries, and warships. The Portuguese and later Europeans came in search of commerce, converts to Christianity, and spheres of influence. Their arrival disrupted indigenous African culture and political relations and presaged Africa's involvement in a new, expanding global trading system dominated by Europeans.

CHAPTER QUESTIONS

HOW DID Islam spread south of the Sahara?

WHAT WERE the four most important states in the Sahel between 1000 and 1600?

WHY DID Christianity gradually disappear in Nubia?

HOW DID the arrival of Europeans affect the peoples of West and Central Africa?

HOW DID Swahili language and culture develop?

HOW DID slavery affect race relations in the Cape Colony?

CHAPTER OUTLINE

- North Africa and Egypt
- The Spread of Islam South of the Sahara
- Sahelian Empires of the Western and Central Sudan
- The Eastern Sudan
- The Forestlands—Coastal West and Central Africa
- East Africa
- Southern Africa

In this chapter we explore, region by region, some salient developments in Africa from 1000 to 1800. While the Atlantic slave trade is treated in Chapter 18, its importance must be kept in mind as we review the period's other developments. We begin with Africa above the equator, where the influence of Islam increased and where substantial empires and kingdoms developed and flourished. Then we discuss west, east, central, and southern Africa and the effects of first Arab-Islamic and then European influence in both regions.

NORTH AFRICA AND EGYPT

WHY WAS no single power able to control North Africa for long?

In politics, this period witnessed the influential dynasties of the Fatimids (909–969 in Tunisia; 969–1171 in Egypt), the Almoravids (1056–1147 in Senegal and the western Sudan; 1062–1118 in Marrakesh and western North Africa; 1086–1147 in Spain), the Almohads (1130–1269 in western North Africa; 1145–1212 in Spain), the Ayyubids (1169–1250 in Egypt), the Mamluks (1250–1517 in Egypt and the eastern Mediterranean); and the Ottomans (from the 14th century) across most of Mediterranean Africa. In general, a feisty regionalism characterized states, city-states, and tribal groups north of the Sahara and along the lower Nile, especially vis-à-vis external power centers, such as Baghdad and Spain. No single power controlled them for long. Regionalism persisted even after 1500, when most of North Africa came under the influence—and often direct control—of the Ottoman Empire.

By 1800, the nominally Ottoman domains from Egypt to Algeria were effectively independent principalities. In Egypt, the Ottomans had established direct rule after their defeat of the Mamluks in 1517, but by the 17th and 18th centuries, power had already passed to Egyptian governors descended from the former ruling Mamluks. The Mediterranean coastlands between Egypt and Morocco were officially Ottoman provinces, or regencies, whether under local governors or Ottoman deputies. By the 18th century, however, Algiers, Tripoli (in modern Libya), and Tunisia were virtually independent of the Ottomans. Morocco was the only North African sultanate to remain fully independent after 1700. Its most important dynasty was that of the Sa'dis (1554–1659).

THE SPREAD OF ISLAM SOUTH OF THE SAHARA

HOW DID Islam spread south of the Sahara?

By 1800, Islamic influence in sub-Saharan Africa affected most of the Sudanic belt and the coast of East Africa as far south as modern Zimbabwe. Typically, Islam did not penetrate beyond the ruling or commercial classes of a region and tended to coexist or blend with indigenous ideas. Nevertheless, Islam and its carriers brought commercial and political changes as well as the Qur'an, new religious practices, and literate culture.

In East Africa, Islamic city-states along the coast from Mogadishu to Kilwa became a major factor. By contrast, in the western and central parts of the continent, Islam penetrated south of the Sahara into the Sudan by overland routes, primarily from North Africa and the Nile valley. Its agents were sometimes traders, but primarily emigrants from the east seeking new land.

From the 1030s, zealous militants known as Almoravids began an overt conversion campaign that extended to the western Sahel and Sahara. This movement eventually swept into Ghana, and finally Kumbi in 1076. Farther west, the Fulbe rulers of Takrur along the Senegal became Muslim in the 1030s and propagated their new faith among their subjects.

SAHELIAN EMPIRES OF THE WESTERN AND CENTRAL SUDAN

WHAT WERE the four most important states in the Sahel between 1000 and 1600?

*U*rbanization and state formation in sub-Saharan Africa did not occur only in response to trans-Saharan trade with the Islamic world, which dates largely from the end of the first millennium. Substantial states had risen in the first millennium C.E. in the Sahel regions just south of the Sahara proper (see Chapter 5). From about 1000 to 1600, four of these developed into notable and relatively long-lived empires: Ghana, Mali, and Songhai in the western Sudan, and Kanem-Bornu in the central Sudan.

GHANA

Ghana was located north of modern Ghana between and north of the inland Niger delta and the upper Senegal. It emerged as a regional power near the end of the first millennium and flourished for about two centuries. Its capital, Kumbi (or Kumbi Saleh), on the desert's edge, was well sited for the Saharan and Sahelian trade networks. Ghana's major population group were the Soninke. (*Ghana* is the Soninke term for "ruler.")

Ghanaian rulers were matrilineally descended. The king was supreme judge and held court regularly to hear grievances. Royal ceremonies were embellished with the full trappings of regal wealth and power appropriate to a king held to be divinely blessed if not semi-divine himself.

Tribute from the empire's many chieftaincies and taxes on royal lands and crops supplemented the duties levied on all incoming and outgoing trade. This trade involved a variety of goods—notably imported salt, cloth, and metal goods such as copper—probably in exchange for gold and perhaps kola nuts from the south. The regime apparently also controlled the gold (and, presumably, the slave) trade that originated in the savannah to the south and west.

Although the king and court of Ghana did not convert to Islam, they made elaborate arrangements to accommodate Muslim traders and government servants in their own settlement a few miles from the royal preserve in Kumbi Saleh. Muslim traders were prominent in the court, literate Muslims administered the government, and Muslim legists advised the ruler. In Ghana's hierarchical society, slaves were at the bottom; farmers and draftsmen above them; merchants above them; and the king, his court, and the nobility on top.

A huge, well-trained army secured royal control and enabled the kings to extend their sway in the late 10th century to the Atlantic shore and to the south as well (see Map 17–1). Ghanaian troops captured Awdaghast, the important southern terminus of the trans-Saharan trade route to Morocco, from the Berbers in 992. The empire was, however, vulnerable to attack from the desert fringe, as Almoravid Berber forces proved in 1054 when they took Awdaghast in a single raid.

Ghana's rulers may have converted to Islam soon after 1100. Ghana's empire was probably

The Great Mosque in Timbuktu. This mud and wood building is typical of western Sudanese mosques. The distinctive tower of the mosque was a symbol of the presence of Islam, which came to places like Timbuktu in central and West Africa by way of overland trade routes.

Werner Forman/Art Resource, N.Y.

MAP EXPLORATION

Interactive map: To explore this map further, go to **http://www.prenhall.com/craig/map17.1**

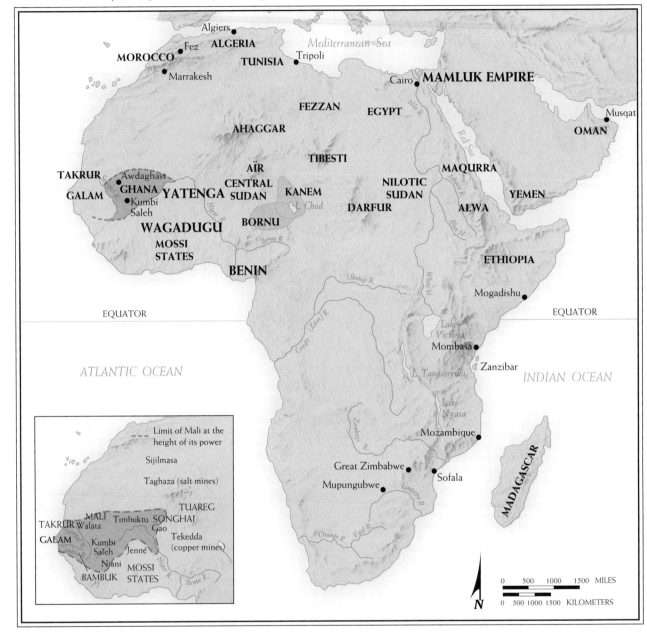

MAP 17–1

Africa ca. 900–1500. Shown are major cities and states referred to in the text. The main map shows the region of West Africa occupied by the empire of Ghana from ca. 990 to ca. 1180. The inset shows the region occupied by Mali between 1230 and 1450.

WHY WAS Ghana's location important for its prosperity?

destroyed in the late 12th century by the militantly anti-Muslim Soso people from the mountains southeast of Kumbi Saleh.

MALI

After the Almoravids brought their reform movement to the western Sahel at the end of the 11th century, their proselytizing zeal led to conversion of many of the region's ruling classes. It was, however, over a half-century after the breakup of

Ghana's empire before anyone in the western Sahel, Muslim or non-Muslim, could reestablish an empire of comparable extent. With Ghana's collapse and the Almoravids' failure to build a new empire below the Sahara (largely because of their focus on North Africa), the western Sudan broke up into smaller kingdoms. The former Ghanaian provinces of Mande and Takrur were already independent before 1076, and in the early 12th century Takrur's control of the Senegal valley and the gold-producing region of Galam made it briefly the strongest state in the western Sudan. Like Ghana, however, it was soon eclipsed by developments to the east, along the upper Niger—first the brief Soso ascendancy and then the rise of Mali.

In the mid-13th century, the Keita ruling clan of a Ghanaian successor kingdom, Mali, forged a new and lasting empire. The Keita kings dominated enough of the Sahel to control the flow of West African gold from the Senegal regions and the forestlands south of the Niger to the trans-Saharan trade routes, and the influx of copper and especially salt in exchange. Because they were farther south, in the fertile land along the Niger, than their Ghanaian predecessors had been, they were better placed to control all trade on the upper Niger and to add to it the Gambia and Senegal trade to the west. They were also able to use war captives for plantation labor in the Niger inland delta to produce surplus food for trade.

Agriculture and cattle farming were the primary occupations of Mali's population and, together with the gold trade, the mainstays of the economy. Rice was grown in the river valleys and millet in the drier parts of the Sahel. Together with beans, yams, and other agricultural products, this made for a plentiful food supply. Fishing flourished along the Niger and elsewhere. Animal husbandry was strongest among pastoralists of the Sahel, such as the Fulani (or Fulbe), but cattle, sheep, and goats were also plentiful in the Niger valley by the 14th century. Many of the Fulani seem to have been attracted by excellent pasturages to the riverine regions. The chief craft specialties were metalworking (iron and gold) and weaving of cotton grown within the empire.

The Malinke, a southern Mande-speaking people of the upper Niger region, formed the core population of the new state. They lived in walled urban settlements typical of the western savannah region. Each walled town was surrounded by its own agricultural land, and held perhaps 1,000 to 15,000 people.

The Keita dynasty had converted early to Islam (ca. 1100). During Mali's heyday in the 13th and 14th centuries, its kings often made the pilgrimage to Mecca. From their travels in the central Islamic lands, they brought back ideas about political and military organization. Through Muslim traders' networks, Islam also connected Mali to other areas of Africa.

Mali's imperial power was built largely by one leader, the Keita King Sundiata (or Sunjaata; r. 1230–1255). Sundiata and his successors, aided by significant population growth in the western savannah, exploited their agricultural resources and Malinke commercial skills to build an empire even more powerful than its Ghanaian predecessor. Sundiata extended his control well beyond the former domains of Ghana, west to the Atlantic coast and east beyond Timbuktu. By controlling the commercial entrepôts of Gao, Walata, and Jenne, he was able to dominate the Saharan as well as the Niger trade. He built his capital, Niani, into a major city. Niani was located on a tributary of the Niger in the savannah at the edge of the forest in a gold- and iron-rich region, well away from the lands of the Sahel nomads and well south of Ghana's capital, Kumbi. Niani had access to the forest trade products of gold, kola nuts, and palm oil; it was easily defended by virtue of its surrounding small hills; and it was easily reached by river.

QUICK REVIEW

Mali

* Keita clan forged Mali in mid-13th century
* Keita kings controlled the flow of West African gold
* Agriculture and cattle farming were primary occupations of Mali's people

11.3
Ibn Battuta in Mali

QUICK REVIEW

King Sundiata (r. 1230–1255)

* Built Mali's imperial power
* Mali's empire was more powerful than its Ghanaian predecessor
* Empire encompassed three major regions: Senegal, the central Mande states, and the peoples of the Niger in the Gao region

The Great Mosque at Jenne. Jenne was one of the important commercial centers controlled by the empire of Mali in the 13th and 14th centuries.

Ann Stalcup.

 11.1

Mansa Musa: The "King Who Sits on a Mountain of Gold"

Mansa Musa, King of Mali. The 14th-century Catalan Atlas shows King Mansa Musa of Mali, seated on a throne. A rider on a camel approaches him.

The Granger Collection.

The empire that Sundiata and his successors built ultimately encompassed three major regions and language groups of Sudanic West Africa: (1) the Senegal region (including Takrur), occupied by speakers of the West Atlantic Niger-Kongo language group (including Fulbe, Tukulor, Wolof, Serer); (2) the central Mande states between Senegal and Niger, occupied by the Niger-Kongo-speaking Soninke and Mandinke peoples; and (3) the peoples of the Niger in the Gao region who spoke Songhai, the only Nilo-Saharan language west of the Lake Chad basin.

Mali was less a centralized bureaucratic state than the center of a vast sphere of influence that included provinces and tribute-paying kingdoms. Many chieftaincies retained much of their independence but recognized the sovereignty of the supreme, sacred *mansa*, or "emperor," of the Malian realms.

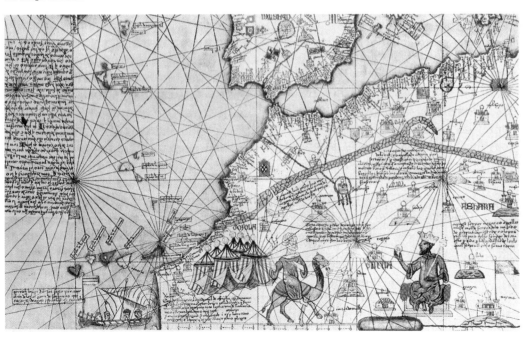

The greatest Keita king proved to be Mansa Musa (r. 1312–1337), whose pilgrimage through Mamluk Cairo to Mecca in 1324 became famous. At home, he consolidated Mali's power, securing peace for most of his reign throughout his vast dominions. Musa's devoutness as a Muslim fostered the further spread of Islam in the empire and beyond. Under his rule, Timbuktu became known far and wide for its *madrasas* (religious schools), libraries, poets, scientists, and architects—making the city the leading intellectual center of sub-Saharan Islam as well as a major trading city of the Sahel.

Mali's dominance waned in the 15th century as the result of competition for its throne. As time went on, subject dependencies became independent, and the empire withered. After 1450, a new Songhai power in Gao to the east ended Mali's imperial authority.

SONGHAI

Gao became an imperial power in the reign of Sonni Ali (1464–1492). Sonni Ali made the Songhai Empire so powerful that it dominated the political history of the western Sudan for more than a century and was arguably the most powerful state in Africa (see Map 17–2).

Askia Muhammad al-Turi (r. 1493–1528) continued Sonni Ali's expansionist policies. Between them, Sonni Ali and Askia Muhammad built an empire that stretched from near the Atlantic into the Sahara and the central Sudan. The ancient caravan trade across the Sahara to the North African coasts provided their major source of wealth. Muhammad al-Turi was an enthusiastic Muslim. He built up the Songhai state after the model of the Islamic empire of Mali. In his reign, Muslim scholars made Timbuktu a major intellectual and legal training center for the whole Sudan. Nevertheless, his reforms failed to Islamize the empire or to ensure a strong central state under his less able successors.

The last powerful Askia leader was Askia Dawud (r. 1549–1583), under whom Songhai economic prosperity and intellectual life peaked. Still, difficulties mounted. Civil war broke out over succession to the throne in 1586, and the empire was divided. The once-great state became only one among many regional competitors in the western Sudan.

KANEM AND KANEM-BORNU

A fourth sizable Sahelian empire, Kanem, in the central Sudan, arose after 1100. Roughly contemporaneous with the Malian Empire to the west, Kanem began as a southern Saharan confederation of the black nomadic tribes known as Zaghawah. Their key leader, Mai Dunama Dibbalemi (r. ca. 1221–1259), was probably the first Kanuri leader to embrace Islam, which appears to have entrenched itself among the Kanuri ruling class during his reign. Dibbalemi used Islam to sanction his rule and provide a rationale for expansion through *jihad*, or holy "struggle" against polytheists. Dibbalemi and his successors expanded Kanuri power to control important trade routes to Libya and Egypt.

Sahelian Empires of the Western Sudan

ca. 990–ca. 1180?	Empire of Ghana
1076	Ghana loses Awdaghast to Almoravids
1180–1230	Soso clan briefly controls the old Ghanaian territories
ca. 1230–1450	Empire of Mali, founded by Sundiata
1230–1255	Reign of Sundiata
1312–1337	Reign of Mansa Musa
1374	Independent Songhai state emerges in Gao after throwing off Malian rule
ca. 1450–1600	Songhai Empire at Gao
1464–1591	Askia dynasty
1464–1492	Reign of Sonni Ali
1493–1528	Reign of Askia Muhammad al-Turi
1549–1583	Reign of Askia Dawud
1590s	Collapse of the Songhai Empire

MAP EXPLORATION

Interactive map: To explore this map further, go to **http://www.prenhall.com/craig/map17.2**

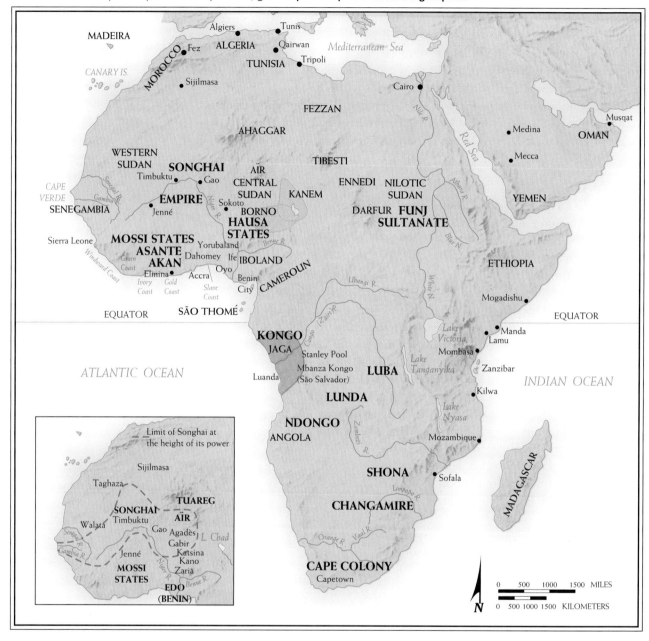

MAP 17–2

Africa ca. 1500–1800.   Important towns, regions, peoples, and states are presented in the main map. The inset shows the empire of Songhai at its greatest extent in the early 16th century.

WHAT WAS Songhai's major source of wealth?

Civil strife, largely over the royal succession, weakened the Kanuri state from the later 14th century, and after 1400, the locus of power shifted from Kanem proper westward, to the land of Bornu, southwest of Lake Chad. Near the end of the 16th century, firearms and Turkish military instructors enabled the Kanuri leader Idris Alawma (r. ca. 1575–1610) to unify Kanem and Bornu. He set up an avowedly Islamic state and extended his rule even into Hausaland, between Bornu and the Niger River. The center of trading activity as well as political power and security now shifted from the Niger bend east to the territory under Kanuri control.

Deriving its prosperity from the trans-Saharan trade, Idris Alawma's regional empire survived for nearly a century, but by 1700, its power had been reduced by the Hausa states to the west.

THE EASTERN SUDAN

The Christian states of Maqurra and Alwa in the Nilotic Sudan, or Nubia, lasted for more than 600 years from their early seventh-century beginnings. Often thought of as isolated, Christian Nubia in fact maintained political, religious, and commercial contact with Egypt, the Red Sea world, and the east-central and even central Sudan. From late Fatimid times onward, both Maqurra and Alwa were subject to growing Muslim minorities. The result was a long-term intermingling of Arabic and Nubian cultures and the creation of a new Nilotic Sudanese people and culture.

Islam spread slowly with Arab immigration into the upper Nile region. A significant factor in the gradual disappearance of Christianity in Nubia was the apparently elite character of Christianity there and its association with foreign Egyptian Coptic Christianity. Maqurra became officially Muslim at the beginning of the 14th century. The Islamization of Alwa came somewhat later, under the Funj sultanate that replaced the Alwa state.

The Funj state flourished from just after 1500 until 1762. The Funj developed an Islamic society whose Arabized character was unique in sub-Saharan Africa. A much-reduced Funj state held out until an Ottoman-Egyptian invasion in 1821.

THE FORESTLANDS—COASTAL WEST AND CENTRAL AFRICA

WEST AFRICAN FOREST KINGDOMS: THE EXAMPLE OF BENIN

Many states had developed in West Africa centuries before the first Portuguese reports of their existence in 1485. Benin, the best known of these kingdoms, reflects, especially in its art, the sophistication of West African culture before 1500.

Benin State and Society   A distinct kingdom of Benin likely existed as early as the 12th century, and the power of the king, or *oba*, at this time was sharply limited by the *uzama*, an order of hereditary indigenous chiefs. Only in the 15th century, with King Ewuare, did Benin become a royal autocracy and a large state of major regional importance.

Ewuare apparently established a government in which he had sweeping authority, although he exercised it in light of the deliberations of a royal council formed from the palace uzama and the townspeople. He gave each chief specific administrative responsibilities and rank in the government hierarchy. Ewuare and his successors engaged in major wars of expansion and claimed for the office of oba an increasing ritual authority.

Central Sudanic Empires

ca. 1100–1500	Kanuri Empire of Kanem
ca. 1220s–1400	Height of Empire of Kanem
1221–1259	Reign of Mai Dunama Dibbalemi
1575–1846	Kanuri Empire of Kanem-Bornu
1575–1610	Reign of Idris Alawma, major architect of the state

WHY DID Christianity gradually disappear in Nubia?

HOW DID the arrival of Europeans affect the peoples of West and Central Africa?

oba   Title of the king of Benin.

uzama   Order of hereditary chiefs in Benin.

In the 17th century, the oba was transformed from a military leader into a religious figure with supernatural powers. Human sacrifice, specifically of slaves, seems to have accompanied the cult of deceased kings. Succession by primogeniture was discontinued, and new obas were chosen by the uzama from any branch of the royal family.

Benin Art   The lasting significance of Benin lies in its court art, especially its famous brass sculptures. The splendid terracotta, ivory, and brass statuary sculpture of Ife-Benin are among the glories of human creativity. These magnificent sculptures, initially realistic or naturalistic and later sometimes highly stylized, seem to be wholly indigenous African products.

The best sculptures are cast bronze plaques depicting legendary and historical scenes. These were mounted on the walls and columns of the royal palace in Benin City. There are also brass heads, apparently of royalty. Similar sculptures have been found both well to the north and in the Niger delta. Recent excavations east of the Niger at Igbo-Ukwu have unearthed stunning terracottas and bronzes that belong to the same general artistic culture, which is dated as early as the ninth century. These artifacts testify to the high cultural level attained in traditional African societies that had little or no contact with the extra-African world.

EUROPEAN ARRIVALS ON THE COASTLANDS

Along the coasts of West and central Africa, many changes occurred between 1500 and 1800, including those connected with trade in West African gold and other commodities and the effects associated with the importation and spread in West and central Africa of food crops, such as maize, peanuts, squash, sweet potatoes, cocoa, and cassava (manioc) from the Americas. The gradual involvement of Africa in the emerging global economic system paved the way for eventual colonial domination of the continent, especially its coastal regions, by the Europeans. The European names for segments of the coastline—the Grain (or Pepper) Coast, the Ivory Coast, the Gold Coast, and the Slave Coast—identify the main exports that could be extracted by ship and vividly indicate the nature of the emerging relationship.

Senegambia   In West Africa, Senegambia—which takes its name from the Senegal and Gambia Rivers—was one of the earliest regions affected by European trade. Its maritime trade with European powers, like the older overland trade, was primarily in gold and products such as salt, cotton goods, hides, and copper. Senegambian states also provided perhaps a third of all African slaves exported during the 16th century. Thereafter, the focus of the slave trade shifted south and east along the coast. Over time, Portuguese-African mulattos and the British came to control the Gambia River trade, while the French won the Senegal River markets.

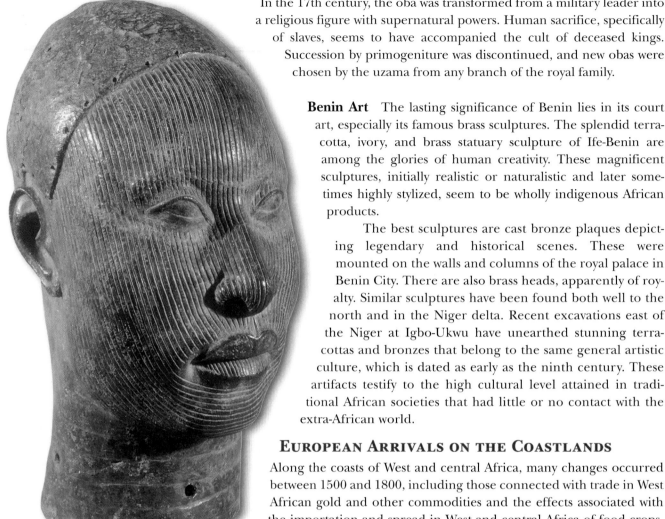

Brass head. This naturalistic brass head (29 cm high), which dates to the 13th century, conveys a serenity remarkably similar to classical Greek sculpture.

© Frank Willet.

Benin

ca. 1100–1897	Benin state
ca. 1300	First Ife king of Benin state
1440–1475	Reign of Ewuare

The Gold Coast   The Gold Coast derives its name from its importance after 1500 as the outlet for West Africa's gold fields. Here, beginning with the Portuguese at Elmina in 1481, European states and companies built coastal forts to protect their trade. The trade encouraged the growth of larger states—like the Akan forest states near the coast and the Gonja state just north of the forest—perhaps because they could better control commerce.

The intensive contact of the Gold Coast with Europeans also led to the spread of American crops, notably maize and cassava, into the region, which contributed to substantial population growth. Slaves became big business here in the late 17th century, especially in the Accra region. The economy was so disrupted by the slave trade that gold mining declined. Eventually more gold came into the Gold Coast from the sale of slaves than went out from its mines.

CENTRAL AFRICA

The vast center of the subcontinent is bounded by swamps in the north, coastal rain forests to the west, highlands to the east, and deserts in the south. Before 1500, these natural barriers impeded international contact and trade with the interior.

The coming of the Portuguese broke down this isolation, albeit slowly. The Portuguese came looking for gold and silver but found none. Instead, they exported such goods as ivory and palm cloth. Ultimately, their main export was slaves, first to the Portuguese sugar plantations on Sao Thomé island in the Gulf of Guinea, then to Brazil.

The Kongo Kingdom   Kongo was the major state with which the Portuguese dealt after coming to central Africa in 1483. Dating from probably the 14th century, the Kongo kingdom was located on a fertile, well-watered plateau south of the lower Zaïre River valley, between the coast and the Kwango River in the east. Here, astride the border between forest and grassland, the Kongo kings had built a central government based on a pyramid structure of tax or tribute collection balanced by rewards for those faithful in paying their taxes. Kongo society was dominated by the king, whose authority was tied to acceptance of him as a kind of spiritual spokesman of the gods or ancestors. By 1600, Kongo was half the size of England and alongside farming boasted a high state of specialization in weaving and pottery, salt production, fishing, and metalworking.

The Portuguese brought Mediterranean goods, preeminently luxury textiles from North Africa, to trade for African goods. Such luxuries augmented the prestige and wealth of the ruler and his elites. However, slaves became the primary export that could be used to obtain foreign luxury goods. Imports, such as fine clothing, tobacco, and alcohol, did nothing to replace the labor pool lost to slavery.

At first the Portuguese put time and effort into education and Christian proselytizing, but the need for more slaves led to their concentrating on exploiting the human

Benin Bronze Plaque. From the palace of the Obas of Benin it dates to the Edo period of Benin culture, 1575–1625. It depicts two Portuguese males, perhaps a father and son, holding hands. It is likely that they represent the traders or government officials who came to the African coasts in increasing numbers from the end of the 15th century on.

Werner Forman, Art Resource, N.Y.

Central Africa

1300s	Kongo kingdom founded
1483	Portuguese come to central African coast
ca. 1506–1543	Reign of Affonso I as king of Kongo
1571	Angola becomes Portuguese proprietary colony

HISTORY'S VOICES

AFFONSO I OF KONGO WRITES TO THE KING OF PORTUGAL

In 1526, Affonso, the Christian African king of Kongo, wrote to the Portuguese monarch ostensibly to complain about the effects of slaving on the Kongo people and economy. But the real issue was that the Portuguese were circumventing his own royal monopoly on the inland slave trade. One of the insidious effects of the massive demand of the Atlantic trade for slaves was the ever-increasing engagement in it of African monarchs, chieftains, and merchants.

HOW HAD the introduction of Portuguese merchants and European goods upset the social and political situation in Kongo? How had these goods tempted Affonso's subjects into the slave trade? How did Affonso wish to change the relationship of his people to Portugal? Was the king more worried about human rights or his economic losses?

Sir, Your Highness [of Portugal] should know how our Kingdom is being lost in so many ways that it is convenient to provide for the necessary remedy, since this is caused by the excessive freedom given by your factors and officials to the men and merchants who are allowed to come to this Kingdom to set up shops with goods and many things which have been prohibited by us, and which they spread throughout our Kingdoms and Domains in such an abundance that many of our vassals, whom we had in obedience, do not comply because they have the things in greater abundance than we ourselves; and it was with these things that we had them content and subjected under our vassalage and jurisdiction, so it is doing a great

harm not only to the service of God, but the security and peace of our Kingdoms and State as well.

And we cannot reckon how great the damage is, since the mentioned merchants are taking every day our natives, sons of the land and the sons of our noblemen and vassals and our relatives, because the thieves and men of bad conscience grab them wishing to have the things and wares of this Kingdom which they are ambitious of; they grab them and get them to be sold; and so great, Sir, is the corruption and licentiousness that our country is being completely depopulated, and Your Highness should not agree with this nor accept it as in your service. And to avoid it we need from those [your] Kingdoms no more than some priests and a few people to teach in schools, and no other goods except wine and flour for the holy sacrament. That is why we beg of Your Highness to help and assist us in this matter, commanding your factors that they should not send here either merchants or wares, because it is *our will that in these Kingdoms there should not be any trade of slaves nor outlet for them.**

Concerning what is referred above, again we beg of Your Highness to agree with it, since otherwise we cannot ... remedy such an obvious damage. Pray Our Lord in His mercy to have Your Highness under His guard and let you do for ever the things of His service. I kiss your hands many times. ...

From *The African Past*, trans. by J. O. Hunwick, reprinted in Basil Davidson (Grosset and Dunlap, The Universal Library), pp. 191–193. Reprinted by permission of Curtis Brown Ltd. Copyright © 1964 by Basil Davidson.

*Emphasis in the original.

resources of central Africa. Regional rulers sought to procure slaves from neighboring kingdoms, as did Portuguese traders who went inland themselves. As the demand grew, local rulers increasingly attacked neighbors to garner slaves for Portuguese traders (see Chapter 18).

The Kongo ruler Affonso I (r. ca. 1506–1543), a Christian convert, began by welcoming Jesuit missionaries and supporting conversion. But in time he broke with the Jesuits and encouraged traditional practices, even though he himself remained a Christian. Affonso had constant difficulty curbing slaving practices and provincial governors who often dealt directly with the Portuguese, undermining royal authority (see "Affonso I of Kongo Writes to the King of Portugal"). Affonso's successor restricted Portuguese activity to Mpinda harbor and the Kongo capital of Mbanza Kongo (São Salvador). A few years later, Portuguese attempts to name the Kongo royal successor caused a bloody uprising against them that led in turn to a Portuguese boycott on trade with the kingdom.

Thereafter, disastrous internal wars shattered the Kongo state. Kongo, however, enjoyed renewed vigor in the 17th century. Its kings ruled as divine-right monarchs at the apex of a complex sociopolitical pyramid that rose from district headmen through provincial governors to

East and Southeast Africa

900–1500	"Great Zimbabwe" civilization
ca. 1200–1400	Development of Bantu Kiswahili language
ca. 1300–1600	Height of Swahili culture
1698	Omani forces take Mombasa, oust Portuguese from East Africa north of the port of Mozambique
1741–1856	United sultanate of Oman and Zanzibar

Fort Jesus, Mombasa, Kenya. Built by the Portuguese in the sixteenth century, it is the most conspicuous reminder of their former presence in East Africa.

Robert Harding World Imagery.

the court nobility and king. Royal power came to depend on a guard of musket-armed hired soldiers. The financial base of the kingdom rested on tribute from officials holding positions at the king's pleasure and on taxes and tolls on commerce. Christianity, the state religion, was accommodated to traditional beliefs. Kongo sculpture, iron and copper technology, and dance and music flourished.

Angola To the south, in Portuguese Angola, the experience was even worse than in Kongo. By 1600, Angola was exporting thousands of slaves yearly through the port of Luanda. In less than a century, the hinterland had been plundered. The Portuguese arrival had brought economic and social catastrophe.

EAST AFRICA

SWAHILI CULTURE AND COMMERCE

HOW DID Swahili language and culture develop?

The participation of East African port towns in the lucrative southern seas trade was ancient. Arabs, Indonesians, and even Indians had trafficked there for centuries. From the eighth century onward, Islam traveled with Arab and Persian sailors and merchants to these southerly trading centers. In the 13th century, Muslim traders from Arabia and Iran began to come in increased numbers and to dominate the coastal cities. Henceforward, Islamic faith and culture were often predominant along the seacoast, from Mogadishu to Kilwa.

By this time, a common language had also developed from the interaction of Bantu and Arabic speakers along the coast. This tongue is called *Swahili*, or *Kiswahili*, from the Arabic *sawahil*, "coastlands." Swahili language and culture probably developed first in the northern towns of Manda, Lamu, and Mombasa, then farther south along the coast to Kilwa. Likewise, the spread of Islam was largely limited to the coastal civilization and did not reach inland. This contrasts with lands farther north, in the Horn of Africa, where Islamic kingdoms developed in the Somali hinterland as well as on the coast.

Swahili civilization reached its apogee in the 14th and 15th centuries. The harbor trading towns were the administrative centers of the local Swahili states, and most of them were sited on coastal islands or easily defended peninsulas. To these ports came merchants from abroad and from the African hinterlands, some to settle and stay. These towns had impressive mosques, fortress-palaces, harbor fortifications, fancy residences, and commercial buildings.

Today, historians recognize that the ruling dynasties of the Swahili states were probably African in origin, with an admixture of Arab or Persian immigrant blood. Swahili coastal centers boasted an advanced, cosmopolitan level of culture. By comparison, most of the populace in the small villages lived in mud houses and sometimes stone houses and earned their livings by farming or fishing, the two basic coastal occupations besides trade. Society consisted of three principal groups: local nobility, commoners, and resident foreigners engaged in commerce. Slaves constituted a fourth class, although their local extent (as opposed to their sale) is disputed.

The flourishing trade of the coastal centers was fed mainly by export of inland ivory. Other exports included gold, slaves, turtle shells, ambergris, leopard skins, pearls, fish, sandalwood, ebony, and local cotton cloth. The chief imports were cloth, porcelain, glassware, china, glass beads, and glazed pottery. Certain exports tended to dominate particular ports: cloth, sandalwood, ebony, and ivory at Mogadishu; ivory at Manda; and gold at Kilwa. Cowrie shells were a

Swahili Language and culture that developed from the interaction of native Africans and Arabs along the East African coast.

OVERVIEW   MAJOR AFRICAN STATES, 1000–1800

North Africa	Sahel	Eastern Sudan	West and Central Africa	East Africa	Southern Africa
Morocco	Ghana	Maqurra	Benin	Zanzibar	"Great Zimbabwe"
Algiers	Mali	Alwa	Kongo		
Tunis	Songhai	Funj			
Tripoli	Kanem				
Egypt					

common currency in inland trade, but coins were used in the major trading centers. The gold trade itself apparently became important only in the 15th century.

THE PORTUGUESE AND THE OMANIS OF ZANZIBAR

The decline of the original Swahili civilization in the 16th century can be attributed primarily to the arrival of the Portuguese and their destruction of the old oceanic trade (in particular, the Islamic commercial monopoly) and the main Islamic city-states along the eastern coast.

In Africa, as everywhere, the Portuguese saw the "**Moors**" as implacable enemies. Many Portuguese viewed the struggle to wrest the commerce and seaports of Africa and Asia from Islamic control as a Christian crusade. The initial Portuguese victories along the African coast led to the submission of many small Islamic coastal ports and states. Still, there was no concerted effort to spread Christianity. Thus, the long-term cultural and religious consequences of the Portuguese presence were slight. After 1660, the eastern Arabian state of Oman ejected the Portuguese everywhere north of Mozambique.

The Omanis soon shifted their home base to Zanzibar, which became a major power in East Africa. Their control of the coastal ivory and slave trade fueled a substantial recovery of prosperity by the later 18th century. The domination of the east coast by Omani African sultans, descendants of the earlier invaders, continued until 1856. Thereafter, Zanzibar and its coastal holdings became independent, and then passed to the British. Still, the Islamic impact on the whole coast survives today.

SOUTHERN AFRICA

SOUTHEASTERN AFRICA: "GREAT ZIMBABWE"

At about the same time that the east-coast trading centers were beginning to flourish, a purely African civilization was enjoying its heyday inland in modern southern Zimbabwe. It was founded in the 10th or 11th century by Bantu-speaking Shona people, who still inhabit the same general area today. It seems to have become a large and prosperous state between the late 13th and the late 15th centuries. We know it only through the archaeological remains of an estimated 150 settlements in the Zambezi-Limpopo region.

QUICK REVIEW

East African Port Towns
- Part of trade with Middle East, Asia, and India
- Tied together by common language, *Swahili*
- Swahili civilization reached its peak in the 14th and 15th centuries

Moors Spanish and Portuguese term for Muslims.

HOW DID slavery affect race relations in the Cape Colony?

14.1
Kilwa, Mombasa, and the Portuguese: Realities of Empire

The most impressive of these ruins is known today as "Great Zimbabwe"—a huge, 60-odd-acre site encompassing two major building complexes. One—the so-called acropolis—is a series of stone enclosures on a high hill. It overlooks another, much larger enclosure that contains many ruins and a circular tower, all surrounded by a massive wall some 32 feet high and up to 17 feet thick. The acropolis complex may have contained a shrine, whereas the larger enclosure was apparently the royal palace and fort. The stonework reflects a wealthy and sophisticated society. Artifacts from the site include gold and copper ornaments, soapstone carvings, and imported beads, as well as china, glass, and porcelain of Chinese, Syrian, and Persian origins.

The state itself seems to have had partial control of the increasing gold trade between inland areas and the east coast. We can speculate that this large settlement was the capital city of a prosperous empire and the residence of a ruling elite. Its wider domain was made up mostly of smaller settlements whose inhabitants lived by subsistence agriculture and cattle raising and whose culture was considerably different from that of the capital. Without written or new archaeological sources, we shall likely never know exactly what allowed this impressive civilization to develop and to dominate its region for nearly 200 years.

THE PORTUGUESE IN SOUTHEASTERN AFRICA

The Portuguese destroyed Swahili control of both the inland gold trade and the overseas trade. Their chief objective was to obtain gold from the interior.

"Great Zimbabwe." The most impressive of 300 such stone ruins in modern Zimbabwe and neighboring countries. These sites give clear evidence of the advanced Iron Age mining and cattle-raising culture that flourished in this region between about 1000 and 1500 C.E. The people, thought to have been of Bantu origins, apparently had a highly developed trade in gold and copper with outsiders, including Arabs on the east coast. As yet, all too little is known about this impressive society.

Robert Aberman and Barbara Heller/
Art Resource, N.Y.

Although the Portugese derived little lasting profit from their enterprise, all along the Zambezi a lasting and destabilizing consequence of their intrusion was the creation of quasi-tribal chiefdoms led by mixed-blood Portuguese landholders, who were descended from the first Portuguese estate holders along the Zambezi. By the late 18th century, they were too strong for either the Portuguese or the regional African rulers to control. They remind us of how diverse the peoples of modern Africa are.

SOUTH AFRICA: THE CAPE COLONY

In South Africa, the Dutch planted the first European colonials almost inadvertently, yet the consequences of their action were to be ultimately as grave and far-reaching as any European incursion onto African soil. The first Cape settlement was built in 1652 by the Dutch East India Company as a resupply point and way station for Dutch vessels on their route between the Netherlands and the East Indies. The support station gradually became a settler community, the forebears of the Afrikaners of modern South Africa.

The local Khoikhoi (see Chapter 5) had neither a strong political organization nor an economic base beyond their herds. They bartered livestock freely to Dutch ships. As company employees established farms to supply the Cape station, they began to displace the Khoikhoi. Conflicts led to the consolidation of European landholdings and a breakdown of Khoikhoi society. Military success led to even greater Dutch control of the Khoikhoi by the 1670s.

The Khoikhoi became the chief source of colonial wage labor, but the colony also imported slaves. Slavery set the tone for relations between the emergent, and ostensibly "white," Afrikaner population and the "coloreds" of other races. Free or not, the latter were eventually identified with slave peoples.

After the first settlers spread out around the company station, nomadic white livestock farmers, or *Trekboers*, moved more widely afield, leaving the richer, but limited, farming lands of the coast for the drier interior tableland. There they contested still wider groups of Khoikhoi cattle herders for the best grazing lands. Again the Khoikhoi lost. By 1700, their way of life was destroyed.

The Cape society in this period was thus a diverse one. The Dutch Company officials (including Dutch Reformed ministers), the emerging Afrikaners (both settled colonists and Trekboers), the Khoikhoi, and the slaves of diverse nationalities played differing roles. Intermarriage and cohabitation of masters and slaves added to the complexity. The emergence of *Afrikaans*, a new vernacular language of the colonials, shows that the

Carving from Great Zimbabwe. This carving (steatite, 40.5 cm high) is thought to represent a mythical eagle that carries messages from man to the gods. It dates to ca. 1200–1400 C.E.

Werner Forman Archive/Art Resource, N.Y.

Trekboers White livestock farmers in Cape Colony.

Afrikaans New language, derived from Dutch, that evolved in the 17th- and 18th-century Cape Colony.

Southern Africa

1652	First Cape colony settlement of Dutch East India Company
1795	British replace Dutch as masters of Cape Colony

Cape Town, with European ships in its harbor. The colony relied on shipping for commercial links with the outside world.

National Archives of South Africa.

apartheid "Apartness," the term referring to racist policies enforced by the white-dominated regime that existed in South Africa from 1948 to 1992.

Dutch immigrants themselves were also subject to acculturation processes. By the time of English domination after 1795, the sociopolitical foundations—and the bases of the *apartheid* doctrine—of modern South Africa were firmly laid.

IMAGE KEY
for pages 414–415

a. Moroccan Coin dating from Songhai Empire
b. Benin plaque
c. Golden rhino found at Mapungubwe
d. Thirteenth-century brass head from Benin
e. Mosque in Janne
f. Mansa Musa early medieval painting
g. The Djinquereber mosque in Timbuktu
h. Benin plaque
i. Fort Jesus, Mombasa, Kenya, Africa
j. "Great Zimbabwe," one of 300 stone ruins
k. Great Zimbabwe carving (stearite, 40.5cm high) representing a mythical eagle carrying messages to the gods.

SUMMARY

North Africa Developments in African history from 1000 to 1800 varied from region to region. In North Africa, the key new factor was the imperial expansion of the Ottoman Empire as far west as Morocco. But regionalism soon rendered Ottoman authority in North Africa purely nominal.

Empires of the Sudan Several substantial states arose south of the Sahara: Ghana, Mali, Songhai, and Kanem. The ruling elites of these states converted to or were heavily influenced by Islam, although most of their populations clung to their older traditions. Much of the wealth of these states was tied to their control of the trans-Saharan trade routes. Farther south, in the coastal forestlands of Central Africa, another substantial kingdom arose in Benin, famous for its brass sculptures.

East Africa On the east coast, Islam influenced the development of the distinctive Swahili culture and language, and Islamic traders linked the region to India and East Asia.

The Coming of the Europeans The key development of the 15th century was the arrival of European traders, missionaries, and warships. The Portuguese and later Europeans came in search of commerce, converts to Christianity, and spheres of influence. Their arrival disrupted indigenous African culture and political relations and presaged Africa's involvement in and exploitation by a new, expanding global trading system dominated by Europeans.

REVIEW QUESTIONS

1. Why did Islam succeed in sub-Saharan and East Africa? How did warfare and trade affect its success?

2. What was the importance of the empires of Ghana, Mali, and Songhai to world history? Why was the control of the trans-Saharan trade so important to these kingdoms? What was the importance of Islamic culture to them? Why did each of these empires break up?

3. How did the Portuguese affect East and central Africa? How did European coastal activities affect the African interior?

4. How did the Portuguese and Dutch differ from or resemble the Arabs, Persians, and other Muslims who came as outsiders to sub-Saharan Africa?

5. Who were the Trekboers and what was their conflict with the Khoikhoi? How was the basis for apartheid formed in this period?

KEY TERMS

Afrikaans (p. 431)
apartheid (p. 432)
Moors (p. 429)

oba (p. 423)
Swahili (p. 428)

Trekboers (p. 431)
uzama (p. 423)

 For additional study resources for this chapter, go to:
www.prenhall.com/craig/chapter17

18 Conquest and Exploitation
The Development of the Transatlantic Economy

CHAPTER HIGHLIGHTS

European Conquest of the New World The contact between the native peoples of the American continents and the European explorers of the fifteenth and sixteenth centuries transformed world history. In the Americas, the native peoples had established a wide variety of civilizations, but until the European explorations, the civilizations of the Americas and Eurasia and Africa had no significant contact with each other.

Within half a century of the landing of Columbus, millions of America's native peoples had encountered Europeans intent on conquest, exploitation, and religious conversion. Because of their technology and the new diseases they brought with them, as well as internal divisions among the native Americans, the Europeans achieved a rapid conquest.

The Transatlantic Economy In both North and South America, economies of exploitation were established. From the mid-Atlantic English colonies through the Caribbean and into Brazil, slave-labor plantations forcibly imported slaves from Africa. The economies and peoples of Europe, Africa, and the Americas were thus drawn into a vast worldwide web of production based on slave labor.

Slavery The impact of slavery in the Americas was not limited to the life of the black slaves. Whites in the New World numbered about 12 million in 1820, compared to some six million blacks. However, only about two million whites had migrated there, compared to some 11 million or more Africans forcibly imported as slaves. Such numbers reveal the effects of brutal slave conditions and the high mortality and low birthrates of slave populations.

None of these statistics, however, enables us to asses the role that slavery has played in the Americas or, in particular, the United States. The United States actually received only a bit more than a quarter as many slaves as did Brazil, yet the consequences of the forced migration of just over a half-million Africans remain massive. The Atlantic slave trade's impact continues to be felt at both ends of the original "trade."

CHAPTER QUESTIONS

WHAT WAS mercantilism?

WHAT ROLES did the Roman Catholic Church play in Spanish America?

HOW WERE sugar production and slavery intertwined in colonial Brazil?

HOW WERE the economies of the French and British North American colonies integrated into the transatlantic economy?

WHY WAS the transatlantic slave trade so economically important?

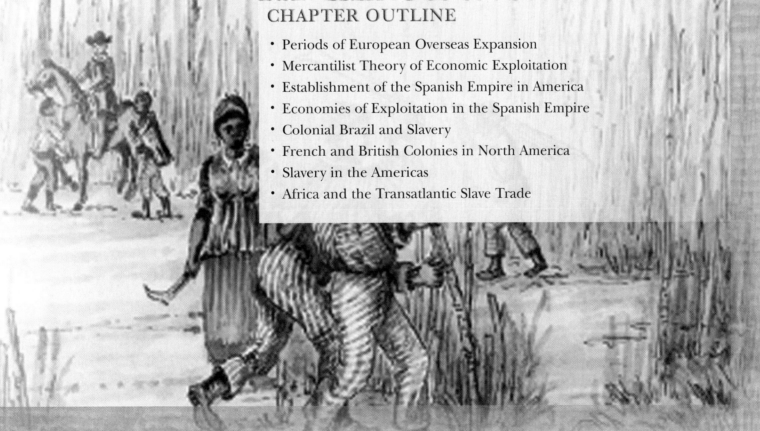

CHAPTER OUTLINE

- Periods of European Overseas Expansion
- Mercantilist Theory of Economic Exploitation
- Establishment of the Spanish Empire in America
- Economies of Exploitation in the Spanish Empire
- Colonial Brazil and Slavery
- French and British Colonies in North America
- Slavery in the Americas
- Africa and the Transatlantic Slave Trade

The European encounter with the American continents in the late 15th century made the region an area where European languages, legal and political institutions, trade, and religion prevailed. These developments in the Americas gave Europe more influence over other world cultures than it would otherwise have achieved.

Within decades of the European voyages of discovery, Native Americans, Europeans, and Africans began to interact in a manner unprecedented in human history. By the end of the 16th century, Europe, the Americas, and Africa had become linked in a vast transatlantic economy that extracted wealth from the American continents largely on the basis of the nonfree labor of impressed Native Americans and imported African slaves in a plantation economy that extended from Maryland to Brazil. The slave trade connected the economy of sections of Africa to the transatlantic economy and devastated the African people and cultures involved in it, but it also enriched the Americas with African culture.

PERIODS OF EUROPEAN OVERSEAS EXPANSION

WHAT IMPACT has European expansion had on the peoples of Asia, Africa, Australia, and the Americas?

Since the late 15th century, Europe's contacts with the rest of the world have passed through four stages. The first was the discovery, exploration, conquest, and settlement of the Americas and commercial expansion elsewhere. The second was an era of trade rivalry among Spain, France, and Great Britain. During this period (to 1820) the British colonies of North America and the Spanish colonies of Mexico and Central and South America broke free from European control. The third period spanned the 19th century and was characterized by the development of European empires in Africa and Asia. Imperial ideology at this time involved theories of trade, national honor, race, religion, and military strength. The last period of European experience with empire occupied the mid-20th century and was a time of decolonization—a retreat from empire.

It was technological advantages, not innate cultural superiority, that enabled Europeans for four and a half centuries to exercise global dominance beyond the proportions of Europe's size and population. However, the legacy of European imperialism—a memory of suffering, abuse, and exploitation—survives to complicate contemporary international relations.

MERCANTILIST THEORY OF ECONOMIC EXPLOITATION

WHAT WAS mercantilism?

The European empires of the 16th through the 18th centuries were based on commerce and were established primarily to promote trade. As a result, extensive trade rivalries sprang up around the world, and competitors developed navies to protect their interests. The empires also relied largely on slave labor. Indeed, the Atlantic slave trade was a major way in which European merchants profited. That trade in turn forcibly thrust the people of Africa into the life and culture of the New World.

If any formal economic theory lay behind these empires, it was **mercantilism**, a system in which governments heavily regulate trade and commerce to increase national wealth. From beginning to end, the economic well-being of the home country was the primary concern of mercantilist writers. They believed that a nation had to gain more gold and silver bullion than its rivals and that one nation's economy could grow only at the expense of others. Governments did this by establishing colonies overseas to provide markets and natural resources for the home country, which furnished military security and

mercantilism Term used to describe close government control of the economy that sought to maximize exports and accumulate as much precious metals as possible to enable the state to defend its economic and political interests.

Batavia. The Dutch established a major trading base at Batavia in the East Indies in the 17th century. Its geographical position allowed the Dutch to dominate the spice trade. Batavia is now Djakarta, capital of modern-day Indonesia.

Bildarchiv Preussicher Kulturbesitz.

political administration for these colonies. The home country and its colonies were to trade exclusively with each other. For decades, both sides assumed that the colonies were the inferior partner in a monopolistic relationship.

Mercantilist ideas were always neater on paper than in practice. By the early 18th century, it was clear that mercantilist assumptions did not correspond with reality. Colonial and home markets did not mesh. Spain, for instance, could not produce enough goods for South America, and manufacturing in the British North American colonies challenged production in England. Colonists of different countries also wanted to trade with one another. Governments could not control all their subjects, and they could be dragged into war by clashes among their colonies. Problems associated with the mercantile empires led to conflicts around the world.

ESTABLISHMENT OF THE SPANISH EMPIRE IN AMERICA

CONQUEST OF THE AZTECS AND THE INCAS

Within 20 years of the arrival of Columbus (1451–1506), Spanish explorers in search of gold had claimed the major islands of the Caribbean and suppressed the native peoples. These actions presaged what was to occur on the continent.

In 1519, Hernan Cortés (1485–1547) landed in Mexico with about 500 men and a few horses. He opened communication with Moctezuma II (1466–1520), the Aztec emperor. Moctezuma hesitated to confront Cortés, attempting at first to appease him with gifts of gold. Cortés forged alliances with subject peoples of the Aztecs. His forces then marched on the Aztec capital of Tenochtitlán (modern Mexico City), where Moctezuma welcomed him. Cortés soon made Moctezuma a prisoner in his own capital. After Moctezuma died from unknown circumstances, the Spaniards were driven from Tenochtitlán. But they returned, and the Aztecs were defeated in late 1521. Cortés proclaimed the Aztec Empire to be New Spain.

In 1532, Francisco Pizarro (c. 1478–1541) landed on the western coast of South America to take over the Inca Empire. His force included about 200 men

WHAT ROLES did the Roman Catholic Church play in Spanish America?

QUICK REVIEW

Francisco Pizarro (c. 1478–1541)

- Invasion force landed in South America in 1532

- Forces included 200 men, horses, guns, and swords

- 1533: Executed the Inca ruler and captured Cuzco

Spanish Conquest of Mexico. A 16th-century Aztec drawing depicts a battle during the Spanish conquest of Mexico. Note how the Spanish are assisted by a far greater number of Indian allies.

Corbis–Bettmann. Archivo Iconografico. S. A./Corbis.

armed with guns, swords, and horses, the military power of which the Incas did not understand. Pizarro lured the Inca ruler, Atahualpa (c. 1500–1533), into a conference, then seized him and had him garroted in 1533. The Spaniards then captured Cuzco, the Inca capital, ending the Inca Empire.

The conquests of Mexico and Peru are among the most dramatic and brutal events in modern world history. Small military forces armed with advanced weapons quickly subdued two advanced, powerful groups. European diseases, especially smallpox, aided the conquerors. Having never been explosed to European diseases, the native populations had no natural immunity to them.

Beyond the drama and bloodshed, these conquests marked a turning point. Whole civilizations with long histories and enormous social, architectural, and technological achievements were destroyed. Native American cultures endured, but European culture had the upper hand.

THE ROMAN CATHOLIC CHURCH IN SPANISH AMERICA

The Spanish conquest of the West Indies, Mexico, and South America opened these regions to the Roman Catholic faith. As it had in the Castilian reconquest of the Iberian peninsula from the Moors, religion played a central role in the conquest of the New World. In both cases, the obligation Christians felt to spread their faith was used to justify military conquest and the extension of political control

OVERVIEW THE COLUMBIAN EXCHANGE

The same ships that carried Europeans and Africans to the Americas also transported animals, plants, and diseases that had never before appeared in the New World. There was a similar transport back to Europe and Africa. Historians call this cross-continental flow "the Columbian exchange." The overall result was an ecological transformation that continues to shape the world.

To the Americas

Animals:	cattle, chickens, goats, horses, pigs, and sheep
Plants:	almonds, apples, apricots, bananas, barley, cabbage, cherries, dandelions, grapes, lemons, mangos, melons, oats, okra, olives, onions, oranges, peaches, pears, plums, radishes, rice, sugar cane, wheat, and other green vegetables
Diseases:	bubonic plague, chicken pox, diphtheria, influenza, malaria, measles, smallpox, typhoid, and typhus

From the Americas

Animals:	turkeys
Plants:	avocados, beans, blueberries, chilis, cocoa, guavas, maize, manioc (tapioca), peanuts, pecans, pineapples, potatoes, pumpkins, squash, sweet peppers, sweet potatoes, tobacco, and tomatoes
Diseases:	syphilis

and dominance. The link between the goals of the church and the state meant that the Roman Catholic Church in the New World worked to protect the interests of the Spanish authorities.

The relationship between political authority and the propagation of religious doctrine was even closer in the New World than on the Iberian peninsula. The papacy recognized that it could not self-support such an extensive missionary effort and turned over much of the control of the church in the New World to the Spanish monarchy. A close relationship between the monarchy and the church was created. The zeal of both institutions increased in the 16th century as the papacy and the Habsburg monarchy attempted to prevent Protestantism from establishing a foothold in America. As a consequence, the Roman Catholicism that spread throughout Spanish America was the zealous faith of the Counter-Reformation.

The Roman Catholic Church, first with the aid of the Franciscans and Dominicans, and later the Jesuits, sought to convert the Native Americans and eradicate Indian religious practices. Religious conversion involved, among other things, an attempt to destroy still other aspects of Native American culture. Converts, however, did not enjoy equality with Europeans; even late in the 18th century there were few Native American Christian priests.

There were some tensions between the early Spanish conquerors and the friars. Without conquest, the church could not convert the Native Americans, but the priests often deplored the harsh treatment native peoples received from their conquerors. The most outspoken clerical critic of the Spanish conquerors was Bartolomé de Las Casas (1474–1566), a Dominican. He contended that conquest was not necessary for conversion, and after 1550 his agitation inspired the royal government to pass legislation aimed at improving conditions for the native peoples. Las Casas's writings inspired the "**Black Legend**," according to which all Spanish treatment of the Native Americans was inhumane. Although substantially true, the Black Legend exaggerated the case against Spain. Certainly the rulers of the native empires—as the Aztec demands for sacrificial victims attest—had often themselves been cruel to their subject peoples.

By the end of the 16th century, the church in Spanish America had become largely an institution upholding the colonial status quo. Although priests did defend the communal rights of Indian tribes, the colonial church prospered through its exploitation of the resources of the New World. Those who spoke for the church did not challenge Spanish domination, and the church only modestly moderated the forces exploiting human labor and material wealth. By the late 18th century, the Roman Catholic Church had become one of the most conservative forces in Latin American society.

ECONOMIES OF EXPLOITATION IN THE SPANISH EMPIRE

Colonial Spanish America had an economy of exploitation in two senses. First, its organization of labor involved dependent servitude or slavery. Second, resources were exploited for the economic advantage of Spain.

VARIETIES OF ECONOMIC ACTIVITY

The early *conquistadores* ("conquerors") had been interested primarily in gold, but by the middle of the 16th century, silver mining provided the chief source of metallic wealth. Great silver mining centers were in Bolivia and northern Mexico.

15.1
The Black Legend of Spain: Bartolomé de Las Casas

Black Legend Argument that Spanish treatment of Native Americans was uniquely inhumane.

HOW WERE sugar production and slavery intertwined in colonial Brazil?

conquistadores Meaning "conquerors." Spanish conquerors of the New World.

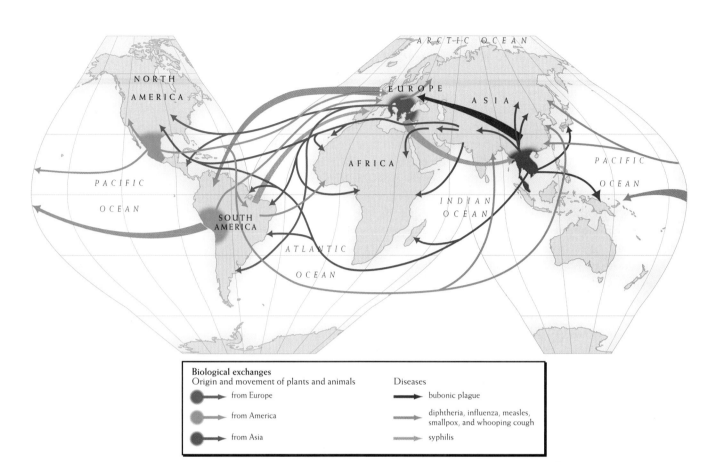

MAP 18–1
Biological Exchanges, 1000–1600 c.e. Though the transfer of plants, animals, and diseases had been going on for centuries, European expansion set in motion a global movement transformed the world.

HOW DID the Columbian exchange alter environments around the world?

The Spanish crown received one fifth of all mining revenues. Silver mining for the benefit of Spaniards and the Spanish crown epitomized the extractive economy on which Latin American colonial life was based.

This extractive economy required labor, but there were too few Spanish colonists to provide it, and most of the colonists who came to the Americas did not want to work for wages. So, the Spaniards turned first to the native population for workers and then to African slaves. Indian labor dominated on the continent and African labor in the Caribbean (see Map 18–1).

Encomienda The Spanish devised a series of institutions to exploit Native American labor. The first was the *encomienda*, a formal grant by the crown of the right to the labor of a specific number of Native Americans for a particular time. The Spanish crown disliked the encomienda system. The monarchy was distressed by reports from clergy that the Native Americans were being mistreated and feared that encomienda holders were becoming a powerful nobility in the New World. Encomienda as an institution declined by the middle of the 16th century.

Repartimiento The passing of the encomienda led to the *repartimiento*, largely copied from the draft labor practices of the Incas. Repartimiento required adult male Native Americans to devote a set number of days of labor annually to

encomienda Grant by the Spanish crown to a colonist of the labor of a specific number of Indians for a set period of time.

repartimiento Labor tax in Spanish America that required adult male Native Americans to devote a set number of days a year to Spanish economic enterprises.

Spanish economic enterprises. The time limitation on repartimiento led some Spanish managers to try to maximize productivity by working teams of men to exhaustion—sometimes to death—before replacing them with the next rotation.

The Hacienda   The *hacienda*, which dominated rural and agricultural life in Spanish colonies on the continent, developed when the crown made grants of land. These grants created large landed estates for ***peninsulares***, whites born in Spain, or creoles, whites born in America. This use of the resources of the New World for royal patronage did not directly burden Native Americans because the grazing that occurred on the haciendas required less labor than did the mines. But laborers on the hacienda were usually in formal servitude to the owner and had to buy goods for everyday living on credit from him. They were rarely able to repay the resulting debts and thus could not leave. This system was known as ***debt peonage***. The hacienda economy produced foodstuffs for mining areas and urban centers, and haciendas became one of the most important features of Latin American life.

THE DECLINE OF THE NATIVE AMERICAN POPULATION

Conquest, exploitation, forced labor, and European diseases decimated the Indian population (see Map 18–1). Beginning in the 16th century, Native Americans began to die off in huge numbers. In New Spain (Mexico) alone, the population probably declined from approximately 25 million to fewer than 2 million within the first century after the conquest. Thereafter, the Indian population began to expand slowly, but the precipitous drop eliminated the easy supply of exploitable labor.

COMMERCIAL REGULATION AND THE FLOTA SYSTEM

Because Queen Isabella of Castile (r. 1474–1504) had commissioned Columbus, the legal link between the New World and Spain was the crown of Castile. The governing of America was assigned to the Council of the Indies, which nominated the viceroys of New Spain and Peru, the chief executives in the New World.

hacienda   Large landed estates in Spanish America.

peninsulares   Persons born in Spain who settled in the Spanish colonies.

debt peonage   Requirement that laborers remain and continue to work on a hacienda until they had paid their debts to the owner for goods bought from him on credit.

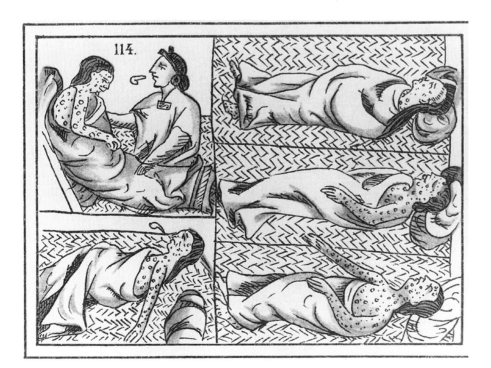

Smallpox.   Introduced by Europeans to the Americas, smallpox had a devastating effect on Native American populations. The disease swept through the Aztec capital of Tenochtitlán soon after the Spaniards arrived, contributing to the fall of the city. This illustration of the effect of the plague in the Aztec capital is from a post-conquest history known as the Florentine Codex compiled for Spanish church authorities by Aztec survivors.

Sixteenth-century drawing of smallpox victims. Atzec original codex Florentino. Courtesy President and Fellows of Harvard College. Courtesy Peabody Museum of Archeology and Ethnology, Harvard University, photograph by Hillel Burger.

Each of the viceroyalties included subordinate judicial councils known as *audiencias*. A variety of local officers presided over municipal councils. Virtually all political power flowed from the top of this political structure downward; there was little local initiative or self-government (see Map 18–2).

Colonial political structures existed largely to support the commercial goals of Spain. But the system of monopolistic trade regulation was often breached. The Casa de Contratación (House of Trade) in Seville regulated all trade with the New World and was the most influential institution of the Spanish Empire. The entire organization was geared to benefit the Spanish monarchy and privileged merchant groups.

A complicated system of trade and bullion fleets administered from Seville maintained the trade monopoly. Each year a fleet of commercial vessels controlled by Seville merchants and escorted by warships carried merchandise from Spain to specified ports in America. These included Portobello, Veracruz, and Cartagena. There were no authorized ports on the Pacific Coast. Areas such as Buenos Aires received goods only after the shipments had been unloaded at one of the authorized ports. After selling their wares, the ships were loaded with silver and gold bullion. They then usually wintered in fortified Caribbean ports before sailing back to Spain. Regulations prohibited Spanish colonists from trading directly with each other and from building their own shipping and commercial industries. Foreign merchants were also forbidden to breach the Spanish monopoly.

COLONIAL BRAZIL AND SLAVERY

In 1494, by the Treaty of Tordesillas, the pope divided the overseas empires of Spain and Portugal by drawing a line west of the Cape Verde Islands. In 1500, a Portuguese explorer landed in present-day Brazil, east of the papal line. This gave Portugal a foothold in South America. Portugal, however, had fewer resources to devote to its New World empire than did Spain. Its rulers, therefore,

Sugar Plantation. Brazil and the West Indies were a major source of the demand for slave labor. Slaves are shown here grinding sugar cane and refining sugar, which was then exported to the consumer markets in Europe.

© Hulton-Deutsch Collection/Corbis.

MAP EXPLORATION

Interactive map: To explore this map further, go to **http://www.prenhall.com/craig/map18.2**

DISPUTED BY ENGLAND, RUSSIA, AND SPAIN

VICEROYALTY OF NEW SPAIN

ATLANTIC OCEAN

EFFECTIVE FRONTIER OF SPANISH SETTLEMENT

Rio Grande

Gulf of Mexico

Mexico City

Veracruz

Santo Domingo

Caribbean Sea

Portobelo

Cartagena

Caracas

VICEROYALTY OF NEW GRANADA

Separated From Viceroyalty of Peru, 1717, 1739

GUIANA

Bogotá

Quito

VICEROYALTY OF PERU

Amazon R.

VICEROYALTY OF BRAZIL

Pernambuco

Bahia

PACIFIC

Lima

OCEAN

Portosi

São Paulo

Rio de Janeiro

VICEROYALTY OF LA PLATA

Separated From the Viceroyalty of Peru, 1776

Santiago

AUDIENCIA OF CHILE

Buenos Aires

Claimed but not settled by Spain

N

MAP 18–2

Viceroyalties in Latin America in 1780. Spain organized its vast holdings in the New World into viceroyalties, each of which had its own governor and other administrative officials.

HOW EFFECTIVE was Spain's control over its New World colonies?

British North America

- Jamestown, Virginia: Became first successful British settlement in 1607
- Religion shaped the organization of British colonies
- English colonies had a complex relationship with Native Americans

HOW WERE the economies of the French and British North American colonies integrated into the transatlantic economy?

The Fur Trade. Europeans and Indians, from an engraving of 1777.

©The Granger Collection, New York.

left exploitation of the region to private entrepreneurs. Because the native peoples in the lands that Portugal claimed were nomadic, the Portuguese, unlike the Spanish, imported Africans as slaves rather than using the native Indian population as their work force.

By the mid-16th century, sugar production had gained preeminence in the Brazilian economy, and the dominance of sugar meant the dominance of slavery. Slavery became even more important when, in the early 18th century, gold was discovered in southern Brazil. Nowhere, except perhaps in the West Indies, was slavery so important as it was in Brazil, where it persisted until 1888.

The taxation and administration associated with gold mining brought new wealth to Portugal's monarchs that strengthened them by allowing them to rule without recourse to Cortés or the parliament for taxation. Through transatlantic trade, the diffusion of Brazilian gold also promoted the economies of all the major trading nations.

FRENCH AND BRITISH COLONIES IN NORTH AMERICA

French explorers moved down the St. Lawrence River valley in Canada during the 17th century. French fur traders and missionaries followed, with the French government sponsoring the missionary effort. By the end of the 17th century, Canada was sparsely populated by the French. Their largest settlement was Quebec, founded in 1608. It was primarily through the fur trade that French Canada functioned as part of the early transatlantic economy.

Beginning with the first successful settlement in Jamestown, Virginia, in 1607, English colonies spread along the eastern seaboard of the future United States. With the exception of Maryland, these colonies were Protestant. The Church of England dominated the southern colonies. In New England, varieties of Protestantism associated with or derived from Calvinism were in the ascendancy. In their religious affiliations, the English-speaking colonies manifested two important traits derived from the English experience. First, much of their religious life was organized around self-governing congregations. Second, their religious outlook derived from those forms of Protestantism that were suspicious of central political authority. In this regard, their cultural and political outlook differed sharply from the cultural and political outlook associated with the Roman Catholics of the Spanish Empire. In a sense, the ideologies of the extreme Reformation and Counter-Reformation confronted each other in the Americas.

The English colonists had complex interactions with the Native American populations. They had only modest interest in missionizing the natives and, as in South America, European diseases took a high toll on the native population. Unlike Mexico and Peru, however, North America had no large Native American cities. The Native American populations were dispersed, and intertribal animosity was intense. The English often used one tribe against another, and the Native Americans also tried to use the English or the French in their own conflicts. From the late 17th century through the American Revolution, however, the Native Americans were drawn into the Anglo-French Wars that were fought in North America as well as Europe (see Chapter 20).

The economies of the English-speaking colonies were primarily agricultural. From New England through the Middle Atlantic states, there were mostly small farms tilled by free white labor; from Virginia southward a plantation economy dependent on slavery predominated. The principal ports—Boston, Newport, New York, Philadelphia, Baltimore, and Charleston—were the chief centers through which goods moved back and forth between the colonies and England and the West Indies. The commercial economies of these cities were all related to the transatlantic slave trade.

Until the 1760s, most Americans, like their English counterparts, were monarchists who were suspicious of monarchical power. Their politics involved patronage and individual favors. Their society was hierarchical. It had an elite that functioned like an aristocracy and many ordinary people who were dependent on that aristocracy. Throughout the colonies during the 18th century, the Anglican church grew in influence and membership. The prosperity of the colonies might eventually have led them to separate from England, but in 1750 few people anticipated that break.

Roanoke. The first successful English colonies in North America in the 17th century were preceded by two failed efforts on Roanoke Island in what is now North Carolina in the late 16th century. John White accompanied both attempts, the second as governor. White was a perceptive and sensitive observer whose watercolor paintings provide invaluable information about Native American life in the coastal Carolina region at the time of contact. This painting shows the Algonquian village of Secoton. The houses were bark-covered. In the lower left is a mortuary temple. Dancers in the lower right are performing a fertility ceremony. The man sitting in the platform in the upper right is keeping birds away from the corn crop.

The Bridgeman Art Library International Ltd.

Both England and France had important sugar islands in the Caribbean, with plantations worked by African slaves. The trade and commerce of the northern British colonies were focused on meeting the needs of these islands.

SLAVERY IN THE AMERICAS

lack slavery was the final mode of forced or subservient labor in the New World. It extended throughout the Americas.

ESTABLISHMENT OF SLAVERY

As the numbers of Native Americans in South America declined, the Spanish and Portuguese turned to African slaves. By the late 1500s, in the West Indies and the cities of South America, black slaves surpassed the white population.

On much of the South American continent dominated by Spain, slavery declined during the late 17th century, but it continued to thrive in Brazil and in the Caribbean. In British North America, it began with the importation of slaves to Jamestown in 1619, and quickly became a fundamental institution.

The spread of slavery in Brazil and the West Indies was promoted by the market for sugar. Only slave labor could provide enough workers for the sugar plantations. As the production of sugar expanded, so did the demand for slaves.

By 1700, the Caribbean Islands were the world center for sugar production. As the European appetite for sugar grew, so did the slave population. By 1725, black slaves may have constituted almost 90 percent of the population of the West Indies. There and in Brazil and the southern British colonies, prosperity and slavery went hand in hand. The wealthiest colonies were those that raised consumer staples, such as sugar, rice, tobacco, or cotton, by slave labor.

THE PLANTATION ECONOMY AND TRANSATLANTIC TRADE

The **plantation economy** encompassed plantations that stretched from Maryland through the West Indies and into Brazil and formed a vast corridor of slave societies. This kind of society—defined by a total dependence on slave labor and racial difference—had not existed before the European discovery and exploitation of the Americas. The social and economic influence of plantation slavery also touched West Africa, Europe, and New England. It persisted from the 16th century through the second half of the 19th century. Every society in which it existed still contends with its effects.

The slave trade was part of the larger system of transatlantic trade that linked Europe, Africa, and the European colonies in the Americas. In this system, the Americas supplied labor-intensive raw materials (tobacco, sugar, coffee, precious metals, cotton, and indigo). Europe supplied manufactured goods (textiles, liquor, guns, metal wares, and beads) and cash. Africa supplied gold,

---

WHICH ECONOMIC factors led to the spread of slavery in the New World?

plantation economy Economic system stretching between Chesapeake Bay and Brazil that produced crops, especially sugar, cotton, and tobacco, using slave labor on large estates.

Slave Auction Notice. Africans who survived the voyage across the Atlantic were immediately sold into slavery in the Americas. This slave-auction notice describes a group of slaves whose ship had stopped at Charleston, South Carolina, and then landed elsewhere in the region to auction its human cargo. Notice the concern to assure potential buyers that the slaves were healthy.

Corbis-Bettmann.

ivory, wood, palm oil, gum, and other products, as well as the slaves who provided the labor to create the American products. By the 18th century, slaves were the predominant African export.

SLAVERY ON THE PLANTATIONS

The American plantations to which the African slaves arrived produced for an overseas market that was part of a larger integrated transatlantic economy. In turn, plantation owners imported virtually all the finished or manufactured goods they consumed.

The conditions of plantation slaves differed from colony to colony. Vast slave holdings were the exception. Black slaves living in Portuguese areas had the fewest legal protections. In the Spanish colonies, the church provided some protection, but devoted more effort to protecting Native Americans. Slave codes in the British and the French colonies provided only the most limited protection. Regulations were designed to prevent slave revolts and favored the master rather than the slave. Masters were permitted to punish slaves by harsh corporal punishment. Slaves were forbidden to gather in large groups lest they plan a rebellion. Slave marriages were usually not recognized by law. Children of slaves were owned by the owner of the parents, and slave families could be separated by sale or inheritance. The death rate among slaves was high. Their lives were sacrificed to the ongoing expansion of the plantations that made their owners wealthy and that produced goods for consumers in Europe.

The African slaves who were transported to the Americas were converted to Christianity: in the Spanish domains to Roman Catholicism, and in the English colonies to Protestantism. In both cases, they were largely separated from African religious traditions. Although slaves mixed Christianity with some African religion, the conversion of Africans to Christianity represented another example of the crushing of non-European cultural values in the New World.

Europeans were also prejudiced against black Africans. Many Europeans thought Africans were savages or looked down on them because they were slaves. These attitudes had been shared by both Christians and Muslims in the Mediterranean world, where slavery had long existed. Furthermore, many European cultures attached negative connotations to blackness. Although racial thinking in regard to slavery became more important in the 19th century, the fact that slaves were differentiated from the rest of the population by race as well as by their status as chattel property was fundamental to the system.

Job Ben Solomon. Captured by Mandingo enemies and sold to a Maryland tobacco planter, Job Ben Solomon accomplished the nearly impossible feat of returning to Africa as a free man. By demonstrating his talents as a Muslim scholar, including his ability to write the entire Qur'an from memory, he astonished his owners and eventually convinced them to let him go home.

"The Fortunate Slave," An Illustration of African Slavery in the early 18th century by Douglas Grant (1968). From "Some Memoirs of the Life of Job," by Thomas Bluett (1734). Photo by Robert D. Rubic/ Precision Chromes, Inc. The New York Public Library, Research Libraries.

AFRICA AND THE TRANSATLANTIC SLAVE TRADE

*T*he establishment of plantations demanding slave labor drew Africa into the heart of the transatlantic economy. As Native Americans were decimated by conquest and disease or proved unsatisfactory as plantation laborers, colonial entrepreneurs began to look elsewhere for workers. The Portuguese first, and then the Spanish, Dutch, French, and English, turned to Africa for slaves. The Atlantic slave trade was not overtly the result of racist principles but of the economic needs of the colonial powers and their willingness (based on tacit racist assumptions) to exploit weaker peoples to satisfy those needs.

The Portuguese were the principal transporters throughout most of the history of the slave trade. During the 18th century, which saw the greatest shipments,

WHY WAS the transatlantic slave trade so economically important?

15.3

Olaudah Equiano, *The Interesting Narrative of the Life of Olaudah Equiano, or Gustavus Vassa, the African*

the French and English carried almost half the total traffic. Americans were avid slavers who managed to make considerable profits even after Britain and the United States outlawed slaving in 1807 (see Map 18–3.)

Slaving was an important part of the massive new overseas trade that financed much of the European and American economic development that so changed the West during the 19th century. This trade, bought at the price of immense human suffering, helped propel Europe and some of its colonial offshoots in the Americas to world dominance.

MAP EXPLORATION

Interactive map: To explore this map further, go to **http://www.prenhall.com/craig/map18.3**

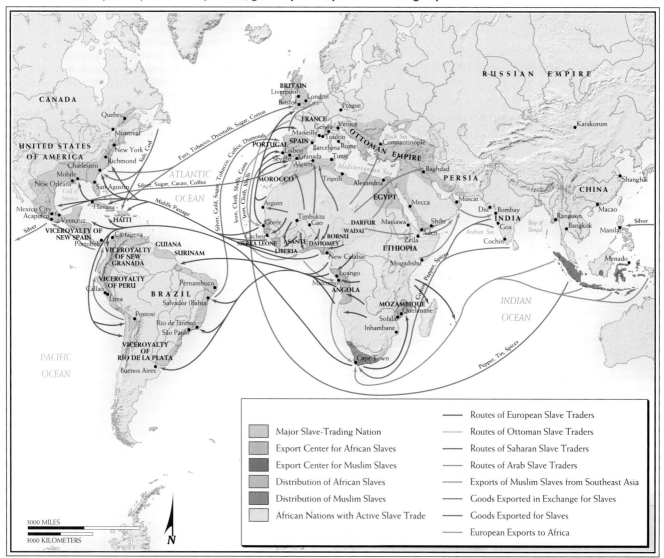

MAP 18–3

The Slave Trade, 1400–1860.   Slavery is an ancient institution and complex slave-trading routes were in existence in Africa, the Middle East, and Asia for centuries, but it was the need to supply labor for the plantations of the Americas that led to the greatest movement of peoples across the face of the earth.

WHY WAS the slave trade so economically important?

THE BACKGROUND OF SLAVERY

Slavery seems to have been a tragic fact of human societies as far back as we can trace it. Although linked to warfare, it cannot be explained by military or economic necessity.

Virtually every premodern state around the globe depended on slavery. The Mediterranean and African worlds were no exception. Slave institutions in sub-Saharan Africa were ancient. The Islamic states of southwestern Asia and North Africa increased this traffic, although they took fewer slaves from Africa than from Eastern Europe and central Asia. (Hence it is not surprising that the word *slave* is derived ultimately from *Slav.*) Both Mediterranean-Christian and Islamic peoples were using slaves—mostly Greeks, Bulgarians, Turkish prisoners of war, and Black Sea Tartars, but also Africans—before the voyages of discovery opened sub-Saharan sources of slaves for the new European colonies.

Not all forms of slavery were as dehumanizing as the chattel slavery in the Americas. Islamic law, for example, ameliorated slavery. All slavery, however, involved the forceful exploitation and degradation of human beings, the denial of basic freedoms, and the sundering of family ties.

Africa suffered immense social devastation when it was the chief supplier of slaves to the world. Societies that were built on the exploitation of African slavery also suffered enduring consequences, not the least of which is racism.

SLAVERY AND SLAVING IN AFRICA

The trade that supplied African slaves to the Islamic lands and Asia has been termed the "oriental" slave trade. The Sudan and the Horn of Africa were the two prime sources of slaves for this trade. The trade managed by Europeans is called the "occidental" slave trade. Voyages beginning in the 15th century by first the Portuguese and then other Europeans made the western coasts of Africa as far south as Angola the prime slaving areas.

Before the full development of the transatlantic slave trade (about 1650), slavery and slave trading had been no more significant in Africa than anywhere else.[1] Indigenous African slavery resembled that of other premodern societies. Estimates suggest that about 10,000 slaves per year, most of them female, were taken from sub-Saharan Africa through the oriental trade.

By about 1650, the newer occidental slave trade of the Europeans had become as large as the oriental trade and for the ensuing two centuries far surpassed it. It affected all of Africa, disrupting especially western and central African

A Slave Coffle. This 18th-century print shows bound African captives being forced to a slaving port. It was largely African middlemen who captured slaves in the interior and marched them to the coast.

North Wind Picture Archives.

 15.2
"Our Kingdom is Being Lost," Nzinga Mbemba (Affonso I)

Estimated Slave Imports into the Americas and Old World by Region, 1451–1870

British North America	523,000
Spanish America	1,687,000
British Caribbean	2,443,000
French Caribbean	1,655,000
Dutch Caribbean	500,000
Danish Caribbean	50,000
Brazil (Portuguese)	4,190,000
Old World	297,000
Total	**11,345,000**

Figures as calculated by James A. Rawley, *The Transatlantic Slave Trade: A History* (New York: W. W. Norton, 1981), p. 428, based on his and other more recent revisions of the careful but older estimates of Philip D. Curtin, *The Atlantic Slave Trade: A Census* (Madison: University of Wisconsin Press, 1969), especially pp. 266, 268.

[1]The summary follows closely that of P. Manning, *Slavery and African Life: Occidental, Oriental, and African Slave Trades* (Cambridge: Cambridge University Press, 1990), pp. 127–140.

Conquest of the Americas and the Transatlantic Slave Trade

1494	The Treaty of Tordesillas divides the overseas empires of Spain and Portugal
1500	The Portuguese arrive in Brazil
1519–1521	Hernan Cortés conquers the Aztec Empire
1531–1533	Francisco Pizarro conquers the Inca Empire
1607	Jamestown, Virginia, first permanent English settlement in North America, founded
1608	The French found Quebec
1619	First African slaves brought to British North America
1650	Transatlantic slave trade becomes bigger than the older oriental slave trade
1700s	More than 6 million slaves imported from Africa to the Americas
1807	Slavery abolished in British domains
1808	The importation of slaves abolished in the United States
1874–1928	Indigenous African slavery abolished
1888	Slavery abolished in Brazil

society. As a result of the demand for young male slaves on the plantations of the Americas, West Africa experienced a sharp drain on its productive male population. Between 1640 and 1690, the number of slaves sold to European carriers doubled, indicating the increasing participation of Africans in the trade. The demand for slaves increased internal warfare in western and central Africa. Moreover, as the external trade destroyed the male-female population balance, an internal market for female slaves arose.

These developments accelerated during the 18th century when African states and slave traders were most heavily involved in the trade. The population declined sharply in the coastal and inland areas hardest hit by the ravages of the trade.

As European and American nations began to outlaw slaving and slavery in the 19th century, the oriental and internal trades increased. Slave exports from East Africa and the Sudan and Horn increased after about 1780, and indigenous African slavery also expanded. This traffic was dominated by the same figures—merchants, warlords, and rulers—who had profited from external trade.

Indigenous African slavery began a real decline only at the end of the 19th century because of the dominance of European colonial regimes and internal changes. The formal end of African indigenous slavery occurred only in 1928 in Sierra Leone.

THE AFRICAN SIDE OF THE TRANSATLANTIC TRADE

Africans were actively involved in the transatlantic slave trade.

European slave traders generally obtained their human cargoes from private or government-sponsored African middlemen along the coast. This situation was the result of both the ability of Africans to control inland trade and the vulnerability of Europeans to tropical disease. Thus, it was largely African middlemen who undertook the capture or procurement of slaves and the difficult task of marching them to the coast. These middlemen were generally either wealthy merchants or the agents of African chieftaincies or kingdoms.

The media of exchange for slaves varied. At first the items were usually gold dust, firearms, or alcohol. Increasingly, they involved monetary payments. This trade drained productive resources (human beings) in return for nonproductive wealth.

The chief West and central African slaving regions provided different numbers of slaves at different times, and the total number of exported slaves varied between periods. When one area could not meet demand, the European traders shifted to other locales. Traders went where population density and African merchant or state suppliers promised the best numbers and prices.

THE EXTENT OF THE SLAVE TRADE

The slave trade fluctuated greatly from period to period. It peaked between 1701 and 1810, accounting for more than 60 percent of the total. The final half-century of slaving (ending in 1870) accounted for more than 20 percent of the total. The Portuguese transported more than a million slaves to Brazil between

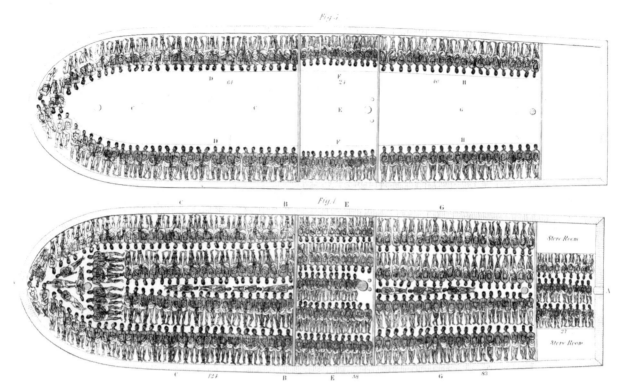

1811 and 1870. It is sobering to contemplate how long it took the "modern" occidental world to abolish the trade in African slaves.

The overall number of African slaves exported during the occidental trade—effectively, between 1451 and 1870—is still debated and must be seen in the larger context of all types of slaving in Africa in the same period. A major unknown is the number of slaves who died under the brutal conditions to which they were subjected when captured and transported overland and by sea. The most reliable estimates pertain only to those slaves who actually landed abroad. As the table on page 443 shows, just those who actually reached an American or Old World destination in the occidental trade totaled more than 11 million.

At a minimum, Africa lost some 13 million people to the Atlantic trade alone. Another 5 million or more were lost to the oriental trade. Finally, according to the estimate of one expert, an additional 15 million people were enslaved within African societies themselves.[2]

CONSEQUENCES OF THE SLAVE TRADE FOR AFRICA

Statistics hint at the massive impact slave trading had on African life, but the actual effects remain in dispute. We do not know for certain if the Atlantic trade brought net population loss or gain to specific areas of West Africa. The rapid spread of maize and cassava cultivation in forest regions after these plants were imported from the Americas may have fueled African population increases that offset regional human loss through slaving. We know, however, that slaving took away many of the strongest young men and, in the oriental-trade zones, most of the young women. Similarly, we do not know if more slaves were captured as byproducts of local wars or from pure slave raiding, but we do know they were captured and removed from their societies (see "Olaudah Equiano Recalls His Experience at the Slave Market in Barbados").

[2]Ibid., pp. 37, 170–171.

Slave Ship. Loading plan for the main decks of the 320-ton slave ship *Brookes*. The *Brookes* was only 25 feet wide and 100 feet long, but as many as 609 slaves were crammed onboard for the nightmarish passage to the Americas. The average space allowed each person was only about 78 inches by 16 inches.

Photographs and Prints Division, Schomburg Center for Research in Black Culture, The New York Public Library, Astor, Lenox, and Tilder Foundations.

HISTORY'S VOICES

OLAUDAH EQUIANO RECALLS HIS EXPERIENCE AT THE SLAVE MARKET IN BARBADOS

O laudah Equiano composed one of the most popular and influential slave narratives of the late 18th and early 19th centuries. He also led a remarkable life. Born in West Africa in what is today Nigeria, he spent his early life among the Ibo. He was captured and sold into slavery, making the dreaded Atlantic crossing. In the passage that follows, Equiano recounts his arrival in Barbados and the experience of cultural disorientation, his sale into slavery, and seeing Africans separated from their families. His life did not end in slavery, the most destructive aspects of which he also described in vivid detail. He achieved his freedom and then had an adventuresome career sailing on various commercial and military ships plying the Caribbean, the Atlantic, and the Mediterranean. Equiano also made a trip to the Arctic Ocean. His account consequently describes not only the life of a person taken from Africa and sold into American slavery, but also the life of a person who, once free, explored the entire transatlantic world. His autobiographical narrative, which first appeared in 1789 and displayed Equiano's wide reading, served two purposes for the antislavery campaign that commenced in the second half of the 18th century. First, it provided a firsthand report of the slave experience in crossing from Africa to America. Second, his powerful rhetoric and clear arguments demonstrated that, if free, Africans could achieve real personal independence. Many defenders of slavery had denied that Africans possessed the character and intelligence to be free.

WHAT WERE the fears of the Africans on the slave ship as they approached the port? How were older slaves in Barbados used to calm their fears? How did the sale of slaves proceed? What happened to African families in the process of the sale?

At last, we came in sight . . . of Barbados, . . . and we soon anchored . . . off Bridgetown. Many merchants and planters now came on board. . . . They put us in separate parcels, and examined us attentively. They also made us jump, and pointed to the land, signifying we were to go there. We thought by this we should be eaten by these ugly men, as they appeared to us; and when, soon after we were all put down under the deck again, there was much dread and trembling among us, and nothing but bitter cries to be heard all the night from these apprehension, insomuch that at last the white people got some old slaves from the land to pacify us. They told us we were not to be eaten, but to work, and were soon to go on land, where we should see many of our country people. This report eased us much. . . . We were conducted immediately to the merchant's yard, where we were all pent up together like so many sheep in a fold, without regard to sex or age. As every object was new to me, everything filled me with surprise . . . and indeed I thought these people were full of nothing but magical arts. . . . We were not many days in the merchant's custody before we were sold after their usual manner which was this: On a signal given (as the beat of a drum), the buyers rush at once into the yard where the slaves are confined, and make choice of that parcel they like best. The noise and clamour with which this is attended, and the eagerness visible in the countenances of the buyers, serve not a little to increase the apprehension of the terrified Africans, who may well be supposed to consider them as the ministers of that destruction to which they think themselves devoted. In this manner, without scruple, relations and friends separate, most of them never to see each other again. I remember in the vessel in which I was brought over, in the men's apartment, there were several brothers who, in the sale, were sold in different lots; and it was very moving on this occasion to see and hear their cries at parting. . . . Surely this is a new refinement in cruelty, which, while it has no advantage to atone for it, thus aggravates distress, and adds fresh horrors even to the wretchedness of slavery.

Source: *The Interesting Narrative of the Life of Olaudah Equiano or Gustavus Vassa, The African, Written by Himself* (first published 1789), as quoted in Henry Louis Gates Jr., and William L. Andrews, eds., *Pioneers of the Black Atlantic: Five Slave Narratives from the Enlightenment, 1772–1815* (Washington, DC: Counterpoint, 1998), pp. 221–223.

Nor do we know if slaving inhibited trade or stimulated it. Commerce in African products from ivory to wood and hides often accompanied that in slaves. Still, we do know that the exchange of productive human beings for money or goods that were not used to build a productive economy was ultimately a loss for African society.

Finally, because we do not yet have accurate estimates of the total population of Africa at different times over the four centuries of the Atlantic slave trade, we cannot determine with certainty its demographic impact. We can, however, make educated guesses. If, for example, tropical Africa had 50 million inhabitants in 1600, it would then have had 30 percent of the combined population of the Americas, the Middle East, Europe, and Africa. If in 1900, after the depredations of the slave trade, it had 70 million inhabitants, its population would have dropped to about 10 percent of the combined population of the same world regions. Current estimates indicate that overall African population growth suffered significantly as a result of the slave trade. Figures like these also give some idea of slavery's probable impact on Africa's ability to keep up with the modern industrializing world.[3]

Even in West and central Africa, which bore the brunt of the Atlantic trade, its impact and the response to it were varied. In a few cases, kingdoms such as Dahomey (the present Republic of Benin) seem to have derived immense economic profit by making slaving a state monopoly. Other kingdoms derived no gain from it. In many instances, including the rise of Asante power or the fall of the Yoruba Oyo Empire, increased slaving was a result as well as a cause of regional change. Increased warfare meant increased prisoners to be sold; however, whether slaving was a motive for war is still unclear.

Similarly, if it can be established, as seems evident, that a major increase in indigenous slavery was a result of the external trade to occident and orient, we have to assume major social consequences for African society. The specific consequences would, however, differ according to regional situations. For example, in West Africa more men were taken as slaves than women, whereas in the Sahelian Sudanic regions, more women than men were taken. In the west, the loss of so many men increased the pressures for polygamy and possibly the use of female slaves, whereas in the Sahelian Sudanic regions, the loss of women may have stimulated polyandry and reduced the birthrate.

Even though slavery existed previously in Africa, the scale of the Atlantic trade was unprecedented and hence had an unprecedented impact. In general, the slave trade changed patterns of life and balances of power in the main affected areas, whether by stimulating trade or warfare, by disrupting market and political structures, by increasing slavery inside Africa, or by disturbing the male-female ratio (and hence the work-force balance and birthrate patterns) and consequently the basic social institution of monogamous marriage.

[3]Ibid., pp. 126–148, 168–176.

Plantation. In the American South, the islands of the Caribbean, and in Brazil, slaves labored on sugar plantations under the authority of overseers.

The Granger Collection.

QUICK REVIEW

Difficulties in Determining Consequences of the Slave Trade
- Do not know how slave trade affected specific West African regions
- Cannot determine number of slaves captured during wars and captured during pure slave raiding
- Do not know how slave trading affected commerce in African products

The overseas slave trade at the least siphoned off indigenous energy and channeled it in counterproductive or destructive directions. This inhibited economic development. The Atlantic slave trade was one of the most tragic aspects of European involvement in Africa.

IMAGE KEY
for pages 434–435

a. Job Ben Solomon, a freed slave who returned to Africa

b. A poster for a slave auction in Charleston

c. John Singleton Copley, "Watson and the Shark," ca. 1778

d. A chunk of silver metal and rock

e. Spanish map showing the seven cities of Cibola and Baja California, 16th century

f. Dried tobacco leaves

g. Slave ship, ca. 1790

h. Samuel Scott, "Old Custom House Quay"

i. Bartolemé de Las Casas

j. Slaves grinding sugar cane and refining sugar

k. Fur traders and Indians

l. Slaves harvest sugar cane on a plantation

SUMMARY

European Conquest of the New World   Contact between the native peoples of the American continents and the European explorers of the 15th and 16th centuries transformed world history. In the Americas, the native peoples had established a wide variety of civilizations. Some of their most remarkable architectural monuments and cities were constructed during the centuries when European civilizations were reeling from the collapse of Roman power. Until the European explorations, the civilizations of the Americas and Eurasia and Africa had no significant contact with one another.

Within half a century of Columbus's landing, millions of America's native peoples encountered Europe's intent on conquest, exploitation, and religious conversion. Because of their advanced weapons, navies, and the diseases they brought with them, as well as internal divisions among the Native Americans themselves, Europeans achieved a rapid conquest.

The Transatlantic Economy   In both North and South America, economies of exploitation were established. In Latin America, various institutions were developed to extract native labor. From the mid-Atlantic English colonies through the Caribbean and into Brazil, slave-labor plantation systems were established. Slaves were forcibly imported from Africa and sold in America to plantation owners. The economies and peoples of Europe, Africa, and the Americas were thus drawn into a worldwide web of production based on slave labor.

Slavery   The impact of slavery in the Americas was not limited to the life of the black slaves. Whites in the New World numbered about 12 million in 1820, compared to some 6 million blacks. However, only about 2 million whites had migrated there, compared to some 11 million or more Africans forcibly imported as slaves. Such numbers reveal the effects of brutal slave conditions and the high mortality and low birthrates of slave populations.

None of these statistics, however, enables us to asses the role that slavery has played in the Americas or, in particular, the United States. The United States actually received only a bit more than a quarter as many slaves as did Brazil alone or the British and French Caribbean regions together, yet the consequences of the forced migration of just over a half-million Africans remain massive. Consider just the American Civil War and the endurance of racism and inequality or, more positively, the African contribution to American industrial development, language, music, literature, and artistic culture. The Atlantic slave trade's impact continues to be felt at both ends of the original trade route.

REVIEW QUESTIONS

1. How were small groups of Spaniards able to conquer the Aztec and Inca Empires?

2. What was the the mercantilist economic theory? How accuately did it describe the relationship between the colonies and their homelands?

3. Why did forced labor and slavery develop in tropical colonies? How was slavery in the Americas different from slavery in earlier societies?

4. What was the effect of the transatlantic slave trade on African societies? What role did Africans themselves play in the slave trade?

KEY TERMS

Black Legend (p. 439)   *encomienda* (p. 440)   **peninsulares** (p. 441)

conquistadores (p. 439)   *hacienda* (p. 441)   **plantation economy** (p. 446)

debt peonage (p. 441)   **mercantilism** (p. 436)   *repartimiento* (p. 440)

 For additional study resources for this chapter, go to:
www.prenhall.com/craig/chapter18

The World in Transition

1500 – 1600   1600 – 1700   1700 – 1800

EUROPE

1500 – 1600	1600 – 1700	1700 – 1800
1517–1555 Protestant Reformation	**618–1648** Thirty Years' War	**1701** Act of Settlement provides for Protestant succession to English throne
1533–1584 Ivan the Terrible of Russia reigns	**1640–1688** Frederick William, the Great Elector, reigns in Brandenburg-Prussia	**1702–1713** War of Spanish Succession
1540 Jesuit Order founded by Ignatius Loyola	**1642–1646** Puritan Revolution in England	**1740–1748** War of Austrian Succession
1543–1727 Scientific Revolution	**1643–1715** Louis XIV of France reigns	**1756–1763** Seven Years' War
1556–1598 Philip II of Spain reigns	**1682–1725** Peter the Great of Russia reigns	**ca. 1750** Industrial Revolution begins in England
1558–1603 Elizabeth I of England reigns	**1688** Glorious Revolution in England	**1772** First partition of Poland
1562–1598 French Wars of Religion	**1690** *Second Treatise of Civil Government* by John Locke	**1789** First French Revolution
1581 The Netherlands declares its independence from Spain		**1793 and 1795** Last two partitions of Poland
1588 Defeat of the Spanish Armada		
1589–1610 Henry IV, founds Bourbon dynasty, France		

NEAR EAST/ASIA

1500 – 1600	1600 – 1700	1700 – 1800
500–1722 Safavid Shi'ite rule in Iran	**1628–1657** Shah Jahan reigns; builds Taj Mahal as mausoleum for his beloved wife	**1700** Sikhs and Marathas bring down Mughal Imperial Power
1512–1520 Ottoman ruler Selim I	**1646** Founding of Maratha Empire	**1708** British East India Company and New East India Company merge
1520–1566 Ottoman ruler Suleiman the Magnificent	**1648** Delhi becomes the capital of Mughal Empire	**1722** Last Safavid ruler forced to abdicate
1525–1527 Babur founds Mughal dynasty in India	**1658–1707** Shah Aurangzeb, the "World Conqueror," reigns in India	**1724** Rise in the Deccan of the Islamic state of Hyderabad
1540 Hungary under Ottoman rule	**1669–1683** Last military expansion by Ottomans: 1669, seize Crete; 1670s, the Ukraine; 1683, Vienna	**1725** Nadir Shah of Afganhistan becomes ruler of Persia
1556–1605 Akbar the Great of India reigns		**1739** Persian invasion of northern India, by Nadir Shah
1571 Battle of Lepanto; Ottomans defeated		**1748–1761** Ahmad Shah Durrani of Afghanistan invades India
ca. 1571–1640 Safavid philosopher-writer Mullah Sadra		**1757** British victory at Plassey, in Bengal
1588–1629 Shah Abbas I of Iran reigns		

EAST ASIA

1500 – 1600	1600 – 1700	1700 – 1800
1500–1800 Commercial revolution in Ming-Ch'ing China; trade with Europe; flourishing of the novel	**1600** Tokugawa Ieyasu wins battle of Sekigahara, completes unification of Japan	**1701** Forty-seven ro-nin incident in Japan
1543 Portuguese arrive in Japan	**1600–1868** Tokugawa shogunate in Edo	**1716–1733** Reforms of Tokugawa Yoshimune in Japan
1568–1600 Era of unification follows end of Warring States Era, Japan	**1630s** Seclusion adopted as national policy in Japan	**1737–1795** Reign of Ch'ien Lung in China
1587 Spanish arrive in Japan	**1644–1694** Bashō Japanese poet	**1742** Christianity banned in China
1588 Hideyoshi's sword hunt in Japan	**1644–1911** Ch'ing (Manchu) dynasty in China	**1784** American traders arrive in China
1592–1598 Ming troops battle Hideyoshi's army in Korea	**1661-1722** K'ang Hsi reign in China	**1787–1793** Matsudaira Sadanobu's reforms in Japan
	1673–1681 Revolt of southern generals in China	**1798** White Lotus Rebellion in China
	1699 British East India Company arrives in China	

AFRICA

1500 – 1600	1600 – 1700	1700 – 1800
1506 East coast of Africa under Portuguese domination	**1600s** English, Dutch, and French enter the slave trade	**1702** Asiento Guinea Trade Company founded for slave trade between Africa and the Americas
1507 Mozambique founded by Portuguese	**1619** First African slaves in North America land in Virginia	**1700s** Transatlantic slave trade at its height
1517 Spanish crown authorizes slave trade to its South American colonies; rapid increase in importation of slaves to the New World	**1652** First Cape Colony settlement of Dutch East India Company	**1741–1856** United Sultanate of Oman and Zanzibar
1554–1659 Sa'did Sultanate in Morocco	**1660–1856** Omani domination of East Africa	**1754–1817** Usman Dan Fodio, founder of sultanate in northern and central Nigeria
1575 Union of Bornu and Kanem by Idris Alawma		**1762** End of Funj Sultanate in eastern Sudanic region
1591 Songhai Empire collapses		

THE AMERICAS

1500 – 1600	1600 – 1700	1700 – 1800
1519 Conquest of the Aztecs by Cortes	**1607** The London Company establishes Jamestown Colony	**1733** Georgia founded as last English colony in North America
1533 Pizarro begins his conquest of the Incas	**1608** Champlain founds Quebec	**1739–1763** Era of trade wars in Americas between Great Britain and the French and Spanish
1536 Spanish under Mendoza arrive in Argentina	**1619** Slave labor introduced at Jamestown (Virginia)	**1763** Peace of Paris establishes British government in Canada
1544 Lima becomes capital of the viceroyalty of Peru		**1776–1781** American Revolution
1584 Sir Walter Raleigh sends expedition to Roanoke Island (North Carolina)		**1783–1830** Simón Bolívar, Latin American soldier, statesman
		1789 U.S. Constitution
		1791 Negro slave revolt in French Santo Domingo
		1791 Canada Constitution Act divides the country into Upper and Lower Canada

Consolidation and Interaction of World Civilizations

500 C.E – 800	800 – 1100	1100 –1300	1300 –1500

EUROPE

500 C.E – 800	800 – 1100	1100 –1300	1300 –1500
511 Death of Clovis, Frankish ruler of Gaul	ca. 800–1000 Invasions of England and the Carolingian Empire (Vikings, Magyars, and Muslims)	1154–115 Frederick Barbarosa invades Italy	1337 Hundred Years' War begins
529 Benedict of Nursia founds Benedictine Order	843 Treaty of Verdun	1182–1226 St. Francis of Assisi	ca. 1340–1400 Geoffrey Chaucer
590–604 Pontificate of Gregory I, "The Great"	910 Cluny Monastery founded	1198–1216 Pontificate of Innocent III	1347–1349 The Black Death
768–814 Charlemagne	1019–1054 Yaroslav the Wise reigns; peak of Kievan Russia	ca. 1100–1300 Growth of trade and towns	1375–1527 The Italian Renaissance
	1054 Schism between Latin and Greek churches	1215 Magna Carta granted	1485 Battle of Bosworth Field; accession of Henry Tudor to the throne of England
	1066 Norman Conquest of England	ca. 1225–1274 St. Thomas Aquinas	1492 Columbus's first voyage to the New World
	1073–1085 Investiture controversy	265–1321 Dante Alighieri	
	1096–1270 The Crusades		

NEAR EAST/ASIA

500 C.E – 800	800 – 1100	1100 –1300	1300 –1500
527–565 Justinian's reign	800–120 Period of feudal overlordship in India	1174–1193 Saladin reigns	1250–1517 Mamluk rule in Egypt
531–579 Reign of Chosroes Anosharvian in Iran	900–1100 Golden age of Muslim learning	1192 Muslim conquerors end Buddhism in India	1366–1405 Timur (Tamerlane) reigns
ca. 570–632 Muhammad	909–1171 Fatimids in North Africa and Egypt	1206–1526 Delhi Sultanate in India	1405–1494 Timurids rule in Transoxiana and Iran
622 The Hijra	945–1055 Buyid rule in Baghdad	ca. 1220 Mongol invasions of Iran, Iraq, Syria, India	1453 Byzantine Empire falls to the Ottoman Turks
616–657 Reign of Harsha	994–1186 Ghaznavid rule in northwestern India, Afghanistan, and Iran	1258 Hulagu Khan, Mongol leader, conquers Baghdad	
651 Death of last Sasanid ruler	1055–1194 Seljuk rule in Baghdad	1260–1335 Il-Khans rule Iran	
661–750 Umayyad dynasty	1071 Seljuk Turks capture Jerusalem		
680 Death of Al-Husayn at Karbala	1081–1118 Byzantine emperor Alexius Comnenus reigns		
ca. 710 First Muslim invasion of India	ca. 1000–1300 Turko-Afghan raids into India		
750–1258 Abbasid dynasty			
786–809 Caliph Harun Al-Rashid reigns			

EAST ASIA

500 C.E – 800	800 – 1100	1100 –1300	1300 –1500
589–618 Sui dynasty reunifies China	856–1086 Fujiwara dominate Heian court	1130–1200 Chu Hsi, Song philosopher	1336–1467 Ashikaga shogunate in Kyoto
607 Japan begins embassies to China	960–1279 Sung dynasty in China	1167–1227 Genghis Khan, founder of Mongol Empire	1368–1644 Ming dynasty in China
618–907 Tang dynasty in China	ca. 1000 *Pillow Book* by Shohōnagon and *Tale of Genji* by Murasaki Shikibu	1185–1333 Kamakura shogunate in Japan	1405–1433 Voyages of Cheng Ho
701–762 Li Po, Tang poet	1037–1101 Su Tung-p'o, Sung poet	1274–1281 Mongol invasions of Japan	1467–1568 Warring States era in Japan
710–784 Nara court, Japan's first permanent capital		1279–1368 Mongol (Yuan) dynasty in China	1472–1529 Wang Yang-ming, Ming philosopher
712 Records of Ancient Matters, in Japan			
713–756 Emperor Hsuan Tsung reigns in China			
755 An Lu-shan rebellion in China			
794–1185 Heian (Kyoto) court in Japan			

AFRICA

500 C.E – 800	800 – 1100	1100 –1300	1300 –1500
ca. 500 States of Takrur and Ghana founded	ca. 800–900 Decline of Aksum	ca. 1100–1897 Kingdom of Benin in tropical rain forest region	1307–1332 Mansa Musa, greatest king of Mali
ca. 500–700 Political and commercial ascendancy of Aksum (Ethiopia)	ca. 900–1100 Kingdom of Ghana; capital city, Kumbi Saleh	1194–1221 Kanem Empire achieves greatest expansion	1490s Europeans establish trading posts on western African coast
ca. 600–1500 Extensive slave trade from sub-Saharan Africa to Mediterranean	ca. 1000–1100 Islam penetrates sub-Saharan Africa	1203 Kingdom of Ghana falls to Sosso people	mid-1400s Decline of Mali Empire; creation of Songhai Empire
ca. 700–800 Ghanians begin to supply gold to Mediterranean	1000–1500 "Great Zimbabwe" center of Bantu Kingdom in southeastern Africa	1230–1255 King Sundiata, first ruler of Mali Empire	1468 Sonni Ali captures Timbuktu
ca. 700–900 States of Gao and Kanem		ca. 1230–1450 Kingdom of Mali Empire	1476–1507 Reign of King Mai Ali of Bornu in central Sudan
ca. 800 Appearance of the Kanur people around Lake Chad			1493–1528 Songhai ruler Askia Muhammed reigns; consolidates Songhai Empire

THE AMERICAS

500 C.E – 800	800 – 1100	1100 –1300	1300 –1500
ca. 150–900 Classic period. Dominance of Teotihuacán in central Mexico, Tikal in southern Yucatán	ca. 600–1000 Middle (Huari/Tiwanaku) Horizon in Andean South America	ca. 800–1400 Chimu Empire on north coast of Peru	1325 Founding of Aztec capital
			1428–1519 Period of Aztec expansion
			1492 European encounter with America
			1519 Cortes conquers Aztec Empire
			ca. 1350–1533 Inca Empire in Peru
			1533 Pizarro executes Inca ruler Atahualpa

STUDY IN TIME

A Chronological Survey of World History

Enlightenment, Revolution, and Modernity

1750 – 1850

1850 – 1914

EUROPE

1756–1763 Seven Years' War
1783 Peace of Paris, ending American Revolution
1789 French Revolution begins
1804–1814 Napoleon's empire
1814–1815 Congress of Vienna
1832 First British Reform Act
1837–1901 Queen Victoria of England
1848 Revolutions across Europe

1854–1856 The Crimean War
1861 Italy unified
1861 Emancipation of Russian serfs
1866 Austro-Prussian War; creation of Dual Monarchy of Austria-Hungary in 1867
1870–1871 Franco-Prussian War; German Empire proclaimed in 1871
1882 Triple Alliance
1905 Revolution in Russia
1914 World War I begins in Europe

NEAR EAST/ASIA

1757 British victory at Plassey, in Bengal
1772–1833 Ram Mohan Roy, Hindu reformer in India
1794–1925 Qajar shahs in Iran
1805–1849 Muhammad Ali in Egypt
ca. 1839–1880 Tanzimat reforms, Ottoman Empire
1839–1897 Muslim intellectual Jamal al-Din Al-Afghani

1857–1858 Sepoy Rebellion, India
1869 Suez Canal completed
1869–1948 Mohandas (Mahatma) Gandhi
1876–1949 Muhammad Ali Jinnah, "founder of Pakistan"
1882 English occupation of Egypt
1886 India National Congress formed
1889–1964 Jawaharlal Nehru
1899 Ottoman sultan grants concession to Germany to extend railway to Baghdad
1908 "Young Turk" Revolt, Turkey

EAST ASIA

1787–1793 Matsudaira Sadanobu's reforms in Japan
1789 White Lotus Rebellion in China
1835–1908 Empress Dowager Tz'u-hsi
1839–1842 Opium War

1850–1873 Taiping and other rebellions, China
1853–1854 Commodore Perry "opens" Japan to the West
1860s Establishment of treaty ports in China
1870s–1890s Self-Strengthening movement in China
1889 Meiji Constitution in Japan
1894–1895 Sino-Japanese War
1898–1900 Boxer Rebellion in China
1904–1905 Russo-Japanese War
1910 Japan annexes Korea
1911 Republican Revolution begins in China

AFRICA

1754–1817 Usman Dan Fodio, founder of Sultanate in northern and central Nigeria
1762 End of Funj sultanate in eastern Sudanic region
1806 British take Cape Colony from the Dutch
1817–1828 Zulu chief Shaka reigns
1830–1847 French invasion of Algeria
1830s Dutch settlers, the Boers, expand northward from Cape Colony
1848–1885 Sudanese Madhi, Muhammad Ahmad

1856–1884 King Mutasa of Buganda reigns
1880s Mahdist revival and uprising in Sudan
1880 French protectorate in Tunisia and the Ivory Coast
1885 British control Nigeria and British East Africa
1894 French annex Dahomey
1899 German East Africa; British in Sudan
1899–1902 Boer War
1900 Nigeria a British Crown colony
1907 Union of South Africa formed
1911 Liberia becomes a virtual U.S. protectorate
1914 Ethiopia the only independent state in Africa

THE AMERICAS

1776 American Declaration of Independence
1791 First ten amendments to U.S. Constitution (Bill of Rights) ratified
1791 Negro slave revolt in French Santo Domingo
1804 Haitian independence
1808–1824 Wars of independence in Latin America
1822 Brazilian independence
1847 Mexican War

1854 Kansas-Nebraska Act
1856 Dred Scott Decision
1859 Raid on Harper's Ferry
1860 Abraham Lincoln elected U.S. president
1861–1865 U.S. Civil War
1862–1867 French invasion of Mexico
1863 Emancipation Proclamation in United States
1865–1877 Reconstruction
1880s Slavery eliminated in Cuba and Brazil
1898 Spanish-American War
1901 Theodore Roosevelt elected U.S. president
1910–1917 Mexican Revolution
1912 Woodrow Wilson elected U.S. president

Empires and Cultures of the Ancient World

3000 B.C.E	1500 B.C.E	500 B.C.E	300 B.C.E	1 C.E.

EUROPE

3000 B.C.E	1500 B.C.E	500 B.C.E	300 B.C.E	1 C.E.
ca. 2500–1100 Minoan civilization ca. 1600–1100 Mycenaean civilization on Greek mainland	ca. 1100–800 Greek "dark ages" 800 Etruscan civilization begins in Italy ca. 750–550 Rise of the polis 594 Solon's legislation at Athens 509 Foundation of the Roman Republic 508 Democracy established in Athens	480–479 Persian invasion of Greece 478 Foundation of Delian League/Athenian Empire 431–404 Peloponnesian Wars 338 Battle of Chaeronia; Macedonian conquest of Greece 336–323 Career of Alexander the Great	264 Rome rules all of Italy 146 Rome destroys Carthage; rules all of western Mediterranean 44–31 Civil wars destroy Roman Republic 31 Rome rules Mediterranean 31 b.c.e.–14 c.e. Principate of Augustus	96–180 The good emperors rule Rome 180–284 Breakdown of the Pax Romana 306–337 Constantine reigns 313 Edict of Milan 325 Council of Nicaea 391 Theodosius makes Christianity the official imperial religion ca. 400–500 The Germanic invasions 426 The City of God, by Augustine 476 The last Western emperor is deposed

NEAR EAST/ASIA

3000 B.C.E	1500 B.C.E	500 B.C.E	300 B.C.E	1 C.E.
ca. 3500–3000 Emergence of Sumerian city–states ca. 3000 Emergence of civilization along the Nile River ca. 2300 Emergence of Harappan civilization in Indus valley 2276–2221 Sargon of Akkad creates the first Mesopotamian Empire ca. 2000 Epic of Gilgamesh 1750 Hammurabi's code	ca. 1500 Aryan peoples migrate into northwestern India 960–933 Rule of Hebrew king Solomon ca. 628–551 Life of Zarathushtra ca. 537–486 Siddhartha Gautama 559–529 Cyrus the Great creates the Persian Empire	ca. 540–468 Vardhamana Mahavira, founder of Jain tradition 334 Alexander begins conquest of the Near East; invades India in 327 321–181 Mauryan Empire in India	ca. 300 Founding of Seleucid dynasty in Anatolia, Syria, and Mesopotamia; Ptolemaic dynasty in Egypt 269–232 Mauryan emperor Ashoka patronizes Buddhism 247 b.c.e.–224 c.e. Parthian dynasty controls Persia 180 b.c.e.–320 c.e. India politically divided	30 Crucifixion of Jesus 70 Romans destroy the Temple at Jerusalem 216–277 Mani ca. 224 Fall of Parthians, rise of Sasanids, in Persia ca. 320–500 Gupta dynasty, India ca. 400 Chandra Gupta conquers western India ca. 450 The Huns invade India

EAST ASIA

3000 B.C.E	1500 B.C.E	500 B.C.E	300 B.C.E	1 C.E.
ca. 4000 Neolithic cultures in China ca. 8000–300 Jōmon culture in Japan ca. 1766–1050 Hang dynasty in China with city–states and writing	1027–771 Western Chou dynasty, China 771–256 Eastern Chou dynasty in China ca. 771 Iron Age territoria states in China 551–479 Confucius in China	ca. 500–200 Rise of Mohist, Taoist, and Legalist schools of thought in China 401–256 Period of the Warring States in China ca. 300 Old Stone Age Jōmon culture in Japan replaced by Yayoi culture	256–206 Ch'in dynasty in China 221 Ch'in emperor unites all of China 206 b.c.e.–8 c.e. Former Han dynasty in China 179–104 Han philosopher Tung Chung-shu 145–90 Han historian Ssu-ma Chien 141–187 Emperor Wu Ti of China reigns	25–220 The Later Han dynasty, China ca. 220–590 Spread of Buddhism in China 220–589 Six Dynasties period in China ca. 300–500 Barbarian invasions of China ca. 300–680 Archaic Yamato state in Japan

AFRICA

3000 B.C.E	1500 B.C.E	500 B.C.E	300 B.C.E	1 C.E.
ca. 3000 Practice of agriculture spreads from Nile river valley to the Sudan ca. 2000 Ivory and gold trade between Kush (Nubia) and Egypt ca. 1500 Practice of agriculture spreads from the Sudan to Abyssinia and the savanna region	750 Kushite king Kashta conquers Upper Egypt ca. 720 Kushite king Piankhy completes conquest of Egypt ca. 600 Meroitic period of Kushan civilization begins		25 Romans sack Kushite capital of Napata 00 b.c.e.–1 c.e. Probable first Indonesian migrations to east African coast	ca. 200 Camel first used for trans-Saharan transport ca. 200–900 Expansion of Bantu people ca. 250 Aksum (Ethiopia) controls the Red Sea trade ca. 300–400 Rise of kingdom of Ghana a. 350 Kush ceases to exist

THE AMERICAS

3000 B.C.E	1500 B.C.E	500 B.C.E	300 B.C.E	1 C.E.
ca. 4000 Maize already domesticated in Mexico	ca. 1500–800 Olmec civilization in Mesoamerica a. 800–200 Chavín (Early) Horizon in Andean South America	ca. 500–20 Founding of Monte Albán		ca. 200–600 Early Intermediate period in Andean South America; Moche and Nazca cultures ca. 150–900 Classic period. Dominance of Teotihuacán in central Mexico, Tikal in southern Yucatán

The Birth of Civilization

8000 B.C.E	3500 B.C.E	1500 B.C.E	1000 B.C.E	500 B.C.
EUROPE				
End of Paleolithic introduction of farming	Copper Age	Bronze Age	624–545 Thales of Miletus ca. 611–546 Anaximander ca. 546 Anaximenes	469–399 Socrates 429–347 Plato 384–322 Aristotle 435–404 Great Peloponnesian War ca. 460–400 Thucydides ca. 400 Hippocrates of Cos 384–322 Demosthenes
NEAR EAST/ASIA				
ca. 8000 Neolithic Revolution, Mesopotamia	ca. 3500 Development of Sumerian Cities ca. 3000 Development of Writing in Mesopotamia ca. 2800–2370 Early Dynastic period of Sumerian city–states ca. 2370 Sargon establishes Akkadian dynasty and empire ca. 2250–1750 Indus (Harappan) civilization; writing first appears in India ca. 2125–2027 Third dynasty of Ur ca. 2000–1800 Establishment of Amorites in Mesopotamia ca. 1800–1500 Aryan peoples invade northwestern India ca. 1792–1750 Reign of Hammurabi ca. 1550 Establishment of Kassite dynasty at Babylon	ca. 1500–1000 Rig-Vedic period, India ca. 1400–1200 Hittite Empire ca. 1100 Rise of Assyrian Power	ca. 1000–961 Reign of King David ca. 961–922 Reign of King Solomon ca. 1000–500 Late Vedic period, India ca. 1000–800/600 Composition of Brahmanas ca. 800–500 Composition of major Upanishads ca. 700–500 Probable reintroduction of writing 732–722 Assyrian conquest of Syria-Palestine 722 Assyrian conquest of Israel (Northern Kingdom) 612 Destruction of Assyrian capital at Nineveh 612–539 Neo-Babylonian (Chaldean) Empire 586 Destruction of Jerusalem fall of Judah (southern kingdom); Babylonian captivity 539 Restoration of Temple; return of exiles 540–ca. 468 Mahavira ca. 566–ca. 486 Siddhartha Gautama, the Buddha	ca. 400 b.c.e.–200 c.e. Composition of great epics, the *Mahabharata* and *Ramayana*
EAST ASIA				
4000 b.c.e. Neolithic Revolution	2205–1766 Xia dynasty 1766 Bronze Age city–states 1766–1050 Shang dynasty	1050–256 Zhou dynasty	771 Iron Age territorial states 551–479 Confucius	500 Age of philosophers 370–290 Mencius **Fourth century** Laozi 221 China is unified under the Qin
AFRICA				
	3100–2700 Early Dynastic period, Egypt ca. 3000 Writing first appears in Egypt 2700–2200 Old Kingdom (III–VI) 2200–2025 First Intermediate period 2025–1630 Middle Kingdom 1630–1550 Second Intermediate period 1550–1075 New Kindom		671 Assyrian conquest of Egypt	
THE AMERICAS				
ca. 4000 Neolithic revolution in Mexico	ca. 2750 Monumental architecture at Aspero	1500–400 The Olmec	800 b.c.e.–200 c.e. Chavin (Early) Horizon	200 b.c.e.–750 c.e. The Classic period in central Mexico 150 b.c.e.–900 c.e. The Classic period of Mayan civilization in the Yucatán and Guatemala

Global Conflict and Change

1914 – 1970   1970 – 2005

EUROPE

1914–1970	1970–2005
1917 Bolsheviks seize power, Russia	**1972** British Impose direct rule on N. Ireland
1919 Versailles Settlement	**1972** Israeli Olympic athletes killed by Arab terrorists
1922 Mussolini seizes power, Italy	**1974** Portuguese dictatorship deposed
1933 Hitler comes to power	**1977** Brezhnev president of USSR
1936 Spanish Civil War begins	**1979** Margaret Thatcher becomes British prime minister
1939 World War II begins	**1980** Solidarity Movement in Poland
1945 World War II ends	**1984** Mikhail Gorbachev introduces *glasnost* in USSR
1948 Berlin blockade and airlift	**1989** Berlin Wall demolished
1949 NATO treaty; Russia detonates atomic bomb	**1990** Germany unified
1955 Warsaw Pact	**1991** Failed coup in Soviet Union; Yeltsin emerges as leader of Russia
1956 Soviets crush Hungarian revolt	**1993** Czechoslovakia divides into two republics
1957 EEC founded	**1995** Dayton Peace Accords end war in Bosnia
1958 Charles de Gaulle comes to power in France	**2000** Putin elected president of Russia
1961 Berlin Wall erected	**2005** Angela Merkl becomes chancellor of Germany
1968 Soviets invade Czechoslovakia	

NEAR EAST/ASIA

1914–1970	1970–2005
1922 British leave Egypt	**1973** Arab-Israeli October War
\1922–1938 Mustafa Kemal first president of Turkey	**1973** OPEC oil embargo
1928 The Muslim Brotherhood founded	**1978** Iranian revolution
1947 Indian Independence; creation of Pakistan	**1979** Egyptian-Israeli Peace Treaty
1949 State of Israel founded	**1979** Iran takes U.S. hostages
1953 Mosaddeq overthrown in Iran	**1979** Soviets invade Afghanistan
1954–1970 Abdel Nasser leads Egypt	**1980–1988** Iran-Iraq War
1956 Suez Crisis	**1981** Egypt's Sadat assassinated
1966 Indira Gandhi becomes prime minister of India	**1982** Israel invades Lebanon
1967 Israeli-Arab June War	**1989** Soviets leave Afghanistan
	1990–1991 Gulf War

EAST ASIA

1914–1970	1970–2005
1919 May 4th Movement in China	**1959–1975** Vietnam War
1925 Universal male suffrage in Japan	**1965–1976** Cultural Revolution devastates China
1928–1937 Nationalist government in China	**1972** President Nixon visits China
1931 Japan occupies Manchuria	**1976** Death of Mao Zedong
1937–1945 Japan at war with China	**1978–1989** New Economic policies of Deng Xiaoping in China
1941 Japan attacks Pearl Harbor	**1988** Japan's GNP second in world
1945 Japan surrenders	**1989** China crushes pro-democracy demonstrations in Beijing
1949 People's Republic of China founded	**1991–1992** Political scandals and plummeting stock market in Japan
1950 N. Korea invades S. Korea	**2004** Tsunami strikes Indian Ocean
1952 U.S. ends occupation of Japan	
1959–1960 Sino-Soviet split	

AFRICA

1914–1970	1970–2005
1919 Pan-African Congress in Paris	**1967–1970** Nigerian Civil War
1935 Mussolini invades Ethiopia	**1974** Drought and famine in Africa
1942–1945 World War II engulfs North Africa	**1974** Emperor Haile Selassie of Ethiopia is deposed
1955–1962 Wars of independence in French Algeria	**1974–1975** Portugal grants independence to Guinea, Angola, Mozambique, Cape Verde
1956 Sudan gains independenc	**1980** Southern Rhodesia (Zimbabwe) gains independence from Britain
1956 Morocco and Tunisia gain independence	**1984** Bishop Desmond Tutu awarded Nobel Peace Prize
1957 Ghana an independent state	**1985** U.S. economic sanctions against South Africa
1960 Belgian Congo granted independence	**1992** Nelson Mandela freed from prison in South Africa
1963 Kenya becomes an independent republic	**1994** Nelson Mandela elected president of South Africa
1965 Revolution in Kenya	**2004** Ellen Johnson–Sirleaf becomes woman president of Liberia

THE AMERICAS

1914–1970	1970–2005
1917 U.S. enters World War I	**1970** Allende elected in Chile
1930–1945 Vargas dictatorship in Brazil	**1972** Nixon visits China and USSR
1932 FDR U.S. president	**1973** Watergate scandal breaks
1938 Mexico nationalizes oil industry	**1973** Perón reelected, Argentina
1941 U.S. enters World War II	**1973** Chile's Allende overthrown
1945 Death of FDR	**1979** Revolution in Nicaragua and El Salvador
1946 Perón elected president in Argentina	**1980** Reagan elected president
1954 U.S. Supreme Court outlaws segregation	**1983** Argentine military government overthrown
1955 Perón overthrown	**1983** End of Mexican oil boom
1956 Montgomery bus boycott	**1988** Major arms agreement between U.S. and USSR
1959 Fidel Castro comes to power in Cuba	**1991** Gulf War
1962 Cuban Missile Crisis	**1992** Clinton elected president
1964 Passage of Civil Rights Act	**1994** Revolt in Chiapas, Mexico
1965 U.S. expands Vietnam commitment	**1998** Pope visits Cuba
1968 Martin Luther King and Robert Kennedy assassinated	**2001** Terrorists attack the U. S.
	2005 New Orleans devastated by Hurricane Katrina

absolutism Term applied to strong centralized continental monarchies that attempted to make royal power dominant over aristocracies and other regional authorities.

Acropolis Religious and civic center of Athens. It is the site of the Parthenon.

Afrikaans New language, derived from Dutch, that evolved in the 17th- and 18th-century Cape Colony.

agape Meaning "love feast." A common meal that was part of the central ritual of early Christian worship.

agora Greek marketplace and civic center. It was the heart of the social life of the polis.

agricultural revolution Innovations in farm production that began in the eighteenth century and led to a scientific and mechanized agriculture.

amir/emir Islamic military commander.

Amitabha Buddha Buddhist Lord of the Western Paradise, or Pure Land.

Annam Chinese term for Vietnam.

Anschluss Meaning "union." Annexation of Austria by Germany in March 1938.

anti-Semitism Prejudice, hostility, or legal discrimination against Jews.

apartheid "Apartness," the term referring to racist policies enforced by the White-dominated regime that existed in South Africa from 1948 to 1992.

apostolic primacy Doctrine that the popes are the direct successors to the Apostle Peter and as such heads of the church.

appeasement Anglo-French policy of making concessions to Germany in the 1930s to avoid a crisis that would lead to war. It assumed that Germany had real grievances and Hitler's aims were limited and ultimately acceptable.

Areopagus Governing council of Athens, originally open only to the nobility. Named after the hill on which it met.

Arianism Belief formulated by Arius of Alexandria (ca. 280–336 C.E.) that Jesus was a created being, neither fully man nor fully God, but something in between.

aristocratic resurgence Eighteenth-century aristocratic efforts to resist the expanding power of European monarchies.

Aryans Indo-European people who invaded India and Iran in the second and first millenia B.C.E.

assignats Government bonds based on the value of confiscated church lands issued during the early French Revolution.

Atman-Brahman The unchanging, infinite principle of reality in Indian religion.

Atomists School of ancient Greek philosophy founded in the fifth century B.C.E. by Leucippus of Miletus and Democritus of Abdera. It held that the world consists of innumerable, tiny, solid, indivisible, and unchangeable particles called atoms.

Augustus Title given to Octavian in 27 B.C.E. and borne thereafter by all Roman emperors.

ausgleich Meaning "compromise." Agreement between the Habsburg emperor and the Hungarians to give Hungary considerable administrative autonomy in 1867. It created the Dual Monarchy, or Austria-Hungary.

Axis Alliance between Nazi Germany and Fascist Italy. Also called the Pact of Steel.

ayatollah Major Shi'ite religious leader.

bakufu "Tent government." Military regime that governed Japan under the shoguns.

bazaari Iranian commercial middle class.

bhakti Hindu devotional movements.

Black Death Bubonic plague that killed millions of Europeans in the 14th century.

Black Legend Argument that Spanish treatment of Native Americans was uniquely inhumane.

Blitzkrieg Meaning "war by lightening strokes." German tactic early in World War II of employing fast-moving, massed armored columns supported by air power to overwhelm the enemy.

bodhisattva A "Buddha to be" who postpones his own nirvana until he has helped all other beings become enlightened.

Bolsheviks Meaning the "majority." Term Lenin applied to his faction of the Russian Social Democratic Party. It became the Communist Party of the Soviet Union after the Russian Revolution.

Boxers Nationalistic Chinese religious society that attacked foreigners and their encroachments on China in the late 19th century.

boyars Russian nobility.

Brahmanas Texts dealing with the ritual application of the Vedas.

Bronze Age The name given to the earliest civilized era, ca. 4000 to 1000 B.C.E. The term reflects the importance of the metal bronze for the people of this age in making weapons and tools.

caliphate Spiritual and temporal rule of the Muslim community.

calpulli Wards into which the Aztec capital, Tenochtitlan, was divided.

cantonments Segregation of areas in which Europeans lived in British-ruled India from those areas inhabited by native Indians.

Catholic emancipation Grant of full political rights to Roman Catholics in Britain in 1829.

Catholic Meaning "universal." The body of belief held by most Christians enshrined within the church.

caudillo Latin American strongman, or dictator, usually with close ties to the military.

Censorate Branch of the imperial Chinese government that acted as a watchdog, reporting instances of misgovernment directly to the emperor and remonstrating when it considered the emperor's behavior improper.

censor Official of the Roman republic charged with conducting the census and compiling the lists of citizens and members of the Senate.

Chartism First large-scale European working-class political movement. It sought political reforms that would favor the interests of skilled British workers in the 1830s and 1840s.

chiaroscuro Use of shading to enhance naturalness in painting and drawing.

chicha Maize beer brewed by the mamakuna for the Inca elite.

chun-tzu The Confucian term for a person who behaves ethically, in harmony with the cosmic order.

civilization A form of human culture marked by urbanism, metallurgy, and writing.

clash of civilizations Political theory, most often identified with Harvard political scientist Samuel P. Huntington, which contends that conflict between the world's religio-cultural traditions or "civilizations" increasingly dominates world affairs.

Cold War Ideological and geographical struggle between the United States and its allies and the USSR and its allies that began after World War II and lasted until the dissolution of the USSR in 1989.

collectivization Bedrock of Stalinist agriculture, which forced Russian peasants to give up their private farms and work as members of collectives, large agricultural units controlled by the state.

conquistadores Meaning "conquerors." Spanish conquerors of the New World.

Consulate French government dominated by Napoleon from 1799 to 1804.

Convention French radical legislative body from 1792 to 1794.

Council of Nicaea Council of Christian bishops at Nicaea in 325 C.E. that formulated the Nicene Creed, a statement of Christian belief that rejected Arianism in favor of the doctrine that Christ is both fully human and fully divine.

Counter-Reformation Sixteenth-century reform movement in the Roman Catholic Church in reaction to the Protestant Reformation.

Creole A person of European descent born in Latin America or the Caribbean.

Crusades Religious wars directed by the church against infidels and heretics.

Cultural Revolution Movement launched by Mao between 1965 and 1976 against the Soviet-style bureaucracy that had taken hold in China. It involved widespread disorder and violence.

culture The ways of living built up by a group and passed on from one generation to another.

cuneiform A writing system invented by the Sumerians that used a wedge-shaped stylus, or pointed tool, to write on wet clay tablets that were then baked or dried (*cuneus* means "wedge" in Latin). The writing was also cut into stone.

Curia Papal government.

daimyo Japanese territorial lord.

Daoism A Chinese philosophy that teaches that wisdom lies in becoming one with the *Dao*, the "way," which is the creative principle of the universe.

debt peonage Requirement that laborers remain and continue to work on a hacienda until they had paid their debts to the owner for goods bought from him on credit.

deism Belief in a rational God who had created the universe, but then allowed it to function without his interference according to the mechanisms of nature and a belief in rewards and punishments after death for human action.

Delian League Alliance of Greek states under the leadership of Athens that was formed in 478–477 B.C.E. to resist the Persians.

demesne Part of a manor that was cultivated directly for the lord of the manor.

devshirme System under the Ottoman Empire that required each province to furnish a levy of Christian boys who were raised as Muslims and became soldiers in the Ottoman army.

dharma Moral law or duty.

diaspora Dispersion of an originally homogeneous people or culture. Among the many diasporas in world history, some of the most famous are the Jewish, the Chinese, the African, the Irish, and the Armenian.

Diet of Worms Meeting of the representatives (diet) of the Holy Roman Empire, presided over by the Emperor Charles V at the German city of Worms in 1521, at which Martin Luther was ordered to recant his ninety-five theses. Luther refused and was declared an outlaw although he was protected by the Elector of Saxony and other German princes.

Diet Bicameral Japanese parliament.

divine right of kings Theory that monarchs are appointed by and answerable only to God.

domestic or putting-out system of textile production Method of producing textiles in which agents furnished raw materials to households whose members spun them into thread and then wove cloth, which the agents sold as finished products.

Duce Meaning "leader." Mussolini's title as head of the Fascist Party.

Duma Russian parliament, after the revolution of 1905.

dynastic cycle Term used to describe the rise, decline, and fall of China's imperial dynasties.

ego According to Freudian theory, the part of the mind that mediates between the impulses of the id and the asceticism of the superego and allows the personality to cope with the inner and outer demands of its existence.

empiricism Use of experiment and observation derived from sensory evidence to construct scientific theory or philosophy of knowledge.

enclosures Consolidation or fencing in of common lands by British landlords to increase production and achieve greater commercial profits. It also involved the reclamation of waste land and the consolidation of strips into block fields.

encomienda Grant by the Spanish crown to a colonist of the labor of a specific number of Indians for a set period of time.

Enlightenment Eighteenth-century movement led by the philosophes that held that change and reform were both desirable through the application of reason and science.

Epicureans School of philosophy founded by Epicurus of Athens (342–271 B.C.E.). It sought to liberate people from fear of death and the supernatural by teaching that the gods took no interest in human affairs and that true happiness consisted in pleasure, which was defined as the absence of pain.

equestrians Literally "cavalrymen" or "knights." In the earliest years of the Roman republic, those who could afford to serve as mounted warriors.

Estado Novo "New state" based on political stability and economic and social progress supposedly established by the dictator Getulio Vargas after 1937.

Etruscans A people of central Italy who exerted the most powerful external influence on the early Romans.

Eucharist Meaning "thanksgiving." Celebration of the Lord's Supper. Considered the central ritual of worship by most Christians. Also called Holy Communion.

euro Common currency created by the EEC in the late 1990s.

European Economic Community Economic association formed by France, Germany, Italy, Belgium, the Netherlands, and Luxembourg in 1957. Also known as the Common Market.

European Union New name given to the EEC in 1993. It included most of the states of Western Europe.

Fabians British Socialists in the late 19th and early 20th centuries who sought to achieve socialism through gradual, peaceful, and democratic means.

family economy Basic structure of production and consumption in preindustrial Europe.

fascism Political movements that tend to be antidemocratic, anti-Marxist, antiparliamentary, and often anti-Semitic. Fascists were invariably nationalists and exhalted the nation over the individual. They supported the interests of the middle class and rejected the ideas of the French Revolution and 19th-century liberalism. The first fascist regime was founded by Benito Mussolini (1883–1945) in Italy in the 1920s.

fealty Oath of loyalty by a vassal to a lord, promising to perform specified services.

feudal society Social, political, military, and economic system that prevailed in the Middle Ages and beyond in some parts of Europe.

fief Land granted to a vassal in exchange for services, usually military.

Fourteen Points President Woodrow Wilson's (1856–1924) idealistic war aims.

Führer Meaning "leader." Title taken by Hitler when he became dictator of Germany.

gentry In China, a largely urban, landowning class that represented local interests and functioned as quasi-bureaucrats under the magistrates.

ghazis Warriors who carried Islam by force of arms to pagan groups.

ghettos Separate communities in which Jews were required by law to live.

glasnost Meaning "openness." Policy initiated by Mikhail Gorbachev in the 1980s of permitting open criticism of the policies of the Soviet Communist Party.

globalization Term used to describe the increasing economic and cultural interdependence of societies around the world.

Glorious Revolution Largely peaceful replacement of James II by William and Mary as English monarchs in 1688. It marked the beginning of constitutional monarchy in Britain.

Golden Horde Name given to the Mongol rulers of Russia from 1240 to 1480.

Grand Mufti Chief religious authority of the Ottoman Empire. Also called "the Shaykh of Islam."

Great Depression Prolonged worldwide economic downturn that began in 1929 with the collapse of the New York Stock Exchange.

Great Leap Forward Mao's disastrous attempt to modernize the Chinese economy in 1958.

Great Purges Imprisonment and execution of millions of Soviet citizens by Stalin between 1934 and 1939.

Great Reform Bill (1832) Limited reform of the British House of Commons and expansion of the electorate to include a wider variety of the propertied classes. It laid the groundwork for further orderly reforms within the British constitutional system.

Great Schism Appearance of two and at times three rival popes between 1378 and 1415.

Great Trek Migration between 1835 and 1847 of Boer pioneers (called *voortrekkers*) north from British-ruled Cape Colony to establish their own independent republics.

guild Association of merchants or craftsmen that offered protection to its members and set rules for their work and products.

Guomindang (GMT) China's Nationalist Party, founded by Sun Zhongshan.

hacienda Large landed estates in Spanish America.

hadith Saying or action ascribed to Muhammad.

Hajj Pilgrimage to Mecca that all Muslims are enjoined to perform at least once in their lifetime.

Harappan Term used to describe the first civilization of the Indus Valley.

Hegira Flight of Muhammad and his followers from Mecca to Medina in 622 C.E. It marks the beginning of the Islamic calendar.

heliocentric theory The theory, now universally accepted, that the Earth and the other planets revolve around the sun. First proposed by Aristarchos of Samos (310–230 B.C.E.).

Helots Hereditary Spartan serfs.

heretics Persons whose religious beliefs differ from the official doctrines of their faith.

hieroglyphics The complicated writing script of ancient Egypt. It combined picture writing with pictographs and sound signs. Hieroglyph means "sacred carvings" in Greek.

Hindu Term applied to the diverse social, racial, linguistic, and religious groups of India.

Holocaust Nazi extermination of millions of European Jews between 1940 and 1945. Also called the "final solution to the Jewish problem."

Holy Roman Empire Revival of the old Roman Empire, based mainly in Germany and northern Italy, that endured from 870 to 1806.

home rule Advocacy of a large measure of administrative autonomy for Ireland within the British Empire between the 1880s and 1914.

hoplite phalanx Basic unit of Greek warfare in which infantrymen fought in close order, shield to shield, usually eight ranks deep.

Huguenots French Calvinists.

humanism Study of the Latin and Greek classics and of the Church Fathers both for their own sake and to promote a rebirth of ancient norms and values.

humanitas Roman name for a liberal arts education.

id According to Freudian psychoanalysis, the part of the mind that consists of amoral, irrational, driving instincts for sexual gratification, aggression, and physical and sensual pleasure.

imam Islamic prayer leader.

impact of modernity Effect of western political, economic, and social ideas and institutions on traditional societies.

imperator Under the Roman republic, the title given to a victorious general. Under Augustus and his successors, it became the title of the ruler of Rome, meaning "emperor."

imperium In ancient Rome, the right to issue commands and to enforce them by fines, arrests, and even corporal and capital punishment.

import substitution Replacement of imported goods with those manufactured domestically.

Indo-European A widely distributed language group that includes most of the languages spoken in Europe, Persian, Sanskrit, and their derivatives.

Indo-Greeks Bactrian rulers who broke away from the Seleucid Empire to found a state that combined elements of Greek and Indian civilizations.

indulgences Remission of the temporal penalty of punishment in purgatory that remained after sins had been forgiven.

Industrial Revolution Mechanization of the European economy that began in Britain in the second half of the 18th century.

intifadah Literally, "shaking." Uprisings by the Palestinians against Israeli occupation.

Islam "Submission." Religion founded by the prophet Muhammad.

Italia Irredenta Meaning "unredeemed Italy." Italian-speaking areas that had been left under Austrian rule at the time of the unification of Italy.

Jacobins Radical republican party during the French Revolution that displaced the Girondists.

Jains Indian religious community that teaches compassion for all beings.

Janissaries Elite Ottoman troops who were recruited through the *devshirme*.

jatis The many subgroups that make up the Hindu caste system.

jihad "Struggle in the path of God." Although not necessarily implying violence, it is often interpreted to mean holy war in the name of Islam.

July Monarchy French regime set up after the overthrow of the Bourbons in July 1830.

Junkers Noble landlords of Prussia.

Ka'ba A black meteorite in the city of Mecca that became Islam's holiest shrine.

Kabuki Realistic form of Japanese theater similar to English Elizabethan drama.

Kalahari A large desert in southwestern Africa that partially isolates southern Africa from the rest of the continent.

kamikaze "Divine winds" that sank a portion of the invading Mongol fleet in Japan in 1281.

karma Indian belief that every action has an inevitable effect. Good deeds bring good results; evil deeds have evil consequences.

Khmer Rouge Meaning "Red Cambodia." Radical Communist movement that ruled Cambodia from 1975 to 1978.

kleindeutsch Meaning "small German." Argument that the German-speaking portions of the Habsburg Empire should be excluded from a united Germany.

Kristallnacht Meaning "crystal night" because of the broken glass that littered German streets after the looting and destruction of Jewish homes, businesses, and synagogues across Germany on the orders of the Nazi Party in November 1938.

La Reforma The 19th-century Mexican liberal reform movement that opposed Santa Ana's dictatorship and sought to foster economic progress, civilian rule, and political stability. It was strongly anticlerical.

laissez-faire French phrase meaning "allow to do." In economics, the doctrine of minimal government interference in the working of the economy.

latifundia Large plantations for growing cash crops owned by wealthy Romans.

LDP Liberal Democratic Party. A conservative party that has dominated postwar Japanese politics.

League of Nations Association of sovereign states set up after World War I to pursue common policies and avert international aggression.

Lebensraum "Living space," Nazi plan to colonize and exploit eastern Europe.

Legalism Chinese philosophical school that argued that a strong state was necessary to have a good society.

levée en masse French revolutionary conscription (1792) of all males into the army and the harnessing of the economy for war production.

liberalism In the 19th century, support for representative government dominated by the propertied classes and minimal government interference in the economy.

liberation theology Effort by certain Roman Catholic theologians to combine Marxism with traditional Christian concern for the poor.

logos Divine reason, or fire, which according to the Stoics, was the guiding principle in nature.

Long Count Mayan calendar that dated from a fixed point in the past.

Long March Flight of the Chinese communists from their nationalist foes to northwest China in 1934.

Luftwaffe German air force in World War II.

madrasa Islamic college of higher learning.

Magna Carta The "Great Charter" limiting royal power, which the English nobility forced King John to sign in 1215.

Magna Graecia Meaning "Great Greece" in Latin. The name given by the Romans to southern Italy and Sicily because there were so many Greek colonies in the region.

Magyars Majority ethnic group in Hungary.

Mahabharata and Ramayana Two classical Indian epics.

Mahayana The "Great Vehicle" for salvation in Buddhism. It emphasized the Buddha's infinite compassion for all beings.

mamakuna Inca women who lived privileged but celibate lives and had important economic and cultural roles.

Mandate of Heaven The Chinese belief that heaven entrusts or withdraws a ruler's or a dynasty's right to govern.

Manichaeism A dualistic and moralistic view of reality in which good and evil, spirit and matter warred with each other.

mannerism A style of art in the mid to late 16th century that permitted artists to express their own "manner" or feelings in contrast to the symmetry and simplicity of the art of the High Renaissance.

manors Village farms owned by a lord.

Marshall Plan U.S. program, named after Secretary of State George C. Marshall, that provided economic aid to Europe after World War II.

Marxism Theory of Karl Marx (1818–1883) and Friedrich Engels (1820–1895) that history is the result of class conflict, which will end in the inevitable triumph of the industrial proletariat over the bourgeoisie and the abolition of private property and social class.

Meiji restoration Overthrow of the Tokugawa *bakufu* in Japan in 1868 and the transfer, or "restoration," of power to the imperial government under the Emperor Meiji.

Mein Kampf Meaning "My Struggle." Hitler's statement of his political program, published in 1924.

Mensheviks Meaning the "minority." Term Lenin applied to the majority moderate faction of the Russian Social Democratic Party opposed to him and the Bolsheviks.

mercantilism Term used to describe close government control of the economy that sought to maximize exports and accumulate as much precious metals as possible to enable the state to defend its economic and political interests.

Mesoamerica Region of North America that extends from the central part of modern Mexico to Central America.

Mesopotamia Modern Iraq. The land between the Tigris and Euphrates Rivers.

Messiah The redeemer whose coming, Jews believed, would establish the kingdom of God on earth. Christians considered Jesus to be the Messiah (Christ means Messiah in Greek).

mestizos Persons of mixed Native American and European descent.

Mexica Aztecs' name for themselves.

mfecane Period of widespread warfare and chaos among Bantu peoples in east-central Africa during the early 19th century.

millets Small self-governing communities within the Ottoman Empire.

Minoan Bronze Age civilization that arose in Crete in the third and second millennia B.C.E.

mita Inca system of forced labor in return for gifts and ritual entertainments.

Mitimaqs Communities whom the Incas forced to settle in designated regions for strategic purposes.

monotheism The worship of one universal God.

Moors Spanish and Portuguese term for Muslims.

Mughals Descendants of the Mongols who established an Islamic empire in India in the 16th century with its capital at Delhi.

mujtahid Shi'ite religious-legal scholar.

mulattos Persons of mixed African and European descent.

Mycenaean Bronze Age civilization of mainland Greece that was centered at Mycenae.

"mystery" religions Cults of Isis, Mithra, and Osiris, which promised salvation to those initiated into the secret or "mystery" of their rites.

nacionalismo Right-wing Argentine nationalist movement that arose in the 1930s and resembled European fascism.

National Studies Japanese intellectual tradition that emphasized native Japanese culture and institutions and rejected the influence of Chinese Confucianism.

nationalism Belief that one is part of a nation, defined as a community with its own language, traditions, customs, and history that distinguish it from other nations and make it the primary focus of a person's loyalty and sense of identity.

natural selection According to Darwin, the process in nature by which only the organisms best adapted to their environment tend to survive and transmit their genes, while those less adapted tend to be eliminated.

neocolonial economy Economic relationship between a former colonial state and countries with more developed economies in which the former colony exports raw materials to and imports manufactured goods from the more developed nations.

Neo-Daoism A revival of Daoist "mysterious learning" that flourished as a reaction against Confucianism during the Han dynasty.

Neolithic Revolution The shift beginning 10,000 years ago from hunter-gatherer societies to settled communities.

New Economic Policy (NEP) Limited revival of capitalism, especially in light industry and agriculture, introduced by Lenin in 1921 to repair the damage inflicted on the Russian economy by the civil war and War Communism.

New Imperialism Extension in the late 19th and early 20th centuries of Western political and economic dominance to Asia, the Middle East, and Africa.

Nicene Creed A declaration of faith that the Council of Nicaea hoped would be endorsed by all Christians.

Nilotic Africa The lands along the Nile River.

ninety-five theses Document posted on the door of Castle Church in Wittenberg, Germany on October 31, 1517 by Martin Luther protesting, among other things, the selling of indulgences.

nirvana In Buddhism the attainment of release from the wheel of karma.

Nō play Highly stylized form of Japanese drama in which the chorus provides the narrative line as in classical Greek plays.

oba Title of the king of Benin.

obsidian Hard volcanic glass that was widely used in Mesoamerica.

occupied territories Land occupied by Israel as a result of wars with its Arab neighbors in 1948–1949, 1967, and 1973.

Old Regime Term applied to the pattern of social, political, and economic relationships and institutions that existed in Europe before the French Revolution.

orthodox Meaning "holding the right opinions." Applied to the doctrines of the Catholic Church.

orthopraxy Correct practice of a religion.

Paleolithic Age The earliest period when stone tools were used, from about 1,000,000 to 10,000 B.C.E. From the Greek meaning "old stone."

Panhellenic Meaning "all-Greek." The sense of cultural identity that all Greeks felt in common with each other.

pan-Islamism Movement that advocates that the entire Muslim world should form a unified political and cultural entity.

Pan-Slavic movement Effort to create a nation or federation that would embrace all the Slavic peoples of Eastern Europe.

Papal States Territory in central Italy ruled by the pope until 1870.

parlement French regional court dominated by hereditary nobility. The most important was the Parlement of Paris, which claimed the right to register royal decrees before they could become law.

Parliamentary monarchy Form of limited monarchy developed in England.

patricians Hereditary upper class of early republican Rome.

peace process Efforts, chiefly led by the United States, to broker a peace between the state of Israel and the PLO.

Peloponnesian Wars Protracted struggle between Athens and Sparta to dominate Greece between 465 and Athens' final defeat in 404 B.C.E.

peninsulares Native-born Spaniards who immigrated from Spain to settle in the Spanish colonies.

perestroika Meaning "restructuring." Attempt in the 1980s to reform the Soviet government and economy.

Perónism Authoritarian, nationalist movement founded in Argentina in the 1940s by the dictator Juan Perón.

pharaoh The god-kings of ancient Egypt. The term originally meant "great house" or palace.

Pharisees Group that was most strict in its adherence to Jewish law.

philosophes Eighteenth-century writers and critics who forged the new attitudes favorable to change. They sought to apply reason and common sense to the institutions and societies of their day.

pipiltin Aztec bureaucrats and priests.

pirs Shi'ite holy men.

plantation economy Economic system stretching between Chesapeake Bay and Brazil that produced crops, especially sugar, cotton, and tobacco, using slave labor on large estates.

plebeians Hereditary lower class of early republican Rome.

plenitude of power Teaching that the popes have power over all other bishops of the church.

pochteca Aztec merchants.

pogroms Organized riots against Jews in the Russian Empire.

polis The basic Greek political unit. Usually, but incompletely, translated as "city-state," the Greeks thought of the polis as a community of citizens theoretically descended from a common ancestor.

polytheism The worship of many gods.

Popular Front Government of all left-wing parties that took power in France in 1936 to enact social and economic reforms.

populares Roman politicians who sought to pursue a political career based on the support of the people rather than just the aristocracy.

positivism Philosophy of Auguste Comte that science is the final, or positive, stage of human intellectual development because it involves exact descriptions of phenomena, without recourse to unobservable operative principles, such as gods or spirits.

Pragmatic Sanction Legal basis negotiated by Emperor Charles VI (r. 1711–1740) for the Habsburg succession through his daughter Maria Theresa (r. 1740–1780).

PRI The Institutional Revolutionary Party, which emerged from the Mexican revolution of 1911 and governed Mexico until the end of the 20th century.

proletarianization Process whereby independent artisans and factory workers lose control of the means of production and of the conduct of their own trades to the owners of capital.

Ptolemaic system Pre-Copernican explanation of the universe, which placed the Earth at the center of the universe.

Punic Wars Three wars between Rome and Carthage for dominance of the western Mediterranean that were fought from 264 B.C.E. to 146 B.C.E.

Pure Land Buddhism Variety of Japanese Buddhism that maintained that only faith was necessary for salvation.

Puritans English Protestants who sought to "purify" the Church of England of any vestiges of Catholicism.

Quechua Inca language.

quipu Knotted string used by Andean peoples for recordkeeping.

Qur'an "A reciting." Islamic bible, which Muslims believe God revealed to the prophet Muhammad.

racism Pseudoscientific theory that biological features of race determine human character and worth.

raja An Indian king.

raj The years from 1858 to 1947 during which India was governed directly by the British Crown.

Ramadan Month when Muslims must fast during daylight hours.

Reconquista Christian reconquest of Spain from the Muslims from 1000 to 1492.

Reformation Sixteenth-century religious movement that sought to reform the Roman Catholic Church and led to the establishment of Protestantism.

regular clergy Monks and nuns who belong to religious orders.

Reichstag German parliament, which existed in various forms, until 1945.

Reign of Terror Period between the summer of 1793 and the end of July 1794 when the French revolutionary state used extensive executions and violence to defend the Revolution and suppress its alleged internal enemies.

relativity Theory of physics, first expounded by Albert Einstein in 1905, in which time and space exist not separately, but rather as a combined continuum.

Renaissance Revival of ancient learning and the supplanting of traditional religious beliefs by new secular and scientific values that began in Italy in the 14th and 15th centuries.

repartimiento Labor tax in Spanish America that required adult male Native Americans to devote a set number of days a year to Spanish economic enterprises.

revisionism Advocacy among 19th-century German Socialists of achieving a humane socialist society through the evolution of democratic institutions, not revolution.

Sahara The world's largest desert. It extends across Africa from the Atlantic to the eastern Sudan. Historically, the Sahara has hindered contact between the Mediterranean and sub-Saharan Africa.

Sahel An area of steppe and semi-desert that borders the Sahara.

samsara The endless cycle of existence, of birth, and rebirth.

samurai Professional Japanese warriors.

Sandinistas Marxist guerrilla force that overthrew the Somoza dictatorship in Nicaragua in 1979.

sans-culottes Meaning "without breeches." The lower-middle classes and artisans of Paris during the French Revolution.

satraps Governors of provinces in the Persian Empire.

savannah An area of open woodlands and grassy plains.

Schlieffen Plan Germany's plan for achieving a quick victory in the West at the outbreak of World War I by invading France through Belgium and Luxembourg.

Scholasticism Method of study based on logic and dialectic that dominated the medieval schools. It assumed that truth already existed; students had only to organize, elucidate, and defend knowledge learned from authoritative texts, especially those of Aristotle and the Church Fathers.

Scientific Revolution Sweeping change in the scientific view of the universe that occurred in the West in the 16th and 17th centuries.

scramble for Africa Late 19th century takeover of most of Africa by European powers.

secular clergy Parish clergy who did not belong to a religious order.

serfs Peasants tied to the land they tilled.

Shaanxi banks Private commercial banks in China under the Manchus.

Shahanshah "King of kings," the title of the Persian ruler.

Shari'a Islamic religious law.

Shi'a Muslims who trace their beliefs to the caliph Ali, who was assassinated in 661 C.E.

Shintō "The way of the gods." The animistic worship of the forces of nature that is the indigenous religion of Japan.

shōgun Military official who was the actual ruler of Japan in the emperor's name from the late 1100s until the mid-19th century.

Silk Road Trade route from China to the West that stretched across Central Asia.

Sophists Professional teachers who emerged in Greece in the mid-fifth century B.C.E. who were paid to teach techniques of rhetoric, dialectic, and argumentation.

soviets Workers' and soldiers' councils formed in Russia during the revolution.

spinning jenny Machine invented in England by James Hargreaves around 1765 to mass-produce thread.

Stele (also Stela) An upright stone or slab within inscribed surface, used as a monument or as a commemorative tablet.

steppe peoples Nomadic tribespeople who dwelled on the Eurasian plains from eastern Europe to the borders of China and Iran. They frequently traded with or invaded more settled cultures.

Stoics Philosophical school founded by Zeno of Citium (335–263 B.C.E.) that taught that humans could only be happy with natural law.

streltsy Professional troops who made up the Moscow garrison. They were suppressed by Peter the Great.

studia humanitatis During the Renaissance, a liberal arts program of study that embraced grammar, rhetoric, poetry, history, philosophy, and politics.

stupa A Buddhist shrine.

suffragettes British women who lobbied and agitated for the right to vote in the early 20th century.

Sufi Movement within Islam that emphasizes the spiritual and mystical.

sultan Muslim royal title that means "authority."

Sunna "Tradition." Dominant Islamic group.

superego According to Freud, the part of the mind that embodies the external moral imperatives and expectations imposed on the personality by society and culture.

Swahili Language and culture that developed from the interaction of native Africans and Arabs along the East African coast.

symposion Carefully organized drinking party that was the center of Greek aristocratic social life. It featured games, songs, poetry, and even philosophical disputation.

syncretism In religion, the equating or combining of deities.

Table of Ranks Official hierarchy established by Peter the Great in imperial Russia that equated a person's social position and privileges with his rank in the state bureaucracy or army.

taille Direct tax on the French peasantry.

Taiping rebellion A 19th-century revolt against China's Manchu dynasty that was inspired by quasi-Christian ideas and that led to enormous suffering and destruction before its collapse in 1868.

tennō "Heavenly emperor." The official title of the emperor of Japan.

tetcutin Subordinate Aztec lords.

tetrarchy Diocletian's (r. 306–337 C.E.) system for ruling the Roman Empire by four men with power divided territorially.

The *Iliad* and the *Odyssey* Epic poems by Homer about the "Dark Age" heroes of Greece who fought at Troy. The poems were written down in the eighth century B.C.E. after centuries of being sung by bards.

theocracy State ruled by religious leaders who claim to govern by divine authority.

Theravada The "Way of the Elders." A school of Buddhism that emphasized the monastic ideal.

Thermidorean Reaction Reaction against the radicalism of the French Revolution that began in July 1794. Associated with the end of terror and establishment of the Directory.

Third Estate Branch of the French Estates General representing all of the kingdom outside the nobility and the clergy.

three-field system Medieval innovation that increased the amount of land under cultivation by leaving only one-third fallow in a given year.

tlatoani An Aztec ruler.

transubstantiation Doctrine that the entire substances of the bread and wine are changed in the Eucharist into the body and blood of Christ.

treaty ports Chinese ports ruled by foreign consuls where foreigners enjoyed commercial privileges and immunity from Chinese laws.

Trekboers White livestock farmers in Cape Colony.

tribunes Roman officials who had to be plebeians and were elected by the plebeian assembly to protect plebeians from the arbitrary power of the magistrates.

Tripartite Pact Alliance between Japan and Nazi Germany and Fascist Italy that was signed in 1940.

ulama "Persons with correct knowledge." Islamic scholarly elite who served a social function similar to the Christian clergy.

Umma Islamic community.

"unequal treaties" Agreements imposed on China in the 19th century by European powers, the United States, and Japan that granted their citizens special legal and economic privileges on Chinese soil.

Upanishads Vedic texts most concerned with speculation about the universe.

Urdu-Hindi Language that combines Persian-Arabic and native Indian elements. Urdu is the Muslim version of the language; Hindi is the Hindu version.

uzama Order of hereditary chiefs in Benin.

varnas The four main classes that form the basis for Hindu caste relations.

vassal Person granted an estate or cash payments in return for accepting the obligation to render services to a lord.

Vedas Sacred texts of the ancient Aryan invaders of India. The Rig Veda is the oldest material in the Vedas.

vernacular Everyday language spoken by the people as opposed to Latin.

Viet Minh Communist-dominated popular front organization formed by Ho Chi Minh to establish an independent Vietnamese republic.

War Communism Economic policy adopted by the Bolsheviks during the Russian civil war to seize the banks, heavy industry, railroads, and grain.

war guilt clause Clause of the Versailles Treaty, which assigned responsibility for World War I solely to Germany.

water frame Water-powered device invented by Richard Arkwright to produce a more durable cotton fabric. It led to the shift in the production of cotton textiles from households to factories.

Weimar Republic German democratic regime that existed between the end of World War I and Hitler's coming to power in 1933.

White Russians Russians who opposed the Bolsheviks (the "Reds") in the Russian Civil War of 1918–1921.

Works Progress Administration New Deal program created by the Roosevelt administration in 1935 that provided relief for the unemployed in the industrial sector during the Great Depression in the United States.

yangban Elite Korean families of the Choson period.

zaibatsu Groups of Japanese companies, or "trusts," that had a common ownership and dominated the economy of prewar Japan.

Zen A form of Buddhism, which taught that Buddha was only a man and exhorted each person to attain enlightenment by his or her own efforts.

Zionism Movement to create a Jewish state in Palestine (the Biblical Zion).

Zoroastrianism A quasi-monotheistic Iranian religion founded by Zoroaster (ca. 628–551 B.C.E.) who preached a message of moral reform and exhorted his followers to worship only Ahura Mazda, the Wise Lord.

CHAPTER 1

General Prehistory

P. BOGUCKI, *The Origins of Human Society* (1999). An excellent summary of recent scholarship on the earliest origins of human societies.

F. BRAY, *The Rice Economies: Technology and Development in Asian Societies* (1986). Still the best authority on the origins of rice cultivation and its effect on the development of ancient Asia.

M. EHRENBERG, *Women in Prehistory* (1989). An account of the role of women in early times.

C. FREEMAN, *Egypt, Greece and Rome: Civilizations of the Ancient Mediterranean* (2004). Good comparative study of Egypt with Greece and Rome.

D. C. JOHNSON and M. R. EDEY, *Lucy: The Beginning of Mankind* (1981). An account of the African origins of humans.

S. M. NELSON, ed., *Ancient Queens: Archaeological Explorations* (2003). Reassesses women rulers and female power in the ancient world.

S. M. NELSON and M. ROSEN-AYALON, *In Pursuit of Gender: Worldwide Archaeological Approaches* (2002). Essays on gender and the archaeology of the ancient world.

D. L. NICHOLS and T. H. CHARLTON, eds., *The Archaeology of CityStates: Cross-cultural Approaches* (1997). One of a growing body of books and essay collections employing cross-cultural and comparative approaches to world history and archaeology.

M. OLIPHANT, *The Atlas of the Ancient World: Charting the Great Civilizations of the Past* (1992). An excellent comprehensive atlas of the ancient world.

P. L. SHINNIE, *Ancient Nubia* (1996). A study of the African state most influenced by Egyptian culture.

Near East

M. E. AUBER, *The Phoenicians and the West* (1996). A new study of an important sea-going people who served as a conduit between East and West.

BEN-TOR, ed., *The Archaeology of Ancient Israel* (1992). A useful and up-to-date survey.

J. BOTTÉRO, *Everyday Life in Ancient Mesopotamia* (2001). Interesting vignettes of ancient Mesopotamian life.

H. CRAWFORD, *Sumer and the Sumerians* (1991). A discussion of the oldest Mesopotamian civilization.

I. FINKELSTEIN and N. A. SILBERMAN, *The Bible Unearthed: Archaeology's New Vision of Ancient Israel and the Origin of its Sacred Texts* (2001). An interesting discussion of the insights of recent archaeological finds on the history of the Bible and ancient Israel.

G. LEICK, *Mesopotamia: The Invention of the City* (2002). Good discussion of the urban history of ancient Mesopotamia.

J. N. POSTGATE, *Early Mesopotamia* (1992). An excellent study of Mesopotamian economy and society from the earliest times to about 1500 B.C.E., helpfully illustrated with drawings, photos, and translated documents.

D. B. REDFORD, *Akhenaten* (1987). A study of the controversial religious reformer.

W. F. SAGGS, *The Might That Was Assyria* (1984). A history of the northern Mesopotamian Empire and a worthy companion to the author's account of the Babylonian Empire in the south.

M. VAN DE MIEROOP, *A History of the Ancient Near East, ca. 3000–323 B.C.* (2004). An up-to-date comprehensive survey of ancient Near Eastern history.

India

D. P. AGRAWAL, *The Archaeology of India* (1982). A fine survey of the problems and data. Detailed, but with excellent summaries and brief discussions of major issues.

C. CHAKRABORTY, *Common Life in the Rigveda and Atharvaveda—An Account of the Folklore in the Vedic Period* (1977). An interesting attempt to reconstruct everyday life in the Vedic period from the principal Vedic texts.

J. R. MCINTOSH, *A Peaceful Realm: The Rise and Fall of the Indus Civilization* (2002). Discusses what archaeologists have managed to unearth so far regarding Harrapan civilization.

W. D. O'FLAHERTY, *The Rig Veda: An Anthology* (1981). An excellent selection of Vedic texts in prosaic but very careful translation, with helpful notes on the texts.

J. E. SCHWARTZBERG, ed., *A Historical Atlas of South Asia* (1978). The definitive reference work for historical geography. Includes chronological tables and substantive essays.

R. THAPAR, *Early India: From the Origins to A.D. 1300* (2003). A comprehensive introduction to the early history of India.

China

M. LOEWE and E. SHAUGHNESSY eds., *The Cambridge History of Ancient China: From the Origins of Civilization to 221 B.C.* (1999). A comprehensive and authoritative history of ancient China.

K. C. CHANG, *The Archeology of Ancient China*, 4th ed. (1986). The standard work on the subject.

K. C. CHANG, *Art, Myth, and Ritual, The Path to Political Authority in Ancient China* (1984). A study of the relation between shamans, gods, agricultural production, and political authority during the Shang and Zhou dynasties.

N. DI COSMO, *Ancient China and its Enemies: The Rise of Nomadic Power in East Asian History* (2002). An excellent study of the relationship between China and nomadic peoples that was a powerful force in shaping Chinese and Central Asian history.

C. Y. Hsu, *Western Chou Civilization* (1988).

D. N. Keightley, *The Origins of Chinese Civilization* (1983).

M. E. Lewis, *Sanctioned Violence in Early China* (1990).

X. Q. Li, *Eastern Zhou and Qin Civilizations* (1986). This work includes fresh interpretations based on archaeological finds.

Americas

R. L. Burger, *Chavín and the Origins of Andean Civilization* (1992). A lucid and detailed account of the rise of civilization in the Andes.

M. D. Coe and R. Koontz, *Mexico: From the Olmecs to the Aztecs* (2002). Good survey of ancient Mexico.

D. Drew, *The Lost Chronicles of the Maya Kings* (1999). Fine introduction to the history of Maya civilization.

V. W. Fitzhugh and A. Crowell, *Crossroads of Continents: Cultures of Siberia and Alaska* (1988). Covers the area where the immigration from Eurasia to the Americas began.

R. Ford, ed., *Prehistoric Food Production in North America* (1985). Examines the origins of agriculture in the Americas.

P. D. Hunt, *Indian Agriculture in America: Prehistory to the Present* (1987). Includes a discussion of preconquest agriculture.

A. Knight, *Mexico: From the Beginning to the Spanish Conquest* (2002). First of a three-volume comprehensive history of Mexico.

C. Morris and A. Von Hagen, *The Inka Empire and Its Andean Origins* (1993). An overview of Andean civilization with excellent illustrations.

M. Moseley, *The Incas and Their Ancestors: The Archaeology of Ancient Peru* (1992). An overview of Peruvian archaeology.

J. A. Sabloff, *The New Archaeology and the Ancient Maya* (1990). A lively account of recent research in Maya archaeology.

I. Silverblatt, *Moon, Sun, and Witches: Gender Ideologies and Class in Inca and Colonial Peru* (1987). A controversial but thought-provoking discussion of Incan ideas about gender.

CHAPTER 2

China

R. Berstein, *Ultimate Journey: Retracing the Path of an Ancient Buddhist Monk who Crossed Asia in Search of Enlightenment* (2001). Discusses the diffusion of Buddhism from India to China.

H. G. Creel, *What Is Taoism? And Other Studies in Chinese Cultural History* (1970).

W. T. de Bary et al., *Sources of Chinese Tradition* (1960). A reader in China's philosophical and historical literature. It should be consulted for the later periods as well as for the Zhou.

H. Fingarete, *Confucius—The Secular as Sacred* (1998).

Y. L. Fung, *A Short History of Chinese Philosophy*, ed. by D. Bodde (1948). A survey of Chinese philosophy from its origins down to recent times.

A. Graham, *Disputers of the Tao* (1989).

D. Hawkes, *Ch'u Tz'u: The Songs of the South* (1985).

D. C. Lau, trans., *Lao-tzu, Tao Te Ching* (1963).

D. C. Lau, trans., *Confucius, The Analects* (1979).

C. Li, ed., *The Sage and the Second Sex: Confucianism, Ethics, and Gender* (2000). A good introduction to gender and ethics in Confucian thought.

B. I. Schwartz, *The World of Thought in Ancient China* (1985).

A. Waley, *Three Ways of Thought in Ancient China* (1956). An easy yet sound introduction to Confucianism, Daoism, and Legalism.

A. Waley, *The Book of Songs* (1960).

B. Watson, trans., *Basic Writings of Mo Tzu, Hsun Tzu, and Han Fei Tzu* (1963).

B. Watson, trans., *The Complete Works of Chuang Tzu* (1968).

H. Welch, *Taoism, The Parting of the Way* (1967).

India

A. L. Basham, *The Wonder That Was India*, rev. ed. (1963). Still unsurpassed by more recent works. Chapter VII, "Religion," is a superb introduction to the Vedic Aryan, Brahmanic, Hindu, Jain, and Buddhist traditions of thought.

W. N. Brown, *Man in the Universe: Some Continuities in Indian Thought* (1970). A penetrating yet brief reflective summary of major patterns in Indian thinking.

W. T. de Bary et al., *Sources of Indian Tradition* (1958). 2 vols. Vol. I, *From the Beginning to 1800*, ed. and rev. by Ainslie T. Embree (1988). Excellent selections from a variety of Indian texts, with good introductions to chapters and individual selections.

P. Harvey, *An Introduction to Buddhism* (1990). Chapters 1–3 provide an excellent historical introduction.

T. J. Hopkins, *The Hindu Religious Tradition* (1971). A first-rate, thoughtful introduction to Hindu religious ideas and practice.

K. KLOSTERMAIER, *Hinduism: A Short History* (2000). A relatively compact survey of the history of Hinduism.

J. M. KOLLER, *The Indian Way* (1982). A useful, wide-ranging handbook of Indian thought and religion.

R. H. ROBINSON and W. L. JOHNSON, *The Buddhist Religion*, 3rd ed. (1982). An excellent first text on the Buddhist tradition, its thought and development.

R. C. ZAEHNER, *Hinduism* (1966). One of the best general introductions to central Indian religious and philosophical ideas.

Israel

A. BACH, ed., *Women in the Hebrew Bible: A Reader* (1999). Excellent introduction to the ways in which biblical scholars are exploring the role of women in the Bible.

BRIGHT, *A History of Israel* (1968), 2nd ed. (1972). One of the standard scholarly introductions to biblical history and literature.

W. D. DAVIES and L. FINKELSTEIN, eds., *The Cambridge History of Judaism*. Vol. I, *Introduction: The Persian Period* (1984). Excellent essays on diverse aspects of the exilic period and later.

J. NEUSNER, *The Way of Torah: An Introduction to Judaism* (1979). A sensitive introduction to the Judaic tradition and faith.

The Oxford History of the Biblical World, M. D. Coogan, ed. (1998).

Greece

The Cambridge Companion to Greek and Roman Philosophy, D. SEDLEY ed., (2003).

G. B. KERFERD, *The Sophistic Movement* (1981). An excellent description and analysis.

J. LEAR, *Aristotle: The Desire to Understand* (1988). A brilliant yet comprehensible introduction to the work of the philosopher.

T. E. RIHIL, *Greek Science* (1999). Good survey of Greek science incorporating recent reseach on the topic.

J. M. ROBINSON, *An Introduction to Early Greek Philosophy* (1968). A valuable collection of the main fragments and ancient testimony to the works of the early philosophers, with excellent commentary.

G. VLASTOS, *The Philosophy of Socrates* (1971). A splendid collection of essays illuminating the problems presented by this remarkable man.

G. VLASTOS, *Platonic Studies*, 2nd ed. (1981). A similar collection on the philosophy of Plato.

G. VLASTOS, *Socrates, Ironist and Moral Philosopher* (1991). The results of a lifetime of study by the leading interpreter of Socrates in our time.

Comparative Studies

(Increasingly world historians are looking at ancient civilizations in relationship to each other rather than as isolated entities to try to understand commonalities and differences in social and cultural development.)

W. DONIGER, *Splitting the Difference: Gender and Myth in Ancient Greece and India* (1999).

G. E. R. LLOYD, *The Ambitions of Curiosity: Understanding the World in Ancient Greece and China* (2002).

G. E. R. LLOYD, *The Way and the Word: Science and Medicine in Early China and Greece* (2002).

T. MCEVILLEY, *The Shape of Ancient Thought: Comparative Studies of Greek and Indian Philosopies* (2002).

CHAPTER 3

The Rise of Greek Civilization

P. CARTLEDGE, *The Spartans* (2003). A readable account of this enigmatic people.

J. CHADWICK, *The Mycenaean World* (1976). A readable account by a man who helped decipher Mycenaean writing.

R. DREWS, *The Coming of the Greeks* (1988). A fine discussion of the Greeks' arrival as part of the movements of the Indo-European peoples.

J. V. FINE, *The Ancient Greeks* (1983). An excellent survey that discusses historical problems and the evidence that gives rise to them.

M. I. FINLEY, *World of Odysseus*, rev. ed. (1965). A fascinating attempt to reconstruct Homeric society.

P. GREEN, *Xerxes at Salamis* (1970). A lively and stimulating history of the Persian War.

D. HAMEL, *Trying Neaira* (2003). A lively account of the events surrounding a famous jury trial that sheds interesting light on Athenian society in the fourth century B.C.E.

V. D. HANSON, *The Western Way of War* (1989). A brilliant and lively discussion of the rise and character of the hoplite phalanx and its influence on Greek society.

V. D. HANSON, *The Other Greeks* (1995). A revolutionary account of the Greek invention of the family farm and its centrality for the shaping of the *polis*.

D. KAGAN, *The Great Dialogue: A History of Greek Political Thought from Homer to Polybius* (1965). A discussion of the relationship between the Greek historical experience and political theory.

W. K. LACEY, *The Family in Ancient Greece* (1984).

J. F. LAZENBY, *The Defense of Greece, 490–479 B.C.* (1993). A new and valuable study of the Persian Wars.

J. F. McGlew, *Tyranny and Political Culture in Ancient Greece* (1993). A recent account of political developments in the Archaic period.

O. Murray, *Early Greece* (1980). A lively and imaginative account of the early history of Greece to the end of the Persian War.

A. M. Snodgrass, *The Dark Age of Greece* (1972). A good examination of the archaeological evidence.

B. S. Strauss, *The Battle of Salamis: The Naval Encounter That Saved Greece and Western Civilization* (2004). A lively account of the major naval battle of the Persian Wars and its setting.

A. G. Woodhead, *Greeks in the West* (1962). An account of the Greek settlements in Italy and Sicily.

W. J. Woodhouse, *Solon the Liberator* (1965). A discussion of the great Athenian reformer.

S. G. Miller, *Ancient Greek Athletics* (2004). The most complete and most useful account of the subject.

Classical and Hellenistic Greece

W. Burkert, *Greek Religion* (1987). An excellent study by an outstanding student of the subject.

J. R. Lane Fox, *Alexander the Great* (1973). An imaginative account that does more than the usual justice to the Persian side of the problem.

Y. Garlan, *Slavery in Ancient Greece* (1988). An up-to-date survey.

P. Green, *Alexander to Actium: The Historical Evolution of the Hellenistic Age* (1990). A remarkable synthesis of political and cultural history.

C. D. Hamilton, *Agesilaus and the Failure of Spartan Hegemony* (1991). An excellent biography of the king who was the central figure in Sparta during its domination in the fourth century B.C.E.

N. G. L. Hammond, *Philip of Macedon* (1994). A new biography of the founder of the Macedonian Empire.

N. G. L. Hammond and G. T. Griffith, *A History of Macedonia*, Vol. 2, *550–336 B.C.* (1979). A thorough account of Macedonian history that focuses on the careers of Philip and Alexander.

R. Just, *Women in Athenian Law and Life* (1988). An account of women's place in Athenian society.

D. Kagan, *The Peloponnesian War* (2003). A narrative history of the war.

B. M. W. Knox, *The Heroic Temper: Studies in Sophoclean Tragedy* (1964). A brilliant analysis of tragic heroism.

D. M. Lewis, *Sparta and Persia* (1977). A valuable discussion of relations between Sparta and Persia in the fifth and fourth centuries B.C.E.

A. A. Long, *Hellenistic Philosophy: Stoics, Epicureans, Sceptics* (1974). An account of Greek science in the Hellenistic and Roman periods.

R. Meiggs, *The Athenian Empire* (1972). A fine study of the rise and fall of the empire, making excellent use of inscriptions.

J. J. Pollitt, *Art and Experience in Classical Greece* (1972). A scholarly and entertaining study of the relationship between art and history in classical Greece, with excellent illustrations.

J. J. Pollitt, *Art in the Hellenistic Age* (1986). An extraordinary analysis that places the art in its historical and intellectual context.

E. W. Robinson, *Ancient Greek Democracy* (2004). A stimulating collection of ancient sources and modern interpretations.

D. M. Schaps, *Economic Rights of Women in Ancient Greece* (1981).

B. S. Strauss, *Athens After the Peloponnesian War* (1987). An excellent discussion of Athens' recovery and of the nature of Athenian society and politics in the fourth century B.C.E.

B. S. Strauss, *Fathers and Sons in Athens* (1993). An unusual synthesis of social, political, and intellectual history.

V. Tcherikover, *Hellenistic Civilization and the Jews* (1970). A fine study of the impact of Hellenism on the Jews.

G. Vlastos, *Socrates, Ironist and Moral Philosopher* (1991). The results of a lifetime of study by the leading interpreter of Socrates in our time.

CHAPTER 4

Iran

M. Boyce, *Zoroastrians: Their Religious Beliefs and Practices* (1979). The most recent survey, organized historically and based on extensive research.

M. Boyce, ed. and trans., *Textual Sources for the Study of Zoroastrianism* (1984). Well-translated selections from a broad range of ancient Iranian materials.

J. M. Cook, *The Persian Empire* (1983). Survey of the Achaemenid period.

J. Curtis, *Ancient Persia* (1989). Excellent portfolio of photographs of artifacts and sites, with a clear historical survey of the arts and culture of ancient Iran.

W. D. Davies and L. Finklestein, ed., *The Cambridge History of Judaism*, Vol. 1, Introduction; "The Persian Period". Good articles on Iran and Iranian religion as well as Judaism.

J. Duchesne-Guillemin, trans., *The Hymns of Zarathushtra*, trans. by M. Henning (1952, 1963). The best short introduction to the original texts of the Zoroastrian hymns.

R. N. Frye, *The Heritage of Persia* (1963, 1966). A first-rate survey of Iranian history to Islamic times: readable but scholarly.

R. Ghirshman, *Iran* (1954). Good material on culture, society, and economy as well as politics and history.

W. W. Malandra, trans. and ed., *An Introduction to Ancient Iranian Religion: Readings from the Avesta and Achaemenid Inscriptions* (1983). Helpful especially for texts of inscriptions relevant to religion.

India

A. L. Basham, *The Wonder That Was India*, rev. ed. (1963). Excellent material on Mauryan religion, society, culture, and history.

A. L. Basham, ed., *A Cultural History of India* (1975). A fine collection of historical-survey essays by a variety of scholars. See Part I, "The Ancient Heritage" (Chapters 2–16).

N. N. Bhattacharyya, *Ancient Indian History and Civilization: Trends and Perspectives* (1988). Covers Mauryan and Gupta times as well as earlier periods, with chapters on political systems, cities and villages, ideology and religion, and art.

W. T. de Bary et al., comp., *Sources of Indian Tradition*, 2nd ed. (1958). Vol. I: *From the Beginning to 1800*, ed. and rev. by Ainslie T. Embree (1988). Excellent selections from a wide variety of Indian texts, with good introductions to chapters and selections.

B. Rowland, *The Art and Architecture of India: Buddhist/Hindu/Jain*, 3rd rev. ed. (1970). The standard work, lucid and easy to read. Note Part Three, "Romano-Indian Art in North-West India and Central Asia."

V. A. Smith, ed., *The Oxford History of India*, 4th rev. ed. by Percival Spear et al. (1981), pp. 71–163. A dry, occasionally dated historical survey. Includes useful reference chronologies.

R. Thapar, *Ashoka and the Decline of the Mauryans* (1973). The standard treatment of Ashoka's reign.

R. Thapar, *A History of India, Part I* (1966), pp. 50–108. Three chapters that provide a basic survey of the period.

S. Wolpert, *A New History of India*, 2nd ed. (1982). A basic survey history. Chapters 5 and 6 cover the Mauryans, Guptas, and Kushans.

Greek and Asian Dynasties

A. K. Narain, *The Indo-Greeks* (1957. Reprinted with corrections, 1962). The most comprehensive account of the complex history of the various kings and kingdoms.

F. E. Peters, *The Harvest of Hellenism* (1970), pp. 222–308. Helpful chapters on Greek rulers of the Eastern world from Seleucus to the last Indo-Greeks.

J. W. Sedlar, *India and the Greek World: A Study in the Transmission of Culture* (1980). A basic work that provides a good overview.

D. Sinor, ed., *The Cambridge History of Early Inner Asia* (1990). See especially Chapters 6 and 7.

CHAPTER 5

P. Bohannan and P. Curtin, *Africa and Africans*, rev. ed. (1971). An enjoyable and enlightening discussion of African history and prehistory and of major African institutions (e.g., arts, family life, religion).

R. Bulliet, *The Camel and the Wheel* (1990). Explains why the camel was chosen over the wheel as a means of transport in the Sahara.

P. Curtin, S. Feiermann, L. Thompson, and J. Vansina, *African History* (1978). Probably the best survey history. The relevant portions are chapters 1, 2, 4, 8, and 9.

T. R. H. Davenport, *South Africa: A Modern History*, 3rd rev. ed. (1987). Chapter 1 gives excellent summary coverage of prehistoric southern Africa, the Khoisan peoples, and the Bantu migrations.

B. Davidson, *The African Past* (1967). A combination of primary-source selections and brief secondary discussions trace sympathetically the history of the diverse parts of Africa.

P. Garlake, *The Kingdoms of Africa* (1978). A lavishly illustrated set of photographic essays that provide a helpful introduction to the various historically important areas of precolonial Africa.

E. Gilbert and J. Reynolds, *Africa in World History* (2004). The best new survey of African history, placing it in a global context.

R. W. July, *Precolonial Africa: An Economic and Social History* (1975). A very readable, topically arranged study. See especially "The Savannah Farmer," "The Bantu," "Cattlemen," and "The Traders" chapters.

H. Loth, *Woman in Ancient Africa*, trans. by S. Marnie (1987). An interesting survey of legal, familial, cultural, and other aspects of women's roles.

R. Oliver, *The African Experience* (1991). A masterly, balanced, and engaging sweep through African history. The chapters on prehistory and early history are outstanding summaries of the results and implications of recent research.

I. Van Sertima, *Black Women in Antiquity* (1984, 1988). Studies of queens, goddesses, matriarchy, and other aspects of the role and status of women in Egyptian, Ethiopian, and other African societies of the past.

CHAPTER 6

From Republic to Empire

R. BAUMANN, *Women and Politics in Ancient Rome* (1995). A Study of the role of women in roman public life.

A. H. BERNSTEIN, *Tiberius Sempronius Gracchus: Tradition and Apostasy* (1978). A new interpretation of Tiberius's place in Roman politics.

T. J. CORNELL, *The Beginnings of Rome: Italy and Rome from the Bronze Age to the Punic Wars, c. 1000–264 B.C.* (1995). A consideration of the royal and early republican periods of Roman history.

T. CORNELL AND J. MATTHEWS, *Atlas of the Roman World* (1982). Much more than the title indicates, this book presents a comprehensive view of the Roman world in its physical and cultural setting.

J-M. DAVID, *The Roman Conquest of Italy* (1997). A good analysis of how Rome united Italy.

A. GOLDSWORTHY, *Roman Warfare* (2002). A good military history of Rome.

A. GOLDSWORTHY, *In the Name of Rome: The Men Who Won the Roman Empire* (2004). The story of Rome's greatest generals in the republican and imperial periods.

E. S. GRUEN, *Diaspora: Jews Amidst Greeks and Romans* (2002). A fine study of Jews in the Hellenistic and Roman world.

E. S. GRUEN, *The Hellenistic World and the Coming of Rome* (1984). A new interpretation of Rome's conquest of the eastern Mediterranean.

W. V. HARRIS, *War and Imperialism in Republican Rome, 327–70 B.C.* (1975). An analysis of Roman attitudes and intentions concerning imperial expansion and war.

A. KEAVENEY, *Rome and the Unification of Italy* (1988). The story of how Rome organized her defeated opponents.

S. LANCEL, *Carthage, A History* (1995). Includes a good account of Rome's dealings with Carthage.

J. F. LAZENBY, *Hannibal's War: A Military History of the Second Punic War* (1978). A careful and thorough account.

F.G.B. MILLAR, *The Crowd in Rome in the Late Republic* (1999). A challenge to the view that only aristocrats counted in the late republic.

M. PALLOTTINO, *The Etruscans*, 6th ed. (1974). Makes especially good use of archaeological evidence.

H. H. SCULLARD, *A History of the Roman World 753–146 B.C.*, 4th ed. (1980). An unusually fine narrative history with useful critical notes.

G. WILLIAMS, *The Nature of Roman Poetry* (1970). An unusually graceful and perceptive literary study.

Imperial Rome

W. BALL, *Rome in the East: The Transformation of an Empire* (2001). A thorough account of the influence of the East on Roman history.

T. BARNES, *The New Empire of Diocletian and Constantine* (1982).

K. R. BRADLEY, *Slavery and Society at Rome* (1994). A study of the role of slaves in Roman life.

P. BROWN, *The Rise of Western Christendom: Triumph and Diversity, 200–1000* (1996). A vivid picture of the spread of Christianity by a master of the field.

A. FERRILL, *The Fall of the Roman Empire, The Military Explanation* (1986). An interpretation that emphasizes the decline in the quality of the Roman army.

K. GALINSKY, *Augustan Culture* (1996). A work that integrates art, literature, and politics.

A. H. M. JONES, *The Later Roman Empire*, 3 vols. (1964). A comprehensive study of the period.

D. KAGAN, ed., *The End of the Roman Empire: Decline or Transformation?* 3rd ed. (1992). A collection of essays discussing the problem of the decline and fall of the Roman Empire.

J. E. LENDON, *Empire of Honor, The Art of Government in the Roman World* (1997). An original and path-breaking interpretation.

E. N. LUTTWAK, *The Grand Strategy of the Roman Empire* (1976). An original and fascinating analysis by a keen student of modern strategy.

R. MACMULLEN, *Roman Social Relations, 50 B.C. to A.D. 284* (1981).

R. MACMULLEN, *Corruption and the Decline of Rome* (1988). A study that examines the importance of changes in ethical ideas and behavior.

R. W. MATHISON, *Roman Aristocrats in Barbarian Gaul: Strategies for Survival* (1993). An unusual slant on the late empire.

J.F. MATTHEWS, *Laying Down the Law: A Study of the Theodosian Code* (2000). A study of the importance of Roman law as a source for the understanding of Roman history and civilization.

W. A. MEEKS, *The Origins of Christian Morality: The First Two Centuries.* An account of the shaping of Christianity in the Roman Empire.

F. MILLAR, *The Emperor in the Roman World, 31 B.C.–A.D. 337* (1977). A study of Roman imperial government.

F. MILLAR, *The Roman Empire and Its Neighbors*, 2nd ed. (1981).

H. M. D. PARKER, *A History of the Roman World from A.D. 138 to 337* (1969). A good survey.

M. I. ROSTOVTZEFF, *Social and Economic History of the Roman Empire*, 2nd ed. (1957). A masterpiece whose main thesis has been much disputed.

V. RUDICH, *Political Dissidence Under Nero, The Price of Dissimulation* (1993). A brilliant exposition of the lives and thoughts of political dissidents in the early empire.

E. T. SALMON, *A History of the Roman World, 30 B.C. to A.D. 138* (1968). A good survey.

R. SYME, *The Roman Revolution* (1960). A brilliant study of Augustus, his supporters, and their rise to power.

R. SYME, *The Augustan Aristocracy* (1985). An examination of the new ruling class shaped by Augustus.

L. A. THOMPSON, *Romans and Blacks* (1989).

CHAPTER 7

D. BODDE, *China's First Unifier* (1938). A study of the Qin unification of China, viewed through the Legalist philosopher and statesman LiSi.

T. T. CH'U, *Law and Society in Traditional China* (1961). Treats the sweep of Chinese history from 202 B.C.E. to 1911 C.E.

T. T. CH'U, *Han Social Structure* (1972).

A. COTTERELL, *The First Emperor of China* (1981). A study of the first Qin emperor.

R. COULBORN, *Feudalism in History* (1965). One chapter interestingly compares the quasi feudalism of the Zhou with that of the Six Dynasties period.

J. K. FAIRBANK, E. O. REISCHAUER, AND A. M. CRAIG, *East Asia: Tradition and Transformation* (1989). A fairly detailed single-volume history covering China, Japan, and other countries in East Asia from antiquity to recent times.

J. GERNET, *A History of Chinese Civilization* (1982). A survey of Chinese history.

D.A. GRAFF AND R. HIGHAM, *A Military History of China* (2002).

C. Y. HSU, *Ancient China in Transition* (1965). On social mobility during the Eastern Zhou era.

C. Y. HSU, *Han Agriculture* (1980). A study of the agrarian economy of China during the Han dynasty.

J. LEVI, *The Chinese Emperor* (1987). A novel about the first Qin emperor based on scholarly sources.

M. LOEWE, *Everyday Life in Early Imperial China* (1968). A social history of the Han dynasty.

J. NEEDHAM, *The Shorter Science and Civilization in China* (1978). An abridgment of the multivolume work on the same subject with the same title—minus Shorter—by the same author.

S. OWEN, ed. and Trans., *An Anthology of Chinese Literature: Beginnings to 1911* (1996).

I. ROBINET, *Taoism: Growth of a Religion* (1987).

M. SULLIVAN, *The Arts of China* (1967). An excellent survey history of Chinese art.

D. TWITCHETT AND M. LOEWE, eds., *The Ch'in and Han Empires, 221 B.C.E.–C.E. 220* (1986). Vol. 1 of *The Cambridge History of China.*

Z. S. WANG, *Han Civilization* (1982).

B. WATSON, *Ssu-ma Ch'ien, Grand Historian of China* (1958). A study of China's premier historian.

B. WATSON, *Records of the Grand Historian of China*, Vols. 1 and 2 (1961). Selections from the *Shiji* by Sima Qian.

B. WATSON, *The Columbia Book of Chinese Poetry* (1986).

F. WOOD, *The Silk Road: Two Thousand Years in the Heart of Asia* (2003). A lively narrative combined with photographs and paintings.

A. WRIGHT, *Buddhism in Chinese History* (1959).

Y. S. YU, *Trade and Expansion in Han China* (1967). A study of economic relations between the Chinese and their neighbors.

CHAPTER 8

General

P. BOL, *This Culture of Ours* (1992). An insightful intellectual history of the Tang through the Song dynasties.

J. CAHILL, *Chinese Painting* (1960). An excellent survey.

J. K. FAIRBANK AND M. GOLDMAN, *China: A New History* (1998). The summation of a lifetime engagement with Chinese history.

F. A. KIERMAN JR., AND J. K. FAIRBANK, eds., *Chinese Ways in Warfare* (1974). Chapters by different authors on the Chinese military experience from the Zhou to the Ming.

Sui and Tang

P. B. EBREY, *The Aristocratic Families of Early Imperial China* (1978).

D. MCMULLEN, *State and Scholars in T'ang China* (1988).

S. OWEN, *The Great Age of Chinese Poetry: The High T'ang* (1980).

S. OWEN, trans. and ed., *An Anthology of Chinese Literature: Beginnings to 1911* (1996).

E. G. PULLEYBLANK, *The Background of the Rebellion of An Lu-shan* (1955). A study of the 755 rebellion that weakened the central authority of the Tang dynasty.

E. O. REISCHAUER, *Ennin's Travels in T'ang China* (1955). China as seen through the eyes of a ninth-century Japanese Marco Polo.

E. H. SCHAFER, *The Golden Peaches of Samarkand* (1963). A study of Tang imagery.

SO. TEISER, *The Ghost Festival in Medieval China* (1988). On Tang popular religion.

D. TWITCHETT, ed., *The Cambridge History of China*, Vol. III: *Sui and T'ang China, 589–906 Part 1*, (1979).

G. W. WANG, *The Structure of Power in North China During the Five Dynasties* (1963). A study of the interim period between the Tang and the Song dynasties.

A. F. WRIGHT, *The Sui Dynasty* (1978).

Song

B. BIRGE, *Women, Property, and Confucian Reaction in Song and Yuan China (960–1366)* (2002). The rights of women to property—whether in the form of dowries or inheritances—were considerable during the Song but declined thereafter.

C. S. CHANG AND J. SMYTHE, *South China in the Twelfth Century* (1981). China as seen through the eyes of a twelfth-century Chinese poet, historian, and statesman.

E. L. DAVIS, *Society and the Supernatural in Song China* (2001).

J. W. HAEGER, ed., *Crisis and Prosperity in Song China* (1975).

R. HYMES, *Statesmen and Gentlemen* (1987). On the transformation of officials into a local gentry elite during the twelfth and thirteenth centuries.

R. HYMES, *Way and Byway: Taoism, Local Religion, and Models of Divinity in Sung and Modern China* (2002).

M. ROSSABI, *China Among Equals* (1983). A study of the Liao, Qin, and Song Empires and their relations.

W. M. TU, *Confucian Thought, Selfhood as Creative Transformation* (1985).

K. YOSHIKAWA, *An Introduction to Song Poetry*, trans. by B. Watson (1967).

Yuan

T. T. ALLSEN, *Mongol Imperialism* (1987).

J. W. DARDESS, *Conquerors and Confucians: Aspects of Political Change in Late Yuan China* (1973).

DE RACHEWILTZ, trans., *The Secret History of the Mongols: A Mongolian Epic Chronicle of the Thirteenth Century* (2003). A new translation of a key historical work on the life of Genghis.

H. FRANKE AND D. TWITCHETT, eds., *The Cambridge History of China*, Vol. VI: *Alien Regimes and Border States, 710–1368* (1994).

J. D. LANGLOIS, *China Under Mongol Rule* (1981).

R. LATHAM, trans., *Travels of Marco Polo* (1958).

H. D. MARTIN, *The Rise of Chingis Khan and His Conquest of North China* (1981).

D. MORGAN, *The Mongol Empire and its Legacy* (1999). Genghis, the several khanates, and the aftermath of empire.

P. RATCHNEVSKY, *Genghis Khan, His Life and Legacy* (1992). The rise to power of the Mongol leader, with a critical consideration of historical sources.

CHAPTER 9

M. ADOLPHSON, *The Gates of Power: Monks, Courtiers, and Warriors in Premodern Japan* (2000). A new interpretation stressing the importance of temples in the political life of Heian and Kamakura Japan.

B.L. BATTEN, *To the Ends of Japan: Premodern Frontiers, Boundaries, and Interactions.* (2003). An interesting treatment of Heian Japan, topic by topic.

C. BLACKER, *The Catalpa Bow* (1975). An insightful study of folk Shinto.

R. BORGEN, *Sugawara no Michizane and the Early Heian Court* (1986). A study of a famous courtier and poet.

D. M. BROWN, ed., *The Cambridge History of Japan: Ancient Japan* (1993). This series of six volumes sums up several decades of research on Japan.

D. BROWN AND E. ISHIDA, eds., *The Future and the Past* (1979). A translation of a history of Japan written in 1219.

The Cambridge History of Japan, D.M. BROWN, ed.; Vol. 1, *Ancient Japan*, W. McCullough and D. H. Shively eds; Vol. 2, *Heian Japan*, K. Yamamura, ed. Vol. 3, *Medieval Japan*. Fine multi-author works.

M. COLLCUTT, *Five Mountains* (1980). A study of the monastic organization of medieval Zen.

T.D. CONLON, *State of War: The Violent Order of Fourteenth Century Japan* (2003). Compare Conlon's account with those of Souyri and Friday.

P. DUUS, *Feudalism in Japan* (1969). An easy survey of the subject.

W. W. FARRIS, *Population, Disease, and Land in Early Japan, 645–900* (1985). An innovative reinterpretation of early history.

W. W. FARRIS, *Heavenly Warriors: The Evolution of Japan's Military, 500–1300* (1992).

W. W. FARRIS, *Sacred Texts and Buried Treasures* (1998). Studies of Japan's prehistory and early history, based on recent Japanese research.

K. F. Friday, *Samurai, Warfare and the State in Early Medieval Japan* (2004). Weapons and warfare in Japan from the tenth to fourteenth centuries.

A. E. Goble, *Gō Daigo's Revolution* (1996). A provoking account of the 1331 revolt by an emperor who thought emperors should rule.

J. W. Hall, *Government and Local Power in Japan, 500–1700: A Study Based on Bizen Province* (1966). A splendid and insightful book.

J. W. Hall and T. Toyoda, *Japan in the Muromachi Age* (1977). Another collection of essays.

D. Keene, ed., *Anthology of Japanese Literature from the Earliest Era to the Mid-Nineteenth Century* (1955).

D. Keene, ed., *Twenty Plays of the Nō Theatre* (1970).

T. Lamarre, *Uncovering Heian Japan: An Archeology of Sensation and Inscription* (2000). The "archeology" in the title refers to digging into literature.

I. H. Levy, *The Ten Thousand Leaves* (1981). A fine translation of Japan's earliest collection of poetry.

J. P. Mass and W. Hauser, eds., *The Bakufu in Japanese History* (1985). Topics in *bakufu* history from the twelfth to the nineteenth centuries.

I. Morris, trans., *The Pillow Book of Sei Shōnagon* (1967). Observations about the Heian court life by the Jane Austen of ancient Japan.

S. Murasaki, *The Tale of Genji*, trans. by A. Waley (1952). A comparison of this translation with that of Seidensticker is instructive.

S. Murasaki, *The Tale of Genji*, trans. by E. G. Seidensticker (1976). The world's first novel and the greatest work of Japanese fiction.

R. J. Pearson et al., eds., *Windows on the Japanese Past: Studies in Archaeology and Prehistory* (1986).

D. L. Philippi, trans., *Kojiki* (1968). Japan's ancient myths.

J. Piggot, *The Emergence of Japanese Kingship* (1997).

E. O. Reischauer, *Ennin's Diary, the Record of a Pilgrimage to China in Search of the Law and Ennin's Travels in T'ang China* (1955).

E. O. Reischauer and A. M. Craig, *Japan: Tradition and Transformation* (1989). A more detailed work covering the sweep of Japanese history from the early beginnings through the 1980s.

H. Sato, *Legends of the Samurai* (1995). Excerpts from various tales and writings.

D. H. Shively and W. H. McCullough, eds., *The Cambridge History of Japan: Heian Japan* (1999).

D. T. Suzuki, *Zen and Japanese Culture* (1959).

H. Tonomura, *Community and Commerce in Late Medieval Japan* (1992).

R. Tsunoda, W. T. de Bary, and D. Keene, comps., *Sources of the Japanese Tradition* (1958). A collection of original religious, political, and philosophical writings from each period of Japanese history. The best reader. A new edition should be out soon.

H. P. Varley, *Imperial Restoration in Medieval Japan* (1971). A study of the 1331 attempt by an emperor to restore imperial power.

A. Waley, trans., *The Nō Plays of Japan* (1957). Medieval dramas.

K. Yamamura, ed., *Cambridge History of Japan: Medieval Japan* (1990).

CHAPTER 10

Iran

M. Boyce, *Zoroastrians: Their Religious Beliefs and Practices* (1979). A detailed survey by the current authority on Zoroastrian religious history. See Chapters 7–9.

M. Boyce, ed. and trans., *Textual Sources for the Study of Zoroastrianism* (1984). A valuable anthology with an important introduction that includes Boyce's arguments for a revision of the dates of Zoroaster's life (to between 1400 and 1200 B.C.E.).

R. N. Frye, *The Heritage of Persia* (1963). Still one of the best surveys, Chapter 6 deals with the Sasanid era.

R. Ghirshman, *Iran* (1954 [orig. ed. 1951]). An introductory survey of similar extent to Frye, but with differing material also.

R. Ghirshman, *Persian Art: The Parthian and Sasanid Dynasties* (1962). Superb photographs, and a very helpful glossary of places and names. The text is minimal.

Geo Widengran, *Mani and Manichaeism* (1965). Still the standard introduction to Mani's life and the later spread and development of Manichaeism.

India

A. L. Basham, *The Wonder That Was India* (1963). The best survey of classical Indian religion, society, literature, art, and politics.

W. T. de Bary et al., comp., *Sources of Indian Tradition*, 2nd ed. (1958), Vol. I, *From the Beginning to 1800*, ed. and rev. by Ainslie T. Embree (1988). Excellent selections from a wide variety of Indian texts, with good introductions to the text selections.

S. Dutt, *Buddhist Monks and Monasteries of India* (1962). The standard work. See especially Chapters 3 ("Bhakti") and 4 ("Monasteries Under the Gupta Kings").

D. G. Mandelbaum, *Society in India* (1972). 2 vols. The first two chapters in Volume I of this study of caste, family, and village relations are a good introduction to the caste system.

B. Rowland, *The Art and Architecture of India: Buddhist/Hindu/Jain*, 3rd rev. ed. (1970). See the excellent chapters on Sungan, Andhran, and other early Buddhist art (6–8, 14), the Gupta period (15), and the Hindu Renaissance (17–19).

V. A. Smith, *The Oxford History of India*, 4th rev. ed. (1981). See especially pages 164–229 (the Gupta period and following era to the Muslim invasions).

R. Thapar, *A History of India, Part I* (1966), pp. 109–193. Three chapters covering the rise of mercantilism, the Gupta "classical pattern," and the southern dynasties to ca. 900 C.E..

P. Younger, *Introduction to Indian Religious Thought* (1972). A sensitive attempt to delineate classical concerns of Indian religious thought and culture.

CHAPTER 11

O. Grabar, *The Formation of Islamic Art* (1973). A critical and creative interpretation of major themes in the development of distinctively Islamic forms of art and architecture.

A. Hourani, *A History of the Arab Peoples* (1991). A masterly survey of the Arabs down through the centuries and a clear picture of many aspects of Islamic history and culture that extend beyond the Arab world.

H. Kennedy, *The Prophet and the Age of the Caliphates: The Islamic Near East from the Sixth to the Eleventh Century* (1986). The best survey of early Islamic history.

I. Lapidus, *A History of Islamic Societies* (1988). A comprehensive overview of the rise and development of Islam all over the world.

F. E. Peters, *Muhammad and the Origins of Islam* (1994). A balanced analysis of the life of Muhammad.

F. Rahman, *Major Themes of the Qur'an* (1980). The best introduction to the basic ideas of the Qur'an and Islam, seen through the eyes of a perceptive Muslim modernist scholar.

F. Schuon, *Understanding Islam* (1994). Compares the Islamic worldview with Catholic Christianity. A dense, but intellectually stimulating, discussion.

M. Sells, *Approaching the Qur'an. The Early Revelations* (1999). A fine introduction and new translations of some of the more common earlier Qur'anic revelations.

B. Stowasser, *Women in the Qur'an, Traditions and Interpretation* (1994). An outstanding systematic study of statements regarding women in the Qur'an.

CHAPTER 12

K. Armstrong, *Muhammad: A Biography of the Prophet* (1992). Strong on religion.

R. Bartlett, *The Making of Europe, 950–1350* (1992). A study of the way immigration and colonial conquest shaped the Europe we know.

M. Bloch, *Feudal Society*, Vols. 1 and 2, trans. by L. A. Manyon (1971). A classic on the topic and as an example of historical study.

P. Brown, *Augustine of Hippo: A Biography* (1967). Late antiquity seen through the biography of its greatest Christian thinker.

J. H. Burns, *The Cambridge History of Medieval Political Thought c. 350–c. 1450* (1991). The best scan.

R. H. C. Davis, *A History of Medieval Europe: From Constantine to St. Louis* (1972). Unsurpassed in clarity.

R. Fletcher, *The Barbarian Conversion: From Paganism to Christianity* (1998). Up-to-date survey.

J. B. Glubb, *The Great Arab Conquests* (1995). Jihadists.

G. Guglielmo, ed., *The Byzantines* (1997). Updates key issues.

D. Gutas, *Greek Thought, Arabic Culture* (1998). A comparative intellectual history.

G. Holmes, Ed., *The Oxford History of Medieval Europe* (1992). Overviews of Roman and northern Europe during the "Dark Ages."

B. Lewis, *The Middle East: A Brief History of the Last 2,000 Years* (1995)

C. Mango, *Byzantium: The Empire of New Rome* (1980).

J. Martin, *Medieval Russia 980–1584* (1995). A concise narrative history.

R. McKitterick, ed., *Carolingian Culture: Emulation and Innovation* (1994). Fresh essays.

J.J. Norwich, *Byzantium: The Decline and Fall* (1995).

J.J. Norwich, *Byzantium: The Apogee* (1997). The whole story in two volulmes.

R.I. Page, *Chronicles of the Vikings: Records, Memorials, and Myths* (1995). Sources galore.

F. Robinson, ed., *The Cambridge Illustrated History of the Islamic World* (1996). Spectacular.

S. Runciman, *Byzantine Civilization* (1970). Succinct, comprehensive account by a master.

P. Sawyer, *The Age of the Vikings* (1962). Old but solid account.

C. Stephenson, *Medieval Feudalism* (1969). Excellent short summary and introduction.

L. WHITE JR., *Medieval Technology and Social Change* (1962). Often fascinating account of how primitive technology changed life.

H. WOLFRAM, *The Roman Empire and Its Germanic Peoples* (1997). Challenging, but most rewarding.

CHAPTER 13

The Islamic Heartlands

L. AHMED, *Women and Gender in Islam. Historical Roots of a Modern Debate* (1992). A good historical survey of the status of women in Middle Eastern societies.

J. BERKEY, *The Formation of Islam. Religion and Society in the Near East 600–1800* (2002). An interesting new synthesis foducing on political and religious trends.

C. E. BOSWORTH, *The Islamic Dynasties: A Chronological and Genealogical Handbook* (1967). A handy reference work for dynasties and families important to Islamic history in all periods and places.

M. A. COOK, *Commanding Right and Forbidding Wrong in Islamic Thought* (2001). A masterful anaylsis of the development of Islamic law.

P. K. HITTI, *History of the Arabs*, 8th ed. (1964). Still a useful English resource, largely for factual detail. See especially Part IV, "The Arabs in Europe: Spain and Sicily."

A. HOURANI, *A History of the Arab Peoples* (1991). The newest survey history and the best, at least for the Arab Islamic world.

S. K. JAYYUSI, ed., *The Legacy of Muslim Spain*, 2 vols. (1994). A comprehensive survey of the arts, politics, literature, and society by experts in various fields.

B. LEWIS, ed., *Islam and the Arab World* (1976). A large-format, heavily illustrated volume with many excellent articles on diverse aspects of Islamic (not simply Arab, as the misleading title indicates) civilization through the premodern period.

D. MORGAN, *The Mongols* (1986). A recent and readable survey history.

J. J. SAUNDERS, *A History of Medieval Islam* (1965). A brief and simple, if sketchy, introductory survey of Islamic history to the Mongol invasions.

India

W. T. DE BARY et al., comp., *Sources of Indian Tradition*, 2nd ed. (1958), Vol. I, *From the Beginning to 1800*, ed. and rev. by Ainslie T. Embree (1988). Excellent selections from a wide variety of Indian texts, with good introductions to chapters and individual selections.

S. M. IKRAM, *Muslim Civilization in India* (1964). The best short survey history, covering the period 711 to 1857.

R. C. MAJUMDAR, gen. ed., *The History and Culture of the Indian People*, Vol. VI, *The Delhi Sultanate*, 3rd ed. (1980). A comprehensive political and cultural account of the period in India.

F. ROBINSON, ed., *The Cambridge History of India, Pakistan, Bangladesh, Sri Lanka, Nepal, Bhutan, and the Maldives* (1989). A very helpful quick reference source with brief but well-done survey essays on a wide range of topics relevant to South Asian history down to the present.

A. WINK, *Al-Hind: The Making of the Indo-Islamic World*, Vol. 1 (1991). The first of five promising volumes to be devoted to the Indo-Islamic world's history. This volume treats the seventh to eleventh centuries.

Southeast Asia

L. ANDAYA, *The World of Maluku: Eastern Indonesia in the Early Modern Period* (1993). A comprehensive view of the formation of what is now Indonesia.

B. W. ANDAYA AND L. ANDAYA, *A History of Malaysia* (1982). A good overiew of Indonesia's smaller but critical northern neighbor.

J. SIEGEL, *Shadow and Sound: The Historical Thought of a Sumatran People* (1979). An excellent analysis tracing the relation between foreign influences and local practice.

CHAPTER 14

B. S. BAUER, *The Development of the Inca State* (1992). An important new work that emphasizes archaeological evidence over the Spanish chronicles in accounting for the emergence of the Inca Empire.

F. F. BERDAN, *The Aztecs of Central Mexico: An Imperial Society* (1982). An excellent introduction to the Aztecs.

R. E. BLANTON, S. A. KOWALEWSKI, G. FEINMAN, AND J. APPEL, *Ancient Mesoamerica: A Comparison of Change in Three Regions* (1981). Concentrates on ancient Mexico.

K. O. BRUHNS, *Ancient South America* (1994). A clear discussion of the archaeology and civilization of the region with emphasis on the Andes.

R. L. BURGER, *Chavín and the Origins of Andean Civilization* (1992). A detailed study of early Andean prehistory by one of the leading authorities on Chavín.

R. M. CARMACK, J. GASCO, AND G. H. GOSSEN, *The Legacy of Mesoamerica: History and Culture of a Native American Civilization* (1996). A survey of Mesoamerica from its origins to the present.

I. CLENDINNEN, *Aztecs: An Interpretation* (1995). A fascinating attempt to reconstruct the Aztec world.

M. D. COE, *Breaking the Maya Code* (1992). The story of the remarkable achievement of deciphering the ancient Maya language.

M. D. Coe, *The Maya* (1993). The best introduction.

M. D. Coe, *Mexico from the Olmecs to the Aztecs* (1994). A wide-ranging introductory discussion.

G. Conrad and A. A. Demarest, *Religion and Empire: The Dynamics of Aztec and Inca Expansionism* (1984). An interesting comparative study.

S. D. Gillespie, *The Aztec Kings* (1989).

R. Hassig, *Aztec Warfare*.

J. Hyslop, *Inka Settlement Planning* (1990). A detailed study.

M. León-Portilla, *Fifteen Poets of the Aztec World* (1992). An anthology of translations of Aztec poetry.

M. E. Miller, *The Art of Mesoamerica from Olmec to Aztec* (1986). A well-illustrated introduction.

C. Morris and A. Von Hagen, *The Inka Empire and Its Andean Origins* (1993). A clear overview of Andean prehistory by a leading authority. Beautifully illustrated.

M. E. Mosely, *The Incas and Their Ancestors: The Archaeology of Peru* (1992). Readable and thorough.

J. A. Sabloff, *The Cities of Ancient Mexico* (1989). Capsule summaries of ancient Mesoamerican cultures.

J. A. Sabloff, *Archaeology and the Maya* (1990). A look at changing views of the ancient Maya.

L. Schele and M. E. Miller, *The Blood of Kings* (1986). A rich and beautifully illustrated study of ancient Maya art and society.

R. S. Sharer, *The Ancient Maya*, 5th ed. (1994). A classic. Readable, authoritative, and thorough.

M. P. Weaver, *The Aztecs, Maya, and Their Predecessors* (1993). A classic textbook.

CHAPTER 15

L. B. Alberti, *The Family in Renaissance Florence*, trans. by R. N. Watkins (1962). A contemporary humanist, who never married, explains how a family should behave.

E. Amt, ed., *Women's Lives in Medieval Europe: A Source-book* (1992). Outstanding collection of sources.

H. Baron, *The Crisis of the Early Italian Renaissance*, Vols. 1 and 2 (1996). New edition of an old, major work, setting forth the civic dimension of Italian humanism.

G. Barraclough, *The Origins of Modern Germany* (1963). Penetrating political narrative.

S. Bramly, *Discovering the Life of Leonard da Vinci* (1991). The man and the genius.

G. Brucker, *Renaissance Florence* (1983). Still one of the best introductions.

G. Bull, *Michelangelo: A Biography* (1995). Recent life in full.

J. Burckhardt, *The Civilization of the Renaissance in Italy* (1867). The famous classic that still has as many defenders as detractors.

S. Flanagan, *Hildegard of Bingen, 1098–1179: A Visionary Life* (1995). A most interesting German woman.

E. Hallam, ed., *Chronicles of the Crusades (1989).* All nine!

D. Herlihy, *Medieval Households* (1985). Survey of Middle Ages that defends the medieval family against modern caricatures.

D. Herlihy and C. Klapisch-Zuber, *Tuscans and Their Families* (1985). Important work based on unique demographic data that gives the reader an appreciation of quantitative history.

G. Holmes, *Renaissance* (1996). An expert's take on the subject.

J. C. Holt, *Magna Carta*, 2nd ed. (1992). The famous document and its interpretation by succeeding generations.

J. Huizinga, *The Waning of the Middle Ages: A Study of the Forms of Life, Thought, and Art in France and the Netherlands in the Dawn of the Renaissance* (1924). A classic study of "mentality" at the end of the Middle Ages.

L. Jardine, *Worldly Goods: A New History of the Renaissance* (1996). The material side of the Renaissance.

M. King, *Women of the Renaissance* (1991). Women's presence and creativity.

W. H. McNeill, *Plagues and Peoples* (1976). The Black Death in a broader context.

R. I. Moore, *The Formation of a Persecuting Society: Power and Deviance in Western Europe, 950–1250* (1987). A sympathetic look at heresy and dissent.

T. Noonan, *Contraception: A History of Its Treatment by the Catholic Theologians and Canonists* (1967). A fascinating account of medieval theological attitudes toward sexuality and sex-related problems.

J. Riley-Smith, ed., *Oxford Illustrated History of the Crusades* (1995) Lucid, gorgeous, and up-to-date.

J. Weisheipl, *Friar Thomas* (1980). Biography of Saint Thomas Aquinas, both the man and the theologian.

CHAPTER 16

M. Brecht, *Martin Luther: His Road to Reformation, 1483–1521* (1985). Best on young Luther.

C. Brown, et al., *Rembrandt: The Master and His Workshop* (1991) A great master's art and influence.

R. Briggs, *Witches and Neighbors: A History of European Witchcraft* (1996). A readable introduction.

E. DUFFY, *The Stripping of the Altars* (1992). Strongest argument yet that there was no deep reformation in England.

H. O. EVENNETT, *The Spirit of the Counter Reformation* (1968). The continuity and independence of Catholic reform.

HANS-JÜRGEN GOERTZ, *The Anabaptists* (1996). Best treatment of minority Protestants.

O. P. GRELL AND A. CUNNINGHAM, *Health Care and Poor Relief in Protestant Europe* (1997) The civic side of the Reformation.

M. HOLT, *The French Wars of Religion, 1562–1629* (1995). Scholarly appreciation of religious side of the story.

J. C. HUTCHISON, *Albrecht Durer* (1990). The life behind the art.

H. JEDIN, *A History of the Council of Trent*, Vols. 1, 2 (1957–1961). Comprehensive, detailed, and authoritative.

M. KITCHEN, *The Cambridge Illustrated History of Germany* (1996). Comprehensive and accessible.

A. KORS AND E. PETERS, eds., *European Witchcraft, 1100–1700* (1972). Classics of witch belief.

W. MACCAFFREY, *Elizabeth I* (1993). Magisterial study.

G. MATTINGLY, *The Armada* (1959). A masterpiece, novel-like in style.

D. MCCOLLOCH, *The Reformation* (2004). No stone unturned, with English emphasis.

H. A. OBERMAN, *Luther: Man Between God and Devil* (1989). Authoritative biography

J. W. O'MALLEY, *The First Jesuits* (1993). Extremely detailed account of the creation of the Society of Jesus and its original purposes.

S. OZMENT, *The Age of Reform 1250–1550: An Intellectual and Religious History of Late Medieval and Reformation Europe* (1980). Broad, lucid survey.

S. OZMENT, *When Fathers Ruled: Family Life in Reformation Europe* (1983). Effort to portray the constructive side of Protestant thinking about family relationships.

S. OZMENT, *The Bürgermeister's Daughter: Scandal in a Sixteenth Century German Town* (1996). What a woman could do at law in the sixteenth century.

G. PARKER, *The Thirty Years' War* (1984). Large, lucid survey.

J. H. PARRY, *The Age of Reconnaissance* (1964). A comprehensive account of explorations from 1450 to 1650.

W. PRINZ, *Durer* (1998). Latest biography of Germany's greatest painter.

J. J. SCARISBRICK, *Henry VIII* (1968). The best account of Henry's reign.

G. STRAUSS, ed. and trans., *Manifestations of Discontent in Germany on the Eve of the Reformation* (1971). A rich collection of sources for both rural and urban scenes.

H. WUNDER, *He Is the Sun, She Is the Moon: Women in Early Modern Germany* (1998). Best study of early modern women.

CHAPTER 17

J. ABUN-NASR, *A History of the Maghrib in the Islamic Period* (1987). The most recent North African survey. Pages 59–247 are relevant to this chapter.

D. BIRMINHAM, *Central Africa to 1870* (1981). Chapters from the *Cambridge History of Africa* that give a brief, lucid overview of developments in this region.

P. BOHANNAN AND P. CURTIN, *Africa and Africans*, rev. ed. (1971). Accessible, topical approach to African history, culture, society, politics, and economics.

P. D. CURTIN, S. FEIERMANN, L. THOMPSON, AND J. VANSINA, *African History* (1978). An older, but masterly survey. The relevant portions are Chapters 6–9.

R. ELPHICK, *Kraal and Castle: Khoikhoi and the Founding of White South Africa* (1977). An incisive, informative interpretation of the history of the Khoikhoi and their fateful interaction with European colonization.

R. ELPHICK AND H. GILIOMEE, *The Shaping of South African Society, 1652–1820* (1979). A superb, synthetic history of this crucial period.

J. D. FAGE, *A History of Africa* (1978). Still a readable survey history.

M. HISKETT, *The Development of Islam in West Africa* (1984). The standard survey study of the subject. Of the relevant sections (Chapters 1–10, 12, 15), that on Hausaland, which is treated only in passing in this text, is noteworthy.

R. W. JULY, *Precolonial Africa: An Economic and Social History* (1975). Chapter 10 gives an interesting overall picture of slaving in African history.

R. W. JULY, *A History of the African People*, 3rd ed. (1980). Chapters 3–6 treat Africa before about 1800 area by area; Chapter 7 deals with "The Coming of Europe."

I. M. LEWIS, Ed., *Islam in Tropical Africa* (1966), pp. 4–96. Lewis's introduction is one of the best brief summaries of the role of Islam in West Africa and the Sudan.

D. T. NIANI, ed., *Africa from the Twelfth to the Sixteenth Century, UNESCO General History of Africa*, Vol. IV (1984). Many survey articles cover the various regions and major states of Africa in the centuries noted in the title.

R. OLIVER, *The African Experience* (1991). A masterly, balanced, and engaging survey, with outstanding syntheses and summaries of recent research.

J. A. RAWLEY, *The Transatlantic Slave Trade: A History* (1981). Impressively documented, detailed, and well-presented survey history of the Atlantic trade; little focus on African dimensions.

A. F. C. RYDER, *Benin and the Europeans: 1485–1897* (1969). A basic study.

JOHN K. THORNTON, *The Kingdom of Kongo: Civil War and Transition, 1641–1718* (1983). A detailed and perceptive analysis for those who wish to delve into Kongo state and society in the seventeenth century.

M. WILSON AND L. THOMPSON, eds., *The Oxford History of South Africa*, Vol. I., *South Africa to 1870* (1969). Relatively detailed, if occasionally dated, treatment.

CHAPTER 18

I. BERLIN, *Many Thousands Gone: The First Two Centuries of Slavery in North America* (1998); *Generations of Captivity: A History of African American Slaves* (2003). Two volumes representing the most extensive and important recent treatment of slavery in North America.

R. BLACKBURN, *The Making of New World Slavery from the Baroque to the Modern 1492–1800* (1997). An extraordinary work.

B. COBO, *History of the Inca Empire* (1979). A major discussion.

N. D. COOK, *Born to Die: Disease and New World Conquest, 1492–1650* (1998) A survey of the devastating impact of previously unknown diseases on the native populations of the Americas.

P. D. CURTIN, *The Atlantic Slave Trade: A Census* (1969). Remains a basic work.

D. B. DAVIS, *The Problem of Slavery in Western Culture* (1966). A brilliant and far-ranging discussion.

H. L. GATES JR. AND W. L. ANDREWS, eds., *Pioneers of the Black Atlantic: Five Slave Narratives from the Enlightenment 1772–1815* (1998). An anthology of autobiographical accounts.

S. GRUZINSKI, *The Conquest of Mexico: The Incorporation of Indian Societies into the Western World, 16th–18th Centuries* (1993). Interprets the experience of Native Americans, from their own point of view, during the time of the Spanish conquest.

L. HANKE, *Bartolomé de Las Casas: An Interpretation of His Life and Writings* (1951). A classic work.

R. HARMS, *The Diligent: A Voyage through the Worlds of the Slave Trade* (2002). A powerful narrative of the voyage of a French slave trader.

J. HEMMING, *The Conquest of the Incas*, (1970). A lucid account of the conquest of the Inca Empire and its aftermath.

J. HEMMING, *Red Gold: The Conquest of the Brazilian Native Americans, 1500–1760* (1978). A careful account with excellent bibliography.

H. KLEIN, *The Middle Passage: Comparative Studies in the African Slave Trade* (1978). A far-ranging overview of the movement of slaves from Africa to the Americas.

M. LEON-PORTILLA, ed., *The Broken Spears: The Aztec Account of the Conquest of Mexico* (1961). A collection of documents recounting the experience of the Aztecs from their own point of view.

P. MANNING, *Slavery and African Life: Occidental, Oriental, and African Slave Trades* (1990). An admirably concise economic-historical synthesis of the evidence, with multiple tables and statistics to supplement the magisterial analysis.

A. PAGDEN, *Lords of All the World: Ideologies of Empire in Spain, Britain, and France* c. 1500–c. 1800 (1995). An effort to explain the imperial thinking of the major European powers.

S. B. SCHWARTZ, *Sugar Plantations in the Formation of Brazilian Society: Bahia, 1550–1835* (1985). A broad-ranging study of the emergence of the plantation economy.

I. K. STEELE, *The English Atlantic, 1675–1740s: An Exploration of Communication and Community* (1986). An exploration of culture and commerce in the transatlantic world.

S. J. STEIN, *Peru's Indian Peoples and the Challenge of Spanish Conquest: Huamanga to 1640* (1983). A work that examines the impact of the conquest of the Inca empire over the scope of a century.

H. THOMAS, *Conquest: Montezuma, Cortés, and the Fall of Old Mexico* (1993). A splendid modern narrative of the event with careful attention to the character of the participants.

H. THOMAS, *The Slave Trade: The Story of the Atlantic Slave Trade: 1440–1870* (1999). A sweeping narrative overview.

J. THORNTON, *Africa and Africans in the Making of the Atlantic World, 1400–1680* (1992). A discussion of the role of Africans in the emergence of the transatlantic economy.

N. WACHTEL, *The Vision of the Vanquished: The Spanish Conquest of Peru Through Indian Eyes, 1530–1570* (1977). A presentation of Incan experience of conquest.

CHAPTER 19

China

D. BODDE AND C. MORRIS, *Law in Imperial China* (1967). Focuses on the Qing dynasty (1644–1911).

T. BROOK, *The Confusions of Pleasure: Commerce and Culture in Ming China* (1988).

C. S. CHANG AND S. L. H. CHANG, *Crisis and Transformation in Seventeenth Century China: Society, Culture, and Modernity* (1992).

P. CROSSLEY, *Translucent Mirror: History and Identity in Qing Imperial Ideology* (1999).

W. T. DE BARY, *Learning for One's Self: Essays on the Individual in Neo-Confucian Thought* (1991). A useful corrective to the view that Confucianism is simply a social ideology.

M. C. ELLIOTT, *The Manchu Way: The Eight Banners and Ethnic Identity in Late Imperial China* (2001). The latest word; compare to Crossley above.

M. ELVIN, *The Pattern of the Chinese Past: A Social and Economic Interpretation* (1973). A controversial but stimulating interpretation of Chinese economic history in terms of technology. It brings in earlier periods as well as the Ming, Qing, and modern China.

J. K. FAIRBANK, ed., *The Chinese World Order: Traditional China's Foreign Relations* (1968). An examination of the Chinese tribute system and its varying applications.

H. L. KAHN, *Monarchy in the Emperor's Eyes: Image and Reality in the Ch'ien-lung Reign* (1971). A study of the Chinese court during the mid-Qing period.

P. KUHN, *Soulstealers: The Chinese Sorcery Scare of 1768* (1990).

LI YU, *The Carnal Prayer Mat*, trans. by P. Hanan (1990).

F. MOTE AND D. TWITCHETT, eds., *The Cambridge History of China: The Ming Dynasty 1368–1644*, Vols. VI (1988) and VII (1998).

S. NAQUIN, *Peking Temples and City Life, 1400–1900* (2000).

S. NAQUIN AND E. S. RAWSKI, *Chinese Society in the Eighteenth Century* (1987).

J. B. PARSONS, *The Peasant Rebellions of the Late Ming Dynasty* (1970).

P. C. PERDUE, *Exhausting the Earth, State and Peasant in Hunan, 1500–1850* (1987).

D. H. PERKINS, *Agricultural Development in China, 1368–1968* (1969).

E. RAWSKI, *The Last Emperors: A Social History of Qing Imperial Institutions* (1998).

M. RICCI, *China in the Sixteenth Century: The Journals of Matthew Ricci, 1583–1610* (1953).

W. ROWE, *Hankow* (1984). A study of a city in late imperial China.

G. W. SKINNER, *The City in Late Imperial China* (1977).

J. D. SPENCE, *Ts'ao Yin and the K'ang-hsi Emperor: Bondservant and Master* (1966). An excellent study of the early Qing court.

J. D. SPENCE, *Emperor of China: A Self-Portrait of K'ang-hsi* (1974). The title of this readable book does not adequately convey the extent of the author's contribution to the study of the early Qing emperor.

J. D. SPENCE, *Treason by the Book* (2001). An account of the legal workings of the authoritarian Qing state that reads like a detective story.

L. A. STRUVE, trans. and ed., *Voices from the Ming-Qing Cataclysm* (1993). A reader with translations of Chinese sources.

F. WAKEMAN, *The Great Enterprise* (1985). On the founding of the Manchu dynasty.

Japan

M. E. BERRY, *Hideyoshi* (1982). A study of the sixteenth-century unifier of Japan.

M. E. BERRY, *The Culture of Civil War in Kyoto* (1994). On the Warring States era.

H. BOLITHO, *Treasures Among Men: The Fudai Daimyo in Tokugawa Japan* (1974). A study in depth.

H. BOLITHO, *Bereavement and Consolation: Testimonies from Tokugawa Japan* (2003). Instances of how Tokugawa Japanese handled the death of a child.

C. R. BOXER, *The Christian Century in Japan, 1549–1650* (1951).

The Cambridge History of Japan, Vol. 4 J.W. Hall (ed.), *Early Modern Japan* (1991). A multi-author work.

M. CHIKAMATSU, *Major Plays of Chikamatsu*, trans. by D. Keene (1961).

R. P. DORE, *Education in Tokugawa Japan* (1965).

G. S. ELISON, *Deus Destroyed: The Image of Christianity in Early Modern Japan* (1973). A brilliant study of the persecutions of Christianity during the early Tokugawa period.

J. W. HALL AND M. JANSEN, eds., *Studies in the Institutional History of Early Modern Japan* (1968). A collection of articles on Tokugawa institutions.

J. W. HALL, K. NAGAHARA, AND K. YAMAMURA, eds., *Japan Before Tokugawa* (1981).

S. HANLEY, *Everyday Things in Premodern Japan: The Hidden Legacy of Material Culture* (1997).

H. S. HIBBETT, *The Floating World in Japanese Fiction* (1959). An eminently readable study of early Tokugawa literature.

M. JANSEN, ed., *The Nineteenth Century*, Vol. 5 in *The Cambridge History of Japan* (1989).

K. KATSU, *Musui's Story* (1988). The life and adventures of a boisterous, no-good samurai of the early nineteenth century. Eminently readable.

D. KEENE, trans., *Chushingura, the Treasury of Loyal Retainers* (1971). The puppet play about the forty-seven rōnin who took revenge on the enemy of their former lord.

O.G. LIDIN, *Tanegashima: The Arrival of Europe in Japan* (2002). The impact of the musket and Europeans on sixteenth-century Japan.

M. MARUYAMA, *Studies in the Intellectual History of Tokugawa Japan*, trans. by M. Hane (1974). A seminal work in this field by one of modern Japan's greatest scholars.

J.L. MCCLAIN, et. al., *Edo and Paris: Urban Life and the State in the Early Modern Era* (1994). Comparison of city life and government role in capitals of Tokugawa Japan and France.

K. W. NAKAI, *Shogunal Politics* (1988). A brilliant study of Arai Hakuseki's conceptualization of Tokugawa government.

P. NOSCO, ed., *Confucianism and Tokugawa Culture* (1984). A lively collection of essays.

H. OOMS, *Tokugawa Village Practice: Class, Status, Power, Law* (1996).

A. RAVINA, *Land and Lordship in Early Modern Japan* (1999). A sociopolitical study of three Tokugawa domains.

I. SAIKAKU, *The Japanese Family Storehouse*, trans. by G. W. Sargent (1959). A lively novel about merchant life in seventeenth-century Japan.

G. B. SANSOM, *The Western World and Japan* (1950).

J. A. SAWADA, *Confucian Values and Popular Zen* (1993). A study of *Shingaku*, a popular Tokugawa religious sect.

C. D. SHELDON, *The Rise of the Merchant Class in Tokugawa Japan* (1958).

T. C. SMITH, *The Agrarian Origins of Modern Japan* (1959). On the evolution of farming and rural social organization in Tokugawa Japan.

P. F. SOUYRI, *The World Turned Upside Down: Medieval Japanese Society* (2001). After a running start from the late Heian period, an analysis of the overthrow of lords by their vassals.

R. P. TOBY, *State and Diplomacy in Early Modern Japan: Asia in the Development of the Tokugawa Bakufu* (1984).

C. TOTMAN, *Tokugawa Ieyasu: Shōgun* (1983).

C. TOTMAN, *Green Archipelago, Forestry in Preindustrial Japan* (1989).

H. P. VARLEY, *The Ō'nin War: History of Its Origins and Background with a Selective Translation of the Chronicle of Ō'nin* (1967).

K. YAMAMURA AND S. B. HANLEY, *Economic and Demographic Change in Preindustrial Japan, 1600–1868* (1977).

Korea

T. HATADA, *A History of Korea* (1969).

W. E. HENTHORN, *A History of Korea* (1971).

KI-BAIK LEE, *A New History of Korea* (1984).

P. LEE, *Sourcebook of Korean Civilization*, Vol. I (1993).

Vietnam

J. BUTTINGER, *A Dragon Defiant, a Short History of Vietnam* (1972).

NGUYEN DU, *The Tale of Kieu* (1983).

N. TARLING, ed., *The Cambridge History of Southeast Asia* (1992).

K. TAYLOR, *The Birth of Vietnam* (1983).

A. B. WOODSIDE, *Vietnam and the Chinese Model* (1988).

CHAPTER 20

F. ANDERSON, *The Crucible of War: The Seven Years' War and the Fate of Empire in British North America, 1754–1766* (2000) A splendid narrative and analysis.

J. BLUM, *Lord and Peasant in Russia from the Ninth to the Nineteenth Century* (1961). Remains a thorough and wide-ranging discussion.

P. BURKE, *The Fabrication of Louis XIV* (1992). Examines the manner in which the public image of Louis XIV was forged in art.

P. BUSHKOVITCH, *Peter the Great: The Struggle for Power, 1671–1725* (2001). Replaces previous studies.

L. COLLEY, *Britons: Forging the Nation, 1707–1837* (1992) A major study of the making of British nationhood.

P. DEANE, *The First Industrial Revolution*, (1999). A well-balanced and systematic treatment.

J. DE VRIES, *European Urbanization 1500–1800* (1984). The most important and far-ranging of recent treatments of the subject.

W. DOYLE, *The Old European Order, 1660–1800* (1992). The most thoughtful treatment of the subject.

R. J. W. EVANS, *The Making of the Habsburg Monarchy, 1550–1700: An Interpretation* (1979). Places much emphasis on intellectual factors and the role of religion.

D. FRASER, *Frederick the Great: King of Prussia* (2001) Excellent on both Frederick and eighteenth-century Prussia.

E. HOBSBAWM, *Industry and Empire: The Birth of the Industrial Revolution* (1999). A survey by a major historian of the subject.

K. HONEYMAN, *Women, Gender and Industrialization in England, 1700–1850* (2000). Emphasizes how certain work or economic roles became associated with either men or women.

O. H. HUFTON, *The Poor of Eighteenth-Century France, 1750–1789* (1975). A brilliant study of poverty and the family economy.

L. HUGHES, *Russia in the Age of Peter the Great* (1998). An excellent account.

D. I. KERTZER AND M. BARBAGLI, *The History of the European Family: Family Life in Early Modern Times, 1500–1709* (2001). A series of broad-ranging essays covering the entire Continent.

S. KING AND G. TIMMONS, *Making Sense of the Industrial Revolution: English Economy and Society, 1700–1850* (2001). Examines the Industrial Revolution through the social institutions that brought it about and were changed by it.

M. KISHLANSKY, *A Monarchy Transformed: Britain 1603–1714* (1996) An excellent synthesis.

P. LANGFORD, *A Polite and Commercial People: England 1717–1783* (1989). An excellent survey of mid-eighteenth-century Britain covering social history as well as politics, the overseas wars, and the American Revolution.

A. LOSSKY, *Louis XIV and the French Monarchy* (1994). The most recent major analysis.

F. E. MANUEL, *The Broken Staff: Judaism Through Christian Eyes* (1992). An important discussion of Christian interpretations of Judaism.

M. A. MEYER, *The Origins of the Modern Jew: Jewish Identity and European Culture in Germany, 1749–1824* (1967). A general introduction organized around individual case studies.

D. UNDERDOWN, *Fire from Heaven: Life in an English Town in the Seventeenth Century* (1992). A lively account of how a single English town experienced the religious and political turmoil of the century.

D. VALENZE, *The First Industrial Woman* (1995). An elegant work exploring the manner in which industrialization transformed the work of women.

J. WEST, *Gunpower, Government, and War in the Mid–Eighteenth Century* (1991). A study of how warfare touched much government of the day.

CHAPTER 21

S. S. BLAIR AND J. BLOOM, *The Art and Architecture of Islam, 1250–1800* (1994). A fine survey of the period for all parts of the Islamic world.

R. CANFIELD, ed., *Turko-Persia in Historical Perspctive* (1991). A good general collection of essays.

K. CHELEBI, *The Balance of Truth* (1957). A marvelous volume of essays and reflections by probably the major intellectual of Ottoman times.

W. T. DE BARY et al., comp., *Sources of Indian Tradition*, 2nd ed. (1958),Vol. I, *From the Beginning to 1800*, ed. and rev. by Ainslie T. Embree (1988). Excellent selections from a wide variety of Indian texts, with good introductions to chapters and individual selections.

S. FAROQI, *Towns and Townsmen of Ottoman Anatolia* (1984). Examines the changing balances of economic power between the urban and rural areas.

C. H. FLEISCHER, *Bureaucrat and Intellectual in the Ottoman Empire: The Historian Mustafa Ali (1541–1600)* (1986). A major study of Ottoman intellectual history.

G. HAMBLY, *Central Asia* (1966). Excellent survey chapters (9–13) on the Chaghatay and Uzbek (Shaybanid) Turks.

R. S. HATTOX, *Coffee and Coffee-Houses: The Origins of a Social Beverage in the Medieval Near East* (1985). A fascinating piece of social history.

M. G. S. HODGSON, *The Gunpowder Empires and Modern Times*, Vol. 3 of *The Venture of Islam*, 3 vols. (1974). Less ample than Vols. 1 and 2 of Hodgson's monumental history, but a thoughtful survey of the great post-1500 empires.

S. M. IKRAM, *Muslim Civilization in India* (1964). Still the best short survey history, covering the period from 711 to 1857.

H. INALCIK, *The Ottoman Empire: The Classical Age 1300–1600* (1973). An excellent, if dated, survey with solid treatment of Ottoman social, religious, and political institutions.

H. INALCIK, *An Economic and Social History of the Ottoman Empire, 1300–1914* (1994). A masterly survey by the dean of Ottoman studies today.

C. KAFADAR, *Between Two Worlds: The Construction of the Ottoman State* (1995). A readable analysis of theories of Ottoman origins and early development.

N. R. KEDDIE, ed., *Scholars, Saints, and Sufis: Muslim Religious Institutions in the Middle East Since 1500* (1972). A collection of interesting articles well worth reading.

M. MUJEEB, *The Indian Muslims* (1967). The best cultural study of Islamic civilization in India as a whole, from its origins onward.

G. NECIPOGLU, *Architecture, Ceremonial, and Power: The Topkapi Palace in the Fifteenth and Sixteenth Centuries* (1991). A superb analysis of the symbolism of Ottoman power and authority.

L. PIERCE, *The Imperial Harem: Women and Sex in the Ottoman Empire* (1993). Ground-breaking study on the role of women in the Ottoman Empire.

D. QUATARERT, *An Economic and Social history of the Ottoman Empire 1300–1914* (1994). The authoritative account of Ottoman economy and society.

J. RICHARDS, *The Mughal Empire*, Vol. 5 of *The New Cambridge History of India* (1993). A impressive synthesis of the varying interpretations of the Mughal India.

S. A. A. RIZVI, *The Wonder That Was India*, Vol. II (1987). A sequel to Basham's original *The Wonder That Was India*; treats Mughal life, culture, and history from 1200 to 1700.

F. ROBINSON, *Atlas of the Islamic World Since 1500* (1982). Brief, excellent historical essays, color illustrations with detailed accompanying text, and chronological tables, as well as precise maps, make this a refreshing general reference work.

R. SAVORY, *Iran Under the Safavids* (1980). A solid and readable survey.

S. J. SHAW, *Empire of the Gazis: The Rise and Decline of the Ottoman Empire, 1280–1808*, Vol. I of *History of the Ottoman Empire and Modern Turkey* (1976). A solid historical survey with excellent bibliographic essays for each chapter and a good index.

CHAPTER 22

D. BEALES, *Joseph II: In the Shadow of Maria Theresa, 1741–1780* (1987). The best treatment in English of the early political life of Joseph II.

M. BIAGIOLI, *Galileo Courtier: The Practice of Science in the Culture of Absolutism* (1993). A major revisionist work that emphasizes the role of the political setting on Galileo's career and thought.

D. D. BIEN, *The Calas Affair: Persecution, Toleration, and Heresy in Eighteenth-Century Toulouse* (1960). Classic treatment of the famous case.

T. C. W. BLANNING, *The Culture of Power and the Power of Culture: Old Regime Europe 1660–1789* (2002). The strongest treatment of the relationship of eighteenth-century cultural changes and politics.

R. DARNTON, *The Literary Underground of the Old Regime* (1982). Classic essays on the world of printers, publishers, and booksellers.

P. DEAR, *Revolutionizing the Sciences: European Knowledge and Its Ambitions, 1500–1700* (2001). A broad-ranging study of both the ideas and institutions of the new science.

I. DE MADARIAGA, *Catherine the Great: A Short History* (1990). A good brief biography.

S. GAUKROGER, *Francis Bacon and the Transformation of Early-Modern Philosophy* (2001). An excellent, accessible introduction.

J. GLEIXK, *Isaac Newton* (2003) The best brief biography.

D. GOODMAN, *The Republic of Letters: A Cultural History of the French Enlightenment* (1994). Concentrates on the role of salons.

I. HARRIS, *The Mind of John Locke: A Study of Political Theory in Its Intellectual Setting* (1994). The most comprehensive recent treatment.

J. L. HEILBRON, *The Sun in the Church: Cathedrals as Solar Observatories* (2000). A remarkable study of the manner in which Roman Catholic cathedrals were used to make astsronomical observations and calculations.

K. J. HOWELL, *God's TwoBooks: Copernican Cosmology and Biblical Interpretqation in Early Modern Science* (2003) Best introduction to early modern issues of science and religion.

J. MELTON, *The Rise of the Public in Enlightenmen Europe* (2001). A superb overview of the emergence of new institutions which made the expression of a broad public opinion possible in Europe.

T. MUNCK, *The Enlightenment: A Comparative Social History 1721–1794* (2000). A clear introduction to the social background making possible the spread of Enlightenment thought.

S. MUTHU, *Enlightenment against Empire* (2003) A study of philosophes who criticized the European empires of their day.

D. OUTRAM, *The Enlightenment* (1995). An excellent brief introduction.

R. PORTER, *The Creation of the Modern World: The Untold Story of the British Enlightenment* (2001) A superb, lively overview.

P. RILEY, *The Cambridge Companion to Rousseau* (2001). Excellent accessible essays by major scholars.

E. ROTHCHILD, *Economic Sentiments: Adam Smith, Condorcet, and the Enlightenment* (2001). A sensitive account of Smith's thought and its relationship to the social questions of the day.

S. SHAPIN, *The Scientific Revolution* (1996). An important revisionist survey emphasizing social factors.

L. STEINBRÜGGE, *The Moral Sex: Woman's Nature in the French Enlightenment* (1995). Emphasizes the conservative nature of Enlightenment thought on women.

P. ZAGORIN, *How the Idea of Religious Toleration Came to the West* (2003) An excellent exploration of the rise of toleration.

CHAPTER 23

R. ANSTEY, *The Atlantic Slave Trade and British Abolition, 1760–1810* (1975). A standard overview that emphasizes the role of religious factors.

B. BAILYN, *The Ideological Origins of the American Revolution* (1967). An important work illustrating the role of English radical thought in the perceptions of the American colonists.

K. M. BAKER, *Inventing the French Revolution: Essays on French Political Culture in the Eighteenth Century* (1990). Important essays on political thought before and during the revolution.

K. M. BAKER AND C. LUCAS, eds., *The French Revolution and the Creation of Modern Political Culture*, 3 vols. (1987). A splendid collection of important original articles on all aspects of politics during the revolution.

R. J. BARMAN, *Brazil: The Forging of a Nation, 1798–1852* (1988). The best coverage of this period.

C. BECKER, *The Declaration of Independence: A Study in the History of Political Ideas* (1922). Remains an important examination of the political and imperial theory of the Declaration.

J. F. BERNARD, *Talleyrand: A Biography* (1973). A useful account.

L. BETHELL, *The Cambridge History of Latin America*, Vol. 3 (1985). Contains an extensive treatment of independence.

R. BLACKBURN, *The Overthrow of Colonial Slavery, 1776–1848* (1988). A major discussion quite skeptical of the humanitarian interpretation.

T. C. W. BLANNING, ed., *The Rise and Fall of the French Revolution* (1996). A wide-ranging collection of essays illustrating the debates over the French Revolution.

J. BROOKE, *King George III* (1972). The best biography.

R. COBB, *The People's Armies* (1987). The major treatment in English of the revolutionary army.

O. CONNELLY, *Napoleon's Satellite Kingdoms* (1965). The rule of Napoleon and his family in Europe.

E. V. DA COSTA, *The Brazilian Empire* (1985). Excellent coverage of the entire nineteenth-century experience of Brazil.

D. B. DAVIS, *The Problem of Slavery in the Age of Revolution, 1770–1823* (1975). A transatlantic perspective on the issue.

F. FEHÉR, *The French Revolution and the Birth of Modernity* (1990). A wide-ranging collection of essays on political and cultural facets of the revolution.

A. FORREST, *The French Revolution and the Poor* (1981). A study that expands consideration of the revolution beyond the standard social boundaries.

M. GLOVER, *The Peninsular War, 1807–1814: A Concise Military History* (1974). An interesting account of the military campaign that so drained Napoleon's resources in western Europe.

J. GODECHOT, *The Counter-Revolution: Doctrine and Action, 1789–1804* (1971). An examination of opposition to the revolution.

A. GOODWIN, *The Friends of Liberty: The English Democratic Movement in the Age of the French Revolution* (1979). A major work that explores the impact of the French Revolution on English radicalism.

L. HUNT, *Politics, Culture, and Class in the French Revolution* (1986). A series of essays that focus on the modes of expression of the revolutionary values and political ideas.

W. W. KAUFMANN, *British Policy and the Independence of Latin America, 1802–1828* (1951). A standard discussion of an important relationship.

E. KENNEDY, *A Cultural History of the French Revolution* (1989). An important examination of the role of the arts, schools, clubs, and intellectual institutions.

M. KENNEDY, *The Jacobin Clubs in the French Revolution: The First Years* (1982). A careful scrutiny of the organizations chiefly responsible for the radicalizing of the revolution.

M. KENNEDY, *The Jacobin Clubs in the French Revolution: The Middle Years* (1988). A continuation of the previously listed study.

H. KISSINGER, *A World Restored: Metternich, Castlereagh and the Problems of Peace, 1812–1822* (1957). A provocative study by an author who became an American secretary of state.

G. LEFEBVRE, *The Coming of the French Revolution* (trans. 1947). A classic examination of the crisis of the French monarchy and the events of 1789.

G. LEFEBVRE, *Napoleon*, 2 vols., trans. by H. Stockhold (1969). The fullest and finest biography.

J. LYNCH, *The Spanish American Revolutions, 1808–1826* (1986). An excellent one-volume treatment.

P. MAIER, *American Scripture: Making the Declaration of Independence* (1997). Stands as a major revision of our understanding of the Declaration.

G. MASUR, *Simón Bolívar* (1969). The standard biography in English.

S. E. MELZER AND L. W. RABINE, eds., *Rebel Daughters: Women and the French Revolution* (1992). A collection of essays exploring various aspects of the role and image of women in the French Revolution.

M. MORRIS, *The British Monarchy and the French Revolution* (1998). Explores the manner in which the British monarchy saved itself from possible revolution.

R. MUIR, *Tactics and the Experience of Battle in the Age of Napoleon* (1998). Examines the wars from the standpoint of the soldiers in combat.

H. NICOLSON, *The Congress of Vienna* (1946). A good, readable account.

T. O. OTT, *The Haitian Revolution, 1789–1804* (1973). An account that clearly relates the events in Haiti to those in France.

R. R. PALMER, *Twelve Who Ruled: The Committee of Public Safety During the Terror* (1941). A clear narrative and analysis of the policies and problems of the committee.

R. R. PALMER, *The Age of the Democratic Revolution: A Political History of Europe and America, 1760–1800*, 2 vols. (1959, 1964). An impressive survey of the political turmoil in the transatlantic world.

C. PROCTOR, *Women, Equality, and the French Revolution* (1990). An examination of how the ideas of the Enlightenment and the attitudes of revolutionaries affected the legal status of women.

A. J. RUSSELL-WOOD, ed., *From Colony to Nation: Essays on the Independence of Brazil* (1975). A series of important essays.

P. SCHROEDER, *The Transformation of European Politics, 1763–1848* (1994). A fundamental treatment of the diplomacy of the era.

T. E. SKIDMORE AND P. H. SMITH, *Modern Latin America*, 4th ed. (1997). A very useful survey.

A. SOBOUL, *The Parisian Sans-Culottes and the French Revolution, 1793–94* (1964). The best work on the subject.

A. SOBOUL, *The French Revolution* (trans. 1975). An important work by a Marxist scholar.

D. G. SUTHERLAND, *France, 1789–1825: Revolution and Counterrevolution* (1986). A major synthesis based on recent scholarship in social history.

T. TACKETT, *Religion, Revolution, and Regional Culture in Eighteenth-Century France: The Ecclesiastical Oath of 1791* (1986). The most important study of this topic.

T. TACKETT, *Becoming a Revolutionary: The Deputies of the French National Assembly and the Emergence of a Revolutionary Culture* (1789–1790) (1996). The best study of the early months of the revolution.

J. M. THOMPSON, *Robespierre*, 2 vols. (1935). The best biography.

D. K. VAN KEY, *The Religious Origins of the French Revolution: From Calvin to the Civil Constitution, 1560–1791* (1996). Examines the manner in which debates within French Catholicism influenced the coming of the revolution.

M. WALZER, ed., *Regicide and Revolution: Speeches at the Trial of Louis XVI* (1974). An important and exceedingly interesting collection of documents with a useful introduction.

I. WOLOCH, *The New Regime: Transformations of the French Civic Order, 1789–1820s* (1994). An important overview of just what had and had not changed in France after the quarter century of revolution and war.

G. WOOD, *The Radicalism of the American Revolution* (1991). A major interpretation.

CHAPTER 24

I. BERLIN, *Generations of Captivity: A History of African-American Slaves* (2003) A major work.

D. BLACKBOURN, *The Long Nineteenth Century: A History of Germany, 1780–1918* (1998). An outstanding survey.

D. G. CREIGHTON, *John A. MacDonald* (1952, 1955). A major biography of the first Canadian prime minister.

D. DONALD, *Lincoln* (1995). Now the standard biography.

R. B. EDGERTON, *Death or Glory: The Legacy of the Crimean War* (2000). Multifaceted study of a badly mismanaged war that transformed many aspects of European domestic politics.

M. HOLT, *The Rise and Fall of the American Whig Party: Jacksonian Politics and the Onset of the Civil War* (2003) An extensive survey of the Jacksonian era.

R. KEE, *The Green Flag: A History of Irish Nationalism* (2001). A vast survey.

W. LACQUER, *A History of Zionism* (1989). The most extensive one-volume treatment.

M. B. LEVINGER, *Enlightened Nationalism: The Transformation of Prussian Political Culture, 1806–1848* (2002). A major work based on the most recent scholarship.

J. M. MCPHERSON, *The Battle Cry of Freedom: The Civil War Era* (1988). An excellent one-volume treatment.

D. MORTON, *A Short History of Canada* (2001). Useful popular history.

J. P. PARRY, *The Rise and Fall of Liberal Government in Victorian Britain* (1994). An outstanding study.

A. PLESSIS, *The Rise and Fall of the Second Empire, 1852–1871* (1985). A useful survey of France under Napoleon III.

D. M. POTTER, *The Impending Crisis, 1848–1861* (1976) A penetrating study of the coming of the American Civil War.

A. SKED, *Decline and Fall of the Habsburg Empire 1815–1918* (2001). A major, accessible survey of a difficult subject.

D. M. SMITH, *Cavour* (1984). An excellent biography.

C. P. STACEY, *Canada and the Age of Conflict* (1977, 1981). A study of Canadian foreign relations.

D. WETZEL, *A Duel of Giants: Bismarck, Napoleon III, and the Origins of the Franco-Prussian War* (2001). Broad study based on most recent scholarship.

CHAPTER 25

M. ADAS, *Machines as the Measure of Men: Science, Technology, and Ideologies of Western Dominance* (1989). The best single volume on racial thinking and technological advances as forming ideologies of European colonial dominance.

A. ASCHER AND P. A. STOLYPIN, *The Search for Stability in Late Imperial Russia* (2000). A broad-ranging biography based on extensive research.

I. BERLIN, *Karl Marx: His Life and Environment*, 4th ed. (1996). A classics volume that remains an excellent introduction.

JANET BROWNE, *Charles Darwin*, 2 vols. (2002) An eloquent, accessible biography.

J. BURROW, *The Crisis of Reason: European Thought, 1848–1914* (2000). The best overview available.

A. D. CHANDLER JR., *The Visible Hand: Managerial Revolution in American Business* (1977). Remains the best discussion of the innovative role of American business.

A. CLARKE, *The Struggle for the Breeches: Gender and the Making of the British Working Class* (1995). An examination of the manner in which industrialization made problematical the relationships between men and women.

W. CRONIN, *Nature's Metropolis: Chicago and the Great West, 1848–1893* (1991) The best examination of any major American nineteenth-century city.

P. GAY, *Freud: A Life for Our Time* (1988). The new standard biography.

R. F. HAMILTON, *Marxism, Revisionism, and Leninism: Explication, Assessment, and Commentary* (2000). A contribution from the perspective of a historically minded sociologist.

S. HAHN, *A Nation under Our Feet: Black Political Struggles in the Rural South from Slavey to the Great Migration* (2003). A major synthesis.

A. HOURANI, *Arab Thought in the Liberal Age 1789–1939* (1967). A classic account, clearly written and accessible to the nonspecialist.

D. I. KERTZER AND M. BARBAGLI, eds., *Family Life in the Long Nineteenth Century, 1789–1913: The History of the European Family* (2002). Wide-ranging collection of essays.

J. T. KLOPPENBERG, *Uncertain Victory: Social Democracy and Progressivism in European and American Thought* (1986). An extremely important comparative study.

J. KÖHLER, *Zarathustra's Secret: The Interior Life of Friedrich Nietzsche* (2002). A controversial new biography.

L. KOLAKOWSKI, *Main Currents of Marxism: Its Rise, Growth, and Dissolution*, 3 vols. (1978). Especially good on the last years of the nineteenth century and the early years of the twentieth.

P. KRAUSE, *The Battle for Homestead, 1880–1892* (1992). Examines labor relations in the steel industry.

D. LANDES, *The Wealth and Poverty of Nations: Why Some Are So Rich and Some So Poor* (1998). A major international discussion of the subject.

M. MCGERR, *A Fierce Discontent: The Rise and Fall of the Progressive Moevement in America l870–1920* (2003). The best recent synthesis.

E. MORRIS, *Theodore Rex* (2002). Major survey of Theodore Roosevelt's presidency and personality.

A. PAIS, *Subtle Is the Lord: The Science and Life of Albert Einstein* (l983). Remains the most accessible scientific biography.

J. RENDALL, *The Origins of Modern Feminism: Women in Britain, France and the United States, 1780–1860* (1985). A well-informed introduction.

R. SERVICE, *Lenin: A Biography* (2002). Based on new sources and will no doubt become the standard biography.

R. M. UTLEY, *The Indian Frontier and the American West, 1846–1890* (1984). A broad survey of the pressures of white civilization against Native Americans.

D. VITAL, *A People Apart: The Jews In Modern Europe, l789–1939* (1999). A deeply informed survey.

CHAPTER 26

S. ARROM, *The Women of Mexico City, 1790–1857* (1985). A pioneering study.

E. BERMAN, ed., *Women, Culture, and Politics in Latin America* (1990). Useful essays.

L. BETHELL, ed., *The Cambridge History of Latin America*, 8 vols. (1992). The single most authoritative coverage, with extensive bibliographical essays.

V. BULMER-THOMAS, *The Economic History of Latin America Since Independence* (1994). A major study in every respect.

E. B. BURNS, *The Poverty of Progress: Latin America in the Nineteenth Century* (1980). Argues that the elites suppressed alternative modes of cultural and economic development.

E. B. BURNS, *A History of Brazil* (1993). The most useful one-volume treatment.

D. BUSHNELL AND N. MACAULAY, *The Emergence of Latin America in the Nineteenth Century* (1994). A survey that examines the internal development of Latin America during the period.

R. CONRAD, *The Destruction of Brazilian Slavery, 1850–1889* (1971). A good survey of the most important problem in Brazil in the second half of the nineteenth century.

R. CONRAD, *World of Sorrow: The African Slave Trade to Brazil* (1986). An excellent survey of the subject.

E. V. DA COSTA, *The Brazilian Empire: Myths and Histories* (1985). Essays that provide a thorough introduction to Brazil during the period of empire.

H. S. FERNS, *Britain and Argentina in the Nineteenth Century* (1968). Explains clearly the intermeshing of the two economies.

M. FONT, *Coffee, Contention, and Change in the Making of Modern Brazil* (1990). Extensive discussion of the problems of a single-commodity economy.

R. GRAHAM, *Britain and the Onset of Modernization in Brazil* (1968). Another study of British economic dominance.

S. H. HABER, *Industry and Underdevelopment: The Industrialization of Mexico, 1890–1940* (1989). Examines the problem of industrialization before and after the revolution.

G. HAHNER, *Emancipating the Female Sex: The Struggle for Women's Rights in Brazil, 1850–1940* (1990). An extensive examination of a relatively understudied issue in Latin America.

C. H. HARING, *Empire in Brazil: A New World Experiment with Monarchy* (1958). Remains a useful overview.

J. HEMMING, *Amazon Frontier: The Defeat of the Brazilian Indians* (1987). A brilliant survey of the experience of Native Americans in modern Brazil.

R. A. HUMPHREYS, *Latin America and the Second World War*, 2 vols. (1981–1982). The standard work on the topic.

F. KATZ, ed., *Riot, Rebellion, and Revolution in Mexico: Social Base of Agrarian Violence, 1750–1940* (1988). Essays that put the violence of the revolution in a longer context.

A. KNIGHT, *The Mexican Revolution*, 2 vols. (1986). The best treatment of the subject.

S. MAINWARING, *The Catholic Church and Politics in Brazil, 1916–1985* (1986). An examination of a key institution in Brazilian life.

M. C. MEYER AND W. L. SHERMAN, *The Course of Mexican History* (1995). An excellent survey.

M. MORNER, *Adventurers and Proletarians: The Story of Migrants in Latin America* (1985). Examines immigration to Latin America and migration within it.

J. PAGE, *Perón: A Biography* (1983). The standard English treatment.

D. ROCK, *Politics in Argentina, 1890–1930: The Rise and Fall of Radicalism* (1975). The major discussion of the Argentine Radical Party.

D. ROCK, *Argentina, 1516–1987: From Spanish Colonization to Alfonsin* (1987). Now the standard survey.

D. ROCK, ed., *Latin America in the 1940s: War and Postwar Transitions* (1994). Essays examining a very difficult decade for the continent.

R. M. SCHNEIDER, *"Order and Progress": A Political History of Brazil* (1991). A straightforward narrative with helpful notes for further reading.

T. E. SKIDMORE, *Black into White: Race and Nationality in Brazilian Thought* (1993). Examines the role of racial theory in Brazil.

P. H. SMITH, *Argentina and the Failure of Democracy: Conflict Among Political Elites. 1904–1955* (1974). An examination of one of the major political puzzles of Latin American history.

S. J. STEIN AND B. H. STEIN, *The Colonial Heritage of Latin America: Essays on Economic Dependence in Perspective* (1970). A major statement of the dependence interpretation.

D. TAMARIN, *The Argentine Labor Movement, 1930–1945: A Study in the Origins of Perónism* (1985). A useful introduction to a complex subject.

H. J. WIARDA, *Politics and Social Change in Latin America: The Distinct Tradition* (1974). Excellent essays that stress the ongoing role of Iberian traditions.

J. D. WIRTH, ed., *Latin American Oil Companies and the Politics of Energy* (1985). A series of case studies.

J. WOLFE, *Working Women, Working Men: São Paulo and the Rise of Brazil's Industrial Working Class, 1900–1955* (1993). Pays particular attention to the role of women.

J. WOMACK, *Zapata and the Mexican Revolution* (1968). A classic study.

CHAPTER 27

General Works

S. COOK, *Colonial Encounters in the Age of High Imperialism* (1996). A good introduction to the imperial enterprise in Africa and Asia.

D. K. FIELDHOUSE, *The West and the Third World. Trade, Colonialism, Depedence and Development* (1999). Addresses whether colonialism was detrimental or beneficial to colonized peoples.

P. HOPKIRK, *The Great Game: The Struggle for Empire in Central Asia* (1992). Focuses on the political and economic rivalries of the imperial powers.

India

A. AHMAD, *Islamic Modernism in India and Pakistan, 1857–1964* (1967). The standard survey of Muslim thinkers and movements in India during the period.

C. A. BAYLY, *Indian Society and the Making of the British Empire, The New Cambridge History of India*, II. 1 (1988). One of several major contributions of this author to the ongoing revision of our picture of modern Indian history since the eighteenth century.

A. GHOSH, *In an Antique Land. History in the Guise of a Traveler's Tale* (1992). An anthropologist traces the footsteps of a premodern slave traveling with his master from North Africa to India. A gripping tale of premodern life in the India Ocean basin and also of contemporary Egypt.

R. GUHA, ed., *Subaltern Studies: Writings on South Asian History and Society* (1982). Essays on the colonial period that focus on the social, political, and economic history of "subaltern" groups and classes (hill tribes, peasants, etc.) rather than only the elites of India.

S. N. HAY, ed., "Modern India and Pakistan," Part VI of Wm. Theodore de Bary et al., eds., *Sources of Indian Tradition*, 2nd ed. (1988). A superb selection of primary-source documents with brief introductions and helpful notes.

F. ROBINSON, ed., *The Cambridge Encyclopedia of India, Pakistan, Bangladesh, Sri Lanka, Nepal, Bhutan, and the*

Maldives (1989). A fine collection of survey articles by various scholars, organized into topical chapters ranging from "Economies" to "Cultures."

Central Islamic Lands

J. J. DONAHUE AND J. L. ESPOSITO, eds., *Islam in Transition: Muslim Perspectives* (1982). An interesting selection of primary-source materials on Islamic thinking in this century.

W. CLEVELAND, *A History of the Modern Middle East,* 3rd ed. (2004). A balanced and well-organized overview of modern Middle Eastern history.

A. DAWISHA, *Arab Nationalism in the Twentieth Century. From Triumph to Despair* (2003). A good overview of the development of Arab nationalism.

S. DERINGIL, *The Well-Protected Domains: Ideology and the Legitimation of Power in the Ottoman Empire, 1876–1909* (1998). An impressive study on nationalism and reform in the Ottoman Empire.

D. F. EICKELMAN, *Knowledge and Power in Morocco: The Education of a Twentieth-Century Notable* (1985). A fascinating study of traditional Islamic education and society in the twentieth century through a social biography of a Moroccan religious scholar and judge.

A. HOURANI, *Arabic Thought in the Liberal Age, 1798–1939* (1967). The standard work, by which all subsequent scholarship on the topic is to be judged.

N. R. KEDDIE, *An Islamic Response to Imperialism* (1968). A brief study of al-Afghani, the great Muslim reformer, with translations of a number of his writings.

B. LEWIS, *The Emergence of Modern Turkey,* 2nd ed. (1968). A concise but thorough history of the creation of the Turkish state, including nineteenth-century background.

J. O. VOLL, *Islam: Continuity and Change in the Modern World* (1982). Chapters 1–6. An interpretive survey of the Islamic world since the eighteenth century. Its emphasis on eighteenth-century reform movements is especially noteworthy.

Africa

A. A. BOAHEN, *Africa Under Colonial Domination, 1880–1935* (1985). Vol. VII of the *UNESCO General History of Africa.* Excellent chapters on various regions of Africa in the period. Chapters 3–10 detail African resistance to European colonial intrusion in diverse regions.

W. CARTEY AND M. KILSON, eds., *The Africa Reader: Colonial Africa* (1970). Original source materials give a vivid picture of African resistance to colonial powers, adaptation to foreign rule, and the emergence of the African masses as a political force.

P. CURTIN, S. FEIERMANN, L. THOMPSON, AND J. VANSINA, *African History* (1978). The relevant portions are Chapters 10–20.

B. DAVIDSON, *Modern Africa: A Social and Political History* (1989). A very useful survey of African history.

J. D. FAGE, *A History of Africa* (1978). The relevant chapters, which give a particularly clear overview of the colonial period, are 12–16.

B. FREUND, *The Making of Contemporary Africa: The Development of African Society Since 1800* (1984). A refreshingly direct synthetic discussion and survey that take an avowedly, but not reductive, materialist approach to interpretation.

T. PAKENHAM, *The Scramble for Africa* (1991). An excellent analysis of the imperialist age in Africa.

A. D. ROBERTS, ed., *The Colonial Moment in Africa: Essays on the Movement of Minds and Materials, 1900–1940* (1986). Chapters from *The Cambridge History of Africa* treating various aspects of the colonial period in Africa, including economics, politics, and religion.

CHAPTER 28

China

P. M. COBLE, *The Shanghai Capitalists and the Nationalist Government, 1927–1937* (1980).

L. E. EASTMAN, *The Abortive Revolution: China Under Nationalist Rule, 1927–1937* (1974).

L. E. EASTMAN, *Seeds of Destruction: Nationalist China in War and Revolution, 1937–1949* (1984).

M. ELVIN AND G. W. SKINNER, *The Chinese City Between Two Worlds* (1974). A study of the late Qing and Republican eras.

J. W. ESHERICK, *The Origins of the Boxer Rebellion* (1987).

S. ETŌ, *China's Republican Revolution* (1994).

J. K. FAIRBANK AND M. GOLDMAN, *China, a New History* (1998). A survey of the entire sweep of Chinese history; especially strong on the modern period.

J. K. FAIRBANK AND D. TWITCHETT, eds., *The Cambridge History of China.* Like the premodern volumes in the same series, the volumes on modern China represent a survey of what is known. Volumes 10–15, which cover the history from the late Qing to the People's Republic, have been published, and the others will be available soon. The series is substantial. Each volume contains a comprehensive bibliography.

J. FITZGERALD, *Awakening China: Politics, Culture, and Class in the Nationalist Revolution* (1996).

C. HAO, *Chinese Intellectuals in Crisis: Search for Order and Meaning, 1890–1911* (1987).

W. C. KIRBY, ed., *State and Economy in Republican China* (2001).

P. A. KUHN, *Rebellion and Its Enemies in Late Imperial China: Militarization and Social Structure, 1796–1864* (1980). A study of how the Confucian gentry saved the Manchu dynasty after the Taiping Rebellion.

P. KUHN, Origins of the Modern Chinese State (2002).

J. LEVENSON, *Liang Ch'i-ch'ao and the Mind of Modern China* (1953). A classic study of a major Chinese reformer and thinker.

LU XUN, *Selected Works* (1960). Novels, stories, and other writings by modern China's greatest writer.

S. NAQUIN, *Peking: Temples and City Life, 1400–1900* (2000).

E. O. REISCHAUER, J. K. FAIRBANK, AND A. M. CRAIG, *East Asia: Tradition and Transformation* (1989). A detailed text on East Asian history. Contains ample chapters on Japan and China and shorter chapters on Korea and Vietnam.

H. Z. SCHIFFRIN, *Sun Yat-sen, Reluctant Revolutionary* (1980). A biography.

B. I. SCHWARTZ, *Chinese Communism and the Rise of Mao* (1951). A classic study of Mao, his thought, and the Chinese Communist Party before 1949.

B. I. SCHWARTZ, *In Search of Wealth and Power: Yen Fu and the West* (1964). A fine study of a late-nineteenth-century thinker who introduced Western ideas into China.

J. D. SPENCE, *The Gate of Heavenly Peace: The Chinese and Their Revolution, 1895–1980* (1981). Historical reflections on twentieth-century China.

J. D. SPENCE, *The Search for Modern China* (1990). A thick text but well written.

M. SZONYI, *Practicing Kinship: Lineage and Descent in Late Imperial China* (2002).

S. Y. TENG AND J. K. FAIRBANK, *China's Response to the West* (1954). A superb collection of translations from Chinese thinkers and political figures, with commentaries.

T. H. WHITE AND A. JACOBY, *Thunder Out of China* (1946). A view of China during World War II by two who were there.

Japan

G. AKITA, *Foundations of Constitutional Government in Modern Japan* (1967). A study of Itō Hirobumi in the political process leading to the Meiji constitution.

G. C. ALLEN, *A Short Economic History of Modern Japan* (1958).

A. E. BARSHAY, *The Social Sciences in Modern Japan: the Marxian and Modernist Traditions* (2004). Different interpretations of history.

J. R. BARTHOLOMEW, *The Formation of Science in Japan* (1989). The pioneering English-language work on the subject.

W. G. BEASLEY, *Japanese Imperialism, 1894–1945* (1987). Excellent short book on subject.

G. M. BERGER, *Parties Out of Power in Japan, 1931–1941* (1977). An analysis of the condition of political parties during the militarist era.

G.L. BERNSTEIN, *Recreating Japanese Women, 1600–1945* (1991).

The Cambridge History of Japan, The Nineteenth Century, M.B. Jansen, ed. (1989); *The Twentieth Century*, P. Duus, ed. (1988). Multi-author works.

A. M. CRAIG, *Chōshū in the Meiji Restoration* (2000). A study of the Chōshū domain, a Prussia of Japan, during the period 1840–1868.

A. M. CRAIG AND D. H. SHIVELY, eds., *Personality in Japanese History* (1970). An attempt to gauge the role of individuals and their personalities as factors explaining history.

P. DUUS, *Party Rivalry and Political Change in Taisho Japan* (1968). A study of political change in Japan during the 1910s and 1920s.

P. DUUS, *The Abacus and the Sword, the Japanese Penetration of Korea, 1895–1910* (1995). A thoughtful analysis.

S. ERICSON, *The Sound of the Whistle: Railroads and the State in Meiji Japan* (1996). An economic and social history of railroads, an engine of growth and popular symbol.

Y. FUKUZAWA, *Autobiography* (1966). Japan's leading nineteenth-century thinker tells of his life and of the birth of modern Japan.

A. GARON, *The State and Labor in Modern Japan* (1987). A fine study of the subject.

C. N. GLUCK, *Japan's Modern Myths: Ideology in the Late Meiji Period* (1988). A brilliant study of the complex weave of late Meiji thought.

A. GORDON, *The Evolution of Labor Relations in Japan: Heavy Industry, 1853–1955* (1985). A seminal work.

B. R. HACKETT, *Yamagata Aritomo in the Rise of Modern Japan, 1932–1922* (1973). History as seen through the biography of a central figure.

I. HALL, *Mori Arinori* (1973). A biography of Japan's first minister of education.

T. R. H. HAVENS, *The Valley of Darkness: The Japanese People and World War II* (1978). Wartime society.

C. IRIYE, *After Imperialism: The Search for a New Order in the Far East, 1921–1931* (1965). (Also see other studies by this author.)

D. M. B. JANSEN AND G. ROZMAN, eds., *Japan in Transition from Tokugawa to Meiji* (1986). Contains fine essays.

W. JOHNSTON, *The Modern Epidemic: A History of Tuberculosis in Japan* (1995). A social history of a disease.

E. KEENE, Ed., *Modern Japanese Literature, An Anthology* (1960). A collection of modern Japanese short stories and excerpts from novels.

F. Y.T. MATSUSAKA, *The Making of Japanese Manchuria, 1904–1932* (2001). On railroad strategies in empire building.

J. W. MORLEY, ed., *The China Quagmire* (1983). A study of Japan's expansion on the continent between 1933 and 1941. (For diplomatic history, see also the many other works by this author.)

R. H. MYERS AND M. R. PEATTIE, eds., *The Japanese Colonial Empire, 1895–1945* (1984).

T. NAJITA, *Hara Kei in the Politics of Compromise, 1905–1915* (1967). A study of one of Japan's greatest party leaders.

K. OHKAWA AND H. ROSOVSKY, *Japanese Economic Growth: Trend Acceleration in the Twentieth Century* (1973).

M. RAVINA, *The Last Samurai: The Life and Battles of Saigo Takamori* (2004). Unlike the movie, this account of the Satsuma uprising is historical.

G. SHIBA, *Remembering Aizu* (1999). A stirring autobiographical account of a samurai youth whose domain lost in the Meiji Restoration.

K. SMITH, *A Time of Crisis: The Great Depression and Rural Revitalization* (2001). An intellectual history of village movements during the 1930s.

J. J. STEPHAN, *Hawaii Under the Rising Sun* (1984). Japan's plans for rule in Hawaii.

R. H. SPECTOR, *Eagle Against the Sun: The American War with Japan* (1985). A narrative of World War II in the Pacific.

E. P. TSURUMI, *Factory Girls: Women in the Thread Mills of Meiji Japan* (1990). A sympathetic analysis of the key component of the Meiji labor force.

W. WRAY, *Mitsubishi and the N. Y. K., 1870–1914* (1984). The growth of a shipping *zaibatsu*, with analysis of business strategies, the role of government and imperialist involvements.

CHAPTER 29

L. ALBERTINI, *The Origins of the War of 1914*, 3 vols. (1952, 1957). Discursive but invaluable.

V. R. BERGHAHN, *Germany and the Approach of War in 1914* (1973). A work similar in spirit to both of Fischer's (see below) but stressing the importance of Germany's naval program.

R. BOSWORTH, *Italy and the Approach of the First World War* (1983). A fine analysis of Italian policy.

S. B. FAY, *The Origins of the World War*, 2 vols. (1928). The most influential of the revisionist accounts.

F. FISCHER, *Germany's Aims in the First World War* (1967). An influential interpretation that stirred a great controversy in Germany and around the world by emphasizing Germany's role in bringing on the war.

F. FISCHER, *War of Illusions* (1975). A long and diffuse book that tries to connect German responsibility for the war with internal social, economic, and political developments.

D. FROMKIN, *Europe's Last Summer: Who Started the Great War in 1914?* (2004). A lively account that fixes on the final crisis in July 1914.

J. N. HORNE, *Labour at War: France and Britain, 1914–1918* (1991). An examination of a major issue on the home fronts.

J. JOLL, *The Origins of the First World War* (1984). A brief but thoughtful analysis.

P. KENNEDY, *The Rise of the Anglo-German Antagonism 1860–1914* (1980). An unusual and thorough analysis of the political, economic, and cultural roots of important diplomatic developments.

W. L. LANGER, *European Alliances and Alignments*, 2nd ed. (1966). A splendid diplomatic history of the years 1871–1890.

W. L. LANGER, *The Diplomacy of Imperialism* (1935). A continuation of the previous study for the years 1890–1902.

D. C. B. LIEVEN, *Russia and the Origins of the First World War* (1983). A good account of the forces that shaped Russian policy.

A. MOMBAUER, *The Origins of the First World War. Controversies and Consensus* (2002). A fascinating survey of the debate over the decades and the current state of the question.

R. PIPES, *A Concise History of the Russian Revolution* (1996). A one-volume version of a scholarly masterpiece.

Z. STEINER, *Britain and the Origins of the First World War* (1977). A perceptive and informed account of the way British foreign policy was made in the years before the war.

H. STRACHAN, *The First World War* (2004). A fine one-volume account of the war.

A. J. P. TAYLOR, *The Struggle for Mastery in Europe, 1848–1918* (1954). Clever but controversial.

S. R. WILLIAMSON, JR., *Austria-Hungary and the Origins of the First World War* (1991). A valuable study of a complex subject.

CHAPTER 30

W. S. ALLEN, *The Nazi Seizure of Power: The Experience of a Single German Town, 1930–1935*, rev. ed. (1984). A classic treatment of Nazism in a microcosmic setting.

J. BARNARD, *Walter Reuther and the Rise of the Auto Workers* (1983). A major introduction to the new American unions of the 1930s.

K. D. BRACHER, *The German Dictatorship* (1970). A comprehensive treatment of both the origins and the functioning of the Nazi movement and government.

A. BULLOCK, *Hitler: A Study in Tyranny*, rev. ed. (1964). The best biography.

M. BURLEIGH AND W. WIPPERMAN, *The Racial State: Germany 1933–1945* (1991). Emphasizes the manner in which racial theory influenced numerous areas of policy.

R. CONQUEST, *The Great Terror: Stalin's Purges of the Thirties* (1968). The best treatment of the subject to this date.

G. CRAIG, *Germany, 1866–1945* (1978). A major survey.

I. DEUTSCHER, *The Prophet Armed* (1954), *The Prophet Unarmed* (1959), and *The Prophet Outcast* (1963). Remains the major biography of Trotsky.

I. DEUTSCHER, *Stalin: A Political Biography*, 2nd ed. (1967). The best biography in English.

B. EICHENGREEN, *Golden Fetters: The Gold Standard and the Great Depression, 1919–1939* (1992). A remarkable study of the role of the gold standard in the economic policies of the interwar years.

E. EYCK, *A History of the Weimar Republic*, 2 vols. (trans. 1963). The story as narrated by a liberal.

M. S. FAUSOLD, *The Presidency of Herbert Hoover* (1985). An important treatment.

G. FELDMAN, *The Great Disorder: Politics, Economics, and Society in the German Inflation, 1914–1924* (1993). The best work on the subject.

S. FITZPATRICK, *Stalin's Peasants: Resistance and Survival in the Russian Village After Collectivization* (1994). A pioneering study.

P. FUSSELL, *The Great War and Modern Memory* (1975). A brilliant account of the literature arising from World War I during the 1920s.

J. K. GALBRAITH, *The Great Crash* (1979). A well-known account by a leading economist.

R. GELLATELY, *The Gestapo and German Society: Enforcing Racial Policy, 1933–1945* (1990). A discussion of how the police state supported Nazi racial policies.

H. J. GORDON, *Hitler and the Beer Hall Putsch* (1972). An excellent account of the event and the political situation in the early Weimar Republic.

R. HAMILTON, *Who Voted for Hitler?* (1982). An examination of voting patterns and sources of Nazi support.

J. HELD, ed., *The Columbia History of Eastern Europe in the Twentieth Century* (1992). Individual essays on each country.

P. KENEZ, *The Birth of the Propaganda State: Soviet Methods of Mass Mobilization, 1917–1929* (1985). An examination of the manner in which the Communist government inculcated popular support.

B. KENT, *The Spoils of War: The Politics, Economics, and Diplomacy of Reparations, 1918–1932* (1993). A comprehensive account of the intricacies of the reparations problem of the 1920s.

D. LANDES, *The Unbound Prometheus: Technological Change and Industrial Development in Western Europe from 1750 to the Present* (1969). Includes an excellent analysis of both the Great Depression and the few areas of economic growth.

B. LINCOLN, *Red Victory: A History of the Russian Civil War* (1989). An excellent narrative account.

M. MCAULEY, *Bread and Justice: State and Society in Petrograd, 1917–1922* (1991). A study that examines the impact of the Russian Revolution and Leninist policies on a major Russian city.

D. J. K. PEUKERT, *Inside Nazi Germany: Conformity, Opposition, and Racism in Everyday Life* (1987). An excellent discussion of life under Nazi rule.

R. PIPES, *The Unknown Lenin: From the Secret Archives* (1996). A collection of previously unpublished documents that indicated the repressive character of Lenin's government.

P. PULZER, *Jews and the German State: The Political History of a Minority, 1848–1933* (1992). A detailed history by a major historian of European minorities.

L. J. RUPP, *Mobilizing Women for War: German and America Propaganda, 1939–1945* (1978). Although concentrating on a later period, it includes an excellent discussion of general Nazi attitudes toward women.

A. M. SCHLESINGER, JR., *The Age of Roosevelt*, 3 vols. (1957–1960). The most important overview.

D. M. SMITH, *Mussolini's Roman Empire* (1976). A general description of the Fascist regime in Italy.

D. M. SMITH, *Italy and Its Monarchy* (1989). A major treatment of an important neglected subject.

A. SOLZHENITSYN, *The Gulag Archipelago*, 3 vols. (1974–1979). A major examination of the labor camps under Stalin by one of the most important contemporary Russian writers.

R. J. SONTAG, *A Broken World, 1919–1939* (1971). An exceptionally thoughtful and well-organized survey.

A. J. P. TAYLOR, *English History, 1914–1945* (1965). Lively and opinionated.

H. A. TURNER JR., *German Big Business and the Rise of Hitler* (1985). An important major study of the subject.

H. A. TURNER JR., *Hitler's Thirty Days to Power* (1996). A narrative of the events leading directly to the Nazi seizure of power.

L. YAHIL, *The Holocaust: The Fate of European Jewry, 1932–1945* (1990). A major study of this fundamental subject in twentieth-century history.

CHAPTER 31

A. ADAMTHWAITE, *France and the Coming of the Second World War,* 1936–1939 (1977). A careful account making good use of the French archives.

E. R. BECK, *Under the Bombs: The German Home Front,* 1942–1945 (1986). An interesting examination of a generally unstudied subject.

R. S. BOTWINICK, *A History of the Holocaust,* 2nd ed., 2002. A brief but broad and useful account of the causes, character and results of the Holocaust.

A. BULLOCK, *Hitler: A Study in Tyranny,* rev. ed. (1964). A brilliant biography.

W. S. CHURCHILL, *The Second World War,* 6 vols. (1948–1954). The memoirs of the great British leader.

A. CROZIER, *The Causes of the Second World War,* 1997. An examination of what brought on the war.

R. B. FRANK, *Downfall: The End of the Imperial Japanese Empire,* 1998. A thorough, well-documented account of the last months of the Japanese empire and the reasons for its surrender.

J. L. GADDIS, *We Now Know: Rethinking Cold War History* (1998). A fine account of the early years of the Cold War making use of new evidence emerging since the collapse of the Soviet Union.

J. L. GADDIS, P. H. GORDON, E. MAY, eds., *Cold War Statesmen Confront the Bomb: Nuclear diplomacy Since 1945* (1999). A collection of essays discussing the effect of atomic and nuclear weapons on diplomacy since WW II.

M. GILBERT, *The Holocaust: A History of the Jews of Europe During the Second World War* (1985). The best and most comprehensive treatment.

A. IRIYE, *Pearl Harbor and the Coming of the Pacific War* (1999). Essays on how the Pacific war came about, including a selection of documents.

J. KEEGAN, *The Second World War* (1990). A lively and penetrating account by a master military historian.

I. KERSHAW, *Hitler: 1889–1936: Hubris* (1999) and *Hitler: 1936–1945: Nemesis* (2001). An outstanding two-volume biography.

W. F. KIMBALL, *Forged in War: Roosevelt, Churchill, and the Second World War,* (1998). A study of the collaboration between the two great leaders of the West based on a thorough knowledge of their correspondence.

W. MURRAY AND A. R. MILLETT, *A War to be Won: Fighting the Second World War,* (2000). A splendid account of the military operations in the war.

R. OVERY, *Why the Allies Won* (1997). An anlysis of the reasons for the victory of the Allies with special emphasis on technology.

N. RICH, *Hitler War Aims,* 2 vols. (1973–1974). The best study of the subject in English.

H. THOMAS, *The Spanish Civil War,* 3rd ed. (1986). The best account in English.

P. WANDYCZ, *The Twilight of French Eastern Alliances,* 1926–1936 (1988). A well-documented account of the diplomacy of central and eastern Europe in a crucial period.

G. L. WEINBERG, *A World at Arms: A Global History of World War II* (1994). A thorough and excellent narrative account.

CHAPTER 32

B. S. ANDERSON AND J. P. PINSSER, *A History of Their Own: Women in Europe from Prehistory to the Present,* Vol. 2 (1988). A broad-ranging survey.

R. BERNSTEIN, *Out of the Blue: The Story of September 11, 2001 from Jihad to Ground Zero* (2002). An excellent account by a gifted journalist.

A. BROWN, *The Gorbachev Factor* (1996). An important commentary by an English observer.

D. CALLEO, *Rethinking Europe's Future* (2003) A daring book by an experienced commentator.

J. L. GADDIS, *What We Know Now* (1997). Examines the Cold War in light of newly released documents.

D. J. GARROW, *Bearing the Cross: Martin Luther King, Jr. and the Southern Leadership Conference 1955–1968* (1986). The best work on the subject.

W. HITCHCOCK, *Struggle for Europe: The Turbulent History of a Divided Continent, 1945–2002* (2003). The best overall narrative now available

D. KEARNS, *Lyndon Johnson and the American Dream* (1976). A useful biography.

J. KEEP, *The Last of the Empires: A History of the Soviet Union, 1956–1991* (1995). A clear narrative.

M. MANDELBAUM, *The Ideas That Conquered the World: Peace, Democracy, and Free Markets* (2002). An important analysis by a major commentator on international affairs.

J. MANN, *The Rise of the Vulcans: The History of Bush's War Cabinet* (2004). An account of the major foreign policy advisors behind the invasion of Iraq.

R. MANN, *A Grand Delusion: America's Descent into Vietnam* (2001). The best recent narrative.

J. McCORMICK, *Understanding the European Union: A Concise Introduction* (2002) Outlines the major features.

N. NAIMARK, *Fires of Hatred: Ethnic Cleansing in Twentieth-Century Europe* (2002). A remarkably sensitive treatment of a tragic subject.

R. SAWKA AND ANNE STEVENS, eds., *Contemporary Europe* (2000). A collection of essays on major topics.

G. STOKES, ed., *From Stalinism to Pluralism: A Documentary History of Eastern Europe Since 1945* (1996). An important collection of documents that are not easily accessible elsewhere.

M. WALKER, *The Cold War and the Making of the Modern World* (1994). A major survey.

CHAPTER 33

China

R. BAUM, *Burying Mao: Chinese Politics in the Age of Deng Xiaoping* (1996).

A. CHAN, R. MADSEN, J. UNGER, *Chen Village under Mao and Deng* (1992).

J. CHANG, *Wild Swans: Three Daughters of China* (1991). An intimate look at recent Chinese society through three generations of women. Immensely readable.

J. FENG, *Ten Years of Madness: Oral Histories of China's Cultural Revolution* (1996).

J. FEWSMITH, *China Since Tiananmen: The Politics of Transition* (2001). Focus is on the rise to power of Jiang Zemin and Chinese politics during the nineties.

B. M. FROLIC, *Mao's People: Sixteen Portraits of Life in Revolutionary China* (1987).

T. GOLD, *State and Society in the Taiwan Miracle* (1986). The story of economic growth in postwar Taiwan.

M. GOLDMAN, *Sowing the Seeds of Democracy in China: Political Reform in the Deng Xiaoping Era* (1994).

A. IRIYE, *China and Japan in the Global Setting* (1992).

D. M. LAMPTON, *Same Bed, Different Dreams: Managing U.S.–China Relations, 1989–2000* (2001).

H. LIANG, *Son of the Revolution* (1983). An autobiographical account of a young man growing up in Mao's China.

K. LIEBERTHAL, *Governing China, from Revolution Through Reform* (2004).

B. LIU, *People or Monsters? and Other Stories and Reportage from China After Mao* (1983). Literary reflections on China.

R. MACFARQUHAR AND J. K. FAIRBANK, eds., *The Cambridge History of China*, Vol. 14, *Emergence of Revolutionary China* (1987), and Vol. 15, *Revolutions Within the Chinese Revolution, 1966–1982* (1991).

L. PAN, *Sons of the Yellow Emperor: A History of the Chinese Diaspora* (1990). A pioneer study that treats not only Southeast Asia but the rest of the world as well.

M. R. RISTAINO, *Port of Last Resort: The Diaspora Communities of Shanghai* (2001).

T. SAICH, *Governance and Politics of China* (2004).

H. WANG, *China's New Order* (2003). Translation of a work by a Qinghua University professor, a liberal within the boundaries of what is permissable in China.

G. WHITE, ed., *In Search of Civil Society: Market Reform and Social Change in Contemporary China* (1996).

M. WOLF, *Revolution Postponed: Women in Contemporary China* (1985).

ZHANG X. AND SANG Y., *Chinese Lives: An Oral History of Contemporary China* (1987).

Japan

G. L. BERNSTEIN, *Haruko's World: A Japanese Farm Woman and Her Community* (1983). A study of the changing life of a village woman in postwar Japan.

T. BESTOR, *Neighborhood Tokyo* (1989). A portrait of contemporary urban life in Japan.

G. L. CURTIS, *The Logic of Japanese Politics: Leaders, Institutions, and the Limits of Change* (1999).

G. L. CURTIS, *Policymaking in Japan: Defining the Role of Politicians* (2002).

M. H. CUSUMANO, *The Japanese Automobile Industry* (1985). A neat study of the postwar business strategies of Toyota and Nissan.

R. P. DORE, *City Life in Japan* (1999). A classic, reissued.

R. P. DORE, *Land Reform in Japan* (1959). Another classic.

S. GARON, *Molding Japanese Minds: The State in Everyday Life* (1997).

S. M. GARON, *The Evolution of Civil Society from Meiji to Heisei* (2002). That is to say, from the mid–nineteenth century to the present day.

A. GORDON, ed., *Postwar Japan as History* (1993).

H. HIBBETT, ed., *Contemporary Japanese Literature: An Anthology of Fiction, Film, and Other Writing Since 1945* (1977). Translations of postwar short stories.

Y. KAWABATA, *The Sound of the Mountain* (1970). Sensitive, moving novel by Nobel author.

J. NATHAN, *Sony, the Private Life* (1999). A lively account of the human side of growth in the Sony Corporation.

D. OKIMOTO, *Between MITI and the Market* (1989). A discussion of the respective roles of government and private enterprise in Japan's postwar growth.

S. PHARR, *Losing Face: Status Politics in Japan* (1996).

E. F. VOGEL, *Japan as Number One: Lessons for America* (1979). While dated and somewhat sanguine, this remains an insightful classic.

Korea and Vietnam

B. CUMINGS, *Korea, The Unknown War* (1988).

B. CUMINGS, *The Origins of the Korean War* (Vol. 1, 1981; Vol. 2, 1991).

B. CUMINGS, *The Two Koreas: On the Road to Reunification?* (1990).

C. J. ECKERT, *Korea Old and New, A History* (1990). The best short history of Korea, with extensive coverage of the postwar era.

C. J. ECKERT, *Offspring of Empire: The Koch'ang Kims and the Colonial Origins of Korean Capitalism, 1876–1945* (1991).

G. M. T. KAHIN, *Intervention: How America Became Involved in Vietnam* (1986).

S. KARNOW, *Vietnam: A History.* rev. ed. (1996).

L. KENDALL, *Shamans, Housewives, and Other Restless Spirits: Women in Korean Ritual and Life* (1985).

K. B. LEE, *A New History of Korea* (1984). A translation by E. Wagner and others of an outstanding Korean work covering the full sweep of Korean history.

T. LI, *Nguyen Cochinchina: South Vietnam in the Seventeenth and Eighteenth Centuries* (1998).

D. MARR, *Vietnam 1945: The Quest for Power* (1995).

C. W. SORENSEN, *Over the Mountains Are Mountains* (1988). How peasant households in Korea adapted to rapid industrialization.

A. WOODSIDE, *Vietnam and the Chinese Model* (1988). Provides the background for Vietnam's relationship to China.

CHAPTER 34

Latin America

P. BAKEWELL, *A History of Latin America: c. 1450 to the Present* (2003). An up-to-date survey.

A. CHOMSKY et al., *The Cuba Reader: History, Culture, Politics* (2004). Very useful, broad-ranging anthology.

J. DOMINGUEZ AND M. SHIFTER, *Contructing Democratic Governance in Latin America* (2003). Contains individual country studies.

G. JOSEPH et al. , *The Mexico Reader: History, Culture, Politics*(2003). Excellent introduction to major issues.

P. LOWDEN, *Moral Opposition to Authoritarian Rule in Chile* (1996). A discussion of Chilean politics from the standpoint of human rights.

J. PRESTON AND S. DILLON, *Opening Mexico: The Making of a Democracy* (2004). Excellent analysis of recent developments in Mexico.

H. WIRARDA, *Democracy and Its Discontents: Development, Interdependence, and U.S. Policy in Latin America* (1995). A useful overview.

Africa

B. DAVIDSON, *Let Freedom Come* (1978). Remains a thought commentary of African independence.

R. W. JULY, *A History of the African People,* 5th ed. (1995). Provides a careful and clear survey of post–World War I history and consideration of nationalism.

J. HERBST, *States and Power in Africa* (2000). Relates current issues of African state-building to those before to the colonial era.

J. H. LATHAM, *Africa, Asia, and South America Since 1800: A Bibliographic Guide* (1995). A valuable tool for finding materials on the topics in this chapter.

N. MANDELA, *Long Walk to Freedom: The Autobiography of Nelson Mandela* (1995). Autobiography of the African leader who transformed South Africa.

L. THOMPSON, *A History of South Africa* (2001). The best survey.

N. VAN DE WALLE, *African Economies and the Politics of Perm anent Crisis, 1979–1999* (2001). Exploration of difficulties of African economic development.

India and Pakistan

O. B. JONES, *Pakistan: Eye of the Storm* (2003). Best recent introduction.

R. RASHID, *Taliban: Militant Islam, Oil and Fundamentalism in Central Asia* (2001). Analysis of radical Isalmist regime in Afghanistan.

R. W. STERN, *Changing India: Bourgeois Revolution on the Subcontinent* (2003). Overview of forces now changing Indian society.

S. WOLPERT, *A New History of India* (2003). The closing chapters of this fine survey history are particularly helpful in orienting the reader in postwar Indian history until the mid-1980s.

Islam and the Middle East

A. AHMED, *Discovering Islam. Making Sense of Muslim Hisotry and Society,* rev. ed. (2003). An excellent and readable overivew of Islamic– Western relations.

J. ESPOSITO, *The Islamic Threat: Myth or Reality,* 2nd ed. (1992). A useful corrective to some of the polemics against Islam and Muslims today.

J. J. ESPOSITO, ed., *The Oxford Encyclopedia of Islam* (1999). A thematic survey of Islamic history, particularly strong in the Modern Era.

D. FROMKIN, *A Peace to End All Peace: The Fall of the Ottoman Empire and the Creation of the Modern Middle East* (2001). Very good on the impact of World War I on the region.

G. FULLER, *The Future of Political Islam* (2003). A very good overview of Islamist ideology by a former CIA staff member.

J. KEAY, *Sowing the Wind: The Seeds of Conflict in theMiddle East* (2003). A balanced account.

N. R. KEDDIE, *Modern Iran. Roots and Results of Revolution* (2003). Chapters 6–12 focus on Iran from 1941 through the first years of the 1978 revolution and provide a solid overview of history in this era.

G. KEPEL, *Jihad: The Trail of Political Islam* (2002). An extensive treatment by a leading French scholar of the subject.

Bronze equestrian statuette of Charlemagne, from Metz Cathedral, 9th–10th c. 3/4 view. Louvre, Paris, France. Copyright Bridgeman-Giraudon/Art Resource, NY; William haranguing his troups for combat with the English army. Detail from the Bayeux tapestry, scene 51. Musee de la Tapisserie, Bayeux, France. Photograph copyright Bridgeman-Giraudon/Art Resource, NY; Ewer with carved flower sprays. China; Yaozhou, Shaanxi province. Northern Song dynasty (960–1127). Porcelain with carved decoration under celadon glaze. H. 9 5/8 in × W. 5 1/4 in × D. 7 3/4 in, H. 24.5 cm × W. 13.4 cm × D. 19.7 cm. Museum purchase, B66P12 © Asian Art Museum of San Francisco. Used by permission; A leaf from a Manichaean Book, Kocho, Temple K (MIK III 6368), 8th–9th century, manuscript painting, 17.2 × 11.2 cm. Museum fur Indische Kunst, Staatliche Museen Preussischer Kulturbesitz, Berlin; Copyright Werner Forman/Art Resource, NY; Odyssey Productions, Inc

Part 3, Timeline, top to bottom, left to right: Art Resource, NY; The Nelson-Atkins Museum of Art, Kansas City, Missouri. (Purchase: Nelson Trust) 50-20; The Granger Collection, NY; Albert Craig; Werner Forman/Art Resource, NY; Templo Mayor CoyoIxauhqui. Aztec Moon Goddess Stone. Aztec, 15th century. Stone, diameter 11'6" (3.5 m).

Chapter 8 a. Corbis/Bettmann; c. CORBIS-NY; d. CORBIS-NY; e. Gift of the Asian Art Museum of San Francisco. The Avery Brundage Collection, B66P12; f. Worcester Art Museum; g. Dorling Kindersley Media Library.

Chapter 9 a. Corbis/Bettmann; c. Araldo de Luca/Corbis/Bettmann; d. Corbis/Bettmann; e. Tokyo National Museum; f. Corbis/Bettmann; g. "Fan-Shaped Sutra" Tokyo National Museum. Image: TNM Image Archives. Source: **http://TnmArchives.jp/**; h. "Scroll w/depictions of the Night Attach on the Sanjo Palace" from Heiji monogatari emaki, 2nd half of the 13th c. Unknown. Japanese, Kamakura Period. Handscroll; ink & colors on paper. 41.3 × 699.7 cm. Fenollosa-Weld C. Courtesy of Museum of Fine Arts, Boston; i. PPS/Pacific Press Service.

Chapter 10 a. Corbis/Bettmann b. Art Resource, NY; c. J. Kershaw/Dorling Kindersley Media Library; d. J. Kershaw/Dorling Kindersley Media Library; e. Corbis/Bettmann; f. © Hulton-Deutsch Collection/CORBIS; g. Sassanid Art. Bottom of a silver bowl with Sassanid relief work. Leningrad Museum. Corbis-Bettmann; h. Borromeo; Art Resource, NY; i. The Nelson-Atkins Museum of Art, Kansas City, Missouri. (Purchase: Nelson Trust) 50-20; j. Paul Almasy; Corbis/ Bettmann; k. J. Kershaw; Dorling Kindersley Media Library.

Chapter 11 a. Courtesy of Freer Gallery of Art, Smithsonian Institution, Washington, DC; b. Bowl. Unidentified. 10th Century, Earthenware painted under glaze H 11.2 × Diam. 39.3 cm. Iran. freer Gallery of Art, Smithsonian Institution, Washington, D.C.: Purchase, F1957.24; c. Mehmet Biber/ Photo Researchers, Inc.; d. Dorling Kindersley Media Library; e. Arabic Manuscript: 30.60 Page from a Koran, 8th–9th century. Kufic script. H: 23.8 × W: 35.5 cm. Courtesy of the Freer Gallery of Art, Smithsonian Institution, Washington, D.C.; f. Werner Forman Archive; Art Resource, NY; g. Library of Congress; h. Scala/Art Resource, NY; i. Adam Lubroth, Art Resource, NY.

Chapter 12 a. Trinity College, Dublin, Ireland/Rev. Raymond Schoder/SuperStock; c. Book of Kells: St. Matthew, Chi Rho initial. Ca. 800 C.E.. Trinity College, Dublin, Ireland, © Art Resource, NY; d. © Werner Forman/Art Resource, NY; e. Scala/Art Resource, NY; f. Bodleian Library, University of Oxford; g. Giraudon/Art Resource; h. Bronze equestrian statuette of Charlemagne, from Metz Cathedral, 9th–10th c. 3/4 view. Louvre, Paris, France. Copyright Giraudon/Art Resource, NY; i. Giraudon/Art Resource, NY; j. Giraudon/Art Resource, NY; k. Kunsthistorisches Museum, Vienna.

Chapter 13 a. "Khusraw at the castle of Shirin" Folio from a manuscript by Nizami. Iran, early 15th century. Opaque watercolor, ink, and gold on paper; 25.7 × 18.4 cm. Courtesy of the Freer Gallery of Art, Smithsonian Institution, Washington DC, Purchase F1931.36. b. Bowl. Iran, late 12th century. Stone-paste painted over glaze with luster; 7.8 × 17.3 cm. Arthur M. Sackler Gallery, Smithsonian Institution, Washington, D.C. Gift of Osborne and Gratia Hauge, S1997.113; c. Adam Woolfitt; Corbis/Bettmann; d. Giraudon/Art Resource, NY; Robert Harding World Imagery; e. Geoff Dann; Dorling Kindersley Media Library; f. Clare Arni; Dorling Kindersley Media Library; g. By permission of the British Library.

Chapter 14 a. Lowell Georgia/NGS Image Collection; b. Siede Preis; Getty Images, Inc.-Photodisc; c. © CONACULTA-INAH-MEX. Authorized reproduction by the Instituto Nacional de Antropologia e Historia; e. Getty Images Inc./Photodisc; f. ©Erich Lessing/Art Resource, NY; g. Robert Frerck/Odyssey Productions, Inc.; h. Sexto Sol/Getty Images Inc. - Photodisc; i. © CONACULTA-INAH-MEX. Authorized reproduction by the Instituto Nacional de Antropologia e Historia; j Robert and Linda Mitchell Photography; k. Robert Frerk/Odyssey Productions; l. © Bettmann/CORBIS.

Chapter 15 a. Dorling Kindersley/The Wallace Collection; b. Cliché des Musees Nationaux, Paris; c. Museo Civico, Bologna, Italy; d. Giraudon/Art Resource, NY; e. Scala/Art Resource, NY; f. Scala/Art Resource, NY; g. Scala/Art Resource, NY; h. Scala/Art Resource, NY; i. Photograph © Erich Lessing/Art Resource, NY; j. Reunion des Musees Nationaux/Art Reesource, NY.

Part 4 Timeline, top to bottom, left to right: Elizabeth I (1558–1603) standing on a map of England in 1592. An astute politician in both foreign and domestic policy, Elizabeth was perhaps the most successful ruler of the sixteenth century. By courtesy of the National Portrait Gallery, London; Sultan Muhammad (active ca. 1501–1545), "Allegory of Worldly and Otherworldly Drunkenness". Leaf from a manuscript of a "Divan" by Hafiz, folio 137r. Opaque watercolor, ink and gold on paper. 11 3/8 × 8 1/2 in. (28.9 × 21.6 cm). Promised Gift of Mr. and Mrs. Stuart Cary Welch, Jr. in honor of the students of Harvard University and Radcliffe College. Partially owned by The Metropolitan Museum of Art and The Arthur M. Sackler Museum, Harvard University, 1988. Copyright 1989, Metropolitan Museum of Art; Library of Congress; The Bridgeman Art Library International Ltd; © Archivo Iconografico, S. A./Corbis.

Part 4 Timeline, top to bottom, left to right: Bridgeman-Giraudon/Art Resource, NY; Francis Wheatley (RA) (1747–1801) "Evening", signed and dated 1799, oil on canvas, 17 1/2 × 21 1/2 in.

(44.5 × 54.5 cm), Yale Center for British Art, Paul Mellon Collection/Bridgeman Art Library (B1977.14.118); Getty Images Inc. - Stone Allstock; Japan Airlines Photo; Unidentified Artist. The Emperor Ch'ien Lung (1736–1795) as a Young Man. Colors on silk. H. 63-1/2 in. W. 30-1/2 in. © The Metropolitan Museum of Art, Rogers Fund, 1942. (42.141.8). Photograph © 1980 The Metropolitan Museum of Art; Embassy of Kenya; © Hulton-Deutsch Collection/CORBIS.

Chapter 16 a. Dorling Kindersley/British Museum; c. Rijksmuseum, Amsterdam; d. Huntington Library; e. Art Resource, NY, The Branch Libraries, The New York Public Library, Astor, Lenox and Tilden Foundations; f. © Art Resource, NY; g. Musee Cantonal Des Beaux Arts, Palais de Rumine, Lausanne; h. Biblioteheque Publique et Universitaire, Geneva; i. National Portrait Gallery, London.

Chapter 17 a. Dorling Kindersley Media Library; c. Mapungubwe Museum; d. © Frank Willet; e. UN/DPI PHOTO/Jeffrey Fox; f. Cliche Bibliotheque nationale de France—Paris; g. Photograph by Eliot Elisofon, National Museum of African Art, Eliot Elisofon Archives, Smithsonian Institution, Washington DC; h. Courtesy Entwistle Gallery, London; j. Robert Aberman and Barbara Heller/Art Resource, NY; k. Werner Forman Archive/Art Resource, NY.

Chapter 18 a. "The Fortunate Slave" An illustration of African Slavery in the early 18th century by Douglas Grant (1968). From "Some Memoirs of the Life of Job," by Thomas Bluett, 1734. Photo by Robert D. Rubic/Precision Chromes, Inc. The New York Times Library, Research Libraries; b. Courtesy, American Antiquarian Society; d. Guy Ryecart/Dorling Kindersley Media Library; e. Courtesy of The University of Texas Archives. The UT Institute of Texan Cultures at San Antonio; f. Chas Howson/Dorling Kindersley Media Library; g. Dorling Kindersley Media Library; h. Samuel Scott, "Old Custom House Quay" Collection. V&A IMAGES, THE VICTORIA AND ALBERT MUSEUM, LONDON; i. The Granger Collection; j. Hulton/Corbis/Bettmann; k. Fur traders and Indians: engraving, 1777. c. The Granger Collection, New York; l. Glenbow Museum.

Chapter 19 a. Dorling Kindersley Media Library; c. Box: Carved lacquer box with cover decorated with scene of sages in a garden. Chinese, Yongle (1403–1429). Carved red lacquer over wood. 7.9 × 26.6 cm. China. freer Gallery of Art. Smithsonian Institution, Washington, D.C.: Purchase, F1953.64a; d. Karaori kimono. Middle Edo period, c. 1700. Brocaded silk. Tokyo National Museum; e. Tai Chin, "Fisherman on an Autumn River", (1390–1460). Painting. Ink and color on paper. 18-1/8 × 291-1/4 in. (46 × 740 cm). Courtesy of the Freer Gallery of Art, Smithsonian Institution, Washington, D.C.; f. Albert Craig; g. Melon-shaped Ewer, Stoneware. Koryo Dynasty, ca. 12th century H. 9" × Diam. 19-1/2" Korea. The Avery Brundage Collection, Asian Art Museum of San Francisco; h. Roger Phillips/ Dorling Kindersley Media Library; i. © Metropolitan Museum of Art, Rogers Fund, 1942, (42.141.8); j. Giraudon/Art Resource, NY; k. © 1996. All rights reserved. Courtesy of Museum of Fine Arts, Boston.

Chapter 20 a. Francois Boucher (1703 – 1770), "Breakfast" Louvre, Paris, France. Copyright Scala/Art Resource; b. Mary Evans Picture Library Ltd.; c. Kunsthistorisches Museum, Vienna; d. Art Resource, NY; e. Dorling Kindersley/The Museum of English Rural Life; f. Art Resource/Musee du Louvre; g. General James Wolfe's expedtion against Quebec in 1759; English engraving. 1760. The Granger Collection, NY; h. By permission of the Master and Fellows of Sidney Sussex College, Cambridge; i. The Granger Collection; j. The Granger Collection.

Part 5 Timeline, top to bottom, left to right: Anonymous, France, 18th century, "Seige of the Bastille, 14 July, 1789." Obligatory mention of the following: Musee de la Ville de Paris, Musee Carnavalet, Paris, France. Bridgeman-Giraudon/Art Resource, NY; Bildarchiv Preubischer Kulturbesitz; Corbis/Bettmann; Bettmann/ Corbis; The Granger Collection, New York.

Part 5 Timeline, top to bottom, left to right: "Col. James Todd on elephant Indian painting" ca. 1880. E.T. Archive, Victoria and Albert Museum; © Hulton-Deutsch Collection/CORBIS; © Christie's Images/Corbis.

Chapter 21 a. Bichitr, "Jahangir Preferring a Sufi Shaikh to Kings", ca. 1660-70. Album page. Opaque watercolor, gold, and ink on paper. 25.3 cmH × 18.1 cm W (10" × 7 1/8"). Courtesy of the Freer Gallery of Art, Smithsonian Institution, Washington, DC.; b. Opaque watercolor, ink, and gold on paper, 34.2 × 21.5 cm, Arthur M. Sackler Gallery, Smithsonian Institution, Washington DC. Lent by the Art and History Trust, LTS 1995. 2,80; c. Mart Nieuwland/Omni Photo Communications, Inc.; d. Getty Images, Inc. – All Stock; e. Tony Sterling © Dorling Kindersley; f. Arifi, "suleymanname," Topkapi Palace Museum, 11 1517, fol. 31b, photograph courtesy of Talat Halman; g. Michel Gotin/Ouzebekistan; h. Super Stock; i. Corbis/Bettmann.

Chapter 22 a. Dorling Kindersley/The Wallace Collection; b. Bildarchiv Preussischer Kulturbesitz; c. Corbis Bettman; d. The Granger Collection; e. © Bettmann/CORBIS; f. Sir Godfrey Kneller, *Sir Isaac Newton*, 1702. Oil on canvas. The Granger Collection; g. The Granger Collection; h. The Granger Collection; e. SuperStock, Inc.; j. The Granger Collection, New York.

Part 6 Timeline, top to bottom, left to right: Bildarchiv Preubischer Kulturbesitz; Bildarchiv Preubischer Kulturbesitz; Corbis/Bettmann; © Hulton-Deutsch Collection/CORBIS; Bridgeman Art Library, London/SuperStock, Inc.; SuperStock, Inc.

Part 6 Timeline, top to bottom, left to right: Bildarchiv Preubischer Kulturbesitz; Shosai Ginko (Japanese, act. 1874–1897), View of the Issuance of the State Constitution in the State Chamber of the New Imperial Palace, March 2, 1889 (Meiji 22), Ink and color on paper, 14 1/8 × 28 3/8 in. The Metropolitan Museum of Art, Gift of Lincoln Kirstein, 1959 (JP3233-3235) Photograph © The Metropolitan Museum of Art; Dorling Kindersley Media Library; The Granger Collection.

Chapter 23 a. Execution of Louis XVI. Aquatint. French, 18th century. Musee de la Ville de Paris, Musee Carnavalet, Paris, France. Giraudon/Art Resource, N.Y.; b. Corbis Bettmann; c. Corbis Bettmann; d. Francisco de Goya, "Los fusilamientos del 3 de mayo, 1808" 1814. Oil on canvas, 8'6" × 11'4" © Museo Nacional del Prado, Madrid; e. The Granger Collection; f. Austrian Archive/Corbis; g. Biblioteque Nationale Paris. France/Giraudon/Art Resource, NY; h. Mary Evans Picture Library, Ltd.; i. Hulton-Deutsch Collection/Corbis; j. The Granger Collection; k. Muse de la Ville de Paris, Musee Carnavalet/Giraudon/Art Resource, NY.

Chapter 24 a. The Art Archive/Picture Desk, Inc./Kobal Collection; b. Library of Congress; c. Library of Congress; d. Corbis/Bettmann; e. Art Resource/Bildarchiv P_reussischer Kulturbesitz; f. The Granger Collection, NY; g. Roger Violett; Getty Images Inc. – Liaison; h. Bildarchiv Preussicher Kulturbesitz/Original: Friedrichsruher Fassung, Bismark Musuem; i. Roger Viollett; Getty Images, Inc.—Liaison; j. The Granger Collection, New York.

Chapter 25 a. Corbis Bettmann; b. Photo RMN/Senice Photographique des Muses Nationaux, Paris; c. Georges Seurat, (French 1859 – 1891), "A Sunday on La Grande Jatte 1884" 1884-86, Oil on canvas, 207.6 × 308 cm. Helen Birch Bartlett Memorial Collection, 1926.224 © The Art Institute of Chicago. All Rights Reserved; d. Corbis Bettmann; e. Oil on canvas, 283 cm × 550 cm. Civica Galleria d'Arte Moderna-Milano. Photo by Marcello Saporetti; f. The Granger Collection, NY; g. Getty Images Inc.; h. Art Resource/Bildarchiv Preussischer Kulturbesitz; i. Leeds Museums and Art Galleries (City Museum) UK/Bridgeman Art Library; j. Mary Evans Picture Library.

Chapter 26 a. Geoff Brightling, Dorling Kindersley Media Library; b. Corbis/ Bettmann; c. Dorling Kindersley Media Library; d. Diego Rivera, "Orgy – Night of the Rich" (La Orgia – La noche de los ricos), 1926. Mural, 2.05 × 1.54 m. Court of Fiestas, Level 3, North Wall. Secretaria de Education Publica, Mexico City, Mexico. Schalkwijk/Art Resource, NY © Banco de Mexico Diego Rivera; e. Geoff Brightling; Dorling Kindersley Media Library; f. Corbis Bettmann; g. © Corbis; h. Corbis Bettmann; i. Corbis Bettmann; j. UPI/Corbis Bettmann.

Chapter 27 a. © Stockbyte; b. Giraud Philippe; Corbis/Sygma; c. Caravan with Ivory, French Congo, (now the Republic of the Congo). Robert Visser (1882–1894). c. 1890–1900, postcard, collotype. Publisher unknown, c. 1900. Postcard 1912. Image No. EEPA 1985-140792. Eliot Elisofon Photographic Archives. National Museum; d. By permission of the British Library; e. AP/Wide World Photos; f. The Granger Collection, New York; g. The Granger Collection; f. Brown Brothers; h. Getty Images Inc.—Hulton Archive Photos.

Chapter 28 a. Jean-Loup Charmet; b. Corbis/Bettmann; c. Coll. Ministry of Foreign Affairs, Tokyo, Japan; d. Shoes for bound feet. China, Asia circa 1900–1910. Qing Dynasty. Silk, leather 9.5 cm high, 12.5 cm. Dora O. Mitchell Collection. Museum of Anthropology, University of Missouri-Columbia. Daniel S. Glover, photographer; e. Hulton Picture Library/Bettman; Corbis/Bettmann; f. Courtesy of the Library of Congress. Gift of Mrs. E. Crane Chadbourne; 1930; g. Stock Montage, Inc./Historical Pictures Collection;h. Martin Plomer; Dorling Kindersley Media Library.

Part 7 Timeline, top to bottom, left to right: The Granger Collection; Pablo Picasso , 'Guernica' 1937, Oil on canvas. 11'5 1/2 × 25'5 3/4. Museo Nacional Centro de Arte Reina Sofia/ © 2004 Estate of Pablo Picasso/Artists Rights Society (ARS), New York; Getty Images Inc. - Hulton Archive Photos; Corbis/Bettmann.

Part 7 Timeline, top to bottom, left to right: Corbis/Sygma; Corbis/Bettmann; Corbis/Bettmann; Getty Images Inc. - Hulton Archive Photos; AP/Wide World Photos.

Chapter 29 a. Karl Shone; Dorling Kindersley Media Library; b. Corbis/Bettmann; c. Imperial War Museum, London; d. Andy Crawford; Dorling Kindersley Media Library; e. Alexander Gerasimov "Lenin at the Tribune" 1930. Tretyakov Gallery, Moscow, Russia. Scala/Art Resource, NY; f. Dorling Kindersley Media Library; g. Richard Ward/Dorling Kindersley Media Library; h. The Granger Collection; i. Musee des Blindes; j. Corbis Bettmann.

Chapter 30 a. © Scheufler Collection/CORBIS; b. Bildarchiv Preubischer Kulturbesitz; c. Corbis/Bettmann; d. The Granger Collection; e. Dorling Kindersley/ The Museum of the Revolution; e. Grosz George (1893–1959) ©VAGA, NY. Stuetzen der Gesellschaft (Pillars of Society), 1926. Oil on Canvas, 200,0 × 108,0 cm. Photo: Joerg P. Anders. Nationalgalerie, Staatliche Museen zu Berlin, Berlin, Germany; f. Getty Images Inc.—Hulton Archive Photos; f. Corbis/Bettmann; g. Bildarchiv Preubischer Kulturbesitz; h. © Leonard de Selva/CORBIS; i. Corbis Bettmann.

Chapter 31 a. © Bettmann/CORBIS; b. Corbis Bettmann; c. Dorling Kindersley/The Imperial War Museum; d. Corbis/Bettmann; e. The Granger Collection; f. Corbis/Bettmann; g. Getty Images Inc.—Hulton Archive Photos; h. Corbis Bettmann.

Chapter 32 a. Dorling Kindersley Media Library; b. Corbis/Bettmann; d. © Owen Franken/CORBIS; e. Telepress Syndicate Agency; Corbis/Bettmann; f. Corbis/Bettmann; g. Van Parys; Corbis/Sygma; h. SuperStock, Inc.; i. Corbis/Sygma; j. Peter Turnley; Corbis/Bettmann; k. Reuters; Corbis/Bettmann.

Chapter 33 a. Clive Streeter/Dorling Kindersley Media Library; b. China Tourism Press/Xie Guang Hui/ Getty Images; c. CORBIS-NY; d. Koren POOL/ Yonhap; AP/Wide World Photos; e. Dave Bartruff/CORBIS; f. Corbis/Bettmann CORBIS-NY; g. Photographer's Mate 3rd Class Todd Frantom; U.S. Navy News Photo; h. Corbis/Bettmann.

Chapter 34 a. Dorling Kindersley Media Library; b. Markus Matzel/Das Fotoarchiv/Peter Arnold, Inc.; c. AP Wide World Photos; d. David Brauchli/AP/Wide World Photos; e. AP/Wide World Photos; f. Roberto & Osvaldo Salas; Getty Images, Inc.—Liaison; f. M & E Bernheim; Woodfin Camp & Associates; g. UPI; Corbis/Bettmann; h. David Guttenfelder; AP/Wide World Photos; i. Masatomo Kuriya, Corbis/Sygma.

Voltaire, 542–43, 544
Voting
    African Americans, 806
    and women, 630, 631
Voting Rights Act of 1965, 806
Vulgate Bible, 150

W

Wagner Act, 769
Wahhabi movement, 650, 679, 683, 694, 695, 853
Walesa, Lech, 809, 811
Wallace, Alfred Russel, 646
Walpole, Robert, 487
Wang Mang, 161–62
War Communism, 754
War guilt clause, 748
War of Jenkins's Ear, 495–96
War of the Austrian Succession, 496, 550
War of the Roses, 367
War of the Spanish Succession, 494
War on Poverty, 807
War on terrorism, 808, 816
Warring States period, 22, 465, 466–68
Wars of Liberation, 571
Wars of Religion, 394–403
Warsaw Pact, 798
Washington, George, 560
Water frame, 507
Water management, 7, 23
Watergate scandal, 807
Waterloo, 573
Watt, James, 507
Wealth of Nations (Smith), 578
Weapons of mass destruction, 816, 859
Webb, Beatrice, 637
Webb, Sydney, 637
Weber, Max, 385, 650
Wei Jingsheng, 829
Weimar Republic, 752, 759–62, 764
Wellesley, Arthur, 571
Wellington, Duke of, 589
Wells, H. G., 637
West Africa, 107, 684–85
West Bank, 855
Western Europe
    Middle Ages, 264–87
Western World
    since World War II, 794–813
Western Zhou period, 22
What is to be Done? (Lenin), 638
Whigs, 590
White Lotus Rebellion, 462
White Russians, 743
Whitney, Eli, 595
Wilkinson, John, 507–8
William I of Germany, 604, 635
William I of Prussia, 605, 606
William II of Germany, 635, 735, 736, 738, 744

William III of England, 487
William IV of England, 590
William of Orange, 397–98, 487
William Pitt, the Elder, 496
William Pitt the Younger, 570
William the Conqueror, 350–51
Wilson, Woodrow, 645–46, 742, 744, 745
Witch hunts, 403–5
Wollstonecraft, Mary, 549, 629
Wolsey, Cardinal, 388
Women
    after World War II, 803–5
    in ancient art, 102–3
    in ancient Egypt, 13
    in Athens, 72–73, 74–75
    in Aztec society, 325–26
    and China's third commercial revolution, 459
    in Eastern Europe, 805
    and education, 626–27
    in 18th and 19th century art, 614–15
    and employment, 627–28, 805
    during the Enlightenment, 548–49
    and family economy, 502
    and feminism, 629–31
    in French revolution, 567
    in Germany, 350
    and Hitler, 788
    and Incas, 330
    and Industrial Revolution, 623–25
    and Islam, 249, 250
    in Japan, 218–19, 713, 823
    in Mesopotamia, 10
    in Middle Ages, 349–50
    in the Middle East, 682–83
    in Nazi Germany, 765–67
    in 19th century Europe, 586, 623–31
    in the Ottoman Empire, 517
    in Paleolithic Age, 6–7
    and property, 625
    during the Renaissance, 361
    right to vote in Europe, 631
    role in French revolution, 563
    and the Scientific Revolution, 540–41
    as slaves, 453
    social disabilities, 625–27
    during Tang dynasty, 178
    Turkish, 544
    in U.S. during World War II, 790
    and voting, 630
    and witch hunts, 404–5
    and working class, 628–29
    as writers of Japanese literature, 213
Women's Congress of Palestine, 683
Women's Social and Political Union, 630
Working class, 632–33, 638
    women, 628–29
Works and Days (Hesiod), 64
Works Progress Administration, 769
World Trade Organization, 827

World War I, 736–42
    America enters, 742
    casualties, 744, 745
    in the east, 740
    end of, 743–48
    1908-1914, 736–37
    outbreak of, 738–39
    at sea, 740–742
    Treaty of Versailles, 744–48
    in the west, 739–40
World War II, 772–93
    and Brazil, 668
    casualties, 787
    1939-1945, 778–90
    preparations for peace, 791–92
    road to war, 774–78
    strategic bombing, 784
    and women, 803–5
Writers, early modern European, 405–9
Writing
    cuneiform, 9–10
    during Han dynasty, 164
    hieroglyphics, 12, 316
    invention of, 7
    Japanese, 210
    Mayan, 318
    Mesoamerican, 24, 316
    Vedic Aryan, 19
Wu Zhao, Empress, 178–79
Wudi, 157–58, 161–62

X

X rays, 647
Xenophanes of Colophon, 43
Xenophon, 45
Xerxes, 69
Xia dynasty, 20
Xianbii, 163
Xinjang, 701
Xiongnu Empire, 158, 161, 162, 163, 476
Xuan Zong, 179–80, 182
Xuanzang, 167
Xunzi, 32

Y

Yahweh, 39, 41
Yalta, 792
Yamagata Aritomo, 711, 714, 717
Yamato state, 206–7
Yang Guifei, 182
Yangban, 477
Yangzi Basin, 188
Yaroslav the Wise, 365
Yathrib (Medina), 246, 247
Yayoi culture, 206–9
Yellow River Valley, 20
Yeltsin, Boris, 812–14
Yom Kippur War, 855

WORLD HISTORY DOCUMENTS CD-ROM

SINGLE PC LICENSE AGREEMENT AND LIMITED WARRANTY

READ THIS LICENSE CAREFULLY BEFORE OPENING THIS PACKAGE. BY OPENING THIS PACKAGE, YOU ARE AGREEING TO THE TERMS AND CONDITIONS OF THIS LICENSE. IF YOU DO NOT AGREE, DO NOT OPEN THE PACKAGE. PROMPTLY RETURN THE UNOPENED PACKAGE AND ALL ACCOMPANYING ITEMS TO THE PLACE YOU OBTAINED THEM.

1. GRANT OF LICENSE AND OWNERSHIP: THE ENCLOSED COMPUTER PROGRAMS <<AND DATA>> ("SOFTWARE") ARE LICENSED, NOT SOLD, TO YOU BY PEARSON EDUCATION, INC. PUBLISHING AS PEARSON PRENTICE HALL ("WE" OR THE "COMPANY") AND IN CONSIDERATION OF YOUR PURCHASE OR ADOPTION OF THE ACCOMPANYING COMPANY TEXTBOOKS AND/OR OTHER MATERIALS, AND YOUR AGREEMENT TO THESE TERMS. WE RESERVE ANY RIGHTS NOT GRANTED TO YOU. YOU OWN ONLY THE DISK(S) BUT WE AND/OR OUR LICENSORS OWN THE SOFTWARE ITSELF. THIS LICENSE ALLOWS YOU TO USE AND DISPLAY YOUR COPY OF THE SOFTWARE ON A SINGLE COMPUTER (I.E., WITH A SINGLE CPU) AT A SINGLE LOCATION FOR ACADEMIC USE ONLY, SO LONG AS YOU COMPLY WITH THE TERMS OF THIS AGREEMENT. YOU MAY MAKE ONE COPY FOR BACK UP, OR TRANSFER YOUR COPY TO ANOTHER CPU, PROVIDED THAT THE SOFTWARE IS USABLE ON ONLY ONE COMPUTER.

2. RESTRICTIONS: YOU MAY NOT TRANSFER OR DISTRIBUTE THE SOFTWARE OR DOCUMENTATION TO ANYONE ELSE. EXCEPT FOR BACKUP, YOU MAY NOT COPY THE DOCUMENTATION OR THE SOFTWARE. YOU MAY NOT NETWORK THE SOFTWARE OR OTHERWISE USE IT ON MORE THAN ONE COMPUTER OR COMPUTER TERMINAL AT THE SAME TIME. YOU MAY NOT REVERSE ENGINEER, DISASSEMBLE, DECOMPILE, MODIFY, ADAPT, TRANSLATE, OR CREATE DERIVATIVE WORKS BASED ON THE SOFTWARE OR THE DOCUMENTATION. YOU MAY BE HELD LEGALLY RESPONSIBLE FOR ANY COPYING OR COPYRIGHT INFRINGEMENT THAT IS CAUSED BY YOUR FAILURE TO ABIDE BY THE TERMS OF THESE RESTRICTIONS.

3. TERMINATION: THIS LICENSE IS EFFECTIVE UNTIL TERMINATED. THIS LICENSE WILL TERMINATE AUTOMATICALLY WITHOUT NOTICE FROM THE COMPANY IF YOU FAIL TO COMPLY WITH ANY PROVISIONS OR LIMITATIONS OF THIS LICENSE. UPON TERMINATION, YOU SHALL DESTROY THE DOCUMENTATION AND ALL COPIES OF THE SOFTWARE. ALL PROVISIONS OF THIS AGREEMENT AS TO LIMITATION AND DISCLAIMER OF WARRANTIES, LIMITATION OF LIABILITY, REMEDIES OR DAMAGES, AND OUR OWNERSHIP RIGHTS SHALL SURVIVE TERMINATION.

4. LIMITED WARRANTY AND DISCLAIMER OF WARRANTY: COMPANY WARRANTS THAT FOR A PERIOD OF 60 DAYS FROM THE DATE YOU PURCHASE THIS SOFTWARE (OR PURCHASE OR ADOPT THE ACCOMPANYING TEXTBOOK), THE SOFTWARE, WHEN PROPERLY INSTALLED AND USED IN ACCORDANCE WITH THE DOCUMENTATION, WILL OPERATE IN SUBSTANTIAL CONFORMITY WITH THE DESCRIPTION OF THE SOFTWARE SET FORTH IN THE DOCUMENTATION, AND THAT FOR A PERIOD OF 30 DAYS THE DISK(S) ON WHICH THE SOFTWARE IS DELIVERED SHALL BE FREE FROM DEFECTS IN MATERIALS AND WORKMANSHIP UNDER NORMAL USE. THE COMPANY DOES NOT WARRANT THAT THE SOFTWARE WILL MEET YOUR REQUIREMENTS OR THAT THE OPERATION OF THE SOFTWARE WILL BE UNINTERRUPTED OR ERROR-FREE. YOUR ONLY REMEDY AND THE COMPANY'S ONLY OBLIGATION UNDER THESE LIMITED WARRANTIES IS, AT THE COMPANY'S OPTION, RETURN OF THE DISK FOR A REFUND OF ANY AMOUNTS PAID FOR IT BY YOU OR REPLACEMENT OF THE DISK. THIS LIMITED WARRANTY IS THE ONLY WARRANTY PROVIDED BY THE COMPANY AND ITS LICENSORS, AND THE COMPANY AND ITS LICENSORS DISCLAIM ALL OTHER WARRANTIES, EXPRESS OR IMPLIED, INCLUDING WITHOUT LIMITATION, THE IMPLIED WARRANTIES OF MERCHANTABILITY AND FITNESS FOR A PARTICULAR PURPOSE. THE COMPANY DOES NOT WARRANT, GUARANTEE OR MAKE ANY REPRESENTATION REGARDING THE ACCURACY, RELIABILITY, CURRENTNESS, USE, OR RESULTS OF USE, OF THE SOFTWARE.

5. LIMITATION OF REMEDIES AND DAMAGES: IN NO EVENT, SHALL THE COMPANY OR ITS EMPLOYEES, AGENTS, LICENSORS, OR CONTRACTORS BE LIABLE FOR ANY INCIDENTAL, INDIRECT, SPECIAL, OR CONSEQUENTIAL DAMAGES ARISING OUT OF OR IN CONNECTION WITH THIS LICENSE OR THE SOFTWARE, INCLUDING FOR LOSS OF USE, LOSS OF DATA, LOSS OF INCOME OR PROFIT, OR OTHER LOSSES, SUSTAINED AS A RESULT OF INJURY TO ANY PERSON, OR LOSS OF OR DAMAGE TO PROPERTY, OR CLAIMS OF THIRD PARTIES, EVEN IF THE COMPANY OR AN AUTHORIZED REPRESENTATIVE OF THE COMPANY HAS BEEN ADVISED OF THE POSSIBILITY OF SUCH DAMAGES. IN NO EVENT SHALL THE LIABILITY OF THE COMPANY FOR DAMAGES WITH RESPECT TO THE SOFTWARE EXCEED THE AMOUNTS ACTUALLY PAID BY YOU, IF ANY, FOR THE SOFTWARE OR THE ACCOMPANYING TEXTBOOK. BECAUSE SOME JURISDICTIONS DO NOT ALLOW THE LIMITATION OF LIABILITY IN CERTAIN CIRCUMSTANCES, THE ABOVE LIMITATIONS MAY NOT ALWAYS APPLY TO YOU.

6. GENERAL: THIS AGREEMENT SHALL BE CONSTRUED IN ACCORDANCE WITH THE LAWS OF THE UNITED STATES OF AMERICA AND THE STATE OF NEW YORK, APPLICABLE TO CONTRACTS MADE IN NEW YORK, EXCLUDING THE STATE'S LAWS AND POLICIES ON CONFLICTS OF LAW, AND SHALL BENEFIT THE COMPANY, ITS AFFILIATES AND ASSIGNEES. THIS AGREEMENT IS THE COMPLETE AND EXCLUSIVE STATEMENT OF THE AGREEMENT BETWEEN YOU AND THE COMPANY AND SUPERSEDES ALL PROPOSALS OR PRIOR AGREEMENTS, ORAL, OR WRITTEN, AND ANY OTHER COMMUNICATIONS BETWEEN YOU AND THE COMPANY OR ANY REPRESENTATIVE OF THE COMPANY RELATING TO THE SUBJECT MATTER OF THIS AGREEMENT. IF YOU ARE A U.S. GOVERNMENT USER, THIS SOFTWARE IS LICENSED WITH "RESTRICTED RIGHTS" AS SET FORTH IN SUBPARAGRAPHS (A)-(D) OF THE COMMERCIAL COMPUTER-RESTRICTED RIGHTS CLAUSE AT FAR 52.227-19 OR IN SUBPARAGRAPHS (C)(1)(II) OF THE RIGHTS IN TECHNICAL DATA AND COMPUTER SOFTWARE CLAUSE AT DFARS 252.227-7013, AND SIMILAR CLAUSES, AS APPLICABLE.

SHOULD YOU HAVE ANY QUESTIONS CONCERNING THIS AGREEMENT OR IF YOU WISH TO CONTACT THE COMPANY FOR ANY REASON, PLEASE CONTACT IN WRITING: LEGAL DEPARTMENT, PRENTICE HALL, 1 LAKE STREET, UPPER SADDLE RIVER, NJ 07450 OR CALL PEARSON EDUCATION PRODUCT SUPPORT AT 1-800-677-6337.